# thepurplebook™

# thepurplebook™

## the definitive guide to
## exceptional online shopping

# 2004 edition

bantam books

# thepurplebook™

Editor-in-chief & Founder
Hillary Mendelsohn

Co-Founder
Lawrence Butler

Author
Ian Anderson

Art Director
Jerome Curchod

Technology Director
Christian Giangreco

THEPURPLEBOOK
A Bantam Book

A Bantam trade paperback  / October 2003

Published by
Bantam Dell
A Division of Random House, Inc.
New York, New York

Library of Congress Cataloging-in-Publication Data is on file with the publisher.

ISBN 0-553-38278-0

Manufactured in the United States of America
Published simultaneously in Canada

RRC 10   9   8   7   6   5   4   3   2   1

This book was made possible with the unending support, encouragement and patience of
my husband Michael,
my kids Max and Gabriella,
my parents Shelley and Ron,
my partner Larry,
my right hand Ian,
and my creative eye Jerome.


"Success is an idea that is realized."

# thepurplebook

## TABLE OF CONTENTS

# foreword

**thepurplebook** exists to provide consumers with an internet shopping directory that is at once comprehensive, objective, incisive, entertaining, reliable, easy-to-use and, above all, informative. It is our sincere hope that the sites listed within these pages will offer some of the best online shopping experiences available, and that our humble book will contribute in some small way to the many conveniences and advantages of e-commerce.

In years to come, we plan to continually improve the book with updated editions, so as to expand and improve our unique collection, both with the addition of new sites and the inclusion of new categories. Hopefully, by cultivating the awareness of discerning shoppers, our books will encourage existing sites to better serve the online shopping population, and we welcome this growth. We believe that the American economy is best served if a wide variety of large and small businesses can fairly compete on a national and global level, and with **thepurplebook** our intention is not only to bring the best available products and services to deserving consumers, but to direct customers to deserving retailers as well.

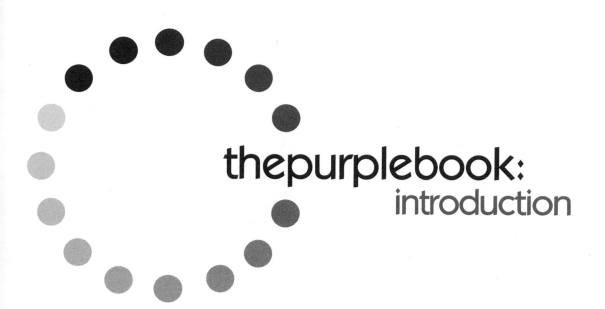

# thepurplebook:
## introduction

**H**ave you ever *actually* tried to find a needle in a haystack? Of course not. The expression only exists to highlight the futility of such pursuits. And yet, every day, tens of millions of people turn to web search engines to help them find the information and merchandise that interest them most. However, suppose you enter a query for the word "needle" on the internet's most powerful search engine. The resulting list features more than 1,200,000 online pages to sort through.

Welcome to the world wide web. With more than one billion pages already, and that number expected to double each year, it's no longer just a matter of finding the needle; the problem is finding the right haystack.

It gets worse. If you type in "shirts," you get almost four million responses. "Wine" gets you nearly six million. Type in "gifts," and you will be presented with more than seven million pages, each of which *might* contain what you're looking for, if you're willing to take the time to find it ...

# ✳ WE TAKE THE GUESSWORK OUT OF ONLINE SHOPPING

**thepurplebook** is the solution to your search engine woes. The way we see it, why waste valuable time looking for an online shop, then waste more time looking for the item you want to purchase, only to discover that you shouldn't have bothered in the first place? Isn't the promise of the internet that it has the power to make our lives both easier and more efficient? Then why must we spend entire afternoons scouring through dozens or hundreds of web sites instead of spending that time at the beach?

We spent over a year cataloging and reviewing every e-commerce site we could track down, whether we found out about it through search engines, advertisements, links from other web sites, community bulletin boards, magazine articles or word of mouth. Of the tens of thousands of online stores we discovered, we had to toss a few out for being detrimental to humanity. The rest we subjected to our own rigorous set of standards, scrutinizing each aspect of the site: *Is it easy to use? Does it have a good selection? Are the prices good? Will it download in less than an hour?*

By the end, we'd whittled down the selection to include only the finest catalogs, the most beautiful web designs, the best bargains and that occasional ingenious purveyor of a product or service of such unique charm that we couldn't possibly leave it out. Our final tally includes brick-and-mortar stores that have established a viable online presence, manufacturers who have done the same, internet juggernauts that have managed to survive the dot-com backlash, and small businesses, often individuals working out of their bedrooms, who've embraced the virtual marketplace in their pursuit of the American Dream. It's a pretty good bunch, capable of fulfilling nearly any online shopping need you may have, and possibly turning you on to something new.

# ✳ WHAT YOU CAN EXPECT...

All of these sites we have assembled into a single collection, printed on actual, as opposed to virtual, pages, indexed and split up into several categories to correspond with the nation's most common shopping needs, as follows:

### ART & COLLECTIBLES
Whether you want to bid on the original masterworks of the century, poster your dorm room or add to your collection of kitsch, we have the online tools to help dress your surroundings in any mode, medium or era, across all price ranges.

### ENTERTAINMENT
Whatever your tastes, we have a listing for just the sort of music, movie or book you may want to find, whether you're seeking old (records, print, video) or new (CD, eBook, DVD) formats. Or, if you prefer a less passive pastime, you can find plenty of puzzles and games, as well as tickets to live performances/events.

### EPICUREAN
Named for the sensuous embrace of luxurious living, this section features stores dedicated to grocery items, gourmet foods, vintage wines and fine cigars. While there's an obvious disparity between listings for health food and tobacco products, we have to figure that it all balances out.

### GADGETS & ELECTRONICS
Improving life from the outside in, this category includes computer hardware and software, along with a lengthy list of electronics for your home or pocket, whether the aim is to enjoy music or hold conversations over great distances. Then there are the whimsical, non-electric devices that can accomplish stuff bare hands just never could.

### HEALTH & BEAUTY
All the convenience of a corner drug store, and all the glamour of a high-priced salon; in this section, you will find the pills, dressings and ointments it takes to keep your body healthy, as well as all the cosmetics, cleansers and fragrances you favor to keep yourself looking and feeling beautiful.

### HOME & GARDEN
From home improvement to making your garden grow, this section comes complete with listings to help furnish any room in the house or landscape your grounds with flowers, latticework and even bodies of water.

### LIFESTYLES & MEGASTORES
These are stores that don't fit the mold. Any of them might offer everything you want to buy in a single location. Some cater to a specific lifestyle or interest you may have, while others have simply assembled a smattering of random merchandise. Either way, the benefits of these shops include wide selections and the optimization of shipping charges.

### MATERNITY
Between special equipment and expert advice, the primary focus of this section has the health of parent and child in mind. On the other hand, a thorough selection of fashionable clothing will help show off the radiance of impending motherhood during nine months of changes. You'll have to see the Epicurean section to satisfy any odd food cravings, though.

### MEN'S APPAREL
Clothes for any event, style or day of the week make for easy browsing with this list of man-friendly stores. If the appropriate dress involves a tie, no problem. If jeans are better suited to the activity, find them here. Whether the aim is to impress a woman, satisfy the boss or while away the days in comfort, you can find your threads in the best way possible: fast.

## MINORS
From infants on through teens, this section caters to children, whether you're doing the shopping for them or they're picking things out themselves. Most likely, toy stores will be at the top of their lists, while parents might prefer the clothes or educational opportunities, any of which span a range of prices and interests.

## PETS
For the animals with the greatest owners, these sites cover all the basics, like food and hygiene, and even manage to include a lot of indulgences, ranging from toys to furniture and even some clothing. A healthy, happy pet is a cinch, whether it walks, flies, crawls, swims or trots.

## SENIORS
The tools and products to be found in this section address the lifestyle changes typically faced by those over the age of 55. Most prominently featured are items that promote independent living, whether by combating the symptoms of a particular physical ailment, or by increasing access to the world of technology.

## SHOES & ACCESSORIES
True style includes every part of the body, from head to toe. With this in mind, this section offers everything from hats to shoes, alongside some jewelry, watches and eyewear, with handbags and wallets to stow it all in. Whatever the accoutrements, men and women alike will find some great ones here.

## SPORTS & OUTDOORS
Physical lifestyles get more active with less effort thanks to these online shops devoted to home gyms, athletic equipment and outdoor gear. Whether you intend to trounce the competition, camp high up in the stratosphere or pursue your own body's limits, these listings will help.

## STATIONERY & GIFTS
The Stationery portions of this section feature anything from personalized letterheads to invitations and greeting cards, while the Gifts that are offered include standards like flowers, baskets and confections, with a few innovative ideas thrown in for those tough-to-shop-for special occasions.

## TRAVEL
Get out of town. Better yet, do it with ease and comfort. Here you can find several different means of booking flights, hotel rooms, car rentals and any other kind of accommodation you might require on your travels. Better still, outfit yourself with the right clothes, luggage and other gear that'll make getting there nearly as fine as being there.

## WEDDINGS
Making the most important day of your life a little easier to plan, these sites can help you establish the costuming, invitations, decorations and catering that may mean the difference between a day to remember and a lifetime to forget. And then there's the best part: the wedding registries.

## WOMEN'S APPAREL
Your wardrobe just got better. In this section you will find an extensive selection of shops, featuring every layer of clothes between the world and your skin. Whether it's lingerie, swimwear, outerwear or a killer evening gown, you may easily find the best designers and/or the greatest bargains.

## CHARITY
Have you got something to give? Here are some fine ways to devote yourself to the betterment of the planet, whether you're improving peoples' lives or saving the environment. If nothing else, in this section you'll discover that helping out is easier and more effective today than ever before.

# ✳ HOW TO USE **thepurplebook**

While we've made every effort to be discriminating, the number of web sites listed in this book does approach 1,700. Though these comprise a mere fraction of the more than 10,000 sites we viewed, we're well aware that it's a lot to handle. With this in mind, we've split the book into 19 categories, and designed a system to make individual sites and products easier to locate. If you are looking for a good place to shop or find a gift, for example, you may browse the alphabetical site listings. If you have something more specific in mind, you may search one of our several indexes for products, companies or key words.

# ✳ BROWSING

Within each category, **thepurplebook** site listings are arranged alphabetically, and presented along with a five- or six-sentence summary that should give you a general idea of what to expect from the site before ever logging on. Alongside these reviews, you will find icons that evaluate the site's service, selection and usability, as well as a list of key words describing the store's product selection.

Using the icons and key words, you may browse each category to find specific product types, or to find stores that offer specific services like gift wrapping or overnight delivery. See the sample site listing below, and the descriptions on the following pages, for further details.

# ✳ SAMPLE SITE LISTING

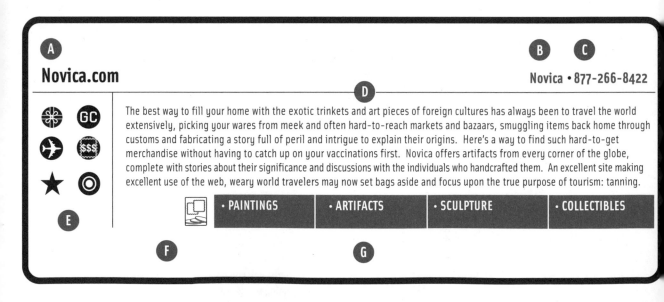

**A**

**Novica.com**

**B** **C**

Novica • 877-266-8422

**D**

The best way to fill your home with the exotic trinkets and art pieces of foreign cultures has always been to travel the world extensively, picking your wares from meek and often hard-to-reach markets and bazaars, smuggling items back home through customs and fabricating a story full of peril and intrigue to explain their origins. Here's a way to find such hard-to-get merchandise without having to catch up on your vaccinations first. Novica offers artifacts from every corner of the globe, complete with stories about their significance and discussions with the individuals who handcrafted them. An excellent site making excellent use of the web, weary world travelers may now set bags aside and focus upon the true purpose of tourism: tanning.

**E**

• PAINTINGS    • ARTIFACTS    • SCULPTURE    • COLLECTIBLES

**F** **G**

#  UNDERSTANDING THE SITE LISTINGS

### A URL

Each site in this book has been listed alphabetically by its URL (internet address). We've left out the standard **http://www.** that precedes each domain name and extension. In other words, to visit **Novica.com**, go to the address bar in your browser and type in **http://www.Novica.com**. We've gone over and over all the sites listed here, which doesn't mean that a few might not have changed. But if you're having trouble reaching a site, double-check to make sure you've added the **http://www.** portion— some sites are more sensitive to it than others.

### B COMPANY NAMES

Especially in the case of exclusively online entities, the company name often does not differ from the site URL. Occasionally, though, a familiar name may turn up here.

### C CUSTOMER SERVICE NUMBERS

Whenever available, we've listed the company's customer service phone number with its site entry. This should help if you cannot log on to the site for some reason, or if you cannot easily find the number listed there (sometimes they like to hide them). Oftentimes, using the web site's human support staff is more productive than sending emails when things go wrong.

### D REVIEW

These reviews are intended to offer some insight into the breadth and scope of the web site at hand, but more often than not, they have deteriorated into base humor and wry observation. This is wholly to be blamed on the writer, who admittedly does not often know a good thing when he sees it.

### E UNIVERSAL ICONS

A set of round Universal Icons depict some of the particularities about each store that may come in handy when deciding where to shop: Shipping Costs, Overnight Shipping, Gift Certificates, Gift Wrapping, User Friendliness, and a Star, to indicate whether a site is particularly useful or unique (see pages 18-19).

### F SECTION ICONS

The rectangular Section Icons have been included to help you distinguish between specific types of stores commonly housed in each category. For example, an icon in the Shoes & Accessories section will pinpoint the shoe stores, whereas one in the Stationery & Gifts section will highlight sites that offer gift baskets.

### G KEY WORDS

Within the strip of orange that lines the bottom of each site listing, you will find a list of key words offering a general description of the types of products available from that store. A quick scan of these words should give you a rough idea of whether a store has what you seek.

# ✳ UNDERSTANDING THE ICONS

### SHIPPING COSTS

A huge consideration when online shopping is the cost of shipping & handling orders. High fees can turn what seemed like a great deal into a waste of cash, whereas a cheap shipping policy can mean the difference between competitive prices.

 **Free, Incentivized or Flat Rate Shipping** – Sites marked by this icon either cover shipping costs, reduce the cost of shipping if you spend more or charge a single, preset amount to cover shipment of your entire order, regardless of cost or weight.

 **Standard Shipping Rates** – Sites covered by this icon either charge the same weight-based amount for shipping as determined by the carrier (usually UPS, FedEx, Airborne Express or the US Postal System) or compute comparable rates based on the value of the purchase.

 **Exorbitant or Unknown Shipping & Handling Fees** – Sites tagged with this icon either charge excessive handling fees designed to pad their profit margins, or do not inform you of an order's shipping charges until after a credit card has been used to make the purchase. A third category of these sites simply ship very large, heavy items that require special companies or even individual trucks, usually at great expense.

### OVERNIGHT SHIPPING

When you see this icon, the site in question offers the option of overnight shipping or next-day delivery, in most cases at an extra charge, and often not on weekends. Bear in mind that sites usually have an early afternoon or morning deadline for one-day delivery, and that time zones may consequently play a big role in your last-minute purchases.

### GIFT CERTIFICATES

This icon only appears when gift certificates are available for purchase in either electronic or paper form. Electronic gift certificates will be sent to the recipient's email address and therefore make excellent last-second gifts.

### GIFT WRAPPING

 We offer an entire section of sites boasting great gift ideas, but really just about any site in this book has the perfect gift for *somebody*. Any site will also send your order in a plain brown box. Some will wrap it up a bit nicer (usually at an extra charge). Such sites are noted by this icon.

## USER FRIENDLINESS

Product selection is the most important aspect to building an online store, but presentation is often what sells, and if using a site to make a purchase is just too much work it may not be worth it. We've ranked each site's performance with the following three icons:

These sites have gone the distance to make sure that you can find the products you need without hassle and order them with minimal difficulty, either through fancy web design or plain common sense. Or the site only has a handful of products to begin with and everything may be viewed or purchased on one page. Either way, we wish all the sites qualified for this rank, but very few did.

Savvy web shoppers are used to the industry standard—a left-side menu of options, with a few more general choices thrown across the top of the page for good measure. Such sites warrant no complaints, as everything you need is laid out logically so that browsing and buying are easy on the mind, and only hard on the mouse-clicking finger.

In some cases, these sites involve dramatic and failed attempts to create the virtual world's best new shopping technique. On the other end of the spectrum are the web designers who simply weren't up to the task. In between, we have the online shopkeepers who simply didn't care, and scattered their products haphazardly across cyberspace for hackers to trip over. Whatever the case, these sites are often impossible to load, browse and/or order from. Ironically, these aberrations wouldn't have made the cut except that they offer something special.

## thepurplebook RECOMMENDS

If you see this star next to a site you know that we found some reason to favor it over the rest. Either it stands out among its field of competitors with excellent offerings and design, or it stands alone by offering something unique and/or innovative in the realm of e-commerce.

## ✳ USING THE INDEXES

These indexes will help you track down specific products, stores and sites of interest in the most efficient manner.

### KEY WORD INDEX
Located in the introduction to each section you will find a key word index that can help you locate which stores carry particular types of products within that category.

### PRODUCT INDEX (PAGE 605)
At the end of the book you will find a detailed listing of products and the corresponding names of sites that carry them. Note that this is not necessarily a comprehensive list, and that you will be able to find some of these products on sites not mentioned in the index. By the same token, using the key word indexes within each section, you are bound to find some products we missed.

### COMPANY NAME INDEX (PAGE 643)
This list of brand and company names, located at the end of the book, is simply meant to help you locate web sites for companies that may not otherwise be readily familiar. For example, if you look up popular chain store Urban Outfitters, you will discover that they reside under the URBN.com URL.

### URL INDEX (PAGE 659)
Also located at the end of the book, this index simply lists each of the site URLs in alphabetical order, regardless of category.


## ✳ FIND ONLY WHAT YOU NEED...

With **thepurplebook** in hand, the huge, looming specter of the internet is broken down a bit, and the futility of searching through its billions of pages eclipsed. Finally, we can conquer the overflow of information, at least a small part of it, and fulfill the potential promised to us by the world wide web. Finally, we can shop.

# Art & Collectibles

Whether you're in it for the sheer aesthetic value, the practical investment, to cover water stains or just to show off your artistic patronage, the procurement of art contributes to a personal sense of culture, and in nearly all cases looks better than bare walls.  From historic masterpieces to experimental contemporary trends, the art world has made little distinction in bringing its wares to e-market.  Posters and prints exist in almost limitless supply, touching upon every school or style, while auction houses and artist forums tap into slightly more original fare.  Whatever your preferred medium, if you're serious about collecting, you may find some great opportunities to build your collection with the work of old favorites or young, emerging talents.

Then again, maybe you aren't after prestige pieces.  After all, some of the sincerest artisans consist of unknown craftsmen and women of foreign cultures whose work would seldom catch notice in the US without the internet as a venue.  From pottery and carvings to traditional painting and etching styles that have been passed down through the ages, these craft pieces serve as authentic reminders that variety existed once upon a time, before American influence put virtually the entire planet in blue jeans.  Of course, the kitschy memorabilia of mass-produced American pop culture proves collectible in its own right, whether you're talking about tin lunchboxes or limited-edition commemorative plates. You'll find them amid lists of antiques of a finer nature, from all eras and cultures, for the serious or casual collector.  Indeed, what they say is true: beauty is in the eye of the beholder.  It just also happens to be in the window of your web browser.

NOTES:

_____

_____

_____

_____

_____

_____

_____

_____

_____

_____

_____

_____

_____

_____

_____

_____

_____

# TIPS ON BUYING ART & COLLECTIBLES ONLINE

These suggestions may help prevent misconception and disappointment.

•**COLOR DISCREPANCIES:** Differences in monitor settings and digital image compression in most cases mean that the image you see online will not match up precisely to the actual colors or dimensions of the painting, print or poster. Usually, this is a trivial difference.

•**CERTIFY AUTHENTICITY:** Original artwork, antiques, collectibles and memorabilia can be a very large investment. Online, as in real life, it is very important that you receive a valid certificate of authenticity with your purchase. Make sure the online seller guarantees such certification before you make your purchase, and definitely make a phone call if you are uncertain.

•**CHECK FRAMING OPTIONS/COSTS:** In some cases, you may anticipate paying a lot for a specific item, and will be ready to make your online purchase. However, some merchants may be in the habit of including default framing options that run up the price of the work. When buying framed artwork, be sure you're not paying more for the frame than you are for the art itself.

•**SHIPPING INSURANCE:** As with any valuable long-distance purchase, you'll want to be sure your merchandise is insured in transit. This section in particular includes a lot of fragile and/or one-of-a-kind pieces, and it's always a safe bet to be covered in case your order shows up *in* pieces. When in doubt, call before ordering.

•**SHIPPING WEIGHT & COSTS:** Heavy frames, bulky materials and odd sizes can significantly drive up the cost of shipping art items. Before you agree to a purchase, take note of the shipping methods and rates offered by your vendor, so you don't find too big a surprise on your credit card bill.

# SITES THAT MAY COME IN HANDY

The following URLs may be useful when you shop.

Determining Art Market Value: http://www.artmarketresearch.com
More Art Valuations: http://www.artfact.com
Antique Appraisals: http://www.antiqueappraisals.net
Antique & Collectibles Price Guide: http://www.kovels.com
Art Directory & Daily Art News: http://www.artnet.com
Fine Art & Collectibles Insurance: http://www.axa-art.com
A Guide to Displaying Artwork in the Home:
http://www.diynet.com/DIY/projectIndexDetail/0,2041,DIYD_643,FF.html
Equipment for Collectible Storage & Display: http://www.containerstore.com

>> SECTION ICON LEGEND

Use the following guide to understand the rectangular icons that appear throughout this section.

### AUCTIONS

Most recognizable original pieces and some antiques are sold at auction (because how else do you put a price on something exquisite?). The same holds true on the web. Some of these auctions are strictly internet based, while some enable you to engage in real-time bidding against a room full of paddle-wielding patrons around the world.

### COLLECTIBLES

Their value may be monetary, sentimental, decorative, based in hobby or invested against the future. The objects denoted by this symbol may be stamps, coins, baseball cards, collector's plates, porcelain figurines or any variety of similar items people see fit to hoard.

### ORIGINAL ARTWORK

This icon is meant to distinguish those sites offering artworks that have actually been crafted by their creators, as opposed to prints, reproductions, replicas, posters or artifacts created in kind along an assembly line.

### POSTERS & PRINTS

The affordable way to fill your walls with the flat images that stir your fancy, posters include photos of athletes and movie stars as well as replicas of famous paintings, pin-up girls and sleek automobiles. Prints usually fare a little better; at least, they tend to feature a higher-quality paper....

## LIST OF KEY WORDS

The following words represent the types of items typically found on the sites listed in this section.

### ANTIQUES

The defining lines of antiques are starting to blur as the era of mass production edges toward the century mark, but that just makes the truly archaic stuff all the more interesting.

### ARTIFACTS

Some artifacts are quite old, made by hands long since dust, named in a language long dead. Some are being made by hand at this moment for sale to tourists on the cheap. The cultural relevance of these crafts and utensils notwithstanding, they usually warrant a look.

### BOOKS & MEDIA

It could be a collection of your favorite artwork or a video documentary about an important movement or era. This key word denotes a site that offers not just the art, but pertinent information about it as well.

### EMERGING ART

You don't know their names, you may never know their faces. But these are the people out there producing art right now, and their work is for sale.

### KITSCH

Some is procured with a sense of irony, some with a sense of history. Kitsch generally consists of items adhering to popular culture; things like cartoon lunchboxes, promotional movie items and old advertisements. This stuff is often as gaudy as it sounds.

### MASTER ARTISTS

Museums want them, poster renditions adorn college dormitories worldwide: These are the works hewn by the great artists of history, and they're going to cost you. Of course, it doesn't get better....

### MEMORABILIA

There's often a fine line between collectibles and memorabilia. Here's how we see it: a baseball card is collectible. An autographed baseball card is memorabilia. These span sports, politics, entertainment and other cultural areas.

### MUSEUM SHOPS

The end of any museum tour lands you in the gift shop, where you're subjected to posters, puzzles, calendars and ties decorated with the art you've just spent the day admiring. You'll find such fare on these sites.

### PAINTINGS

Oil, acrylic, watercolors: these are the real things, paints laid upon canvas with an artist's tender brush strokes.

### PHOTOGRAPHY

Especially with digital scanning technology, it's pretty tough to maintain the authenticity of fine photography, but the good stuff shows a keen eye, superior light control and excellent developing techniques.

### SCULPTURE

Carved from rock, molded from clay, wrought together with controlled flames and molten metal; sculptures consist of three-dimensional art pieces assembled from any variety of materials, even some you might not want to know about (ah, the quirks of experimental art).

### SKETCHES & NOTES

The original sketches and notes of an artist can offer amazing insight into the objectives and labors of a particular piece, whatever the medium. This stuff is quite valuable on many levels, and rare to find.

# KEY WORD INDEX

Use the following lists to locate online retailers that sell the Art & Collectibles you seek.

## ANTIQUES

AntiqNet.com
Antiques.co.uk
CollectorOnline.com
iCollector.com
RubyLane.com
TIAS.com

## ARTIFACTS

AncientArt.co.uk
AntiqNet.com
Antiques.co.uk
Eziba.com
MagellanTraders.com
Novica.com
PopHouse.com
PrintSellers.com
RubyLane.com
Tapestries-Inc.com
TheAfricaStore.com
TheOrigins.com
TIAS.com
Yokodana.com

## BOOKS & MEDIA

Alibris.com
AnselAdams.com
ArtRepublic.com
Guggenheim.org
HeritageComics.com
LilliputMotorCompany.com
Louvre.fr
MetMuseum.org
MoMAStore.org
MuseumCompany.com
NGA.gov
ObeyGiant.com
ShagMart.com
UrsusBooks.com
WarholStore.com

## COLLECTIBLES

AHS.com
Alibris.com
AntiqNet.com
Antiques.co.uk
Cartoon-Factory.com
CoinLand.com
CoinWire.com
CollectiblesToday.com
CollectorOnline.com
DavidHall.com
DoWahDiddy.com
EntertainmentEarth.com
FastFoodToys.com
FranklinMint.com
FritzGifts.com
HeritageCoin.com
HeritageComics.com
iCollector.com
JamesMcCusker.com
LilliputMotorCompany.com
Novica.com
OnlineSports.com
PopHouse.com
PrintSellers.com
RubyLane.com
StampFinder.com
Steuben.com
TheOrigins.com
TIAS.com
USMint.gov
VintageVending.com

## EMERGING ART

Art4Sale.com
ArtCanadiana.ca
ArtCanyon.com
ArtfulStyle.com
EyeStorm.com
Guild.com
iTheo.com
MixedGreens.com

NextMonet.com
PaintingsDirect.com
PicassoMio.com

## KITSCH

AllPosters.com
AntiqNet.com
Art.com
ArtRock.com
Cartoon-Factory.com
ClassicPhotos.com
CollectiblesToday.com
CollectorOnline.com
DoWahDiddy.com
EntertainmentEarth.com
FastFoodToys.com
FranklinMint.com
FritzGifts.com
LilliputMotorCompany.com
MovieGoods.com
NightOwlBooks.com
ObeyGiant.com
PopHouse.com
RubyLane.com
ShagMart.com
Streamlined-Prints.com
TIAS.com
VintageVending.com
WarholStore.com

## MASTER ARTISTS

AnselAdams.com
iCollector.com
WarholStore.com

## MEMORABILIA

AntiqNet.com
ArtRock.com
ClassicPhotos.com
CollectorOnline.com
DoWahDiddy.com

MovieGoods.com
OnlineSports.com
RoslynHerman.com
RubyLane.com
VintageVending.com

## MUSEUM SHOPS

Guggenheim.org
Louvre.fr
MetMuseum.org
MoMAStore.org
MuseumCompany.com
NGA.gov
WarholStore.com

## PAINTINGS

Art4Sale.com
ArtCanadiana.ca
ArtCanyon.com
ArtfulStyle.com
ArtOnCanvas.com
BasilStreet.com
EyeStorm.com
Guild.com
HandColoredArt.com
iCollector.com
iTheo.com
MastersCollection.com
MixedGreens.com
NextMonet.com
Novica.com
PaintingsDirect.com
PicassoMio.com

## PHOTOGRAPHY

AnselAdams.com
Art4Sale.com
ArtCanadiana.ca
ArtCanyon.com
ArtfulStyle.com
ClassicPhotos.com

Corbis.com
EyeStorm.com
Guild.com
HandColoredArt.com
iCollector.com
iTheo.com
MixedGreens.com
NextMonet.com
PicassoMio.com

## POSTERS & PRINTS

AllPosters.com
AnselAdams.com
AntiqNet.com
Art.com
Art4Sale.com
ArtCanadiana.ca
ArtExpression.com
ArtInAClick.com
ArtInside.com
ArtRepublic.com
ArtRock.com
ArtSelect.com
BareWalls.com
Chisholm-Poster.com
Corbis.com
Guggenheim.org
Louvre.fr
MetMuseum.org
MoMAStore.org
MovieGoods.com
MuseumCompany.com
NGA.gov
NightOwlBooks.com
ObeyGiant.com
PosterShop.com
PrintSellers.com
ShagMart.com
Streamlined-Prints.com
WarholStore.com

## SCULPTURE

Antiques.co.uk
Art4Sale.com
ArtCanadiana.ca
ArtfulStyle.com
Guild.com

iCollector.com
iTheo.com
Louvre.fr
MetMuseum.org
MixedGreens.com
MuseumCompany.com
NextMonet.com
NGA.gov
Novica.com
PicassoMio.com

## SKETCHES & NOTES

iCollector.com
iTheo.com

## AHS.com

**The American Historic Society • 818-442-0324**

The American Historic Society has some stamps, and a few sports collectibles, but the bulk of this catalog consists of money— not the kind you save but the kind you keep, if you can dig the difference. From long-since obsolete Confederate coins and bank notes to MPCs (Military Payment Certificates) and even the newest state quarter editions, pretty much the entire history of the US Mint may be traced here on any given day. Then there are some novelty entries, such as "the world's luckiest coin" and a colorized two-dollar bill, along with ancient and foreign currency that just looks like funny money.

·COLLECTIBLES

## Alibris.com

**Alibris • 877-254-2747**

We'll get to the actual selection maintained by this retailer of "books you thought you'd never find" in a moment. However, our favorite thing about this site is the Glossary of Book Terms. This comprehensive list of words defines for the neophyte such terms as Armorial Binding, Buckram, Deckle Edges and Yapp (ten bucks says you have to go to the site to see what all of these are). Getting to it, though, this knowledge becomes imperative to understanding this collector-oriented shop. Though it tends to operate kind of slow online, this store proves itself to be more than just a fancy dictionary.

·BOOKS & MEDIA  ·COLLECTIBLES

## AllPosters.com

**AllPosters.com • 888-654-0143**

Somewhere between wallpaper and paintings ... are posters. You can't find a less expensive way to fill your walls with the indelible images of great artists, and this is a specialty retailer that knows how to make it easy for you to find them. Of course, it's not all high culture here, as there're plenty of movie posters, celebrity glamour shots and spectacular athletic moments captured on film, each equally easy to locate. Finally, there are harder-to-categorize images, like pictures of cookies, and of people sewing, and yet somehow even these may be found without difficulty. Good site.

·KITSCH  ·POSTERS & PRINTS

## AncientArt.co.uk

**Ancient Art Online • 011-44-208-882-1509**

This site is your chance to get a hold of "authentic ancient artifacts." Pretty cool, huh? The selection ranges from Roman coins and Greek swords to the handwritten pages of a medieval Bible. Lest you think the selection strictly Eurocentric, you can also find Egyptian beads and Chinese pottery dating from the Ming, Yuan, Han or Tang dynasties. And if that makes you wonder just how ancient these artifacts get, look to the Fossils category, where you'll find such desirable dinosaur items as eggs, bones and dung— all right, so not all of this stuff is expressly beautiful, but it's never less than fascinating.

·ARTIFACTS

## 888-361-7622 • The Ansel Adams Gallery

### AnselAdams.com

In the unlikely event that the name doesn't ring a bell, you're undoubtedly familiar with at least one of the images captured by this most prolific landscape photographer. Adams gained fame taking beautiful pictures of natural sites such as Yosemite National Park and Alaska's Mt. McKinley. Likewise, all the photographers featured in this shop offer landscape portraits in natural settings; here in the form of posters, calendars and original photography. The only way to get a better glimpse of the beautiful world around us is to go out and take a look for yourself.

| ·PHOTOGRAPHY | ·BOOKS & MEDIA | ·MASTER ARTISTS | ·POSTERS & PRINTS |
|---|---|---|---|

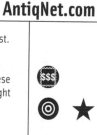

## 888-959-1605 • AntiqNet.com

### AntiqNet.com

As years go by, the definition of what constitutes an antique continually expands to include more and more items from eras past. It's therefore not surprising that more antique stores exist than anyone would care to count. AntiqNet strives to bring these thousands of stores together on the web so that antique hunters out there can track down rare items in one easy place. To this end, they succeed, with more than 5,000 vendors contributing every imaginable kind of searchable item. However, most of these vendors do not have e-commerce capability, so while the site might help you track a piece down, getting it into your hands might be another story.

| ·ANTIQUES ·COLLECTIBLES | ·ARTIFACTS ·POSTERS & PRINTS | ·KITSCH | ·MEMORABILIA |
|---|---|---|---|

★

## 011-44-207-286-7803 • Antiques.co.uk

### Antiques.co.uk

Maybe it's their European origins, maybe it's because a lot of this stuff is very old, but for some reason the items sold by this UK antique retailer are extremely expensive, ranging from armor helmets to ornate 17th century cupboards. Most of it is pricey for a reason, but even some of the pre-assembly-line merchandise will make you scratch your head in wonder, especially given that prices are listed in pounds.

| ·ANTIQUES | ·ARTIFACTS | ·COLLECTIBLES | ·SCULPTURE |
|---|---|---|---|

## 800-952-5592 • Art.com

### Art.com

What do you get from the art site with the easiest-to-remember name? For starters, over 100,000 posters, prints and photographs bearing some quite memorable images rendered by some of this and every century's greatest, all at quite competitive prices. Oh yeah, some of these are actually posters and 8x10 glossy photos celebrating top sports figures, pop stars, actors and less easily categorized personalities (Einstein, anyone?). Does the inclusion of these alternatives to wallpapering a teenager's bedroom besmirch the good name of "Art"? We can only hope.

| ·KITSCH | ·POSTERS & PRINTS | | |
|---|---|---|---|

# Art4Sale.com

Art4Sale.com • 561-392-7220

If you take a good look at this site you are almost guaranteed to eventually come across something so vile, so despicably heinous that it gives you cause to wonder if maybe this whole art thing is a waste of time altogether. But don't blame the gallery; they're just trying to offer a great variety of art contributed by known and emerging artists, to account for all tastes and styles. And they do this well. Actually, for every bad piece listed here, there are probably six amazing paintings, sculptures, photographs and animation cels available elsewhere on the site.

| ·PAINTINGS ·POSTERS & PRINTS | ·PHOTOGRAPHY | ·SCULPTURE | ·EMERGING ART |
| --- | --- | --- | --- |

# ArtCanadiana.ca

ArtCanadiana.ca • 866-888-5556

Welcome to "the exciting world of Canadian art." What distinguishing features constitute Canadian art? Well, if we knew that, this site would become obsolete. Here we see a variety of paintings, photography, sculpture and mixed media, both originals and reproductions, covering a range of subjects and themes. Canada does have a very rich natural environment, which we suspect is why there's no dearth of landscapes here, and a lot of animal portraits as well. Hey, when you see how much less these pieces cost in American dollars, how can you pass them up?

| ·PAINTINGS ·POSTERS & PRINTS | ·PHOTOGRAPHY | ·SCULPTURE | ·EMERGING ART |
| --- | --- | --- | --- |

# ArtCanyon.com

Artcanyon • 404-254-6562

If you view art as an investment, here is the place to find fresh work at relatively cheap prices. Featuring contemporary and emerging artists, none of these works is incredibly well known, but as these pieces speak for themselves, some most assuredly will be. Browsing can be quite the entertaining afternoon here, and there's even a few price categories to check out, though if you limit your search too much you'll miss some fantastic stuff. The only real remaining question: Can you spot the next great masterpiece?

| ·PAINTINGS | ·PHOTOGRAPHY | ·EMERGING ART | |
| --- | --- | --- | --- |

# ArtExpression.com

Artexpression • 800-398-4335

A comprehensive selection of posters and prints awaits you at this site, which otherwise has little to entice you away from other, similar online art retailers. A list of categories allows you to sift through sections of Abstract, Architectural, Landscapes and other types of images, but this organization makes little sense from there. More reliable is to search alphabetically by artist or title, though this will result in a daunting number of pages for any bandwidth. This one's good for finding stuff you already know you want.

| ·POSTERS & PRINTS | | | |
| --- | --- | --- | --- |

**877-939-7270 • Artful Style**

**ArtfulStyle.com**

On a mission to "bring artist and audience together," this site does so with aplomb. A bevy of talented and creative artists has contributed works to this online dealer, whether paintings, sculptures, photographs, objets d'art, furniture or even rugs. While browsing will lead to some beautiful views of some fabulous stuff, there's enough here to warrant a bit of patience if you intend to look straight through it (which you should, and keep looking because the talent here runs deep). The good news is, if you see a piece you particularly like, you may easily view all the works by that artist, and even send the artist an email encouraging more to come. Here's hoping this one's around for a long time.

| ·PAINTINGS | ·PHOTOGRAPHY | ·SCULPTURE | ·EMERGING ART |  |

**888-799-7888 • ArtInAClick.com**

**ArtInAClick.com**

Seemingly slapped together by a team of art historians who possess web-programming capabilities, the most important thing to remember when viewing this site is that the frame typically comprises well over fifty percent of the price. There's little actual mention of this per se, but they do offer a See/Buy Unframed option on most pieces, at which point it all becomes clear. Now, they do offer a variety of framing options, including a Mix and Match feature allowing you to see any piece with the available styles and colors, but losing the frame can mean the difference between several hundreds of dollars and a couple dozen. Framing aside, there are some great prices on a decent selection of posters here.

| ·POSTERS & PRINTS | | | | |

**800-638-0008 • ArtInside.com**

**ArtInside.com**

This site refers to itself as the "premier online home art store for everyone," which only really makes it distinguishable from other art print retailers in that it offers the option to browse by Room, so that you must only look at prints, for example, that will adapt well to a Bathroom setting, if not a Kitchen one. If, on the other hand, you think you can make such a determination for yourself, you may browse by Color, which includes options like Sea Tones, Sepia and Pastels, to find works that fit your home's motif.

| ·POSTERS & PRINTS | | | | |

**877-463-3266 • ARTonCANVAS.com**

**ArtOnCanvas.com**

If you need an elegant reproduction of a classic master painting and you need it fast, this isn't the place for you. If you can wait for a few weeks, however, this might just be the shop you're looking for. It "specializes in museum style, framed canvas oil reproductions," built to order, covering various celebrated pieces as well as less cerebral images, such as puppies sitting under an umbrella.

| ·PAINTINGS | | | |

## ArtRepublic.com

artrepublic • 011-44-127-372-4829

This UK site offers many of the things most of its US competitors do in terms of posters. But these guys do it a little better, with an additional selection of art books and a whole section devoted to educating the novice art fan. All in all, the only drawback might be the shipping costs of having a framed print flown in from England ... except that they offer free shipping. Ironic, but these guys might on occasion do it cheaper than the local sites.

| | ·BOOKS & MEDIA | ·POSTERS & PRINTS | | |
|---|---|---|---|---|

## ArtRock.com

ArtRock Online • 415-777-5736

Some posters just hang; others rock! This is a retail site for just such posters. Most of them are the colorful; psychedelic and/or cartoonish concert posters that make each performance seem like a special, if somewhat demented, occasion. Primarily, there are a lot of classic rock performances represented—Led Zeppelin at the Fillmore, Jimi Hendrix in Stuttgart and The Beatles all over the place, just to name a few—but some contemporary alternative and punk bands may be found. If only the browsing function made it easy....

| | ·KITSCH | ·MEMORABILIA | ·POSTERS & PRINTS | |
|---|---|---|---|---|

## ArtSelect.com

Art Select • 888-686-4254

Here's a great site for people looking to complement their living space with posters and prints that contribute to a general atmosphere rather than paying homage to a particular icon (like sports figures, sex symbols or artists). For example, in Decorative Art you'll find images where the focus isn't the picture, but how it complements a room. You can also browse Art Styles, various vintage collections and a healthy assortment of subjects like Cityscapes, Botanicals and Lighthouses. Of course, on top of all this you may still shop by artist; but only if you have varied tastes.

| | ·POSTERS & PRINTS | | | |
|---|---|---|---|---|

## BareWalls.com

BareWalls.com • 800-455-3955

Like a tabula rasa, bare walls offer us an unlimited realm of options, space to fill. That seems to be the general idea here, anyway, as this art print and poster seller is set up to provide you with options upon options, which lead to, you guessed it, more options. It starts when you browse for an image by subject. A long list of categories as general as Still Life and as particular as Smoking will each in turn show a long list of subcategories that will lead you to a collection of images to peruse. Once you select a piece, though, the choosing doesn't stop; rather, you then have several framing options and in some instances the choice to have the print transferred to canvas, and then to (if you want) have brush strokes added by hand.

| | ·POSTERS & PRINTS | | | |
|---|---|---|---|---|

## 800-525-9661 • Basil Street Gallery

## BasilStreet.com

Representing the Basil Street Gallery of London, this snooty-sounding dealer offers "framed oil replicas on canvas." In other words, you can get some of the greatest paintings history has to offer for mere hundreds of dollars; they just happen to be painted by some kid out of art school rather than the original artist. Actually, they employ a "sophisticated replication process" called oleography (not that we know what that is, exactly), which apparently stays true to the original right down to the surface texture. Experts will surely see the difference, but the rest of us may report you for art theft.

·PAINTINGS

## No Service Number • The Cartoon Factory

## Cartoon-Factory.com

Boasting "the largest selection of animation art cels on the internet," we should point out that the actual selections here are limited. But by "limited" we don't mean that you can't find the goods from Disney, Hanna-Barbera and Warner Brothers, just that your options within each category are limited. You'll also likely find Dr. Seuss characters, Ren & Stimpy, Beavis & Butthead, the Peanuts gang, The Simpsons and Fat Albert. And we won't even get into the commercial characters. One thing to watch out for: some links will appear to be broken. Keep hitting the Refresh or Reload button on your browser, and the pages should eventually show up.

·KITSCH   ·COLLECTIBLES

## 212-741-1703 • Chisholm Larsson Gallery

## Chisholm-Poster.com

This site proves as frustrating as it is wonderful. The bottom line is there's no better source for vintage posters, which is what makes it worthwhile to delve into this often confusing, disorganized catalog; to suffer the invariable "Availability: 0" notice after having scoured dozens of images to find the one you like. See, one of the problems is that, in order to browse images, you must utilize the Other Features pull-down menu on the home page. This will allow you to browse Russian Political Posters, World War II Posters, Spanish Civil War Posters and other equally intriguing and international fare. However, ordering requires another page and another procedure, and the two do not often mesh well. Good luck—you'll want it and need it with these outstanding images.

·POSTERS & PRINTS

## 218-365-6219 • ClassicPhotos.com

## ClassicPhotos.com

Here's a great place to find those photographs that, over the years, have burned their images into our cultural awareness. Whether it's Muhammad Ali standing over a knocked-out Sonny Liston, The Beatles performing on the Ed Sullivan Show, Sophia Loren glaring at the cleavage of Jayne Mansfield or the Wright brothers taking flight at Kitty Hawk, there's a great chance the 8x10 glossy is for sale here, amidst celebrity and cultural archives. It's entertaining enough if you don't plan to buy; just browse the images and bask in the warmth of familiarity.

·PHOTOGRAPHY   ·KITSCH   ·MEMORABILIA

# CoinLand.com

CoinLand.com • 866-327-2165

Welcome to "America's Family Friendly Coin Web Site," which lacks any of the smut and anti-government rhetoric the other coin sites are known to propagate. Of course, we're joking. The fact is, we're not sure why these guys deem themselves particularly family oriented, but the site does seem to be really easy to browse. Their out-front selection includes Sacagawea dollars, Buffalo nickels, Mercury dimes, Indian Head pennies, Walking Liberty half-dollars and the new state quarters. There's not much in the way of foreign mint, but there's a lot of weird domestic stuff. This one's decake.

·COLLECTIBLES

# CoinWire.com

CoinWire.com • 877-415-4435

What this coin dealer lacks in pictures, it makes up for in variety. Unlike most of the online US coin dealers we've found, this one features foreign coins and currency, for starters, and plenty of options in domestic mint to make it worth your while. Since images often are lacking, you would need to know what the rating codes for serious collectors mean; rather, you would if these guys didn't just give them descriptions like "good," "fine" or "very fine." Far from perfect, if this site didn't have some pretty cool items for sale, it would be worth skipping.

·COLLECTIBLES

# CollectiblesToday.com

CollectiblesToday.com • 877-268-6638

The category list of collectibles featured on this site is so long that many of them slip into the realm of the absurd. Including sections devoted to door corners (we didn't know what they were either), mouse pads and cookie jars, the real focus of this collection is brand name collectible manufacturers like Berta Hummel, Waterford Crystal and Thomas Kincaid, among others. Let us not forget Barbie and Elvis specialty sections, nor all the Coca-Cola merchandise you've been looking for but unable to find. Clear out some shelf space, because you are about to hit the jackpot.

·KITSCH    ·COLLECTIBLES

# CollectorOnline.com

Collector Online • 800-546-2941

Here's a site that is "dedicated to serving people with a passion for the handmade products of yesterday and today," meaning simply that you can find a lot of antiques and collectibles. As it turns out, these guys operate a little differently from most online stores, acting as a centralized location for a huge variety of scattered dealers and retailers. We're not entirely sure to what extent these guys have direct access to these other stores' inventories, but the shopping function seems to take place on a single server, so the end result seems to be that you can scour thousands of pieces from hundreds of shops from this one site. Ideal? Far from it, but valuable nonetheless.

·ANTIQUES    ·KITSCH    ·MEMORABILIA    ·COLLECTIBLES

## 888-829-0722 • Corbis

## Corbis.com

This is a huge site that offers thousands of images for publishing and design purposes, as well as some to suit your decorating needs. Thus, it gets awkward and confusing, even possessing a few technical flaws to further slow you down. Here's a tip: go straight to Shopping and then select Prints from the Decorate menu, from here you can choose either Art or Photography, select a category, and from there filter your browsing with the Refine Results option. Occasionally, you may come across a link that doesn't work—don't fret, just keep refreshing the page and it should show up. The good news is that once you actually get to an image, you have some options in terms of framing, matting and size.

| ·PHOTOGRAPHY | ·POSTERS & PRINTS | | |  |

## 800-759-7575 • David Hall Rare Coins

## DavidHall.com

If you're interested in seeing a retailer charge thousands of dollars for a single penny, you should check out this dealer of rare and memorable coins. It sounds like a bad investment, but it turns out these are "gem quality coins," which means that they're worth significantly more than nickels and dimes, despite any values the coins themselves might have minted on them. You can check out a Price Guide to see what the valuation of these pieces should be, as well as those differences in designations and gradings that affect the collector's price.

| ·COLLECTIBLES | | | | |

## 602-957-3874 • Do Wah Diddy

## DoWahDiddy.com

This "Home of 20th Century Pop Culture Collectibles" promises "all items are in excellent condition ... you will find NO dents, rust, wear, chips, cracks, tears or other annoying problems." Well, you might, but they'll be sure to tell you first. Sometimes that's just the price you have to pay to get your hands on this kitschy merchandise from the '40s, '50s and onward. We're talkin' lunchboxes, vintage *TV Guides,* pin-up calendars, flamingo lawn ornaments and whatever else the manufacturing age has made memorable. Of course, you have to fill out the order form manually; a drag, man.

| ·KITSCH | ·MEMORABILIA | ·COLLECTIBLES | | |

## 818-255-0095 • Entertainment Earth

## EntertainmentEarth.com

Basically, this is a toy store for sci-fi fanatics. You'll see a range of action figures for everything from *X-Men* to *Buffy the Vampire Slayer*. There's also plenty of kitschy collectibles like games, masks, and cardboard cutouts of your favorite cult figures. But the items of most value to serious collectors may be found in the appropriately named Really Cool Expensive Stuff category. Here you'll find movie costumes, full-size statues and replica weapons like Rambo's knife or Darth Vader's light saber (don't get excited, it's not a working model). But yes, what about *Star Wars* stuff? It's here in droves, whether in the form of a Boba Fett helmet or life-sized replicas of R2D2 and C3PO. Can a land speeder be far behind?

| ·KITSCH | ·COLLECTIBLES | | | |

## EyeStorm.com

Eyestorm • 866-393-4278

Either one of the best domain names we've seen or one of the worst (it's really hard to say), Eyestorm makes a good argument for itself with a slick, beautiful website full of unorthodox design elements and some pretty intriguing original art. Though the coding here sometimes proves too slick for its own good, and the layout offers the occasional browsing hardship (mostly to do with inconsistent patterns), you get great, big looks at these paintings and photographs, which may be viewed by "theme" or by artist. Chances are, if you glance at this one, you'll stick around for a while.

| | ·PAINTING | ·PHOTOGRAPHY | ·EMERGING ART | |
|---|---|---|---|---|

## Eziba.com

Eziba • 888-404-5108

While anybody may enjoy this site, its presentation seems to be particularly attuned to those who mistakenly think elegance is strictly a western notion. Rather, this retailer of arts, crafts and creative furniture delivers a selection whose origins spans the globe, and doesn't mind telling you the what-and-where of it all. "We'll never promise you the world," they explain to the curious yet uninformed potential customer, "but we'll use our understanding to select the most exquisite crafts the planet has to offer." Experienced collectors might object to these "translators" and their quasi-condescension, but no amount of language will detract from the luster of these wares, nor from their glossy appeal.

| | ·ARTIFACTS | | | |
|---|---|---|---|---|

## FastFoodToys.com

Aunt Linda's Fast Food Toys • 419-332-3901

Most of us still revile the notion that fast food could possibly contribute anything of lasting worth to our culture (other than clogged arteries and love handles). This site, however, would posit its collection of toys that have for decades been distributed with Happy Meals, fun meals, kids' meals and any other incarnation of the cardboard-box-with-toy-included meal. Some are tied-in to movies or athletics, some involve particular colorful franchise characters and some are sealed in the original packaging. Where these items are concerned, heaven forefend that there be a more comprehensive retailer than this.

| | ·KITSCH | ·COLLECTIBLES | | |
|---|---|---|---|---|

## FranklinMint.com

The Franklin Mint • 877-843-6468

What better way to sell collectible items than to make them yourself? At least, this seems to be the feeling behind this world-leading manufacturer of manufactured collectibles. Eggs, plates, dolls, tankards and figurines mark some of the standard fare to be found here. They usually honor or commemorate some celebrity (like the John Wayne pocket watch), sport (a die-cast stock car model, for example) or classic era (such as the western-themed bowie knife). Other browsing themes include Dragons, Myths & Fantasies; Princesses, Royalty & Icons; Military Icons; and Harley-Davidson. After all, somebody had to make this stuff.

| | ·KITSCH | ·COLLECTIBLES | | |
|---|---|---|---|---|

**800-266-8029 • FritzGifts.com**                                    **FritzGifts.com**

Do you like figurines? How about crystal? Well, you better like one or the other if you're going to log on to this site, or you'll simply be wasting your time. As for the rest of us, well this may be a waste of time, regardless, but if so it's not for lack of selection. See, for these collectible genres of limited appeal, this site does an excellent job for browsing and viewing the works of mainstays like M.I. Hummel, Emmett Kelly and Waterford Crystal, among others, ranging from cutesy to the sublime. "Delightful!"

| ·KITSCH | ·COLLECTIBLES | | | |
|---------|---------------|---|---|---|

**800-329-6109 • The Guggenheim Museum**                    **Guggenheim.org/store**

Much like the famous architecture of its branches in New York, Bilbao, Venice and Berlin, the items for sale in the Guggenheim online store are rarely less than ... interesting. Much of the merchandise is a celebration of the work of architect Frank O. Gehry, in the form of posters, models and ... um, fruit baskets. The Guggenheim likeness is similarly transposed into the kitschy splendor of yo-yos and luggage tags, among other sundries. Artists get the treatment as well, with scarves based on the work of Gustav Klimt, jewelry inspired by Edgar Degas, and an umbrella actually designed by Robert Rauschenberg. If you absolutely love the Guggenheim, there's no other place to shop.

| ·BOOKS & MEDIA | ·MUSEUM SHOPS | ·POSTERS & PRINTS | |
|----------------|---------------|------------------|---|

**877-344-8453 • Guild.com**                                          **Guild.com**

This "source of the finest artists and their work" is a bit busy, visually, but it has a great selection of original art pieces from an extensive list of contemporary artists like Jeremy Cline, Shuji Ikeda and Edy Pickens; artists you may not know offhand, but whose work could easily invigorate your environment. The great thing is, this stuff isn't limited to paintings, or even photography. All manner of visual representation has a place here, whether it be of wood, metal, plaster or any other physical form. Ranging from lovely to edgy, this site provides a great way to decorate your surroundings while making an investment in the future of art.

| ·PAINTINGS | ·PHOTOGRAPHY | ·SCULPTURE | ·EMERGING ART | |
|------------|--------------|------------|---------------|---|

**847-821-5405 • HandColoredArt.com**                        **HandColoredArt.com**

Here's a site with a peculiar niche: an entire selection of black-and-white photography enhanced with hand-painted colors. Most of these are only very subtly tinted, typically with pastels, resulting in a look made familiar by the movie *Pleasantville*. It's a little weird, sometimes kind of cool. What really makes it work is that some of the images are interesting regardless of color, ranging anywhere from stark landscapes to mid-performance classic rockers. On the flipside, some of these images would be abysmally boring were it not for the intriguing textures offered by just a touch of paint in the right spot ... yeah, it's an unusual art form, but worth a glance.

| ·PAINTINGS | ·PHOTOGRAPHY | | |
|------------|--------------|---|---|

# HeritageCoin.com

This is probably the easiest place to shop for collectible US coins and currency, if not the best place to find such items. See, while the site is thoroughly organized and exquisitely programmed, enough to easily handle a great selection, relatively speaking we didn't find a whole lot here, though this could change. That being said, they do have their fair share of in-demand items, so a serious collector with a mind for great finds shouldn't take this site lightly. Sometimes for sale, sometimes for auction and sometimes consisting of ancient coins from foreign cultures, this catalog is quietly one of the best.

·COLLECTIBLES

# HeritageComics.com

Comic books may be the most unlikely of the collectible ilk, but they are easily some of the best appreciated. Divided into ages (Platinum 1897–1937, Golden 1938–1955 and so on), this selection features some of the most coveted items from more than a century of publishing. From *Superman* original editions to the goofball antics of *Mad Magazine*, they've got a healthy selection of favorites as well as those merely with historical appeal (say, *Captain America*), cult faves (*Weird Tales*) and lesser-known oddities (anybody know who Airboy is?). Any drawbacks of this site may be summed up in one word: slow.

·BOOKS & MEDIA ·COLLECTIBLES

# iCollector.com

Most art retail sites on the web can't offer you the big stuff; sure, you can get a Picasso poster, print or even reproduction, but the real thing? Not so much. This site makes it possible—in its own, very complicated way. We strongly recommend you read the FAQ before getting started, but the gist of it is that you can gain electronic access to hundreds of dealers, galleries and auction houses and, more important, to a schedule of international auctions. Then you have the option to enter absentee bids on your most desired lots, or in some cases even engage in live bidding, real-time through your browser; here's hoping your connection speed can keep up with the action.

·PAINTINGS ·SKETCHES/NOTES | ·ANTIQUES ·COLLECTIBLES | ·PHOTOGRAPHY ·MASTER ARTISTS | ·SCULPTURE

# iTheo.com

Named for a van Gogh (not Vincent of course, but Theo, who apparently supported and promoted many artists of his day), this site also endorses a great variety of "emerging artists and their work." The best part would be the sort of fanciful way in which this is done, with creative categories like Urban Apartment, Nooks & Crannies and Under $300 doing well to complement typical organization techniques, and helpful search filters enabling you to veer away from anything you might not want to see. Not that there's much of that here....

·PAINTINGS ·EMERGING ART | ·PHOTOGRAPHY | ·SCULPTURE | ·SKETCHES/NOTES

**800-852-0076** • James T. McCusker, Inc.

**JamesMcCusker.com**

Any first-day cover collectors out there?  If not, you may be unaware that FDCs are canceled US stamps that have been postmarked on the same date they were initially released to the public, which usually takes place in one specific location, on a date relevant to the stamp (i.e., in a politician's hometown, on his/her birthday).  It's a singular hobby, to be sure, but these of course turn out to be a bit more rare than regular stamps, and as they are usually marked on special cards, or cachets, part of the fun is finding the same stamp on a different cachet. Pregnant women and those with heart conditions should maybe skip this ride.

| ·COLLECTIBLES | | | |  |
|---|---|---|---|---|

---

**800-846-8697** • Lilliput

**LilliputMotorCompany.com**

Featuring an array of "toys from the pre-digital era" these guys may just be onto something.  These are collectible, original-issue wind-up toys, miniatures, toy boats, electric trains, robots (non-working—remember this is "pre-digital"), ornaments, music boxes and toy soldiers.  Selections vary as much as the years of manufacture, and while browsing can be kind of a pain, the images and details are typically quite good, and some of the selections just plain hilarious. (A Space Cream Robot? Too funny.) For the big spenders, a handy One-of-a-Kind section truly delivers some gems.

| ·BOOKS & MEDIA | ·KITSCH | ·COLLECTIBLES | | |
|---|---|---|---|---|

---

**011-33-1-40-13-41-07** • The Louvre

**Louvre.fr**

There's really not a whole lot that this online representation of the world's most famous museum has to offer; certainly, it's a far, far cry from actually going there.  However, we'd be remiss to skip it, so now you know where to find it (the dot.fr might have slowed you down).  Once inside, you may of course find a poster of the *Mona Lisa,* as well as a smattering of the museum's other incredibly famous paintings, and some small replica sculptures as well (think *Venus de Milo*).  Otherwise, this is the standard museum gift shop fare, highlighted by some impressive coffee-table and postcard books.  *C'est tout.*

| ·SCULPTURE | ·BOOKS & MEDIA | ·MUSEUM SHOPS | ·POSTERS & PRINTS | |
|---|---|---|---|---|

---

**520-622-4968** • Magellan Traders

**MagellanTraders.com**

Behind the proclamation, "We Bring the World to You," what this site actually will deliver is "authentic, handmade functional and decorative art from Africa, New Guinea, the Orient and South America."  While origins vary, consistency may be found in the presentation of these crafts, with excellent photos and informative item descriptions, whether for a range of African masks, Mexican glassware or figurines from all over.  Particularly interesting is the variety of Nativity scenes, each imbued with the originating culture's interpretation and traditions.  How often can an e-commerce site claim to offer any anthropological relevance?

| ·ARTIFACTS | | | |
|---|---|---|---|

## MastersCollection.com

**The Masters' Collection • 800-222-6827**

Here's a spot to find "affordable reproductions of masterpieces," framed oil paintings copied from some of the most celebrated works of the last several hundred years. A lengthy list of artists includes Monet, Degas, Da Vinci and van Gogh, as well as some lesser-known names responsible for some not-so-lesser-known works (as well as a few that make you wonder). None of this stuff is terribly modern, mostly portraits and landscapes from the Romantic and Impressionist schools, but the price is right.

| ·PAINTINGS | | | |
|---|---|---|---|

## MetMuseum.org

**The Metropolitan Museum of Art • 800-662-3397**

This web site for the Metropolitan Museum of Art of New York City showcases 3,500 of its 2 million or so art pieces in a spectacular online format, with many of the works to be found in their equally impressive store. A long list of posters from artists like Manet, Monet, Kandinsky and Matisse actually represents the lower end of the spectrum. Framed prints and limited-edition reproductions of all manner of art, enough to make it almost daunting, can be easily purchased, for a price. Facsimile sketchbooks and portfolios of such renowned artists as Jackson Pollock are also available, if you get to them in time, as well as replica ornaments and jewelry covering both ends of the 5,000 years of culture represented in the museum.

| ·SCULPTURE | ·BOOKS & MEDIA | ·MUSEUM SHOPS | ·POSTERS & PRINTS |
|---|---|---|---|

## MixedGreens.com

**Mixed Greens • 212-331-8888**

"Get Smart. Buy Art," says this site's opening page. Cheeky? Yeah, a little, but in this case it's warranted, if only because they go the distance to present you with a truly intelligent selection. Simply follow the Art & Artists link and you will find a list of people you've probably never heard of. However, unlike most such lists, this one features pop-up samples of the artists' work when you roll over their names. Hence, you can get a glimpse of each one's personal style without having to click around endlessly. This makes browsing especially quick and easy, allowing you to actually find some amazing images in no time. If you were an artist, this is how you'd want it to be.

| ·PAINTINGS | ·PHOTOGRAPHY | ·SCULPTURE | ·EMERGING ART |
|---|---|---|---|

## MoMAStore.org

**Museum of Modern Art • 800-793-3167**

New York's Museum of Modern Art puts its gift shop online with a wide assortment of art-related goods. Posters include familiar works by Picasso, Dali, van Gogh and some ever-so-slightly lesser-known artists. If you're feeling more adventurous, a selection of accessories ranges from the sublime (a Bauhaus ashtray) to the absurd (a Frank Lloyd Wright tie). Best for broadening your artistic horizons, however, is the Books section, which features exhibition catalogs, MoMA collections, and assorted works compiled by artist, era or style, any of which are guaranteed to increase a coffee table's aesthetic appeal.

| ·BOOKS & MEDIA | ·MUSEUM SHOPS | ·POSTERS & PRINTS | |
|---|---|---|---|

**866-279-2403 • Movie Goods**        **MovieGoods.com**

Film buffs may ultimately prefer good movies, but for the purposes of home and office decoration, this, "the single largest online movie poster art product inventory anywhere," proves particularly satisfying.  Aside from new and recent releases, these guys offer a healthy selection of vintage posters, either in reproductions/replica, or occasionally original, form.  Browsing is a lot easier if you have particular films in mind, though the categorical separation of movies by genre, actor, director or year should get you closer to what you like.

| ·KITSCH | ·MEMORABILIA | ·POSTERS & PRINTS | |
|---------|--------------|-------------------|---|

**877-305-7201 • MuseumCompany.com**        **MuseumCompany.com**

You don't typically expect the words "Museum" and "Company" to be seen together.  Likewise, you don't typically expect van Gogh's celebrated painting, *Starry Night,* to show up on a cutting board.  And yet, here we are.  See, this site specializes in selling great artwork that has been incorporated into everyday items.  Hence, Frank Lloyd Wright coasters, Monet-infused umbrellas, and M.C. Escher ties.  For our purposes here, though, we would point you to their collection of reproductions, most notably in the Sculpture section, which features the contemporary, classic and ancient works of many cultures from around the planet.

| ·SCULPTURE | ·BOOKS & MEDIA | ·MUSEUM SHOPS | ·POSTERS & PRINTS | |
|------------|----------------|--------------|-------------------|---|

**888-914-5050 • NextMonet.com**        **NextMonet.com**

We usually buy art in response to a visceral reaction we have upon viewing it.  This means that for an online art retailer, in particular, determining which art is visible to the consumer is extremely important.  That is why this site turns out to be one of the best dealers of original art online, regardless of the quality of its selection.  Here, you may browse the catalog by artistic Subject, Style, Price, Artist and Medium, with search filters that can account for the item's color and/or physical dimensions on top of everything else.  Probably nowhere else is art so thoroughly categorized for our viewing ease.  Oh yeah, the selection? It's outstanding.

| ·PAINTINGS | ·PHOTOGRAPHY | ·SCULPTURE | ·EMERGING ART | |
|------------|--------------|------------|---------------|---|

**800-697-9350 • National Gallery of Art**        **NGA.gov**

You'd hardly expect a dot-gov site to offer much in the way of … well, anything really.  But this site represents the National Gallery of Art in Washington, DC.  Look in the Gallery Shop and you will find an assortment of posters and reproductions based on the museum's permanent collections, plus a few that are simply known to sell.  Otherwise, it's your typical gift shop fare here, with plenty of stationery and coffee mugs to make the art history books look extra-classy.  Check here to see your art-loving tax dollars at work.

| ·SCULPTURE | ·BOOKS & MEDIA | ·MUSEUM SHOPS | ·POSTERS & PRINTS | |
|------------|----------------|--------------|-------------------|---|

## NightOwlBooks.com

**Night Owl Books • 703-590-2966**

As of this writing, this site offered not a single book for sale. This may have changed, but undoubtedly they still have to offer what we found: cult and vintage movie posters. That's right, if you're in the hunt for posters advertising such memorable cinema as *The Brain That Wouldn't Die, Glory Stompers!* or *How To Stuff a Wild Bikini*, here's where you look. They have special sections for Elvis Presley movies, Martial Arts films, Westerns and Blaxploitation flicks, as well as a general Cult section, in which the titles are bound to be obscure even to cult fans.

| ·KITSCH | ·POSTERS & PRINTS | | |
|---|---|---|---|

## Novica.com

**Novica • 877-266-8422**

The best way to fill your home with the exotic trinkets and art pieces of foreign cultures has always been to travel the world extensively, picking your wares from meek and often hard-to-reach markets and bazaars, smuggling items through customs and then fabricating a story full of peril and intrigue to explain their origins. Here is a way to find such hard-to-get merchandise without having to catch up on your vaccinations first. Novica offers artifacts from every corner of the globe, complete with stories about their significance and discussions with the individuals who handcrafted them. An excellent site making excellent use of the internet, weary world travelers may now set their bags aside and focus upon the true purpose of tourism: tanning.

| ·PAINTINGS | ·ARTIFACTS | ·SCULPTURE | ·COLLECTIBLES |
|---|---|---|---|

## ObeyGiant.com

**Obey Giant • No Service Number**

To some of you, this will be the answer to a great mystery—specifically, "What is up with all those Giant posters?" Graphic designer Shephard Fairey has done something unique in marketing an image that has no commercial value (other than his own self-promotion, perhaps), and making it recognizable in metropolitan areas worldwide. The image in question is a likeness of the rather large, French pro wrestler Andre the Giant (deceased), usually with the word "Giant," or alternately, "Obey" printed beneath it. Stickers and posters bearing this image (available here) show up in the damnedest places, posted by fans on blank walls, the backs of billboards and anywhere else that might attract your gaze.

| ·BOOKS & MEDIA | ·KITSCH | ·POSTERS & PRINTS | |
|---|---|---|---|

## OnlineSports.com

**OnlineSports.com • 800-856-2638**

This site may just offer the widest price range discrepancy ever seen in the online sale of basketballs. See, you can buy a ball here for a measly five bucks. Or you can buy one autographed by Michael Jordan, and suddenly the price shoots up to nearly $2000. That's how it goes in the world of sports memorabilia, and Jordaniana, or basketball collectibles for that matter, is just the tip of this site's enormous iceberg. You can browse this stuff by sport, team, item (ranging from trading cards to jerseys, autographed or otherwise) or by specific athlete. And it's not limited to pro teams sports, either, but includes items pertaining to all sorts of racing, women's sports, college and amateur competitions. How huge a fan are ya?

| ·COLLECTIBLES | ·MEMORABILIA | | |
|---|---|---|---|

**212-504-8151 • PaintingsDirect.com**

## PaintingsDirect.com

You generally don't want to gather 500 artists under the same roof (for a host of reasons), but on the internet it proves nothing less than beneficial. Here, artists from 40 different countries offer their work for sale. While it's a fine opportunity for them to gain exposure and bring their pieces to market, it's also a great way for the rest of us to find original art at decent prices in support of artists that might otherwise escape notice. The site layout contributes to the notion that you can find a winner here, allowing searches by subject (landscapes or portraits, for example), style (abstract, impressionist and so forth), or technique (oils, pastels, sculpture, photograph, etc.).

| ·PAINTINGS | ·EMERGING ART | | |
|---|---|---|---|

**877-212-5879 • PicassoMio**

## PicassoMio.com

This site's "juried selection of thousands of one-of-a-kind and limited-edition artworks … is sourced from over a thousand artists and art dealers, across Europe, Americas and worldwide." This gives them bragging rights to a snootiness their competitors just can't match. What's more is that it may be justified, as this selection of contemporary pieces doesn't just fill a web site but is oftentimes even exciting. Excellent browsing and searching capabilities are icing on the cake.

| ·SCULPTURE | ·PAINTINGS | ·PHOTOGRAPHY | ·EMERGING ART |
|---|---|---|---|

**888-515-2327 • House Pop-Culture Artifacts**

## PopHouse.com

Boasting "Pop Culture Artifacts" and "Hard to Find Cool Stuff," this kitschy retailer has a mad and hilarious assortment of both timeless and dated materials, depending on your point of view. With merchandise ranging in subject from the Smurfs to Ronald Reagan, with a dab of Schoolhouse Rock in between, you can be sure that these lunchboxes, trading cards, dolls and salt & pepper shakers will have you shaking your head and/or clicking furiously at the Add to Cart button. In search of a Peter Frampton belt buckle? Look no further.

| ·ARTIFACTS | ·KITSCH | ·COLLECTIBLES | |
|---|---|---|---|

**No Service Number • PosterShop.com**

## PosterShop.com

If you're looking to decorate your space with those indelible images of pop culture that can only be adequately captured within the confines of everybody's favorite tack-up, the poster, this site will probably have what you want. Celebrity images abound, whether in movie posters, athletic action shots, in the midst of a musical performance or striking those promotional poses that best capture their pearly whites. A great quantity of art posters, from ancient to modern works, can also be easily found, if you so desire. But their selection's not limited to paper. Artist prints are also sold here, as well as a few reproductions on silk, T-shirts and even mouse pads.

| ·POSTERS & PRINTS | | | |
|---|---|---|---|

# PrintSellers.com

PrintSellers.com • 800-669-7843

Ever wonder where old maps go when they become obsolete? This may be the place. Now, these maps go just a little farther back than the days when Myanmar was still known as Burma, or the Republic of Congo, Zaire. No, these maps date as far back as the 16th century, and only as recently as the 19th. Hence, their charms lie in the fact that they are generally wrong, wrong, wrong (and not just in the shapes and scales; some, for example, show California to be an island—isn't it, though?). While these are infinitely fascinating and beautiful, bear in mind that they are actually mere reproductions of the original inaccurate maps, which, presumably in the hands of seafaring explorers, no doubt ended up on the bottom of the ocean somewhere.

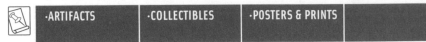

| ·ARTIFACTS | ·COLLECTIBLES | ·POSTERS & PRINTS | |
|---|---|---|---|

# RoslynHerman.com

Roslyn Herman & Co. • 718-846-3496

Offering "Authentic Celebrity Apparel," which means that all of this stuff was at one time owned by somebody famous, this site's wares include certificates of authenticity to prove it. Thus you may find items like Charlie Chaplin's cufflinks, Cary Grant's wallet, a fur worn by Bette Davis and one of Joan Crawford's pillboxes (no wire hangers, though). Consisting mostly of jewelry and other fashion accessories, you may find cause to question many of these legends' sense of style, but then, in many cases that's exactly why these items are intriguing to begin with.

| ·MEMORABILIA | | | |
|---|---|---|---|

# RubyLane.com

Ruby Lane • 415-864-4563

Ruby Lane serves as a virtual street where you can find a wide dispersement of unique fine art, crafts and antiques dealers, easily accessible through one site and commerce engine. Of course, things can get a little complicated and confusing, and to be frank, we're still not entirely sure how it's all organized, just that it generally works and you can definitely buy stuff here. Not only that, but some of these things are great finds, to boot. If you do manage to find your way to something great, and manage to buy it, let us know.

| ·ANTIQUES ·COLLECTIBLES | ·ARTIFACTS | ·KITSCH | ·MEMORABILIA |
|---|---|---|---|

# ShagMart.com

ShagMart • 949-764-0068

Here's another site that doesn't offer the huge selection we've come to expect from art shops. Actually, this features just one artist, who goes by the name of Shag, and at any given time most of his scant few selections are sold out. But that only goes to show the appeal of his designs, which look like a somewhat demented (it would have to be) blend of cubism and Looney Tunes. While perhaps not appropriate for all environments, these will certainly attract notice and appreciation from even casual viewers. Get it if you can.

| ·KITSCH | ·POSTERS & PRINTS | ·BOOKS & MEDIA | |
|---|---|---|---|

**No Service Number • Stamp Finder**

**StampFinder.com**

You must really be devoted to philately to put yourself through this one, or at least know what it is. That's because this site operates exclusively for the stamp collector, whether a collection is strictly domestic or includes postage from all over the planet. The irony of some of these stamps is that they don't cover current postal rates, and wouldn't get a letter to its destination, but here they sell for sometimes exponentially more than the cost to send a first-class flat. A complicated and thorough search feature holds this site together, but as it turns out, photos are miserably lacking. Know what you're here for going in, or put it off.

·COLLECTIBLES

**800-424-4240 • Steuben**

**Steuben.com**

Having spent nearly 100 years "at the forefront of glass design," it's little surprise that Steuben offers a variety of exquisite creations, whether sculpted from molten crystal or cut from cooled glass. They have beautiful bowls, vases, candleholders and hand coolers (holdovers from the 17th/18th centuries), plus a list of miscellaneous products ranging from paperweights to clocks. These dazzling wares prove ironic: who'd have thought one could spend so much time looking at something you can actually see through?

·COLLECTIBLES

**877-771-6848 • Streamlined**

**Streamlined-Prints.com**

Here's a site that invites you to "take a journey back in time … to an era of style, elegance and imagination." If you're not insulted by the implication that contemporary times somehow lack these positive traits, then you're likely to be dazzled by this selection of "Early 20th Century Art Prints." Mostly prewar (World War II) images, mainly advertising airline, ocean and rail travel, the binding forces here are classic and art deco trends in design, meaning a lot of clean lines and geometric shapes. Are these emblematic of classier days gone by, or reminiscent portents of an advertising age to come…?

·KITSCH | ·POSTERS & PRINTS

**800-699-6836 • Heirloom European Tapestries**

**Tapestries-Inc.com**

Operating out of northern California, this company imports fine hanging tapestries from Belgium, France and Italy and distributes them, along with free hanging rods. Most of the tapestries constitute reproductions of classic palace and museum pieces that date back as far as the 12th century, ranging from hanky-size to massive. Knights, hunting dogs, and women with flowers ornament many of these hand-woven lengths of cloth, and special sections instruct you in how best to care for and display such regal fineries. If you're not entirely convinced by the richly colored images that greet you in their Gallery, they'll offer you interest-free installment plans and a 30-day money-back guarantee.

·ARTIFACTS

## TheAfricaStore.com

The Africa Store • No Service Number

This site has about as much to teach you as to sell you about "the tradition, beauty and heart of Africa." Along with the plethora of carvings, statues, paintings, masks and other sundry traditional items one might naturally expect to find in such a store, is delivered a wealth of succinct information not only about various African nations, but also in regard to specific African tribes, from the Ashanti of Ghana to the Zulus of South Africa. While this site is a far cry from making you an expert, it may at least provide you with an appropriate response to offer guests who will inevitably ask about these objects.

| ·ARTIFACTS | | | |
|---|---|---|---|

## TheOrigins.com

The Origins • 800-978-4776

If modern art leaves you weary, you might consider checking out a site like this, which devotes its resources to "preserving cultural heritage around the world." Everything they sell has either "been created through artistic traditions handed down for generations," or replicates cultural benchmarks. The varied selection covers different continents and countries, and includes things like pottery, sculpture, baskets, masks and even weapons. An inspiring mix of craftsmanship and early technologies, it takes us back to a moment long since past, when we could conceivably imbue a sense of being into the tools we use in life (aside from changing the colors in your windows display). Well worth a visit.

| ·ARTIFACTS | ·COLLECTIBLES | | |
|---|---|---|---|

## TIAS.com

TIAS.com • 888-653-7883

This site houses an enormous conglomeration of shops from all over the western hemisphere, each offering its own, unique selection of antiques and collectibles. The result is an original and extensive, although very convoluted, design. The only real problem is that while all stores reside on the TIAS server, you can only purchase from them one by one. So, if you want to buy a Kiss lunchbox and a vintage doorknob all at once, you're out of luck. If, on the other hand, you're open to buying trinkets from these shops, one at a time, a massive search engine makes it ultimately worthwhile.

| ·ANTIQUES | ·ARTIFACTS | ·KITSCH | ·COLLECTIBLES |
|---|---|---|---|

## UrsusBooks.com

UrsusBooks.com • 212-627-5370

Here's a rare books dealer with a specialty: art. You can find a wealth of tomes devoted to artistic movements, cultural artifacts, gardens and architecture. Rather, you can if you look in the right place. The more obvious links to browsing will do nothing for you here, as you must use the search feature to find what you want. At the time we viewed the site at least, the best way to scour their unusual selection was to follow the Search link (as opposed to the search box), and then find the View by Categories button. This will get you started; after that, what you already know about the art itself will come into play.

| ·BOOKS & MEDIA | | | |
|---|---|---|---|

## 800-872-6468 • The United States Mint

### USMint.gov

Interested in buying some money? Why not go straight to the source? Here you may find commemorative coins, first-edition coins, uncut currency and plenty of money-related memorabilia such as coin jewelry, collector's spoons and our favorite, the Mixed Quarters Bag (you never know what you're going to get!). In typical government fashion, they manage to charge you more than the actual money is worth as legal tender, but many of us will be surprised to find that the site is well designed, attractive to view and actually quite efficient.

| ·COLLECTIBLES | | | | |
|---|---|---|---|---|

## 888-242-6633 • Vintage Vending

### VintageVending.com

Offering "the coolest retro gifts for you and anyone else," most of the stuff for sale on this site would fit in to the general décor of a Fifties diner. With classic jukeboxes, tiki bars, neon clocks and old-time candy vending machines, this is as much for preservationists as it is for collectors (if there's a difference). Of course, we advocate visiting any store with a section titled Cool Stuff, and this one's no different. It could be done better, but then, if it were too slick it would lose some of its charm. Check this one out even if you're only reading this by accident.

| ·COLLECTIBLES | ·KITSCH | ·MEMORABILIA | |
|---|---|---|---|

## 877-492-7465 • The Warhol Store

### WarholStore.com

One can only wonder where the brain of Andy Warhol might have taken us with the advent of the internet; perhaps he would have sold us cash at a discount (plus shipping and handling, of course). At the very least, this store can sell us some of the stuff he incurred upon the happy world he delighted in provoking. Here, it's mostly posters and photographs, alongside some bizarre films he made and some Warhol-themed stuff that he surely would have wholeheartedly endorsed. In a strange universe, this man made a strange mark. Here, this mark resides in a digital format.

| ·BOOKS & MEDIA ·POSTERS & PRINTS | ·MUSEUM SHOPS | ·KITSCH | ·MASTER ARTISTS |
|---|---|---|---|

## 800-987-2926 • Yoko Trading

### Yokodana.com

When we think of antiquing, the conjured image is usually of long drives through the New England countryside to find quaint, cluttered shops run by white-haired, eccentric locals. This is only because a Sunday drive to Japan is out of the question. Fortunately, this shop offers an incredible wealth of prewar Japanese items, ranging from bamboo umbrellas to decorative prints, with a lot of amazing vintage kimonos and fabrics in between. The great drawback is that you have to manually enter catalog numbers into the order form; assuming you can find it. If all else fails, go to the Site Map, then click on Order Form and finally Secure SSL Ordering. It's a hassle, but worth it.

| ·ARTIFACTS | | | |
|---|---|---|---|

NOTES:

_____

_____

_____

_____

_____

_____

_____

_____

_____

_____

_____

_____

_____

_____

_____

_____

_____

_____

_____

# Entertainment

It's all about how we fill our free time (not that we have a lot). In this section, we've assembled some of the better places to find those modern-day masterpieces that inspire us to dance, stir up our imaginations or simply motivate us to sit on the sofa for another few hours at a time, staring at the TV screen. Or if you prefer to be entertained outside of the home, some of these sites offer movie, game and show tickets. The best part is that many of these stores sell a little bit of everything, so you can keep shipping costs low and your absorption of culture high.

**Music**   Current estimates indicate that two hours of music is recorded for every hour that goes by in a day, making it official: you cannot possibly hear it all. Therefore, you may want to take advantage of our listings of specialty retailers that offer unerring knowledge and devotion to specific genres.

**Books** - Books don't just make you look smart, they entertain you for hours and hours. All the top web booksellers are represented here, as well as a few independents we think do it just as well or better.

**Movies** - Many of the DVD and video retailers we've listed here offer great databases that make it easy to cross-reference your favorite directors, actors, screenwriters and genres.

**Games** – Board games, puzzles and cards have kept people out of trouble for ages. And none of these ever packed the punch of a videogame. Whether you're skilled with your brains or with your thumbs, find your poison in this section.

NOTES:

_____

_____

_____

_____

_____

_____

_____

_____

_____

_____

_____

_____

_____

_____

_____

_____

_____

_____

_____

TIPS ON BUYING ENTERTAINMENT ONLINE

These suggestions may help prevent boredom and disappointment.

•**BUYING TICKETS:** Events tickets will often be easier to purchase online than anywhere else (it's often the only way to avoid endless voicemail menus).  However, keep an eye out for the excessive add-on fees sometimes charged for this service, and be sure to take note whether the tickets will be mailed to you or made available at the Will-Call Window (usually, you will have a choice).

•**BUYING MUSIC:** In most cases the internet makes it possible to actually listen to a piece of music *before* you buy it.  This is all but essential these days, as there's a lot of bad music out there.  If you can't listen to an album on one site, you may want to look around—chances are, you can sample the music elsewhere.

•**BUYING MOVIES:** Seeing as you can rent a movie for a fraction of the cost, it rarely makes sense to purchase a film you haven't seen yet.  If you decide to, take advantage of the consumer review areas posted on many sites, and try to view a trailer and/or clips from the movie as well, just so you know what you're getting into.  Additionally, some DVD editions offer additional special features, so you may want to see all that are available and at what prices before committing to one edition or another.

•**BUYING USED AUDIO & VIDEO:** It's often possible to find used copies of the CD, DVD, record, VHS or cassette you wish to purchase.  Sometimes, it's the only way to find rare and out-of-print stuff.  Make sure the site offers a guarantee that the item will play before you buy.

 SITES THAT MAY COME IN HANDY

The following URLs may be useful when you shop.

Information on Music Artists, including Biographies and Samples: http://www.UBL.com

Information on Videogames:  http://www.gamespot.com

Information on Films, Television Shows, Casts and Crews:  http://www.imdb.com

Books Research & Reference:  http://www.libraryspot.com

Restaurant Reservations:  http://www.opentable.com

Local Club, Event and Restaurant Guides:  http://www.citysearch.com

Local Movie Listings & Times:  http://www.moviefone.com

Movie Trailers, Past & Present:  http://www.trailersworld.com

Theater and Performing Arts Guide:  http://www.culturefinder.com

## >> SECTION ICON LEGEND

Use the following guide to understand the rectangular icons that appear throughout this section.

### BOOKS

By and large, books still consist of pages bound between a cardboard cover, but here we include comic books, magazines, audio books and downloadable eBooks in addition to traditionally formatted works of fiction and nonfiction.

### MUSIC

The mediums of music have changed almost as often as the styles, and recently added to the list of vinyl, 8-track, cassette, CD and DAT formats is downloadable MP3. Finding an 8-track cassette, on the other hand, may prove difficult.

### MOVIES

As with music, home movie formats have changed over the years, and here we find a smattering of them all. Not just DVD and VHS; occasionally in these sites you'll come across Video Disc and Beta cassettes. You won't just find films, either, but also television shows, professional sports, performing arts and other recorded events.

### GAMES

Games of chance, games of skill and games that let you put your brain on hold for hours at a time; if it can be played this icon will indicate it's for sale in one of these shops. Board games, videogames and puzzles merely scratch the surface.

## LIST OF KEY WORDS

The following words represent the types of items typically found on the sites listed in this section.

### AUDIO BOOKS

Audio books on cassette have given way to CDs, and are now available for MP3 download. Many of our sites offer books in an audio format in one way or another.

### BOARD GAMES

For one-on-one or designed for a party, a bevy of board games are available these days. From Chess and Monopoly to Trivial Pursuit and Boggle, this ever-expanding selection turns dice, wheels, cards and hourglasses into hours of fun.

### COMICS

Not just made to inspire motion pictures, Comic Books and Graphic Novels exist for collecting and investing, but primarily to please the reader. Editions old and new are for sale from a variety of online sellers.

### KARAOKE

Singing along to your favorite tunes is fun, but when you remove the original vocalist from the mix, the spotlight's on you. These catalogs of Karaoke CDs and CDGs cover contemporary tunes and pop classics.

### MAGAZINES

Sure, if you order from a clearinghouse you may increase your chances at winning the multimillion-dollar prize, but magazine subscriptions are quite easy and cheap to order online, for yourself or as a gift. Check these sites for all major titles.

### RARE

We cover a lot of stores that specialize in hard-to-find books, movies or music, whether the items are first edition, autographed, limited edition or simply out-of-print. Look for this key word to locate sites with rare titles and editions.

### RENTALS

At first, the idea of renting a video or audio book online and waiting for it to find you through the mail seems inefficient. But when you take away late fees and include postage-paid return envelopes, you'll see that these sites have found ingenious ways to make online renting easier and better than any other type.

### TICKETS

Whether you're seeking admission to a sporting event, concert, play or movie, you can now order tickets online as soon as they're available, and can usually get a good look at seating charts.

### USED

Entertainment fans on a budget can easily find used video, audio, videogames and books for sale from a variety of stores. Sites denoted by this key word offer used versions, and usually guarantee that they work.

### VIDEOGAMES

Videogames aren't just for kids; children just happen to play them better than the rest of us. The sites listed with this key word usually sell games across platforms, for home consoles or handhelds.

### VINYL

Many vinyl fetishists will tell you that records still beat CDs for a high-fidelity sound, and many collectors simply don't care. Whether you're a DJ or just old school, look for this key word to find vinyl retailers.

# >> KEY WORD INDEX

Use the following lists to locate online retailers that sell the Entertainment you seek.

## AUDIO BOOKS

1BookStreet.com
A1Books.com
AbeBooks.com
Amazon.com
Audible.com
AudioEditions.com
BarnesAndNoble.com
BooksAMillion.com
BooksOnTape.com
CommonReader.com
Powells.com
RecordedBooks.com

## BOARD GAMES

4APuzzle.com
Amazon.com
AreYouGame.com
BitsAndPieces.com
BoardGames.com
CheapAss.com
CompletelyPuzzled.com
PuzzleHouse.com
RecRooms.com
Spilsbury.com
YesAsia.com

## BOOKS

1BookStreet.com
A1Books.com
AbeBooks.com
Alibris.com
Amazon.com
BarnesAndNoble.com
BookPool.com
BooksAMillion.com
BookSoup.com
CCVideo.com
CommonReader.com
eCampus.com

eFollett.com
ElephantBooks.com
GEMM.com
HamiltonBook.com
HeritageComics.com
MedBookStore.com
NetLibrary.com
PBS.org
Powells.com
ScriptCity.com
UrsusBooks.com
VarsityBooks.com
VintageLibrary.com
WordsWorth.com
YesAsia.com

## COMICS

GEMM.com
HeritageComics.com
Powells.com
VintageLibrary.com
YesAsia.com

## KARAOKE

ColonyMusic.com
KaraokeWH.com
YesAsia.com

## MAGAZINES

Amazon.com
BooksAMillion.com
HeritageComics.com
MagazineOutlet.com
Magazines.com
VintageLibrary.com
YesAsia.com

## MOVIES

ActionSportsVideos.com
Amazon.com
AnimeDVDStore.com
BarnesAndNoble.com
Biography.com
Blockbuster.com
CafeDVD.com
CCVideo.com
CDUniverse.com
DVDPlanet.com
Fandango.com
GEMM.com
MoviesUnlimited.com
MovieTickets.com
NetFlix.com
PBS.org
TowerRecords.com
YesAsia.com

## MUSIC

Amazon.com
ArtistDirect.com
BarnesAndNoble.com
Biograph.com
BlueNote.com
BopShop.com
BreakbeatScience.com
CalabashMusic.com
CaravanMusic.com
CCMusic.com
CDUniverse.com
Cheap-CDs.com
CountryOnly.com
Descarga.com
Djangos.com
DustyGroove.com
eMusic.com
GEMM.com
HipHopSite.com
InterPunk.com

MiddlePillar.com
MosaicRecords.com
MP3.com
MusicSpace.com
OtherMusic.com
PastPerfect.com
PBS.org
RecordRunnerUSA.com
ReggaeCD.com
Rhino.com
SatelliteRecords.com
TowerRecords.com
VenerableMusic.com
YesAsia.com

## RARE

AbeBooks.com
Alibris.com
BooksAMillion.com
BookSoup.com
BopShop.com
CalabashMusic.com
CaravanMusic.com
Djangos.com
DustyGroove.com
ElephantBooks.com
GEMM.com
HeritageComics.com
InterPunk.com
MiddlePillar.com
MoviesUnlimited.com
OtherMusic.com
PastPerfect.com
Powells.com
RecordRunnerUSA.com
ReggaeCD.com
Rhino.com
SatelliteRecords.com
TowerRecords.com
UrsusBooks.com
VenerableMusic.com
VintageLibrary.com

## RENTALS

BooksOnTape.com
CafeDVD.com
NetFlix.com
RecordedBooks.com
RedOctane.com

## TICKETS

Fandango.com
MovieTickets.com
MurraysTickets.com
StubHub.com
TicketMaster.com
TicketWeb.com

## USED

AbeBooks.com
Blockbuster.com
BooksOnTape.com
BopShop.com
CafeDVD.com
Djangos.com
EBGames.com
eCampus.com
eFollett.com
ElephantBooks.com
GameStop.com
GEMM.com
Powells.com
RedOctane.com
TowerRecords.com
VarsityBooks.com

## VIDEOGAMES

Amazon.com
BitsAndPieces.com
Blockbuster.com
CDUniverse.com
CheapAss.com
CompletelyPuzzled.com
EBGames.com
GameStop.com
GoGamer.com
RedOctane.com
YesAsia.com

## VINYL

BlueNote.com
BopShop.com
BreakbeatScience.com
CalabashMusic.com
CCMusic.com
Djangos.com
DustyGroove.com
GEMM.com
HipHopSite.com
InterPunk.com
MiddlePillar.com
MosaicRecords.com
OtherMusic.com
RecordRunnerUSA.com
SatelliteRecords.com
TowerRecords.com

# 1BookStreet.com

This mail-order catalog turned web seller (sadly, they have no actual Book Street address) initially specialized in mysteries and romance novels, as well as a more general listing of bargain books. They've since expanded, with special sections for kids and cooks, but they actually now boast more than three dozen sections with such particular interests as Idiot Guides, Irreverent Travel and Large Print. They also offer audio books and a few errant video titles, but generally the printed word, in all conceivable forms, reigns here, and although you won't find every imaginable text, sometimes a little less choice can be a good thing.

| | ·BOOKS | ·AUDIO BOOKS | | |

# 4APuzzle.com

Imagine your face, carved into hundreds of tiny interlocking pieces, scattered across a tabletop in no discernable order. Okay, that sounds grim, but bear in mind we're talking about taking the images your family holds dear and transferring them onto a custom-made, wood-carved puzzle. Ordering these personalized puzzles can be quite complicated, and you may need to email the guy who makes them for a little assistance (yes, it's one man with a band saw), but most likely you can handle the entire procedure online and he'll do the rest.

| | ·BOARD GAMES | | |

# A1Books.com

With over 700,000 titles, it's a pretty sure bet that you'll find the book you're looking for here. Now where it can get confusing is that you'll often come across multiple editions of the same book. For example, a search for *Tom Sawyer* yielded several dozen results, including paperbacks, hardbacks, audio books and special editions. This sounds fine at the outset, but the detail offered is scant, so you can't necessarily tell what the differences are between selections. Of course, when in doubt, you can be assured that the more cheaply priced options should include every written page. At least, we hope so.

| | ·BOOKS | ·AUDIO BOOKS | | |

# AbeBooks.com

This site offers "millions of used, rare, second-hand and out-of-print books ... at your fingertips." Actually, in this case "at your fingertips" refers mostly to the literal fact that you access the site with a keyboard and mouse. Despite the presence of a Browse button, sifting through this site is an awful task, which should be reserved for only the most deservedly wicked. Basically, don't show up hoping you'll stumble across something great; you really have to have an idea or two of what you want from the outset. If you do, this place is almost guaranteed to satisfy the literary connoisseur.

| | ·BOOKS | ·AUDIO BOOKS | ·RARE | ·USED |

## 800-992-7442 • ActionSportsVideos.com

**ActionSportsVideos.com**

The action sports referred to here are those that aren't often represented on your major sports networks, instructional or otherwise. While surfing, skiing and even motocross occasionally find themselves on the tube, rarer are wakeboarding, snowboarding, skateboarding and BMX biking, and almost never seen are snowmobiling, rock climbing, inline skating and base jumping. To use the parlance of our times, these videos depict extreme action sports to the max. After all, how many sports video stores can you find that feature "bone crushing slam" sections?

| ·MOVIES | | | | |
|---|---|---|---|---|

## 877-254-2747 • Alibris

**Alibris.com**

We'll get to the actual selection maintained by this retailer of "books you thought you'd never find" in a moment. However, our favorite thing about this site is the Glossary of Book Terms. This comprehensive list of words defines for the neophyte such terms as Armorial Binding, Buckram, Deckle Edges and Yapp (ten bucks says you have to go to the site to see what all of these are). Getting to it, though, this knowledge becomes imperative to understanding this collector-oriented shop. Though it tends to operate kind of slow online, this store proves itself to be more than just a fancy dictionary.

| ·BOOKS | ·RARE | | | |
|---|---|---|---|---|

## 800-201-7575 • Amazon.com

**Amazon.com**

The first name in internet retail has come a long way from its origins as strictly a bookseller. Its expansion started, logically, with music and videos, but has gone on to plenty else. But it's a continued mastery of entertainment media that keeps us coming back. Here you may listen to music samples, read book samples and read customer reviews of just about anything. There are plenty of reasons these guys are number one, and you probably don't want to read about them here. Suffice to say, if for some strange reason you've never visited, check it out.

| ·BOOKS<br>·AUDIO BOOKS | ·MOVIES<br>·VIDEOGAMES | ·BOARD GAMES<br>·MAGAZINES | ·MUSIC | |
|---|---|---|---|---|

## No Service Number • AnimeDVDStore.com

**AnimeDVDStore.com**

Anime devotees won't care what we have to say about this culturally pervasive cartoon art form native to Japan, so we'll direct all comments to those who're at best only dimly aware of the genre famous for its large-eyed characters and explosive animation. Basically, as much anime is geared towards adults as for children, featuring sophisticated plots and three-dimensional characters. Serials and TV shows somehow manage to combine everyday life with fantasy, with features decidedly more epic. Long since a cult phenomenon in the US, anime's influence on American mainstream culture is evident in children's programs like *Dragonball Z* and *Ugemon,* and the box office successes of *Princess Mononoke* and the Oscar-winning *Spirited Away.*

| ·MOVIES | | | | |
|---|---|---|---|---|

# AreYouGame.com

This "largest game and puzzle store on the planet" has such a large selection that it not only includes all the standby favorites, but even sells stuff that nobody likes. Categories like Brain Teasers, Magic, and Dinosaurs make it easy to find great stuff for kids, or even fun-minded adults. If you're looking for games that are educational, no problem, but there's also plenty that require almost no brain cells at all. More or less, though, it's all about passing time in entertaining and social ways, without resorting to the word "video."

 ·BOARD GAMES

# ArtistDirect.com

If you're the type of fan who likes to delve into the backgrounds of your favorite pop artists, discuss their comings and goings with other fans and get a hold of rare and special editions of their music or merchandise, this may just be your next bookmark. There're rare recordings, picture discs, tour dates, listening rooms, exclusive downloads, links to informative web sites and a community of press agents who will try to turn you on to other acts by pretending to be other fans. Of course, there are other fans out there as well, and occasionally the musicians themselves, who check in just long enough to touch base with the people before gliding back to their giant castles hidden deep in some majestic hills.

 ·MUSIC

# Audible.com

Here you'll find a healthy selection of audio books ready for download. Now, these aren't books on cassette or CD, the distinction being that you can only listen to these over your computer, or on a portable electronic device that works with your computer (like an MP3 player, handheld, etc.). If you don't have such a device, you may find them here, available with a discount should you opt to sign up for a monthly subscription. Otherwise, simply browse the titles (which include speeches, interviews and short radio-type pieces as well as books) and listen away.

 ·AUDIO BOOKS

# AudioEditions.com

For your listening pleasure, this will prove the place most likely to possess that audio book title you've been looking for. Rather, as books on cassette and/or CD are this retailer's specialty, it'll be easier to find it here than most other online shops (or brick-and-mortar stores for that matter). Follow the Browse link and you'll see a list of very distinctive categories (they even distinguish between UFOs and UFOs/Paranormal). Another convenient section, Audio Samples, might get you hooked on a few titles you weren't expecting. Just remember, actually reading is still rewarding.

 ·AUDIO BOOKS

## 877-275-2626 • Barnes & Noble

### BarnesAndNoble.com

In fact, you've probably already purchased a book from one of the retail locations they have posted in your local shopping malls, or open-air promenades. Don't think so? Well, they also own Doubleday's, Scribner's, BookStop, Book Star, and B Dalton bookstores, so chances are you've enjoyed their services under one name or another. Essentially anything you'll find in any of them can be purchased here, online. Not only that, but they've expanded their selection to include music, video/DVD and videogrames, as well as college textbooks, eBooks and lengthy articles that may be downloaded for a fee. All without exposing yourself to a food court.

| ·BOOKS | ·MUSIC | ·MOVIES | ·AUDIO BOOKS |
|--------|--------|---------|--------------|

## No Service Number • Biograph

### Biograph.com

This music catalog was founded in 1967 "to preserve music that has its roots in America—Jazz, Ragtime and Blues." Adding Folk and music originating in New Orleans to the roster, this preservation is accomplished by highlighting roots classics and promoting new artists who relish and expand upon them. Presently a little small by music store standards, this selection reaps the benefits with great organization and thorough detail. You may view liner notes, listen to audio samples and search by Artist, Song Title or even Instrument. This is some good work.

| ·MUSIC | | | |
|--------|--|--|--|

## No Service Number • Biography Channel

### Biography.com

If you're a fan of cable television's Arts & Entertainment Network or The History Channel, you're already familiar with the documentaries, docudramas and dramatizations that regularly air on these channels, A&E's Biography chief among them. Here, in the Shop section you may find them on video and DVD. Virtually every notable person (politician, artist, celebrity), event (historical moments, cultural events, mysteries) and civilization imaginable has been or will be eventually covered by this vast array of programming, which usually entertains as much as educates. More important than a Marx Brothers film, less dreary than a Marx Manifesto, this is television at its best.

| ·MOVIES | | | |
|---------|--|--|--|

## 800-884-2637 • Bits and Pieces

### BitsAndPieces.com

Here's a fun site that's whole-heartedly devoted to ... well, fun. The chief components: puzzles and games, puzzles mostly. Sorted by the number of bits and pieces (Under 1000, 1000, and 1500 Pieces and Up), this selection even includes Novelty Jigsaws and Jigsaw Accessories (these won't help you assemble it, but will enable you to preserve the finished product). A section devoted to Brainteasers will put your mind in a twist, but the real goods may be found in the Online Games area, which features Flash-based games that will positively kill your workday.

| ·BOARD GAMES | ·VIDEOGAMES | | |
|--------------|-------------|--|--|

## Blockbuster.com

We're pretty sure you know pretty much all there is to know about this renter/retailer of videos, DVDs and videogames (of all platforms), but it's interesting to know where the word "blockbuster" came from. Obviously, this store is so named in reference to a movie that dominates all box offices and is viewed by nearly all moviegoers, earning loads of money in the bargain. But that word initially came about during World War II to describe bombs that were actually powerful enough to bust, or destroy, entire city blocks. Interesting, huh?

| | ·MOVIES | ·USED | ·VIDEOGAMES | |
|---|---|---|---|---|

## BlueNote.com

Blue Note is that classic jazz record label that once played home to legends like Miles Davis, John Coltrane and Cannonball Adderly. Lest you think them past their prime (they do still offer some of the best jazz albums of all time), they've kept at it through contemporary times, adding to their roster some of the more exciting and talented artists of today. Whether it's legend in his own time Herbie Hancock; heir apparent Charlie Hunter; dynamic trio Modeski, Martin & Wood; the rhythmically infused St. Germain or much-celebrated vocalist Norah Jones, Blue Note keeps its legacy afloat with some excellent music.

| | ·MUSIC | ·VINYL | | |
|---|---|---|---|---|

## BoardGames.com

Surely, this will be the easiest-to-remember place to buy games online, but how does it stand up to our whimsical scrutiny? Well, if it's any indication, there's an entire section here devoted to Monopoly in all its variant forms (including the *X-Men* edition, the *Wizard of Oz* edition and the *Simpsons* edition). As if that weren't enough, there are sections devoted to Party Games and to Adult Games, not to mention Brainteasers, Mindbenders & More. When in doubt, go to the index, where just about all the games you can think of (including several more *Simpsons*-themed) may be found alphabetically.

| | ·BOARD GAMES | | | |
|---|---|---|---|---|

## BookPool.com

The exciting focus of this retailer is "Discount Technical Books." To be fair, it's better that these books have a discount than not, right? Besides, as dull as categories like Databases, Programming Languages, Distributed Computing or Graphics & Multimedia might make these books sound, imagine how confusing a world without them might be. Particularly useful here are consumer reviews, which tend to be less subjective than those reviewing fiction. In this case it's a matter of whether the book served its function as an instructional manual or guide. Besides, the reviews may prove more interesting reading than the books themselves.

| | ·BOOKS | | | |
|---|---|---|---|---|

## 800-201-3550 • Books-A-Million
### BooksAMillion.com

With an established chain or two of brick-and-mortar booksellers, this online entity claims to be the third largest bookstore in the nation. All we know for sure is that they sell a great variety of fiction and nonfiction, with magazines, eBooks and books on tape to boot. You can even join their free Book Preview club, wherein you'll be emailed chapters of selected works so you can actually get started reading before you decide to buy (read, get hooked). Best is their Millionaire's Club: for a trifling annual fee you get additional discounts to what are already some of the lowest prices on the web. Then, we may just be high on finding a "Millionaire's Club" that will accept us as members.

| ·BOOKS | ·MAGAZINES | ·AUDIO BOOKS | ·RARE | |
|--------|------------|--------------|-------|--|

## 800-521-7925 • Books On Tape
### BooksOnTape.com

If you have a bigger appetite than budget for audio books, check out this site that offers them in CD, MP3 and cassette tape formats, not only for sale but for rent as well. Buy new or used tapes for great prices, or simply rent them for thirty days before sending them back in the postage-paid return sleeve. While their unabridged selection isn't particularly easy to browse, searches by title, author and even reader (if you have a favorite) should suffice, and the occasional audio sample may illuminate something worthwhile, or at least good enough to rent.

| ·AUDIO BOOKS | ·USED | ·RENTALS | | |
|--------------|-------|----------|--|--|

## 800-764-2665 • Book Soup
### BookSoup.com

Billing itself as "a 'must see' on any tour of LA," this "bookseller to the great and infamous" does cater to regular folk as well as superstars. While it specializes in the sort of cultural tomes apropos to its Hollywood home, stuff like art, drama, music and film, its general selection should suit most needs, and the Signed Books section alone offers a fairly wide variety of popular titles. For more ignominious selections, just head straight for the Visit Our Online Store Now!! link from the home page.

| ·BOOKS | ·RARE | | | |
|--------|-------|--|--|--|

## 585-271-3354 • BopShop.com
### BopShop.com

This independent seller of records stakes a place online direct from Rochester, NY, promising "10,000 choice albums [of] luxurious black vinyl." Featuring loads of used, hard-to-find and out-of-print stuff, they prove particularly focused on "Blues, Jazz and American Roots Music styles like Soul, Rockabilly, Surf Rock & Doo-Wop," with some English and domestic folk to give it all a rounded edge. It sounds like a lot just describing it. Never a bad stop for the vinyl fetishist.

| ·MUSIC | ·VINYL | ·RARE | ·USED | |
|--------|--------|-------|-------|--|

## BreakbeatScience.com

Breakbeat Science • 212-995-2592

Drum n' Bass, aka Jungle, is arguably the most markedly innovative form of music to come about since Hip Hop achieved international popularity in the 1980s—and Breakbeat Science is the best place to find it online. In just more than a decade, Jungle's dance-driven compositions of erratic beats and floor-shaking bass lines have spawned a whole array of sub-genres and legions of fans around the globe, and this store's been dishing it proper all the while. You'll find the best-available selection of tracks on vinyl or CD, presented to you by some of NYC's top DJs.

| | ·MUSIC | ·VINYL | | |
|---|---|---|---|---|

## CafeDVD.com

CafeDVD.com • No Service Number

What makes this source of new & used, rented or sold DVDs worth mentioning isn't its overwhelming selection or shockingly low prices. Here it's all about the product presentation. Featuring various browsing lists, you can find titles here by perusing the oeuvres of Foreign Directors, various Film Festival Selections and either Top DVD Titles by Genre or Decade. Sure, they sell just about as many lousy DVDs as other sites, but use this site to its full potential and you can be relatively assured of finding decent popular and/or critical successes without having to look too hard.

| | ·MOVIES | ·RENTALS | ·USED | |
|---|---|---|---|---|

## CalabashMusic.com

Calabash Music • No Service Number

It would seem that the term "World Music" would be a pretty all-encompassing notion. But, as there is more than half a world of music out there that goes largely ignored by western markets, it's come to signify the natively produced work of different countries and cultures from typically overlooked sections of the globe. Aside from a rousing international community and various musical resources, this shop touches upon some great gospel, blues, folk and jazz recordings, as well as an incredibly deep World Music catalog. You can browse by different geographic region to find hundreds of titles in, for example, Indian music, several different Middle Eastern styles and many choices from the expanses of Africa and Asia.

| | ·MUSIC | ·VINYL | ·RARE | |
|---|---|---|---|---|

## CaravanMusic.com

Caravan Music • 210-525-9562

Whether you're hooked on merengue, mariachi, mambo, cumbia, rumba, samba, salsa or bossanova, your favorite Latin music is well represented on this colorful but clunky specialty site. You can browse their selection of New Titles, Recommended Titles, New & Recommended Titles (presumably to save time) and Essential Titles to find some of the freshest and inspiring Latin music from points international. Or, if you're looking for something a little more specific, the Alternative Search lets you search by specific style or country of origin. Unfortunately, after that, you're pretty much on your own, as the catalog offers little in terms of detail and forces you to manually enter the names and catalog numbers of those things you wish to order. *¡Que lástima!*

| | ·MUSIC | ·RARE | | |
|---|---|---|---|---|

## 800-993-6344 • Collector's Choice Music

**CCMusic.com**

As with its Critic's Choice Video sister site, this one offers its fair share of new and popular titles, but it will direct your focus more toward its collection of vintage and classics. It does, after all, devote entire sections to Dean Martin and The Beatles, as well as featuring Old Radio Shows, Comedy and Big Band. It's ultimately a decent place to find CDs and LPs, but will be most truly appreciated by those wishing to avoid the virtual planet's over-saturation with images of pop mini-divas and boy bands.

| ·MUSIC | ·VINYL | | |  |

## 800-993-6357 • Critic's Choice Video

**CCVideo.com**

Boasting "over 50,000 films ... from the newest releases to the most obscure cult classics," the whole "critic's choice" distinction kind of just flies out the window. To be fair, though, this site began as a mail-order catalog back in 1987, when the world wide web could only have evoked the image of some giant alien spider come to conquer the planet... but we digress. Today, Critic's Choice includes a load of books with their films, and several standard ways to browse for each; though surely with such a giant catalog, a search will get you checked out much faster.

| ·MOVIES | ·BOOKS | | |  |

## 800-231-7937 • CD Universe

**CDUniverse.com**

Technically misnamed, as there are plenty of movies and videogames here as well as CDs, these guys do tend to keep their focus on disc formats. The layout is generally unimaginative, the selection typical and occasionally a link will falter, requiring you to hit the Reload button of your browser. On the bright side, they offer a lot of audio samples and an easy-to-use alternative to the similarly priced media mega-sellers out there that will inevitably do something to lose your business.

| ·MUSIC | ·MOVIES | ·VIDEOGAMES | |  |

## No Service Number • Cheap-CDs.com

**Cheap-CDs.com**

Okay, so you know what you want and you want it for cheap, and you don't want to waste any time wading through the glitz and glamour of some online superstore to find it. Well, then, this no-frills website is for you. Simply enter an artist, album, or song into the search engine, and it responds with an entry that includes a track listing (often with audio samples), informative links, and artists with the same fan-base. A low handling fee consists of the site's only profit over wholesale prices, while a flat shipping rate on orders of 3 or more entices you to buy in bulk. If you want to pay for pretty, go somewhere else; this e-merchant only deals in fast, cheap and ugly.

| ·MUSIC | | | | |

## CheapAss.com
**Cheap Ass Games • 206-526-1096**

Not just a hilarious name, Cheap Ass Games will tell you they are "aware of two basic facts about games: they cost too much, and they are at some level all the same." In other words, if you take away the manufacturing costs of interchangeable items like game pieces, fake money and dice, most board games could be made and sold for less money. Thus, they offer the basic elements of all games in a cheap ass kit, following with an ever-growing collection of unique (and alarmingly fun) games that require a minimal investment for only the pieces that you don't already have. Some games even ask you to scrounge the deep recesses of your home for parts, and some "are even free!" Now that's pretty cheap.

| ·BOARD GAMES | ·VIDEOGAMES | | |
|---|---|---|---|

## ColonyMusic.com
**Colony Music • 212-265-2050**

Nothing says wild party better than karaoke, and what's wilder to sing along to than showtunes? Well, here is the spot where these two avant-garde musical formats come together into one happy-go-lucky retailer. Buy either the original cast recordings of your favorite Broadway musicals, or try your hand at a variety of popular favorites across genres with nothing but a microphone, a musical soundtrack and your ability to read and sing simultaneously. Practically everything you need is here; just add liquor.

| ·KARAOKE | | | |
|---|---|---|---|

## CommonReader.com
**A Common Reader • 800-832-7323**

Initially a monthly catalog featuring new books, articles and reviews, the Common Reader has evolved online to become a somewhat editorial bookseller. See, they don't offer every book that gets published (they haven't a single Stephen King title, for example). Instead, they offer books that their staff deems valuable or important for a more erudite crowd, whether newly published or out of print and requiring resuscitation by the Common Reader press. Ironically, the books you'll find here through various means of recommendation or categorization aren't common reads at all, but they may be good ones, nonetheless.

| ·BOOKS | ·AUDIO BOOKS | | |
|---|---|---|---|

## CompletelyPuzzled.com
**Completely Puzzled • 888-750-2209**

For the kind of adult fun that doesn't know the meaning of the word "erotic," this site offers some classic games and puzzles that may usually be referred to without fear of trademark infringement. Which isn't to say that these chess and backgammon sets aren't backed up by more contemporary fare like How to Host a Murder and Travel Games. Brain teasers, magic tricks, CD-ROMs and 3-D puzzles also bolster this catalog that might bore a child, but should entertain a fun-loving grown-up.

| ·BOARD GAMES | ·VIDEOGAMES | | |
|---|---|---|---|

**No Service Number • Country Only**

**CountryOnly.com**

Where can you find more than 700 country & western musicians all in one place? It's not Nashville, or even Branson, Missouri. It's Delaware. More precisely, it's this Delaware-based retailer that provides an exhaustive collection of country CDs and cassettes. From legends like Johnny Cash, Merle Haggard and George Jones to new favorites like Faith Hill, Shania Twain and the Dixie Chicks, it's easy to find the artists you desire via a highly functional search feature. Just a warning, though, you won't find a whole lot of information about each album here, so if you're not sure what you want, you might have better luck at a bigger, fancier online retailer. If you're a country music enthusiast, however, this site is really all you need.

| ·MUSIC | | | | |
|--------|--|--|--|--|

**800-377-2647 • Descarga.com**

**Descarga.com**

This one's not a great site, but it sure is a great niche retailer, specializing in "Tropical Afro-Latin" music. After all, how can you fault such an upbeat, multicultural selection of music that stems from one island paradise or another? You simply can't. There are various search options available from this store (whose name means "discharge"), but if you don't have a particular artist or song in mind, the most fun can be had browsing in sections like Cumbia Vallenato, Merengue Bachata and Latin Soul Boogaloo.

| ·MUSIC | | | | |
|--------|--|--|--|--|

**503-241-6584 • Djangos**

**Djangos.com**

Named for outstanding gypsy jazz guitarist Django Reinhardt, this store knows its jazz. In fact, it seems to know a lot about every type of music. Every entry you find will lead you to a list of new and used titles available, both on CD and vinyl, along with audio samples, artist bios and links to related artists, similar albums, roots and influences. It's a lot, but not in a burdensome way; these guys have more information to impart than just about anyone, and yet manage to arrange the gamut of musical teachings with more ease and convenience than a bookmobile. Where else, for example, can you find an extensive collection of Zydeco resources without need of a Cajun translation guide?

| ·MUSIC | ·VINYL | ·RARE | ·USED |
|--------|--------|-------|-------|

**888-387-8947 • Dusty Groove America**

**DustyGroove.com**

If you live in Chicago, it must be quite convenient to stop into this multifaceted music dealer to satisfy your eclectic tastes before stepping out for some deep-dish pizza. The rest of us have to settle for this regularly updated site that, while not spectacular, makes the store's spectacular catalog available. Whether trying to track down the Now Sound (vintage and contemporary lounge and exotica), the Out Sound (experimental 20th century recordings) or any number of international styles from French Pop to an array of Central and South American rhythms, getting lucky is fairly common here. But the real dish is in their jazz, soul and funk selection, which can keep you browsing for hours—and it only gets deeper every week.

| ·MUSIC | ·VINYL | ·RARE |
|--------|--------|-------|

## DVDPlanet.com

DVD Planet • 800-624-3078

This site leaves us with one burning question: who is Ken Crane? Apparently, he's the guy who started the store, in brick-and-mortar form, at some unspecified time, in some unspecified place. At any rate, Ken Crane's DVD Planet, as it is called, offers VHS and the elusive Laserdisc in addition to the newest media formats, and the selection is rather extensive. Fortunately, the Power Search feature offers a lot of different filters by which to narrow your options, including some pertaining to special features and MPAA ratings, handy these days as some DVD releases offer differently rated editions.

·MOVIES

## EBGames.com

EB Games • 877-432-9675

"EB" stands for "Electronics Boutique," which is kind of a funny thing to imagine. However, this site isn't that funny; it's actually quite serious about videogames. Its passion is such that it's contagious, and we suddenly find ourselves derelict for not having the highest speed processor, top-end video card or latest, greatest gaming console platform. Then there are the special controllers, expansion packs and other obliquely necessary accessories, which up until moments ago seemed overindulgent. And let us not forget the games; games for Sega, Sony, Nintendo, Mac and PC, each of which hold the promise that fun may be returned to our suddenly dreary lives.

·VIDEOGAMES     ·USED

## eCampus.com

eCampus.com • 888-388-9909

Built to be a college bookstore online, these guys have surely captured the true purpose of most campus booksellers: selling college-brand merchandise. They seem to have misplaced their focus on selling textbooks, but if you have a reading list to work with you should be able to find most of the required titles. Otherwise, backpacks, baseball caps and sweatshirts featuring all of your favorite major university logos and mascots abound, threatening to distract any course of study with allegiance to the alma mater.

·BOOKS     ·USED

## eFollett.com

eFollett.com • 800-381-5151

Staking its claim as "The Official Online Bookstore of over 1,000 college and university campuses nationwide," this site makes it easy to see just why. Particularly impressive is the ability to seek out your exact course's reading list, made available on one page, with the option to choose between new and used titles (when available). This way you can skip both the distractions and long chattering lines of a campus bookstore to focus on more important things, like staying in and browsing the internet. Well, anyway, now there's a choice.

·BOOKS     ·USED

**No Service Number • ElephantBooks.com**   **ElephantBooks.com**

These guys claim to be "your primary source of out-of-print, rare, and used books." Of course, almost by definition such hard-to-find titles tend to require checking various sources, or they'd be easy to find. As it turns out, though, between the thousands of signed books, hundreds of categories of Rare Books (43 under Literature alone, including Fables, Correspondences, Essays and Chinese Lit) and loads of first editions, this site does turn out to be a great place to start, and quite possibly end, your hunt.

| ·BOOKS | ·RARE | ·USED | |
|---|---|---|---|

**858-623-7021 • eMusic**   **eMusic.com**

MP3, we're told, is the musical format of the future—fast, immediate and cheap—a music revolution. Well, eMusic certainly thinks so, making available hundreds of thousands of albums and individual tracks, providing the instant gratification of having high-quality digital music as quick as your computer can download it. Whether they're new hits, old favorites, exclusive live tracks or relatively unknown, they all go for about a dollar each, with royalties going to the musicians and publishers (unlike certain other popular MP3 services of the past). If you're planning to come by often, though, it makes sense to start a subscription.

| ·MUSIC | | | | |
|---|---|---|---|---|

**866-857-5191 • Fandango**   **Fandango.com**

Going to a movie theater, parking and waiting in line for tickets is fine—unless you get to the front of the line only to find that the show you're looking to see is sold out. Instead of settling for your second choice or waiting two hours for the next show time, you can now buy tickets ahead of time online through this growing retailer that, in some cases, allows you to print out tickets at home (otherwise you'll have to go to the Will Call window). Unfortunately, at this writing most theaters don't participate, meaning your favorite neighborhood movie house may still require you to purchase tickets the old-fashioned way.

| ·MOVIES | ·TICKETS | | |
|---|---|---|---|

**817-424-2200 • GameStop.com**   **GameStop.com**

Hardcore gamers generally have their own ideas about where the best places to find games are. Of course, this usually means the closest place with the shortest lines. If, however, you'd care to venture online to research game titles, this place should do you right. Between new and used games across a variety of platforms, you'll find in these pages plenty of detail, good screen captures and customer reviews that you can take or leave. It's all so quick and easy, just how a videogame junky likes it.

| ·VIDEOGAMES | ·USED | | |
|---|---|---|---|

## GEMM.com

Chances are, if you type an incoherent jumble of letters and numbers into the address bar of your browser, you'll stumble onto an e-tailer that is prepared to sell you a copy of the latest teen pop CD, at a "discounted" price, of course. Fortunately for people with more complex cravings, there's the Global Electronic Music Marketplace, whose powerful search engine scours a worldwide collaboration of retailers, collectors, record labels, importers and artists, returning a satisfying list of results. Offering your desired item in different formats, different editions, new or used and at various prices, this is perfect for collectors, or anyone who's having trouble finding rare or out-of-print music.

| | | | ·BOOKS | ·MUSIC | ·MOVIES | ·COMICS |
|---|---|---|---|---|---|---|
| | | | ·VINYL | ·RARE | ·USED | |

## GoGamer.com

Keeping up with videogame advancements gets tougher each year. This site doesn't actually offer the hardware involved in home gaming consoles, but if a game is available they'll almost always have it. Sections are split between PC, Mac, X-Box, PlayStation2 and GameCube, with subsections devoted to Sport, Race, Shoot, Fight and Action games. Also, individual game titles, mostly popular and new releases, are listed in menu form. However, text descriptions featuring sales rhetoric aside, there's not a lot of information on these games available, such as screen shots or customer ratings, which makes it a better place to find a game you already know you must have.

| ·VIDEOGAMES | | | |
|---|---|---|---|

## HamiltonBook.com

This is not the book retailer to turn to if you want the hot new titles and bestsellers. It is, however, a good place to find really cheap books that other people don't necessarily want. See, most of these titles are what are known as Remainders, which means they're book editions that were either overprinted or undersold (depending on how you look at it). The good news is that you'll get great discounts on books you do want, which may mostly be those popular titles which the public has forgotten about or, if you're lucky, a decent title sold here because it got a little frayed on display in a bookstore. Because, hey, we know a book is still readable even if it's tattered.

| ·BOOKS | | | |
|---|---|---|---|

## HeritageComics.com

Comic books may be the most unlikely of the collectible ilk, but they are easlily some of the best appreciated. Divided into ages (Platinum 1879–1937, Golden 1938–1955 and so on), this selection features some of the most coveted items from more than a century of publishing. From *Superman* original editions to the goofball antics of *Mad Magazine,* they've got a healthy selection of favorites as well as those merely with historical appeal (say *Captain America*), cult faves (*Weird Tales*) and lesser-known oddities (anybody know who Airboy is?). Any drawbacks of this site may be summed up in one word: slow.

| ·BOOKS | ·COMICS | ·MAGAZINES | ·RARE |
|---|---|---|---|

## 702-933-2123 • Hip Hop Site

### HipHopSite.com

The Hip Hop Site is a cluttered magazine site, probably due to the incredibly thorough nature of its content. As it turns out, their Store is equally thorough, featuring a wide selection of contemporary and classic CDs, LPs and 12-inch vinyl, from both major and independent labels. You can learn a lot here about hip hop as it lunges into its third decade, reading some decent (if opinionated) articles and listening to occasional sound clips. A Search by Producer function can also prove very rewarding, as frequent collaborations between different artists and producers provide for some of the best music available. East Coast, West Coast, all quality hip hop has a voice here, because, as this site says, "It ain't where ya from, it's where ya @."

| ·MUSIC | ·VINYL | | |  |

## No Service Number • Interpunk

### InterPunk.com

Usually a product of the do-it-yourself philosophy, Punk Rock embraces amateurish production, simple song structure, and the emotive screeching of coarse voices in sweaty, low-slung bars. So how come this is the best genre-specific music store online? Distributing music from hundreds of indie labels across the globe (if you've never heard Brazilian punk, now's your chance), this vast and constantly growing catalog of punk, hardcore, emo and ska music offers great detail and audio samples for recordings in all formats. They even sell the hair dye, buttons, stickers, posters and 'zines that round out any punk scene, and clue you into the local sounds of any region; punk is not dead.

| ·MUSIC | ·VINYL | ·RARE | |  |

## 800-645-8401 • Karaoke Warehouse

### KaraokeWH.com

Welcome to the Karaoke Warehouse, a good source for bolstering your karaoke song library (or you can just go on singing "Stand By Your Man" for another ten years). Available in CDG (CD plus Graphics), Video CD and DVD formats, these tunes may be sought by the names of songs or artists, but in the world of karaoke it's all about the song packs, available in disc sets like the '70s Pack, the Country Pack and the slumber party fave Teen Pack. All you need then is the equipment, which they have here as well.

| ·KARAOKE | | | | |

## 800-884-3350 • MagazineOutlet.com

### MagazineOutlet.com

They will tell you they're, "the best magazine provider on the internet," but with so many out there, who can say for sure? They all tend to offer mostly the same selection (with a few differences), generally tend to be similar in price and never seem to make it too difficult on the user. If we were forced to point out the best, though, we would take note that this one offers you fourteen issues in a subscription instead of the typical twelve, and without any increase in price. Hey, for two extra issues, the word "best" is close enough.

| ·MAGAZINES | | | | |

## Magazines.com

Magazines.com • 800-929-2691

Another in a spate of magazine subscription retailers, what makes this one stand out (only barely) is that it's got a few more titles to choose from than most. At least, there are some here we aren't used to seeing elsewhere. Aside from that, this "Your Subscription Headquarters" offers nothing particularly special, save for a few incentives that may be found and browsed easily in the Special Values and Magazines with Free Gifts sections. Oh, that and their name is really easy to remember.

·MAGAZINES

## MedBookStore.com

MedBookStore.com • 800-554-1325

From Acupuncture to Urology, this specialty book retailer offers texts on everything known to the medical universe about the health and treatment of human beings (and occasionally animals, to be found in the Veterinary section, of course). Many of these books will prove to be way over your head if you are not a medical professional (or if you're not a particularly good one), but there are plenty of books that should be beneficial to the layman, most of which probably fall under the Alternative Medicine section.

·BOOKS

## MiddlePillar.com

Middle Pillar Distribution • 888-763-2323

Life might be nice if all music was imbued with the bouncy and colorful glee of a Burt Bacharach tune; then again, such a world might drive people to wear all black and take a keen interest in death. Then they might start shopping at this store, which specializes in gothic, dark and industrial music. You can browse the entire catalog alphabetically, check out new releases or just head straight to the New World Serpent section for rare and limited-edition items. This is for those with fringe aesthetics to say the least, but hey, somebody's got to keep a balance against the piping insincerity of elevator music.

·MUSIC    ·VINYL    ·RARE

## MosaicRecords.com

Mosaic Records • 203-327-7111

Mosaic Records is all about Jazz. This selection is limited to boxed collections of some of the great jazz musicians and composers of all time, including Miles Davis, Duke Ellington, Charlie Parker and Django Reinhardt. Of course, these guys are easy to find anywhere. Better is that this site can turn you on to some of the great lesser-knowns who may be revered in jazz circles, but have fallen short of mainstream radar. Thanks to audio samples and some great bios, this site is an essential visit for budding jazz enthusiasts.

·MUSIC    ·VINYL

## 800-668-4344 • MoviesUnlimited.com

### MoviesUnlimited.com

Movies Unlimited may not be the perfect video retailer, but it's an absolutely devoted one. Its deep catalog offers some very handy browsing techniques, pertinent to each category. For example: in the Comedy section you can browse by subjects including Beach Films, Bill Murray and Police Academy (okay, so not all of them are entirely worthwhile). To add to the atmosphere, they offer a hilarity-inspiring collection of campy cult and B movies, complete with raucous plot summaries. Another helpful feature links you to all Academy Award winners (and nominees) by year, in case the B movies leave you wanting a little more substance (warning: you may not find this in some of the more recent Oscar picks).

## 888-440-8457 • MovieTickets.com

### MovieTickets.com

Built specifically with movie fanatics in mind, this site enables you to buy tickets (with a very small service charge) for premieres ahead of time to avoid long lines and sell-outs, and gives you all the information you might want about the film, including trailers, release dates, ratings, running times, cast lists and synopses. Simply enter your zip code, and a list of participating nearby theaters will turn up complete with showtimes and featured amenities (including wheelchair access, digital sound and stadium seating). Some even allow printable tickets, though most will be picked up at automated vendors at the theater. Good stuff for movie, film and cinema buffs alike.

## 858-623-7000 • MP3.com

### MP3.com

If you've grown disillusioned with major label music, it's maybe time to check out this forum where artists can receive international attention without ever coming close to signing a deal. These musicians are passionate about their creative work; you can tell because you haven't heard of anybody here. However, message boards, chat rooms and streaming radio may lead you to the next great talent of a generation for a quick digital download. Think of it as like crashing a party: you don't know anybody when you get there, but if you're lucky, by the time you leave maybe you've found somebody worth taking home.

## 800-542-4466 • Murray's Tickets & Tours

### MurraysTickets.com

When the search for tickets to that sold-out concert, play or sporting event becomes an act of desperation, there are a few things you can do. 1) Try to win tickets from your local radio station by being the 57th caller. 2) Engage in an all-out bidding war on eBay competing for the title of Ultimate Uberfan. 3) Go to the event with a wad of cash in pocket and present it to the shadiest character around in hopes he's a scalper. 4) Check out this site for very expensive but usually very desirable tickets available up to the last minute. Prices on 2) and 3) won't wind up being all that great, with the added concern of counterfeit tickets. Good luck with the radio station, but otherwise, this is your last, best bet.

# MusicSpace.com

MusicSpace.com • 800-581-4515

Here you'll find "the best hit collections ... as seen on TV!" That's right, here's the website you can visit to find all those music compilations made famous in the sort of television ads known to turn the phrases, "Wow! All those great songs in one collection!" "Wow, I love the [insert decade], how do I order?" and "All for one low, low price!" Appropriately split by decade and then by genre (like Monster Ballads or Easy Rock), you will know virtually all of these songs already, but they offer audio samples just in case. Pretty cheesy, but kinda fun in a nauseating sort of way.

# NetFlix.com

NetFlix.com • No Service Number

Forget everything you ever knew about renting movies; these guys do it better. Here's how it works: you devise a list of films (from "nearly every DVD ever published") on this site (a rather entertaining activity in itself). NetFlix will then send you the first three available titles from the list, to be viewed at your leisure. When you are done with a particular DVD, simply slide it into the provided postage-paid envelope and drop it into a mailbox. Once they've received it, you will be sent the next title from your list, and so on with each return, so that at any time you can have up to three discs at your disposal. Your end of the bargain is a regular (and modest) monthly membership charge. If you still doubt that ingenuity can exist on the web, check this one out.

# NetLibrary.com

Net Library • No Service Number

Where will you find the best prices on electronic books anywhere? Right here. Yes, Net Library has all the perks of the regular kind of library; it's free. With more than 3,500 Public Collection titles available, you simply need to register online and start downloading. Sure, you won't find a lot of new stuff, but nearly all the works of Shakespeare are available, and so are most of the other classics you'll remember not reading in high school (and a few they never bothered to mention). Browse these excellent cultural works online, or download them to print, depending on whether you'd rather save trees or prevent blindness.

# OtherMusic.com

Other Music • 212-477-8150

This online version of a decidedly hip New York City music store may be confusing at first, as the category names are weird and all seem to lead you nowhere. A little patience and exploration can prove quite valuable, though, and the About This Genre links will let you know just what may be found in categories named In, Out, Decadance, Groove and Psychadelia. All in all, it's definitely not the perfect musical shopping experience, but with this breadth of product, we feel the web would be lacking without it.

## 011-44-186-932-5052 • Past Perfect

### PastPerfect.com

Taking a somewhat altruistic approach to selling music, this series of collections from the '20s, '30s and '40s promises "Original Sound, Today's Clarity." Essentially, this is a project devoted to cleaning up and restoring to high quality the original recordings of some American classics. Using computers to remove hiss and scratches (with all attempts made to keep from altering the original sound quality), the results are clear renditions of the original artists and their work. The limited but fine collection should appeal to those with a love of Big Band, Jazz, Swing, Showtunes and even Humor from a nearly lost era.

| ·MUSIC | ·RARE | | |
|---|---|---|---|

## 877-727-7467 • PBS

### PBS.org

Even if you're not a big fan of public television, it's tough to deny the quality of PBS programming. Whether it's a documentary, news show or depiction of a cultural event, these programs usually favor substance over glitz and glamour. While this doesn't make them ratings leaders, they keep making the stuff anyway, due to its inherent worth to the American public. Featured here is nearly everything that you probably missed in original broadcast: all the Ken Burns documentaries, plenty of plays and musical performances, nature shows, educational kid's programming (as opposed to loud, grating, silly and fruitless cartoons) and financial shows, etc.

| ·BOOKS | ·MUSIC | ·MOVIES | |
|---|---|---|---|

## 800-291-9676 • Powell's City of Books

### Powells.com

How often does a bookshop become a tourist attraction? Located in downtown Portland, Oregon, Powell's fills four stories and an entire city block with books covering over 100 subject areas, plus rooms devoted to rare and out-of-print volumes, and a used section that just doesn't quit. Every day thousands of people pass through their doors, some to buy books, some to sell and some just to soak in coffee and atmosphere. Surely, Powell's has done the book thing properly in real life; but what about the web site? Let's just say that over a million books have never been so easily browsed. In fact, as the brick-and-mortar store stocks shelves to the ceiling, the ladder-free online experience may be easier, if not as fun.

| ·BOOKS ·RARE | ·AUDIO BOOKS | ·COMICS | ·USED |
|---|---|---|---|

## 877-924-6895 • PuzzleHouse.com

### PuzzleHouse.com

This site houses what may be the best niche puzzle retailer online. With "over 750 jigsaw puzzles" to choose from, you can probably fill a lifetime with this selection alone. Should you not have such time to devote to your puzzle merriment, they make it easy to track down the right sort of jigsaw for you, with eight different categories split by number of pieces (ranging from under 500 to over 6,000). Additionally, you will see sections devoted to Glow in the Dark puzzles, [MC] Escher Puzzles and Mystery Puzzles (wherein you won't know what the image is until you finish the puzzle), among others. Good stuff.

| ·BOARD GAMES | | | |
|---|---|---|---|

## RecordedBooks.com

RecordedBooks.com • 800-638-1304

The gist of recorded books is that people who don't like to read can still get some reading done. In this case, you can buy some fresh or used titles or, since you'll probably only listen to them once anyway, rent them. It's pretty simple, through and through, even though some of the sorting options don't always work. Really, it doesn't matter too much what you choose within each particular genre, as, on a long car trip, you tend not to care too much what you're listening to as long as it's something.

| | ·AUDIO BOOKS | ·RENTALS | | |
|---|---|---|---|---|

## RecordRunnerUSA.com

Record Runner • 212-255-4280

While this site makes no mention of any particular devotion to genre or era, there seems to be a rather large selection of 1980's pop—surprisingly large, actually. We imagine this might have been what one of the larger music retail sites might have looked like if they'd existed fifteen years ago. Available in CDs, and in 7", 10" or 12" vinyl, this selection will also keep you updated with what popular '80s artists are up to these days, or reacquaint you with the out-of-print picture discs that you were maybe too young to afford back in the day.

| | ·MUSIC | ·VINYL | ·RARE | |
|---|---|---|---|---|

## RecRooms.com

Rec Rooms Direct • 800-890-3010

Here you'll find for sale exactly what you'd expect to find in a rec room: games, big games. We're talking the kind of games you need to move furniture out of the way to make space for. From billiards, air hockey and foosball tables to convertible card tables, pretty much all of your general four-legged game furniture is covered. Then there are dartboards, jukeboxes and skeeball setups, without which no game room is complete. Just sprinkle some sawdust on the floor and you can have your very own dive bar.

| | ·BOARD GAMES | | | |
|---|---|---|---|---|

## RedOctane.com

Red Octane • 888-737-8038

Videogamers on a limited budget will really like this site, which offers game rentals for a monthly fee. Take out two games at a time, and keep them as long or short as you like before returning them in the postage-paid envelopes and then receive the next one in only a few days. Covering all major gaming platforms and keeping up-to-date with new releases, this is a great way to see if you like a game before buying it, and especially to play the sort of adventure game that you play for a few weeks, finish and then never play again. Good stuff.

| | ·VIDEOGAMES | ·USED | ·RENTALS | |
|---|---|---|---|---|

## 718-763-4685 • ReggaeCD.com

**ReggaeCD.com**

Reggae is right. These guys sell, you guessed it, CDs: a great big catalog of CDs for fans of the music Bob Marley showed to the world, and all of its variations. Reggae gospel, reggae jazz, and even reggae x-mas tunes find a place here, alongside dub, dancehall, ska and rock steady, just to name a few. You can even find a healthy dose of calypso and a good quantity of African music, if you keep your eye out. If they don't have what you seek, emailing a request will motivate them to track it down (they're diligent that way), and if they do have the goods to satisfy your Rastafarian hunger (which they likely will) some great bulk buys should be enough to keep you jammin' for a long, long time.

·MUSIC    ·RARE

## 800-432-0020 • Rhino

**Rhino.com**

It's odd to find a music retailer with a social mission (something about raising awareness and encouraging activism), but here it is, and it's not a bad store either. Its limited but eclectic selection highlights some truly intriguing recordings across most known genres, sectioned off into categories like Masters of the Old Soul (R&B, Funk, Disco and Hip Hop) and Smooth Sounds (Jazz and Lounge). With so much good stuff so close to the surface of these shopping pages, chances are everybody can find something they'll really like within minutes of logging on.

·MUSIC    ·RARE

## 866-318-9556 • Satellite

**SatelliteRecords.com**

If you've been to a dance club recently, you may have heard the DJ play a particular track that got everybody gleefully booty-shaking and bobbing their heads to the beat. You'd love to get a recording of this music so that you can recreate the experience in your living room. Only problem is that you have no idea who made the record, and of course you won't exactly hear it on the radio anytime soon. That's where Satellite Records comes in. Specializing in the House, Techno and Trance music that packs clubs all over the country, they offer more music than you'll ever be able to sift through, with a boasted 300 new titles every week.

·MUSIC    ·VINYL    ·RARE

## 800-676-2522 • Script City

**ScriptCity.com**

Somewhere between avid readers and film buffs resides the audience for this site, which sells the scripts of most popular movies and television shows. Their selection is remarkably extensive, including TV Miniseries, Treatments, Storyboards and Continuities (the more accurate postproduction scripts used by projectionists and subtitlers). In fact, as you sift through their alphabetical listings, you won't recognize many of the titles available between your favorites. Generally about $15 apiece, the one thing to watch for is that these are an absolute pain to order; only truly worthwhile for the dedicated fan.

·BOOKS    ·MOVIES

## Spilsbury.com

Spilsbury • 800-285-8619

Some stores strive to deliver the widest possible selection in their product range, stocking warehouses full of merchandise, featuring as many brands as possible, trying to cover all the bases. This is not one of those stores. Instead, what you'll find with this game and puzzle retailer is just about the oddest collection of such stuff anywhere. Between the Jumping and Screaming Cow, Virtual Reality Hunting (better than the real thing, at least so the deer say) and a backyard ice rink (freezing temperatures required), this site's smattering of products is great enough to ignore all other possibilities.

·BOARD GAMES

## StubHub.com

Stub Hub • 866-788-2482

Less a ticket seller than a ticket re-seller, this site takes advantage of peoples' occasional inability to attend events they've already purchased tickets for, by offering a marketplace to sell them at a (usually) fair price. Thus, sports team season ticket holders can recoup the cost of their seats on missed games and those with extra concert tickets can sell them to desperate fans. We're not sure what the distinction is between this and scalping, other than the inevitable middleman charge accrued by the web site, but this is a way to purchase tickets ahead of time, and without actually having to meet sketchy individuals face-to-face.

·TICKETS

## TicketMaster.com

Ticketmaster • 213-639-6100

Educating us all in the ways of charging order processing fees plus convenience charges for concert, theater and sporting event tickets is this ubiquitous virtual box office. While most of us will and do rail against the additional charges levied on already expensive event tickets, there's usually no other place to buy them, especially for fast-selling events wherein the actual venue box office can only sell a small fixed amount before Ticketmaster's automated system sells the rest. Ordering here is easier than by phone, as you will generally be able to read and click much faster than voice-mail menus operate. There's no use claiming that this will be a pleasant experience, however; supplication never is.

·TICKETS

## TicketWeb.com

Ticket Web • No Service Number

One of the only event ticket retailers out there, this would be the one that you'd have to consider the underdog (in the unlikely event that you would view such things in the context of a competitive free market). You will come across some less-than-enthralling events here, including some you might never have known about if browsing elsewhere, but this isn't to say there aren't some great finds. It's just a matter of taste, really, and the determination of different venues as to where their event tickets might be more marketable. We recommend checking this one out, if only for historical clarification.

·TICKETS

## 800-275-8693 • Tower Records

**TowerRecords.com**

With franchises in more than a dozen countries, as well as more than a hundred US locations, it's safe to say that the sun never sets on Tower Records' musical empire.  Not that it matters, as this site offers a better selection than you're likely to find in any of their brick-and-mortar stores, especially in the video/DVD section.  Back to the music though; you may be surprised to know that behind the global rock/pop veneer is a gigantic and thorough catalog of classical music recordings, so big in fact that it warrants its own, excellently organized section.  Nevertheless, the best reason to shop Tower is the spectacular assortment of popular recordings in every modern genre imaginable.

| ·MUSIC ·USED | ·MOVIES | ·VINYL | ·RARE |
|---|---|---|---|

## 212-627-5370 • UrsusBooks.com

**UrsusBooks.com**

Here's a rare books dealer with a specialty: art.  You can find a wealth of tomes devoted to artistic movements, cultural artifacts, gardens and architecture.  Rather, you can if you look in the right place.  The more obvious links to browsing will do nothing for you here, as you must use the Search feature to find what you want.  At the time we viewed the site at least, the best way to scour their unusual selection was to follow the Search link (as opposed to the search box), and then find the View by Categories button.  This will get you started; after that, what you already know about the art itself must come into play.

| ·BOOKS | ·RARE | | |
|---|---|---|---|

## 877-827-2665 • VarsityBooks.com

**VarsityBooks.com**

The books for sale here aren't too likely to show up on any bestseller lists, but they do offer something your typical book-of-the-month club titles don't: education, instruction and enlightenment.  These are your general academic texts, arranged by subj no, wait a second.  As much sense as it might make to arrange them by subject, they arrange these books by college, allowing you to select a region, and locate the applicable school from a lengthy list.  Then ... well, you don't get to browse, but must enter search terms.  We are forced to wonder what's the point of selecting a school, but then, presuming a college student is doing the searching here, he/she should be intelligent enough to handle it.

| ·BOOKS | ·USED | | |
|---|---|---|---|

## 770-207-6966 • Venerable Music

**VenerableMusic.com**

Once upon a time, and a very good time it was, recorded music was sold exclusively on records that were to be played at 78rpm. At speeds that fast, those old-time recordings didn't tend to last very long.  Fortunately, these guys are dedicated to the preservation of these pre-1960 recordings.  What?  You don't own a turntable that plays 78rpm?  Relax, these have been transferred to CD and cassette for posterity.  While you must browse by artist alphabetically, bluegrass, folk, gospel, blues and jazz styles are split into easier-to-view sections.  In particular, this is probably the best place to find the original big band, swing and bebop recordings that excited those youngsters of another era.

| ·MUSIC | ·RARE | | |
|---|---|---|---|

# VintageLibrary.com

This is not a slick site, neither is it glamorous, but then, neither is its subject matter. After all, this is a site devoted to pulp fiction. From hard-boiled detective fiction to weird tales, monster stories, fan zines, westerns and sci-fi, this retailer has a surprising abundance of tattered paperbacks and comics, many long since out of print, most having to do with the legendary and/or fantastic. Some of these titles seem like they should cost more than they do, some less, but all are off the beaten path, touting the gritty charms of the likes of Mickey Spillane, Zorro and Girls of the Slime God. Cool stuff.

| ·BOOKS | ·MAGAZINES | ·COMICS | ·RARE |
|---|---|---|---|

# WordsWorth.com

Lest you forget, this site will keep reminding you that Words Worth's, located in Cambridge, Massachusetts, is an independent bookseller. Indeed, this is an important distinction, as most retailers of books on the web pay homage to a centralized corporate authority of some sort or another. Something else they might brag about is that they offer nearly everything made that pertains to Curious George. What they won't likely mention is that their search feature is the only half-decent way to find their fiction and nonfiction as, aside from their own in-store bestseller list and a few recommendations, they don't offer much categorization for browsing. Still, not bad for a bookstore alone in the world.

| ·BOOKS | | | |
|---|---|---|---|

# YesAsia.com

This site covers a lot of entertainment media, from music and videos to books and even videogames. The one unifying factor? It's all of Asian origins. Specifically, these items hail from China, Korea and Japan, and may be viewed based on origin. Or you can browse stuff based on language, including Mandarin, Cantonese, Taiwanese and even English. Mostly, though, you can view categories as specific as Karaoke, Comics, Magazines and Anime. You'll never find most of this stuff in your local bookshop.

| ·BOOKS ·VIDEOGAMES | ·MUSIC ·MAGAZINES | ·BOARD GAMES ·COMICS | ·MOVIES ·KARAOKE |
|---|---|---|---|

# Epicurean

The best things in life may just be edible. This section focuses on those fine foods and spices that make the day-to-day task of living worth its while. Whether it's gourmet foodstuffs you're after, exquisite chocolate, international flavors, baked goods or strictly healthy fare, you can find easy purchase of these most sensual treats, usually for immediate delivery. You may also encounter some fantastic pre-prepared meals, alongside foods that suit special diets (kosher, for example) and freshly cut meats.

Of course, not everything we ingest fits under the term "sustenance," and so we've also included sellers of your favorite vices, like coffee, liquor and the occasional tobacco product (cigars and pipe tobacco, no cigarettes). These sites are set up to cater only to those old enough to legally purchase such products (be wary of crafty youngsters—the easiest of internet frauds takes place under your own roof), and restrictions make it tough for them to cater to every location. Still, for many of us these sites will provide access to higher-quality merchandise than we could geographically imagine.

Between fine wines and cheeses and other items not necessarily found in your local grocery store, we've tried to cover all bases here, and met with fair success (if we do say so ourselves). Thanks to the wonders of web commerce, we can feast on Russian caviar, Belgian truffles and authentic Cajun cuisine wherever we happen to live, and while sitting in front of our computers, at that (we won't mention all the snacks). We sought out the best, and have gained weight just looking at it all. If your mouth doesn't water just from reading some of these sites' descriptions, you may need to have your glands checked.

NOTES:

_____

_____

_____

_____

_____

_____

_____

_____

_____

_____

_____

_____

_____

_____

_____

_____

_____

_____

## TIPS ON BUYING FOOD & DRINK ONLINE

These suggestions may help prevent spoilage and other dissatisfactions.

•**NOTE DELIVERY TIME:** Most perishable items are delivered overnight in special packaging, and with good reason. Make sure somebody will be around to accept delivery, or you could return home to find some expensive food spoiling on your doorstep. [Note: some items, like chocolate, can melt during transit in the summer and require special considerations. Make sure the retailer knows this going in].

•**SPECIAL EVENTS & CATERING:** When ordering a lot of food for a big event, it is best to order well ahead of time. Most retailers are willing to send the stuff on a specified date, but it's a good idea to use ordering "Comments" boxes and customer service phone numbers to ensure punctual delivery.

•**FROZEN VS. FRESH:** When ordering meat & fish, make sure to note whether the product you're ordering is being delivered fresh or frozen.

•**FOOD ALLERGIES:** International food orders may include unlisted or differently named ingredients. If you suffer from food allergies, take precautions.

•**INSURING FINE WINES:** Simple rule: if it comes in a bottle, it can break during delivery. Make sure big investments are insured in transit.

## SITES THAT MAY COME IN HANDY

The following URLs may be useful when you shop.

FDA Food Safety Guidelines: http://www.foodsafety.gov

Nutrition & Food Guide Pyramid: http://www.nal.usda.gov/fnic/Fpyr/pyramid.html

Nutritional Analysis Tool: http://www.nat.uiuc.edu

Measurements Converter: http://onlineconverters.com/index.html

Cigar Friendly Establishments: http://www.cigarfriendly.com

Wine Guide: http://www.winespectator.com

## >> SECTION ICON LEGEND

Use the following guide to understand the rectangular icons that appear throughout this section.

### ALCOHOL
Fairly self-explanatory, most of the sites that offer alcohol focus on wine, but a few of the international grocery stores offer beers worthy of note, and the general hard liquor supply is punctuated by some fine whiskies.

### GOURMET
We use this icon to cover a wide range of high-quality foods, from chocolates to fungi, including in-fused oils, caviar, exotic meats, cheeses, wines, coffees and all manner of ingredients.

### PRE-PREPARED
These dishes don't necessarily arrive at your doorstep ready-to-eat, but they do require only a minimal effort, usually the application of a little heat. Selections include appetizers, gourmet meals, Chicago pizza and full clam bake kits.

### TOBACCO
Smokes come in many forms, but here we're strictly dealing in cigars and pipe tobacco, and the appropriate accessories.

# >> LIST OF KEY WORDS

The following words represent the types of items typically found on the sites listed in this section.

## APPETIZERS

Hosting a party, preparing a multicourse family meal or secretly eating a plate of finger food alone in your apartment; appetizers and hors d'oeuvres are here.

## BAKERY

You'll miss the smell of fresh baking, but get the bread, pies, cakes, pastries and cookies from these sites.

## CONDIMENTS

Sauces, dressings, gravies, relishes, garnishes, jams or spreads; whatever form they take, if they enhance your meal and/or come in a jar, they get labeled with this key word.

## GROCERY

The basic staples of your standard diet, generally anything that might come in a can gets the Grocery label.

## HOT DRINKS

Either coffee or tea, you'll find beans, grounds, teabags or loose tea at sites marked in this fashion.

## MEAT & FISH

If it's the flesh of an animal you seek, look for this indicator that the store sells beef, lamb, venison, pork, chicken, turkey, game foul, shellfish and any other land or seafood.

## OILS & SPICES

Rich, subtle or just plain hot, these can improve the flavor of whatever you're cooking, if not mask it completely.

## ORGANIC

The FDA occasionally updates the defining qualities, but generally, organic food is culled from a farm that uses tried-and-true methods in preference to chemicals.

## RECIPES

Some sites offer recipes for regional fare or favored cuisines; others offer entire cookbooks.

## REGIONAL

Many of our sites specialize in food and drink from a specific country, culture or geographic location. Whether foreign lands are the subject of the shop or particular parts of this nation, this is how you'll recognize them.

## SNACKS

Chips, crackers, nuts and dozens of other between-meal snacks show up in many of our shops. Whether healthy or junk food, we went ahead and listed this word next to them.

## SPECIAL DIETS

Dietary constraints catered to by these stores include food items suitable for the following diets: kosher, sugar-free, vegan, vegetarian and low fat.

## SPIRITS

Take them neat, on the rocks or in a variety of mixed combinations; these drinks include gin, rum, tequila, vodka and whisky, among others. Just for fun, we also included beer in this group.

## SWEETS

Whether candy, confections, cake or breath mints, if it's something you have to control a child's access to, it's probably sweet and fits into this group.

## WINES

Whether or not you take notice of things like vintage or appellation, wines exist on the web in great variety of price and taste. Find them here.

## >> KEY WORD INDEX

Use the following lists to locate online retailers that sell the Epicurean items you seek.

### APPETIZERS

AllenBrothers.com
ComtesseDuBarry.com
HolidayFoods.com
Kosher.com
OmahaSteaks.com
StonewallKitchen.com
The-Golden-Egg.com

### BAKERY

AllenBrothers.com
AndersonButik.com
BittersweetPasteriesDirect.com
BuyLebanese.com
ByrdCookieCompany.com
Cakes-Online.com
CollinStreetBakery.com
DiamondOrganics.com
DivineGluuttony.com
EliCheesecake.com
FlyingNoodle.com
FultonFishDirect.com
Gambinos.com
GermanDeli.com
Kosher.com
LittlePieCompany.com
Polana.com
RussianFoods.com
Stahmanns.com
VeryVera.com
Zigermans.com

### CONDIMENTS

AGFerrari.com
AsiaMex.com
AuntSue.com
AvalonWine.com
CajunGrocer.com
ChefShop.com
ChileToday.com

Citarella.com
CooksNook.com
DeanDeluca.com
DiabeticFriendly.com
DiamondOrganics.com
DiBruno.com
Earthy.com
ElPasoChile.com
FlyingNoodle.com
FreshPasta.com
Friedas.com
GermanDeli.com
GritLit.com
GusGallucci.com
iGourmet.com
iKoreaPlaza.com
ILovePeanutButter.com
Katagiri.com
KeyWestSeafood.com
LeVillage.com
MexGrocer.com
MoHotta.com
OmahaSteaks.com
OrientalPantry.com
Peck.it
PreserveCompany.com
RussianFoods.com
SalsaExpress.com
StonewallKitchen.com
ThaiGrocer.com
The-Golden-Egg.com
Tienda.com
VermontGoldUSA.com
VillageOrganics.com
Zingermans.com

### GOURMET

AGFerrari.com
ALaZing.com
AvalonWine.com
Bissingers.com
BittersweetPasteriesDirect.com
BridgewaterChocolate.com
ByrdCookieCompany.com

Caviar-Direct.com
CheeseExpress.com
Cheese-Online.com
ChefShop.com
ChocolateGarden.com
ChocolateSource.com
Citarella.com
ComtesseDuBarry.com
CooksNook.com
DeanDeluca.com
DiBruno.com
DinnerDirect.com
DivineGluttony.com
Earthy.com
FlyingNoodle.com
FreshPasta.com
GusGallucci.com
HolidayFoods.com
iCaviar.com
IceCreamSource.com
IdealCheese.com
iGourmet.com
LaMaisonDuChocolat.com
LeVillage.com
MurraysCheese.com
Papanicholas.com
Peck.it
Plantin.com
PreserveCompany.com
SalsaExpress.com
Scharffen-Berger.com
SimonJohnson.com
StonewallKitchen.com
Sugar-Plum.com
The-Golden-Egg.com
VeryVera.com

### GROCERY

AfricanHut.com
AndersonButik.com
AsiaMex.com
BuyLebanese.com
CajunGrocer.com
DiamondOrganics.com

Earthy.com
EthnicGrocer.com
Friedas.com
GermanDeli.com
GritLit.com
GusGallucci.com
iKoreaPlaza.com
Katagiri.com
Kosher.com
MexGrocer.com
OrientalPantry.com
RussianFoods.com
ThaiGrocer.com
Tienda.com
VillageOrganics.com

### HOT DRINKS

AllTea.com
CooksNook.com
DeanDeluca.com
DiBruno.com
EconomyCandy.com
GermanDeli.com
GusGallucci.com
iKoreaPlaza.com
Papanicholas.com
Peck.it
SimonJohnson.com
SpecialTeas.com
Starbucks.com
Tealuxe.com
ThaiGrocer.com
VillageOrganics.com

### MEAT & FISH

AllenBrothers.com
AndersonButik.com
AsiaMex.com
CajunCrawfish.com
CajunGrocer.com

Caviar-Direct.com
Citarella.com
ClamBakeCo.com
ComtesseDuBarry.com
CooksNook.com
CrabBroker.com
DeanDeluca.com
DiamondOrganics.com
DiBruno.com
FultonFishDirect.com
GermanDeli.com
iCaviar.com
iGourmet.com
iKoreaPlaza.com
JamisonFarm.com
KeyWestSeafood.com
Kosher.com
LeVillage.com
LiveLob.com
NimanRanch.com
Nueske.com
OmahaSteaks.com
OrientalPantry.com
PikePlaceFish.com
Polana.com
RussianFoods.com
Seafoods.com
SimonJohnson.com
SmithfieldHams.com
SmokeHouse.com
The-Golden-Egg.com
Tienda.com
TillamookJerky.com

## OILS & SPICES

AsiaMex.com
BuyLebanese.com
CajunGrocer.com
ChefShop.com
ChileToday.com
Citarella.com
DeanDeluca.com
DiamondOrganics.com
DiBruno.com
Earthy.com
FlyingNoodle.com
Friedas.com
GritLit.com
GusGallucci.com
iGourmet.com

iKoreaPlaza.com
Katagiri.com
LeVillage.com
MexGrocer.com
MoHotta.com
OrientalPantry.com
Peck.it
SalsaExpress.com
SimonJohnson.com
StonewallKitchen.com
ThaiGrocer.com
The-Golden-Egg.com
TheSpiceHouse.com
Tienda.com
VillageOrganics.com
Zingermans.com

## ORGANIC

DiamondOrganics.com
JamisonFarm.com
NimanRanch.com
VillageOrganics.com

## PRE-PREPARED

ALaZing.com
AllenBrothers.com
CajunGrocer.com
Citarella.com
ClamBakeCo.com
ComtesseDuBarry.com
DinnerDirect.com
ElPasoChile.com
FultonFishDirect.com
HolidayFoods.com
JamisonFarm.com
Kosher.com
KosherMeal.com
LeVillage.com
LouToGo.com
NoMeat.com
Nueske.com
OmahaSteaks.com
Seafoods.com
SmokeHouse.com
StonewallKitchen.com
The-Golden-Egg.com
VeryVera.com

## RECIPES

AGFerrari.com
CajunCrawfish.com
CajunGrocer.com
ChefShop.com
ChileToday.com
ChocolateSource.com
Citarella.com
DeanDeluca.com
DiabeticFriendly.com
Earthy.com
ElPasoChile.com
EthnicGrocer.com
FlyingNoodle.com
Friedas.com
GourmetGuides.com
GritLit.com
GusGallucci.com
LeVillage.com
MexGrocer.com
OrientalPantry.com
PikePlaceFish.com
Plantin.com
Scharffen-Berger.com
SimonJohnson.com
SmithfieldHams.com
ThaiGrocer.com
The-Golden-Egg.com

## REGIONAL

AfricanHut.com
AGFerrari.com
AndersonButik.com
AsiaMex.com
BuyLebanese.com
CajunCrawfish.com
CajunGrocer.com
ClamBakeCo.com
CooksNook.com
EthnicGrocer.com
FlyingNoodle.com
Gambinos.com
GermanDeli.com
GritLit.com
GusGallucci.com
HomeTownFavorites.com
iKoreaPlaza.com
Katagiri.com

LeVillage.com
LouToGo.com
MexGrocer.com
OrientalPantry.com
Peck.it
Polana.com
RussianFoods.com
SmithfieldHams.com
ThaiGrocer.com
Tienda.com
VermontGoldUSA.com
VeryVera.com

## SNACKS

CasaDeFruta.com
ChileToday.com
DiamondOrganics.com
EconomyCandy.com
eSnacks.com
GermanDeli.com
GritLit.com
HomeTownFavorites.com
Katagiri.com
KosherMeal.com
MexGrocer.com
MoHotta.com
Stahmanns.com
Sugar-Plum.com
ThaiGrocer.com
Tienda.com
TillamookJerky.com

## SPECIAL DIETS

Bissingers.com
CandyWarehouse.com
CheeseExpress.com
DiabeticFriendly.com
DiamondOrganics.com
EconomyCandy.com
FlyingNoodle.com
FudgeKitchens.com
Kosher.com
KosherMeal.com
NoMeat.com
Sugar-Plum.com

## SPIRITS

877Spirits.com
BeerOnTheWall.com
ParkAveLiquor.com
Peck.it
RussianFoods.com
Sherry-Lehman.com

## SWEETS

AGFerrari.com
AndersonButik.com
BenJerry.com
Bissingers.com
BittersweetPastriesDirect.com
BridgewaterChocolate.com
BulkCandyStore.com
BurdickChocolate.com
BuyLebanese.com
ByrdCookieCompany.com
CajunGrocer.com
Cakes-Online.com
CandyDirect.com
CandyWarehouse.com
ChefShop.com
ChocolateGarden.com
ChocolateSource.com
Citarella.com
CollinStreetBakery.com
ComtesseDuBarry.com
CooksNook.com
DeanDeluca.com
DiabeticFriendly.com
DiamondOrganics.com
DivineGluttony.com
EconomyCandy.com
EliCheesecake.com
FudgeKitchens.com
Gambinos.com
GermanDeli.com
HarborSweets.com
HomeTownFavorites.com
IceCreamSource.com
iGourmet.com
ILovePeanutButter.com
JellyBelly.com
Katagiri.com
KeyWestSeafood.com

Kosher.com
LaMaisonDuChocolat.com
LeVillage.com
LittlePieCompany.com
MintShop.com
OldTimeCandy.com
OmahaSteaks.com
OrientalPantry.com
Peck.it
Polana.com
RussianFoods.com
Scharffen-Berger.com
Sees.com
SimonJohnson.com
SmithfieldHams.com
Stahmanns.com
Sugar-Plum.com
The-Golden-Egg.com
Tienda.com
VeryVera.com
WhoopeeCushion.com
Zingermans.com

## TOBACCO

Cigar.com
CigarsInternational.com
GetCubans.com
JRCigars.com
NetCigar.com
OnlineHumidors.com
TobacoDirect.com

## WINES

301Wines.com
877Spirits.com
AfricanHut.com
AGFerrari.com
AmbrosiaWine.com
AvalonWine.com
Citarella.com
DiBruno.com
GusGallucci.com
Kosher.com
MorrellWine.com
ParkAveLiquor.com
Peck.it
RussianFoods.com
Sherry-Lehman.com
Tienda.com
Wine.com

NOTES:

_____
_____
_____
_____
_____
_____
_____
_____
_____
_____
_____
_____
_____
_____
_____
_____
_____
_____

## 301Wines.com

301 Wine Shop & Club • 707-445-0311

Don't be misled; this site features well more than 301 different bottles of wine, and fortunately they're almost all good ones. Shopping is simple and direct: first you choose between red wines, white wines and so forth. Then you select particular varieties like Pinot Noir, Shiraz, Cabernet Sauvignon, Beaujolais, Chardonnay, Chablis and dozens of others. At this point, however, you're going to have to know a little something about what you want or you will be lost, as there's no help in choosing one variety or another, or even descriptions to distinguish between them. Good luck.

| ·WINES | | | |
|---|---|---|---|

## 877Spirits.com

877Spirits • 877-774-7487

Should you feel the need to order liquor online for some reason, the selection of this site will make you smile, if only drunkenly. Vodka, Tequila, Rum and Gin head up the list, with specific sections for Scotch, Canadian Whisky, Tennessee Whisky and Single Malt breaking it down for the whisky fan. The cost of shipping is included in the prices, which still may not excuse the expense. Basically, it's only worthwhile to look here if you live in a place where you cannot buy locally, though in such cases you may want to check their "Unable To Deliver To" list first.

| ·SPIRITS | ·WINES | | |
|---|---|---|---|

## AfricanHut.com

eAfrican Hut • 888-323-3889

Have a taste for some bacon kips? How about some chakalaka and samp invicta? Okay, maybe you prefer to have your morning toast spread with a bit of fig jam? Chances are, if any of this sounds the least bit appetizing or even familiar, you've probably spent time in South Africa. Once better known for its racial divisions than its beer, now we can order six packs of Castle Lager and plenty of other regional grocery items from this store based in ... Laguna Beach, CA? Count this one as evidence that the world is shrinking.

| ·REGIONAL | ·GROCERY | ·WINES | |
|---|---|---|---|

## AGFerrari.com

A.G. Ferrari Foods • 877-878-2783

The proprietor of this site "scours the Italian countryside several times a year in his relentless pursuit of the best that Italy has to offer." Some of the results: pastas, olive oils, wines and cheeses are predictable, even if of higher quality than we may be used to seeing. But there's a richer variety than one might expect, and a Browse by Region feature even offers a bit of cultural education on the different parts of Italy and their culinary differences (for example, the site tells us that eggplant is the most popular ingredient in Sicily, while the best salami comes out of Umbria). Go ahead, try to do better than this without knowing how to speak Italian.

| ·REGIONAL ·GOURMET | ·SWEETS ·CONDIMENTS | ·WINES | ·RECIPES |
|---|---|---|---|

## 888-959-9464 • A La Zing

**ALaZing.com**

A fine meal involves a lot of thought and planning. One must select the proper ingredients, considering complementary flavors and nutritional values. Then, there's a matter of having suitable equipment. This site claims to have it all figured out for you, offering to send a ready-to-cook meal to your home overnight, for either one or two people. They promise to take less than a half hour to make, usually with multiple cooking options and tips on presentation (even which sort of wine to serve); you may want to start with the wine, just to be on the safe side.

| ·GOURMET | ·PRE-PREPARED | | |
|---|---|---|---|

## 800-548-7777 • Allen Brothers

**AllenBrothers.com**

These "purveyors of the finest meats" originate out of Chicago—a town that knows its meats. All kinds of meats. Hence, here you will find steaks, roasts, grounds, pork, chicken, veal, game meats, seafood and jerky. Except for the jerky, you might have reservations about eating meat that's been through the postal service. There's no need to worry about that with these guys, though; they freeze, vacuum-pack and box these meats in dry ice to ensure freshness.

| ·BAKERY | ·MEAT & FISH | ·APPETIZERS | ·PRE-PREPARED |
|---|---|---|---|

## 415-382-1146 • AllTea.com

**AllTea.com**

If you think all teas are the same, you only have to take a look at the categories here to realize you've a lot to learn: Green Teas, Black Teas, Decaf Teas, Iced Teas, Oolong Teas, Chai, Herbal Teas, Medicinal Teas, Maté, White Teas, Organic and Rooibos. We'll only tell you that Rooibos is a tea brewed from *aspalathus linearis*, a plant found native to South Africa. The rest you're going to have to find out for yourself. Hey, what do you want? Tea is cheap; try them all and see for yourself.

| ·HOT DRINKS | | | |
|---|---|---|---|

## 800-435-2225 • Ambrosia

**AmbrosiaWine.com**

From America's wine country itself—Napa, California—we get this family-founded venture that offers the region's wares to the world with easy Price Range and Type browsing. They also have included for your convenience a Wine Finder, which asks you a series of questions pertaining to your wine preferences, including such traits as Sweetness, Intensity, Acidity, Complexity and Body (along with a Glossary should you be unclear on any of these terms). A good site for the wine novice, especially if you don't want to spend a lot on an import.

| ·WINES | | | |
|---|---|---|---|

## AndersonButik.com

Anderson Butik Swedish Imports • 800-782-4132

In the pre-internet world, it was tough for someone here in the US to find such Swedish drinks as Julmust, Saft and Glögg. This site changes all that. Yes, you can find these delicious(?) beverages as well as sweets like Pepparkaker, Läkerol and Gille Havreflarn (no, we are not making these names up). You may also find (mostly goat) cheeses ranging from Bond Ost and Havarti to Gjetost. Finally, what Swedish selection would be complete (and this site's selection is complete) without some herring fillets?

| ·REGIONAL ·BAKERY | ·SWEETS | ·GROCERY | ·MEAT & FISH |
|---|---|---|---|

## AsiaMex.com

Pacific Island Market • 877-274-2639

This one's simply your typical schizophrenic grocery store, the Pacific Island Market. Boasting edible goods from Asia, Latin America, the Middle East and West Africa, geographically you'd expect to find the store headquartered somewhere in the mid-Atlantic, or on a Pacific island as the name would suggest. Well, you're both wrong. Somehow, these guys come to you from the very locus of Middle America: Missouri. Weird, and not too pretty to look at, the site nevertheless has its high points, like sections devoted entirely to Ginseng, Sushi, Mole and Coconut, in addition to more common categories found under the Main Grocery link.

| ·REGIONAL ·CONDIMENTS | ·GROCERY | ·MEAT & FISH | ·OILS & SPICES |
|---|---|---|---|

## AuntSue.com

Aunt Sue's • 800-553-5753

Who exactly is "Aunt Sue" and just what the heck is it that she's doing with pears, tomatoes, ginger and cinnamon? Well, we can't exactly figure out the answer to the first question, but we have been able to ascertain that she's using these ingredients in what seems to be a bizarre reinterpretation of old-world preservation. A small selection of jellies, vinegars, dressings and … chutneys(?) derived from simple combinations of these fruits and spices proves easier to shop for than understand, but for those with adventurous tastes, they could prove newly traditional.

| ·CONDIMENTS | | | |
|---|---|---|---|

## AvalonWine.com

Avalonwine.com • 541-752-7418

A scattered but charming site plays host to the online version of this "Pacific NW Wine and Gourmet" shop out of rural Oregon. Under categories named Big Reds and Pinot Noir you will find wines from Washington and Oregon, respectively, both in various red and white appellations (ours is not to question the naming, only to try to understand it). In the Gourmet section you'll find unique items like Jerky of the Gods, a slew of marionberry products (not to be confused with the former mayor of Washington, DC) and a host of pickled vegetables (and a few mushrooms as well). Apparently, the store was founded to give rural Oregonians access to stuff that could only be found in big cities. Makes you wonder what they think city folk are really eating.

| ·WINES | ·GOURMET | ·CONDIMENTS | |
|---|---|---|---|

## 888-840-2337 • Beer On The Wall

**BeerOnTheWall.com**

On the verge of being crass, this site that was founded by a local skateboarder/beer-lover makes up for any unsavory language by offering a fantastic selection of California micro-brews. Better yet, you can assemble your own six- or twelve-pack from the available beers, and even devise your own custom labels to adorn them (more of a novelty, and, if you plan to drink the beer and recycle the bottle, it will be a short-lived one at that). The best bet may be the Beer of the Month Club, which will keep you abreast of seasonal developments, and a little drunk (minors need not apply).

·SPIRITS

## 866-254-4387 • Ben & Jerry's Ice Cream

**BenJerry.com**

In a quarter-century of operation, this company has created terms almost guaranteed to put a smile on your face: Cherry Garcia, Chubby Hubby, Chocolate Chip Cookie Dough and Chunky Monkey, just to name a few. Of course, why do we tantalize with mention of such famous flavors; you can't mail ice cream—or can you? Ben & Jerry's will, packed in dry ice, in reusable coolers, sent overnight. Can't wait that long? Select your favorite flavor and this site will tell you the closest place you can buy it yourself. We all just got a little heavier.

·SWEETS

## 800-325-8881 • Bissinger French Confections

**Bissingers.com**

What's more enticing: an offer for a free pound of chocolate with the first purchase, a picture of chocolate dipped strawberries or the term "French Confections"? Well, all three greeted us when we encountered this site, the result being a chocolate feeding frenzy the likes of which should not be seen again. These guys are simply out to make you drool with talk of "luscious chocolate-covered fresh fruits, decadent truffles and hand-crafted chocolate confections." It's best that those with weak wills refrain from viewing the pictures; it's all just too much.

·SWEETS | ·SPECIAL DIETS | ·GOURMET

## 800-537-7791 • Bittersweet Pastries Direct

**BittersweetPastriesDirect.com**

Boasting "Award Winning Desserts," it only takes a glance at these sweet things to see just why they're so revered. If you need to know more before you look, consider these delicious sounding items: Marbled Chocolate Truffle Cheesecake, White Chocolate Lace Cake, Cranberry Walnut Cheese Tart, Raspberry Rugelach and a cake of Chocolate Satin. Once only available in hotels and restaurants, having such stuff delivered direct to your home could be detrimental to your diet, but it will change your definition of "cake."

·SWEETS | ·BAKERY | ·GOURMET

## BridgewaterChocolate.com

**Bridgewater Chocolate • 800-888-8742**

Bigger than your average confection, this line of candies offers more snackworthy sizes of caramels, toffees, nuts, truffles, and dipped fruits, and some cookies besides. The century-old Connecticut sweetmaker doesn't offer a wide range of products, but what it does show on the website is enough to make us scramble for the Order button. Of course, a long history of mail order hasn't quite prepared them for the intricacies of the internet, so it takes quite a few clicks before you can actually make it to the Order Page. Consider it a cooling-off period.

| ·SWEETS | ·GOURMET | | |
|---------|----------|---|---|

## BulkCandyStore.com

**Bulk Candy Store • 561-615-8646**

For those of us who prefer to take our candy in half-pound increments, this store delivers. Basically, you can find the typical variety of sweets that you're used to scooping out of giant bins, as well as assorted candy bars and 10-ounce bags. Either way, any store that offers category names like Big Lollipops, Jawbreakers, Candy Sticks and Gummis is going to attract the interest of sweet-tooths young and old alike. Sort of like an online cavity, we can only hope this site gets kickbacks from your dentist.

| ·SWEETS | | | |
|---------|---|---|---|

## BurdickChocolate.com

**L.A. Burdick Handmade Chocolate • 800-229-2419**

The selling point of these chocolates is that they're handmade. While the pictures make it easy to imagine Lucille Ball stuffing half-made confections into her mouth to avoid the wrath of her supervisor, most of these chocolates are more enticing than hilarious. Possible exceptions would be the chocolate penguins, cigars and mice (not as creepy as they sound). But, as the site points out, even these handmade chocolates are "more delicate than those made with molds," so despite the fact ordering isn't as easy as we'd like, these confections, pastries, dipped fruits and nuts sound better than a laugh track.

| ·SWEETS | | | |
|---------|---|---|---|

## BuyLebanese.com

**Buy Lebanese • 011-961-3-602405**

This site isn't just out to tell you to buy Lebanese, they mean for you to buy from Lebanon, straight out of Beirut. Beginning with authentic Baba Ghannouge and including Borghol Khechen Asmar, Balah bil Lawz, Debs el Remman, Halawa bi Shokola, Hommos bi Tahini and Kadami, this selection remains true to age-old traditions and native "taste and savour." Okay, if you don't know what most of this stuff is, then all the more reason to check out the site. Browsing will be confusing, but in the product descriptions you'll find out everything you need to know.

| ·REGIONAL ·BAKERY | ·SWEETS | ·GROCERY | ·OILS & SPICES |
|-------------------|---------|----------|----------------|

## 800-291-2973 • Byrd Cookie Company

**ByrdCookieCompany.com**

Can simple strings of words make your mouth water? Let's try it with a few of the varied selections of cookies, biscuits, salad dressings, jams and salsas available from this gourmet specialty store devoted to "the fine art of taste." Jalapeño Cheese Biscuits. Artichoke Parmesan Biscuits. Key Lime Salsa. Didn't do it? Okay, maybe you have a sweet tooth. Raspberry Tart. Butter Thins cookies. Cinnamon Pecan Biscuits. If these product's names don't get you, we're betting their pictures will; they look delicious.

| ·SWEETS | ·GOURMET | ·BAKERY | |
|---|---|---|---|

## 888-254-8626 • Moe's Cajun Crawfish

**CajunCrawfish.com**

Crawfish aren't pretty. In fact, they look more than just a little creepy. But the purveyors of this site are smart; understanding that you can put the word "Cajun" in front of just about anything to make it sound more appetizing. Still not convinced? How about this: their "History of Crawfish" page (located in the Humor section for some reason) explains that crawfish came to be when French colonials brought lobsters to Louisiana from Canada: the lobsters survived, but were not so robust. Hence, when you think about it, crawfish are nothing more than "little lobsters," which makes them sound much more appealing. Believe what you will, just don't be surprised if their claws and spindly legs are still kicking upon receipt—these guys send them fresh!

| ·REGIONAL | ·MEAT & FISH | ·RECIPES | |
|---|---|---|---|

## 888-272-9347 • CajunGrocer.com

**CajunGrocer.com**

Louisiana might just be the most creative region in the nation when it comes to culinary concoctions, and not just because they eat things like alligator burgers and crawfish pies. A cursory glance of this all-Louisiana retailer indicates that they have these, but also plenty of other Cajun and Creole delicacies. You may be familiar with any manner of gumbo, stuffed breads and jambalaya, but how about tur-duc-ken? This is a dish involving a chicken smeared with crawfish dressing, stuffed in a shrimp-slathered duck and then crammed inside a turkey. When in doubt, just order a king cake.

| ·REGIONAL<br>·OILS & SPICES | ·SWEETS<br>·RECIPES | ·GROCERY<br>·CONDIMENTS | ·MEAT & FISH<br>·PRE-PREPARED | |
|---|---|---|---|---|

## 866-263-2253 • Cakes-Online.com

**Cakes-Online.com**

If the idea of ordering a cake online and then having it sent through the mail seems ludicrous to you, you should see some of the other things the post office is willing to deliver. Ha ha. Seriously, this site doesn't intend to pack a freshly frosted cake into a cardboard box and simply stamp the word Fragile across the top. Operating from a network of bakeries across the country, they're set up so that you can customize a cake with some simple menu options (including flavor, filling, frosting and a personalized message), which will then be baked locally and hand-delivered to your door, with no messy hilarity whatsoever.

| ·SWEETS | ·BAKERY | | |
|---|---|---|---|

## CandyDirect.com

CandyDirect.com • 619-827-7377

From Almond Roca to Zagnuts and Abba Zabba to Zero Bars, this site offers a great range of popular and sometimes bizarre candies, easily browsed alphabetically with pictures or, assuming you're an old hand at this and are well familiar with all the candy names and flavors, on an Easy Order list that fits everything on one page (we recommend shopping this way for expediency's sake). Now, before you go off half-cocked, these guys aren't charging twenty dollars per candy bar—this candy is sold by the box, so be sure to note what quantities it is you'll be purchasing.

·SWEETS

## CandyWarehouse.com

Candy Warehouse • 626-480-0899

In case you need 2,500 Pixy Stix for some reason, or other large candy orders, this place has it all. You can shop by delicious category, or through more than 60 brands, ranging from popular candy makers like Nestlé, Willy Wonka and Jolly Rancher to lesser knowns Trolli, Candy Tech and Andy Wertz. Otherwise, you can shop by candy occasion, which features some of the perennial candy holidays like Halloween, Easter, Mother's Day and… St. Patrick's Day? Well, truth be known, candy tastes good every day of the year, and buying bulk from a place like this will ensure that every occasion leads to a sugar-rush.

·SWEETS  ·SPECIAL DIETS

## CasaDeFruta.com

Casa de Fruta • 800-543-1702

Representing a cluster of California orchards that have been in operation for nearly a hundred years, this site does well to offer a selection of items representative of California itself: fruits and nuts, some of them candied. Dried fruits include apricots, cranberries, raisins, dates and prunes, whereas the nuts sold here include some of the best: pistachios and cashews. You'll find these guys stationed in kiosks off highways in the northern and central regions of the state, but if for some reason you can't make it out there this year, this site will do it just as well, with freshness guaranteed.

·SNACKS

## Caviar-Direct.com

Caviar Direct • 800-650-2828

There's not much to be said about this site; they sell caviar. Choose among Russian, American and Iranian caviar, each in several varieties (like beluga, sevruga and osetra). They generally come in different-sized tins, ranging from 2 oz. to a full pound. Oh yeah, and there are some other sundry items, like lox, sliced fish of different kinds, and foie gras. It's all on one page, so you'll see the entire inventory as you scroll toward the order form. Talk about taking the word "Direct" to an extreme.

·GOURMET  ·MEAT & FISH

## 888-530-0505 • Cheese Express
### CheeseExpress.com

Around forty years ago, these guys drove trucks around the San Francisco Bay Area delivering milk in glass bottles on a daily basis. While milkmen are long since a thing of the past, these guys are back in the home delivery business; though don't expect any glass milk bottles dropped off at your doorstep. They pretty much stick to cheese these days, and they do it well, offering categories like Goudas, Bries and Fetas, alongside some American standards, as well as the option to shop by other countries of origin. With appetizing details (and crackers too), this visually oriented site should easily win you over.

| ·SPECIAL DIETS | ·GOURMET | | | |
|---|---|---|---|---|

## 011-33-47-66-17-17 • Fromages.com
### Cheese-Online.com

Do you know enough about cheese? Thanks to the Cheese Library of this site, the answer to this question may someday be "yes." See, it will decipher the many difficult-to-pronounce cheese names, offering essential information, including which wine best suits the selection and even the best "season for indulging." Only at this point will you feel fully qualified to enjoy one of this retailer's fine and rapturous cheeses, each of which has been "selected with the help of a renowned French cheesemaster." Yes, this site features one of the greatest and most difficult-to-come-by traits of a web seller: unintentional hilarity.

| ·GOURMET | | | |
|---|---|---|---|

## 877-337-2491 • Chefshop.com
### ChefShop.com

The proprietors of this site state unequivocally that fine ingredients are the most important element to gourmet cooking, with recipe and skill showing up somewhere farther down the list. As such, this is a great site to easily find good, relatively inexpensive raw materials. That being said, they also maintain that there are certain ingredients that must be procured locally to assure quality and consumed immediately, whereas others that may be purchased in quantity and stored in a pantry. This selection belongs in a pantry. Hence, you'll find no meats or produce, except the sort that is stewed and/or preserved in jars or cans.

| ·SWEETS ·CONDIMENTS | ·OILS & SPICES | ·RECIPES | ·GOURMET | |
|---|---|---|---|---|

## 800-468-7377 • Chile Today – Hot Tamale
### ChileToday.com

The full name of this one, "Chile Today – Hot Tamale," takes a second to appreciate, and will elicit groans soon thereafter. Conversely, their product selection wastes no time in provoking a response. As "the gourmet source for hot and spicy products," the chile peppers, powders, salsas and snacks proffered here may burn a hole through your tongue before you can say the word "spicy." What else would you expect from "the Heat Brothers," stepbrothers turned business partners, who may be seen on the About Us page standing in a vat of hot peppers? Their manic desire to spice up a few meals is contagious, and the heat itself … well that's just plain addictive.

| ·OILS & SPICES | ·RECIPES | ·CONDIMENTS | ·SNACKS |
|---|---|---|---|

## ChocolateGarden.com

**The Chocolate Garden • 269-468-9866**

Some chocolates are made according to the finest European traditions, with the French, Belgian and Swiss chocolates of legend foremost among them. The handmade truffles you'll find on this site, however, were not. These are the result of a little American experimentation, and they're terrific. While we could have easily listed these in our Gifts section (they make fine ones), we ultimately figured there was no point—you'd just end up eating them all yourself anyway. These are strictly for personal use.

| | ·GOURMET | ·SWEETS | | |
|---|---|---|---|---|

## ChocolateSource.com

**ChocolateSource.com • 800-214-4926**

Bearing chocolate in just about all of its splendiferous forms, the primary advantage offered by this site is ease of use, because when you've gotta get your chocolate fix, you don't want to waste any time browsing. Of course, if you're in the midst of a heavy craving, the internet can't help you achieve instant gratification. But, if there are any guarantees in life, one is that you'll want chocolate again, and here you can shop by Type (baking chocolate, candy bars, cocoa, confections or spread), Brand or Price. Here's to planning ahead!

| | ·SWEETS | ·RECIPES | ·GOURMET | |
|---|---|---|---|---|

## Cigar.com

**Cigar.com • 800-357-9800**

If you're already a cigar smoker, and know what you like, you'll almost certainly find it here (unless, of course, you like Cuban cigars, and who doesn't?). Otherwise, the impossibly long list of available brands to be found under this site's Shop link might just be enough to keep you from picking up the habit. Humidors and accessories are a little bit easier to sift through, and the occasional picture will actually help you make a decision, but a novice smoker's best bets show up in various recommendation pages, bestseller lists, samplers and a five-stogie "Cigar of the Month Club."

| | ·TOBACCO | | | |
|---|---|---|---|---|

## CigarsInternational.com

**Cigars International • 888-244-2790**

Wading through this poorly organized site's Big List of Brands is only made bearable by the excitement inspired by its many products—that is, if cigars excite you for some reason. But to some, a cigar is just a smoke, and if you know what you're on the lookout for, the "big list" might just serve your purposes. To laymen, though, this site's core offering is a burdensome catalog of unfamiliar (mostly Spanish) names and none-too-helpful photos. A beginner's only hope might be the Starter Kit, although we find it hard to understand why someone would want to start such a habit with an online purchase.

| | ·TOBACCO | | | |
|---|---|---|---|---|

## 212-874-0383 • Citarella
### Citarella.com

One of the advantages to living in New York City is the fantastic selection of foods available to its citizens. The good news is, more and more of the venerable New York stores that provide this luxury are taking their business online. Here's another one, this time of the gourmet variety. Whether it's foie gras you're after, a fantastic selection of meats (including fish, fowl and game) or one of their ready-to-make meals (quiches and pot pies are only the beginning), the gourmand allure of the Big Apple may be diminished, as the rest of us have been granted access to some of the best.

| ·SWEETS <br> ·RECIPES | ·MEAT & FISH <br> ·GOURMET | ·OILS & SPICES <br> ·CONDIMENTS | ·WINES <br> ·PRE-PREPARED |
|---|---|---|---|

## 800-722-2526 • Clambakes to Travel
### ClamBakeCo.com

When it's time for a good old-fashioned clambake, you can do no better than to visit this new-fangled specialty retailer. What's a clambake? Well, as these guys have it, it's a shindig that involves steamed lobster, mussels, vegetables, Portuguese sausage and, of course, clams. Yes, it sounds like a lot to prepare, but that's the great thing about this site: they send you a prepacked steamer pot, loaded with ingredients. You simply add water, put over a flame and twenty minutes (or so) later you have a full-fledged clambake for as many people as you need. It couldn't be easier, and you get to keep the pot.

| ·REGIONAL | ·MEAT & FISH | ·PRE-PREPARED | |
|---|---|---|---|

## 800-292-7400 • Collin Street Bakery
### CollinStreetBakery.com

Even your cartoon-watching kids probably already know that the fruitcake is the perennial joke of all the gift foods, seemingly recycled year after year, as nobody admits to eating them and most of us figured they stopped selling them decades ago. Well, if it turns out you're actually looking to buy one, whether for yourself or for another, here's the only place worth looking. With a wider than expected selection that actually promises to taste good, a fruitcake purchased here makes for something more than a gag gift.

| ·SWEETS | ·BAKERY | | |
|---|---|---|---|

## 011-33-5-62-67-98-12 • Comtesse du Barry
### ComtesseDuBarry.com

When you consider that the French culinary tradition is considered among the best in the world, if not *the* best, one has to assume that an online shop devoted to traditional French cuisine is going to have the most delectable, appetizing selection of meals available to mankind. Well, it does, and it doesn't. First you have to get past the abject gastronomic creativity responsible for stuffed duck necks and pork head paté among these authentic ready-made meals. Once you do this, however, you are certainly rewarded with chocolate soufflés, coq au vin, scallop flan, duck breast ravioli and all the foie gras you could shake a liver at. Sophisticated palates, take note.

| ·SWEETS <br> ·MEAT & FISH | ·GOURMET | ·APPETIZERS | ·PRE-PREPARED |
|---|---|---|---|

## CooksNook.com

Cook's Nook • 888-557-8761

This "emporium of fine and unusual gourmet foods" offers scattered selections of stuff like pastas, sauces, seafood and condiments, some of which prove entirely unpredictable (unless you're expecting to track down a marionberry barbecue sauce). Most appealing, though, is the site's selection of coffees and teas—if you can handle the navigation. The Coffee Shop, in particular, boasts some great roasts, but is such a tangle as to almost deter you from even checking them out. Cooler heads will prevail, but we suspect you'll tire of the disorganization fairly quick, so check out those fruity BBQ sauces first.

| ·REGIONAL ·CONDIMENTS | ·SWEETS ·MEAT & FISH | ·HOT DRINKS | ·GOURMET |
|---|---|---|---|

## CrabBroker.com

The Crab Broker • 888-454-2722

If the thought of fresh crab overnighted to you from such legendary fishing locations as Alaska, Australia and Texas makes you drool, wait until you see what else this site has to offer. Namely, there's plenty of lobster, scallops, prawns, oysters, halibut, salmon, shrimp and even crawfish, all sold in fixed quantities. That's where you really want to pay attention, as frozen and fresh are listed together, and if you're not careful you may find yourself with ten pounds of last season's draw. A word of advice: don't be distracted by the dancing crab.

| ·MEAT & FISH | | | |
|---|---|---|---|

## DeanDeluca.com

Dean & Deluca • 877-826-9246

The proprietors of this store, based in the artsy SoHo neighborhood of NYC, "want to share [their] passion for food of incomparable quality and taste." Well, sure, it sounds great until you factor in the goose liver (foie gras) and fish roe (caviar). Seriously, though, this is fine gourmet stuff that will permanently spoil fast food for you (this is a good thing). Meats, cheese, grains, sauces, fish, herbs and assorted fungi are just a sampling of what's available, and the site offers a slew of recipes to give you ideas about what to do with it all.

| ·SWEETS ·RECIPES | ·HOT DRINKS ·GOURMET | ·MEAT & FISH ·CONDIMENTS | ·OILS & SPICES |
|---|---|---|---|

## DiabeticFriendly.com

DiabeticFriendly.com • 614-478-8341

In most cases, the candy stores we've listed in this section will go ignored by those living with diabetes. Admittedly, it's almost cruel to describe the rich chocolates, tangy candies and rapturous cookies of a dozen web sites to a group unable to freely enjoy the unholy decadence of sugar. Which is why we hope this site will satisfy a lot of sweet-tooths out there. Diabetic friendly chocolate, hard candies, cookies and peanut butter treats—all are easy to find on this simply conceived and orchestrated site. Let's hope it's not habit forming.

| ·SWEETS | ·RECIPES | ·SPECIAL DIETS | ·CONDIMENTS |
|---|---|---|---|

## 888-674-2642 • Diamond Organics
### DiamondOrganics.com

Staking its claim as "The Freshest Site Online," this fantastic shop offers nothing less than organic fruits and vegetables, available seasonally and delivered fresh. Of course, you may want to eat this stuff quick, as a general lack of preservatives, combined with delivery time, may allow for early spoilage. This shouldn't be too much of a problem though, as you'll most likely wait impatiently at the door for your order to arrive. Additional sections like Soy Dairy, Mushrooms, Macrobiotics and Herbs should entice health food lovers and gourmet connoisseurs alike, though we're not exactly sure what segment of the population will be drawn to the Edible Flowers category.

| ·ORGANIC<br>·OILS & SPICES | ·SWEETS<br>·BAKERY | ·GROCERY<br>·CONDIMENTS | ·MEAT & FISH<br>·SNACKS |
|---|---|---|---|

## 888-322-4337 • Di Bruno Bros.
### DiBruno.com

With over four hundred cheeses from nearly a dozen countries (and a few homemade wedges and spreads), this Philadelphia gourmet grocer will not disappoint, either with selection, price or attitude. While you're there, you can maybe check out their other sundry food items, like some mortadella, prosciutto, chorizo sausage, patés, terrines, mousses, olives, vinegars, caviar, foie gras, coffee, pastas, fish and ... well, you get the picture. It may not be the finest gourmet catalog, per se, but it might be the friendliest.

| ·HOT DRINKS<br>·CONDIMENTS | ·OILS & SPICES<br>·MEAT & FISH | ·WINES | ·GOURMET |
|---|---|---|---|

## 888-999-3196 • Dinner Direct
### DinnerDirect.com

Maybe you're too lazy to cook, maybe you simply lack the faculties. Hey, we're not here to judge. With these ready-to-make meals it doesn't matter either way. Under Classic Entrées you'll find such filling options as Beef Wellington, Stuffed Santa Fe Chicken and Turkey En Croute; just take them out of the freezer and follow instructions to heat in the oven. Still too complicated? Under Fast Pouch Entrées, you can make yourself Beef Stroganoff or Sesame Chicken with no more effort than to boil some water.

| ·GOURMET | ·PRE-PREPARED | | |
|---|---|---|---|

## 800-851-0660 • Divine Gluttony
### DivineGluttony.com

Primarily, Divine Gluttony wishes to serve as "an elegant reminder of European Patisseries and Boulangeries." Don't let this deter you. See, this site has more than just a cool name. They sell some mouth-watering "sinful delicacies"; cookies, brownies, cakes and other pastries. Their use of words like "decadence" and "forbidden" only further spurs your patronage, as if the pictures weren't enough. You can buy these chocolate, nutty and/or fruity sundries by the box, or set up a customized sampling, which is highly recommended.

| ·SWEETS | ·GOURMET | ·BAKERY | |
|---|---|---|---|

## Earthy.com

A little complicated, this store is a great resource nonetheless, lending merit to its claim to be "Where Great Chefs Buy." To start shopping, click on the Fern icon in the top left corner of the home page, then on Products. An animated menu becomes the site's saving grace at this point, leading you to Mushrooms & Truffles (not just portabella or shitake), Fresh Produce (including edible flowers and microgreens), Spices & Flavors (from sea salt to fennel pollen) and plenty of other gourmet ingredients.

| | •GROCERY •CONDIMENTS | •OILS & SPICES | •RECIPES | •GOURMET |
|---|---|---|---|---|

## EconomyCandy.com

Originally an old-time candy shop, with bins and everything, this independent retailer from Manhattan's Lower East Side has managed to survive through the years by its willingness to adapt to the times. By this, we mean they've expanded to include coffees, teas, dried fruit and nuts in their repertoire, and upped the quality of it all to gourmet standards, whatever those may be. Still, the bulk candy remains, with some popular halvah and sugar-free options, so you can sneak a few (pounds) of tasty treats in with your tasteful ones.

| •SWEETS | •SPECIAL DIETS | •SNACKS | •HOT DRINKS |
|---|---|---|---|

## EliCheesecake.com

As if it wasn't enough that this site tempts you to no end with a brilliant selection of easy-to-order cheesecakes, they have to take it all beyond reason by offering a Create a Cheesecake feature. Beginning with a plain or chocolate chip cheesecake, you are given the chance to add up to three additional garnishes, from marshmallows and Heath Bar to peanut butter cups, fruit, nuts, caramel and gummy bears. Do yourself a favor and skip this one unless you already know for sure you want a cheesecake; otherwise the images on this site comprise the virtual equivalent of a mugging.

| •SWEETS | •BAKERY | | |
|---|---|---|---|

## ElPasoChile.com

Walking a somewhat different path from your run-of-the-mill salsa maker, this home-grown company bolsters its kicking selection of spice with dips, sauces, condiments and preserves. Names like Hellfire and Damnation (hot sauce), Chickpea and Chipotle Bean Dip, Sizzling Sicilian Spicy Caponata, Snake Bite Salsa and Beer BBQ Sauce offer some tantalizing insight that things here are maybe not as they should be, but given the creativity involved, we'd call it a good thing. Make sure to keep some water handy.

| | •RECIPES | •CONDIMENTS | •PRE-PREPARED |
|---|---|---|---|

888-762-2534 • eSnacks.com

**eSnacks.com**

Truly, the last thing you need while planted in front of your computer, gazing into the deep currents of the internet, is easy access to snacks … but we do want to be thorough. From beef jerky to cookies, candies and nuts, there are snacks enough here to make your belt burst just by looking at them. Simply pick your hankering, whether yours be a salty or a sweet tooth, and wade through the selection. Not to encourage such behavior, but shipping costs more than some of these items, so it makes more sense to order a lot.

866-438-4642 • EthnicGrocer.com

**EthnicGrocer.com**

If you're sick of American food, already, you may take delight in this internationally themed online grocer. Shopping by product, which we've long since learned is an online standard, will turn up interesting categories like Beans, Grains, Rice and Edible Wrappings. Or, you can shop by country, a long list of which includes India, Japan, Turkey, the Philippines, Vietnam, Korea, Thailand, Mexico, Poland and several other European nations. You may become perplexed by some of the unusual items to be found inside, but a list of recipes and featured cookbooks should have you preparing the exotic dishes you long for in no time. Take that, meatloaf and mashed potatoes.

800-566-0599 • Flying Noodle

**FlyingNoodle.com**

Generally, when you think of quality pasta, you think of Italy, and justifiably so. Actually, most of the high-end pasta sites online owe much of their catalogs to the Mediterranean country from whence sprung the word "primavera." Conversely, the proprietor of this site has little interest in the origins of the noodles, just that they and the sauce that covers them are fantastic: "I don't care if they come from Milan or Hoboken. They just have to exceed some exacting standards—all natural ingredients, beautifully pleasing flavors and made by professionals who love what they are doing." Authenticity just took a hit, but if you're a fan of the bottom line, this is *sufficiènte*.

·RECIPES ·CONDIMENTS ·REGIONAL ·BAKERY
·SPECIAL DIETS ·OILS & SPICES ·GOURMET

800-747-2782 • FreshPasta.com

**FreshPasta.com**

Simply follow the Online Store link from this site's home page to find easy access to a slew of—you guessed it—fresh pastas. Rare as it is we're willing to say this—it's even easier than it sounds! On one page you may view a list of linguinis, fettuccinis, spaghettinis and gnocchis, each fresh and delectable. Lest you doubt it, take a look at the extensive list of raviolis, stuffed with vegetables, cheeses and seafood (especially their lobster selections) and just try to refrain from ordering. If you're having trouble deciding (as you most certainly will), check their selection of sauces to determine just which pasta/sauce combinations prove the most complementary.

·GOURMET ·CONDIMENTS

## Friedas.com

Friedas.com • 800-241-1771

Sometimes, you don't know what you're missing—literally. Take the selection of this "specialty produce" retailer, for example. Without taking a look through this site, you might never realize that your own grocery store is lacking in atemoya, calabaza and peppadew, let alone arrowroot. Sure, odds are against any of us knowing what the stuff is, or how to cook it, but thanks to the informative descriptions and recipe pages, you can soon add some new items to your palate's vocabulary. Just follow the Shop@Frieda's link.

| ·GROCERY | ·OILS & SPICES | ·RECIPES | ·CONDIMENTS |
|---|---|---|---|

## FudgeKitchens.com

The Fudge Kitchens • 800-233-8343

This site, whose name sounds like part of the Willy Wonka factory, has a fairly unsurprising goal: to sell their "world famous whipped cream fudge" by the pound. What could be better than fudge? How about chocolate chip, chocolate peanut butter, chocolate marshmallow and vanilla coconut fudges, for starters? No less than eighteen flavors are available, and that's not even considering the sugar-free options or assorted confections. Operated by a family out of New Jersey (not Oompa Loompas) these kitchens may be the worst thing ever to happen to your waistline.

| ·SWEETS | ·SPECIAL DIETS | | |
|---|---|---|---|

## FultonFishDirect.com

Fulton Fish Direct • 866-275-2722

New York's Fulton Street market seems to feed a city of fish lovers, so why not the rest of us? The proprietors of this site make daily visits to the market in search of worthy shellfish, fillets, shrimp, squid and a variety of other saltwater denizens, promising to get their selections to you as fresh as possible. Of course, as always when ordering fish, here you walk a fine line: you must purchase a lot in order to take advantage of the site's pricing structure, but not so much that you jeopardize the potential freshness of the fare.

| ·BAKERY | ·MEAT & FISH | ·PRE-PREPARED | |
|---|---|---|---|

## Gambinos.com

Gambino's • 800-426-2466

The first thing you'll notice here is that Gambino's is the "King of King Cakes," a king cake being a particularly sweet aspect of Mardi Gras (behind the costumes, parades and, um, beads of course). Anyway, if you're going to try a king cake, it might as well be one of these. Actually, they also prove a good source for various decidedly Southern offerings, like Doberge and Red Velvet cakes, and they definitely make handy use of pecans. Then there are some more typical cakes, some cookies, confections and so on. If you're gonna get it from the south, it might as well show.

| ·SWEETS | ·BAKERY | ·REGIONAL | |
|---|---|---|---|

## 877-437-6269 • GermanDeli.com

### GermanDeli.com

Yes, this online German grocery store is an excellent place to find liverwurst, sauerkraut, fleischkäse, schinken, kassler and sausage. Actually, you can find all kinds of wursts, plus plenty of German sweets and bakery products to go with their plethora meats and seafoods. Animated menus usually make it easy, but the occasional volatility will make you wish you had some German beer. Sadly, this Texas-based retailer doesn't offer any, but otherwise your own authentic Oktoberfest is merely a home delivery away.

| ·REGIONAL ·MEAT & FISH | ·SWEETS ·BAKERY | ·HOT DRINKS ·CONDIMENTS | ·GROCERY ·SNACKS |
|---|---|---|---|

## 888-297-6653 • Castro's Cuban Cigar Store

### GetCubans.com

So, this site is problematic for many reasons, foremost being the fact that a US embargo against Cuba prevents us from being able to buy Cuban cigars in this country. Then there's the name of this shop, Castro's Cuban Cigars, not likely to win the support of staunch American patriots. Not that these guys are concerned, as they operate out of Canada. And yet they claim to ship Cuban cigars to the USA with bands on and in sealed boxes. We're not here to opine on foreign affairs, we're just telling you the site is there; what you and they decide to do on your own time is none of our business.

| ·TOBACCO | | | |  |
|---|---|---|---|---|

## 800-413-3327 • Gourmet Guides

### GourmetGuides.com

This gourmet site leaves it to you to find ways to stock your pantry with the truffles, charcuterie and other fine ingredients favored by elite eaters. Their concern is that you will prepare it properly; hence, they sell cookbooks. If you follow their Book Search link you can sort through books based on region (Mediterranean, Asian, French and so on), type (Vegetarian and Low Fat, for example) or occasion, whether you're entertaining or want something quick and easy. These are good prices on good cookbooks; so who needs restaurants?

| ·RECIPES | | | | |
|---|---|---|---|---|

## No Service Number • GritLit.com

### GritLit.com

If you're fond of those peculiar foods particular to the south, but aren't in range of a Piggly Wiggly, fear not, as this site promises, "more southern food than you can shake a stick at." We're referring to stuff like pickled watermelon rinds, boiled peanuts and succotash. If that stuff scares you, there's plenty of chicory coffee, jambalaya mix and of course grits to satisfy the less-tempered tongue, including all manner of Cajun, Southern BBQ and soul food. If you're not sure what something is, you can check the eternally enlightening Glossary, and then find cookbooks to help you replicate the experience.

| ·REGIONAL ·CONDIMENTS | ·GROCERY ·SNACKS | ·OILS & SPICES | ·RECIPES |
|---|---|---|---|

## GusGallucci.com

Gallucci's Italian Foods • 888-425-5822

The company behind this site describes itself as "a fine purveyor of Italian and imported gourmet foods, serving Ohio and the greater Cleveland area." Well, before you start to wonder just why the heck Ohio should be so lucky, take a moment to remember that, thanks to this online presence, Clevelanders are no longer the only ones privy to these fine Italian grocery items. Sure, there's a lot of pasta, and sauces as well, but let us not forget about the infused oils, meats, produce, cheeses, wines, spices and espresso beans. Finally, we can all eat as well as the Italians and Ohioans do.

| ·REGIONAL ·WINES | ·HOT DRINKS ·RECIPES | ·GROCERY ·GOURMET | ·OILS & SPICES ·CONDIMENTS |
|---|---|---|---|

## HarborSweets.com

Harbor Sweets • 800-243-2115

So it turns out, Salem, Massachusetts, has produced more than witchcraft would let on. Specifically, in this case, we're talking about chocolates. While some items are fairly peculiar (peanut butter lobsters—need we say more?), most of it could simply be categorized as "original." The gift boxes are sometimes as elaborate as the confections themselves, but if you're purely in it for expedient consumption, keep your eyes open for the Home Packs, which offer you a fair amount of candy in a no-frills box, at a reduced price, of course.

| ·SWEETS | | | |
|---|---|---|---|

## HolidayFoods.com

Holiday Foods • 800-877-7434

Here's a site the caterers of the world do not want you to know about. Particularly useful for those big, extravagant fêtes, the sort that usually necessitate tuxedoed servers bearing plates full of hors d'oeuvres, this one puts the catering power in your hands. All you have to do is choose from selections of cheese puffs, mini quiches, lobster strudel triangles, almond-stuffed dates wrapped in bacon and crab rangoons (as well as some others), and navigate one of the worst ordering systems online (start with the Catalog Sales link). As for the serving staff ... dress up the kids; who'll know the difference?

| ·GOURMET | ·APPETIZERS | ·PRE-PREPARED | |
|---|---|---|---|

## HomeTownFavorites.com

Hometown Favorites • 888-694-2656

Assembling a catalog of "Old-Time Favorites and Regionally Exclusive Foods," this site has definitely done something right. This is the kind of stuff city folk find "quaint" in rural areas, or that rural folk are surprised not to find in major metropolises. Or, it may just be stuff that has been around seemingly forever, but for some reason or another is tough to track down wherever you live. This proves to be an excellent manifestation of the internet, allowing us to stock up on those foodstuffs we've grown to miss, like Kenyons Clam Cake & Fritters Mix, Moxie soda or Booberry cereal. You're almost guaranteed to find delight in some of this stuff, whatever town you call home.

| ·REGIONAL | ·SWEETS | ·SNACKS | |
|---|---|---|---|

## 800-521-4491 • Caviar Assouline

## iCaviar.com

There's nothing terribly exciting about this site, the online extension of the Caviar Assouline Catalog. Nothing, that is, unless you're excited by the eats of elite feasts. Beginning with caviar (domestic and imported) and continuing with truffles, foie gras and other so-called "acquired tastes," the Catalog Directory link takes you into a small treasure trove of gastronomical delights. Sure, fish roe isn't the first thing most of us think of when we're feeling peckish, but at several hundred dollars a tin, there must be something to it.

| ·MEAT & FISH | ·GOURMET | | | |
|---|---|---|---|---|

## 920-495-1668 • IceCreamSource.com

## IceCreamSource.com

With enough different ice cream flavors that you could try a new one every weekday of the year (no shipping on weekends, as the product would melt en route), this site can keep you in heaven, pint by pint. Ben & Jerry's, Baskin Robbins, Häagen-Dazs and Carvel are just some of the brand names you might recognize, the other dozen or so might require a little research, such as the Out of a Flower brand, which actually includes flowers and seed pods in its ingredients. There's only one minor hitch to all this—you have to order a minimum of six pints or not at all. Like that's such a horrible thing.

| ·SWEETS | ·GOURMET | | | |
|---|---|---|---|---|

## 800-382-0109 • Ideal Cheese Shop

## IdealCheese.com

Whether you want a half-pound of cheese from France or you want five pounds of stinky cheese, this site can make it happen. In fact, they offer fine cheeses from a long list of countries, including Australia, Canada and a slew of European nations. While the varieties are near endless, the site doesn't really accommodate the cheese browser, as pictures are in limited supply and the cheese descriptions never say too much. Certainly, you'll fare better if you're somewhat of a connoisseur or, at least, a cheese adventurer.

| ·GOURMET | | | | |
|---|---|---|---|---|

## 877-446-8763 • iGourmet.com

## iGourmet.com

This site goes into tremendous detail when describing its gourmet food items, offering mouth-watering photos, recipes, serving tips and links to complementary or related items. Still a bit uncertain what you're getting yourself into? In that case, they offer resources such as the iGourmet Library and Encyclopedia of Cheese, each of which will let you know (among other things) why you should like these foods. Thus, this purveyor of delicacies leaves you with the most unusual of sensations: an educated appetite.

| ·SWEETS ·CONDIMENTS | ·MEAT & FISH | ·OILS & SPICES | ·GOURMET | |
|---|---|---|---|---|

# iKoreaPlaza.com

iKoreaPlaza.com • No Service Number

In all probability the only web shop with entire sections devoted to both Kimshi and Ramen, this site is always authentic, all the time, right down to the gummies.  Actually based in Oakland, California, they nevertheless have replicated the Korean grocery experience with products like Ilhua Chunyeon cider, Yamasa Kamaboko, Shirakiku fish sausage and Pyongyang Naengmyun.  We don't really know what this stuff is, but as always we really enjoy the fact that it's out there, and available to us over the internet.

| ·REGIONAL ·OILS & SPICES | ·HOT DRINKS ·CONDIMENTS | ·GROCERY | ·MEAT & FISH |
| --- | --- | --- | --- |

# ILovePeanutButter.com

Peanut Butter & Co. • 886-456-8372

Used to be, the biggest, most stratifying choice to be made in peanut butter selection was simple: creamy versus crunchy.  This site takes it to the next level.  Peanut butter variations in this site's Online Store include white chocolate, dark chocolate, spicy and cinnamon raisin.  As for what you use to complement the PB on your sandwich, try Marshmallow Fluff, Strawberry Marshmallow Fluff or Nutella.  You're going to need some milk, because this site is enough to keep your mouth sticky for days.

| ·SWEETS | ·CONDIMENTS | | |
| --- | --- | --- | --- |

# JamisonFarm.com

Jamison Farm • 800-237-5262

Here's a site for those of us who embrace the delectability of the other red meat: lamb.  Simply click on the Order Your Lamb Now link and select between shanks, chops, racks, stews, sausages and kabobs, all tender, juicy and presumably delicious.  In fact, deciding which of these cuts of lamb looks most appealing is the only hard part of ordering (to enjoy other parts of the lamb, see our Apparel and Accessories sections).

| | ·MEAT & FISH | ·PRE-PREPARED | ·ORGANIC | |
| --- | --- | --- | --- | --- |

# JellyBelly.com

Jelly Belly • 800-522-3267

The best jellybean maker on the planet has set up this store to sell Jelly Belly-themed merchandise like hats, T-shirts and candy dispensers.  But you're here for the beans, and possibly the jellybean "recipes."  All forty "official" flavors are available here, along with several new selections for a grand total of more than fifty, not even including their sour assortment.  We did notice a few fringe flavors missing; we can only hope they show up when we go back for more, again, and again, and again.

| ·SWEETS | | | |
| --- | --- | --- | --- |

## 888-574-3576 • JRCigars.com

### JRCigars.com

If you're going to buy tobacco, you might as well buy it from people in a position to know what they're talking about. No, not Cubans: North Carolinians. From deep in tobacco country, JR Cigars offers a wide selection of stogies, both hand rolled and machine rolled, each of which has dozens of brands to choose from, including most of the high-quality Central American favorites. If you're lucky, you might just run across JR Alternatives, which amount to the same stuff, just packaged cheaper and under a different name. Then there's pipe tobacco, split into Imported or Domestic sections, although, no pipes to smoke it with. You will, however, find cigar cutters, humidors and ashtrays; just not from Cuba.

| ·TOBACCO | | | | |
|---|---|---|---|---|

## 212-755-3566 • Katagiri & Co.

### Katagiri.com

Between the horrible site design, the abysmal layout, the complicated ordering process and the numerous translation difficulties (the proprietors are definitely Japanese nationals), one look at this site is enough to scare you away. On the other hand, if you know the charms of such distinctly Japanese products as Lotte Gum, canned UCC Ice Coffee, Calbee Shrimp Chips and Pocari Sweat (it's a soft drink), you and a little patience will find a great amount of food products from the planet's most distinctive island nation.

| ·REGIONAL ·CONDIMENTS | ·SWEETS ·SNACKS | ·GROCERY | ·OILS & SPICES |
|---|---|---|---|

## 800-292-9853 • Key West Seafood

### KeyWestSeafood.com

A popular tourist destination, in part because of its excellent deep-sea fishing, Key West seems like a natural location to look to for fresh fish. Armed with coolers and iced gel packs, this site delivers it fresh, whether it's mussels, shellfish, shrimp or large game fish like grouper, wahoo or mahi mahi (all available on a seasonal basis). Off-season, you may opt to have it sent frozen, and any time, of course, you can find yourself some delectable Key Lime Pie. We can only assume that the pies and fish are packaged separately.

| ·SWEETS | ·MEAT & FISH | ·CONDIMENTS | |
|---|---|---|---|

## 866-567-4379 • Kosher.com

### Kosher.com

That's right, you already know what to expect, but we'll tell you anyway. This is a kosher supermarket, online. All of these products are certified kosher, from the many cuts of meat to wines and even vitamins. Matzoh is only the beginning: you'll find all the traditional holy-day menu items, and even some greeting cards for bar and bat mitzvahs. Additionally, you can buy plenty of prepared meals if you're cooking for one or just don't want to mess up the kitchen. Keeping kosher was never so difficult to avoid.

| ·SWEETS ·SPECIAL DIETS | ·MEAT & FISH ·APPETIZERS | ·WINES ·PRE-PREPARED | ·BAKERY ·GROCERY |  |
|---|---|---|---|---|

## KosherMeal.com

KosherMeal.com • No Service Number

If you think a good, pre-prepared kosher meal is hard to come by, you haven't seen this web site. Then again, maybe you have. While this offers a great selection of certified kosher meals and snacks to be sent to your home or even shipped to a hotel you plan to stay in (for those who like to plan ahead), the site does very little to make the ordering process easy. In fact, they warn you that some orders may be "delayed up to twelve hours in cyberspace" (meaning you should plan way ahead). When you finally follow the Order Now link, find the link that says I Agree To All the Terms & Conditions ... Let Me Order Already, and do so. It should work, and should be worth it.

| ·SPECIAL DIETS | ·PRE-PREPARED | ·SNACKS | |
|---|---|---|---|

## LaMaisonDuChocolat.com

La Maison du Chocolat • 800-988-5632

In a quote attributed to "master of ganache" and La Maison du Chocolat founder Robert Linxe, we are told: "Chocolate is alive ... I battle with chocolate. It does not follow obediently like other ingredients. But when you capture it, you have it right there, alive, where you want it." Well, this site is similarly disobedient, with challenging navigation and occasional inconsistencies. Start by following the Our Chocolates link, then links to Classics, Specialties or Les Plaisirs du Palais as you like (other links bear no e-commerce), then select whichever product looks the tastiest (the toughest part). Sometimes prices are in dollars, sometimes in Euros. The chocolate should be dead by the time it arrives.

| ·SWEETS | ·GOURMET | | |
|---|---|---|---|

## LeVillage.com

Le Village • 888-873-7194

Is there any better gourmet than French gourmet? If you think not, you'll probably enjoy this specialty site that caters to would-be nouveau and/or haute cuisine chefs. Maybe you want some raviolis stuffed with pheasant, rabbit or wild boar. Perhaps you just want the meat of these wild game creatures. It's simple enough to find this all among the patés, truffles, coffees, confections and pastries you'd expect from any French store. Oh yeah, if you're crazy enough to eat escargots, you can find that here as well. Just don't kid yourself: it's still snail.

| ·REGIONAL ·RECIPES | ·SWEETS ·GOURMET | ·MEAT & FISH ·CONDIMENTS | ·OILS & SPICES ·PRE-PREPARED |
|---|---|---|---|

## LittlePieCompany.com

Little Pie Company • 877-872-7437

Begging the question, "How little can a pie company stay when it starts delivering all across the US?" this store centered in a theater district of Manhattan offers pies made with all-natural ingredients and no preservatives. Granted, they don't stay hot during shipping, but they'll be fresh, assuming you plan to wolf them down immediately upon receipt. Standbys like apple pie, cherry, key lime and pecan will satisfy your pie lust, while cheesecake, Mississippi Mud and their special sour cream apple walnut pies do plenty to fill in the gaps.

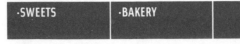

| ·SWEETS | ·BAKERY | | |
|---|---|---|---|

## 800-548-3562 • Lobster Gram

## LiveLob.com

What's better than lobster? Fresh lobster. There are several sites that offer fresh lobster, but let's face it—however fresh it may be when your order is placed, it's going to lose something during its long voyage through the US parcel system. Unless, of course, the lobster is still alive when you open the box. That's what this site delivers: lobster that is still snapping its claws when it gets to you. Whether you know what you're doing going in or stand likely to recreate the famous scene from *Annie Hall,* the dirty work is left to you. If you can manage, the results will melt in your mouth. If not, they're relatively easy pets to care for.

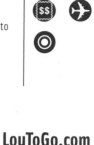

| ·MEAT & FISH | | | |
|---|---|---|---|

## 800-568-8646 • Lou Malnati's Pizzeria

## LouToGo.com

Finally, true Chicago deep-dish pizza has made it out of Illinois, courtesy of Lou Malnati's Pizzeria. Of course, the pizzas are frozen, but only because they haven't yet figured out how to deliver a steaming hot pie through the mail. Your order will be made fresh, then flash frozen, packed in dry ice and sent out. Really, if you just get a glimpse of the pictures on this site, you'll be sold. Just don't look at the About the Pizza section, or you'll be unable to bear the overnight delivery time.

| ·REGIONAL | ·PRE-PREPARED | |  |
|---|---|---|---|

## 877-463-9476 • MexGrocer.com

## MexGrocer.com

No more flying down to Mexico for horchata; now you may simply order it online courtesy of this retailer of non-perishable items from south of the border. It's not that we can't find an abundance of Mexican food just about everywhere we look in this country, it's just that the odds of it being authentic drop dramatically the farther north you go. Based in San Diego, these guys are about as close to the real thing as many of us are going to get. Sure, there's nothing wrong with the hard shells, ground beef, cheese and lettuce of "gringo tacos," but once you get a taste for the real thing, you will never look back.

| ·REGIONAL ·CONDIMENTS | ·GROCERY ·SNACKS | ·OILS & SPICES | ·RECIPES |
|---|---|---|---|

## No Service Number • Mintshop

## MintShop.com

A big fan of fresh breath? You could brush your teeth, or you could pop a few powerful mints. The proprietors of this site "have scoured the earth in search for the latest powerful mints." The results: tins of mints with names like: Blitz, Titanic, Usher. Why the latest, most powerful mints are named for armed invasions, a ship that sank and a house that fell, respectively, is hard to figure. But there're certainly plenty to choose from, including cinnamon, cherry and coffee flavors, as well as some caffeinated options. Your mouth won't know what hit it.

| ·SWEETS | | | |
|---|---|---|---|

## MoHotta.com

Mo Hotta Mo Betta • 800-462-3220

Yes, the name of this spicy condiment specialty store means "more hotter." In other words, as the site says, "no crybabies." To give you a clearer idea, the categories come with names like Scarrry Hot Sauces, Habañero Hot Sauces and Jamaican Jerk. You can find spicy salsas, barbeque sauces and plenty else, if you're up for it. Otherwise, simply look for the mildest of entries and work your way up. A warning, though—hot spices can be addictive; if you start now, you could find yourself trekking a long, hot road down which you will inevitably burn your tongue.

·OILS & SPICES    ·CONDIMENTS    ·SNACKS

## MorrellWine.com

Morrell & Company • 800-969-4637

From "the most wonderful wine shop in America"—located in, of all places, NYC—comes this low-tech online shop. Certainly their real store is gorgeous, with glistening racks full of merlots and whatnot. The website translation, however, leaves a lot to be desired. What it does do right, though, is divide wines based on country and then type and vintage. Sold by the bottle or by the case, it should therefore serve collectors as well as provide some pleasant opportunities for those inclined towards hosting a tasting. If, on the other hand, you don't know anything about wines ... don't buy by the case.

·WINES

## MurraysCheese.com

Murray's Online • 888-692-4339

These guys won't just sell you a wheel or wedge of cheese, they'll tell you how it was made, what it was made of, what type of wine best complements its flavor, how its flavor is defined, how its consistency is defined, how to serve it, how to store it and generally how it is you might like to eat it. Well, this may all be appreciated, as long as it doesn't get in the way of convenient shopping. As it turns out, it doesn't; the cheeses are easily organized by country of origin and listed with pictures and descriptions so that you can simply follow your craving to checkout.

·GOURMET

## NetCigar.com

CigarGold.com • 888-452-4427

According to these guys, the legendary quality of Cuban cigars is a bit overrated. Rather, the quality is there, as the whole concept of cigars sprung out of America's tiny and volatile island neighbor. However, over the years, the reputation of these cigars have been inflated by the very embargo that keeps them out of our hands in this country; as these guys put it, "we want what we cannot have." The solution? Well, apparently the Dominican cigars of today meet and even surpass the expectations we have in the concept of fine Cuban cigars, having been grown from Cuban seeds, mimicked in rolling process and over time improved. Who are you going to believe?

·TOBACCO

## 510-808-0340 • Niman Ranch          NimanRanch.com

To the carnivores among us, merely to mention a great selection of ribs, roasts, steaks, chops and braising cuts is mouth-watering enough.  So we almost hate to imagine what the results of invoking "the finest tasting meat in the world" cut from "livestock [that] are never given growth hormones or sub-therapeutic antibiotics" might be.  From the sound of it, this is meat as pure as it gets, and to be sure this beef, pork and lamb, culled from a "sustainable" ranch in Northern California, will arrive about as fresh and tasty as the postal system allows.  If you live next to a slaughterhouse, you're set.  Otherwise, this one's worth considering.

| ·ORGANIC | ·MEAT & FISH | | |
|---|---|---|---|

## 770-234-6931 • NoMeat.com          NoMeat.com

Offering "virtually every manufactured meat substitute item available," this is a fantastic site for those who'd like to eat vegetarian but don't want salads or grilled vegetables for every meal.  Made with such stuff as soy and vegetable proteins, you can find meatless alternatives to Breakfast Meats, Hot Dogs, Burgers & Steaks, Sandwich Meats and Fish.  Eggs and poultry also get the veggie workout here, ensuring that you stay meat free and still enjoy Buffalo Wings, sort of.  Obviously, these foods are a bit different from the originals, but slather a lot of fake mayo on them and you won't know the difference.

| ·SPECIAL DIETS | ·PRE-PREPARED | | | |
|---|---|---|---|---|

## 800-720-1153 • Nueske's          Nueske.com

"Home of famous applewood-smoked meats," Nueske's Farm says it has for sixty years been offering a fine array of cured meat and fowl, including a Texas-style beef brisket that's smoked "for more than 122 hours."  Delectable by the sound of it, these cuts are vacuum-sealed, sometimes fresh, sometimes precooked, each with a little embellishment to the meat's natural flavors—generally with the help of brown sugar and honey.  Both savory and sweet, this stuff will give any competitive barbecuer a leg up.

| ·MEAT & FISH | ·PRE-PREPARED | | | |
|---|---|---|---|---|

## 440-243-2355 • Old Time Candy Company          OldTimeCandy.com

Nostalgia and your sweet tooth come crashing together with this specialty retailer that offers all "the candy you ate as a kid."  We're talking Willy Wonka candies, Jujyfruits, Jawbreakers, Atomic Fireballs, Wax Lips and Candy Necklaces, among others.  These classics of the sugar kingdom are available here by the box (the display boxes used in stores), in a three-pound assorted bag (featuring at least 35 different candies) and in a Pack Your Own Bag feature.  The latter is the obvious best choice, allowing you to scroll through all your old favorites, adding quantities as you go.  You'll be just like that kid you used to be in a candy store, except this time you'll have more than a nickel to spend.

| ·SWEETS | | | |
|---|---|---|---|

## OmahaSteaks.com

Omaha Steaks • 800-960-8400

The selection of this shop is so extensive that it warrants a disclaimer: animals were harmed in the making of this web site. Packed into cardboard coolers with dry ice, these guys will send you cuts of meat from such popular animals as cows, chickens, pigs, lamb and a whole slew of seafaring fish. In some cases, you can even double up on the meat content, with bacon-wrapped filet mignon for example. For those who shudder at the notion of all this meat, take solace in the fact that you'll find not one ounce of flesh in the Exquisite Desserts section.

| | ·SWEETS ·PRE-PREPARED | ·MEAT & FISH | ·APPETIZERS | ·CONDIMENTS |
|---|---|---|---|---|

## OnlineHumidors.com

Online Humidors • 888-595-7676

Whether you're a longtime devotee of the aromatic, fabled world of cigar smoking or have only recently taken the leap, you know that this musky, flavorful lifestyle isn't nearly as elegant as they say unless you have all the proper accoutrements. We're of course referring to ashtrays, cutters, lighters, cases and, most important of all, the humidors necessary to keep your stogies fresh. Because stale cigars and scattered ashes are a drag, and the rest, well the rest just kinda makes you look cooler, and you'll need all the help you can get what with all those people deriding your "nasty habit."

| | ·TOBACCO | | | |
|---|---|---|---|---|

## OrientalPantry.com

The Oriental Pantry • 978-264-4576

These guys "offer hard-to-find oriental foods, exotic spices, and savory sauces of the finest quality," and on and on, etc., etc. Sure, their selection of Groceries is fine, but more memorable is their fortune cookie selection. Well, less the cookies and more the fortunes you write yourself. Yes, you may now take over the destinies of others for your own amusement with such pithy phrases as "There's something stuck between your teeth," "Avoid the Pork" and "The person beside you will accomplish great things."

| | ·REGIONAL ·RECIPES | ·SWEETS ·CONDIMENTS | ·GROCERY ·OILS & SPICES | ·MEAT & FISH |
|---|---|---|---|---|

## Papanicholas.com

Papanicholas Gourmet Coffee • 888-727-2645

For over one hundred years, this family-operated business located outside of Chicago has devoted its energies to the making of fine coffee culled from beans grown in points international. Shopping narrows it down to Dark Roast, Mild Roast, Flavored and Decaffeinated coffees, and from there it's easy to choose from 10 oz. bags of whole beans. Of course, you'll need a grinder before you can start brewing, but you'll find one here, as well as a few other coffee accessories. We wouldn't automatically think of Chicago when contemplating coffee, but as with all things ingested, it's a matter of taste.

| | ·HOT DRINKS | ·GOURMET | | |
|---|---|---|---|---|

## 212-685-2442 • ParkAveLiquor.com          ParkAveLiquor.com

Once you've proven to this web site that you are indeed of age to purchase alcohol in this country, you'll eventually be led to the online store, which will dazzle you with its extraordinarily extensive selection. Actually, if you follow the Browse link, you'll come face-to-face with an incredibly long list of liquor brands, from A. Conterno to Zwack, with some more familiar names like Bombay Sapphire, Courvoisier and Rémy Martin arranged alphabetically. Unfortunately, beyond that, there's no mechanism (even in their search function) to browse by type of spirit ... unless you're a whisky fiend. You're best bet is the Scotch Search, which enables you to search based on age and distilleries of origin (including more Glens than you can shake a pike at).

| ·SPIRITS | ·WINES | | |
|---|---|---|---|

## 011-39-02-3890-4214 • Peck          Peck.it

The name of this web site is amusing in a couple of ways. The first, of course, comes in simply reading it out loud. Then there's the aspect that the .it extension places the site's origin in Italy, whereas Peck is a distinctly non-Italian name. There's a reason for this—one Francesco Peck, a German immigrant to Italy, originally founded the store as a German deli in Milan over one hundred years ago. So, are we suggesting you shop from an Italian store for German deli items? No. Over the years, the product selection has shifted, now offering mostly Italian gourmet and deli items. Confusing? A little, but the site itself is not, and there's no confusion as to the quality of the food (it's good).

| ·REGIONAL ·OILS & SPICES | ·SWEETS ·WINES | ·HOT DRINKS ·GOURMET | ·SPIRITS ·CONDIMENTS |
|---|---|---|---|

## 888-802-9945 • Picnic-Baskets.com          Picnic-Baskets.com

The word "picnic" evokes imagery of men in striped hats wooing courtly young ladies in white summer dresses who sit daintily upon checkered blankets twirling their parasols. Always in the center is a full, portable spread, complete with classy utensils and a wicker basket. Of course, in time this sight has diminished in favor of a small cooler and plastic sporks—but no more! This site offers plenty of baskets, as well as some fantastic basket kits for two or four people, each elegantly self-contained for picnicking the way it was meant to be. Additionally, you can find picnic backpacks, portable chairs and wine duffels to add to the experience.

## 888-802-9945 • PicnicBaskets2Go.com          PicnicBaskets2Go.com

We know what you're thinking; here's yet another entry to the already overcrowded picnic basket market. Actually, the same company is responsible for this and the other picnic site we found, the discernible difference seeming only to be in the models available. This one appears to have a slightly more modern take on the art of eating outdoors; it offers a selection of both insulated baskets and portable coolers, so the sun can warm your face and not your egg salad, and who wouldn't want that?

## PikePlaceFish.com

Pike Place Fish Market • 800-542-7732

From what appears to be the most fun-loving seafood market in the Pacific Northwest, if not the world, comes this site, complete with pictures of a ragtag group of employees holding up fish carcasses and mugging for the camera. Now, if you enter the Store, you do get better pictures than this of the selection, which includes fresh shrimp, salmon, crab, halibut, swordfish, marlin and trout. Choices also include some live clams, oysters and mussels, which of course don't tend to comply so well with the photographer's directions.

| ·MEAT & FISH | ·RECIPES | | |
|---|---|---|---|

## Plantin.com

Plantin • 201-867-4590

If you're of the mindset that mushrooms are more than just a pizza topping, take a good look at this fungi site that has joint offices in France and, uh, New Jersey. Of course, the delicacies in question come from the French branch, in particular selections of white and black seasonal truffles, which are shipped weekly to maintain consistent freshness. Also found here are some morels, porcinis and a small variety of miscellaneous mushrooms, which also hail from France; New Jersey's known more for a different kind of fun guy.

| | ·RECIPES | ·GOURMET | | |
|---|---|---|---|---|

## Polana.com

Polana • 888-765-2621

It's not all headcheese and tripe soup. This gourmet Polish market offers some of the finest cured meats and baked goods this side of Krakow. In particular, the sausage selection is certain to please, with Cyganska sausage, Zywiecha sausage, Krakowska sausage and of course kielbasa. If you don't know the differences between these, just look at this site as a good excuse to taste them out. While you're here, you might as well pick up a few pierogies, blintzes, potato pancakes and babkas. Hey, it couldn't hurt.

| ·REGIONAL | ·SWEETS | ·MEAT & FISH | ·BAKERY |
|---|---|---|---|

## PreserveCompany.com

Prince Edward Island Preserve Company • 800-565-5267

Are you beginning to tire of the old standbys like strawberry preserves, raspberry jam and grape jelly? Thanks to this family-run business from the northeast, you can put a little bit of zest back into your preserves-loving palate. Flavors like black currant, strawberry & Grand Marnier and wild blueberry & lemon should get you properly started, and there's a lot more. Aside from fruit preserves, there're also interesting assortments of mustards, salsas, marmalades, chutneys and maple syrups. Dry toast is no longer an option.

| | ·GOURMET | ·CONDIMENTS | | |
|---|---|---|---|---|

212-421-0017 • RussianFoods.com

**RussianFoods.com**

Apparently, the Georgian wineries of Russia employ "one of the world's oldest wine making traditions, dating back to 3000 BC." This is only one of the many things you can find out on this site, with a host of facts on topics ranging from Russian cuisine to women. Of course, primarily there's the bevy of Russian products, beginning with some of that Georgian wine, and extending through meats, bread and fish. Find out what rybets, shad and siomga are, and wash them all down with some refreshing kvas.

| ·REGIONAL ·SPIRITS | ·SWEETS ·WINES | ·GROCERY ·CONDIMENTS | ·MEAT & FISH ·BAKERY |
|---|---|---|---|

---

800-437-2572 • Salsa Express

**SalsaExpress.com**

We don't know what it is about salsa in particular, but among all foodstuffs it seems to inspire the most creative naming. Take some of the wares of this spice-loving site: Dave's Insanity Salsa, Lawyer's Breath Sauce, Toxic Waste and Redneck Gormay Sweat Thang Sauce [sic]. As it happens, the extensive sauce and condiment variety found here gets creative with more than just the naming, offering such intriguing and peculiar submissions as Lobster Salsa, Peanut Chipotle Salsa and Mango Thai Chile Chutney. Featuring most of the brands featured elsewhere, and plenty more, this is easily one of the better places to singe and delight your taste buds.

| ·OILS & SPICES | ·GOURMET | ·CONDIMENTS | |
|---|---|---|---|

---

800-884-5884 • Scharffen Berger

**Scharffen-Berger.com**

Even in this country, you would be hard-pressed to find a chocolatier that hasn't been doing it for more than a decade at least, or even more than a century. When you consider the esteemed chocolate makers of continental Europe, well the notion of eating chocolate whose recipe didn't exist long before you were born seems almost laughable. Then these guys come along. Founded in only 1996, this brand is barely an infant in terms of chocolate time, and yet they must be doing something right, as their chocolate is phenomenally popular, both for baking and for eating, and is giving the age-old tradition of waxy American chocolate bars a run for its money.

| ·SWEETS | ·RECIPES | ·GOURMET | |
|---|---|---|---|

---

877-710-3467 • Seafoods.com

**Seafoods.com**

Either fresh or frozen, this is a good place to find (what else?) seafood. There are plenty of places to find most of this stuff: lobster, crab, oysters, halibut, etc. But these guys have pretty much everything you can imagine and some you might not even believe exist. For example, look under Exotic Shellfish and you'll find langostinos and cockles, which you may have to learn how to cook. Under Exotic Fin Fish, haddock and shark may not surprise you, but how about agria, corvine or rouget barbet? See anything you like? Well, don't fill up too fast; there are still some frog's legs to order.

| ·MEAT & FISH | ·PRE-PREPARED | | |
|---|---|---|---|

## Sees.com

West Coasters will no doubt immediately recognize the name of this old-time chocolate shop mainstay. As for the rest of you, pay attention, because you're going to like it. Featuring all the confections you could want, like buttercreams, caramels, nougats, truffles, fruits, nuts and their classic chocolate-covered molasses chips, you can order samplers to figure out which are your favorites. If you've already got a notion, you can build a custom box with no trouble at all, made all the easier by some mouth-watering imagery (they show you the insides). This is good stuff.

| ·SWEETS | | | |
|---|---|---|---|

## Sherry-Lehman.com

This highly lauded NYC wine shop offers a fantastic search function so that aficionados may easily find bottles that run the gamut of varieties. This is particularly good as the selection is huge (as you can tell by browsing through the Go Shopping section). Those relatively new to the wine purchasing game may make good use of the search tool as well, shopping by price (almost always high), vintage (the year it was made), country (France is good), region and/or appellation (whatever that actually is).

| | ·SPIRITS | ·WINES | |
|---|---|---|---|

## SimonJohnson.com

If you're looking for a food supplier that has earned the trust of renowned international chefs, this is the site for you. Featuring raw cooking materials from such varied and exotic origins as Iran, Tunisia and Madagascar, this Australia-based source of fine ingredients is worth the trouble—and it is a bit of trouble. See, browsing is set up through a complex system of pull-down menus that will keep you busy enough if you're not sure what you want. If, however, you know you want some mushrooms, you will have to determine ahead of time that the different varieties of fungi are located in the Dry Goods section, or risk hunting through a dozen pages to view all of your options. A steep learning curve with this one, but a huge payoff.

| | ·SWEETS ·RECIPES | ·HOT DRINKS ·GOURMET | ·MEAT & FISH | ·OILS & SPICES |
|---|---|---|---|---|

## SmithfieldHams.com

If you dig on swine, then consider this: Southerners know their pigs. That's what makes this "Distinctive Southern Foods" retailer out of southern Virginia worthwhile; their huge selection of cured, smoked and aged ham is probably second to none. Then, of course, there's plenty of pork, bacon and sausage interspersed throughout the catalog, easily mouthwatering in the right light. They also smoke turkey and seafood, but should your sweet tooth feel left out (which is undeniably better than your sweet tooth falling out), just look to their startlingly creative array of pound cakes. It's enough to bring you back.

| ·REGIONAL | ·SWEETS | ·MEAT & FISH | ·RECIPES |
|---|---|---|---|

## 800-705-2323 • Burgers' Smokehouse

### SmokeHouse.com

These guys have been curing meats since back when doing so was actually necessary. The full name is Burgers' Smokehouse, but don't start to think that beef is the only thing these guys have to offer. Actually, they're selection is probably the most extensive we've seen, including categories stocked full of veal, game birds, buffalo, catfish and the somewhat enigmatic and disturbing jowl (described as "more flavorful and less expensive" than bacon). All of this in addition to your carnivorous mainstays, and even some heat-and-serve omelets—it's enough to cause a vegetarian to flee.

| ·MEAT & FISH | ·PRE-PREPARED | | |
|---|---|---|---|

## 888-365-6983 • SpecialTeas

### SpecialTeas.com

This fantastic tea site offers just about everything, from Earl Grey and Oolong to Chai and everything tea in between, including herbals, flavored, scented, caffeine-free and decaffeinated (we're not entirely sure what the distinction would be). Several handy search filters make it easy to narrow down your browsing by qualities like grade (broken leaf, pressed and powdered, for example), characteristic (such as flowery, nutty or spicy) or region/nation of origin. This one has the potential to keep you sipping with variety for years to come.

| ·HOT DRINKS | | | |
|---|---|---|---|

## 800-654-6887 • Stahmann's Country Store

### Stahmanns.com

The key word to remember when logging on to this New Mexico "Country Store" is this: pecans. In this catalog you'll find caramel pecan popcorn, assorted pecan pies and cakes, pralined pecans, baking pecans and pecan brittle. Oh yeah, you can also just find plenty of regular pecans—you know, for eating. Almost as an afterthought, they've included a section devoted to Fruits and Meats, which consists mostly of oranges, and some brisket. They sum it up as "Tasteful Gifts from the Land of Enchantment."

| ·SWEETS | ·SNACKS | ·BAKERY | |
|---|---|---|---|

## 800-782-7282 • Starbucks

### Starbucks.com

Sure, it seems silly to shop online from Starbucks. After all, there's no doubt a store just down the street from where you're sitting right now, and another two or three that you pass on the way to work every day. Still, if you just feel the need to import your own espresso roast beans, as it were, and the equipment necessary to brew your own Double Tall Mocha Latte, well, maybe there's reason enough to check out the site. After all, it's a nice-looking site, with plenty of easy shopping features. Anyway, check it out if you will; then, drink locally.

| ·HOT DRINKS | | | |
|---|---|---|---|

# StonewallKitchen.com

Stonewall Kitchen • 800-207-5267

These guys hooked up a decade ago to create flavors "made for the crisp, clear days of Autumn" and "as vibrant as the leaves of Maine … at their colorful and flavorful peak." Sounds pretty, but exactly how do the leaves of Autumnal Maine taste? Tough to say, but the actual relishes, syrups, chutneys, garnishes, jams, dressings and condiments make you want to figure it out. And, while the distinction between condiments and dressings may never be firmly established, these guys also offer some breakfasts and the occasional lobster dinner that should make attempts to do so a delicious effort. Just click on Site Map to get a good look at it all.

| | | ·OILS & SPICES ·PRE-PREPARED | ·GOURMET | ·APPETIZERS | ·CONDIMENTS |
|---|---|---|---|---|---|

# Sugar-Plum.com

Sugar Plum • 800-447-8427

There are no ifs and buts with regard to this site. It's got all sorts of gourmet treats, from chocolates and bulk candies to nuts and, should the regular kind not live up to expectations, candied nuts. Heck, there's even a wily assortment of stuff like infused oils, jams, biscotti, marinades and other sundry items that could only fit under the Gourmet mantle. While there aren't any actual sugarplums listed (at least, at this writing), there's plenty of other stuff to dance in your head.

| | ·SWEETS | ·SPECIAL DIETS | ·SNACKS | ·GOURMET |
|---|---|---|---|---|

# Tealuxe.com

Tealuxe • 888-832-5893

Some of the more interesting things on this site include a Glossary of Tea Terms (a good read) and an interactive World Tea Map that allows you to click on a highlighted region to view the available selection from exotic places like Malaysia, Tanzania and Sikkim. As neat as this all is, and as cool as the site looks, the big question remains: what about the teas? We figure that, among their list of "over 100 teas from around the world" you're bound to find some teas that are right for you.

| ·HOT DRINKS | | | |
|---|---|---|---|

# ThaiGrocer.com

Thai Grocer • No Service Number

This online grocer is pretty much exactly what you'd expect it to be, except that it doesn't feature any Thai alphabet, and seems to be geared towards English-speaking Americans. Which isn't to say the selection isn't authentic. You'll find all the rice noodles, coconut milk soups and Pad Thai you're looking for, along with anything else you might need to cook a great Thai meal. Don't know how to cook one? They've thought of that too, with the ThaiGrocer Cooking School offering instruction and recipes that should be enough to prevent you from having to order out anymore.

| ·REGIONAL ·RECIPES | ·HOT DRINKS ·CONDIMENTS | ·GROCERY ·SNACKS | ·OILS & SPICES |
|---|---|---|---|

## 650-961-4996 • The Golden Egg

**The-Golden-Egg.com**

Where on the internet can you turn these days when you need to roast a whole kid (the goat, of course)? The answer is this no-frills, no-nonsense gourmet food site that also sells such unusual butcher items as a suckling pig, wild boar and rabbit. Want duck? Mallard or Muscovy? You may also find venison, buffalo, quail, grouse, woodpigeon, ostrich, partridge and something called a squab, which we think is also a bird. We're not sure how the stuff is packaged, sent or even where it comes from exactly, but we're reasonably sure that goat will be dead and stripped of fur when it arrives.

| ·SWEETS ·GOURMET | ·MEAT & FISH ·CONDIMENTS | ·OILS & SPICES ·PRE-PREPARED | ·RECIPES ·APPETIZER |
| --- | --- | --- | --- |

## 847-328-3711 • The Spice House

**TheSpiceHouse.com**

Here's a surprisingly bland site, given its product selection. However, you will find hundreds of spices listed alphabetically, from Adobo Seasoning to Zanzibar Whole Cloves, and all the sweet, hot and peppery flavors between. Health watchers can make it easy on themselves by viewing all the salt-free spices alphabetically (to take out the guesswork). As if that wasn't enough, each item has a pretty thorough product description, as well as links to recipes that contain that particular spice. Good stuff if your rack is lacking.

| ·OILS & SPICES | | | |
| --- | --- | --- | --- |

## 888-472-1022 • Tienda.com

**Tienda.com**

You may be surprised to find out that this store, whose name is Spanish for "store," actually deals in products from Spain, as opposed to Mexico or South America. Emphasis of this fact turns up in the form of an entire section devoted to paella. As it turns out, the site carries other things besides just Spanish food, but primarily this is what makes the shop worthwhile. That being said, a visit to the Cookbooks section will almost certainly be necessary as, other than paella, who knows what the Spanish eat? Well, judging by the other category names, stuff like jamón (ham) and tapas (Spanish for "snacks").

| ·REGIONAL ·OILS & SPICES | ·SWEETS ·WINES | ·GROCERY ·CONDIMENTS | ·MEAT & FISH ·SNACKS |
| --- | --- | --- | --- |

## 800-325-2220 • Tillamook Country Smoker

**TillamookJerky.com**

If you're like most people, every day you wonder, "How can I get more meat sticks into my diet?" Well, look no further, friends; this site is your answer! All things even remotely jerky-like are probably found in here somewhere, whether it's your standard, Natural Style, the morsel-sized Jerky Chews or the easier to eat (if tough to swallow) Soft and Tender Style. Also, let us not forget the aforementioned Meat Sticks, which are promised to be "a lot longer on quality than hot dogs." A more ringing endorsement we could not imagine.

| ·MEAT & FISH | ·SNACKS | | |
| --- | --- | --- | --- |

## TobaccoDirect.com

In response to the popular epithet, "you can put that in your pipe and smoke it," you will of course be needing a pipe. This site's only too happy to oblige, whether you're content with the cheap atrocity of a corn cob pipe or opt for one of the infinitely more stylish handmade, imported models. This site's catalog runs the gamut, with more shapes, colors and styles than we care to get into. As it turns out, this selection is overshadowed by an even larger array of tobaccos, in tins or in bulk. All metaphors aside, these you actually can put into your pipe and smoke.

| ·TOBACCO | | | |
|---|---|---|---|

## VermontGoldUSA.com

The About Us page of this site begins, "There is a mystique that is Vermont…." Well, it certainly makes you wonder. Fortunately, the end of the About Us page cinches it all into one finger-snapping answer: "Experience the Magic of Maple." Yes, it all becomes clear; from the land of maple comes this specialty retailer devoted to maple syrup. Actually, it's not just syrup, but maple butter and both pancake and waffle mixes. And we'd be remiss not to mention the maple syrups that come in other flavors. All this maple might cause the state of Vermont to lose some of its mystical luster, but hey, wouldn't you rather have a sweet-tasting breakfast?

| ·REGIONAL | ·CONDIMENTS | | |
|---|---|---|---|

## VeryVera.com

Most of us have never been exposed to traditional, down-home Georgia cooking, with recipes that have been passed from generation to generation. Some of us may even wonder, "Where's Georgia again?" It's inconsequential now, because thanks to this site we can all finally figure out what the fuss is about (assuming you were previously privy to any fuss). With pound cakes and layered cakes, cookies and confections, the family recipes that were passed along to company founder Vera from her grandmother, also named Vera, may be tasted by the lot of us, wherever we may live.

| ·REGIONAL ·BAKERY | ·SWEETS | ·GOURMET | ·PRE-PREPARED |
|---|---|---|---|

## VillageOrganics.com

Even as it's getting tougher and tougher these days to avoid foodstuffs that have been chemically treated, mixed with animal byproducts or genetically engineered somehow, online shops like this one are making it easier to find those that haven't. "All of the products we offer contain no artificial preservatives or additives, no hydrogenated oils and are completely vegetarian," says this site, which is honest enough to point out to you when they're uncertain of just how organic ingredients of certain products might be. To be so sensitive to its customers' needs, this one must be family-owned. Yup.

| ·ORGANIC ·CONDIMENTS | ·HOT DRINKS | ·GROCERY | ·OILS & SPICES |
|---|---|---|---|

**802-375-3015 • The Fun Shop**                                      **WhoopeeCushion.com**

Congratulations, jellybean lovers!  By browsing all the way back into the "W" part of this section, you have saved yourself a little money on your favorite jellybean candies.  While this site looks terrible, and lacks all the recipes and fun facts to be found on the official Jelly Belly site, they offer all of the available flavors and the option to buy then in smaller quantities.  It still pays to order a lot, when you figure in the shipping fees, but the same goes for the official site, so this one wins for those of you diligent enough to find it.

| ·SWEETS | | | |
|---|---|---|---|

**877-289-6886 • Wine.com**                                          **Wine.com**

The products available on this site differ from state to state, but if used properly you shouldn't notice.  See, this one's exquisitely organized, with powerful search filters, copious winemaker's notes, easily identifiable icons and buying guides that should help even the most bumbling of novices to find at a glance the great beverages that are usually only tasted by snooty connoisseurs.  If you happen to be one of the snooty connoisseurs, don't disdain—you should still be able to maintain exclusive access to the finest selections available, as the catalog is quite extensive, and only the happiest of accidents will see the finest of bottles fall into the hands of those unable to fully appreciate it.

| ·WINES | | | | |
|---|---|---|---|---|

**877-665-3213 • Zingermans.com**                                    **Zingermans.com**

It's tough to say whether this online deli's following proclamation pays a bigger compliment to itself or its patronage: "We have always believed that our customers can tell the difference between mediocre and marvelous."  One way to find out would be to try some of the great bread selections available.  Take your pick from loaves of rye, chaleh, poilâne and pumpernickel.  Of course, you'll want all the ingredients necessary to build a sandwich with these breads, starting with a fine selection of cheese and spreads (by the looks of it, you'll have to add your own meat), and maybe finish with a babka.

| ·SWEETS | ·OILS & SPICES | ·BAKERY | ·CONDIMENTS |
|---|---|---|---|

NOTES:

_____

_____

_____

_____

_____

_____

_____

_____

_____

_____

_____

_____

_____

_____

_____

_____

_____

_____

# Gadgets & Electronics

How familiar is this scenario? You want to make a big money purchase on some high-tech items but don't know a lot about the technology. You figure with a little help from a friendly salesperson you can make a decision in no time at all and head home with the best combination of price and function. Then you meet the salesperson, who winks and smiles, and has been trained never to take "no" for an answer. Suddenly, you're on your way home with last year's retread and a payment plan that even your bank finds laughable, while the "friendly" salesperson retires to his luxury yacht. Better luck next time.

Except now you don't need luck. You can find everything you need to know about the newest electronics items, from computers to home theater, with just a little research on the web. You may custom-build your own computer so when it's delivered you can simply plug it in and get down to business. Camera buffs find enough traditional tools to build a dark room, or digital tools that make it unnecessary. Home entertainment becomes a true test of restraint, with TV screens getting bigger and flatter, video recorders getting smarter and audio systems likely to soon exceed the acoustics of real life. Meanwhile, home automation and security products allow you to remotely control other parts of the house.

Of course, wireless technology escalates on almost a daily basis. Then again, some of the non-electronic gadgets out there are ingenious enough to appear on any *Star Trek* episode, or at least *Batman*. If your utility belt's not up to par, you probably need to sit down and spend a good amount of time going through the sites in this section. Hey, it's starting to look like the future is now, and if you're not ahead of the game, you're falling behind.

NOTES:

_____

_____

_____

_____

_____

_____

_____

_____

_____

_____

_____

_____

_____

_____

_____

_____

_____

_____

TIPS ON BUYING ELECTRONICS ONLINE

These suggestions may help prevent frustration and obsolescence.

•**INSURE SHIPMENTS:** As always, when a big purchase is involved you'll want to make sure that your product is insured during shipment. Electronics, in particular, consist of some very fragile merchandise.

•**COMPARISON SHOP:** The site where you find the perfect electronics equipment may be different from the best place to buy this equipment. Use **thepurplebook** to find other sites that sell your product, to compare prices and options. Also, it may be a good idea to check out the manufacturer's web site, when available.

•**COMPATIBILITY CHECK:** If you're buying a new component for your home theater, computer, phone or any other electronics systems, make sure the product you're ordering works in conjunction with the products, you already own. If not, you may be able to find a viable adaptor, or you may just have to find another product.

•**WARRANTIES:** The warranty may be as valuable as the equipment it protects. Check to see that your product is covered if something goes wrong, especially if you're buying it refurbished or at a discount, then (and this is very important) don't lose the warranty documents!

•**INSTALLATION & SUPPORT:** Electronic devices have the power to make life a little easier, but assembling and installing them can send you over the edge. When in doubt, try to stick to products that offer good instructional and technical support, and be patient.

•**BATTERIES:** It sounds silly, but check to see that the personal electronic devices you order come with batteries, especially if they're product specific. On request, some sites will make sure the batteries are charged when they arrive.

 SITES THAT MAY COME IN HANDY

The following URLs may be useful when you shop.

Definitions for Computing Terms:  http://www.whatis.com
Glossary for Internet Terms:  http://www.netlingo.com
Computing Info & Product Reviews:  http://www.zdnet.com
Personal Electronics Info & Product Reviews:  http://www.consumerreview.com
Home Theater Info & Tips:  http://members.aol.com/htbasics
More Reviews of All Products:  http://www.cnet.com

## ≫ SECTION ICON LEGEND

Use the following guide to understand the rectangular icons that appear throughout this section.

### COMPUTERS

Stores devoted to computers (desktops, laptops, network servers, etc.) may be found under this icon, whether they offer hardware, software, peripherals, accessories or, as is typically the case, all of the above.

### HOME THEATER

Home theater equipment, including all audio and video components and accessories, is covered by this icon.

### PERSONAL ELECTRONICS

Any portable electronic devices such as cell phones, personal music players, handheld recorders, videocameras, videogames or any combination fall under this icon.

## >> LIST OF KEY WORDS

The following words represent the types of items typically found on the sites listed in this section.

### A/V ACCESSORIES

Cables, adaptors, batteries, discs, tapes and racks; anything that can connect, power or house your home theater components and make them work properly gets lumped under this term.

### AUTOMATION (& SECURITY)

This site covers the sort of electronics devices that get wired into your walls, whether they're protecting your home from the outside (security), or automating the processes that take place inside.

### CAMERAS

Digital, video, digital video, instant, disposable or traditional 35mm stills; any cameras or camera accessories may be found with this label, including developer, photo quality paper, lenses, tripods, straps, cases, memory and film.

### GADGETS

They may open bottles, point you north, clip your nails or all three at once. Here, gadgets are defined as objects of any size that use ingenuity and engineering to perform any variety or combination of tasks with ease, anything from pocket-knives to massage aids and collapsible chairs.

### GAMING

Videogames cover a lot of ground, and may also be found in the Entertainment section. Generally, sites in this section that include games sell home gaming consoles, portable games, game software, joysticks and other relevant accessories.

### HARDWARE

In this case, computer hardware, meaning machines, printers, keyboards, mice, monitors, scanners, webcams, microphones, speakers, disk drives, servers, networking devices and any other pertinent piece of compatible equipment.

### PHONES

A good chunk of these sites pertain to mobile phones, including service, but also included are home cordless phones, multiline phone systems, answering machines, calling cards, phone accessories and even your basic rotary dialers.

### SOFTWARE

Your computer is nothing without it, and there's more out there than any of us really know what to do with. Software includes programs designed to run an office, create multimedia projects, play media, educate children, store information and any other human task that can be condensed into programming language.

## KEY WORD INDEX

Use the following lists to locate online retailers that sell the Gadgets & Electronics you seek.

### A/V ACCESSORIES

AVConnect.com
Batteries.com
BestBuy.com
BHPhotoVideo.com
Bose.com
Buy.com
CableWholesale.com
CircuitCity.com
Crutchfield.com
DishOnline.com
eBatts.com
eCost.com
ElectroShops.com
eTronics.com
GoodGuys.com
HammacherSchlemmer.com
HiFi.com
HTMarket.com
Kodak.com
LANBlvd.com
LapTopProducts.com
LapTopTravel.com
MPSuperStore.com
MusiciansFriend.com
OrbitCommunications.com
Outpost.com
PlanetMiniDisc.com
RadioShack.com
SHarbor.com
SmartHome.com
SonyStyle.com
TotalMedia.com
Vanns.com
WireCloset.com

### AUTOMATION

BestBuyPCs.com
LetsAutomate.com
RadioShack.com
SharperImage.com
SmartHome.com

### CAMERAS

BestBuy.com
BestBuyPCs.com
BHPhotoVideo.com
Buy.com
BuyDig.com
CDW.com
CircuitCity.com
eBatts.com
eCost.com
eTronics.com
GoodGuys.com
HPShopping.com
Kodak.com
MPSuperStore.com
Outpost.com
PCConnection.com
PlanetMiniDisc.com
RadioShack.com
RitzCamera.com
SonyStyle.com
UniquePhoto.com
Vanns.com

### GADGETS

Brookstone.com
DeLorme.com
GadgetShop.com
GadgetUniverse.com
HammacherSchlemmer.com
iGadget.com
LaptopTravel.com
SharperImage.com
SmartHome.com
WristWatch.com

### GAMING

Buy.com
BuyKensington.com
Outpost.com
RadioShack.com

### HARDWARE

ADSTech.com
Apple.com
BestBuy.com
BestBuyPCs.com
BHPhotoVideo.com
Buy.com
BuyKensington.com
BuyLogitech.com
CableWholesale.com
CDW.com
Chumbo.com
CircuitCity.com
ClearanceClub.com
Crucial.com
Dell.com
eCost.com
eLinux.com
Gateway.com
HammacherSchlemmer.com
HPShopping.com
IBM.com
iGo.com
InkFarm.com
Insight.com
LANBlvd.com
LapTopProducts.com
LaptopTravel.com
MicronPC.com
Minotaur.com
MobilePlanet.com
MonitorOutlet.com
MPSuperStore.com
MusiciansFriend.com
Outpost.com
PCConnection.com
Priceless-Inkjet.com
RadioShack.com
SHarbor.com
SonyStyle.com
Vanns.com
Warehouse.com
WireCloset.com

### HOME THEATER

BestBuy.com
BestBuyPCs.com
BHPhotoVideo.com
Bose.com
Brookstone.com
Buy.com
BuyDig.com
CircuitCity.com
Crutchfield.com
DishOnline.com
DTVExpress.com
eCost.com
ElectroShops.com
etronics.com
GetConnected.com
GoodGuys.com
HammacherSchlemmer.com
HiFi.com
HTMarket.com
Kodak.com
MonitorOutlet.com
MPSuperStore.com
OrbitCommunicatons.com
Outpost.com
PlanetDTV.com
PlanetMiniDisc.com
PlasmaOutlet.com
ProjectorPeople.com
RadioShack.com
SharperImage.com
SimplyWireless.com
SmartHome.com
SonyStyle.com
TotalMedia.com
Vanns.com

### PERSONAL

Apple.com
Batteries.com
BestBuy.com
BestBuyPCs.com
Brookstone.com

Buy.com
BuyDig.com
CDW.com
Chumbo.com
CircuitCity.com
Crutchfield.com
DeLorme.com
eBatts.com
eCost.com
eTronics.com
GadgetUniverse.com
GoodGuys.com
HammacherSchlemmer.com
Handango.com
HiFi.com
IBM.com
iGo.com
Insight.com
LaptopTravel.com
LetsTalk.com
MobilePlanet.com
MPSuperStore.com
MusiciansFriend.com
OrbitCommunicatons.com
Outpost.com
Palm.com
PlanetMiniDisc.com
RadioShack.com
SharperImage.com
SmartHome.com
SonyStyle.com
Vanns.com
Warehouse.com

## PHONES

BestBuy.com
Buy.com
CDW.com
CircuitCity.com
Crutchfield.com
eBatts.com
GetConnected.com
iGo.com
Insight.com
LetsTalk.com
MPSuperStore.com
OrbitCommunicatons.com
RadioShack.com
SimplyWireless.com
SmartHome.com
Vanns.com
Vialta.com
WaveShield.com

## SOFTWARE

Adobe.com
Apple.com
BestBuy.com
BestBuyPCs.com
BHPhotoVideo.com
Buy.com
CDW.com
Chumbo.com
Dell.com
DeLorme.com
DownloadStore.com
eCost.com
eLinux.com
Handango.com
IBM.com
Insight.com
McAfee.com
MobilePlanet.com
MusiciansFriend.com
Outpost.com
Palm.com
PCConnection.com
ScanSoft.com
SHarbor.com
Symantec.com
UniquePhoto.com
Vanns.com
VirtualSoftware.com
Warehouse.com

## Adobe.com

Adobe • 888-724-4508

The first name in graphic design, Adobe's products have long served as industry leaders, led primarily by the oft-revered Photoshop. This is just the sort of software that makes all modern photography suspect, as it is powerful enough to seamlessly doctor any photo, making no image an impossibility. For example, using this software, you could graft your own head onto anybody else's body, show your family picnicking with aliens or create a picture of yourself slam dunking over Shaquille O'Neal. Here, seeing is believing, but only with regard to the software.

 ·SOFTWARE

## ADSTech.com

ADS Technologies • 800-888-5244

This is a company that specializes in products designed to give your computer a little more oomph (that's a technical term). Lending a bit of versatility to older machines, or newer ones that happen to be unequipped with newer technologies, the products here enable you to operate via firewires and USB ports, for example, even if you can't do it internally. Also available are Ethernet cards and other internet stream adaptors, and a bevy of equipment that will facilitate video capture, streaming and editing. Bookmark it.

·HARDWARE

## Apple.com

Apple Computers • 800-692-7753

It's almost odd that Apple Computers should use this domain to house their online presence; after all, the Macintosh brand name has long since eclipsed the Apple brand in popular recognition. Nevertheless, here is the spot to find all currently available Mac products, like iMacs, iBooks, Power Macs, G4 Cubes and whatever other colorful package they may soon invent. Aside from computers, and other compatible hardware/ accessories, you may find here an extensive list of both proprietary Apple software and that of other leading brands. Still better than PCs in most multimedia applications, the name may have changed, but the quality has not.

 ·HARDWARE ·SOFTWARE ·PERSONAL

## AVConnect.com

Dreamz, Etc. • No Service Number

Once your home is full of electronics equipment, you run the risk of losing control of your living space. For example, your TV must be placed on the side of the room closest to the cable hook-up, your speakers won't stray far from the amplifier and your audio receiver strains to be closer to the DVD player because the cable connecting them just barely reaches.... Then you introduce a new component into an already complex system only to realize there are more plugs than sockets and not enough cable to go around—what's to be done!? This is a dramatization of what life might be like without audio, video and power cables of the right length and capacity, which you'll find here.

 ·A/V ACCESSORIES

## 888-288-6500 • Batteries.com

### Batteries.com

How many different kinds of batteries can you name? Let's see: there's 9-Volt, C, D, AA, AAA, AAAAs … then there are rechargeable versions of all these, and those tiny ones made for watches. What's that, about a dozen or so? Well, as this site is prepared to show us, there are thousands of batteries out there, powering things like cell phones, laptops, camcorders, PDAs, power tools and any number of toys, tools and electronic devices. You can shop by device or by battery number (as if we knew they were numbered) and then by brand name and model number. So even if yours is the most obscure, discontinued model Panasonic videocamera, you can probably power it here.

| ·PERSONAL | ·A/V ACCESSORIES | | |
|---|---|---|---|

## 888-237-8289 • Best Buy

### BestBuy.com

You're probably quite familiar with this national electronics outlet store that generally delivers on its promise of savings and selections. Chances are, you even live near one of their brick-and-mortar locations, or near enough that paying postage for online orders doesn't make much sense. Adding to the reasons not to shop online is the enjoyment of simply playing with the computers, home theater products and other electronics in the store, what with all the shiny buttons and dials. But here are the reasons to check out this site first: you can get all of your product research out of the way ahead of time, familiarize yourself with any sales or rebates the store can offer and order any item for pickup at your own convenience.

| ·HARDWARE ·PHONES | ·SOFTWARE ·A/V ACCESSORIES | ·PERSONAL ·CAMERAS | ·HOME THEATER |
|---|---|---|---|

## 877-692-3787 • BestBuyPCs.com

### BestBuyPCs.com

Even if this site only did carry PCs, we'd list it here by virtue of its better-than-competitive prices and a selection that wants nothing to do with poor quality merchandise. As it turns out, they don't even offer desktop PCs, only a few notebooks. Nice of them, then, to carry a great deal of home theater, digital photography, video and home security equipment as well, including some valuable digital video editing suites and intriguingly high-tech surveillance gear. A bit of personal electronic gadgetry rounds out the selection, but will be easily forgotten when you get a gander at the TVs....

| ·HARDWARE ·CAMERAS | ·SOFTWARE ·AUTOMATION | ·PERSONAL | ·HOME THEATER |
|---|---|---|---|

## 800-606-6969 • B&H

### BHPhotoVideo.com

This store claims to be "the world's largest dealer of imaging equipment at discount prices," and who are we to prove them wrong? Though not ideal, they do offer an incredible amount of traditional and high-tech gear, both for novice and pro levels, still and video photographers. So, if you're looking to light up a studio, set up a darkroom or edit video sequences on your computer, no problem. They also have an equally well-rounded selection of pro audio gear, so you can realistically shoot a feature film, edit and score it, entirely with items found on this site. Not bad, huh?

| ·HARDWARE ·CAMERAS | ·SOFTWARE | ·HOME THEATER | ·A/V ACCESSORIES |
|---|---|---|---|

# Bose.com

Bose • 800-999-2673

This manufacturer of audio equipment has made a name for itself largely by designing products that can fill your home with a full, rich sound without taking up much physical space. Between Surround-Sound speaker systems that are tiny enough as to be nearly invisible, subwoofers that tuck neatly under or behind furniture and sleekly designed digital components, this gear offers some fine-quality home audio without cluttering up your home with a lot of clumsy equipment.

| | ·HOME THEATER | ·A/V ACCESSORIES | | |
|---|---|---|---|---|

# Brookstone.com

Brookstone • 800-846-3000

Seen in malls across America, you might think of Brookstone as gadget central, or at least as the home of the Shiatsu Lounger. Whatever term you prefer, it's certainly a good place to find fanciful inventions that make life easier or better in completely nonessential ways. Whether it's personal grooming devices, office toys, travel aids, automobile gizmos or any number of funky tools you're after, you can find interesting things in this place where ingenuity takes precedence.

| | | ·PERSONAL | ·HOME THEATER | ·GADGETS | |
|---|---|---|---|---|---|

# Buy.com

Buy.com • 800-800-0800

With already more than one million items to speak of, we're starting to think that the proprietors of this site won't be happy until they're actually selling every high-tech retail product on the planet. As it stands, it seems they sell a little bit of everything or—failing that—a lot of everything, from computers to books about computers. Particularly sizeable are their Electronics and Computers sections, with competitive pricing on most merchandise, and some particularly enticing deals on mobile technology. Their most valuable feature, though, is the excellent navigation/organization. Just imagine trying to organize a million things yourself and you'll see what we mean.

| | | | ·HARDWARE ·PHONES | ·SOFTWARE ·A/V ACCESSORIES | ·PERSONAL ·CAMERAS | ·HOME THEATER ·GAMING |
|---|---|---|---|---|---|---|

# BuyDig.com

Worldwide Direct • 800-617-4686

Here's the sort of site that won't impress you until you've already used it. Sure, you'll recognize that you've gotten a great value as soon as the ordering process is complete. Then, once the product has been delivered and installed, you'll be quite taken with it. It's when you realize that you could have spent a lot more time shopping elsewhere and wound up paying higher prices for lesser merchandise that you'll sing the praises of this personal electronics, photography, home theater and video retailer.

| | | ·PERSONAL | ·HOME THEATER | ·CAMERAS | |
|---|---|---|---|---|---|

## 800-235-6708 • Kensington
**BuyKensington.com**

If you've checked out any of the sites we've listed that offer custom PCs, you may have noticed that the Kensington brand name pops up from time to time. That's due to their prominence it the world of computer accessories, namely stuff like trackball mice, screen filters, carrying cases, surge protectors and keyboards. They also have gaming accessories, as well as computer security devices and some other stuff less easy to categorize. If you're currently using a standard mouse or wearing out your eyes on an unfiltered monitor, be careful, this site will make you feel entirely business class.

| ·HARDWARE | ·GAMING | | | |
|---|---|---|---|---|

## 702-269-3457 • Logitech
**BuyLogitech.com**

Designer accessories for your computer may initially seem like a waste of money—heck, it may seem that way upon further consideration. But design isn't always about style. For example, some of Logitech's products, like trackball mice or ergonomic keyboards, make prolonged and repetitive use of your machine a little easier on your hands and wrists. They also offer things like webcams, joysticks and speakers, stuff which may not make your life healthier, but can make it more fun. Either way, it's easy to browse their small selection, and most of these products work pretty well (just happening to look kind of cool in the process).

| ·HARDWARE | | | | |
|---|---|---|---|---|

## 888-212-8295 • CableWholesale.com
**CableWholesale.com**

Cables, switchboxes, adaptors: these are the things that can make a computer system look like a tangled mess of confusion to the casual observer. Of course, these same items are absolutely necessary if you intend to expand your computing capacity, which is why advanced users will immediately appreciate this selection—which isn't to say the rest of us can't benefit. Aside from an extension cable here or surge protector there, inexperienced users can easily find stuff like joysticks and trackball mice that make interfacing with the motherboard both easier and more fun, if you catch our drift. It's not pretty to look at, and some of these products require opening up the guts of your CPU to install, but otherwise this is an extraordinarily useful shop.

| ·HARDWARE | ·A/V ACCESSORIES | | | |
|---|---|---|---|---|

## 800-840-4239 • CDW Computer Centers
**CDW.com**

These guys have a lot to offer, with all kinds of networking hardware and software, A/V electronics, cell phones, PDAs and service plans for your local area. Probably their greatest strength, however, lies in matching a computer system, desktop or portable, Mac or PC, to your own specifications based on price, performance and power. Add-ons and accessories can be tinkered with, the price adjusted and software installed. When it's over, you can easily order a top-brand machine at a fair price, and be reasonably sure that it will handle even your most excessive demands.

| ·HARDWARE ·CAMERAS | ·SOFTWARE | ·PERSONAL | ·PHONES | |
|---|---|---|---|---|

# Chumbo.com

Chumbo.com • 612-343-7086

These guys' claim to be "the ultimate source in software and hardware" is dubious, given the number of similar retailers out there, especially when you consider that a lot of their competitors feature bigger selections. However, this one's more likely to have the good stuff, and not buried in the middle of a lot of useless products. Here you will be able to track down powerful software and valuable hardware without any trouble or even expertise (you can pick that up later). We may never know what the word "chumbo" has to do with anything, though.

| ·HARDWARE | ·SOFTWARE | ·PERSONAL | |
|---|---|---|---|

# CircuitCity.com

Circuit City • 800-843-2489

These guys never seem to tire of offering incentives to capture your business—as their Specials and Rebates sections will attest. As to whether it's worth it? The only convincing answer would be: "occasionally." However their selection fares for any given product (too numerous to mention, though few options for each), shopping on this site is quite simple, aided by pop-up sub-menus (we like those) and thorough categorization. They also offer computer customization (a must) that will suit most casual shoppers, but a relative lack of options will again frustrate finicky know-it-alls. Basically, it boils down to this: if you're easy, so is Circuit City.

| ·HARDWARE<br>·A/V ACCESSORIES | ·PERSONAL<br>·CAMERAS | ·HOME THEATER | ·PHONES |
|---|---|---|---|

# ClearanceClub.com

Clearance Club • 877-855-0230

If you're through trying to hunt down that perfect notebook or desktop computer, complete with all the particular features you fancy, and then hoping, crossing your fingers that it will have a decent price, make a note of this site. First, you can find some great prices on clearance models that stand a slim chance of meeting your needs. Otherwise, click on the Build a System link and set up the parameters for the machine you so ardently desire. The catch? Well, generally you'll run into a little word called "refurbished." Basically, if you buy something here, make sure it's covered by a manufacturer's warranty.

| ·HARDWARE | | | |
|---|---|---|---|

# Crucial.com

Crucial Technology • 800-336-8915

Has your computer grown sluggish? Is it holding you back? It's probably not your machine that's changed, but the amount of space new software applications take up in your Random Access Memory (RAM). Fortunately, most PCs (desktops and notebooks) sold over the past few years are expandable, featuring slots where additional memory may be easily inserted (like a cartridge). All you need to do is know your make and model, and this site will offer a selection of RAM upgrades that, in most cases, will improve performance. It can even help you out if you don't understand any of this.

| ·HARDWARE | | | |
|---|---|---|---|

## 888-955-6000 • Crutchfield.com

### Crutchfield.com

If you're one of those nitpicky online shoppers who values things like selection, detailed information, ease of navigation and great prices, you may finally have found an electronics retailer worthy of your time here. Somehow, these guys have managed to bundle loads of information onto each page without making it impossible to decipher and, while not every portable and home electronics product you might want exists in great supply, most of the big items give you plenty of options and enough detail to distinguish between them. Special sections for AV-equipped computers, outlet items and Scratch & Dent discounts round out this stellar home theater specialist. If you find better, do let us know.

| ·PERSONAL | ·HOME THEATER | ·PHONES | ·A/V ACCESSORIES |
|-----------|---------------|---------|------------------|

## 800-999-3355 • Dell Computers

### Dell.com

This gargantuan PC manufacturer makes its headquarters in Texas, so right away you know it's poised for global domination. As a matter of fact, at this writing, the site makes mention of its number-one position in the world market. Much of this, of course, is due to the wide range of products it pumps out year after year, from desktops and laptops to handhelds and all manner of accessories. While their online store is a bit daunting, a little patience will lead you to a pretty decent search engine that enables you to configure a product to your specifications, and for a reasonable price at that.

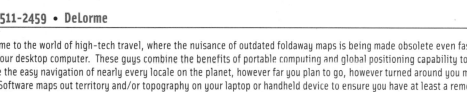

| ·HARDWARE | ·SOFTWARE | | |
|-----------|-----------|---|---|

## 800-511-2459 • DeLorme

### DeLorme.com

Welcome to the world of high-tech travel, where the nuisance of outdated foldaway maps is being made obsolete even faster than your desktop computer. These guys combine the benefits of portable computing and global positioning capability to enable the easy navigation of nearly every locale on the planet, however far you plan to go, however turned around you may feel. Software maps out territory and/or topography on your laptop or handheld device to ensure you have at least a remote idea of the right direction, whereas GPS receivers will pinpoint your exact location on the map, so you may see exactly how lost you've gotten.

| ·SOFTWARE | ·PERSONAL | ·GADGETS | |
|-----------|-----------|----------|---|

## 888-834-1999 • Dish Direct

### DishOnline.com

Lest you think this is an online community for gossip about celebrities, this dish refers to the kind that receives satellite transmissions. It's pretty easy to get started, though familiarizing yourself with the different equipment and terminology might take some time. Whether you're open to installing a large object on the roof of your home, or opt for the smaller model dishes, you should be able to find a good deal on getting the world of entertainment into your home and even captured for posterity on a selection of digital video recorders, which makes it easier to hear what people halfway around the world have to say about your favorite celebrities.

| ·HOME THEATER | ·A/V ACCESSORIES | | |
|---------------|------------------|---|---|

# DownloadStore.com

Is there such a thing as too much software? Maybe so. This site offers a fantastic wealth of downloadable software, meaning unlike most of the other products purchased online, you can get what you buy here almost immediately. The problem is that each category, ranging from anti-virus software to clip-art selections, is well divided but disorganized, offering hundreds of choices, even when you use the Search feature. Consequently, shopping takes longer than delivery, which is almost never true anywhere else.

 ·SOFTWARE

# DTVExpress.com

Digital TV, we are told, is the way of the future. If so, this site probably provides the best view of new technology at its finest, particularly embracing the advent of wide aspect ratio screens (16:9, similar to most feature films) that will rid us of letterboxes forever. You can achieve this through several options, the least of which are a high-end line of HD compatible (High Definition Television) CRT TVs, projection TVs and digital projectors, all fine products, truly. However, the real stuff is in the Plasma Displays, which deliver incredible viewing while thin enough to be hung from a wall like a picture frame. Either way, this stuff isn't for the faint of pocketbook.

 ·HOME THEATER

# eBatts.com

The world of portable electronics would be worthless without batteries, whether for phones, camcorders, laptop computers or otherwise. This site offers batteries for use with any of these items, compatible with any of dozens of different manufacturers and models. It's a good spot to check out if you want longer life or a quicker recharge, and also if you're just looking for a decent AC adapter to plug your device into a wall socket. It's not pretty, though, with long lists of model numbers that can be daunting, but it works, and should free your machines from the bonds of wall sockets.

 ·CAMERAS  ·PERSONAL  ·PHONES  ·A/V ACCESSORIES

# eCost.com

For a dot-com that's built its brand name around the notion of "cost," it's hard to get a bead on these guys' prices as they change them often, sometimes more than once a day. The result is an all-around electronics superstore that probably offers its best incentives at times when the market is better conditioned to buyers than sellers. As such, it may prove worthwhile to check any purchases from other stores against the prices here. Since they offer a pretty elastic selection of computing hardware, software, portable and home electronics, you can get a pretty good idea of what's available and what it's worth, assuming you can see past the hectic exterior.

·HARDWARE ·SOFTWARE ·PERSONAL ·HOME THEATER
·A/V ACCESSORIES ·CAMERAS

866-243-1001 • ElectroShops.com

**ElectroShops.com**

Even if you've embraced the concept of replicating the movie-going experience in your own home, this one may prove a bit scary. Through this site, you can convert any room in your house into one of the poshest viewing theaters in the world, right down to velvet ropes to keep out the rabble. Granted, any good home theater starts with high-quality audio and video, and you'll have to find things like DVD players and audio receivers elsewhere. You can find great wireless and wall-mount speakers, though, and all the tools and hardware needed to set it up properly (you'll need help). In the meantime, it's worth a look if just to imagine setting up marquees, concession stands and theater seating (complete with cup holders) where your Barca lounger used to be.

| ·HOME THEATER | ·A/V ACCESSORIES | | | |
|---|---|---|---|---|

877-395-4689 • eLinux

**eLinux.com**

If you don't already know what Linux is, you probably won't make much use of this site. If, however, you understand the power that this open source coding and its penguin mascot represent, you might make use of the server hardware, software and other gear for sale here. If you know it quite well, however, then you'll probably ignore it anyway. Looks like this one has a slim market, but it's a good place to get started, if nothing else, on learning about this still-young operating system and its many benefits.

| ·HARDWARE | ·SOFTWARE | | | |
|---|---|---|---|---|

800-323-7669 • etronics.com

**eTronics.com**

Actually known to proclaim, "Discount is our middle name," this site would be laughable if it wasn't so darn good. Extremely thorough, this is that rare electronics store that will satisfy the photo gearhead, home theater enthusiast, communications geek, techno outdoorsman and the professional DJ, both in prices and in selection. Excellent navigation makes it all the sweeter, enabling you to narrow down the field if you know what you're doing, or helping you to figure out what you want if you don't. Truly "plugged into the world of electronics," bookmark this one, because you will be back.

| ·PERSONAL | ·HOME THEATER | ·A/V ACCESSORIES | ·CAMERAS | |
|---|---|---|---|---|

011-44-148-259-5100 • gadgetshop.com

**GadgetShop.com**

Offering no dearth of fun stuff for the weirdo gadget freak, this UK-based site seems to have really gone out of its way to cultivate a unique selection. If it's any indication, check out some of the category names: Beer Monster, Kinky, Plasma & Light, Spaced Out, Street Cred and Robodogs & Accessories. For the extreme fan, they even have The Simpsons as its own section, with such unexpected items as a Sideshow Bob Foil Cutter (it's best not to ask why). This may be the best evidence that the world's gone mad.

| ·GADGETS | | | | |
|---|---|---|---|---|

## GadgetUniverse.com

**Gadget Universe • 800-872-6250**

**GC**
**$$**

Yes, gadgets are well represented here, from the tiny electronic gizmos that are necessary for any self-respecting utility belt, to new versions of everyday products that have been tweaked ever so slightly to add new, innovative functionality and/or comic appeal. Imagine walking your robot dog while your robot lawn mower cuts the grass until your talking watch lets you know it's time to watch the game on your other watch. Suddenly, regular life seems so bland.

| ·PERSONAL | ·GADGETS | | |
|-----------|----------|--|--|

## Gateway.com

**Gateway • 800-846-4208**

**GC**
**$$**

Gateway, with its Holstein-patterned boxes, offers a pretty thorough and well-stocked store here, where you can customize desktop and notebook systems, and even arrange to make monthly payments. They also offer accessories and a selection of palmtop computers, as well as plenty of special offers, trade-in deals and rebates. It's not the easiest of sites to use, but getting the hang of it shouldn't take long and the deals you can find might be worth it (assuming you like their products). Just a tip: some of the add-ons they offer may be procured for less elsewhere.

| ·HARDWARE | | | |
|-----------|--|--|--|

## GetConnected.com

**Get Connected • 800-775-2506**

**$$$**

Here is a fine site for setting up service plans in your local area and buying the products needed to utilize them. Whether you seek access to the internet (DSL, dial-up or otherwise), phone service (local, long distance or wireless), TV (cable or satellite) or a plan for your PDA, you can find and compare local rates from different companies and for different products. Rebates and special offers show up almost everywhere you look, so it's worthwhile to take your time here and research all your options. Ironically, when all is said and done, you may not have uttered a single word, and most likely will have saved money in the process.

| ·HOME THEATER | ·PHONES | | |
|---------------|---------|--|--|

## GoodGuys.com

**Good Guys • 888-937-7004**

If you're a longtime customer of the Good Guys, you'll find everything you'd expect from their brick-and-mortar stores here, without the alternately aggressive and invisible sales staff to deal with. For new customers, what you'll find here is free shipping (at least at this writing), no sales tax and a low price guarantee (though this last is tougher to implement online). Otherwise, there's not a whole lot of enjoyment to be taken from the site, despite good items at decent prices. Not that there's anything particularly wrong here—if you have something specific in mind it might even be worth a look.

| ·PERSONAL | ·HOME THEATER | ·A/V ACCESSORIES | ·CAMERAS |
|-----------|---------------|------------------|----------|

## 800-321-1484 • Hammacher Schlemmer

**HammacherSchlemmer.com**

This upscale retailer promises "products as unique as [its] name," and delivers in a big way. Quick perusal of this site might turn up such wild items as a floating trampoline, a watch/MP3 player, a personal submarine and a plethora of other things "that either solve problems or further [your] lifestyle." They place an emphasis on having top-quality merchandise and provide a Tested As Best section to show just how good it can get. If some of this stuff seems a little out there, just remember that Hammacher Schlemmer was the first store to sell electric dry shavers, pop-up toasters and microwave ovens. This bodes well for the future of submarine sales.

| ·HARDWARE ·GADGETS | ·PERSONAL | ·HOME THEATER | ·A/V ACCESSORIES |
|---|---|---|---|

---

## 817-280-0129 • Handango

**Handango.com**

As PDAs and the wireless internet grow in popularity, it's not too surprising that sites like this one would spring up. With an unwavering devotion to all things handheld, whether of the Palm, Pocket PC or other operating systems, you can find software for download, accessories (from cases to collapsible keyboards) and, yes, even a variety of the devices themselves. With such a narrow focus, you'd think navigation would be a cinch: not so. Returning to the home page is the only way to cross between platforms, and the Home link won't do it. Instead, click on the Handango icon; after all, it's got to mean something.

| ·PERSONAL | ·SOFTWARE | | |
|---|---|---|---|

---

## 800-945-4434 • Cambridge Soundworks

**HiFi.com**

If you're really quite serious about outfitting your home with high fidelity audio and video, this neatly laid out site offers a variety of products and a relatively easy shopping experience. For example, aside from the to-be-expected product categories like Audio, Video and Home Theater, you can browse by brand or utilize a Shop by Room feature, in case you were wondering which type of audio equipment was best suited to your bathroom, for instance. Basically, if it can enhance your home-viewing experience, you will find it here, right alongside some portable electronics which prove that, with the help of a little technology, you can take it with you.

| ·PERSONAL | ·HOME THEATER | ·A/V ACCESSORIES | |
|---|---|---|---|

---

## 888-999-4747 • Hewlett-Packard

**HPShopping.com**

The HP here stands for Hewlett-Packard, manufacturer of computers, digital cameras and plenty of other high-tech items. Primarily, though, HP is regarded as the top printer manufacturer, with myriad models of ink jet, laser and color printers, and some items that combine the functions of a printer, copier, fax machine and more into one design. This is also a good place, should you happen to own an HP product already, to find accessories such as replacement toner cartridges, photo-quality paper or memory cards for their digital cameras. Prices aren't ideal, but you can be confident you're getting the right product, straight from the source.

| ·HARDWARE | ·CAMERAS | | |
|---|---|---|---|

## HTMarket.com

The Home Theater Marketplace • 888-764-9273

HT in this context stands for Home Theater, and these guys take that distinction quite literally, going so far as to offer not just one, but a selection of popcorn popping machines such as you would find at your local multiplex (as if you needed more melted butter in your life). They also offer lighted movie marquees, theater-esque lighting/seating, and racks/mounts for all of your electronics equipment. Of course, it's said electronics gear that caught our attention. While audio systems are notoriously absent here (despite a thorough selection of cables and speaker stands), wide aspect ratio plasma screens and digital projectors abound, ripe for the HT connoisseur.

| ·HOME THEATER | ·A/V ACCESSORIES | | |
|---|---|---|---|

## IBM.com

IBM • 800-426-4968

AKA, International Business Machines. Yes, the company that released computers upon the hapless human populace so many decades ago is still at it, and here they offer their wares for online purchase. It's a decent site, given how expansive their products and services are. In addition to custom-built PCs, they offer many kinds of software, hardware and networking systems, each readily available, if difficult to browse. The days are long since past that these guys were innovators, but there's still a lot going on here, so it's worth checking, even if just to spectate.

| ·HARDWARE | ·SOFTWARE | ·PERSONAL | |
|---|---|---|---|

## iGadget.com

iGadget.com • 877-287-1358

If you think that the height of technological splendor has been achieved in the confines of your CPU, then you have got to take a moment to look at this site. From extraordinarily high-tech to downright kitschy, these guys have got toys and utilities the likes of which once existed only in science fiction. Take, for example, a small digital device that completely disguises your voice over a telephone, or a wristwatch that takes digital photographs. While not everything here specifically fits the "gadget" label, with plenty of products for personal grooming, day-to-day living and sheer fun, your shiny, sparkling future has arrived.

| ·GADGETS | | | |
|---|---|---|---|

## iGo.com

iGo • 888-205-0064

For those of us who just can't sit still, technology has found a way that we may stay connected wherever we care to venture. At least, that's what these guys are counting on, selling all sorts of mobile technologies like cell phones, PDAs and laptop computers. They'll even hook you up with wireless plans for your phone or internet needs, as well as interesting accessories like foldaway keyboards that serve to combine mobility and comfort. Whether you just feel like there's not enough time in the day, or you just want to stay abreast of all technology has to offer, these products will make it forever impossible to just "leave it at the office."

| ·HARDWARE | ·PERSONAL | ·PHONES | |
|---|---|---|---|

## 800-465-3276 • Inkfarm Dot Com

**InkFarm.com**

These guys serve one purpose: replacing your printer's toner and ink cartridges. After all, you're bound to run out eventually, and they figure if they make it easy enough you'll look to them when you do. They make it rather easy, offering a menu of product manufacturers and, subsequently, model numbers, so you can simply follow a path to the correct printer and make your purchases. It works the same way if you're looking for paper, whether of regular stock or something better. You may want to pause and take wonder at the ridiculous costs of such things, but then, you'd do that anyway.

| ·HARDWARE | | | |
|---|---|---|---|

## 800-467-4448 • Insight

**Insight.com**

Good prices come and go with this site, but if you're looking for good deals on higher-end computing products, you might want to include these guys in your research. Not that these prices are overwhelmingly good, but for those willing to spend a little extra, here you might also spend a little less. Paradoxical to be sure, but you pretty much have to check it out on a model-by-model basis to get the full picture. As to other aspects of the site, it's cleanly laid out, with good selections of hardware, software and networking solutions from most major brands, and a side-by-side comparison feature doesn't hurt.

| ·HARDWARE | ·SOFTWARE | ·PERSONAL | ·PHONES |
|---|---|---|---|

## 800-235-6325 • Kodak

**Kodak.com**

From the brand name that has become synonymous with photography, this site doesn't readily let you know there's a store to be found. If you do manage to find the Shop@Kodak link, it will lead you to a shop fully stocked with all sorts of (motion and still) film, cameras and other such gear that has made Eastman Kodak a favorite of professionals spanning three centuries. Lest you think, though, that they've fallen behind with the times, take a look at their quite advanced selection of digital imaging tools, including cameras, scanners, printers, imaging software and much more. They've already captured your soul, now let them capture your heart.

| ·HOME THEATER | ·A/V ACCESSORIES | ·CAMERAS | |
|---|---|---|---|

## 877-246-7059 • Lanblvd.com

**LANBlvd.com**

Local Area Networking is usually the sort of thing businesses do; after all, it's not like you generally need to connect multiple computers in your home. Still, in case you have the urge, or develop the need (say, to run multiple machines through one DSL line), this site exhibits a steadfast devotion to all things LAN. From routers, switches and hubs to cables, PC cards and wireless modems, these guys make finding the right equipment simple, given you know what any of this stuff is in the first place.

| ·HARDWARE | ·A/V ACCESSORIES | | |
|---|---|---|---|

## LapTopProducts.com

Connect Globally, Inc. • 888-878-9327

As the name would suggest, this site serves to make it easy to find parts, add-ons, upgrades and accessories for your laptop computer. Thing is, when you get a glimpse of its home page, any notion of simplicity is sucked away by an incredibly busy design. If you can sort through the clutter (following the Products link, if you can find it, should help), it will get easier, but not by much. Still, diligence will turn up things like cellular modems, DVD drives, batteries, ethernet cards, port replicators, scanners, printers and literally dozens of other laptop-specific items that should make mobile computing easier ... eventually.

| | ·HARDWARE | ·A/V ACCESSORIES | | |
|---|---|---|---|---|

## LaptopTravel.com

Laptop Travel • 888-527-8728

If the very thought of wireless communications makes you drool like a hound at a pig roast, this is the site for you, as it is plum full of those little gadgets and cables that make mobility as fun as it is futuristic. From infrared adaptors that can turn your cell phone into a wireless modem, to portable computing accessories, this site really offers just about anything you might imagine you need when you're in the middle of nowhere and wish to phone, email, fax, scan, print, download or rip whatever it is that's distracting you from nature. Topped off by foreign power adaptors and supplies, should you leave the country, bring a comfortable set of clothes on your trip, because there won't be room for much else.

| | ·HARDWARE | ·PERSONAL | ·GADGETS | ·A/V ACCESSORIES |
|---|---|---|---|---|

## LetsAutomate.com

Let's Automate • 011-44-175-358-0516

If you revel in the ultimate and unyielding power that is push-button remote control, you will be primed to enjoy this site, which offers several home automation solutions. Basically, the concept takes advantage of your home's internal wiring structure so that you can centralize command of systems like lighting, security and climate control. Then, in conjunction with motion detectors, timers and even your computer, you can act like a true omnipotent master of your domain, even when away, ensuring that your home never rests on its laurels. Be careful, though, this company ships from the UK, and it can be quite expensive.

| | ·AUTOMATION | | | |
|---|---|---|---|---|

## LetsTalk.com

LetsTalk.com • 877-825-5460

What we're talking about in this case is wireless communications—specifically, cell phones, pagers and the wireless internet. From web-enabled PDAs and cell phones to the service plans that make them go, you can do a little quick comparison shopping through this site and be set up with mobile service for years to come (and let's not forget accessories). Plenty of rebates and other incentives will pop up all over this site, and excellent search functions use your home zip code and user preferences to narrow it all down to just a few easy choices, each listed in exquisitely thorough detail, making this a great place to start looking, if not buy. Good customer service, as well.

| | ·PERSONAL | ·PHONES | | |
|---|---|---|---|---|

## 408-992-8100 • McAfee

### McAfee.com

One of the industry leaders in virus protection, these guys offer software that can detect and remove most of the malicious programming propagated by ruthless hackers, whose dastardly devotion seems to be the destruction of our data. Without this software, chances are high that an email attachment will corrupt your computer. Even with the protection it could happen, but to a lesser extent, and with the availability of downloads to fix the problem, if possible. The moral of the story is that you should get software protection, but you should also back up all of your important documents on a CD or floppy disk.

| •SOFTWARE | | | | |
|---|---|---|---|---|

## 888-224-4247 • MicronPC

### MicronPC.com

This PC manufacturer offers a fairly thorough custom-building process for desktops, notebooks and servers, and while these machines certainly look pricey, that's often because they're built to be powerful even before you select additional parts or accessories (they do offer cheaper alternatives). Aside from a (somewhat refreshing) straightforward site design, novice users can also take advantage of solid technical support (always a quick phone call away, plus hours of hold time), and many series of online tutorials that will get you squared away on hundreds of topics as your usage becomes more advanced.

| •HARDWARE | | | | |
|---|---|---|---|---|

## 703-406-8622 • Minotaur Technologies

### Minotaur.com

If you fancy yourself somewhat of a PC expert and demand that your machine be built from scratch, this site allows you to do just that, right down to the motherboard, processor, multimedia cards and even case. Every single option has multiple items from several different manufacturers, so you can piece things together at your whim, or preferably from knowledgeable experience, in most cases saving money. You can even opt to assemble all the pieces yourself, making it easy to substitute any preferred hardware they fail to offer. Like the site's mythical namesake, the result will be a monstrous and powerful machine, assuming, of course, you know what you're doing.

| •HARDWARE | | | | |
|---|---|---|---|---|

## 800-675-2638 • Mobile Planet

### MobilePlanet.com

Sure, the greatest mobility exists for those equipped with a high-limit credit card, a backpack and a permanent vacation. However, this site focuses on the mobility afforded to those of us who want to get around but also have to get things done. Whether you're in need of a laptop computer, a PDA and/or the wireless applications that make them truly worthwhile, this site can hook you up with varying degrees of success. Primarily, what this site lacks is any information pertinent as to why you might want any of these products, but if you can find this information elsewhere, the prices might be enough to bring you back.

| •SOFTWARE | •PERSONAL | •HARDWARE | |
|---|---|---|---|

## MonitorOutlet.com

The Monitor Outlet • 888-478-6161

Home computer monitors have come a long way from the tiny amber or green on black displays of early IBMs just a couple of decades ago. Now, of course, full-color monitors are the norm, some even with high-enough resolution for viewing television and video. Here, you'll find them all, in varying sizes and technologies, including flat-screen (LCD or plasma) displays, wide aspect ratio screens (16:9, similar to most feature films) and even some touch screen models, for those who prefer a hands-on computing experience.

| ·HARDWARE | ·HOME THEATER | | |
|---|---|---|---|

## MPSuperStore.com

Marine Park • 800-300-0615

What makes a store super? Well, in this case, it doesn't just sell computers, but also all the whistles and bells that make them extra fun. Or, if you're into photography, you can find all kinds of digital and film photography equipment, whether you're into stills or video. You can even find some good editing hardware and software so you can put it all together. Not just a mild-mannered store without the glasses, this site comes complete with pull-down menus and pop-up images to make your experience more enjoyable than it would otherwise seem.

| ·HARDWARE<br>·A/V ACCESSORIES | ·PERSONAL<br>·CAMERAS | ·HOME THEATER | ·PHONES |
|---|---|---|---|

## MusiciansFriend.com

Musician's Friend • 800-391-8762

You might get caught up in the pictures of guitars available on this site, or drums or DJ gear. But look under Recording and you'll see one of the web's best selections of audio hardware and software for your home recording studio, whether your hard disk recording ambitions revolve around MIDI or digital audio. Selection, price and ease of use are the things we always look for in a web site, and this one goes over well in all three categories. The only drawback is that, with all these guitars, online you never have a chance to pick one up to jam.

| ·HARDWARE | ·SOFTWARE | ·PERSONAL | ·A/V ACCESSORIES |
|---|---|---|---|

## OrbitCommunications.com

Orbit Communications • 978-440-8899

If your cable company hasn't been living up to your expectations, or if you simply live out of range of cable wiring or broadcast signals, you may be ready for the world of satellite television. This site can help you do this, though to be honest it's tough to say how. The Site Map might help, and following the Products link will be necessary to form an elementary understanding of what you might want, but ultimately you should probably take advantage of their live sales assistance. Shopping through their selection of computer accessories, phones, portable electronics and home theater items is a little easier … but not by much.

| ·HOME THEATER | ·A/V ACCESSORIES | ·PHONES | ·PERSONAL |
|---|---|---|---|

## 877-688-7678 • Frye's Electronics — Outpost.com

This massive (and we don't use the term lightly) online store is so big that we fear at any moment it might topple over. To be sure, occasionally a link will lose itself in the strain of their servers to keep up, but generally everything works. What will you find? Well, it really depends upon what you're looking for. You begin by following any of the category links, like PC Computers (& Software), Macs, Electronics (including Home Theater), Cameras, Games, Handhelds and Innovations, each of which leads to so many other options that really anything you could imagine might turn up.

| ·HARDWARE ·A/V ACCESSORIES | ·SOFTWARE ·CAMERAS | ·PERSONAL ·GAMING | ·HOME THEATER |
|---|---|---|---|

## 800-881-7256 • Palm — Palm.com

Pockets are in short supply these days, as the customary keys and wallets have been crowded by pocketknives, mobile phones and, of late, electronic handheld organizers. To give you an idea of how popular this particular brand is, its name has become almost synonymous with pretty much any of the wireless handheld products. In truth, though, this is merely one of several options, and the site doesn't seem interested in explaining why you should choose it over the rest, other than to market all its software and hardware options. Needless to say, were it equipped with a bottle opener, screwdriver and tweezers, it might free up some pocket space.

| ·SOFTWARE | ·PERSONAL | | |
|---|---|---|---|

## 888-213-0607 • PC Connection — PCConnection.com

Despite the name, these guys don't limit themselves to strictly PC gear, offering pretty much any type of computer product you're willing to pay for, whether system hardware, software, servers and accessories. Prices stick pretty close to what the market will bear, with overnight delivery being the standard (although you can opt for slower, cheaper shipping). Layout is typical, nearly identical actually to about a hundred other sites we've reviewed. Generally, we couldn't really find anything special about this one. But it seems to be pretty successful, so we've included it here, to stand its middle ground.

| ·HARDWARE | ·SOFTWARE | ·CAMERAS | |
|---|---|---|---|

## 800-851-1356 • PlanetDTV.com — PlanetDTV.com

Televisions are different in the 21st century, and this somewhat off-kilter site manages to do a fine job of showing you the future. Between the high-definition television, LCD flat screen, wide aspect ratio and plasma screen technologies at work here, you may find yourself uncertain as to which future to embrace. Adding HDTV receivers, HDTV projectors and DVD recorders to the mix won't help a bit, and to be sure if these guys had their way you'd buy it all. Of course, new technologies don't come cheap, and getting a jump on the Joneses in this case may take a little extra research on your part.

| ·HOME THEATER | | | |
|---|---|---|---|

## PlanetMiniDisc.com

**Planet Mini Disc • 877-463-4327**

It may be premature to consider the cassette tape a thing of the past, but if you're still listening to music in this format, one question must surely reside in the back of your mind: "Why?" See, somewhere between DAT and CD exists this easily portable, recordable and (more importantly) re-recordable hi-fidelity media format. And this site has it all over: portable players/recorders, in-dash car stereo devices or component systems for your home. This data format seems to offer the best of all worlds, at least for the time being. At least, it's a better idea than 8-track.

·PERSONAL    ·HOME THEATER    ·A/V ACCESSORIES    ·CAMERAS

## PlasmaOutlet.com

**PlasmaOutlet.com • 800-646-4574**

As the name would imply, these guys will try to get you a good deal on a plasma screen TV. In fact, you may even save a hundred dollars over other shops, which sounds like a lot until you see the astronomical prices we're talking about (any price conjecture, of course, is flimsy at best and subject to possibly drastic changes). At any rate, if they do manage to beat their online competitors, it's most likely due to the obvious disregard they show towards site design; ironic that one should view something so dismal in order to view images as fabulous as these high definition plasma and LCD flat screens offer.

·HOME THEATER

## Priceless-Inkjet.com

**Price-Less Inkjet Cartridge • 877-408-3652**

These guys have figured out a way to lower the costs of replacement ink and toner cartridges for your printer. Of course, there is a catch: technically, these aren't the cartridges recommended by printer manufacturers. See, most printer manufacturers keep cartridge costs up in order to keep printer costs down; after all, a printer becomes useless without ink. What these guys offer are "remanufactured" (those which have been used, cleaned and refilled) and "compatible" cartridges (which fit specific makes and models, but were not made by the original printer manufacturer). How well these things work is debatable, but with great prices and guarantees, the site is worth your interest.

·HARDWARE

## ProjectorPeople.com

**ProjectorPeople.com • 888-248-0675**

If you're a believer in home theater—we mean, in actually making your home theater big and magnificent—this site can help you achieve new levels of quality viewing. First of all, there are the 16:9 aspect ratio digital and high-definition television screens (the same ratio as movie theater screens), many of which utilize the wildly exciting plasma screen technology (the TV screens thin and light enough to hang on your wall like a framed painting). But even these have size limits. That is why the focus here is on projectors. These guys offer digital projectors that can take your television or DVD/video signal and cast it onto a blank wall or movie screen (also available here) so you can achieve bigger-than-life images for true home theater viewing.

·HOME THEATER

## 800-843-7422 • Radio Shack

**RadioShack.com**

That's right, the ubiquitous electronics store now ventures to sell all manner of Tandy merchandise online. A more-complicated-than-necessary search feature makes it difficult to find what you're looking for, so you're better off finding the View by Category link and reading through the names of subsections until you see a winner. As you would expect, you can get all the electronic components necessary to invent your own gear or, for the less industrious individual, you can simply purchase whatever sort of device you need, whether it's home theater gear, computer related, games, personal organization tools, climate control equipment, communications devices or home automation kits.

| ·HARDWARE ·PHONES | ·PERSONAL ·A/V ACCESSORIES | ·HOME THEATER ·CAMERAS | ·AUTOMATION ·GAMING |
|---|---|---|---|

## 877-690-0177 • Ritz Camera

**RitzCamera.com**

Interested in capturing those memorable images of a lifetime? Whether you're an amateur videographer, a shutterbug of the traditional sort or have embraced the versatility of digital imaging, Ritz has useful information and a well-priced selection of goods. They've got underwater cameras, disposable cameras, photo-specific printers, zoom lenses, instant cameras, straps, cleaners, albums, batteries, frames—are we leaving anything out? Yes. But as extremely long lists are quite boring when you can't click on them, you'll have to check for yourself.

| ·CAMERAS | | | |
|---|---|---|---|

## 800-654-1187 • ScanSoft

**ScanSoft.com**

Some of us speak to our computers out of frustration, some with tender encouragement, some simply for the companionship. Ironically, this shop offers software that enables your machine to understand human speech directives. Thus, you can give your fingers a rest and simply tell your computer to OPEN, SAVE, RUN, CLOSE and, when times get tough, to GO TO HELL, and it might understand you. Other software includes something that will read the words on scanned documents. Basically, this stuff can give your computer eyes and ears.

| ·SOFTWARE | | | |
|---|---|---|---|

## 262-548-8120 • Safe Harbor Computers

**SHarbor.com**

This is a somewhat clumsy, difficult-to-fathom site. Why, then, do we waste your time with it? Simple. It specializes in multimedia hardware, software and storage devices. If you have an interest in utilizing computer technology for music and/or movie production, for example, here you can find pre-configured systems that should optimize your efforts, or simply some popular software that will make the process easier. Creative individuals may find the process of buying this gear stifling, but using it opens up plenty of possibilities (while at the same time adding a stifling computer interface to your efforts).

| ·HARDWARE | ·SOFTWARE | ·A/V ACCESSORIES | |
|---|---|---|---|

## SharperImage.com

The Sharper Image • 800-344-5555

The products on this site will go a long way into turning your abode into the Home of the Future, as envisioned in 1950's film reels. Not just a store, but an interesting index of how far we've come, you can find things like robot dogs, pens that do more than write and watches that have their own lifestyles, as well as bizarre climate control items (like a Personal Cooling System that air conditions your entire body from a key position behind the neck) and some unique entertainment gizmos.

## SimplyWireless.com

SimplyWireless.com • 888-449-8484

Seemingly complicated at first, this site actually lives up to its promise of "making communication simple," at least if you're looking to match up available wireless service plans in your area to cell phones that match your preferences. In fact, you can start by looking for the service that makes sense to you from a variety of options and carriers, then selecting phones that fit, or you can first find the phone that looks or acts the way you want it to and then select an appropriate plan. After that, it's simply a matter of accessorizing your new device (after all, you don't want to be gauche this season).

## SmartHome.com

Smarthome • 800-762-7846

Sure, your computer allows you mastery of all within your own virtual domain, but what about your physical domain; that is, your home? Well, it turns out you can control this, too, with burgeoning technology. Of course, you're probably familiar with central climate control and home security systems. Well, this site offers so much more, like motorized door and window controls; fully integrated and automated home theater components; automated garden systems; weather, motion and sound sensors to control it all internally and remote controls that'll let you operate it from outside the house. Here you can spruce up your lazy home so that you may never again have to lift a finger to get things done ... except maybe to push a button.

## SonyStyle.com

Sony • 877-865-7669

While you may ultimately dispute just how stylish Sony merchandise may be, it's tough to call the quality of their products into question. From their super-skinny VAIO laptops to a wide array of audio and video electronics, they've long been a world leader in a range of markets for the techno enthusiast. If you're a fan, this site won't let you down, as it offers all their top gear, with varying degrees of customization (in computers especially) and easy navigation throughout. If you hate Sony, prepare to hate them more, because they've now officially conquered the internet.

## 877-255-7907 • Symantec

Considering all of the web surfing you're no doubt embarking upon, there's a very real threat of which you must be wary: viruses. One virus can corrupt your entire computer's software configuration, and if it runs deep enough it can necessitate scratching everything and starting over, meaning you'll lose all the music, photo and text documents you've spent so much time and money accumulating. Anti-virus software can't always protect you against the technological advances of hackers, but frequent online updates can keep you clear of most of the threats, and do a lot to clean/fix your machine post-infection. Think of it as antibiotics for your hardware, and for sale here.

| ·SOFTWARE | | | |
|---|---|---|---|

## 800-355-4400 • Total Media, Inc.

How do you store your data? Sure, it sounds like the sort of question that might be asked in a science fiction plot, but in reality it's nothing new. We're all used to storing data of one sort or another in any number of digital and/or analog formats. This store has a firm grasp on pretty much all of them: audio (cassettes, DAT, open reel, mastering tape, mini discs, CD-R), video (VHS, betamax, digital 8, digital beta, writable DVD) and your computer (zip disks, jaz carts and every sort of floppy disc you can possibly think of). Typically, you'll only need three or four types of these products, ever. But it's cool to know these guys are here providing options.

| ·HOME THEATER | ·A/V ACCESSORIES | | |
|---|---|---|---|

## 800-631-0300 • UniquePhoto.com

As you might expect from the name, this place is set up to sell you cameras and the accessories that will allegedly help you catch that memorable one-of-a-kind shot. Cleanly presented and well organized, you can easily browse sections devoted to digital cameras (along with printers, scanners and software) or the kind that use film (including film, chemicals and dark room equipment). Then there's stuff like tripods, batteries, meters, lenses and all the other little things that make pictures turn out right (assuming your thumb doesn't get in the way).

| ·SOFTWARE | ·CAMERAS | | |
|---|---|---|---|

## 800-769-5668 • Vanns.com

You'll have to scroll down the page to see the entire menu of product categories offered by this retail behemoth, as it covers just about every area of computing, communications and electronics one could fathom. It's surprising, then, that it turns out to be an easy shopping experience, each menu item in turn opening up to a page of cleanly laid out products and a submenu enabling you to peruse different brands, models and product types. Generally, this is due to a relative lack of options per category, but as most of these items tend to be made by the most popular and/or top-quality brands, you may not mind. At least your shopping won't be impeded by that pesky decision-making process.

| ·HARDWARE ·PHONES | ·SOFTWARE ·A/V ACCESSORIES | ·PERSONAL ·CAMERAS | ·HOME THEATER |
|---|---|---|---|

## Vialta.com

Beamer • 877-963-8383

This store couldn't be simpler. They offer one specific product: a videophone. Of course, as a single videophone is useless on its own, they also offer two videophones for sale. While the point is exposed that you won't be able to project or receive video unless the person at the other end of the line also has the same brand of videophone, it's the sort of thing that would be great for new grandparents who want to see they're grandkids grow up over a long distance. Of course, if somebody tells them about webcams and the internet, this site may be in trouble.

| ·PHONES | | | |
|---|---|---|---|

## VirtualSoftware.com

The Virtual Software Store • 919-847-1857

What's great about this site? Well, you can have some new software installed onto your computer within minutes of reading this, for starters. That's because all the software you can purchase is here for download, so you don't have to wait for anything to come in the mail (which, let's face it, is the greatest and most excruciating drawback of online shopping). Ergo, you don't have to pay shipping charges, or even packaging costs. There is a small "transaction processing fee" applied to all orders, but we suppose we can live with that.

| | ·SOFTWARE | | | |
|---|---|---|---|---|

## Warehouse.com

Micro Warehouse • 800-397-8508

Is this yet another, run-of-the-mill computer hardware and software superstore? Yes. This one just happens to be set up a little more tidily than most, making it seem almost like they don't have a whole lot to offer. Do not be mistaken. The selection is as wide as their semblance is deceiving, and the prices, typically standard, occasionally dip into lower realms on some of the lower-end merchandise, meaning you might find a good deal if you're not looking for anything too great. Not that you should get your expectations up.

| | | ·HARDWARE | ·SOFTWARE | ·PERSONAL | |
|---|---|---|---|---|---|

## WaveShield.com

Waveshield • 561-989-9147

Capitalizing on (the probably well-founded) fears that use of cell phones exposes us to harmful radiation, this site sells exactly two products. Actually, they sell two variations of the same product: a small shield that apparently cuts nearly all of the offending rays before they can affect your brains. Designed to fit any phone, the shield focuses on protecting your ear canal, and customer testimonials show it to prevent the dizziness, headache, fatigue and "other abnormal symptoms" often associated with excessive mobile usage. Scare tactics aside, the alternative would be to ditch your cell phone. Yeah, right.

| | ·PHONES | | | |
|---|---|---|---|---|

## WireCloset.com

All kinds of wires and cables fill the pages of this store. You know, the stuff that clutters up the corners of your living room, tangles and clumps behind your entertainment system? If you want higher-fidelity cables for your home theater, longer extensions to meet the demands of your new satellite setup or even some that meet the strict THX criteria, they should be easy enough to find here, if you've got something in mind. If you're browsing, you might get thrown off track by repetition of the words "monster cable."

| ·HARDWARE | ·A/V ACCESSORIES | | | |
|---|---|---|---|---|

800-264-3610 • WristWatch.com

## WristWatch.com

What does your wristwatch do? If your answer is that it does little more than tell you the time and date, we're pretty sure this site will put it to shame. Browse by Activity here and you may distinguish between designs for swimming, photography (which include built-in digital cameras) and survival (which may include internal GPA units). Or shop by Function, which has a list including items like a compass, illuminated face, barometer, thermometer or tide graph, should you need such things in a timepiece.

| ·GADGETS | | | | |
|---|---|---|---|---|

NOTES:

# Health & Beauty

You would think, with the widespread popularity of the internet, that we'd finally find some measure of relief from the constant pressure to put our best faces forward. After all, we can hold a meeting, take a class or go shopping in cyberspace, so what's to keep us from sporting ragged sweatpants, unkempt hair and pores clogged with motor oil while we do it?

Nothing—if you're a hermit. But, while the rest of us may be content to supplement our lives with the perks of the information age, quality of life still demands that we conduct our important affairs the traditional way: face-to-face. In fact, by heightening our exposure to glamorized media images, and by providing greater access to superior products, the web has only raised the bar on our standards for individual beauty. And, since health is pretty much beauty from the inside out, our infatuation with image must necessarily start with a soundness of mind and body. Yes, vanity can be a demanding habit.

To that end, we've assembled this section to accommodate anybody's need for personal health, hygiene, cosmetics or rejuvenating treatment products, whether the purpose is to enhance and maintain your finer features, or to eradicate and obscure those of which you're not so fond. These are the items that populate your medicine cabinet, the stuff you don't want to be without on a long trip and, often, the things that you'd rather not be seen with at the checkout counter. Whether in the area of preventative treatment, the evaluation of symptoms or disease awareness, your health should only get better with the advent of the information age ... provided you step away from the computer from time to time.

NOTES:

_____

_____

_____

_____

_____

_____

_____

_____

_____

_____

_____

_____

_____

_____

_____

_____

_____

## TIPS ON BUYING HEALTH & BEAUTY ONLINE

These suggestions may help prevent frustration and adverse effects.

•**CONSULT YOUR PHYSICIAN:** The reliability of information on the web is sketchy, to say the least, so you'll definitely want to keep the lines of communication open with a licensed physician before you embark on any course of treatment afforded online.

•**CHECK FOR BEAUTY PRODUCT SAMPLES:** Some bath, body and skin care products can run high in price. Many of the online retailers offer to send you sample or travel-size portions of the product. Take them up on this and try it out before committing to a big jar of the stuff. Same goes for fragrances, which alter in reaction to your skin chemistry.

•**MAKE SURE SKIN PRODUCTS ARE RIGHT FOR YOU:** Everybody's skin works in different ways, and certain products may not be right for you. When in doubt, consult the customer service of the site offering the product. If they cannot help you, seek counsel elsewhere, either through a dermatologist, esthetician or other knowledgeable source. In any case, try new skin products on a small patch of skin on your arm before applying to large patches of skin on your face and body, to make sure you suffer no reactions.

## SITES THAT MAY COME IN HANDY

The following URLs may be useful when you shop.

Medical News: http://www.ivanhoe.com
Doctor Finder: http://www.ama-assn.org/aps/amahg.htm
Health Insurance Resource Center: http://www.healthinsurance.org
Vision Info & Resources: http://www.allaboutvision.com
Medical Info & Definitions: http://www.medicinenet.com
Local Pollen Forecasts: http://www.pollen.com/Pollen.com.asp
FDA Consumer Warnings & News: http://www.fda.gov/oc/buyonline/tips_warnings.html
Children's Health Info: http://www.kidshealth.org
Local Alternative Health Care Directory: http://www.holisticnetwork.org
Alternative Health Info: http://healing.about.com

## >> SECTION ICON LEGEND

Use the following guide to understand the rectangular icons that appear throughout this section.

### ALL-NATURAL PRODUCTS

Many products available in this section have been made without the inclusion of any artificial agents. This icon makes them easier to find.

### MEN'S PRODUCTS

Most of the Beauty sites and some of the Health-oriented shops focus on products designed specifically for women. To make it easier for men, this icon lets you know when male products are also available.

### PHARMACY

Several sites allow you to order prescription medications, provided you include the proper documentation. This icon pinpoints drug stores equipped to do so.

### SKIN CARE

Scrubs, masks, cleansers, peels, exfoliates, lotions, ointments and the list goes on. There are myriad products out there designed to keep your skin healthy, clean and clear, and a lot of sites that carry them.

# LIST OF KEY WORDS

The following words represent the types of items typically found on the sites listed in this section.

## ALTERNATIVE

Medical science is usually your best bet, but some ancient and traditional therapies continue to be popular, and work. Locate them with this key word.

## AROMATHERAPY

Oftentimes, products may be infused with herbs and other scents that are said to have a relaxing and/or therapeutic effect. Find more at these sites.

## BATH & BODY

Soaps, body washes, lotions and bath oils are just some of the soothing and cleansing products typically found in a Bath & Body shop. Such products are listed here.

## COSMETICS

Make-ups of all kind fall under this moniker, including lipstick, lip liner, mascara, eyeliner, eye shadow, foundation, rouge, blush, cover-up, nail polish and more.

## DIET

Finding a healthy way to lose weight can be difficult, but hopefully some of the products found on these web sites can help.

## DRUG STORE

Most of us know what it is we're looking for when we go to the drug store. In these shops you will find it (not to be confused with pharmacies, despite a heavy overlap).

## FRAGRANCES

Not restricted to perfumes and colognes, though these do comprise the bulk of the listings, fragrances will also turn up as incense, body sprays and some soaps.

## HAIR CARE

This is fairly self-explanatory, and includes shampoos and conditioners, as well as curling irons, hair dryers, bleaches, dyes, depilatories, gels, mousses, sprays, brushes, combs and other hair accoutrements.

## MEDICATION

Medication may include pills, suppositories, topical treatments and injections, whether prescription or over-the-counter.

## PERSONAL CARE

From tweezers to shaving cream, with some nail clippers in between, this key word denotes grooming and care tools, cleansers and ointments that go into our everyday beauty and health routines.

## SEXUAL CARE

One of the foremost adult health concerns of our times, sexual health is punctuated here by condoms and other forms of contraception.

## SUPPLEMENTS

This indicates that a site offers a selection of nutritional supplements, either vitamins, herbs or compounds that claim to contribute to the body's nutritional make-up. Usually either a pill or a powder.

## >> KEY WORD INDEX

Use the following lists to locate online retailers that sell the Health & Beauty products you seek.

### ALTERNATIVE

AWorldofGoodHealth.com
Drugstore.com
Health4Her.com
NaturoPathica.com
OnlineMagnets.com
StressLess.com
VitaCost.com

### AROMATHERAPY

AromaLeigh.com
AWorldofGoodHealth.com
BeautyHabit.com
BlissWorld.com
BlueMercury.com
CarolsDaughter.com
Caswell-Massey.com
CosmeticsMall.com
eBubbles.com
Elemis.com
Fresh.com
FrontierCoOp.com
Jurlique.com
NaturoPathica.com
Occitane.com
Sephora.com
SpaCadet.com
StressLess.com
TonyTina.com

### BATH & BODY

Apothia.com
AromaLeigh.com
Avon.com
BallBeauty.com
Beauty.com
BeautyHabit.com
BeautySampling.com
BenefitCosmetics.com
BlissWorld.com
BlueMercury.com

BobbiBrownCosmetics.com
BraveSoldier.com
BurtsBees.com
CarolsDaughter.com
Caswell-Massey.com
CCB-Paris.com
Cosbar.com
CosmeticsMall.com
CrabtreeAndEvelyn.com
CVS.com
DermaDoctor.com
DiamondBeauty.com
Drugstore.com
E6Apothecary.com
eBubbles.com
Elemis.com
FlorisOfLondon.com
Fragrance.net
Fresh.com
Gloss.com
GoSoak.com
Health4Her.com
HistoiresDeParfums.com
JoeyNewYork.com
Jurlique.com
Kiehls.com
LauraMercier.com
LushCanada.com
MakeUpMania.com
MoltonBrown.com
NaturoPathica.com
Occitane.com
Origins.com
Perfumania.com
Philosophy.com
ScarlettCos.com
Sephora.com
Sesto-Senso.com
ShopAccaKappa.com
SimoneFrance.com
SpaCadet.com
TonyTina.com

### COSMETICS

Anastasia.net
Apothia.com
Avon.com
BallBeauty.com
Beauty.com
BeautySampling.com
BenefitCosmetics.com
BlissWorld.com
BlueMercury.com
BobbiBrownCosmetics.com
BurtsBees.com
CCB-Paris.com
Cosbar.com
CosmeticsMall.com
CVS.com
DermaDoctor.com
DiamondBeauty.com
E6Apothecary.com
EsteeLauder.com
Fresh.com
Gloss.com
GoSoak.com
JoeyNewYork.com
Jurlique.com
LauraMercier.com
LippmanCollection.com
MACCosmetics.com
MakeUpMania.com
MoltonBrown.com
Origins.com
Perfumania.com
Philosophy.com
ScarlettCos.com
Sephora.com
SpaCadet.com
StrawberryNet.co.uk
Temptu.com
TonyTina.com

### DIET

CVS.com
Drugstore.com
Health4Her.com
MuscleSoft.com
VitaCost.com
VitaminShoppe.com

### DRUG STORE

CVS.com
Drugstore.com
Health4Her.com
StressLess.com
VitaminShoppe.com

### FRAGRANCES

Apothia.com
Beauty.com
BeautyHabit.com
BeautySampling.com
BlissWorld.com
BlueMercury.com
BobbiBrownCosmetics.com
BurtsBees.com
CarolsDaughter.com
Caswell-Massey.com
CCB-Paris.com
Cosbar.com
CosmeticsMall.com
CrabtreeAndEvelyn.com
DiamondBeauty.com
E6Apothecary.com
eBubbles.com
EsteeLauder.com
FlorisOfLondon.com
Fragrance.net
Fresh.com
Gloss.com
HistoiresDeParfums.com
LauraMercier.com
MoltonBrown.com

NaturoPathica.com
Occitane.com
Origins.com
Perfumania.com
Philosophy.com
ScarlettCos.com
Sephora.com
ShopAccaKappa.com
SpaCadet.com
StrawberryNet.co.uk

## HAIR CARE

AfroWorld.com
Avon.com
BallBeauty.com
Beauty.com
BeautyHabit.com
BeautySampling.com
BlissWorld.com
BlueMercury.com
BurtsBees.com
CarolsDaughter.com
Caswell-Massey.com
CCB-Paris.com
CosmeticsMall.com
CVS.com
DermaDoctor.com
DiamondBeauty.com
Drugstore.com
Elemis.com
Fresh.com
GoSoak.com
HairCountry.com
Health4Her.com
Jurlique.com
LushCanada.com
MakeUpMania.com
MoltonBrown.com
Origins.com
Perfumania.com
Philosophy.com
ScarlettCos.com
Sephora.com
ShopAccaKappa.com
SpaCadet.com

## MEDICATION

CVS.com
DermaDoctor.com
Drugstore.com
FootSmart.com

## PERSONAL CARE

1800Wheelchair.com
Anastasia.net
Arc-Vision.com
BackWorks.com
BallBeauty.com
Beauty.com
BlissWorld.com
BlueMercury.com
BobbieBrownCosmetics.com
Caswell-Massey.com
CosmeticsMall.com
CrabtreeAndEvelyn.com
CVS.com
DentalDepot.com
DermaDoctor.com
DiamondBeauty.com
DrLeonards.com
Drugstore.com
E6Apothecary.com
eBubbles.com
eHealthInsurance.com
Elemis.com
eShave.com
FootSmart.com
Gloss.com
GoSoak.com
Kiehls.com
LensMart.com
MakeUpMania.com
MoltonBrown.com
NationalAllergySupply.com
PeepersContacts.com
RelaxTheBack.com
ScarlettCos.com
Sephora.com
Sesto-Senso.com
SimoneFrance.com
Sneeze.com
StressLess.com
VitaminShoppe.com

## SEXUAL CARE

Condomania.com
CVS.com
DiscreetCondoms.com
DrLeonards.com
Drugstore.com
Health4Her.com

## SUPPLEMENTS

FrontierCoOp.com
Health4Her.com
LEF.org
MuscleSoft.com
StressLess.com
VitaCost.com
VitaminShoppe.com

## 1800Wheelchair.com

1-800-Wheelchair.com • 800-320-7140

First things first: this site does not strictly sell wheelchairs; they actually offer a pretty thorough selection of other stuff, including general health items and products meant to enhance independent living for those of limited abilities. That being said, there's not a terrific selection of these things, so the reason you'll want to shop here does turn out to be the wheelchairs (and scooters). Apart from a great selection, both of powered and manually driven chairs, there are some handy accessories (including a fishing rod attachment) that simply improve upon quality of life.

| ·PERSONAL CARE | | | |
|---|---|---|---|

## AfroWorld.com

Afro World • 800-228-9424

For women of African origins, hair styling has become at once an art form and a science unto itself. Of all styles, probably the easiest of which to cultivate is the afro, which, contrary to the name, is not accommodated here. Rather, categories like Weaving, Bonding and Fusion Supplies feature hair extensions in a wide assortment of colors, shapes and textures, while elsewhere on the site you can find products and information to aid in braids, twists, dreadlocks or any combination thereof, as well as some general shaving and skin care items. Unfortunately, ordering exists in a separate, Buy On-line portion of the site, so you'll have to write down your desired items and enter them manually. Of course, the real hard part comes after delivery.

| ·HAIR CARE | | | |
|---|---|---|---|

## Anastasia.net

Anastasia Beverly Hills • 888-409-2769

What you might not realize about Anastasia Soare is that she's not just a beauty expert, she's an artist, and you've probably seen much of her work. Her medium? The eyebrows of the stars. She has sculpted the brows of some of the more visible celebrities out there, from Elle MacPherson and Claudia Schiffer to Penelope Cruz and Jennifer Lopez. Her fine work notwithstanding, the purpose of this site is to market cosmetic tools and supplies. Obviously, the category for brows warrants the most attention, but Face, Lips and Eyes also deserve a look, with anything from eyeliner to waxing kits enabling you to craft your own features into a work of art.

| ·COSMETICS | ·PERSONAL CARE | |
|---|---|---|

## Apothia.com

Apothia • 877-276-8442

The Apothia brand name grew out of seminal Los Angeles shopping haven, Fred Segal. While it's got no proprietary items, what it has to offer is an editorial selection of the best and newest in both women's and men's cosmetics, beauty and grooming products, usually capitalizing upon hip, new products before you've even heard of them. As they put it, "the newest, hippest and up-and-coming brands start out at APOTHIA, before the others catch on." Part pretension, in part an excellent place to find everything your beauty-loving heart desires without the added distraction of inferior products to choose from, this site will do you right if you can handle it.

| | ·COSMETICS | ·BATH & BODY | ·FRAGRANCES | |
|---|---|---|---|---|

## 888-821-5588 • La Forty d'Afflelou

### Arc-Vision.com

If you're squinting right now as you read this, it'll be all too easy to blame our purple ink. However, closer to the truth is that you may need reading glasses. Fortunately, this site happens to carry an incredibly wide array of just that, available in nine levels of quarter-increment correction. It's really remarkable how many models they've amassed, including rimless, folding, metal and plastic frames. Better yet, they even offer a special collection specifically designed to reduce eyestrain when looking at a computer. You'll still have to squint while ordering, but thanks to a simple design, it won't take long.

| ·PERSONAL CARE | | | | |
|---|---|---|---|---|

## 877-894-2283 • Aromaleigh.com

### AromaLeigh.com

Here's a store featuring "aromatherapy remedies and products for pampered humans" where "every product is 100% natural, and contains ingredients you can actually pronounce." Sounds nice, huh? It all comes to you in a colorful site with just this sort of sense of humor interspersed throughout. Though it is visual in nature, it isn't necessarily set up in a way that you can spot products with a casual glance. Yes, even on the world wide web utopia is still a fanciful notion ... but this gets us closer.

| ·BATH & BODY | ·AROMATHERAPY | | | |
|---|---|---|---|---|

## 800-527-2866 • Avon

### Avon.com

Long gone are the days when you would sit at home in the afternoon, waiting, hoping that the doorbell would sound along with the words that invariably followed: "Avon calling." Good. While buying make-up from your friends and neighbors might have seemed like a good idea at the time, it just doesn't compare to shopping online. All of your favorite product lines, like Skin-So-Soft or Anew, can be found on this well-made site. It offers complete product descriptions, 100% guarantees and full ingredients lists, in case you know exactly what iodopropynyl butylcarbamate is.

| ·COSMETICS | ·BATH & BODY | ·HAIR CARE | | |
|---|---|---|---|---|

## No Service Number • A World of Good Health

### AWorldOfGoodHealth.com

For years now, the specter of alternative treatment has haunted the absolute authority of scientific medical practices; the traditional beliefs of ancient cultures in particular. For most of us, alternative health has been somewhat of a curiosity, an exotic unknown. Until now. This site not only gives you a rousing extent of knowledge about Chinese medicine, aromatherapy, yoga, Ayurveda, acupuncture, Tibetan medicine and tai chi, it also sells natural products relevant to the practice of these healing arts. Whether you wish to discover your dosha, or you just want to avoid the chemicals prevalent in "traditional" drug treatments, this will prove an excellent source in demystifying the tenets of medical awareness that have existed for thousands of years.

| ·ALTERNATIVE | ·AROMATHERAPY | | | |
|---|---|---|---|---|

## BackWorks.com

Back Works • 800-361-7788

Been lifting with your back again? Well, unfortunately, severe back problems usually require the attention of a medical professional. Of course, someone with chronic back problems will want to give their aching spine all the help it can get to avoid, and/or recover from, pain. That's where this site can help. Between seat pads, braces, supports and massage items, all the products for sale here promote better back health in one form or another. It's easy to find the right product, whether you intend to sleep on it or wear it to the gym. If you order now, it might just get there by the time you can sit up again.

| ·PERSONAL CARE | | | |
|---|---|---|---|

## BallBeauty.com

Ball Beauty • 323-655-2330

Since 1950, Ball Beauty has sold professional beauty supplies at discount prices. So here is a good place to find good prices on the products and equipment used at salons everywhere ... if you have patience. The site looks like a Crayola box that exploded, and can be very disorienting, even to our experienced eyes. The problem is, even when you do figure out how one section of the site works, others may not operate the same way. The best thing to do is remain calm, look first at the top and then the bottom of the pages, make good use of your browser's Back button and repeat to yourself over and over, "Discount prices, Discount prices." Eventually, you can find excellent hair and nail products that will have you looking professionally done day after day.

| ·COSMETICS | ·BATH & BODY | ·PERSONAL CARE | ·HAIR CARE |
|---|---|---|---|

## Beauty.com

Beauty.com • 800-378-4786

If you know what you're looking for, you may have a shot at narrowing down the hundreds of brands for sale on this massive and confusing site. When you do find your favorite product, there's plenty of information about it, with pictures, descriptions and an exhaustive transcription of every word listed on the package. Browsing will get you recommendations on a plethora of skin care, hair care, make-up, fragrances, bath & body products and even select men's stuff, and eventually you can view a complete listing of products (or go blind trying). Expert advice is available from the type of folks you might recognize from *The Oprah Winfrey Show* and other such venues, so when it comes time to choose from everything under the sun, you'll maybe have a little help.

| ·COSMETICS ·HAIR CARE | ·BATH & BODY | ·FRAGRANCES | ·PERSONAL CARE |
|---|---|---|---|

## BeautyHabit.com

BeautyHabit.com • 800-377-8771

The implication would be that this "simply addicting" array of beauty products might be habit forming. Well, these guys seem to take the theme to heart. Like a dealer hooking a junkie, each order comes with complimentary samples of other products for which you may soon find yourself exhibiting a dire need. See, they know that once you hit upon a beautifying product that does the trick, whether it be for your face or hair, in cream, lotion or elixir form, you'll keep coming back for more. Look at it as the gilded gateway to a whole new world of beauty, or as the ultimate test of will against vanity; either way, just don't let it get out of control, okay?

| ·BATH & BODY | ·FRAGRANCES | ·AROMATHERAPY | ·HAIR CARE |
|---|---|---|---|

**877-726-7591 • BeautySampling.com**

**BeautySampling.com**

This self-proclaimed "educated buyer's choice" is actually just like any other beauty and skin care retailer, with one exception: all these products come in teeny little portions. The concept is simple; rather than buy a tremendously expensive product you've never tried before, here you can spend a fraction of the cost on just enough to figure out whether you actually like it. It's a good way to avoid that medicine cabinet full of products you never use, or simply a convenient place to find travel sizes of your favorite lotions and creams.

| ·FRAGRANCES | ·BATH & BODY | ·HAIR CARE | ·COSMETICS |
|---|---|---|---|

---

**800-781-2336 • Benefit Cosmetics**

**BenefitCosmetics.com**

Based on the original Benefit line of cosmetics and hygiene products, this site's about as wacky as the names of its items. That's right, here you'll find the Honey Snap Out of It scrub, the Touch Me Then Try to Leave Me cream and the But Officer color of lipstick, among others. This is quality merchandise to say the least, and with text like "Gabbi Glickman got grabbed by Glitz'N'Shine … Go Gabbi Go!" you'll do your shopping, have a few laughs, and stock up on Glitzerama as you go. Just try not to hurt yourself.

| ·COSMETICS | ·BATH & BODY | | |
|---|---|---|---|

---

**888-243-8825 • BlissOut**

**BlissWorld.com**

If you're a fan of spas, but just can't seem to get away these days, leave it to the internet to bring the cleansing and relaxing features of a spa to you. Based on Bliss Resorts, located on the East Coast, the BlissOut Store features products that you might be subjected to should you enroll for one of their body or skin care treatments. You will also find a selection of make-up and beauty tools designed to keep you looking hip and beautiful. The site isn't entirely easy to use, but when you compare it to the utter indulgence you could be experiencing in a day spa, really, what could possibly match up?

| ·COSMETICS<br>·PERSONAL CARE | ·BATH & BODY<br>·HAIR CARE | ·FRAGRANCES | ·AROMATHERAPY |
|---|---|---|---|

---

**800-355-6000 • BlueMercury**

**BlueMercury.com**

Blue Mercury was "created to enhance the lifestyle of the time-starved woman." That is, once you have these products, they may save you time; unfortunately ,this site may not. See, with all the lotions, gels, fragrances, masks, emulsions and conditioners (et al.) featured here, you may actually browse only the 20 or so brand names carried. While this is convenient enough if you already have a favorite maker of, say, Ivy Milk, it doesn't bode well if you're curious as to what else is out there. Unless, of course, you've got way too much time on your hands.

| ·COSMETICS<br>·PERSONAL CARE | ·BATH & BODY<br>·HAIR CARE | ·FRAGRANCES | ·AROMATHERAPY |
|---|---|---|---|

## BobbiBrownCosmetics.com

Bobbi Brown Cosmetics • 877-310-9222

Beauty expert Bobbi Brown has applied make-up to enough models and actresses that she has become somewhat of a celebrity in her own right, recognizable from appearances on the Today Show and known for being a top choice of major fashion designers and photographers. Here, she offers tips on achieving a variety of looks along with her own beauty line, an array of products aimed at giving you the "classic yet modern" style to which she owes her success. If you're looking for her make-up, brushes, skin care products or fragrances, this no-nonsense site helps you easily find what you want, saving you a trip to a department store.

| ·COSMETICS | ·BATH & BODY | ·FRAGRANCES | ·PERSONAL CARE |
|---|---|---|---|

## BraveSoldier.com

Brave Soldier • 888-711-2728

For those who worry that using stuff like shower gel and moisturizer might prompt revocation of their "rugged" status, this site offers a small but impressive line of "athletic skin care" products that may change your mind. Initial offerings consisted of antiseptics used to curb road rash on long bicycle trips, but the line has expanded to include shaving creams, aftershaves and sunblock, all formulated from natural products. If you're tough, who are you going to trust other than a company who actively pursues "technical advances such as moist wound healing"?

| ·BATH & BODY | | | |
|---|---|---|---|

## BurtsBees.com

Burt's Bees • 800-849-7112

While, granted, these "Earth friendly personal care products" are pretty cool, the packaging of these products might make you wonder. Each label is affixed with a sketch drawing of the somewhat nefarious-looking Burt, which doesn't seem the wisest choice of branding for a company favored by skin care devotees. However, this line of goods that ranges from bath salts and facial care items to shaving products and fragrances proves to be top-notch. In fact, on top of the ecologically sound selections, it turns out these guys contribute millions of dollars' worth of profits to the preservation of American forests. That'll teach us to judge a book by its cover.

| ·COSMETICS | ·BATH & BODY | ·HAIR CARE | ·FRAGRANCES |
|---|---|---|---|

## CarolsDaughter.com

Carol's Daughter • 718-857-0282

Described as a "labor of love," this homegrown line of beauty products started as one woman's experiments making perfume in her kitchen. Well, the experiments apparently smelled too good to resist and now, thanks to the advent of online business, it's expanded into a family-and-friend-operated venture, selling unique self-made bath treatments, multiple fragrances, massage oils, aromatherapy items and plenty of products for hair and skin. Not as notable as, say, Chanel, but why smell like everybody else, anyway?

| ·BATH & BODY | ·FRAGRANCES | ·AROMATHERAPY | ·HAIR CARE |
|---|---|---|---|

## 866-227-9355 • Caswell-Massey

### Caswell-Massey.com

These "oldest chemist and perfumers in America" reputedly sold cologne to the likes of George Washington. While our founding fathers obviously didn't shop online, you can get through this clumsy but well-meaning site in no time at all. Some of the products seem practically antiquated, but no one could deny the character of an old-fashioned shaving brush or the allure of rose water. Besides, modern treatments are available as well and, anyway, there's something to be said for items that have been tried and true for more than 200 years.

| ·BATH & BODY ·HAIR CARE | ·FRAGRANCES | ·AROMATHERAPY | ·PERSONAL CARE |
|---|---|---|---|

## 800-758-1337 • Le Club des Créateurs De Beauté

### CCB-Paris.com

CCB stands for "le Club des Créateurs de Beauté." What this translates to is tough to say, precisely, as sometimes it's just not sufficient to understand French in order to understand the French. What we can tell you is that here you can find "age defying makeup innovations," such as can only exist in the space age. We're talking about firming and toning creams; unique skin, hair and body treatments; and some pretty advanced make-up. In other words, if you're looking to firm your breasts, tone your tummy or reduce the size of your thighs, these guys claim to have the solution, literally.

| ·COSMETICS | ·BATH & BODY | ·FRAGRANCES | ·HAIR CARE |
|---|---|---|---|

## 800-926-6366 • Condomania

### Condomania.com

In case you're unclear, this site has nothing to do with a fanaticism for condominiums. Yes, this is the sort of site where words like "sensitivity," "texture," "size" and "novelty" cannot be stressed enough. These words also comprise some of the browsing techniques available for prophylactics here, along with the robust-sounding "extra strength." You may also find lubrication, and a variety of other products that either promote sensuality, or make light of the whole process (that clock does what?!). Wait until you see the gift baskets.

| ·SEXUAL CARE | | | |
|---|---|---|---|

## 800-722-8982 • Cosbar

### Cosbar.com

The online manifestation of a well-known Aspen store, you may want to shop here if you want to make sure your skin, beauty and fragrance products will withstand the rough elements of mountain life. Heck, even some of us at low altitudes have a lifestyle that well enough simulates the effects of mountain living. Simply put, these are good brands, sold for fair prices (that is, as fair as some of these incredibly expensive high-end products get) from this small and therefore easy-to-shop store.

| ·COSMETICS | ·BATH & BODY | ·FRAGRANCES |
|---|---|---|

# CosmeticsMall.com

Like a well-stocked drugstore, this compendium of merchants gives you access to a deep selection of everyday items, as well as some high-end merchandise for more discerning cosmetic fans. The framed layout can be messy at times, and certainly confusing. Your best bet is to check the A-Z Store Directory, which opens a pop-up window listing all available brands and categories, including specific sub-categories. Leaving this open on your desktop will make it easier to continue finding what you're looking for. Once you've entered into a category (or brand), you can also use pull-down menus on the bottom of the page to find whichever brands exist within your selection (or whichever categories your brand has items in). Yes, there's a learning curve.

| ·COSMETICS ·PERSONAL CARE | ·BATH & BODY ·HAIR CARE | ·FRAGRANCES | ·AROMATHERAPY |
|---|---|---|---|

# CrabtreeAndEvelyn.com

From the world-renowned purveyors of English style comes a simple but clean site that offers all manner of bath and body products, along with some odds and ends for around the house. Like many competitors, Crabtree & Evelyn features several browsing options, including Bath & Body Care, Home Fragrances and a better-than-average For Men section. One unique browsing option you may appreciate is the Shop by Fragrance and Range link, which allows you to seek out a particular scent you are fond of, Damask Rose for example. The search then returns to you a selection of items, ranging from body creams to potpourris, that all bear that distinctive aroma. Thus, in just a short amount of time, your entire home and body can smell exactly the same.

| ·BATH & BODY | ·FRAGRANCES | ·PERSONAL CARE |
|---|---|---|

# CVS.com

This is like having a corner pharmacy crammed into the back of your computer. While not too different, functionally, from a lot of other on line drug stores, this site's simple construction should allow you to find everything you look for, as well as show you a few areas of interest you might not have considered. A panel of experts is on hand to serve you articles and updates about a variety of illness and general fitness topics, while message boards provide a forum for you to compare experiences with other health-minded individuals or to air your grievances about the current state of healthcare. Hell, if you're that grumpy, there's even a section where you can research other health plans or find a new doctor. Now, if you could only download medicine.

| ·MEDICATION ·PERSONAL CARE | ·DRUG STORE ·HAIR CARE | ·COSMETICS ·DIET | ·BATH & BODY ·SEXUAL CARE |
|---|---|---|---|

# DentalDepot.com

Probably not many people genuinely enjoy visiting the dentist. In fact, it's safe to say that to most of us it's a terrifying and painful prospect. If you're looking to avoid another lecture on how you can better maintain the hygiene of your mouth (followed by up to an hour of poking, prodding and drilling), here's a place to stock up on equipment. Toothbrushes are just the beginning; you can also find electric toothbrushes, brushes for the gums and tongue, waterpicks for all points between, floss, tape, treatments for a dry mouth and a cure or two for halitosis. All is buried underneath a sort of goofy and clumsy veneer, which you may find irritating. If frustration starts to occur, just compare using this site to sitting in your dentist's chair. That should do it.

| ·PERSONAL CARE | | | |
|---|---|---|---|

## 877-337-6237 • DermaDoctor.com

### DermaDoctor.com

The focus of this site does not strictly pertain to the epidermis, but it definitely stays close to the human body's surface. From hair care to toe care, the store offers a cream, salve, ointment, gel, lotion, cleanser or scrub for just about every part of the body and any itch, rash, fungus, wart, burning, peeling, flaking, discoloration or other common ailment that can usually be treated without doctor's care (obviously, if symptoms persist, professional medical attention should be sought). The site doesn't always work as it should, but when it does, browsing is pretty easy.

| ·BATH & BODY ·MEDICATION | ·COSMETICS | ·HAIR CARE | ·PERSONAL CARE |
|---|---|---|---|

## 800-669-6638 • Diamond Beauty

### DiamondBeauty.com

If you've ever looked at a celebrity and wondered, "How does she manage to look like that?" you might be able to find out on this site. With hundreds of brands available, you can search through them each and find out what famous faces fancy their products, or you can search through an extensive list of celebrities and click on those that have made you wonder. The site is a little hectic at first, but it's easy to figure out where everything is, whether you want to peruse the Glossary of Beauty Terms or learn about the past 100 years of Beauty History. Finally, you can take part in regular chat sessions, so you can talk about it all with experts and gossip with fellow beauty fans.

| ·COSMETICS ·HAIR CARE | ·BATH & BODY | ·FRAGRANCES | ·PERSONAL CARE |
|---|---|---|---|

## 253-351-5001, ext. 146 • eCondoms.com

### DiscreetCondoms.com

A little embarrassment about buying prophylactics from your local drug store shouldn't keep you from having safe sex. Welcome to the modern age. Here you'll find a tremendous selection not only of condoms, but also lubricants and, uh … rubber gloves. Then there are the condoms, which range in size, color and, yes, flavor. Some are pre-lubricated, some made out of polyurethane, and some even for females, which are easily worth a try, at least. Of course, they won't be able to deliver for those last-minute, late-night "something's suddenly come up" situations, so you better make that order now.

| ·SEXUAL CARE | | | |
|---|---|---|---|

## 800-455-1918 • Dr. Leonards

### DrLeonards.com

If you're shopping around for sexual aids, girdles or sturdy support bras, the name Dr. Leonard may not exactly strike confidence into your heart. Don't be quick to judge, though; "America's Leading Discount Healthcare Catalog" has plenty to offer, and not just by way of improving your sex life or your posture. You'll also find sleeping aids, household items for sufferers of arthritis, blood pressure monitors and some special apparel for the incontinent. You may also find some odd inclusions, like a set of collectible silver dollars, a heated ice scraper and a titanium drill bit set. We don't know what this Dr. Leonard is up to, but it ain't all bad.

| ·PERSONAL CARE | ·SEXUAL CARE | | |
|---|---|---|---|

# Drugstore.com

Drugstore.com • 800-378-4786

Band-aids, aspirin, antacid, rubbing alcohol, contraceptives: if you were to walk through every aisle in a drug store you would probably find a whole lot of little items that could come in handy during those urgent moments. But what a waste of time. This comprehensive online pharmacy and drug store is set up to help you find your desired products fast, whether they be prescription medications or less vital items like shampoo and moisturizing lotion. Specialty stores even enable quick browsing for all-natural ingredients, weight management products and a slew of other special-interest areas.

| ·MEDICATION ·PERSONAL CARE | ·DRUG STORE ·HAIR CARE | ·BATH & BODY ·SEXUAL CARE | ·ALTERNATIVE ·DIET |
|---|---|---|---|

# E6Apothecary.com

E6 apothecary • 800-664-6635

"Before E6 … beauty junkies only had the traditional outlets for their shopping needs." So, you see how this store might be "pure heaven for anyone interested in the latest and greatest in must-have beauty products." Actually, some of the lines they offer aren't well distributed in the United States, so maybe traditional outlets won't do it if you're looking for Becca, Biotherm, Mavala, Mustela, Tarte or Too Faced … it's tough to say. What's easy to say is that this site carries a fine array of high-end beauty products for the discerning cosmetic and skin care consumer.

| ·COSMETICS | ·BATH & BODY | ·FRAGRANCES | ·PERSONAL CARE |
|---|---|---|---|

# eBubbles.com

eBubbles.com • 888-403-8701

It's all about the bubble bath … well, and other forms of pampering yourself. The most serious items available here involve shaving and other skin treatment. Mostly, though, you'll find a long list of spa products, massage products, aromatherapy, candles and more stuff to make your bath luxurious than you can probably imagine (careful, you will want to leave room for water). The site itself is almost fragrant in its own right, and quite likely to convince you that you haven't been spoiled enough, and that you're nowhere near comfortable enough at this very moment. This may be dangerous to go into alone….

| ·BATH & BODY | ·FRAGRANCES | ·AROMATHERAPY | ·PERSONAL CARE |
|---|---|---|---|

# eHealthInsurance.com

eHealthInsurance.com • 800-977-8860

Health insurance is by no means a perfect concept. After all, it tends to be disliked by patients, caregivers and businesses alike. However, as it remains the only thing separating us and the entirety of our doctors' boat payments, the business perseveres, and we can only hope to find the best coverage at the lowest personal costs. To this end, here's a site that offers you many options in most (if not all) US regions. Enabling you to view a variety of plans from different "leading companies" in your area on one page, you can quickly determine what the market will bear and, with a little research, find the least egregious means of protecting against the high medical costs of disaster.

| ·PERSONAL CARE | | | |
|---|---|---|---|

## 800-423-5293 • Elemis

**Elemis.com**

Here's the home site of a successful European spa product brand that is "retailed in many of the top Health Farms in Europe, the Orient and the Middle East." Using natural products and aromatherapeutic principles, these products cleanse, tone, protect, refresh, exfoliate, moisturize, smooth, boost, detoxify, nourish and generally serve with care all other interests of skin with high-end aplomb. Just think: your daily regimen can be just like those offered on health farms, only without the farmer.

| ·AROMATHERAPY | ·BATH & BODY | ·HAIR CARE | ·PERSONAL CARE |
|---|---|---|---|

## 800-947-4283 • eShave.com

**eShave.com**

"Developed to bring superior performance and elegance to the daily ritual of shaving," these guys have a pretty narrow focus, which as usual makes for a pretty successful site. In other words, you'll find some quality razors, shaving brushes, shaving creams and aftershaves here in no time at all. In fact, were it not for the lack of those big, straight razors and leather sharpening straps, you might have all the makings for a good, old-fashioned shave on your hands here. Drats to these new-fangled designs anyway.

| ·PERSONAL CARE | | | |
|---|---|---|---|

## 877-311-3883 • Estée Lauder

**EsteeLauder.com**

In terms of finding Estée Lauder products available and in stock, your troubles are over, thanks to this proprietary site from one of beauty's most recognized names. Between pictures of Liz Hurley and monthly trend features you'll find all those prized items that waste no time in disappearing from department store shelves; from compacts and perfumes to moisturizers and eyeliners, they're always here. We can't actually tell what the "Virtual Fragrance Gallery" is, exactly, but with several helpful features to guide you through purchases, buying products this fine seems like reason enough for a visit.

| ·COSMETICS | ·FRAGRANCES | | |
|---|---|---|---|

## 800-535-6747 • Floris of London

**FlorisOfLondon.com**

A family operated London perfumery since 1730, the fragrances of Floris have adorned several generations of British royalty and gentry. Classic and elegant, these scents stem from hundreds of recipes originating either in the Mediterranean or from formulas custom-made for centuries' worth of aristocrats. The surviving selections are those which have proven quite popular over the years. Men's No. 89 is even said to be the personal choice of 007 himself, James Bond. Finding the fragrance that best suits you should be easy given the site's navigation and the often poetic descriptions, which vividly explore the aromatic formula (i.e., bergamot, sandlewood, etc), from "top notes" that waft in a breeze to "base notes" that comprise the scent's essence.

| ·BATH & BODY | ·FRAGRANCES | | |
|---|---|---|---|

## FootSmart.com
Foot Smart • 800-230-4077

While feet are, of course, the focal point for this specialty health retailer, it actually promises to cover "everything for lower body health," with attention to your ankles, knees, shins, thighs, hips and lower back as well. You can shop by ailment, such as athlete's foot, bunions and hammertoes, or you can browse through products like insoles, toenail files and arthritis relievers. Thanks to an excellent layout, rooting through these pages will be easy on your clicking fingers, too (they are apt to get sore). If only there was a site like this for every part of the body.

·PERSONAL CARE    ·MEDICATION

## Fragrance.net
Fragrance.net • 800-987-3738

With "more than 1200 brand name fragrances," free shipping, gift wrapping and free gifts with each purchase, there are plenty of reasons to buy perfume and cologne from this site, if you're going to buy online at all. Boasting "no knock-offs," this might just be the most thorough selection of original fragrances anywhere. What's more is that they offer a wide array of mini sizes as well. This may be a good idea, as you can buy a selection of samples to try out before spending big money on the regular sizes. Finally, a decent way to avoid the guerilla tactics of perfume counters.

·BATH & BODY    ·FRAGRANCES

## Fresh.com
Fresh • 800-373-7420

Made from natural products, this beauty line includes everything from make-up to skin care, with some fragrances thrown in for the heck of it. Actually, the smells are what you'll remember most, with unique perfumes and unisex colognes covering a range of fresh and natural blends to match a variety of moods and characters. Often with aroma-therapeutic results, some of these fragrances also apply to candles and incense, which can create a delightful and relaxing atmosphere. Try scents like wisteria or calendula for a pleasant change from aromatic standards, or get more adventurous with the smells of pomegranate anise or galbanum patchouli. Whatever your mood, this elegant and easy-to-use site can set your environment to match.

·COSMETICS  ·HAIR CARE    ·BATH & BODY    ·FRAGRANCES    ·AROMATHERAPY

## FrontierCoOp.com
Frontier Natural Brands • 800-669-3275

These guys have been around selling all-natural and organic products for a quarter century, meaning they were doing it long before it became faddish. In that time, they've developed a rather thorough bit of information, some of which they're willing to share here, though most of your time is best spent in the Aromatherapy and Herbs & Supplements sections. Interestingly, the CoOp element involves the potential to purchase shares in ratio to your purchases so that every year you qualify for a return based on your earned percentage of profits. It's kind of complicated, and we don't entirely understand it, but it basically appears you can get rebates, which are always nice.

·AROMATHERAPY    ·SUPPLEMENTS

## 888-550-4567 • GLOSS

**Gloss.com**

We were somewhat surprised to find a small but valuable stash of men's hygiene and fragrance products on this site, as it initially seems as feminine as can be. Generally laid out by brand (you may have to look under Gifts to find the guy stuff), women will find cosmetics, skin care and bath & body items by the likes of Chanel, Estée Lauder, Clinique, M-A-C and Origins, among others. Essentially, the site will save you a trip to the drug or department store to get some of the more popular beauty products available.

| ·COSMETICS | ·BATH & BODY | ·FRAGRANCES | ·PERSONAL CARE |
|---|---|---|---|

## 877-968-7625 • Go Soak

**GoSoak.com**

If you love a bath—we're talking about a real, deeply satisfying soak in water that is soft, warm and bubbly—here is the site for you. Based on a real-life Virginia store, this online retailer carries only the finest of bath and body products. They also feature an assortment of make-up, and several advisors who offer advice on everything from how to treat itchy skin to the proper way to apply foundation. It may take you a little time to root through different brands for specific items (a search for "bubble bath," for example, returns more than 50 different scented results), but the avid bather will surely find the stuff that life is made of.

| ·COSMETICS | ·BATH & BODY | ·PERSONAL CARE | ·HAIR CARE |
|---|---|---|---|

## 800-720-1303 • HairCountry.com

**HairCountry.com**

A message to anyone who is losing his/her hair: before you stock up on hats, check out this site. Between its treatments, covering options and hair replacement information, there's likely to be something here to remedy the situation. You can also keep updated on any hair-loss-related news that may pop up from time to time, or check out postings on a message board to find out what sort of stuff works for others. They even sell an herbal alternative to Viagra; but that's a whole other ballgame.

| ·HAIR CARE | | | |
|---|---|---|---|

## 800-960-7797 • Health4Her.com

**Health4Her.com**

Catering to the various specific health needs of women, the question isn't about whether a site like this should exist; the question is why aren't there more like it? A wealth of information is available here about a lot of common female health issues, and even about a few lesser-known problems. Many of the remedies here have even been designed to compliment the delicate hormonal balance that makes gynecology such a complicated field. Shopping is easy: just select the area of health you want to cover, from cellulite to menopause to osteoporosis, and go.

| ·DRUG STORE<br>·HAIR CARE | ·BATH & BODY<br>·DIET | ·ALTERNATIVE<br>·SEXUAL CARE | ·SUPPLEMENTS |
|---|---|---|---|

## HistoiresDeParfums.com

HistoiresDeParfums.com • 877-972-7386

Sure, perfumes and body oils almost always smell good, but how many of them look this good? This Paris-based perfumery is "dedicated to creating prestige fragrances according to the finest traditional French methods." If you can judge a fragrance by its cover, this looks like about the best you can buy. Of course, it doesn't work that way, but we're willing to run with the assumption that these scents make sense. Why? Because the traditional techniques they speak of stem from a time in France where people didn't bathe very often—their *parfums* had to be good.

| ·BATH & BODY | ·FRAGRANCES | | |
|---|---|---|---|

## JoeyNewYork.com

Joey New York • 800-563-9691

This therapeutic skin care line could use a better website to market its wares, but it does work well enough to display its skin, lip, hair, eye, pore and general body care products. Once you've browsed through the items in their Store, you should probably check out the Product List section before buying, as you will have to enter the size, item number and price of your purchases while ordering. Still, all the hassle may be worth it once you've clarified, corrected and moisturized yourself into a satisfied customer.

| ·COSMETICS | ·BATH & BODY | | |
|---|---|---|---|

## Jurlique.com

Jurlique • 404-262-9382

"No chemicals and no compromise" is the motivating motto behind this company's holistic approach to skin care. All-natural products are infused with minerals, herbs and all manner of ingredients that promote a healthy skin and body; everything from cleansers, moisturizers, cosmetics and aromatherapy oils. Yes, homeopathy has come a long way on this somewhat difficult but functional site that boasts "the purest skin care on earth." If you're looking to boost your body's natural aversion to aging, Jurlique might be a winner.

| ·BATH & BODY | ·AROMATHERAPY | ·HAIR CARE | ·COSMETICS |
|---|---|---|---|

## Kiehls.com

Kiehl's • 800-543-4572

If you take a keen interest in skin in its best incarnation, then without a doubt take a gander at this site. Kiehl's has been around for more than 150 years, enough time to get it right, and they have like few others. To begin with, they bring together a vast wealth of medicinal, herbal and cosmetic knowledge to concoct gentle treatments comprised largely of all-natural ingredients. Cleansers, moisturizers, sun screen, shaving creams and plenty more are then packaged into recyclable containers and sold for prices uninflated by advertising costs (they don't feel the need to). Men will benefit from this site at least as much as women do, and if there's any doubt, they've got a longstanding tradition of providing sample sizes to hesitant customers. Great stuff.

| ·BATH & BODY | ·PERSONAL CARE | | |
|---|---|---|---|

## 888-637-2437 • Laura Mercier
**LauraMercier.com**

Laura Mercier was initially trained as a painter, eventually shifting her medium from canvas to the human face. In the time since, she has done make-up for the covers of *Vogue*, *Glamour* and plenty of the other top fashion magazines, developing her "flawless face" techniques on such oh-so-tough-to-make-pretty mugs as Gwyneth Paltrow, Julia Roberts and Kim Basinger. Here she uses her expertise to back "a line of cosmetics and skin care that [will] provide every woman the opportunity to achieve her full beauty potential." That is, if you want your face to be a work of art.

| ·COSMETICS | ·BATH & BODY | ·FRAGRANCES | |
|---|---|---|---|

## 800-544-4440 • Life Extension Foundation
**LEF.org**

It turns out LEF stands for the Life Extension Foundation, which is a tough concept to argue with. Unfortunately, while they have a plethora of great items geared towards this goal, your life could wither away while trying to find them on this complicated website. Here's the fastest way to shop: follow the Order Products Online link, choose Advisor from the top menu, then select from one of the many alphabetically listed topics like Acne, Allergies, or Alcohol Induced Hangover Prevention (and that's just part of the A section). This will take you directly to products you're interested in, without actually requiring you to understand exactly what they are.

| ·SUPPLEMENTS | | | |
|---|---|---|---|

## 800-693-8246 • Lensmart
**LensMart.com**

This site is all about contact lenses. It starts with disposables, includes vial lenses and even some toric options (the kind used to treat astigmatism). Then there's the array of colored lenses (including green, aqua and violet ... though you can't necessarily see color samples) and kooky options like cat's eye, spiral, white and wolfish. There's also the option to shop by brand name, which is particularly helpful if this is the sort of product where you prefer one product to another. The site could look better, though.

| ·PERSONAL CARE | | | |
|---|---|---|---|

## 888-929-9950 • Lippman Collection
**LippmanCollection.com**

Deborah Lippman has a pretty solid résumé, having manicured the likes of Cher and Mariah Carey, as well as countless models for high-class fashion magazine shoots. It stands to reason, then, that her line of nail polish and treatments are capable of giving your keratin a glossy sheen worthy of the most glamorous individuals on the planet. Then again, these products are generally named after songs; so don't put too much stock in reason when you enter this site. What you'll need to do is follow the link to View Products to find out, for example, what color Lady is a Tramp corresponds to, then click on Shop Online to make your purchase. It's not ideal, but then neither is cuticle care.

| ·COSMETICS | | | |
|---|---|---|---|

## LushCanada.com

Lush • 888-733-5874

Here's a crazy, off-kilter site; but what else would you expect from a country whose greatest export in the past few decades has been comedians? As it turns out, their collection of soaps, creams, conditioners and other beautifying/clarifying products are no less interesting; they even offer some hot hair treatments. Truly, this may be the only site we've found that offers both dusting powders and solid shampoos, so if you're in the market for such stuff, by all means, get your Canadian currency converter ready.

| ·BATH & BODY | ·HAIR CARE | | |
|---|---|---|---|

## MACCosmetics.com

MAC Cosmetics • 800-588-0070

Not too many cosmetics lines would be confident enough to feature a man as its spokesmodel. Yet, Make-up Art Cosmetics does exactly this, with the planet's best-known cross-dresser, RuPaul, heavily featured on this kinetic and ultra-modern site that promises "make-up for all." The product is good, just so you know what you're suffering for in a product search. Otherwise, the high-paced video and animation might make browsing a dizzying affair. Diehards, however, will eventually come to enjoy the roller coaster speed menus and special feature sections that will make you wonder, "If RuPaul looks that good, imagine how MAC will look on me."

| ·COSMETICS | | | |
|---|---|---|---|

## MakeUpMania.com

MakeUpMania.com • 800-711-7182

Cartoonish graphics and colorful language contribute to the wacky atmosphere of this site that was created by cosmetic and movie industry make-up artists. It features a selection of professional grade make-up along with tips on how best to use it, as well as hair, body and nail care products that can turn up the glamour in any environment. Of course, the real fun starts when you start browsing through the special effects categories, where prosthetic noses, fake scars and Kryolan severed heads are offered for sale beside wigs and fake mustaches. Search by brand or outlandish category to find whichever of these items you might use to achieve those new levels of beauty once only dreamt about.

| ·COSMETICS | ·BATH & BODY | ·PERSONAL CARE | ·HAIR CARE |
|---|---|---|---|

## MoltonBrown.com

Molton Brown • 011-44-207-625-6550

This is a very cool site, especially within the cosmetics spectrum. Skin care, hair products, bath & body items, cosmetics and the tools with which to apply them are simply purchased by using the animated Shop menu, or you can follow the more esoteric thematic categories to find complementary products. It doesn't matter so long as you know these are excellent high-end products, which they are, and that free travel-size samples will be included with your order, even if your order is made up exclusively of travel-size samples.

| ·COSMETICS ·HAIR CARE | ·BATH & BODY | ·FRAGRANCES | ·PERSONAL CARE |
|---|---|---|---|

## 888-811-4286 • MuscleSoft.com

**MuscleSoft.com**

If you buy into the use of hormones, powerbars, protein powders and other such stuff to improve your strength and tone, then this place will seem to you a musclebound playground. All of a bodybuilder's favorite supplements can be found here, whether you're looking to lose weight or add bulk. There are also sections devoted to Anti-Aging products, sleep aids, "Brain Boosters" and hair loss (presumably the prevention of). If you like biotechnology to keep you beautiful and fit, check here and eat creatine to your heart's content.

| ·SUPPLEMENTS | ·DIET | | |
|---|---|---|---|

## 800-522-1448 • National Allergy Supply, Inc.

**NationalAllergySupply.com**

Like a cool breeze on a sweltering day, this site offers a means of absolute relief to the most misunderstood of sufferers: the allergic. The key term to remember here is "environmental control," meaning that these products turn your home into a virtual allergen-free haven from all the dust, spores, pollen and dander that pollute your breathing space. With special bedding supplies to HEPA filters, you can stop the sneezing and wheezing before it starts, whereas asthma aids keep current problems from worsening. Lastly, an assortment of hypoallergenic cleaners and personal care products enable the sensitive soul to live like a moderner for a change.

| ·PERSONAL CARE | | | |
|---|---|---|---|

## 800-669-7618 • Naturopathica

**NaturoPathica.com**

Featuring tinctures, compounds, homeopathic remedies, teas, infusions and floral remedies (to balance moods and emotions), this place operates as a source of all-natural healing products that border on placebic, but genuinely offer relief to more Americans than many comparable side-effect-inducing medicines. Categories divide items between Herbalism, Botanical Skin Care, Aromatherapy and For the Bath (sure to be popular). Check here for all-natural defenses against the soot, smoke and other toxins of the concrete world.

| ·BATH & BODY | ·FRAGRANCES | ·AROMATHERAPY | ·ALTERNATIVE |
|---|---|---|---|

## 888-623-2880 • L'Occitane

**Occitane.com**

This line's founder had it in mind to capture the essence of his home, the beautiful Provence region of France, where the sea meets the Alps in rolling green hills and the wine flows as freely as the water. Hence, most of these beauty, fragrance and skin care products contain ingredients extracted from flowers native to the region. Indeed, it seems as if he's managed to actually capture the air of his cherished homeland in bottles, to be delivered to the rest of the world. Oh yeah, shipping can cost almost as much as the products themselves, so you may want to settle for more local airs.

| ·BATH & BODY | ·FRAGRANCES | ·AROMATHERAPY | |
|---|---|---|---|

## OnlineMagnets.com

The word is, magnetic therapy has the potential to reduce pain, accelerate healing and improve circulation. Sounds good, if it's true. If you're curious, this is a decent site to check out. Aside from bits of information about this burgeoning treatment, you'll find magnetic products that range from elbow and knee braces to mattress overlays. Pretty much every part of the body is covered by one product or another, whether it's used during exercise or while you rest. They even claim that wearing a magnetic facial mask can reduce the appearance of wrinkles and keep the skin clear. Our question: what happens then if you reverse the polarity?

| ·ALTERNATIVE | | | |
|---|---|---|---|

## Origins.com

The proprietors of Origins take a somewhat different approach to looking and feeling good. Espousing such things as reflexology (the application of pressure to reflex points on your feet), daily affirmations and mandala ring meditation, they promote relaxation and a stress-free lifestyle. They also feature a selection of original products for the skin, hair or nose, and particularly the sorts of sensory-therapeutic items that provide the sort of relief your whole body can benefit from. So run a bath, throw in some salts, prepare a full-body scrub and find respite from the daily grind that's made your hair a tangled mess (foot masseuse optional).

| ·COSMETICS | ·BATH & BODY | ·FRAGRANCES | ·HAIR CARE |
|---|---|---|---|

## PeepersContacts.com

Trying to find a contact lens in the real world can be a remarkable test of patience and diligence—never mind the ironic humility of scrounging around on your knees to look for an invisible object that is meant to help you look for things. Fortunately (and myopic or not, you saw this coming), this online retailer makes finding contacts simple. Whether the lenses you want are disposable, tinted, extended or daily wear, you can find them without trouble under one of several popular national brand name categories. All you really need to know is your prescription.

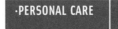

| ·PERSONAL CARE | | | |
|---|---|---|---|

## Perfumania.com

Contrary to its name, you can find more than just fragrances here; there's also plenty of cosmetics, skin care, hair, bath & body products here, too. Shopping is fairly typical of such sites, as unfortunately browsing is limited to brand names. Do not be fooled by the Fragrance Navigator, it's absolutely useless, though Our Perfumer Recommends will be of help if only to narrow down your hundreds of options. Obviously, you can't download any smells, so this site's really only worthwhile if you've already got something in mind.

| ·BATH & BODY | ·FRAGRANCES | ·COSMETICS | ·HAIR CARE |
|---|---|---|---|

## 800-568-3151 • Philosophy
**Philosophy.com**

If you're into conceptual beauty products, you've probably already discovered Philosophy. Otherwise, you might as well make your first impression through this mildly peculiar, yet entirely accessible site. Their popular skin care, hair care, fragrance and bath products are easy to sort through, and they occasionally offer some helpful browsing techniques. If you are a fan, this may be the only place you can find their complete line of products, at least, as they offer no print catalog, it's the only place where you can tell for sure anyway.

| ·COSMETICS | ·BATH & BODY | ·FRAGRANCES | ·HAIR CARE |
|---|---|---|---|

## 800-222-5728 • Relax the Back
**RelaxTheBack.com**

Whether your daily routine consists of scouring the internet for the best in online retail, or something less strenuous like heavy construction, it's quite likely that at the end of the day you could use a little recuperative therapy on the old back muscles. This site hears the creaking of your spine and has the answer ... well, several answers really. From braces and supports to massage products and ergonomic furniture, many of these products seem to have been specifically designed to elicit sighs. You can't go wrong.

| ·PERSONAL CARE | | |
|---|---|---|

## 800-862-2311 • Scarlett
**ScarlettCos.com**

Offering quality cosmetics and personal care products across the board, this helpful site offers more alluring products than most of us will know what to do with. Men have it easier, as products are by definition limited in range and scope, but whoever you are you can be fairly assured that the brands featured here are worth the effort of at least a glance. Products are arranged by purpose (Hair Care, Skin Care, Cosmetics, etc.) but then listed by brand, so from time to time you'll need to do a little digging to find the product right for you. If in doubt, though, take advantage of the Ask Scarlett feature to get guidance without a lot of clicking.

| ·COSMETICS ·HAIR CARE | ·BATH & BODY | ·FRAGRANCES | ·PERSONAL CARE |
|---|---|---|---|

## 877-737-4672 • Sephora
**Sephora.com**

With a different color of lipstick for every day of the year, the Sephora line of beauty products has grown internationally in the past few years, largely due to the success of non-aggressive salesmanship in its stores. They offer the same sense of tact online, with this somewhat busy, but ultimately functional, site. Basically, thousands of products are at your disposal, and not just the manufacturer's own. Some of the finest and best-known beautifying brands on the globe are represented and, in its own consumer friendly tradition, Sephora offers them at prices you'll like. In particular, if you're a fan of French cosmetics, you can find them here at drugstore prices. *Chouette!*

| ·COSMETICS ·HAIR CARE | ·BATH & BODY ·PERSONAL CARE | ·FRAGRANCES | ·AROMATHERAPY |
|---|---|---|---|

## Sesto-Senso.com

Sesto Senso • 888-239-0003

Literally translated as "sixth sense," the products sold here actually serve to please at least one of the first five senses, while at the same time cleaning and beautifying your skin. Brand-name shopping is the clearest feature here, and they feature a lot of European brands, as well as some edgy items like Blue Q's Dirty Girl, Wash Away Your Sins and Sex/Money lines. But if the dozens of brand choices don't help, simply scroll to the bottom of the home page and you'll find it easier to browse categories like Bath, Body, Baby, Home, Men and Just for Fun. And if that isn't enough, check out a book or video on sensual massage. After all, it's not likely to hurt.

| | | ·BATH & BODY | ·PERSONAL CARE | |
|---|---|---|---|---|

## ShopAccaKappa.com

Acca Kappa • 888-551-0225

Acca Kappa, hailing from Italy, is one of the few beauty lines we've encountered that includes Hair Care, Body Care, Skin Care, Fragrances and Dental Care in its repertoire. Better yet, they include a men's line, as well as some soap (this last seems almost redundant these days). More than thorough, they offer some pretty good products with some quite simple shopping, aside from a few excessively deep links to products, and even offer the election of professional grade or all-natural products from time to time.

| | | | ·BATH & BODY | ·FRAGRANCES | ·HAIR CARE | |
|---|---|---|---|---|---|---|

## SimoneFrance.com

Simone France • 877-746-6633

Simone France is a skin care expert who has treated some of the top supermodels in the world, among others, to her own particular brand of facials. Here, her own line of products is featured to cleanse and care for your skin; after all, she can't give a hands-on approach to everyone. She does, however, offer advice on why skin treatments you've used in the past might not have worked, and how you can make them work in the future. She would, of course, recommend that these products might serve you better than others, especially when used properly. To this end, she has formulated special kits designed to treat different kinds of skin, and each one is equipped with explicit directions.

| | ·BATH & BODY | ·PERSONAL CARE | |
|---|---|---|---|

## Sneeze.com

Sneeze.com • 800-469-6673

If sneezing and wheezing is more common to you than a cold, you're probably plagued with nature's curse upon mankind: allergies. If so, this store can be a fantastic resource to help take control of your environment, thus preventing the symptoms of allergies and, in extreme cases, even the asthma that can result. Beginning with air filters and including hypoallergenic bedding supplies, this stuff will help you sleep and breathe easier, whether pet dander, pollen or dust mites have contaminated your environment. Score another one for mankind.

| ·PERSONAL CARE | | |
|---|---|---|

**888-868-5477** • SpaCadet.com

## SpaCadet.com

"You can always count on SpaCadet.com to bring you the hard-to-find, trendy, eclectic beauty treasures that you read about in all the fashion and beauty magazines." That's right, these guys are even wordier than **thepurplebook** writer. Still, this funky and colorful site offers plenty of funky and colorful products in the realm of cosmetics, hair and skin care, whether it's something like Dogfish Head Soap or Lipnotic Kissing Serum. Products are likely to change with the seasons, so waste no time if you wish to keep up.

| ·COSMETICS ·HAIR CARE | ·BATH & BODY | ·FRAGRANCES | ·AROMATHERAPY |
|---|---|---|---|

---

**No Service Number** • StrawberryNet

## StrawberryNet.co.uk

This site claims to be "the largest worldwide discounter of skin care, makeup and fragrance." Truly, they (at this writing, at least) offer free shipping to anywhere on the planet, as well as the additional incentive of 5% discounts for orders of 3 or more products. Their only visible flaw would be a gigantic selection backed by no real mechanism to help you sift through it all, save for a lackluster designation by brand name. The good news is that if you're already hooked on a set list of items, they're sure to have them for a great price.

| ·COSMETICS | ·FRAGRANCES | | |
|---|---|---|---|

---

**800-555-3783** • Stress Less

## StressLess.com

On certain days it seems this might just be the greatest website ever devised by mankind. Indeed, they offer "over 1,300 stress-reducing products and programs." By "programs," they generally mean interactive, downloadable tutorials on stress management, online counseling sessions and a series of Vent/Discussions pages, generally bulletin boards where you can air your many gripes to the world. You can avoid all this, though, by just clicking the Products link, which leads you to a selection of ergonomic devices, massagers and environmental controls meant to help you, oh yes, relax. Also found are books on nutrition, exercise and stress reduction that should keep you from coming back to the site ... at least until you watch the news again.

| ·DRUG STORE ·PERSONAL CARE | ·ALTERNATIVE | ·SUPPLEMENTS | ·AROMATHERAPY |
|---|---|---|---|

---

**800-972-9682** • Temptu Body Art

## Temptu.com

For those of us who know tattoos are cool but still can't find our way to embrace their permanence, this site comes through in a big way. With tattoo outlines in black, and body paints with which to color them in (if you want), these aren't the lick'm and stick'm temporary tattoos you got out of candy machines as a kid. Tribal designs, heart shapes, animals, flowers, insects and midriff-based designs are just a few of many featured options, as well as a line of Mehndi henna kits. These tats look as tough as the real thing, but wash away in a few days so that your parents never have to know.

| ·COSMETICS | | | |
|---|---|---|---|

## TonyTina.com                    Tony & Tina • 888-866-9846

Taking a somewhat New Age approach to beautification, the Tony & Tina art project works on your chakra to help you look good. They do this through "Vibrational Remedies," designed to align your energy centers through use of colors and aromas. It all may sound a bit weird (and it is), but basically they combine therapeutic aromas and herbs with vibrant colors and creative designs to make a line of high-quality make-up and cleansers. All of these items evolve around a specific art project that adds a funky twist to the form and function of a regular cosmetic routine. For example, their Millennium Key nail polish, designed to rest between your fingers as you apply the polish, owns the distinction of being the only nail polish bottle featured in the Museum of Modern Art.

| ·COSMETICS | ·BATH & BODY | ·AROMATHERAPY | |

## VitaCost.com                    VitaCost • 800-793-2601

These guys have been busy, buying up other would-be **thepurplebook** sites in their conquest of all things supplemental. Aside from traditional vitamins, they offer all-natural and alternative therapies, ranging from herbs and minerals to homeopathy and sports nutrition. Shopping by Product Category will turn up sections like Body Care (lotions, etc.), Low Carb and Food Bars, on top of the expected supplemental pages, while Health Concerns enables browsing through the likes of Immune System, Vision and Weight Management to suit your particular health needs. While they've expanded their range and influence, they don't seem to have done much to develop the site accordingly. Ultimately, though, we don't care, as they "guarantee wholesale prices."

| ·ALTERNATIVE | ·SUPPLEMENTS | ·DIET | |

## VitaminShoppe.com                    Vitamin Shoppe • 800-223-1216

Not just vitamins, ye olde shoppe (in cyberspace) offers a variety of nutritional supplements ranging from herbs, minerals and body-building powders to personal care items. Unfortunately, with the enormous list of products all of this entails, browsing is not a pleasant experience, as the bulk of these products are separated into long alphabetical lists. The one saving grace is that you can reorder these lists by the cost, strength and sizes of the products; otherwise, don't expect to find anything you don't already want.

| ·DRUG STORE | ·SUPPLEMENTS | ·DIET | ·PERSONAL CARE |

# Home & Garden

The dispute lingers on as to whether your home is better defined by the people you share it with or the objects contained within. We've decided to go with the latter, as you can't easily buy a family online (in most states), but whether you live with a crowd or alone in a mansion, house, condo, cottage, villa, loft, apartment, shack or lean-to, you'll be needing to furnish it.

Whether you want furniture, decorations, kitchen appliances, linens, window treatments, storage, hardware, tableware or lighting, there is an absolute abundance of sites out there offering an incredible variety. You can be into modern styles, prefer the whole rustic vibe or simply embrace the uninspired polygons of mass production—it doesn't matter. If it's to be had, you will almost certainly find it here. And that's just the *inside* of your home. Your yard and garden open up a whole new array of items to covet, and not just patio furniture or gazebos, either. If you fancy a bit of landscaping, you'll find a slew of ornaments and tools, and pretty much anything to make your garden grow (including the garden). Or, you can wipe out the lawn altogether in favor of a hot tub. Or, maybe a full-size swimming pool? A few well-placed clicks and you can turn even the dankest of weed-ridden mud pits into a veritable oasis.

Simply put, this section is a gateway to everything that fills our drawers and tops our tables, that gets stowed up in the attic or stacked high in boxes at the back of the garage. Sometimes we put it on display for guests to envy. Sometimes we hide it away, protectively. Often, we get stuff to match other stuff, and yet more stuff to clean it. Year after year, it piles up around our ears. It's home.

NOTES:

_____

_____

_____

_____

_____

_____

_____

_____

_____

_____

_____

_____

_____

_____

_____

_____

_____

TIPS ON BUYING HOME & GARDEN PRODUCTS ONLINE

These suggestions may help prevent frustration, but not poor taste.

•**SHIPPING CHARGES:** This section contains a lot of very heavy furniture, and shipping costs may be high accordingly. Some of the better deals may be found on sites that have local affiliations with stores that may drive a truck to your home. If you're paying a lot, see about White Glove service, which includes delivery and any setup/assembly.

•**SHIPPING INSURANCE:** With large and delicate items in particular, make sure the site insures your purchases before they undergo the many potential ravages of shipment.

•**SEASONAL & REGIONAL PLANTS:** Some varieties of plant are only available in certain seasons, while others can only thrive in certain environments. Check to make sure any plants you may order are ready for shipment and can survive in your planting zone.

•**PRECISE MEASUREMENTS:** Window treatments and other customizable home fixtures typically require very precise measurements in order to fit. These can be very expensive, so you'll want to get it right the first time around. It may be necessary to call a store's customer service line.

SITES THAT MAY COME IN HANDY

The following URLs may be useful when you shop.

Home Improvement Resource: http://www.doityourself.com
Home Décor Resource: http://www.bhg.com
Gardening Guide: http://www.gardenguides.com

>> **SECTION ICON LEGEND**

Use the following guide to understand the rectangular icons that appear throughout this section.

### HARDWARE

This icon includes tools, power tools, screws, nuts, bolts, nails, hooks, fasteners, decorative hardware and plenty of other materials that hold your home together and keep it operating properly.

### INDOOR

This icon indicates the sale of furniture, furnishings, décor, accents, lighting and miscellany that goes into assembling and decorating the interior of your home (even if it involves indoor plants).

### OUTDOOR

Whether garden-related or more for the lawn, pool or patio, this icon illuminates the sites that offer flora, furniture and all kinds of accessories for the outdoors including but not limited to stoneware, fencing, fertilizer, spas and outdoor grills.

### TABLEWARE

From fine china to simple barware, this icon indicates a selection of serving tools like plates, glasses and silverware.

 LIST OF KEY WORDS

The following words represent the types of items typically found on the sites listed in this section.

**ACCENTS**

This loosely defined term generally refers to the nonessential items used to add a little decorative charm.

**APPLIANCES**

Those sold online tend to be small (like vacuums or microwaves); though larger units can be ordered for local delivery.

**BED & BATH**

Towels and linens constitute most of these listings, along with shower curtains, bathmats and towel racks.

**CLEANING**

Cleaning supplies include everything from mops, brooms and sponges to solvents and detergents.

**ECO-FRIENDLY**

These sites offer environmentally sound means for energy generation/consumption, and nontoxic cleaning agents.

**FURNITURE**

Quite self-explanatory, this key word turns up whether the furniture is intended for indoor or outdoor use.

**GARDEN**

Garden supplies for everything from pest control to bulbs, including garden structures, stepping stones, tools, gloves and fertilizer.

**IMPROVEMENT**

Home improvement tools and supplies, including woodwork, cabinet handles, light switches, plumbing and other fixtures.

**KITCHEN**

Ranging from pots and pans to oven mitts, sites marked with this key word usually focus on cooking items.

**LANDSCAPING**

Keeping your outdoors manicured, these sites offer anything from lawn mowers to latticework, and a complete set of sundry items that apartment dwellers have never imagined.

**LIGHTING**

Sconces, chandeliers, track lighting and other fixtures are listed here along with lamps, and of course bulbs.

**ORGANIZATION**

From shelves and racks to space-saving contraptions and safes, these sites offer plenty of storage options to keep your tucked-away stuff well tucked away.

**PERSONALIZATION**

You can monogram your towels or put a plaque with your name on it in front of your home. These and other personalization options are available on these sites.

**POOL & SPA**

One of the bigger surprises about online shopping is the ordering availability of Jacuzzis and swimming pools. Also included here are saunas and ponds.

**REGISTRY**

Any of the sites that offer bridal registry services get listed under this key word.

**SECURITY**

Motion sensor lights, alarms and pointy fences. There are different ways to protect your home, and some are here.

# ≫ KEY WORD INDEX

Use the following lists to locate online retailers that sell the Home & Garden supplies you seek.

## ACCENTS

AngelaAdams.com
AnnieGlass.com
Anthropologie.com
AvalonGarden.com
BallardDesigns.com
BedBathAndBeyond.com
Bellacor.com
BlindsGalore.com
BombayCo.com
BraidedRugs.com
Chiasso.com
ColonialBrass.com
Comina.com
CrateBarrel.com
DeadlyNightShades.com
DecorateToday.com
DelawareRiverTrading.com
DesignerStencils.com
DesignStand.com
DomenicaRosa.com
DresslerStencils.com
DWR.com
ExposuresOnline.com
Exterior-Accents.com
Eziba.com
FrontGate.com
GivingTreeOnline.com
GraciousStyle.com
GreatWindows.com
Guild.com
HomeDecorators.com
HomeFiresUSA.com
ICanDigIt.net
IndoorWaterFountains.com
Laura-Ashley.com
MarimekkoFabric.com
MarthaByMail.com
MaxwellSilverNY.com
MelinaMade.com
MossOnline.com
Organize-Everything.com
Palazzetti.com
Pier1.com
PierreDeux.com

PlowHearth.com
PotteryBarn.com
RestorationHardware.com
RetroModern.com
RueDeFrance.com
SmithAndHawken.com
SmithAndNoble.com
SouthwestCountry.com
Spiegel.com
SurLaTable.com
TotemDesign.com
Umbra.com
UncommonGoods.com
UnicaHome.com
UproarHome.com
URBN.com
VintageWoodWorks.com
YowlerSheppsStencils.com
zGlow.com

## APPLIANCES

AltEnergyStore.com
ApplianceAccessories.com
Appliances.com
BathClick.com
BBQGalore-Online.com
BedBathAndBeyond.com
Bodum.com
ChefStore.com
CompactAppliance.com
FrontGate.com
IdeaWorksOnline.com
KitchenEtc.com
RepairClinic.com
Russell-Hobbs.com
SafeHomeProducts.com
Spiegel.com
StacksAndStacks.com
SurLaTable.com
TableTools.com
Williams-Sonoma.com

## BED & BATH

ABed.com
Anthropologie.com
BallardDesigns.com
BathClick.com
BedBathAndBeyond.com
Blankets.com
BombayCo.com
Chiasso.com
CrateBarrel.com
CuddleDown.com
DelawareRiverTrading.com
DomenicaRosa.com
Fortunoff.com
FrontGate.com
GarnetHill.com
GivingTreeOnline.com
HomeDecorators.com
Laura-Ashley.com
LinenPlace.com
MarimekkoFabric.com
MarthaByMail.com
MaxwellSilverNY.com '
Pendleton-USA.com
Pier1.com
PlowHearth.com
PotteryBarn.com
RetroModern.com
RueDeFrance.com
SchweitzerLinen.com
Spiegel.com
StacksAndStacks.com
TheCompanyStore.com
TotemDesign.com
UncommonGoods.com
Urbn.com

## CLEANING

BedBathAndBeyond.com
Caldrea.com
CasaBella.com
Ecos.com
IdeaWorksOnline.com
RestorationHardware.com
SafeHomeProducts.com
StacksAndStacks.com

## ECO-FRIENDLY

AltEnergyStore.com
CasaBella.com
Ecos.com
GardensAlive.com
SafeHomeProducts.com
SeedsOfChange.com

## FURNITURE

AngelaAdams.com
AvalonGarden.com
BallardDesigns.com
BombayCo.com
Chiasso.com
Circa50.com
CrateBarrel.com
CuddleDown.com
DelawareRiverTrading.com
DesignStand.com
DWR.com
Exterior-Accents.com
FineGardenProducts.com
FransWicker.com
Frontera.com
FrontGate.com
GardenSide.com
GarnetHill.com
Guild.com
HomeDecorators.com
ItalyDesign.com
Laura-Ashley.com

LostCityArts.com
MarthaByMail.com
NotABeanBag.com
Palazzetti.com
Pendleton-USA.com
Pier1.com
PierreDeux.com
PlowHearth.com
PotteryBarn.com
RealTeak.com
RestorationHardware.com
RetroModern.com
RueDeFrance.com
SmithAndHawken.com
SouthwestCountry.com
Spiegel.com
StacksAndStacks.com
TheCompanyStore.com
TheKnollShop.com
TidewaterWorkshop.com
TotemDesign.com
Umbra.com
UnicaHome.com
UproarHome.com
Urbn.com
zGlow.com

## GARDEN

AvalonGarden.com
Banana-Tree.com
BrentAndBeckysBulbs.com
Durpee.com
CornerHardware.com
DansDahlias.com
DelawareRiverTrading.com
Exterior-Accents.com
FineGardenProducts.com
GardenGuides.com
GardensAlive.com
HomeDepot.com
ICanDigIt.net
IdeaWorksOnline.com
LilyPons.com
MarthaByMail.com
Mellingers.com
OESCOInc.com
Ponds2Go.com
RestorationHardware.com
SeedsOfChange.com
SmithAndHawken.com

WhiteFlowerFarm.com
WildSeedFarms.com
WindowBox.com

## HARDWARE

Anthropologie.com
BathClick.com
CoastalTool.com
ColonialBrass.com
CornerHardware.com
HomeDepot.com
PoolProducts.com
PoolWarehouse.com
RepairClinic.com
RestorationHardware.com
TooHome.com
ToolsPlus.com
Umbra.com

## IMPROVEMENT

AltEnergyStore.com
Anthropologie.com
ApplianceAccessories.com
AvalonGarden.com
BathClick.com
BlindsGalore.com
CornerHardware.com
DecorateToday.com
DesignerStencils.com
DresslerStencils.com
GreatWindows.com
Homedecorators.com
HomeDepot.com
IdeaWorksOnline.com
Laura-Ashley.com
MarimekkoFabric.com
MelinaMade.com
PierreDeux.com
RepairClinic.com
SmithAndNoble.com
Spiegel.com
TooHome.com
ToolsPlus.com
Umbra.com
VintageWoodWorks.com
YowlerSheppsStencils.com

## KITCHEN

ApplianceAccessories.com
Appliances.com
BallardDesigns.com
BathClick.com
BBQGalore-Online.com
BedBathAndBeyond.com
Bodum.com
ChefStore.com
Chiasso.com
CompactAppliance.com
Cooking.com
CrateBarrel.com
FrontGate.com
HomeDecorators.com
HomeDepot.com
KitchenEtc.com
MarthaByMail.com
MaxwellSilverNY.com
MossOnline.com
Pier1.com
PotsAndPans.com
RetroModern.com
RueDeFrance.com
Russell-Hobbs.com
Spiegel.com
StacksAndStacks.com
SurLaTable.com
TableTools.com
UnicaHome.com
URBN.com
Williams-Sonoma.com
zGlow.com

## LANDSCAPING

AvalonGarden.com
DansDahlias.com
DelawareRiverTrading.com
Exterior-Accents.com
FineGardenProducts.com
FrontGate.com
GardenGuides.com
GardensAlive.com
LilyPons.com
Mellingers.com
OESCOInc.com
Ponds2Go.com
SmithAndHawken.com
WhiteFlowerFarm.com

## LIGHTING

AmericanLightSource.com
Anthropologie.com
BallardDesigns.com
BathClick.com
Bellacor.com
Chiasso.com
Circa50.com
CrateBarrel.com
DeadlyNightShades.com
DecorateToday.com
DWR.com
Exterior-Accents.com
FrontGate.com
Guild.com
HomeDecorators.com
HomeDepot.com
ItalyDesign.com
LampStore.com
Laura-Ashley.com
LightingCenter.com
LostCityArts.com
LouieLighting.com
MaxwellSilverNY.com
PierreDeux.com
PlowHearth.com
PotteryBarn.com
RestorationHardware.com
RetroModern.com
RueDeFrance.com
SouthwestCountry.com
Spiegel.com
StacksAndStacks.com
TooHome.com
TotemDesign.com
UncommonGoods.com
UnicaHome.com
UproarHome.com
URBN.com
zGlow.com

## ORGANIZATION

BathClick.com
BedBathAndBeyond.com
CasaBella.com
Chiasso.com
ContainerStore.com
CornerHardware.com
CrateBarrel.com
HomeDecorators.com
HomeDepot.com
MarthaByMail.com
Organize-Everything.com
Pier1.com
Spiegel.com
StacksAndStacks.com

## PERSONALIZATION

BallardDesigns.com
ColonialBrass.com
DomenicaRosa.com
GarnetHill.com
GivingTreeOnline.com
GraciousStyle.com
MarthaByMail.com
PlowHearth.com
PotteryBarn.com
SafeSmith.com
SchweitzerLinen.com
TheCompanyStore.com
TidewaterWorkshop.com

## POOL & SPA

DirectSpas.com
FrontGate.com
PoolProducts.com
PoolWarehouse.com
TooHome.com

## REGISTRY

BedBathAndBeyond.com
Chiasso.com
Cooking.com
CrateBarrel.com
Fortunoff.com
KitchenEtc.com
MarthaByMail.com
MaxwellSilverNY.com

Pfaltzgraff.com
Pier1.com
PotteryBarn.com
RestorationHardware.com
RetroModern.com
SurLaTable.com
TableTools.com
UnicaHome.com
Williams-Sonoma.com

## SECURITY

HomeDepot.com
SafeHomeProducts.com
SafeSmith.com
SecurityAndMore.com

## TABLEWARE

AnnieGlass.com
Anthropologie.com
BallardDesigns.com
BathClick.com
BedBathAndBeyond.com
Chiasso.com
Comina.com
Cooking.com
CrateBarrel.com
DelawareRiverTrading.com
DesignStand.com
DiningWare.com
DomenicaRosa.com
Eziba.com
Fortunoff.com
GraciousStyle.com
Guild.com
KitchenEtc.com
MaxwellSilverNY.com
MossOnline.com
Pfaltzgraff.com
Pier1.com
PierreDeux.com
PotteryBarn.com
Replacements.com
RetroModern.com
RueDeFrance.com
SchweitzerLinen.com
SurLaTable.com
TableTools.com
UncommonGoods.com
UnicaHome.com
URBN.com

Wedgwood.com
Williams-Sonoma.com
zGlow.com

NOTES:

## ABed.com

These guys, of course, sell beds: waterbeds, foam beds, adjustable beds, travel beds and air mattresses. Unfortunately, while some sell online, some don't, and you really have to kind of get there before you know for sure. They also sell some bedding, and even offer a service wherein they'll connect you via email to a "Sleep Expert" who promises to tell you which of the beds will help if you suffer any mild sleeping disorders. We don't know exactly what constitutes a sleep expert, but we know what a salesman looks like.

·BED & BATH

## AltEnergyStore.com

The "Alt" here stands for "Alternative," as in Alternative Energy Store. Yes, this altruistic retailer may be your best source for energy-responsible "solar panels, windmills, inverters, batteries, refrigerators, charge controllers, panel mounts, meters and much, much more." All right, so we don't know exactly what all of this stuff is, either. But that's the point: here's a place where we can turn our eco-friendly lip service into actual, environmentally sound progress. Best of all, some states offer up to 50% discounts on some of these items that will, ultimately, render your energy bill obsolete.

·APPLIANCES    ·IMPROVEMENT    ·ECO-FRIENDLY

## AmericanLightSource.com

If the standard light fixtures in your home leave you feeling empty or unsatisfied, you either will be interested in the lighting options found here, or require weekly therapy. If it's the former, this entire selection of imported products, including fixtures for chandeliers, foyer lanterns, ceiling fans, wall sconces, track lighting, hanging pendants and exterior lanterns will light up your nights (but may do nothing to brighten your day). You may not know specifically what everything here is at first, but the site is easy to use and most items prove to be fairly self-explanatory. Installation; now that's another story.

·LIGHTING

## AngelaAdams.com

Artist/designer Angela Adams hails from a small island off the coast of Maine, so from her point of view the term "boondocks" actually indicates a location that's probably a bit closer to town. Similar is the insistence that her "patterns and designs are not retro or vintage" when they quite visibly are so, particularly of a Mod-cum-Tiki influence. See; from her perspective the outstanding rugs, ultrasuede pillows and hip glassware that highlight this selection constitute good, contemporary design. Judging by this timeline, she'll start selling love beads sometime next year. Use the e-shopping link to order.

·ACCENTS    ·FURNITURE

## 888-761-0050 • Annie Glass
### AnnieGlass.com

When you hear a term like, "handcrafted sculptural glass dinnerware," you might not immediately be able to visualize what it means. Well, this term refers to the creations of Santa Cruz, CA artist Ann Marhauser, and her dinnerware, serving pieces and accessories are cool enough to impress even those who would settle for paper plates. Utilizing interesting glass and metal blends, Ann's work is both chip-proof and dishwasher friendly. More importantly, it's gorgeous; in particular some of the colored glass and slab series. But all of this stuff is brilliant, and worthy of at least a good, envious look.

| ·ACCENTS | ·TABLEWARE | | |  |
|---|---|---|---|---|

## 800-309-2500 • Anthropologie
### Anthropologie.com

The study of mankind, however you spell it, will often bring you closer to understanding that creative spark that has guided humanity since the origins of civilization. For the purposes of this ceaselessly expanding retailer, this means scouring the antique shops, estate sales and flea markets of the world for interesting items and designs. These wares are then used as inspiration by Anthropologie designers who are charged with the task of incorporating the rich variety of international culture into exclusive home furnishings and décor. The result is a fluid line of limited edition designs that range from functional to flashy, and manage to stay current for an astounding amount of time.

| ·HARDWARE  °  ·BED & BATH | ·LIGHTING  ·TABLEWARE | ·IMPROVEMENT | ·ACCENTS | |
|---|---|---|---|---|

## 888-222-8608 • Appliance Accessories
### ApplianceAccessories.com

One of the more interesting developments in online retail has been in the development of new niche merchandising. We see this in effect here with a store that specializes in, like it says, appliance accessories. For starters, you can find things like clothes dryer vents, trash compactor bags and air conditioner air filters; extra and replaceable parts for major and minor household appliances that may be otherwise hard to find. Then, if you can master the simple but inconsistent navigation, you'll find time- and space-saving accessories for said appliances (including refrigerators, dishwashers and the like). Finally, you can find some actual appliances, like garbage disposals, and even some replacement front panels for your big machines, for beauty's sake.

| ·APPLIANCES | ·IMPROVEMENT | ·KITCHEN | |
|---|---|---|---|

## 888-543-8345 • Appliances.com
### Appliances.com

When the machines inevitably rise up in violent revolt against humankind, it probably won't be advisable to have a house filled with blenders, slicers, grinders and strainers. Until then, however, it's a fantastic idea to do just that, and this outstanding site can help. Every conceivable kitchen appliance is here, from refrigerators to waffle irons, and that's to say nothing of the laundry, climate control and cleaning equipment. Finding what you may or may not need could not be easier, and reasonable prices easily make it the best place to shop for functional electrics. It's almost a little too convenient....

| ·APPLIANCES | ·KITCHEN | | |
|---|---|---|---|

# AvalonGarden.com

AvalonGarden.com • 800-854-0880

According to legend, when Arthur had fought his last battle as King of England, he was magically returned to the island of Avalon, said to be a mystical place of healing and retreat, where he would patiently await his return to the throne. Well, to date, he hasn't shown up, and one can presume that he's just too deliriously happy where he is. At least, that's probably the image this retailer of outdoor and garden furniture intends to promote. At any rate, the high-quality fountains, statues, porch swings and gardening tools should go a long way in making any garden or patio a place of retreat in its own right.

| ·IMPROVEMENT ·GARDEN | ·ACCENTS | ·FURNITURE | ·LANDSCAPING |

# BallardDesigns.com

Ballard Designs • 800-367-2775

Founded by one-time Home of the Year winner Helen Ballard Weeks, it's not surprising that this company has some very fine home and office furnishings for sale. If you have something specific in mind, like a throw pillow or valenza, you can quickly find it in a simple search, or by category, but probably more effective is the Room Search, which lets you browse through various categories pertaining to the different rooms of your home. It's easy to find elegant items for the bathroom, bedroom or boudoir, though you may find some of it ugly. No worry; this purveyor of the best of the best will change the fabric on any original design to one of your liking, even sending you swatches to make sure something matches your home before you commit to an order.

| ·LIGHTING ·BED & BATH | ·ACCENTS ·TABLEWARE | ·FURNITURE ·PERSONALIZATION | ·KITCHEN |

# Banana-Tree.com

The Banana Tree • 610-253-9589

On this site you will find a great, big catalog of seeds, bulbs and plants ranging from the local to the exotic, including tropicals, edibles, cacti, palms and protea. Sounds good, don't it? Well, the catch is this: they don't offer any pictures. Nope. A giant selection such as this, and you are forced to determine which of said plants you'd prefer based on their textual descriptions. To be fair, these are well worded, and usually get the point across. But in this visually savvy medium we find it disappointing. Unless you know your plant life or have an excruciatingly slow modem speed, you might want to find your selection elsewhere; assuming you can.

| ·GARDEN | | | |

# BathClick.com

HomeClick.com • 800-643-9990

These guys will be the first, and only, people to tell you, "America is having a love affair with the bath and kitchen." Does this sound delusional? Well, the upshot is that they've parlayed this belief into a web shop devoted to all parts of your bath and kitchen, whether you're into a spot of home improvement, or just want better lighting to showcase all that you can accomplish with tiles and chrome. And when we say "all parts," we mean all parts. Turns out, you can order a shower off the internet now—not just a shower head, but an entire shower. So, what do you think: is this love, or more just a physical lust?

| ·HARDWARE ·KITCHEN | ·APPLIANCES ·BED & BATH | ·LIGHTING ·TABLEWARE | ·IMPROVEMENT ·ORGANIZATION |

**800-752-3085 • BBQ Galore**                    **BBQGalore-Online.com**

For those who like to play with fire... Outdoor cooking enthusiasts in particular will appreciate this site devoted to the mainstay of American summertime: the barbeque. You can shop by fuel type (propane, coal, etc.), price, brand and even cooking area (for those bigger cuts of meat). One brilliant category, Tailgating, will amply supply the chef on the go. Supplies aren't limited to grills, though; they offer smokers, rotisseries, a bevy of cooking tools and everything else you'll need, down to the eternally hilarious "Danger: Men Cooking" apron.

| ·APPLIANCES | ·KITCHEN | | |
|---|---|---|---|

---

**800-462-3966 • Bed Bath and Beyond**                    **BedBathAndBeyond.com**

Style makes your home look good, but does it make your home work? Well, sometimes you're bound to be looking for some object, like a blender or a CD rack, that isn't going to look good, but damn well better be functional. For such times as these we have Bed, Bath and Beyond, a commonly known store with a commendable online presence. Its excellent navigation is hampered only by its somewhat slow speed, the result of a thorough online gallery that depicts exquisitely practical items. Which isn't to say anything here lacks taste. Let's just say that the site's vast selection of home furnishings, small appliances and accessories values function over form, making it a perfect venue for the BBB online Bridal Registry.

| ·ACCENTS ·ORGANIZATION | ·KITCHEN ·CLEANING | ·BED & BATH ·REGISTRY | ·TABLEWARE ·APPLIANCES |
|---|---|---|---|

---

**877-723-5522 • Bellacor**                    **Bellacor.com**

With more than 500,000 items to choose from, you'd think finding something suitable to your taste and finances might be difficult with this retailer of furnishings for the home and garden. Actually, it's simple: stick to Lighting, conveniently located right at the top of the left-hand menu. It's by far the best stuff on the site, and the track lighting, sconces, chandeliers and lamps come with free shipping. So does the rest of the site's products, but you might want to leave some of those in the dark.

| ·LIGHTING | ·ACCENTS | | |
|---|---|---|---|

---

**888-248-7568 • Blankets.com**                    **Blankets.com**

A domain like this always proves kind of easy and memorable, so it's nice when the site lives up to its promise. Here you can shop through categories like Bedding and Lap Throws, then sift through items comprised of Acrylic Blends, Fleece, Down and then some. Rounding out the selection are blankets with sports teams insignia (college and pro) and utility blankets (the kind commonly found in moving trucks). The truly picky among us will fail to see the charm, but nobody can claim this site's made poor use of its name.

| ·BED & BATH | | | |
|---|---|---|---|

# BlindsGalore.com

Whether you're looking for cornices, roller shades or cordless blinds, this online specialty store has your number. You can browse for specific window-related products, or root through your favorite (if you have any) brand names. You can also use the site's Blinds Finder feature, which allows you to filter items by product category, size and price range. If you're not sure, you may be able to get preview swatches sent to you, to help prevent the hanging of Roman Shades where Woven Wood blinds are clearly more appropriate.

| | ·IMPROVEMENT | ·ACCENTS | | |
|---|---|---|---|---|

# Bodum.com

Making and selling their own tabletop items, cooking tools and small appliances, these guys are proficient at both. Whether it's coffee machines, fondue pots or plat ménages, these products and this web site are equally slick, with clean lines and exquisitely functional design. Best may be their Coffee and Tea sections, featuring grinders, kettles and cups, but honestly all of the sections should satisfy, despite the fact that the selection is slim and that you may not think you like this sort of thing.

| | ·APPLIANCES | ·KITCHEN | | |
|---|---|---|---|---|

# BombayCo.com

Here's a good one. This company began in New Orleans in the 1970s as a mail order company devoted to selling unassembled reproductions of 18th and 19th century English furniture. While its inexpensive products were popular, the company was never really successful until it moved into retail stores and away from mail order. Ironically, the retail company has moved back into the long-distance order game and hopes for continued success with this easy-to-use site. They've also expanded into some original designs, though all adhere to the distinctive British Colonial style that the original Bombay Company founder admired. Hey, any excuse to avoid the mall, right?

| | ·ACCENTS | ·FURNITURE | ·BED & BATH | |
|---|---|---|---|---|

# BraidedRugs.com

Just like it sounds, this web site sells braided rugs. With a variety of shapes and sizes, including chair pads and stair treads, you can quickly browse through every single product in the catalog, selecting between the different colors and fabrics, probably finding just the sort of rug you remember from your grandmother's living room. Just a warning, though, the ordering engine isn't quite up to par with other e-commerce sites, so you'll have to fill in all the ordering information yourself, including rug number, shape, size and price, which is a drag.

| | ·ACCENTS | | | |
|---|---|---|---|---|

## 877-661-2852 • Brent & Becky's Bulbs

### BrentAndBeckysBulbs.com

Brent and Becky are a couple of perennial flower farmers from coastal Virginia who proffer seasonal bulbs for some of your favorite blossoms, as well as some rare and unusual bulbs you may not be able to find anywhere else. You can browse by season, hoping that what you seek isn't sold out, or you can check out some of their expertly designed collections. You may also run a search by name, family, color and height, as well as some other fields which will be best understood by flower experts. Still, selection is limited, so you should maybe just follow the Click Here To Only See Items Currently Available link at the top of the home page to save yourself a little bit of heartbreak.

| ·GARDEN | | | | ☼ |
|---|---|---|---|---|

## 888-333-5808 • Burpee

### Burpee.com

In over 100 years in business, perhaps the greatest advancement by this seller of seeds has been to move online. Now, they can offer you the Garden Wizard, a software entity prescribed with one major task: "find your perfect plant." Merely answer a sequence of relevant questions, and the site will recommend plants suitable to your desires and living situation. You can also check out their Online Garden School, take a 3-D tour of the Virtual Garden or learn what edible things can grow out of your ground in the Burpee Nutritional Guide.

| ·GARDEN | | | | ☼ |
|---|---|---|---|---|

## 877-576-8808 • Caldrea

### Caldrea.com

These guys claim to be "completely devoted to helping you make your household chores more enjoyable." Sadly, we checked, and they don't send a lingerie maid service over to your home. What they do instead is sell various aromatherapeutic cleaning agents (again these are solvents, not people). The selection is quite limited, but you won't find any of this stuff anywhere else. So, rather than flee your chemical-laden home in terror after a good scrubbing session, now you can sit around and smell your way to bliss. You still have to do the work yourself though.

| ·CLEANING | | | |
|---|---|---|---|

## 800-841-4140 • Casabella

### CasaBella.com

Not that you're overly into the stuff, or anything, but... you wanna see some pretty cool mops and brooms? This place offers some of the more interesting home cleaning supplies you're likely to come across, whether it's a Duck Dustpan, Get Bent Cleaner or Magnet Broom. Actually, most of this stuff sounds weirder than it is, and though these are somewhat more than your run-of-the-mill designs, at the root of it they have some functional cleaning tools, and one strange-looking site.

| ·ORGANIZATION | ·CLEANING | ·ECO-FRIENDLY | | 💡 |
|---|---|---|---|---|

## ChefStore.com

You couldn't say that this site has a lot of different categories so much as it lists a categorical menu of all its products. The drawback of this is that, for those of us who might not know exactly what a Mandoline, Mezzaluna or a Windsor Pot is, there's going to be a lot of clicking back and forth. Fortunately, most of these items are self-explanatory, meaning you can browse the list and only bother following relevant links to products you actually want to see. It's a nice looking site, with slick wares.

| ·APPLIANCES | ·KITCHEN | | |

## Chiasso.com

Chiásso (the Italian word meaning "uproar") promises "formfunctionfun." Well, the fun is subjective, but so far as form and function are concerned, this site hits the mark. What appear to simply be cute little icon illustrations in the top left of the screen turn out to offer animated menus upon rollover, delivering an array of subsections across categories like Décor, Kitchen, Tabletop and Bath. Pretty much all of these lead to a genuinely cool selection of products, with the Novelties sections sure to attract the most attention.

| ·LIGHTING ·BED & BATH | ·ACCENTS ·TABLEWARE | ·FURNITURE ·ORGANIZATION | ·KITCHEN ·REGISTRY |

## Circa50.com

It's tough to make sense of this convoluted site, what with their bizarre organization and inconsistent navigation. These products are generally too cool to skip, however, featuring ultra-hip furniture designs by the likes of Herman Miller, Modernica and a host of others. If you're willing to embrace these expensive, confounding waters, there is sort of a game to be made out of locating the Ultra Lounge section. It's buried deep in there somewhere; can you find it?

| ·LIGHTING | ·FURNITURE | | |

## CoastalTool.com

The most important thing to note in regard to this thoroughly well-stocked tool retailer is that their shipping policy is based on the price of the order, not the weight of it. This, if for no other reason, makes this place a necessary stop when doing price comparisons with other shops, as the shipping costs on heavy power tools elsewhere can prove prohibitive to say the least. As for actually shopping here, you should generally go away happy, unless you ultimately utilize these wares to destroy rooms in your home.

| ·HARDWARE | | | |

## 800-549-8670 • Colonial Brass

## ColonialBrass.com

The Colonial Brass Company has pretty much been selling sundials since they were the best time-keeping technology available. While times have certainly changed, the nonfunctional aspects of a sundial remain, making them a great centerpiece to a lawn or garden. Here, you can have them custom-made to include special tributes, family names, dates or any other epithet you'd like to see engraved for the ages. Other than sundials, you can get the same personalized service for home or desktop nameplates, plaques and door knockers. Finally, if you'd like to bestow upon yourself the highest of community honors, you can buy here a key to the city. Who said you had to earn it anymore?

| ·HARDWARE | ·ACCENTS | ·PERSONALIZATION | |
|---|---|---|---|

## 866-266-4621 • Comina

## Comina.com

This site is simply Brillante. That is, all the wares we saw have been hand-crafted from the high-quality aluminum, Brillante, usually into fancifully shaped serving ware such as an ice cream cone-shaped ice cream scoop or a seahorse serving dish. The stuff is shiny and lovely to look at, with much more character than one is used to seeing in such items. Shopping may have its tedious moments, but should usually run smooth, even when the shop's promise to add wrought-iron furniture and chandeliers is fulfilled.

| ·ACCENTS | ·TABLEWARE | | |
|---|---|---|---|

## 800-297-6076 • CompactAppliance.com

## CompactAppliance.com

Despite the name, these guys actually offer some appliances as uncompact as refrigerators, dishwashers and washer/dryers. And despite the high costs associated with having any sizable appliance sent through the mail, their selection might inspire you. Basically, whether it's rotisserie ovens, induction cooktops, steam vacuums or beer coolers, these guys have a variety to choose from, despite the fact that some of these products simply aren't available for purchase online.

| ·APPLIANCES | ·KITCHEN | | |
|---|---|---|---|

## 888-266-8246 • Container Store

## ContainerStore.com

The gist of this site is that if a product can hold your various household utensils and other material possessions, you can probably find it here. Behind the Shop Online link you'll encounter a simply parsed selection of categories, each laden with their own subcategories, and all devoted to products defined only by the term "storage." You get a good look at the products (many of which will require some amount of assembly or other work on your part) and generally pay a fair price.

| ·ORGANIZATION | | | |
|---|---|---|---|

# Cooking.com

You get the feeling, as you look over all the various resources of this rather large site, that its proprietors would take it as an effrontery to find out there was a cooking tool they'd somehow left out of their catalog. After all, they feature an entire section devoted to Egg Tools, so they obviously take it all very seriously. Well, a few things are probably missing, but unless you're quite the experienced cook you may never know. If you're relatively new to the kitchen, the site proves especially helpful, offering recipes, tips and general know-how articles. Feast your eyes on this one, and your stomach will follow.

| | | ·KITCHEN | ·TABLEWARE | ·REGISTRY | |
|---|---|---|---|---|---|

# CornerHardware.com

These guys seem to have missed the fact that the attraction of the corner hardware store is that it's, well, just around the corner. Nevertheless, they've taken to this hardware thing with the zeal of a carpenter. However neatly arranged they might be, it actually makes us tired to think about all the tools, electrical gear, lawn and garden equipment, plumbing supplies and decorative hardware here (dozens upon dozens of wall sconces, for example). This turns out to be a good thing, though, if you need a lot of stuff, as prices are structured to save you a lot of money on large orders.

| | ·HARDWARE | ·IMPROVEMENT | ·GARDEN | ·ORGANIZATION |
|---|---|---|---|---|

# CrateBarrel.com

Like its products, this furniture and home accessories site is slick and modern, finding a subtle form of elegance in its simplicity. Barware, tableware, kitchen tools and furniture selections for every room in or out of the house are neatly organized into readily defined categories, complete with enticing images and intriguing write-ups for each item. Like window-shopping come to life, the open display marketing that made Crate & Barrel a national phenomenon is well represented here.

| | ·LIGHTING ·BED & BATH | ·ACCENTS ·TABLEWARE | ·FURNITURE ·ORGANIZATION | ·KITCHEN ·REGISTRY |
|---|---|---|---|---|

# CuddleDown.com

The proprietors of this site know how imperative comfortable bedding is to a heavenly night's sleep. For years, they've been selling down comforters to keep people warm on long winter nights, and now they bring their selection of high-quality sleeping gear to this very slick and welcoming site. Initially, they merely imported comforters in larger sizes so that people could really stretch out and get comfy. Of course, this created a need for larger duvet covers. Well, since they started producing their own made-to-fit covers, the product line has only expanded to include pillows, sheets, feather beds, towels, mattress pads, sleepwear, bed skirts and anything else you can imagine that could keep you feeling warm and cuddly when the sandman calls.

| | ·FURNITURE | ·BED & BATH | | |
|---|---|---|---|---|

**360-482-2406** • **Dan's Dahlias**  **DansDahlias.com**

It wouldn't seem that a site devoted exclusively to dahlias would be all that interesting. However, Dan Pearson, founder of Dan's Dahlias, has been running this business for going on two decades now—since he was ten! This award-winning grower really knows what he's doing, and the result is a wide variety of incredible flowers; we're talkin' dahlias that look sort of like other flowers, dahlias that are ball-shaped, dahlias that are pointy like a cactus, dahlias with dozens of petals and some rounded with just a few. All this is to say nothing of the different colors. Check this site out and let Dan open your eyes to what he's known for practically his whole life: a dahlia is a beautiful thing.

| ·LANDSCAPING | ·GARDEN | | |
|---|---|---|---|

**336-376-9250** • **Deadly Nightshades**  **DeadlyNightShades.com**

Welcome to what may be the scariest-sounding store online. In truth, it's not all that terrifying, despite a potentially confusing ordering process. See, these guys offer customized lampshades; and pretty cool ones at that. Once you've looked around, and gotten a feel for these offerings, find the Order Stuff Now link, then hit the Place Order button. Here, you'll find a series of nine or ten questions about your shade preferences (it's a good idea to know exactly what you want at this point). Finally you can stop staring at that bare bulb.

| ·LIGHTING | ·ACCENTS | | |
|---|---|---|---|

**800-575-8016** • **American Blind & Wallpaper**  **DecorateToday.com**

Obviously, even with the increased proliferation of overnight service, if you go shopping online here you won't actually be able to decorate today. Still, this mildly confusing but ultimately functional site can give you a good start on adding to your home's aesthetic appeal. With wallpaper, blinds, rugs, lighting, art and "home accents," there can be a lot to sort through before you find the objects of your desire. However, in each product category you'll find a spate of options designed to help you narrow down your selection. Not enough? Well, add free shipping to the equation, and you might decide you're ready after all to decorate … soon.

| ·LIGHTING | ·IMPROVEMENT | ·ACCENTS | |
|---|---|---|---|

**800-732-4791** • **Delaware River Trading Co.**  **DelawareRiverTrading.com**

Proclaiming itself "perfect for your lifestyle," this site is of course being a bit presumptuous. It also tends to be a little too visually snappy, which ultimately gets in the way of convenient shopping. It could just be that these guys are just plain eager to get you excited about their oddball selection of indoor and garden furniture which, perfect or not for your lifestyle, is kind of cool. Then again, if stuff like sheepskin rugs, bamboo dinnerware and hand-forged iron gazebos leave you wanting more, feel free to skip this one.

| ·ACCENTS<br>·BED & BATH | ·FURNITURE<br>·TABLEWARE | ·LANDSCAPING | ·GARDEN |
|---|---|---|---|

## DesignerStencils.com

Designer Stencils • 800-822-7836

If you're looking for an easy and inexpensive way to spruce up the flat surfaces of your home, this family-owned-and-operated business asks you to consider their wide variety of stencils and paints to do the job. Basic stenciling can, of course, substantially reduce the likelihood that any designs you paint on your walls will give your children nightmares. Some of these stencils even get quite intricate, essentially allowing you to replicate familiar images and/or lettering at your own convenience. Designs range from wacky to classic, often featuring flowers, animals or architecture, each with a set of paints all set up to keep you from getting the colors wrong.

| | ·IMPROVEMENT | ·ACCENTS | | |
|---|---|---|---|---|

## DesignStand.com

DesignStand.com • 800-763-6767

If you live on the cutting edge of design, or if you feel like you want to, this site is here to hook you up. It promises "the best that international design has to offer," and delivers a selection of unique furniture and accessories that fit snugly into the modern nooks of your life. Some of these designs are famous (like the Dr. No chair), and some are too new to be known. Either way, Design Stand's sister sites, DesignLog.com and DesignZine.com are ready to educate and advise you on the hip directions in furniture design and how you can be a part of it. Here's hoping the cutting edge is comfortable enough for you.

| | ·ACCENTS | ·FURNITURE | ·TABLEWARE | |
|---|---|---|---|---|

## DiningWare.com

DiningWare.com • 888-371-7511

In terms of software savvy, these guys offer an interesting feature in their Online Workbook, which allows you to view pieces of their glassware, flatware and dinnerware selections on a variety of surfaces, so you can mix and match with ease. It's the kind of thing you don't see much anymore (post-internet fallout), and the reason why may be seen in their relative lack of selection. Slight as it might be, you won't find anything terribly run-of-the-mill here, which is always a plus in our eyes.

| | ·TABLEWARE | | | |
|---|---|---|---|---|

## DirectSpas.com

Hydro Spa • 877-237-8772

It's probably the ultimate home fantasy: return from a long, hard day's work, pour a couple of glasses of champagne, and join your significant other for an intimate evening in the hot tub. Well, now the dream is just clicks away as you can actually order yourself a fully functional whirlpool spa online for delivery to your home (what a time to be alive!). What's more is that through this site you are ordering direct from the manufacturer, so you get a great deal on top of the ordering convenience. Of course, this doesn't mean it comes cheap (we are talking about Jacuzzis here), but if you can't afford it now, this simple selection of spas will surely inspire you to put in some overtime at the office (to be rewarded later by a lifetime of massaging bubbles).

| | ·POOL & SPA | | | |
|---|---|---|---|---|

## 888-354-9388 • Domenica Rosa

**DomenicaRosa.com**

In the pursuit of creating the finest dining forum your home can manage, you should be sure to check out this jumbled but well-meaning site. With top-notch table linens, chair covers, napkins and accents, you can almost increase the elegance of your table setting just by browsing. Between their original silks, linens and brocades, and a plethora of high-end brands featured here, you probably need not resort to custom table-fitting. However, this is an option, and well worth considering. Go ahead and have it custom-made to shape, size, color and material, and monogram everything while you're at it. Just be careful not to spill.

| •ACCENTS | •BED & BATH | •TABLEWARE | •PERSONALIZATION |
|---|---|---|---|

## 888-656-4515 • Dressler Stencils

**DresslerStencils.com**

If you haven't already inferred from the URL, yes these guys sell stencils. Not just ordinary stencils, though; these are "quality laser cut stencils for home decoration." This means these stencils can get quite intricate, allowing for some pretty complicated artwork on your walls by the time you're done with them. You can still find some more cartoonish designs as well, and a wide range listed in categories like Under the Sea, Medieval Magic, Kitchen Kitsch, African Savanna, Sultan's Oasis and the perennial favorite, Cuddly Critters. Stencil-specific paint kits make it quite easy to replicate the artwork you see here, and give those drab, blank walls of yours a little pizzazz.

| •IMPROVEMENT | •ACCENTS | | |
|---|---|---|---|

## 800-944-2233 • Design Within Reach

**DWR.com**

Are you ready for a slick design? That's what there is to be found at DWR, aka Design Within Reach, a San Francisco-based seller of European furniture designs. Apparently, Europeans have a finer grasp and/or appreciation of fine designs, and these guys want to change that. Featuring designs by (and biographies about) top furniture designers, their list of contributors include architecture's two most famous Franks (Frank O. Gehry and Frank Lloyd Wright), among others. The furniture? Yes, it's cool too, with an array of seating options, beds, tables, lighting and office furniture, the likes of which you may never have seen before. Oh so very slick.

| •LIGHTING | •ACCENTS | •FURNITURE | |
|---|---|---|---|

## 800-335-3267 • Earth Friendly Products

**Ecos.com**

Okay, so this site won't make the cleaning of your house any more enjoyable, but these Earth-friendly cleaning products might make the process less hazardous to your health. Made from 100% natural ingredients, the cleansers, stain removers, air fresheners and laundry detergents may face the stigma of being less thorough than their chemical counterparts, but the truth is that your stuff will still be clean, just not toxically so. Add to the mix recycled paper towels, and you've got yourself a nice progressive site here.

| •CLEANING | •ECO-FRIENDLY | | |
|---|---|---|---|

## ExposuresOnline.com

Exposures • 800-572-5750

What better way to decorate your home than with pictures of yourself and your loved ones, right? Well, this site brings you "products... especially designed to safeguard irreplaceable memories." Forget about keeping them between your ears; here you'll find frames, albums, picture storage, displays and even mirrors to help remind you what future memories of your current self might one day look like. We haven't even gotten to the Fun options, like that of having a picture of your pet's face grafted onto the body of a 17th century nobleman in courtly attire. Sound crazy? What if we told you that it could then be printed onto a throw pillow?

·ACCENTS

## Exterior-Accents.com

Exterior Accents • 866-595-9164

A more imaginative garden will be the result of shopping from this seemingly bland North Carolina–based site. Unique versions of garden-variety items like stone fountains, miniature lighthouses, arbors and obelisks are all over the place, along with wind chimes, footbridges and an unusual selection of weather vanes. Most of this stuff is quite beautiful, and will require hours of deliberation on which to buy. Of course, if you have the means you could just buy their entire selection of metal dog statues (50 breeds are represented), but then, chances are you'll find something better.

·LIGHTING ·GARDEN | ·ACCENTS | ·FURNITURE | ·LANDSCAPING

## Eziba.com

Eziba • 888-404-5108

While anybody may enjoy this site, its presentation seems to be particularly attuned to those who mistakenly think elegance is strictly a western notion. Rather, this retailer of arts, crafts and creative furniture delivers a selection whose origins spans the globe, and doesn't mind telling you the what-and-where of it all. "We'll never promise you the world," they explain to the curious yet uninformed potential customer, "but we'll use our understanding to select the most exquisite crafts the planet has to offer." Experienced collectors might object to these "translators" and their quasi-condescension, but no amount of language will detract from the luster of these wares, nor from their glossy appeal.

·TABLEWARE | ·ACCENTS | ·LIGHTING | ·FURNITURE

## FineGardenProducts.com

FineGardenProducts.com • 888-949-2999

Expressing one of the sweetest sentiments on the whole world wide web, this site's tag line claims, "We want you to be happy." Well, it's a wonderful thing to say, but unless happiness comes to you in the form of garden décor or door knockers they're simply not equipped to make it happen. If, however, some garden furniture and other landscaping ornaments do elate you, then by all means take a look here, as the selection is unmatched... enough so that even the occasional garden scrooge will enjoy it.

·FURNITURE | ·LANDSCAPING | ·GARDEN

## 800-367-8866 • Fortunoff

### Fortunoff.com

From modest beginnings as a neighborhood housewares store in Brooklyn, Fortunoff shops have expanded over nearly 8 decades to finally bring their selection of old school furnishings and great prices online. The site is well set up to help you find what you're looking for, whether by department or manufacturer, though it can really take a while before you actually click through to a product. If you have some idea of what you're looking for, you might want to stick to the advanced search so you can filter out any of hundreds of items that might otherwise distract you. On the other hand, if you're getting married, you might just want to take your time, as a Fortunoff Bridal Registry is now available online, and you definitely don't want to miss anything here.

| ·BED & BATH | ·TABLEWARE | ·REGISTRY | |
|---|---|---|---|

## 888-999-2629 • Fran's Wicker

### FransWicker.com

Fran has a brick-and-mortar store in New Jersey, but why go there when you can find all the wicker and rattan furniture you'll ever need on the store's no-frills web site? We're talkin' wicker chairs, tables, entertainment centers, hampers and even a wicker chaise lounge. You can browse through it all pretty easily, and click on the thumbnail images to check out some of the largest and most detailed pictures of furniture we've seen online. In fact, if you notice on the large view that you're not pleased with the fabric of a seat cushion or ottoman, don't fret, just check out the online swatch book to find the right alternative for special order. Looks like this site has some frills after all.

| ·FURNITURE· | | | |
|---|---|---|---|

## 800-762-5374 • Frontera

### Frontera.com

It's hard to say what passes for "traditional" these days, but whatever you imagine it to be, in terms of furniture there's a good chance it's here. The only problem may be finding it. The navigation can be a little confusing, but it works with patience, and actually offers you several different ways to find what you're after. The easiest would be to select the site's Indoor, Outdoor or Accessories options at the top of the home page. You then select a style (e.g., Rustic, Colonial, Contemporary, etc.) and then the room you're trying to furnish. The left side of the page actually features a bunch of different navigations that might work faster, but faster's not always better.

| ·FURNITURE· | | | |
|---|---|---|---|

## 800-626-6488 • Frontgate

### FrontGate.com

Now this is living. Frontgate is a vendor of high-end "lifestyle accessories"; basically the kinds of furnishings and furniture pieces that everybody has, but better versions. This stuff is sleek, chic and hard to beat, and of course it is typically expensive. The site is also high quality, offering you thorough and well-defined categories for browsing, then allowing you to narrow your hunt down by material, style and/or price range. If you somehow find yourself uncertain about which items are the tops in their field, the site gives you the option of contacting one of its product specialists (read: salesmen) for questioning. However, luxurious items abound, and detailed pictures will entice you enough that, have you the means, you'll be able to decide for yourself.

| ·POOL & SPA<br>·FURNITURE | ·APPLIANCES<br>·LANDSCAPING | ·LIGHTING<br>·KITCHEN | ·ACCENTS<br>·BED & BATH |
|---|---|---|---|

# GardenGuides.com

Garden Guides • 800-274-0824

Once you've tilled the soil and positioned the garden gnomes, it's just a matter of what to plant in your garden. As knowledgeable and imaginative as you might be, chances are good that your ideas don't stray too far from the roses, tulips and daisies ilk. This site's a good place to look to expand your understanding of how rich and varied a garden can be. Aside from its phenomenal assortment of flowers, vegetables and herbs (with options for seeds, bulbs and organic seeds), they feature a broad range of articles on topics like optimum planting times and how to deal with pests. It's all a little more than you probably need, but nice to know that it's there.

| | ·LANDSCAPING | ·GARDEN | | |
|---|---|---|---|---|

# GardensAlive.com

Gardens Alive • 513-354-1483

What does it take to make your garden grow? Obviously, there's water, sunlight and fertile soil, but what nature gives nature can take away in the form of insects, fungi and other botanical threats. The tendency is to add chemicals to the mix. But come on, plant life flourished for millennia without the help of pollutant artificial supplements, so why should they stop now? Instead, check this site's "environmentally responsible products that work" for beneficial insects, nonchemical fungicides and other nature-friendly products to aid and protect your lawn and garden.

| | ·LANDSCAPING | ·GARDEN | ·ECO-FRIENDLY | |
|---|---|---|---|---|

# GardenSide.com

Gardenside • 415-380-8325

In a word: teak. This outdoor furniture specialist sticks strictly to the weather-resistant wood with benches, chairs, loungers, parasols, tables and planters to accentuate your deck, patio, lawn and garden. Browsing is easier than selecting specific designs, and while shipping seems a bit pricey, when you consider that it's rather sizable wood furniture going through the mail, the prices suddenly seem quite reasonable. Good stuff.

| | ·FURNITURE | | | |
|---|---|---|---|---|

# GarnetHill.com

Garnet Hill • 800-870-3513

Cool, casual bedding with classic colors and simple patterns are the main focus of this web site that stemmed from the Garnet Hill Catalog Company. You'll find lamps, rugs, towels and other household items as well, but the best selection and highest quality exists in its sheets, comforters, quilts and any other term you can come up with for a blanket. The site is well designed and well maintained, with good pictures and easy ordering, so that the hardest part of your visit here will be deciding what to buy.

| | ·FURNITURE | ·BED & BATH | ·PERSONALIZATION | |
|---|---|---|---|---|

## 888-678-0068 • Giving Tree — GivingTreeOnline.com

For a store with an inventory consisting almost exclusively of textiles, the category list here is astonishingly long. To mention that they sell pillows, quilts, table linens, comforters, towels, bed skirts, blanket covers and duvets would be almost misleading, as it would only scratch the surface. Perhaps they go a little overboard distinguishing between characteristics such as Fine Linens and French Bed Linens, but as this provides the only easy part to this navigational system, we're going to go ahead and say it's a good thing.

| ·ACCENTS | ·BED & BATH | ·PERSONALIZATION | ·TABLEWARE |
|---|---|---|---|

## 888-828-7170 • Gracious Style — GraciousStyle.com

This purveyor of table linens, silverware, porcelain china and crystal wares has the goal to "inspire discerning clients to create the perfect settings for celebrating a life of luxury, elegance and sophistication." As if that weren't enough of a mouthful, they intend to do this by capturing "the essence of fine living with its exquisite collection of tabletop accessories." Sounds to us like you've been issued a challenge. If you fancy yourself a "discerning client," check out their merchandise and see if you can resist, or if you'd prefer to celebrate some luxury elsewhere.

| ·ACCENTS | ·TABLEWARE | ·PERSONALIZATION | |
|---|---|---|---|

## 800-556-6632 • Next Day Blinds — GreatWindows.com

This site is brought to you courtesy of Next Day Blinds; of course, this is the internet, so the use of "next day" would be misleading. Regardless, you can order custom-sized blinds here quite easily—it's just a matter of entering your measurements and a few easy particulars. Of course, first you must choose the blinds, shades or cornices, and that's the hard part, because there are a lot of good-looking products to choose from. It only really gets tricky doing price comparisons, though, as you must view pop-up charts and calculate a cost based on size for each particular selection. Then, it's all sort of pricey anyway; what do you expect? We're talkin' custom blinds here.

| ·IMPROVEMENT | ·ACCENTS | | |
|---|---|---|---|

## 877-344-8453 • Guild.com — Guild.com

If it'll give you any indication of the type of home furnishings you may find here, you should know that this site's primary purpose is to sell art. So, you can imagine, the furniture and home accents here haven't been just haphazardly slapped together. They are, in fact, so utterly imaginative you might sometimes confuse these pieces for something you'd see in a cartoon, or Impressionist painting. Browsing is pretty typical, with one beneficial twist: when you enter a category, Tables, for example, you can then have the option of filtering it down to just wood tables (or metal, glass and ceramic).

| ·LIGHTING | ·ACCENTS | ·FURNITURE | ·TABLEWARE |
|---|---|---|---|

## HomeDecorators.com

Home Decorators Collection • 800-240-6047

It's tough to pinpoint a defining style for this furniture and accents store, but with such an interesting variety of items we just couldn't leave it out, despite the clumsy navigation. See, we found a bunch of odd items here, like dozens of pedestals. Delving deeper, we noticed that there's also a lot of screens, chimeneas (small, portable outdoor fireplaces) and vanity stools (these differ from barstools mainly in height, and have a plusher, flowery look). But, then, just at the point we noticed a collection of coat racks, we came upon the word "switchplate." It turns out, they sell decorative plates to replace the regular, colorless ones that cover your light switches. Who comes up with this stuff?

| | ·LIGHTING<br>·BED & BATH | ·ACCENTS<br>·ORGANIZATION | ·FURNITURE<br>·IMPROVEMENT | ·KITCHEN |
|---|---|---|---|---|

## HomeDepot.com

Home Depot • 800-430-3376

If you're not fortunate enough to live near one of this franchise's behemoth brick-and-mortar stores ... this won't necessarily help. See, they've really set up their online shopping presence as a means of ordering deliveries from their localized warehouse fixtures. Even if the place is just around the corner, though, this can be a legitimate use of the web as it'll save you a potentially mile-long walk down their typically crowded aisles, and set up delivery of all items to your home, especially handy as a great percentage of their merchandise is much bigger than you.

| | ·HARDWARE<br>·KITCHEN | ·LIGHTING<br>·ORGANIZATION | ·IMPROVEMENT<br>·SECURITY | ·GARDEN |
|---|---|---|---|---|

## HomeFiresUSA.com

Home Fires • 800-749-4049

These home fires consist of what you call decorative gas coal fireplaces, which don't necessarily sound authentic but look amazing and prove easy to light. The site only recently made these wares available for delivery in the US, and it may be worth a look simply because you probably never considered such an item for your home. Made of polished iron or brass, these range from fluidly functional to ornate, but you'll find that every single one will properly accompany a snifter of brandy and a stately pipe.

| | ·ACCENTS | | | |
|---|---|---|---|---|

## ICanDigIt.net

ICanDigIt.net • 513-248-8500

A testimony to the power of creativity, this quirky site was founded by a couple of women who met while volunteering at their children's school. What began as a common interest in crafts projects they could share with their kids quickly turned into an organized effort to infuse gardening with an adventurous imaginative spirit. The gardening tools and decorations here are designed to make gardening both easier and more fun, a feat accomplished with colorful items and labor-saving gadgetry. Isn't this what gardening's all about anyway? Do you dig?

| | ·ACCENTS | ·GARDEN | | |
|---|---|---|---|---|

## 800-622-0089 • Ideaworks

**IdeaWorksOnline.com**

This peculiar little shop boasts a catalog of "ideas that make life a little easier." This boils down to some innovative cleaning supplies; stuff like bizarre vacuum cleaner attachments, gutter cleaners and flood alarms. The assortment of "whimsical driveway reflectors" and other such products might make you laugh, which can at least be a nice break from shopping. Otherwise, we figure this stuff must hold a certain amount of appeal for some people or they wouldn't market it... right?

| ·APPLIANCES | ·IMPROVEMENT | ·GARDEN | ·CLEANING |
|---|---|---|---|

## 805-773-2855 • Indoor Water Fountains

**IndoorWaterFountains.com**

These guys really don't mince words, so neither will we. They sell indoor water fountains. Your choices are between Wall Fountains, Floor Fountains and Tabletop Fountains, though there are multiple options in each of these categories. Some are made of glass, some are not, but each consists of a vertical design that lets water trickle its way down into the fountain's base. Trickle, trickle, trickle... or something like that. A word to the wise: never install one too far away from a working toilet.

| ·ACCENTS | | | |
|---|---|---|---|

## 510-420-0383 • ItalyDesign.com

**ItalyDesign.com**

One has to imagine that, in Italy, everyone's home features the most stylish of interior designs with the sleekest furniture imaginable. At least, that's the impression given by this web site devoted to Italian furniture. Its bar furniture and seating in particular would be the envy of any hipster in search of that perfect lounge, and all the other tables, curios and other items pretty much follow suit. A note to the impatient: keep clicking on the type of furniture you want to see—eventually you will get to the photos and product descriptions. After that, resistance is futile.

| ·LIGHTING | ·FURNITURE | | |
|---|---|---|---|

## 800-232-4070 • Kitchen Etc.

**KitchenEtc.com**

Never mind the "etcetera," the important thing to remember in regard to this site is the "kitchen." With cookware, gadgets, electrics, tons of aprons and kitchen storage, they have this room covered and then some. A lot of clicking is unavoidable, as they have whole subsections devoted to things like rolling pins, pasta machines and pressure cookers. But it shouldn't slow you down too much, because everything's visually laid out so that even an inept cook could find his or her way—not that we're implying anything.

| ·APPLIANCES | ·KITCHEN | ·TABLEWARE | ·REGISTRY |
|---|---|---|---|

## LampStore.com

LampStore.com • 888-874-2676

Been bumping your shins on furniture in the dimly lit corners of your home? Well, these guys would rather sell you a lamp than curse your darkness, and so have embraced the great advantage maintained by all specialty retailers: selection. There are only lamps for sale here, but in every traditional design you could imagine, as well as a few odd ones you couldn't. A simple, illustrative design makes it easy to browse—you can shop by room (for example, kids' rooms, rec rooms or studies) or style (anything from Victorian to casual to contemporary). The lack of a search feature might keep you from immediately finding the lampshade shaped like a stuffed shirt, but if your tastes are so specific, you're probably patient enough to find it on your own.

| | ·LIGHTING | | | |
|---|---|---|---|---|

## Laura-Ashley.com

Laura Ashley • 800-463-8075

Now, for those special souls who simply demand good taste in their home décor, here comes a Laura Ashley online store to satisfy your ardent needs. While the Laura Ashley name is most commonly associated with patrician women's clothing, more interesting is the brand's take on traditional furniture and home accents. Once you get past the somewhat annoying menu, the bedding, painted furniture and all kinds of bric-a-brac are easy to root through, and even at its worst is quite nice. But, then, this merchandise is meant for those occasions when "nice" just doesn't cut it.

| | ·LIGHTING ·FURNITURE | ·IMPROVEMENT | ·ACCENTS | ·BED & BATH |
|---|---|---|---|---|

## LightingCenter.com

LightingCenter.com • 888-815-4519

Discount lighting fixtures and ceiling fans are what you'll find here in droves, along with, for some reason, a quirky selection of untraditional weather vanes. Who can say why they do the things that they do? Ours is only to explain how, and that they do it. In this case, it's with a somewhat clumsy, shabby-looking site whose uninspiring design best serves to punctuate the low prices asked for this merchandise. But there's a great selection here, most easily viewed by checking out the Table of Contents page and cozying up to the Back button on your browser. It won't always be easy, but it may pay off in the end.

| | ·LIGHTING | | | |
|---|---|---|---|---|

## LilyPons.com

Lilypons Water Gardens • 800-999-5459

If you've ever looked across the broad landscape of your yard and thought that a small body of water was just what it needed, you're in luck, because this site will set you up. Choose between a selection of premade ponds (in natural or geometric shapes), or get a length of flexible liner to set your own dimensions. Once you've dug your pond and filled it with water, you'll want to add water plants, statuary or maybe even a birdbath. If you're quite daring, you'll opt for a fountain, a footbridge or a waterfall—these can all be ordered online quite simply. And for the finishing touch, populate your pond—live fish will arrive within 48 hours (if you can believe it), probably aching to swim.

| | ·LANDSCAPING | ·GARDEN | | |
|---|---|---|---|---|

**212-629-0300** • Linenplace.com

**LinenPlace.com**

According to these guys, the "mission" of this site is to "revolutionize the way people buy home furnishings." Somebody should maybe tell them how many home furnishing sites there are in our pages alone. Aside from a potentially unrivaled shower curtain selection, there's not a lot to see here, so you can skip any of their advanced search features. Just select Bed or Bath and you'll find a pleasant, decently priced assortment of high-quality towels, bedding and related accessories.

·BED & BATH

**212-375-0500** • Lost City Arts

**LostCityArts.com**

Modeled after a 1950s vision of futuristic and modern furniture design, the furniture for sale here offers a look that is simple and clean, just like the site itself. Loungey and hip, you can browse through your choice of new designs and vintage items that promise to decorate any living room or home office with an enviable chic. Chairs, tables and lamps make up the bulk of this ultra-cool catalog, while sofas, desks, clocks and some angular art pieces await your perusal. Expensive and glamorous, this stuff may not look especially comfortable, but if you're looking to impress, who cares?

·FURNITURE    ·LIGHTING

**877-385-2104** • Louie Lighting

**LouieLighting.com**

Thanks to a popular 19th-century invention that enabled us to create and trap light within an encapsulation of glass, we may in the present day (with the help of electricity) illuminate our homes from the ceilings, walls and floors using the most creative, decorative styles imaginable. Perhaps this site's creators aren't as important in this process as Thomas Edison, but they offer a quite good shop that was complexly assembled, yet proves easy to use. Sconces, chandeliers and other fixtures (even ceiling fans) abound, usually with an array of custom options, and plenty of lamps also demonstrate our collective yearning for a fashionable source of light.

·LIGHTING

**888-343-7285** • Marimekko Fabrics

**MarimekkoFabric.com**

Listen, we're not going to tell you what to do with these fabrics; make curtains, design your own dresses, we don't care. But the "bold designs and vivid colors" of this by-the-yard selection really comprise some of the coolest textiles you'll find anywhere. If you don't feel so inclined to just make stuff, you can still take advantage of these hip looks in the form of towels, and probably the swingingest shower curtains on the planet (warning, these may also be the most expensive shower curtains on the planet).

·IMPROVEMENT    ·ACCENTS    ·BED & BATH

# MarthaByMail.com
**Martha By Mail • 800-950-7130**

Straight from Martha Stewart, "America's most trusted guide to stylish living," comes this site devoted to the beautification of your home and garden. The former model and stockbroker has, of course, risen to prominence as an author, publisher and television host, creating a lifestyle out of home economics. Here, you'll find the sorts of crafts and projects Stewart is best known for, as well as a long list of decorations and accessories for the bedroom, living room, bathroom or kitchen. From hot water bottles to pressed glass, and things like a wreath of dried gourds, everything is easy to locate on this tastefully decorated site, though it might take a little digging before you get to an actual product; then more digging to make your garden grow.

| ·ACCENTS ·BED & BATH | ·FURNITURE ·ORGANIZATION | ·GARDEN ·REGISTRY | ·KITCHEN ·PERSONALIZATION |
|---|---|---|---|

# MaxwellSilverNY.com
**Maxwell-Silver New York • 212-799-1711**

What originally was assembled as an innovative bridal registry can now be appreciated by all, thanks to this site that combines the offerings of "an exclusive network of New York boutiques" into one convenient storefront. You can shop by boutique, if you know them by name (Jonathan Adler, Apartment 48 and Shi, for example), or you can browse by price range. Of course, as usual, the best way to find what you seek is by category. As for what you'll find, it can range from furniture and tableware to kitchen appliances and decorating accessories. You may even find one-of-a-kind items without trouble, if you're into that sort of thing. Otherwise, you may find yourself owning the same stuff as some New York High Society types. Try to live that one down.

| ·LIGHTING ·TABLEWARE | ·ACCENTS ·REGISTRY | ·KITCHEN | ·BED & BATH |
|---|---|---|---|

# MelinaMade.com
**Melina Made • 415-860-1363**

Ditch those squarish wallpaper patterns, man. Here you can find the sickest collection of retro 1950s designs, stuff like Tiki Forest, that give stripe and floral patterns a bad name. Or, get it in fabric form and make curtains or tablecloths. Either way, it's hip, just not exactly set up in an ideal way. View all the patterns first, under Fabrics and/or Wallpaper, then go to Market for shopping by the roll or by the yard. Oh yeah, you can't dress your house up this well without payin' the price; this ain't no cheapie.

| ·IMPROVEMENT | ·ACCENTS | | |
|---|---|---|---|

# Mellingers.com
**Mellinger's • 800-321-7444**

It doesn't look like it right away, but this is a superb site. Why? Because thousands of products—gardening tools, plants, flowers, trees, shrubs, grasses, fungi, mulches, greenhouses, arbors, trellises, (deep breath) lights, garden accents, irrigation kits, fertilizer and composters, just to name a few—can be found in just a few mouse-clicks. They even have some things that make gardening exciting, like plants that eat insects, insects that eat insects, topiary and bonsai trees (and kits). Whether or not you have a green thumb, you'll be able to find something here that makes you want to give botany a shot, even if just to wage war on the insects.

| ·LANDSCAPING | ·GARDEN | | |
|---|---|---|---|

**866-888-6677 • Moss**

**MossOnline.com**

Upon entering this whimsical site, you will be faced with a slowly rolling cityscape. Show no fear. Click on the door as it passes by. You will then be tested by a riddle questioning the nature of your moral principles. Agree to whatever you are asked. A helpful man shaped like a men's room sign will then greet you. Tell him to get lost. Only then will you be privy to the tidy selection of furnishings available for perusal and play on this site. You want to be privy. It's so fun, it almost doesn't matter that the products are slick and cool, or that you maybe never dreamt you would want them (like a series of miniature sculptures that commemorate various global disasters). Bizarre? Yes. Don't miss it.

| ·ACCENTS | ·KITCHEN | ·TABLEWARE | |
|---|---|---|---|

**616-361-1100 • Not-A-Beanbag.com**

**NotABeanBag.com**

You see, it may look like a beanbag, and it may act like a beanbag, but folks, if there's one thing this store wants you to know, it's that its primary product is not a beanbag. Welcome to the "Home of the World-Famous Polymorphic Poof Chair"—not as famous as its bean-filled cousin, it seems. The great and important distinction being made here is that these chairs, pillows and couches aren't filled with polystyrene pellets but with malleable foam that meets the contours of your body and yet manages to retain its original shape. The great benefit to your family's household? Flop-ability.

| ·FURNITURE | | | |
|---|---|---|---|

**800-634-5557 • OESCO Inc.**

**OESCOInc.com**

Much like its name, this is a very unseemly, clumsy, impossible to understand site. That being said, it's probably the only place on the web to track down some of this hardware for your lawn and garden. That being said, we couldn't begin to tell you all the stuff they have to offer, or how to piece together their abominable attempts at site navigation. They do list some categories as Hand Tools, Spraying Equipment and Orchard Supplies, but knowing that will barely help. Instead, look under Catalog and then Search Alphabetically and browse through a list long enough to haunt your grandchildren's children. Good luck, that being said.

| ·LANDSCAPING | ·GARDEN | | |
|---|---|---|---|

**800-600-9817 • Organize Everything**

**Organize-Everything.com**

This site is an obsessive-compulsive's dream come true. As you may have gleaned from the name, here you will find the means to put a little organization into your household. The site's pretty well organized, too, sectioning off different categories that offer storage containers for the kitchen or bathroom, drawers and closets, files for the office and some general chests and shelves that'll do anywhere. There's also plenty of stuff for your data collections—CDs, DVDs, and videotapes—and there's some pretty convenient travel packs with which you can take your new, organized self on the road. After you've bought everything you can manage to on other retail sites, come here for a place to put it.

| ·ACCENTS | ·ORGANIZATION | | |
|---|---|---|---|

# Palazzetti.com

As we embrace the new millennium, we must come to accept the blurring of lines between categories that are endemic to the times. Thus, without irony, we find furniture for sale here to be simultaneously modern and classic. How else can we define an unparalleled selection of classy sofa beds, or a big, cushy chair that is shaped like a giant baseball mitt? Some of these furniture designs find creative ways to buck the fine line between familiarity and newness, like Japanese washi paper lanterns that deviate from the traditional round shape, or area rugs patterned after popular artistic styles. While the site design doesn't live up to such standards, if you like what you see perhaps you too exist in the harmonious contradiction of timeless style.

| ·ACCENTS | ·FURNITURE | | |
|---|---|---|---|

# Pendleton-USA.com

If you're a fan of Native American-inspired products, rugs and blankets in particular, this site from Oregon has something for you. Simply look in the Blankets and Home section and browse through the furniture and accessories until you see something you like (it won't take long). You can also buy fabric by the yard, so if you see a woven pattern you particularly like you can turn it into a motif by reupholstering sofas, chairs, etc. The web site isn't very helpful in much of this, but the online ordering works. Now, if you can only escape the irony of that USA tag in the URL....

| ·FURNITURE | ·BED & BATH | | |
|---|---|---|---|

# Pfaltzgraff.com

Pfaltzgraff started back in early 19th century Pennsylvania when a group of German immigrants started manufacturing salt-glazed stoneware for dinner settings. In the nearly 200 years since, the company has expanded and grown in size, yet they still stick to doing what they do best—making dinnerware. Several great designs are available for perusal here, though if you want to buy online, you will be limited to the selection listed in the Collectors Corner. If you are looking for a new set of dishes, this place is definitely worth the 5 minutes it will take to check out their entire selection.

| ·TABLEWARE | ·REGISTRY | | |
|---|---|---|---|

# Pier1.com

"Filled with unique, quality merchandise from over 50 countries," Pier 1 Imports promises "casual home furnishings at a great value." Baby Boomers might particularly enjoy this store (if you don't already) as it originated as a place for flower children to find bean bags, love beads and incense, and has since paid very careful attention to change in accordance to the changing interests, styles and economic status of Boomers over the decades. The result is an ever-updating catalog of home furniture and décor, ranging from barstools and director's chairs to things like colored bottles in fanciful shapes. Somehow straddling the line between luxurious and practical, this stuff serves to satisfy those who find happiness in their possessions.

| ·ACCENTS ·TABLEWARE | ·FURNITURE ·ORGANIZATION | ·KITCHEN ·REGISTRY | ·BED & BATH |
|---|---|---|---|

## 888-743-7732 • Pierre Deux

### PierreDeux.com

As a style, French Country aims to promote *l'art de bien vivre*, the good life. Whether you describe it as "quaint," "charming" or "comfortable," this classic style almost always impresses, and will discourage houseguests from making a mess. In the Products menu, you may choose Product Type (furniture, decorative items, and the like) or select Decorate by Color, which helps narrow the selection down to your favorite hues. You can similarly shop for fabrics, if you're looking to rehaul your décor in damask, velvet, etc. Or, if table settings be what you seek, the Create a Table section offers interchangeable virtual table settings that let you mix and match crystal and stoneware until your settings are elegant enough to satisfy Le Cordon Bleu cooking.

| ·LIGHTING ·TABLEWARE | ·IMPROVEMENT | ·ACCENTS | ·FURNITURE |
|---|---|---|---|

## 800-494-7544 • Plow & Hearth

### PlowHearth.com

If you're one of those rare few who understands the differences between rustic, farmhouse, cottage and country Victorian furniture styles, then chances are good that you'll want to shop from this merchant devoted to "Country Living." If you only have a vague awareness that there are differences, don't be discouraged; there's enough information available on this hectic site to educate anyone on the nuances of traditional and rural designs. So, while you can browse by style here, it's easier to search departments like Fireplace & Hearth, Outdoor Living and Country Home, each neatly subdivided into categories. All kinds of furniture, furnishings and housewares are here; even a few peculiar items that might cause city folk to wonder....

| ·LIGHTING ·PERSONALIZATION | ·ACCENTS | ·FURNITURE | ·BED & BATH |
|---|---|---|---|

## 877-752-0889 • Ponds2Go

### Ponds2Go.com

This site has everything you need to build, install and maintain a pond on your property, from hardware and plant life to decorations. Sound difficult? Well, you should also be able to find some helpful hints and interesting ideas to make the process relatively easy and somewhat fun, once you get the hang of browsing the site. Still not inspired? Well, just imagine relaxing in a chaise lounge, drinking a beer and watching the sunset as you lie beside a body of water that you've named after yourself. Now imagine the jealous faces of your neighbors as they look over the fence, and then the fun of planning to build a higher fence. Oh yeah, building can be fun.

| ·LANDSCAPING | ·GARDEN | | |
|---|---|---|---|

## 888-764-7665 • Specialty Pool Products

### PoolProducts.com

Category headings like Above Ground, Inground, Ponds, Spa & Hot Tub and Sauna & Steam get the point across: this site is about turning your home into an oasis of soothing respite from the harsh, cruel, dry world. Well, not so fast, there, lazybones. Much of this selection is actually here to remind you that these household havens require cleaning and upkeep, and there are plenty of products here that pump, heat, sanitize, filter, blow and mainly just make everything function properly. Replacement parts and chemicals aside, you may order saunas, spas and some bodies of water here to take your mind off the confounding web design.

| ·POOL & SPA | ·HARDWARE | | |
|---|---|---|---|

## PoolWarehouse.com

**Pool Warehouse • 866-766-5932**

The most astounding thing about this site isn't that it can sell you a swimming pool online—we have, after all, seen a willingness of 'e-tailers' to sell anything and everything over the internet. No, the real surprise here is just how many options you have in purchasing a pool, not to mention things like diving boards, slides and spas. First of all, you have pool-building kits, perfect for the industrious do-it-yourself homeowner. Second, there are some easier-to-set-up aboveground pools. Finally, and this is great, you can have an entire fiberglass pool, available in dozens of different shapes and sizes, delivered to your home on a truck. Sure to make the neighbors jealous.

| ·POOL & SPA | ·HARDWARE | | |
|---|---|---|---|

## PotsAndPans.com

**PotsAndPans.com • 800-450-0156**

With this site, you can pretty much determine what they sell, so we'll just mention how well they do it. First off is the Shop By Shape page, which is great because you can just point and click without too much thinking to find the sort of pot or pan you want. Shop By Material takes you in a different direction where the toughest choice is whether stainless steel or nonstick aluminum sounds easier to clean. Finally, Help Me Shop gets all the important questions (like price, handle and nonstick options) out of the way straight off, leaving you with a worthy choice of cookware.

| ·KITCHEN | | | |
|---|---|---|---|

## PotteryBarn.com

**Pottery Barn • 888-779-5176**

Combining classic American styles with influences from the world over, the Pottery Barn's in-house designers have been creating home furniture and furnishings with enduring charm for more than half a century. Here, their exclusive line of products is available online for both enthusiasts and newcomers to the brand's sturdy simplicity and reasonable prices. Coming from a franchise that has expanded with the ferocity of Starbucks, you may worry that these items lack originality. Sure, but the more practical of these products, especially, will probably stand the test of time and fit seamlessly into the deliberate expression of your own style, however eclectic.

| ·LIGHTING ·TABLEWARE | ·ACCENTS ·REGISTRY | ·FURNITURE ·PERSONALIZATION | ·BED & BATH |
|---|---|---|---|

## RealTeak.com

**Midlothian • 800-806-1983**

So you like teak furniture, but you're tired of the same old "classic" designs that populate the back porches of all your teak-loving friends? Don't fret; this site by the Atlanta-based Midlothian Furniture Sellers doesn't just feature unique and beautiful teak designs, it also offers some of the best prices you'll find anywhere. Ordering can be a bit tricky, but there's not a huge selection so it shouldn't take too long. Look at Products & Specifications for illustrations of all their chairs, benches and tables (click on any drawing for an actual photo). Then, be sure to remember the names of the items you want before you follow the How To Order link.

| ·FURNITURE | | | |
|---|---|---|---|

## 800-269-2609 • Repair Clinic

### RepairClinic.com

If you've ever been face-to-face with a broken appliance and just thought to yourself, "will this fit in the garbage can?" you need to view this site. It turns out, whatever the problem with your microwave, dryer, dishwasher, refrigerator or whatever home appliance is on the fritz, it's probably just a matter of replacing one or two parts. It just so happens; this is the perfect place to find a replacement part. All you really need to know is the make and model of your little machine and … well, enough of an understanding of it to know what's broken. Fortunately, they offer some diagnostic advice, some repair directions and a handy Part Detective to help you through this. Then, you can sit face-to-face with your broken appliance and the part needed to heal it.

·HARDWARE ·APPLIANCES ·IMPROVEMENT

## 800-737-5223 • Replacements, Ltd.

### Replacements.com

In some cultures, appreciation for a good meal may be expressed by smashing the plates it was served on in a wine-fueled display of satiation. Too good a meal, and you may even see all your best china and flatware decimated by a feisty cadre of guests. Or, just invite some children over and something's bound to be smashed. Point is, you can only protect it so much, but your sets will undoubtedly be missing some pieces before too long. The genius of this site is that you may buy individual pieces from "over 175,000 patterns," keeping your tableware intact in spite of the occasional dinnertime violence.

·TABLEWARE

## 800-762-1005 • Restoration Hardware

### RestorationHardware.com

It sounds impossible, but here it is: a selection of merchandise that is at the same time unique and so familiar as to be ingrained into the cultural consciousness of anybody born into the 20th century. That's Restoration Hardware all over, with a myriad of classic, often retro but modern, designs that you just can't find anywhere else. Take, for example, a bathroom mirror attached to an accordion wall fixture that is inspired by 1920s vintage British bath fittings, or a telescopic ostrich feather duster that adds elevation to your housework. Some of these cleaning utensils don't just work; they actually look cool enough to just leave lying around the house.

·HARDWARE ·LIGHTING ·ACCENTS ·FURNITURE
·GARDEN ·CLEANING ·REGISTRY

## 877-724-0093 • RetroModern.com

### RetroModern.com

It can be presumed that the term "retro modern" here either refers to an attempt to emulate contemporary home styles of the past, or simply to take a look back at the styles themselves. In this case both are accurate, as both vintage and new furniture pieces harking back to the postwar era are on keen display by this site that wants to encourage a deeper understanding of and appreciation for 20th century design. Simply select your favorite designer from their list, and enjoy his/her masterworks. Don't know who those people are? Well, you can shop by more conventional methods, browsing through categories, price range and looking at pictures, lots of pictures. The vintage section alone will have you yearning for a higher credit card limit.

·LIGHTING ·ACCENTS ·FURNITURE ·KITCHEN
·BED & BATH ·TABLEWARE ·REGISTRY

## RueDeFrance.com

Rue De France • 800-777-0998

For those of us who can never get enough of France into our lives, this homey little site offers a modest selection of French-themed merchandise, ranging from furniture and window dressings to table linens and wall décor. There's really little to it; a few categories, the occasional monkey pillow. But you'll soon find that this site's charm lies in what it has got, not what it hasn't, so if it seems a little small, don't worry about it. Maybe the French think you're a little big.

| | | ·LIGHTING<br>·BED & BATH | ·ACCENTS<br>·TABLEWARE | ·FURNITURE | ·KITCHEN |
|---|---|---|---|---|---|

## Russell-Hobbs.com

Russell Hobbs • 888-462-2720

Does this scenario sound like you—after spending months of hard searching and thousands of dollars on beautiful and stylish furniture with which to decorate your home, it turns out that the inelegance of your kitchen appliances just brings down the whole house? Well, if so, then you'll be happy to know that Russell Hobbs is here to sell you fine and dandy kitchen equipment like teakettles, toasters and percolators that will not only satisfy, but also possibly improve the aesthetic standards of your living space. One can only hope that once your new kitchenware has arrived, you don't feel the need to start over with the rest of the place.

| | ·APPLIANCES | ·KITCHEN | | |
|---|---|---|---|---|

## SafeHomeProducts.com

SafeHomeProducts.com • 888-607-9902

While not an ideal site, this one falls under the category "good enough" for its selection of home safety devices; stuff like smoke (and other) detectors, air monitors and emergency response kits. It's really tough to gauge exactly what you may find here, and tough enough to find it. Many of these products are environmentally safe, or at least helpful in maintaining environmental safety. We would have to except from this distinction, however, their electric tortilla maker.

| | ·APPLIANCES | ·CLEANING | ·SECURITY | ·ECO-FRIENDLY |
|---|---|---|---|---|

## SafeSmith.com

Safesmith • 866-249-8700

Paranoid about a covetous world of gadabouts who lurk in the shadows just waiting for the opportunity to take your stuff? This site offers ways to keep your valuable personal effects your own. This of course involves safes: electronic safes, combination safes, key safes or combination electronic-key-combination safes. Some have actually been designed to hide behind paintings, others to sit on your closet floor. There are even hollowed-out books to hide stuff in your library and, because sometimes even a safe isn't safe enough, paper shredders to eliminate those incriminating files. Best of all is a custom safe wizard, which is oddly more fun than it sounds.

| ·SECURITY | ·PERSONALIZATION | | |
|---|---|---|---|

## 800-554-6367 • Schweitzer Linen

### SchweitzerLinen.com

For those of us who demand that only the finest of fineries should come into contact with our persons, this Manhattan-based luxury retailer offers a dazzling array of bedding, table linens, towels, rugs and robes that should satisfy even the most discerning tastes. However, finding these items may be a tad confounding. If you're here to browse, your best bet is to select your desired category, and then head straight for the Product List option at the bottom of the page. If you have something very specific in mind, however, you can check out products by Fabric & Features, or by product name, or choose the search option from the menu to narrow things down a bit.

| ·BED & BATH | ·TABLEWARE | ·PERSONALIZATION | |
|---|---|---|---|

## 800-863-7109 • SecurityAndMore.com

### SecurityAndMore.com

Ever wonder what it is that goes bump in the night? With some of the security and surveillance equipment available from this site you can detect and record the late night happenings on your premises without having to be around or awake for them. Alarm systems and safes will keep you and yours out of the grasp of those who would lurk in the shadows, giving you peace of mind, while the high-tech camera equipment will show you that it's probably just raccoons doing the lurking, and rooting through your garbage.

| ·SECURITY | | | | |
|---|---|---|---|---|

## 888-762-7333 • Seeds Of Change

### SeedsOfChange.com

The greatest thing about this site is that all of its products are ecologically sound, promoting the preservation of genetic diversity in all manner of plants. Primarily, seeds are for sale here. But these seeds are the result of natural, open-pollinated plants, grown without chemical or genetic manipulation. The result is a selection of healthy, natural seeds for plants, flowers and herbs that will seed themselves once mature (most nonorganic seeds sold commercially come from nonreproducing hybrids). There's a lot of environmentally conscience gear here, like watering timers and composting equipment. If you want your garden to be Earth-friendly, this is the first place you should look.

| ·GARDEN | ·ECO-FRIENDLY | | | |
|---|---|---|---|---|

## 800-940-1170 • Smith & Hawken

### SmithAndHawken.com

Dispelling the notion that a garden requires merely plants and dirt, the Smith & Hawken catalog and retail stores have long featured traditional tools, accessories and structural items inspired by the country quaintness of English gardens. Here, they've made it all available online, including an expansion into furniture and décor, all ready to order from this self-explanatory site. You might be surprised to know that you can order a greenhouse over the internet and have it delivered to your home, but it's par for the course here. Everything from trellises to fountains, birdbaths and a light-festooned gazebo make it into their inventory; anything to improve the beauty, grace and tranquility of the three-dimensional space a garden is meant to encompass.

| ·ACCENTS | ·FURNITURE | ·LANDSCAPING | ·GARDEN | |
|---|---|---|---|---|

## SmithAndNoble.com

Smith And Noble • 800-560-0027

All right. You've done everything to create the perfect interior design for your home—installed a new carpet, changed the light fixtures, redone the wallpaper and even replaced your switchplates. Everything lines up just right, and you have proven yourself a decorating genius ... except for those pesky windows. Well, these guys will customize your window treatments, from blinds and shades to cornices and even shutters. From start to finish, they'll help you measure all the necessary dimensions, and even give you a glossary of terms so you can figure out exactly what the heck is going on. By the time you're through, you'll know a heck of a lot about windows, and you can finally achieve absolute perfection from floor to ceiling. Now if you could only fix the view....

| | ·IMPROVEMENT | ·ACCENTS | | |
|---|---|---|---|---|

## SouthwestCountry.com

Southwest Country • 800-472-6341

Before you do anything else on this site you're going to want to stop the awful, awful music by clicking Stop on your browser. Actually, we recommend you locate the Stop button before you attempt to log on, or you might find yourself frantically clicking in all directions trying to make it end. After all, it's bad enough that this site is no fun to look at, and not particularly easy to use. Unfortunately, it's pretty much the best place to find Southwestern style home furnishings (think Cowboys). The selection is pretty cool, from time to time bordering on wacky. Funny how the actual store is located not in someplace like Arizona or New Mexico, but in Los Angeles's San Fernando Valley.

| | ·LIGHTING | ·ACCENTS | ·FURNITURE | |
|---|---|---|---|---|

## Spiegel.com

Spiegel • 800-527-1577

The Spiegel catalog features a thorough selection of merchandise for your home, all well categorized and subcategorized for your amusement. For example, in the Running the Home section, subcategories like Sewing or Garment Care will lead to such items as vacuums, irons, sewing machines and several other appliances invaluable to the smooth operation of your household. The Kid's Resource also stands out as a fine place to find bedroom furnishings, decorations and the like. Okay, so it's not so funny; it's a well-arranged store offering high quality at decent prices—odds are good you can't go wrong.

| | ·APPLIANCES ·FURNITURE | ·LIGHTING ·KITCHEN | ·IMPROVEMENT ·BED & BATH | ·ACCENTS ·ORGANIZATION |
|---|---|---|---|---|

## StacksAndStacks.com

Stacks And Stacks • 800-761-5222

Offering "homewares... for your storage and organizational needs," this site is full of crates, carts, boxes, cabinets, shelves, racks and every other conceivable home storage utility. True to form, the site's excellently organized in conjunction with its products with a healthy list of animated menus (our favorite kind) making it quite easy to delve into categories without actually having to look. Of course, this helps you realize that they have a lot more than just storage here, with some surprisingly quirky furnishings and useful cleaning supplies.

| | ·APPLIANCES ·BED & BATH | ·LIGHTING ·ORGANIZATION | ·FURNITURE ·CLEANING | ·KITCHEN |
|---|---|---|---|---|

## 866-328-5412 • Sur La Table

### SurLaTable.com

Boasting "over 13,500 items from more than 900 vendors worldwide," burgeoning national retailer Sur La Table (French for "on the table") aims to be "a reliable source for top-quality cookware and kitchen tools." Do they succeed? Boy howdy. Their Appliances selection, anything from blenders to rice cookers and ice cream makers, handily complements the skillets, pressure cookers and fondue pots available in their Cookware section. Then there's your choice of bakeware, knives, tabletop items, cleaning aids and just about any kind of tool/device that will make your attempts at culinary mastery easier, if not better tasting.

| ·APPLIANCES ·REGISTRY | ·ACCENTS | ·KITCHEN | ·TABLEWARE |
|---|---|---|---|

## 888-211-6603 • TableTools.com

### TableTools.com

Billing itself as "the place for unique, innovative products for your table, kitchen and bar," the scope of this site is not so broad that it ignores the basics. Actually, this proves its best use, as simple shopping and a simple selection allow you to enjoy great prices on stuff you'll actually use on a daily basis. Still, for the lover of odd items, there're always the Kitchen Gadgets and Bar Accessories sections for the procurement of egg tools, lemon zesters, salad spinners and martini shakers in funny shapes.

| ·APPLIANCES | ·KITCHEN | ·TABLEWARE | ·REGISTRY |
|---|---|---|---|

## 800-323-8000 • The Company Store

### TheCompanyStore.com

For the lonely online furniture shopper, here's a site that speaks to you, literally. Simply click on Play at the top left portion of the home page and a soothing voice offers you assistance to make shopping easy and convenient. Of course, this is almost necessary due to the jumbled disorganization that will have you confused from the get-go. You may just want to follow the Shop Online Enter link at the bottom-right part of the page. This will call up a menu of discernible wares, like bedding, pillows and bath-related items, any of which will likely impress. There's also a lot of great furniture, but you'll only find it if you follow the Home Accessories link. Keep your eyes open when visiting The Company Store; otherwise you might just miss something.

| ·BED & BATH | ·PERSONALIZATION | ·FURNITURE | |
|---|---|---|---|

## 877-615-6655 • Knoll

### TheKnollShop.com

If you've gotta have designer furniture—that is, if you want to be able to respond to the question, "Wow, what kind of chair is that?" with a name like Frank Gehry, Pepe Cortez or Vico Magistretti—this will be the site for you. While their selection of high-end furniture is smallish by comparison, it's undeniably cool stuff. Whether you view it in illustrated or photographic form (both of which are featured here) it won't take long for you to clue into just why these prices are so outrageous.

| ·FURNITURE | | | |
|---|---|---|---|

## TidewaterWorkshop.com

**Tidewater Workshop • 609-965-5127**

White Cedar was the type of wood this company used a hundred years ago to build boats for rum smugglers, and later to build faster boats for the Coast Guard so that they could catch the smugglers. As technology surpassed the boat builders, wooden vessels became more and more obsolete, and the skills that had once made their watercrafts so popular were turned towards furniture manufacture, specifically for the outdoors. Thus, here is an excellent selection of cedar furniture, including tables, chairs, porch swings and planters. The site's a little tricky, so you may want to scroll down to the menu on the left side of the screen. Otherwise, get your rum ready; this could take you awhile.

·FURNITURE ·PERSONALIZATION

## TooHome.com

**Too Home • 800-878-6021**

The homepage of this site tells you to "shop for your home from your home." Um, good idea. This place is all about home improvement—you know, that thing you do when you look around your pad and say to yourself, "Hmmm, what could be better...?" Indeed, they've got it all, from patio and garden decorations and supplies to lighting, plumbing, cabinet hardware and decorative trim. They even have stuff that can improve on stuff you may not even have yet, like saunas, steamers, spas and even, uh, bidets. In the future, perchance you can shop for your bidet from your toilet? Good idea? Or no?

·HARDWARE ·POOL & SPA ·LIGHTING ·IMPROVEMENT

## ToolsPlus.com

**Tools-Plus • 800-222-6133**

If you've got tools on the brain, this site's collection of Air Powered Tools, Hand Tools, Cordless Tools, Abrasives and Power Tools is sure to get you a little excited. If you don't, well you've got to buy your tools somewhere, and as this site's a self-proclaimed "discount tool store," the prices may excite you (though in truth, the discounts are often hard to spot). Some things are bit more important than savings though, and topping the selection here is something nobody ever finds exciting, but never regrets owning: safety gear.

·HARDWARE ·IMPROVEMENT

## TotemDesign.com

**Totem Design • 212-925-5506**

The people behind Totem Design believe that we can all enhance our personal existence with the objects we keep in our lives. As such, they have gathered here a wily collection of ultra-high-concept designs that range from coasters to sofas to spiky lamps, each of which (we imagine) has been tailored to make every moment of your day a little bit brighter. It seems to work. You're sure to find something you like here (in theory at least), and once you follow the Shop Totem link in the upper left corner of the screen, it's pretty easy to browse through any type of furniture you wish, in any order.

·LIGHTING ·ACCENTS ·FURNITURE ·BED & BATH

## 800-387-5122 • Umbra

**Umbra.com**

When you enter a room, you're apt to notice any number of things right away: large furniture, wall hangings, lighting fixtures. But what about the minutia of tiny details that fill out a room? Things like clocks, picture frames, knobs and trash cans tend to get second billing in any home, but this doesn't mean you need to take them for granted. At least, that's what the proprietors of this site would tell you. They offer a cool little selection of household accents on slick display, the kinds of finishing touches that can freshen up a modern décor by adding flashes of color and funk to otherwise dreary parts.

| •HARDWARE | •ACCENTS | •FURNITURE | •IMPROVEMENT |
|---|---|---|---|

## 888-365-0056 • Uncommon Goods

**UncommonGoods.com**

This is no site for squares. Lighting, bedding, dining ware and other such home furnishing products may be easily found using colorful, if standard, navigation. But make no mistake; these items are not by any means typical! You might find glassware with a Holstein cow decor, an umbrella-shaped lamp or a fish stapler. If you find browsing a drag, you can use their Serious Search to narrow it down by style, material, color and price range, along with any key words. This will be the best way to find a scattered offering of great accessories made from recycled materials, such as some hip bottle openers crafted out of old bicycle chains, or a colorful desk clock made from compact discs. There're plenty of less flashy items, but nothing short of funky.

| •LIGHTING | •ACCENTS | •BED & BATH | •TABLEWARE |
|---|---|---|---|

## 888-898-6422 • Unica Home

**UnicaHome.com**

The upshot of filling your home with decorative accessories and functional furnishings is that you have to look at these items every day of your life. In the interest of making it all more interesting, here's a fine selection of intriguing ultramodern designs that should keep things fresh whether you're entertaining or just sitting around enjoying all your stuff. You can shop by room, or browse between new and vintage products that range from floor mats to barware and some especially hip lamps. Various designers and companies contribute items to this eclectic selection crafted to convince you that even something as boring as a tape dispenser can look cool.

| •LIGHTING •TABLEWARE | •ACCENTS •REGISTRY | •FURNITURE | •KITCHEN |
|---|---|---|---|

## 212-614-8580 • UproarHome.com

**UproarHome.com**

For those of us who've seen everything, here's a site where "the choices are endless, really." Not literally, of course, but with an ever expanding and frequently changing selection, there is a good chance that you will find something new from time to time. Mostly, though, you'll find plush seating, elegant lighting and stately wood pieces. Then there's an array of gorgeous accessories, things like beaded baskets and faux mink throws, that can lend an air of luxuriance to any room. Most memorable, though, may be the site's entertaining product descriptions. Sure, it's ultimately just sales technique, but with words so effusive, it's hard to believe they don't mean it.

| •LIGHTING | •ACCENTS | •FURNITURE | |
|---|---|---|---|

## URBN.com

Urban Outfitters has made a name for itself in the past few years, with franchise stores secured as mainstays in busy shopping districts wherever young people may yearn for butterfly chairs, disco balls or colorful floor pillows. Just go to the Apartment section from the front page, and you'll easily find your way through any of their varied and vibrant wares, all suitable to modern lifestyles. As the name would suggest, all of their products are infused with a metropolitan vibe; this is hard to shake, especially when you're subjected to the pseudo-pop music piped into any one of their international store locations. To simulate this experience, they've thoughtfully opted to broadcast this music online as well. Fortunately, on the web site you can turn it off.

| | | ·LIGHTING ·BED & BATH | ·ACCENTS ·TABLEWARE | ·FURNITURE | ·KITCHEN |
|---|---|---|---|---|---|

## VintageWoodWorks.com

If you know what corbels are, or spandrels, brackets, bead boards, gable decorations, headers or running trims, find them in Fine Design and Supply here. If you don't know, these are items used to give a house that old-time woody, fancy feeling. It's hard to describe, so you'll just have to check out the site to see. If it makes it any easier, though, there are also some incredible screen doors here, along with some well-crafted shingles, porch posts, balusters, signs and rails aplenty. While outfitting your home with everything you can find here might just be overdoing it, this stuff can give it a look rarely seen since Emily Dickinson's day.

| | | ·IMPROVEMENT | ·ACCENTS | | |
|---|---|---|---|---|---|

## Wedgwood.com

Founder Josiah Wedgwood, an 18th-century English potter who curried the favor of both British aristocracy and American revolutionaries, as well as some of the renowned progressive, scientific thinkers of his time, combined these variable interests into his products. The creations thus sparked recognition of beauty and refinement, at the same time striving for that heady realm of technical advancement, a quality still inherent in Wedgwood products. From our modern perspective, however, this collection of flatware, vases and serving accessories simply seems classic, testimony to the standards old Josiah's work set.

| | ·TABLEWARE | | | |
|---|---|---|---|---|

## WhiteFlowerFarm.com

It was the intent of White Flower Farm founder Amos Pettingill that gardening should become an intellectual and cultural pursuit, meant to evolve in ways similar to art and romance; but don't be so quick to agree. See, Pettingill is simply an alias carried over from the farm's original husband-and-wife owners, journalists-turned-garden-enthusiasts who fled New York City in the 1940s seeking respite from the hustle 'n' bustle, only to find that the fecund glory of nature proved a far greater distraction to their writing endeavors. The payoff comes in the form of a rich supply of gardening supplies: tools, seeds, bulbs and décor, all of which we too can use to pretend that this botanical distraction from our work is not only justified, but culturally rewarding.

| | ·LANDSCAPING | ·GARDEN | | |
|---|---|---|---|---|

## 800-848-0078 • Wild Seed Farms
### WildSeedFarms.com

It may seem a tad ironic selling wildflower seeds to be grown in private gardens. Nevertheless, this flower farm located deep in Texas does exactly that, selling dozens of different wildflowers and herbs known to grow naturally in different regions across the US. In fact, while you can quite easily browse through pictures of individual flowers, you may also opt for seed mixes of flowers native to the same region. Keep an eye out for some helpful planting and growing products listed among the brightly colored flowers and herbs—you never know what may happen if you let them grow on their own.

**·GARDEN**

---

## 877-812-6235 • Williams-Sonoma
### Williams-Sonoma.com

If you've attended a wedding for dear friends who're excited about tossing out all their old housewares and furnishings in favor of the superabundance of elegant items on the Williams-Sonoma gift registry, then you probably don't need to know any more about the fine merchandise listed here. On the other hand, it's worth pointing out that common kitchen electrics get a tasteful workout if they're to live up to this prestigious catalog's standards—stuff like blenders that normally act in antithesis to style show up with smooth curves and beautiful craftsmanship. This is pretty much true of all the cookware, home accents and small furniture, any of which will be easy to locate on the site's standard navigational design, especially if you're shopping for two.

**·APPLIANCES** | **·KITCHEN** | **·TABLEWARE** | **·REGISTRY**

---

## 888-427-3362 • WindowBox.com
### WindowBox.com

Here's a site for those of us who lack one of the more important components of a home garden: land to grow it on. High-rise dwellers can find flowery relief in this site that caters to fans of potted plants and window gardens, starting with its selection of handcrafted window boxes, hanging baskets and planters. There're also many small garden tools, as well as the requisite herb, plant and flower seeds. If you're new to the indoor planting game, the site's Floracle feature will make recommendations based on your gardening diligence and local environment. If you still don't feel ready for the real thing, practice on a virtual plant in the Plant Game, "the slowest game on the internet."

**·GARDEN**

---

## 800-292-5060 • Yowler Shepps Stencils
### YowlerSheppsStencils.com

This mother-and-daughter outfit out of Pennsylvania wants you to know that "more detailed stencils" do not mean "more difficult stencils." They sell a lot of sophisticated, multicolored stencil designs, some inspired by nature, some by architecture and some just made to look fun. These stencils can be used to border ceilings and floors, or as elements in full wall murals. Basically, this is a creative way to decorate a room (especially with the kids) without the added hassle and expense of wallpaper.

**·IMPROVEMENT** | **·ACCENTS**

# zGlow.com

Boasting "affordable multi-purpose furniture, alternative storage solutions, creative lighting products and stylish house wares," it could be said that this product selection "serves the practical needs of urban living." But, oh yeah, what do we think? Well, it's pretty cool, unique stuff (especially in the Lighting and House sections) and really easy to shop for. It gives you detailed images, interesting product descriptions and reasonable prices. Hey— this one may be as good as it thinks it is!

| ·LIGHTING ·TABLEWARE | ·ACCENTS | ·FURNITURE | ·KITCHEN |

# Lifestyles & Megastores

We've done our best to relegate the myriad sites we've researched into conveniently browsed sections, but some sites simply defy categorization. In a few instances we have found shops that offer two or three different specializations (say, clothes, accessories and furnishings) and have placed them all in appropriate sections so you won't miss them. But this gets tiring. See, many sites offer a range of products wide enough to suit more than three sections. Rather than force our lazy writers to review them again and again, we created this category.

Shopping at these far-reaching shops has its benefits, the greatest of which have to do with shipping. Say you want to order several different types of items: shoes, books and garden tools, for instance. If you purchase each from a different web merchant, you will pay shipping charges for each separate order. But if you find all of these products in a single location, all would be combined into one order, which should save you a few bucks on each item. Also, gift certificates never made so much sense.

You'll surely recognize some of the department stores listed here, but we also found a bevy of lifestyle-oriented shops that feature selections devoted to areas like cowboy/western themes, Asian cultures, modern designs and luxury items. Another set of shops provide wholesale or outlet prices on all manner of products, giving you direct access to everything under the sun, and cheap. While many of the stores in this section don't offer the extensive variety or quality of selections possessed by niche retailers, for most nonpersonalized items, they will do to satisfy your consumer needs and then some.

## >> SECTION ICON LEGEND

Use the following guide to understand the rectangular icons that appear throughout this section.

### DEPARTMENT STORES

Many of these are stores you're used to seeing attached to your local mall. They usually center on home and personal fashion products, but many deal in merchandise from across the spectrum.

### INTERNATIONAL MARKETS

Some of these sites offer a breadth of merchandise related only by national or regional origin. In other words: products of all kinds from everywhere.

### LIFESTYLE SHOPS

Whether you're a cowboy or simply a fashionista, we found a range of stores that cater to many walks of life, selling enough variety of products as to defy categorization.

# >> LIST OF KEY WORDS

The following words represent the types of items typically found on the sites listed in this section.

## ACCESSORIES

These sites offer everything from hats to shoes, alongside some jewelry, watches and eyewear with handbags and wallets to stow it all away.

## APPAREL

Shirts or blouses, slacks or trousers, underwear or lingerie, and blue jeans; whatever you call them, a selection of clothes may be found on these sites.

## ART/COLLECTIBLES

The original masterworks of the century, posters for your dorm room or collections of kitsch, these stores include decorations and/or decorative investments.

## ELECTRONICS

Computer hardware, software, and/or electronics for your home or pocket, plus the whimsical, nonelectric devices that can accomplish stuff bare hands just never could.

## ENTERTAINMENT

This indicates a presence of music, movies and/or books; or possibly puzzles and games, as well as event tickets.

## EPICUREAN

Refers to grocery items, gourmet foods, vintage wines and fine cigars, among other ingestible delights.

## GIFTS

Anything from personalized letterheads, invitations and greeting cards to flowers, baskets and confections.

## HEALTH & BEAUTY

The pills, dressings and ointments it takes to keep your body healthy, as well as all the cosmetics, cleansers and fragrances you favor to keep you looking and feeling beautiful.

## HOME & GARDEN

From home improvement to gardening, this may include furniture, household tools or a bounty of landscaping gear.

## MINORS

From infants on through teens, these sites cater to children, from clothes and toys to furniture and educational products.

## PETS

May not cover all the basics, like food and hygiene, but there'll be something worthwhile for a variety of animals.

## SPORTS

Includes home gyms, athletic equipment or outdoor gear, though sport-specific stores are often a better way to go.

## TRAVEL

Booking a vacation may not be what these sites have in mind (there are exceptions), but luggage is pretty sure to be found.

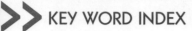

# >> KEY WORD INDEX

Use the following lists to locate online retailers that sell the type of products you seek.

## ACCESSORIES

Ashford.com
AsSeenOnScreen.com
BlueFly.com
Boscovs.com
BrandsMall.com
CatalogCity.com
Coat.com
CoolestShop.com
CorralWest.com
Costco.com
DreamRetail.com
eBay.com
Efendos.com
eLuxury.com
FireBox.com
GlobalMart.com
GoodCatalog.com
GorsuchLtd.com
Half.com
HSN.com
iQVC.com
Language-NYC.com
ModHaus.com
Namaste.com
NeimanMarcus.com
Nordstrom.com
Overstock.com
RentonWW.com
SaksFifthAvenue.com
Sears.com
Spiegel.com
SundanceCatalog.com
Swell.com
Tangs.com
Target.com
ThinkWorld.net
UpNorthGeneralStore.com
UrbanStyle.com
VermontCountryStore.com
Wal-Mart.com
Woolrich.com

## APPAREL

Amazon.com
AsSeenOnScreen.com
BlueFly.com
Boscovs.com
CatalogCity.com
Coat.com
CoolestShop.com
CorralWest.com
EddieBauer.com
eLuxury.com
FireBox.com
GorsuchLtd.com
HSN.com
iQVC.com
LandsEnd.com
Language-NYC.com
LLBean.com
ModHaus.com
Namaste.com
NeimanMarcus.com
Nordstrom.com
Orvis.com
Overstock.com
RentonWW.com
SaksFifthAvenue.com
Sears.com
Spiegel.com
SundanceCatalog.com
Swell.com
Tangs.com
Target.com
ThinkWorld.net
UpNorthGeneralStore.com
UrbanStyle.com
VermontCountryStore.com
Woolrich.com

## ART/COLLECTIBLES

BrandsMall.com
CoolestShop.com
Disney.com
eBay.com

Efendos.com
GoodCatalog.com
Half.com
HSN.com
iQVC.com
ModHaus.com
Namaste.com
NeimanMarcus.com
SamsClub.com
Send.com
ThinkWorld.net
UpNorthGeneralStore.com
UrbanStyle.com

## ELECTRONICS

Amazon.com
Ashford.com
AsSeenOnScreen.com
Boscovs.com
BrandsMall.com
Costco.com
Damianco.com
DreamRetail.com
DynaDirect.com
eBay.com
Efendos.com
eFunctional.com
FireBox.com
GlobalMart.com
GoodCatalog.com
Half.com
HSN.com
iQVC.com
ModHaus.com
NetMarket.com
NewYorkFirst.com
Overstock.com
SafetyCentral.com
SamsClub.com
Sears.com
Spiegel.com
Tangs.com
Target.com
Wal-Mart.com

## ENTERTAINMENT

Amazon.com
Costco.com
Disney.com
eBay.com
FireBox.com
Half.com
iQVC.com
Namaste.com
NetMarket.com
Overstock.com
SamsClub.com
Wal-Mart.com

## EPICUREAN

Damianco.com
eLuxury.com
Namaste.com
NewYorkFirst.com
Send.com
ThinkWorld.net
VermontCountryStore.com

## GIFTS

Amazon.com
Ashford.com
AsSeenOnScreen.com
BlueFly.com
Boscovs.com
BrandsMall.com
CatalogCity.com
CorralWest.com
Costco.com
Disney.com
EddieBauer.com
Efendos.com
eLuxury.com
FireBox.com
GlobalMart.com
HSN.com
iQVC.com

LandsEnd.com
Language-NYC.com
ModHaus.com
Namaste.com
NeimanMarcus.com
NewYorkFirst.com
Nordstrom.com
RentonWW.com
SaksFifthAvenue.com
SamsClub.com
Sears.com
Send.com
Spiegel.com
SundanceCatalog.com
UpNorthGeneralStore.com
UrbanStyle.com
VermontCountryStore.com
Wal-Mart.com
YouCanSave.com

## HEALTH & BEAUTY

Amazon.com
Ashford.com
AsSeenOnScreen.com
Boscovs.com
BrandsMall.com
CatalogCity.com
Coat.com
Costco.com
Damianco.com
DreamRetail.com
DynaDirect.com
Efendos.com
eFunctional.com
eLuxury.com
Gaiam.com
HSN.com
iQVC.com
KokoGM.com
Language-NYC.com
Namaste.com
NeimanMarcus.com
NetMarket.com
NewYorkFirst.com
Nordstrom.com
SafetyCentral.com
SaksFifthAvenue.com
Tangs.com
VermontCountryStore.com
YouCanSave.com

## HOME & GARDEN

Amazon.com
Ashford.com
BlueFly.com
Boscovs.com
BrandsMall.com
CatalogCity.com
Coat.com
CoolestShop.com
Costco.com
Damianco.com
Disney.com
DreamRetail.com
DynaDirect.com
eBay.com
EddieBauer.com
Efendos.com
eFunctional.com
FireBox.com
Gaiam.com
GlobalMart.com
GoodCatalog.com
GorsuchLtd.com
Half.com
iQVC.com
KokoGM.com
LandsEnd.com
Language-NYC.com
LLBean.com
ModHaus.com
NeimanMarcus.com
NetMarket.com
NewYorkFirst.com
Nordstrom.com
Orvis.com
Overstock.com
SafetyCentral.com
SaksFifthAvenue.com
SamsClub.com
Sears.com
Send.com
Spiegel.com
SundanceCatalog.com
Swell.com
Tangs.com
Target.com
ThinkWorld.net
UrbanStyle.com
VermontCountryStore.com
Wal-Mart.com
Woolrich.com
YouCanSave.com

## MINORS

Amazon.com
BlueFly.com
Boscovs.com
CatalogCity.com
Coat.com
CorralWest.com
Damianco.com
Disney.com
DynaDirect.com
eBay.com
Efendos.com
GlobalMart.com
GoodCatalog.com
GorsuchLtd.com
Half.com
KokoGM.com
LandsEnd.com
LLBean.com
Nordstrom.com
RentonWW.com
Sears.com
Spiegel.com
Target.com
UrbanStyle.com
VermontCountryStore.com
Wal-Mart.com
Woolrich.com
YouCanSave.com

## PETS

CatalogCity.com
DynaDirect.com
Gaiam.com
GoodCatalog.com
KokoGM.com
NewYorkFirst.com
Orvis.com
SamsClub.com
Send.com
Target.com
UpNorthGeneralStore.com
UrbanStyle.com
Woolrich.com

## SPORTS

BrandsMall.com
CoolestShop.com
Costco.com
DreamRetail.com
DynaDirect.com
eBay.com
eFunctional.com
FireBox.com
Gaiam.com
GlobalMart.com
GoodCatalog.com
Half.com
HSN.com
LLBean.com
NetMarket.com
Orvis.com
Overstock.com
SafetyCentral.com
SamsClub.com
Sears.com
Send.com
Swell.com
Target.com
UpNorthGeneralStore.com
Wal-Mart.com
Woolrich.com
YouCanSave.com

## TRAVEL

Ashford.com
BrandsMall.com
CatalogCity.com
Coat.com
Costco.com
Disney.com
DynaDirect.com
eBay.com
EddieBauer.com
Efendos.com
eFunctional.com
FireBox.com
Gaiam.com
GoodCatalog.com
LandsEnd.com
LLBean.com
Orvis.com
Overstock.com
SafetyCentral.com
SamsClub.com
UpNorthGeneralStore.com
Wal-Mart.com

# Amazon.com

Amazon.com • 800-201-7575

The first name in internet retail has come a long way from its origins as strictly a bookseller. Its expansion started, logically, with music and videos, but has gone on to include electronics, home and garden stuff, baby gear, toys and even cars (these last through partnerships with industry leaders). As it happens, these guys literally own the patent on "1-Click" shopping and personal pages offer you suggestions based on previous purchases. Of course, if you start taking recommendations from a computer you'll likely end up with multiple copies of *Tron*.

| ·MINORS ·ENTERTAINMENT | ·APPAREL ·HEALTH & BEAUTY | ·GIFTS ·HOME & GARDEN | ·ELECTRONICS |
|---|---|---|---|

# Ashford.com

Ashford • 888-922-9039

This site claims to offer "quality products from over 300 world class brands," which makes them seem somewhat pandering, or at least pompous. The funny thing, though, is that they're not. Actually, they offer everything they promise, and more. You can find accessories, apparel and home décor just for starters, and it's all great, high-end stuff. Better yet, the site organization is terrific, with several browsing options and thoroughly categorized universal menus (keep an eye on the red strip across the top for subheadings). Best of all, they offer free shipping on purchases exceeding $100—which, with such a distinguished catalog, is almost a certainty.

| ·ACCESSORIES ·HEALTH & BEAUTY | ·GIFTS ·HOME & GARDEN | ·TRAVEL | ·ELECTRONICS |
|---|---|---|---|

# AsSeenOnScreen.com

asSeenonScreen • No Service Number

Whether spotted in TV or film, or just on your favorite celebrity during a public appearance, this site aims to offer items worn by world-famous people and characters alike. You can shop by celebrity, TV show, film or product type (mostly sunglasses and other accessories), or you can sort through a list of popular designers to find out who wears their wares where. We found stuff like the "Bad Motherf****r" wallet from *Pulp Fiction*, uniforms from *Star Trek* (both original and *Next Generation*) and a rhinestone cowboy hat made popular by Madonna. But, as with our cultural tastes, the selection changes often, so get it while you can.

| ·ACCESSORIES ·ELECTRONICS | ·HEALTH & BEAUTY | ·APPAREL | ·GIFTS |
|---|---|---|---|

# BlueFly.com

Bluefly.com • 877-258-3359

Whatever Blue Fly means is not important. What's important is that this site is an online outlet store, and that means that whatever you see here will be cheaper than it should be. Why? Who cares? Whether you're shopping for T-shirts, table linens, baby gifts, handbags or jewelry, you can find it here. And not just knock-off, fake-label items either—whether it's Adidas, Tommy Hilfiger or Armani, you can find it. Especially with the excellent organization that lets you browse by designer or category, then narrow down the results on the basis of price, color or size.

| ·ACCESSORIES ·HOME & GARDEN | ·MINORS | ·APPAREL | ·GIFTS |
|---|---|---|---|

## 800-284-8155 • Boscov's
## Boscovs.com

This primarily Pennsylvania department store may not be as well known as Sears, but it could easily be mistaken for the behemoth mall retailer. Covering all ranges of men's, women's and children's apparel, they also boast full coverage of cosmetics, accessories, electronics and home furnishings, including major appliances. They even offer to book some vacation packages, cruises in particular, though it's probably better to settle for the luggage selection. As with most department stores, this collection veers away from any extreme, so style is never flashy or chic, but prices will most likely bring you back.

| ·ACCESSORIES ·GIFTS | ·ELECTRONICS ·HOME & GARDEN | ·APPAREL ·HEALTH & BEAUTY | ·MINORS |
|---|---|---|---|

## 877-568-3272 • Brandsmall.com
## BrandsMall.com

Proclaiming, "Brand Names for Less!" and, "Save up to 60% off retail prices every day!" it's hard to tell just how serious these guys are about their savings. Fortunately, their navigation is a no-brainer–almost so easy it hurts–so the site at the very least turns out to be a good, quick one to use when comparison shopping on commonly found brand-name items. At it's best, you'll find one of its many product subcategories to have a thorough selection at prices you like, unhindered by anything like creativity.

| ·ACCESSORIES ·SPORTS | ·GIFTS ·ELECTRONICS | ·TRAVEL ·HEALTH & BEAUTY | ·ART/COLLECTIBLES ·HOME & GARDEN |
|---|---|---|---|

## No Service Number • CatalogCity.com
## CatalogCity.com

Promising "easy access to the world's best products," Catalog City delivers, offering a section for just about every category you'll find in **thepurplebook**, each filled with hundreds, if not thousands of items. As it turns out, they even managed to come up with a few subsections we'd never have thought of, like Wigs & Turbans, Incontinence Supplies and Make Believe Toys, which makes it remarkably easy to avoid products you don't want to see. On the other hand, if you happen to be looking for such things as Decorative Eggs, you can find a whole lot of them in no time.

| ·ACCESSORIES ·TRAVEL | ·MINORS ·HEALTH & BEAUTY | ·APPAREL ·HOME & GARDEN | ·GIFTS ·PETS |
|---|---|---|---|

## No Service Number • Burlington Coat Factory
## Coat.com

All right, it's pretty easy, given the domain here, to figure out what you'll find, especially as this is the site for the Burlington Coat Factory. The thing is, while coats are indeed in abundance, there's more to this site than just simple outerwear. For one thing, they have plenty of clothes for men, women and children, as well as gloves, shoes and some luggage. None of this may seem too far removed from coats, but there's more. Specifically some home décor and fragrances for men and women, priced as well as all of the other merchandise. Coats indeed.

| ·ACCESSORIES ·HEALTH & BEAUTY | ·TRAVEL ·HOME & GARDEN | ·APPAREL | ·MINORS |
|---|---|---|---|

# CoolestShop.com

Coolest Shop • 541-431-0494

These guys have a bold name, and consequently we were ready to tear them down, fault by uncool fault. Um, as it turns out, we're not able to. They kind of won us over with a persistently hip selection of apparel, wall art, home décor and especially shoes. Even their Sports section is cooler than most, including only stuff like skateboards, off-road toys and other, weird, often electric vehicles. It will of course be difficult to refrain from checking the Gadgets section as well, as some items are just plain cool to begin with.

| ·ACCESSORIES ·HOME & GARDEN | ·SPORTS | ·APPAREL | ·ART/COLLECTIBLES |
|---|---|---|---|

# CorralWest.com

Corral West • 800-688-9888

These guys offer both Ranch Wear and Western Wear, and if you know the difference, you will be stoked. Whether you are an aspiring country singer, a disco cowboy or legitimately plan to ride the range, the hats, boots, belt buckles and bolos you might expect fill these pages, with plenty of fringe and lots of suede. You may feel a little shy about appearing in public dressed in full cowboy/cowgirl regalia; if so, that's what children are for. Just check the Kid's section for cowpokification.

| ·ACCESSORIES | ·APPAREL | ·MINORS | ·GIFTS |
|---|---|---|---|

# Costco.com

Costco • 800-774-2678

If you're already a member of Costco, you'll pretty much know what to expect from this online store. Those of you not so well acquainted should know a couple of things before you start shopping. See, in order to take advantage of their wholesale prices, you'll need to purchase membership, usually for an annual fee. Otherwise, when you purchase from the site, you'll be assessed an additional surcharge. As a result, while there is a limited range of large and/or electronic items, membership really makes sense if you want to shop here repeatedly for grocery and day-to-day items.

| ·ACCESSORIES ·ELECTRONICS | ·GIFTS ·ENTERTAINMENT | ·TRAVEL ·HEALTH & BEAUTY | ·SPORTS ·HOME & GARDEN |
|---|---|---|---|

# Damianco.com

Damianco.com • 866-707-0220

Based largely on a "strict return policy," meant to "control the amount of fraud that is causing you high process," these guys will be the first to tell you that this web site is "only for serious buyers." While such words may not instill in you much confidence, here's a good place to spot a variety of technological items ranging across several categories, things like appliances, electronics, water filters, telescopes and aboveground swimming pools. It's not an easy bunch to figure out, so take your time with this one.

| ·MINORS ·HOME & GARDEN | ·EPICUREAN | ·ELECTRONICS | ·HEALTH & BEAUTY |
|---|---|---|---|

## No Service Number • Disney

**Disney.com**

What can we say about Disney that hasn't been said before, or won't infuriate their lawyers? Basically, you know their cartoon characters, and are probably familiar with the company's penchant for pumping out character-themed merchandise (from painted T-shirts to toys, toys, toys). Most likely, your family knows exactly what it wants, and it's probably a lot. Well, good news! You should be able to find any of it here by following the Shopping link. It's pretty easy as it goes... almost Mickey Mouse you could say (can we say that?).

| ·MINORS ·ENTERTAINMENT | ·GIFTS ·HOME & GARDEN | ·TRAVEL | ·ART/COLLECTIBLES |
|---|---|---|---|

## 250-382-1538 • DreamRetail

**DreamRetail.com**

Begging the question, "can there be too much information on one page?" a lot of things can get confusing on this site, but one thing is quite clear—if you see a product listed, you will know for sure it's in stock. This handy feature will let you avoid placing an order only to wait for weeks and weeks for your product while the web company orders it, has it delivered, processes it and (finally) sends it out to you. What you may find here is a bunch of home, personal and electronics products, ranging from toys to watches.

| ·ACCESSORIES ·HOME & GARDEN | ·SPORTS | ·ELECTRONICS | ·HEALTH & BEAUTY |
|---|---|---|---|

## 877-438-3962 • DynaDirect.com

**DynaDirect.com**

These guys sell from a wide range of categories; at least, if computers, electronics, sports, travel and housewares constitutes a wide range. The site is well designed, well enough anyway to browse easily through a great selection that actually isn't all that awe inspiring. But the prices are great, sometimes, so you can occasionally get some decent deals. Really, it seems the best reason to shop here may be that they ship from warehouses scattered across the US, so on most items the shipping costs should be somewhat reduced. Well, by a little bit.

| ·MINORS ·HOME & GARDEN | ·SPORTS ·PETS | ·ELECTRONICS ·TRAVEL | ·HEALTH & BEAUTY |
|---|---|---|---|

## No Service Number • eBay

**eBay.com**

Yes, this is the big one. Many general auction sites have risen and fallen in the past few years, but eBay has absolutely maintained its dominance. It may seem counter to the American capitalist spirit, but really it's better this way, with one central location where anyone can find anything—literally. In fact, each day there are uncounted millions of products offered for sale across every imaginable category (a few human organs have even been known to pop up from time to time). Sure, the fear is that you'll log on only to find a bunch of crap that somebody else didn't like in the first place. But this site was built around the premise that one person's trash is another's treasure.

| ·ACCESSORIES ·SPORTS | ·MINORS ·ELECTRONICS | ·TRAVEL ·ENTERTAINMENT | ·ART/COLLECTIBLES ·HOME & GARDEN |
|---|---|---|---|

## EddieBauer.com

Eddie Bauer • 800-625-7935

A day free of work is a wonderful thing, by definition, but it can sometimes give us the feeling that we're just not making the most of it. At least, it feels that way if you compare it to the endless frolicking of those happy weekenders in an Eddie Bauer catalog. Will wearing these durable clothes make your days off better? Will the comfortable linens improve your night's sleep? Dubious, but shopping here beats ordering over the phone any day. Besides, if you're not satisfied when your order arrives, you can easily return them to any store located near you. Why not just go to the store to begin with? Because that's no way to spend a weekend.

| ·HOME & GARDEN | ·APPAREL | ·GIFTS | ·TRAVEL |
|---|---|---|---|

## Efendos.com

Efendos • 877-644-0784

What does efendos mean? We have no idea. What it stands for, though, is a different matter. Following the motto, "If we can't do it better, we won't do it!" they promise to cut prices by sending orders straight to the manufacturers or distributors of products, rather than paying to maintain a warehouse and shipping facility of their own. While this may slow down the arrival of your orders, the shipping is free, so you can't complain too much. As for the what of it all, you'll find all kinds of stuff in categories that don't give their contents justice, including mopeds, rotisserie grills, patio umbrellas and handcrafted African art.

| ·ACCESSORIES ·ART/COLLECTIBLES | ·MINORS ·ELECTRONICS | ·GIFTS ·HEALTH & BEAUTY | ·TRAVEL ·HOME & GARDEN |
|---|---|---|---|

## eFunctional.com

eFunctional.com • 435-752-1992

For fairly good prices on a fairly good selection of products, this site offers a generally predictable list of brand names and products, things like portable electronics, small household appliances and camping gear. Then, all of a sudden you come across something like a radar detector, towel warmer or an electronic fishfinder and you don't quite know what to make of it. Then you notice an entire DJ Pro Shop section and are forced to wonder, "what the heck are these guys trying to do?" Whatever it is, they do it all right.

| ·TRAVEL ·HOME & GARDEN | ·SPORTS | ·ELECTRONICS | ·HEALTH & BEAUTY |
|---|---|---|---|

## eLuxury.com

eLuxury • 877-890-7171

You would probably define a luxury item as something that induces great pleasure but is not generally essential in and of itself. Well, you won't find much of that here—you will positively need to own probably half of the top-notch designer items you'll come across, whether it's killer lingerie, ultrastylish clothes, beauty supplies, home décor or gourmet groceries. The site is as slick as its wares, with a gratifying Shopping by Price Range browsing option, as well as a dizzying 3-D Shopping feature that really isn't necessary, making it really the only true luxury item here to be found.

| ·ACCESSORIES ·HEALTH & BEAUTY | ·EPICUREAN | ·APPAREL | ·GIFTS |
|---|---|---|---|

**011-44-208-678-6112 • Firebox.com**                **FireBox.com**

We're all probably more than familiar with the sort of "lad mags" that populate entire corners of news stands; magazines like *Maxim, Gear* and *FHM* flout models on their covers and fill their pages with a mix of electronics, home furnishings and other suave gear for the bachelor in embrace of the high life. This site takes this lifestyle and makes it available online, with clothes, games, gadgets and furniture the (not necessarily) discerning young man can use to keep up with the times and (probably not so much) impress the ladies. Highlights include a refrigerator that links to the internet and preorders for a car that flies (that may never be released). As fun and wild as the net gets, everybody's got to see this one.

| ·ACCESSORIES ·SPORTS | ·APPAREL ·ELECTRONICS | ·GIFTS ·ENTERTAINMENT | ·TRAVEL ·HOME & GARDEN |
|---|---|---|---|

**877-989-6321 • Gaiam.com**                **Gaiam.com**

Derived from the ancient term "Gaia" (Mother Earth) and the common modern phrase "I am," Gaiam.com is intended to promote environmental awareness and alternative lifestyles, complete with an e-magazine and online community. Of course, it's mostly the shop that interests us. This encompasses a great selection of organic and hypoallergenic items, often involving alternatives to chemical products. Their catalog is constantly expanding, including health and home items as well as interesting travel opportunities and pet supplies. Basically, they should eventually be fully stocked against a high-tech world that doesn't necessarily put the health of the planet or humanity ahead of profit.

| ·TRAVEL ·PETS | ·SPORTS | ·HEALTH & BEAUTY | ·HOME & GARDEN |
|---|---|---|---|

**435-755-9266 • Global Mart**                **GlobalMart.com**

Not altogether different from a department store, this strictly online shop boasts "fiscally responsible" e-commerce, which generally refers to their own profit margins rather than your frugality (you won't typically find great deals here). The selection varies, depending on the product line, so whereas there aren't many different types of hats, for example, you can find a surprising number of solar panels or mandolins. Ultimately, you might be just as well served for everyday items in their Outlet section, but it's all worth a check if you've got bizarre tastes.

| ·ACCESSORIES ·ELECTRONICS | ·MINORS ·HOME & GARDEN | ·GIFTS | ·SPORTS |
|---|---|---|---|

**831-649-2489 • Good Catalog**                **GoodCatalog.com**

Enticing with the notion of "unique ideas for you and your home," these guys are little more than an upscale boutique of tasteful items that range across a lot of categories. They give you excellent looks at stuff like a canoe coffee table, holistic teddy bears, crystal pineapples and a great snow shovel. In other words, this isn't the type of place you'd go to find exactly what you're looking for, unless you're quite unusual. Rather, it's the sort of place you turn to when you don't know what the heck you want but you sure do want to spend some money. We guess that makes for a good catalog.

| ·ACCESSORIES ·SPORTS | ·MINORS ·ELECTRONICS | ·TRAVEL ·HOME & GARDEN | ·ART/COLLECTIBLES ·PETS |
|---|---|---|---|

## GorsuchLtd.com

Gorsuch Ltd • 800-525-9808

Here's a site that begs the question: how much are you willing to spend on a sweater? Well, how good's the sweater? Gorsuch offers an outstanding selection of cold weather and ski apparel, including boots, clogs and vests, for men, women and children. These items are well-featured on the web site, with elegant models wearing the glamorous clothes amidst beautiful high mountain surroundings, sitting on the occasional piece of living room furniture. The housewares, however, are all photographed indoors.

| ·ACCESSORIES | ·APPAREL | ·MINORS | ·HOME & GARDEN |
|---|---|---|---|

## Half.com

Half.com • No Service Number

Like a giant yard sale, this site is similar to eBay in that regular people from around the planet offer used products for purchase online. Unlike eBay (which actually owns Half.com), these prices aren't negotiated by auction, but are fixed by the seller and sold to the first buyer—an easy enough concept. The weird thing (which is actually totally unrelated to shopping) is that this site somehow managed to convince a town called Halfway, Oregon to change its name. It is now officially known, we kid you not, as Half.com, Oregon. Talk about marketing.

| ·ACCESSORIES ·ELECTRONICS | ·MINORS ·ENTERTAINMENT | ·ART/COLLECTIBLES ·HOME & GARDEN | ·SPORTS |
|---|---|---|---|

## HSN.com

Home Shopping Network • 800-933-2887

That's right, the Home Shopping Network has moved beyond your television screen and onto your computer. With all kinds of stuff with appeal to the insomniac couch potato, you can now make your late-night shopping forays over the internet, leaving you with plenty of time to spend conversing in chat rooms with some loon from Finland. Should you find yourself missing the high-pressure buys of the TV channel, you can make your way to the Click or Miss section, where it's always "your last chance to order at … fantastic savings."

| ·ACCESSORIES ·SPORTS | ·APPAREL ·ELECTRONICS | ·GIFTS ·HEALTH & BEAUTY | ·ART/COLLECTIBLES |
|---|---|---|---|

## iQVC.com

QVC • 888-345-5788

Even if you've watched the TV channel, you probably didn't realize that the letters stand for "Quality, Value, Convenience." Well, one can't help but question the quality of this stuff when it's all too easy to find things like Richard Simmons collectible dolls or Joan Rivers body lotion. Most of the fashion, furnishings, electronics and other personal products are fairly practical, however, or at least aesthetically pleasing. Navigation is pretty easy too, which makes the web site far superior to the network: never again will you have to sit through the Simmons Beauty Rest Hour.

| ·ACCESSORIES ·ELECTRONICS | ·APPAREL ·ENTERTAINMENT | ·GIFTS ·HEALTH & BEAUTY | ·ART/COLLECTIBLES ·HOME & GARDEN |
|---|---|---|---|

**800-210-0202 • Kokopelli's Green Market**          **KokoGM.com**

Short for Kokopelli's Green Market, these guys offer environment-friendly products to "detoxify your body" and "detoxify your world." Both seem to be good ideas, and between all-natural soaps, household cleaners, water filters and baby care products, it seems to be fairly well executed. Except that the web site doesn't look so hot, seeming proof that they didn't waste a lot of time and money dressing it up. Basically, if these prices weren't great, this would be the wrong kind of green market.

| ·MINORS | ·HEALTH & BEAUTY | ·HOME & GARDEN | ·PETS | |
|---|---|---|---|---|

---

**800-963-4816 • Lands' End**          **LandsEnd.com**

Lands' End actually started out as a mail-order yacht supply company (it turns out the misplaced apostrophe was initially a typo). Somehow, they ended up selling clothes, luggage and home furnishings, though how this happened is poorly documented. Nevertheless, sell it all they do, in a huge selection and with a consistent, subtle style. There's even an Overstock section, which on any given day offers great savings. The site's layout is not ideal, but if you keep your eye out for a View All link, you'll notice the selection is much bigger than you first thought. Probably, the owners had a similar reaction once they realized they'd gone from selling boat parts to Capri pants. Weird.

| ·TRAVEL ·HOME & GARDEN | ·APPAREL | ·MINORS | ·GIFTS | |
|---|---|---|---|---|

---

**888-474-5566 • Language**          **Language-NYC.com**

Here's a department store that may be a cut above the rest, in terms of hipness. Featuring some of the fresher fashions available in the Big Apple (at least, that aren't sold exclusively elsewhere), a pull-down menu offers navigation that pays as much or more attention to the names of designers than to its House & Home, Gift, Fashion (for women only), Beauty and Accessories categories. Slick, funky and ultimately appealing, this is certainly a far cry from the department stores you're likely to find at your local mall.

| ·ACCESSORIES ·HOME & GARDEN | ·APPAREL | ·GIFTS | ·HEALTH & BEAUTY | |
|---|---|---|---|---|

---

**800-441-5713 • L.L. Bean**          **LLBean.com**

Right about now you might be thinking, "L.L. Bean? Don't they make those goofy sweaters?" Well, it's time to clarify your thinking—they make a lot of goofy things. If you check out the Home & Garden section, you'll see more than just a staggering selection of bird feeders and hammocks, but loads of indoor furniture as well, perfect for outfitting lakeside cabins, or just making your apartment look like one. Then there's a bunch of travel and sporting gear that almost make you want to take this stuff seriously. Of course, it's the outdoor gear that makes you realize that you wouldn't mind this goofy garb if you were standing two feet deep in snow with a minus 30 degree wind chill.

| ·SPORTS ·HOME & GARDEN | ·APPAREL | ·MINORS | ·TRAVEL | |
|---|---|---|---|---|

# ModHaus.com

ModHaus.com • 617-822-9183

Do you feel cool? Do you want to? This site specializes in "the Mod," meaning vintage designer items from the 1950s–1970s that were ultra-hip in their own time, and have lost little or no luster with age, even in the 21st century. With sections devoted to jewelry, fashion, art, furniture and the aptly named Other Far Out Stuff, you can now easily decorate your life to look like a Fellini film (well, maybe not that far out). Current designs struggle to be as way cool as this stuff, so why bother with the new when the old mod out-hips us all, man?

| ·ACCESSORIES ·ART/COLLECTIBLES | ·APPAREL ·ELECTRONICS | ·HOME & GARDEN | ·GIFTS |
| --- | --- | --- | --- |

# Namaste.com

Namaste.com • 866-438-4642

Desis will delight in this site, whose name loosely translated means, "I bow to the divine in you." What's a Desi? Well, if you have to ask, the name probably doesn't apply to you, but that doesn't mean you can't enjoy this store devoted to Indian products of all kinds. Really, though, its best use lies in a bevy of community resources, which can connect South Asians with local communities and organizations, offers special deals on things like international calling cards and makes it easy to order gifts for friends and family members in India without incurring high shipping costs. Great use of the web.

| ·ACCESSORIES ·ART/COLLECTIBLES | ·APPAREL ·ENTERTAINMENT | ·EPICUREAN ·HEALTH & BEAUTY | ·GIFTS |
| --- | --- | --- | --- |

# NeimanMarcus.com

Neiman Marcus • 888-888-4757

High-end designer items abound on this site, as in the brick-and-mortar stores, in particular in their unparalleled selection of fine apparel, gifts and ladies' shoes. Then there's jewelry, cosmetics and home décor, none less than stellar. Hell, you can even buy a Mercedes G-Wagon if you look hard enough. But there lies the rub. While shopping by category, designer or trend starts off easy enough; a somewhat clunky, frustrating navigation could lead you to give up easily. Shop here if you're absolutely hungry for the good stuff.

| ·ACCESSORIES ·ART/COLLECTIBLES | ·APPAREL ·HEALTH & BEAUTY | ·HOME & GARDEN | ·GIFTS |
| --- | --- | --- | --- |

# NetMarket.com

Netmarket • 888-696-2753

Their catch phrase is "Save time. Save money. Save your sanity." No, they aren't selling antipsychotic medications, they mean that you can shop here without going crazy thinking about prices and selection and so forth. Only, the site is kind of overwrought with a seemingly endless supply of stuff, with options all over the place and the occasional link to somewhere else and menus that roll on and off and there is just so much to look at—well, suffice it to say that browsing through everything would make any nut crack. When in doubt, check the Flea Market section.

| ·SPORTS ·HOME & GARDEN | ·ELECTRONICS | ·ENTERTAINMENT | ·HEALTH & BEAUTY |
| --- | --- | --- | --- |

## 607-277-0152 • The New York First Company

**NewYorkFirst.com**

This site aims to replicate the New York City shopping experience, right down to the navigation, which treats each shopping section as an elevator stop. Thus, the ninth floor is the Gotham Grocery (the "best of New York restaurants and specialty food shops") and the sixth the Curiosity Shop (toys, tools & gadgets), all the way down to the Bargain Basement. They have pretty much a little bit of everything, from bicycle parts to barware and furniture, and even a few items that defy categorization, like the Groucho Marx ventriloquist dummy we found. We like it, but to paraphrase Groucho; who are you going to believe, us or your own eyes?

| ·EPICUREAN ·HOME & GARDEN | ·GIFTS ·PETS | ·ELECTRONICS | ·HEALTH & BEAUTY |
|---|---|---|---|

## 888-282-6060 • Nordstrom

**Nordstrom.com**

This store was founded on capital gleaned from the Alaskan Gold Rush, back at the turn of the last century. While its founder certainly never dreamed of this thing we call the internet, his successors have managed to assemble a pretty well-made site here. Navigation leads you quite simply into the shoes, clothes, gifts, home items and accessories available from the Seattle-based retailer, and excellent images tell you plenty about these items' quality (you don't even need to know the brand names).

| ·ACCESSORIES ·GIFTS | ·HOME & GARDEN ·HEALTH & BEAUTY | ·APPAREL | ·MINORS |
|---|---|---|---|

## 888-235-9763 • The Orvis Company

**Orvis.com**

We would like to explain to you the unlikely transformation of this store from fly fishing shop to a pets, apparel and home furnishings retailer, and it might even be possible to do so. However, it would take a lot more space than we have here, so let's just say that they offer a good selection on all fronts, most reliably when the product relates in some way to hunting or fishing (such as some great travel opportunities). However, as you may feel the need to display your dead animal, even the Home section offers an array of furniture and furnishings to complement your trophies.

| ·HOME & GARDEN ·PETS | ·APPAREL | ·TRAVEL | ·SPORTS |
|---|---|---|---|

## 800-989-0135 • Overstock.com

**Overstock.com**

This site may just be as great as it sounds. Wherever a manufacturer has made too much of a product, or a new technology has been eclipsed by a newer technology, these guys catch what falls through the cracks and offer them to you at low prices. Sure, it may not be the most highly sought after or cutting-edge stuff on the planet, but it's all unused merchandise, in many cases under warranty. Sure, you'll come across the occasional dud item (the kind of thing nobody wanted to begin with, like XFL merchandise), but with categories for everything, it's well worth a browse.

| ·ACCESSORIES ·ENTERTAINMENT | ·TRAVEL ·HOME & GARDEN | ·SPORTS ·APPAREL | ·ELECTRONICS |
|---|---|---|---|

## RentonWW.com
### Renton Western Wear • 888-273-7039

This western-wear outfitter was founded in Seattle, Washington, by a Greek who immigrated to the US by way of Africa. Okay, so his initial business plan didn't involve cowboy hats and boots, but sometimes a store evolves over the years in ways that are inexplicable to a humble internet shopping guide. Nevertheless, time has been kind to this shop, which features a bevy of first-rate products, beginning with apparel and including blankets, bolo ties, kid stuff and a comprehensive list of wedding supplies. This is what cowboys are referring to when they talk about style.

| ·ACCESSORIES | ·MINORS | ·APPAREL | ·GIFTS |

## SafetyCentral.com
### Preparedness Industries, Inc • 406-222-3171

This is a site that's intriguing from top to bottom, beginning with its primary focus: home safety and preparedness. Emergency food storage, power generators and multiband radios would've gone over well during the Y2K craze, and antiterrorism protection equipment (gas masks and such) probably will stir some imaginations today. Not all of this stuff is so dire, though, and the best of it consists of spy gadgets, outdoor/camping gear and some rather useful travel items. Whatever the case, you can feel prepared.

| ·TRAVEL ·HOME & GARDEN | ·SPORTS | ·ELECTRONICS | ·HEALTH & BEAUTY |

## SaksFifthAvenue.com
### Saks Fifth Avenue • 877-551-7257

The famous New York City department store stakes a great presence on the world wide web with this sharp-looking site. While slow image downloads can prove irritating at times, the quality of the merchandise goes a long way towards arguing forgiveness. Their clothes, accessories, home and gift items are all top-notch, with easy shopping by item or by designer boutique. Of course, some of us will recoil in horror when we get a look at the prices, but that's just why their sales are so popular.

| ·ACCESSORIES ·HEALTH & BEAUTY | ·HOME & GARDEN | ·APPAREL | ·GIFTS |

## SamsClub.com
### Sam's Club • No Service Number

The fact that there's an entire section of this site devoted to Embroidery can kind of draw your attention away from its true worth: wholesale values. Of course, this Walton family warehouse store chain is membership driven, meaning that in order to enjoy these values you must pay your dues. While the selection is much wider than it is deep (which is true of any store offering across-the-board discounts), specific items are priced way better than comparable products at better-stocked specialty retailers. Fortunately, you don't have to be a member to scour the selection and figure out which of their deals might make a membership worth it to you.

| ·GIFTS ·ELECTRONICS | ·TRAVEL ·ENTERTAINMENT | ·ART/COLLECTIBLES ·HOME & GARDEN | ·SPORTS ·PETS |

# Lifestyles & Megastores

## 800-349-4358 • Sears — Sears.com

Probably the most familiar department store in the country, this company made its name selling merchandise on the cheap through mail-order catalogs more than 100 years ago. Nowadays, we associate the name more with our local shopping malls, but here Sears returns to its roots, in a way, just in a much more high-tech manner. The prices? Well, let's just say they probably wouldn't have risen to national prominence with their current cost structure, but they have a lot to offer for a reasonable charge, particularly in the Appliances and Tools sections. There are worse ways to avoid the mall.

·ACCESSORIES ·GIFTS | ·SPORTS ·ELECTRONICS | ·APPAREL ·HOME & GARDEN | ·MINORS

## 609-419-1190 • Send.com — Send.com

Prepare to witness a good idea gone amok. This site's name may seem to convey the gist of their service to us, the consumers: it's a place that will send you stuff. For people troubled with the concept, however, they've chosen to split various sections into various URL's. Hence, you see SendGifts, SendAirplanes, SendLiquor, SendCorsages, SendSalmon, SendStainedGlass and... well, you get the point. If nothing else, this site proves that one little page on the internet can front a rather huge undertaking, and that all the good domain names are taken.

·EPICUREAN ·HOME & GARDEN | ·GIFTS ·PETS | ·ART/COLLECTIBLES | ·SPORTS

## 800-527-1577 • Spiegel — Spiegel.com

Having survived well more than a century as a successful Chicago department store and catalog, this online entity promises to maintain a long-existing standard of customer satisfaction. Offering such perks as delayed billing and upgraded substitutions for out-of-stock items, chances are that you'll find this a reliable retailer, whether you're browsing one robust section or another. Highlights include the Fashion and Home stores, but generally there are no surprises and few, if any, let downs.

·ACCESSORIES ·GIFTS | ·APPAREL ·ELECTRONICS | ·HOME & GARDEN | ·MINORS

## 800-422-2770 • sundance — SundanceCatalog.com

Perhaps for many of us, just to know that this is Robert Redford's store will be enough to warrant a visit. Those less impressed with celebrity will have to check the store out for another reason: the fantastic merchandise. Clothes comprise the best of the catalog, with durable and rugged looks arriving somewhere akin to stylish, especially the coats and jackets. Jewelry, footwear and home furnishings take on the Southwest mountain influences that inspired the store in the first place, owing a lot to the area's native cultures. Like the film festival that shares its name, this one should turn out a lot of hits.

·ACCESSORIES | ·APPAREL | ·GIFTS | ·HOME & GARDEN

# Swell.com

**Swell • 866-255-7873**

The word "surf" has been all but usurped by waves of internet users coming online to download, fileswap and/or chat, but on this particular web site it reverts to its traditional meaning; you know, the one involving the ocean. No boards may be found here, but just about every other accoutrement to the surfer lifestyle may be acquired. In other words, you can pick up plenty of gear. Clothes, sunglasses, wetsuits, watches—even some Home Décor pops up here, along with videos of the best water sport on the planet. This one rips.

| | ·SPORTS | ·ACCESSORIES | ·APPAREL | ·HOME & GARDEN |

# Tangs.com

**C.K. Tang Limited • 011-65-6737-5500**

This site is the online representation of Singapore's top department store, which was founded more than half a century ago by a Chinese expatriate. Sound interesting? It is. Here you may find a funky and/or exotic collection of crisply cool clothes and accessories, as well as some beauty, home and electronics products. Good looks and easy navigation abound (at least, once you figure out that the Techno Bay section leads to electronics), making this a great alternative to comparable domestic department stores.

| | ·ACCESSORIES ·APPAREL | ·ELECTRONICS | ·HEALTH & BEAUTY | ·HOME & GARDEN |

# Target.com

**Target • No Service Number**

There's something distinctly American about the sort of merchandise you find at a Target store: nothing too exotic, but plenty of basics that appeal to both the very wealthy and money-minded alike. It may sound less than glamorous, sure, and the site may run a little slow. But the beach chairs, white undershirts and alkaline batteries you can find in this everything-under-the-sun kind of retailer practically define us as a nation.

| | ·ACCESSORIES ·SPORTS | ·ELECTRONICS ·HOME & GARDEN | ·APPAREL ·PETS | ·MINORS |

# ThinkWorld.net

**Think World • No Service Number**

Well, currently the word "world" is a bit excessive, as the site only, as of this writing, offers selections devoted to Italy and Israel. However, if the wines, accessories, gourmet foods, fashion, home furnishings and religious supplies that can be found from these two nations are any indication, the expansion of the site could prove worthwhile indeed... if they last. It remains to be seen if shops devoted to France and Australia will come about, or whether this site will fold like so many other e-merchants. It's a good idea anyway.

| | ·ACCESSORIES ·HOME & GARDEN | ·APPAREL | ·EPICUREAN | ·ART/COLLECTIBLES |

## 763-522-3839 • Up North General Store

### UpNorthGeneralStore.com

Do you see yourself as rugged as the denizens of the Great White North? The gear on this site was intended for use in the frozen wilderness of North America, but its durability translates into other climes with ease, so long as you don't wear your thermal underwear to the Caribbean or something. As lifestyles go, this one seems to revolve around low temperatures and the wilderness, and across all categories this sort of stuff pops up as a theme. Not quite easy to use, this site would be a novelty if its wares weren't by definition so darned functional.

| ·ACCESSORIES ·TRAVEL | ·ART/COLLECTIBLES ·SPORTS | ·APPAREL ·PETS | ·GIFTS |
|---|---|---|---|

## No Service Number • Urban Style

### UrbanStyle.com

Featuring an ever-growing conglomeration of stylish boutiques, the wide base of categories featured here may be inconsistent in variety, but it's generally pretty faithful to its urban fashion sense. Basically, you have what amounts to a selection lying just shy of fringe; stuff that's pretty cool yet not totally uncommon or unheard of. In other words, this stuff should prove accessible to those of cosmopolitan tastes, so long as they don't ascribe to one extreme or another. Yeah, it gets confusing, but hey—so is urban fashion.

| ·ACCESSORIES ·GIFTS | ·ART/COLLECTIBLES ·HOME & GARDEN | ·APPAREL ·PETS | ·MINORS |
|---|---|---|---|

## 802-362-8499 • The Vermont Country Store

### VermontCountryStore.com

Self-described as "purveyors of practical, functional, and hard-to-find products," the items that stand out most on this site tend to be sweet and tasty, and therefore not practical at all. But, as any mother will tell you, don't fill up on treats. There's plenty else to be found here that qualifies as functional and, better still, charming. Clothes, housewares, accessories and a reliable supply of personal care products (see the Apothecary section) are just the tip of the iceberg of this regional store with a universal vision.

| ·ACCESSORIES ·EPICUREAN | ·GIFTS ·HEALTH & BEAUTY | ·APPAREL ·HOME & GARDEN | ·MINORS |
|---|---|---|---|

## 800-966-6546 • Wal-Mart

### Wal-Mart.com

You know this store. After all, it's the largest retailer in the nation, offering extensive shopping opportunities from coast to coast, and you can't stay away. There's just something about being able to find all of life's accoutrements under one roof that is eminently appealing. And here it all is, on one web site, thoroughly organized for easy perusal and (occasionally) slow loading. A visit to one of their huge stores will certainly give you more exercise, but either way, there will be too much here to find in one visit.

| ·ACCESSORIES ·SPORTS | ·MINORS ·ELECTRONICS | ·GIFTS ·ENTERTAINMENT | ·TRAVEL ·HOME & GARDEN |
|---|---|---|---|

## Woolrich.com

This "Original Outdoor Clothing Company" stocks a good supply of durable outerwear to go with sweaters, vests and warm shirts for men, women and children alike, often available in camouflage. It's a remarkably simple site to navigate, which is why you'll easily find other things as well; for the home, for your pet or for general outdoors activities. Liking this site may very well hinge upon whether or not you condone the hunting of ducks, as that seems to have a lot to do with why the store exists. However, hunters and animal activists alike should be aware that these garments and materials are of excellent quality, and will serve well even the casual passerby to nature.

| ·ACCESSORIES ·HOME & GARDEN | ·MINORS ·PETS | ·APPAREL | ·SPORTS |
|---|---|---|---|

## YouCanSave.com

This "As Seen on TV Headquarters" is loaded with those innovative and remarkable products that fill commercial spots particularly on late-night cable TV (you know, in between the phone sex ads). Basically, if it sells for a special offer, including a bonus set of Ginsu knives, and all for a low, low price of only $19.95, you'll find it here. Actually, from The Clapper to the Ab Slide, these guys promise better prices than you may get from ordering over the phone, and you don't even have to "Call Now!"

| ·MINORS ·HOME & GARDEN | ·GIFTS | ·SPORTS | ·HEALTH & BEAUTY |
|---|---|---|---|

# Maternity

Before your family can grow, your belly must, and this will require a change in wardrobe. But, unless you're prepared to simply rotate various colors of muumuus throughout the week, finding quality maternity clothes can be a difficult and pricey proposition. At least, it used to be. Over the past few years many clothing brands and designers seem to have come to the same realization all at once: there were no fashionably acceptable options out there for the pregnant woman. This is no longer a problem, as evidenced by the selection of apparel retailers we've uncovered—and almost every single maternity line has made an impact on the web.

Now there's incredible designer wear, suits for the office, evening gowns, swimsuits and even some spicy lingerie. Never have pregnant women had so many clothing options. If you doubt it, check out some of the pictures on these sites. It's enough to make a woman wonder why she *isn't* pregnant. Truly, if you are expecting, this apparel can be seen as a continuous string of opportunities as your body changes.

Of course, the birth of your child brings even more change. Nursing mothers, in particular, can find some clothing and equipment to make the natural feeding of a child easier and less physically demanding, not to mention publicly viable. And for those concerned with the proper care of a new baby, both here and in our *Minors* section, plenty of nursery gear and dynamic surroundings can be found for any, bright-eyed tot.

NOTES:

_____

_____

_____

_____

_____

_____

_____

_____

_____

_____

_____

_____

_____

_____

_____

_____

_____

## TIPS ON BUYING MATERNITY ITEMS ONLINE

These suggestions may help prevent frustration and discomfort.

•**SIZING UP APPAREL:** The sizes for maternity clothing are set in parallel to a women's original size; in other words, a size 8 will find size 8 maternity selections. However, during pregnancy a woman may possibly expect to increase in size in addition to the room allowed for an expanding belly. As a pregnant woman's body is consistently changing, this is nearly impossible to determine. When in doubt, it's a safe bet to buy a size you can grow into.

•**STOCK UP ON WARDROBE BASICS:** Part of the benefit of online shopping is easier access to updated styles in maternity wear. If you plan multiple pregnancies though, take advantage of selections that feature classic styles and wardrobe staples, stuff that you'll feel comfortable adding back into your rotation on the next pass.

•**CHECK OUT THE *MINORS* SECTION:** In this section, we've included sites that bring a pretty good focus on items and materials offered for a new or expecting mother. To this end, there is a bit of overlap between this and the Babies portion of our Minors section, which focuses more on stuff for the child. Nevertheless, look there for some Parenting Tools that may come in handy.

•**FEEL BEAUTIFUL:** Comfort will be high on the list of priorities for any pregnant woman. However, this includes a positive self-image. Despite the fact that most of humankind immediately sees the exquisite beauty inherent in a mother-to-be, physical changes can be daunting, and it may sometimes be difficult for a mother to see this beauty in herself. Ranging from sexy lingerie to glamorous evening gowns, there is plenty of clothing, as well as some beauty products, contained within this section that will make a pregnant woman's implicit appeal impossible to ignore. Take advantage of this.

## SITES THAT MAY COME IN HANDY

The following URLs may be useful when you shop.

Pregnancy Info, Resources & Checklists: http://epregnancy.com/tools
Nursing Info & Tips: http://www.nursingbaby.com
Baby Name Resource: http://www.babynamer.com
Maternity Bra Fitting Guide: http://www.medela.com/NewFiles/brafit.html
Lamaze Class Directory: http://www.lamaze.org/2000/home.html
Doula Locator: http://www.dona.org/findingdoula.htm
Midwife Info & Directory: http://www.midwifeinfo.com

>> **SECTION ICON LEGEND**

Use the following guide to understand the rectangular icons that appear throughout this section.

### APPAREL

Ranging from stylish frocks to utilitarian wardrobe basics, the clothing featured in this section promises to keep a woman well dressed through all nine months of pregnancy, in any season.

### EQUIPMENT

This icon refers to the equipment essential to a new mother for the purposes of nursing, hygiene and general small baby care.

### HEALTH

During pregnancy, myriad particular health issues may arise. These sites offer items to promote optimum health in expecting mothers, from skin care products to prenatal vitamins.

## >> LIST OF KEY WORDS

The following words represent the types of items typically found on the sites listed in this section.

### ACCESSORIES

For the most part, new fashion accessories aren't required for the mother-to-be. New mothers, however, do suddenly find need of diaper bags, baby carriers and the like.

### BEAUTY

Beauty options for the pregnant woman include products designed for the special needs of a changing body. Find them here.

### CAREER DRESS

Before the maternity leave kicks in, you'll want to maintain your professional appearance at the office. Here's some professional attire to keep you well dressed on the job.

### CASUAL WEAR

There may be no more valuable commodity for the expecting mom than comfort. So far as you can find it in attire, this stuff is it.

### DESIGNER

What do pregnant women wear to make other pregnant women envious? This stuff.

### EVENING WEAR

A night out can be as glamorous for the pregnant woman as it was before the belly started to grow. Here's some elegant maternity attire.

### FITNESS

Obviously, strenuous exercise isn't often recommended for the expecting mother, but continued personal fitness definitely is. These sites offer exercise equipment and apparel, and stuff like jogging strollers for after the baby has arrived.

### NURSING

These products are specifically intended to promote a healthy nursing process for both mother and child, ranging from pumps to skin care.

### PERSONALIZATION

As always, this key word denotes shops that offer to personalize items through stitching or engravings, usually with monogramming.

### SPECIALTY SIZES

Maternity sizes are special in themselves, but a wider range of sizes and shapes of women may outfit themselves with these sites.

### SWIMWEAR

For swimming or tanning, this bathing attire accommodates the mother-to-be with either modesty or sex appeal.

### UNDERWEAR

Some of it is functional, including nursing bras and support hose. A lot of it is a bit steamier, intended for the bedroom.

## >> KEY WORD INDEX

Use the following lists to locate online retailers that sell the maternity products you seek.

### ACCESSORIES

BabyBecoming.com
BeforeBaby.com
ChantelRenee.com
ChicAndShowing.com
ConceptionStore.com
JustBabies.com
LittleKoala.com
MomsNightOut.com
MothersBest.com
Motherwear.com
OneStopBaby.com
PumpStation.com

### BEAUTY

BeforeBaby.com
BellaMama.com
ErbaViva.com
eStyle.com
JustBabies.com
LittleKoala.com
OneStopBaby.com
PumpkinMaternity.com
TummiesMaternity.com

### CAREER DRESS

AnnaCris.com
APeaInThePod.com
BabyBecoming.com
BloomingMarvellous.co.uk
ChicAndShowing.com
eStyle.com
iMaternity.com
JapaneseWeekend.com
LizLange.com
Maternity-Clothing-
    Fashions.com
MaternityOutfitters.com
MommyChic.com
Motherhood.com

Motherwear.com
OneCoolMama.com
OneHotMama.com
PumpkinMaternity.com
TummiesMaternity.com
ZoeeMaternity.com

### CASUAL WEAR

AnnaCris.com
APeaInThePod.com
BabyBecoming.com
BloomingMarvellous.com
BreastFeedingStyles.com
CadeauMaternity.com
ChantelRenee.com
ChicAndShowing.com
eStyle.com
FitMaternity.com
Gap.com
GarnetHill.com
GirlShop.com
iMaternity.com
JapaneseWeekend.com
LittleKoala.com
LizLange.com
Maternity-Clothing-
    Fashions.com
MommyChic.com
Motherhood.com
Mothers-In-Motion.com
Motherwear.com
NicoleMaternity.com
OldNavy.com
OneCoolMama.com
OneStopBaby.com
PumpkinMaternity.com
PumpStation.com
TummiesMaternity.com
ZoeeMaternity.com

### DESIGNER

APeaInThePod.com
eStyle.com

LizLange.com
Maternity-Clothing-
    Fashions.com
OneHotMama.com
PumpkinMaternity.com
TummiesMaternity.com
ZoeeMaternity.com

### EQUIPMENT

Am-I-Pregnant.com
ConceptionStore.com
eStyle.com
FitMaternity.com
LittleKoala.com
MothersBest.com
Motherwear.com
OneStopBaby.com
PumpStation.com
Puronyx.com

### EVENING WEAR

AnnaCris.com
APeaInThePod.com
BabyBecoming.com
BloomingMarvellous.co.uk
eStyle.com
GirlShop.com
iMaternity.com
JapaneseWeekend.com
LizLange.com
Maternity-Clothing-
    Fashions.com
MaternityOutfitters.com
MommyChic.com
MomsNightOut.com
Motherhood.com
NicoleMaternity.com
OneCoolMama.com
OneHotMama.com
PumpkinMaternity.com
TummiesMaternity.com
ZoeeMaternity.com

### FITNESS

AnnaCris.com
APeaInThePod.com
BloomingMarvellous.co.uk
ChicAndShowing.com
eStyle.com
FitMaternity.com
Gap.com
LittleKoala.com
Maternity-Clothing-
    Fashions.com
Motherhood.com
Mothers-In-Motion.com
OldNavy.com
OneCoolMama.com
OneHotMama.com
PumpkinMaternity.com
SupportSockShop.com

### HEALTH

Am-I-Pregnant.com
BellaMama.com
ConceptionStore.com
ErbaViva.com
eStyle.com
JustBabies.com
Puronyx.com

### NURSING

AnnaCris.com
APeaInThePod.com
BabyBecoming.com
BloomingMarvellous.co.uk
BravadoDesigns.com
BreastFeedingStyles.com
eStyle.com
iMaternity.com
JapaneseWeekend.com
JustBabies.com
LittleKoala.com
MommyChic.com
Motherhood.com

MothersBest.com
Motherwear.com
OneCoolMama.com
OneHotMama.com
OneStopBaby.com
PumpStation.com
Puronyx.com

## PERSONALIZATION

HappyStork.com
StorkAvenue.com
Storkie.com

## SPECIALTY SIZES

BabyBecoming.com
BreastFeedingStyles.com
Maternity-Clothing-
  Fashions.com
Motherhood.com
MothersBest.com
Motherwear.com
OneHotMama.com
TummiesMaternity.com

## SWIMWEAR

APeaInThePod.com
BabyBecoming.com
BloomingMarvellous.co.uk
FitMaternity.com
iMaternity.com
JapaneseWeekend.com
LizLange.com
Maternity-Clothing-
  Fashions.com
Motherhood.com
Mothers-In-Motion.com
Motherwear.com
OldNavy.com
OneHotMama.com
TummiesMaternity.com

## UNDERWEAR

AnnaCris.com
APeaInThePod.com
BabyBecoming.com
BloomingMarvellous.co.uk
BravadoDesigns.com
FitMaternity.com
GarnetHill.com
iMaternity.com
JapaneseWeekend.com
JustBabies.com
LittleKoala.com
LSRMaternity.com
Maternity-Clothing-
  Fashions.com
Motherhood.com
MothersBest.com
Motherwear.com
OneCoolMama.com
OneHotMama.com
OneStopBaby.com
PumpStation.com
SupportSockShop.com
TummiesMaternity.com

## Am-I-Pregnant.com

A little different from the other shops in this section, this glued-together-looking site doesn't offer any mothering accessories or clothes, but it might outfit you with a paternity suit. See, it focuses on the home technology of reproduction. The "Am I Pregnant?" obviously refers to a spate of home pregnancy tests, whereas fertility monitors track ovulation, enabling planning parents to pick just the right moment to... well, you know. Unplanned pregnancies may, however, require turning to the third general product for sale: home DNA tests; they're expensive, but, when notarized, should hold up in court. Will wonders never cease?

| ·HEALTH | ·EQUIPMENT | | |
|---|---|---|---|

## AnnaCris.com

This maternity boutique features many popular brands, as well as its own exclusive line of apparel, on a site nearly as cute as its wares. Seasonal selections are split into Business, Weekend and Casual sections, with clothes ranging from classic to funky. Additionally, there is lingerie and athletic gear, depending on the sport you favor most, and plenty of designs created specifically with the nursing mother in mind. Pretty much, a glance at this site highlights the fact that motherhood requires a restocking of your wardrobe. Fortunately, the great prices here may help you afford it.

| ·EVENING WEAR ·FITNESS | ·CASUAL WEAR ·NURSING | ·UNDERWEAR | ·CAREER DRESS |
|---|---|---|---|

## APeaInThePod.com

Answer to the question, "Where do people like Catherine Zeta-Jones, Cindy Crawford and Madonna shop for maternity clothing?" acclaimed maternity shop A Pea in the Pod offers some pretty sassy stuff. Top designs from the likes of Anna Sui, Nicole Miller and Vivian Tam have been known to surface in this shop, which offers everything from swimwear and lingerie to party dresses and professional attire. With the philosophy, "Maternity clothing for the fashion inspired," this is the place to go if you want to expose your child early to fine fabrics and expert stitching.

| ·EVENING WEAR ·SWIMWEAR | ·CASUAL WEAR ·FITNESS | ·UNDERWEAR ·NURSING | ·CAREER DRESS ·DESIGNER |
|---|---|---|---|

## BabyBecoming.com

We sure won't be the ones to dispute this site's claim that, "large women are the most beautiful pregnant women in the world." The smiles on these women's faces say it all, as they wear a selection of charming, comfortable and affordable clothing fit expressly for the plus-sized mommy-to-be. Though not a terrific-looking site, the design works well enough, offering easy shopping and bolstered by friendly, conversational tones in its product descriptions. You may be most pleased, however, by the size chart (locate it alphabetically in the menu, then follow Click to View), as here a size 18 becomes a size 1, which makes this shopping all the more gratifying.

| ·EVENING WEAR ·SWIMWEAR | ·CASUAL WEAR ·ACCESSORIES | ·UNDERWEAR ·NURSING | ·CAREER DRESS ·SPECIALTY SIZES |
|---|---|---|---|

**877-566-4969** • **Before Baby**                    **BeforeBaby.com**

A plethora of odds and ends related to pregnancy and motherhood are available on this site, things like books on the subject, a prenatal yoga video, weird mom-related jewelry and some occasionally useful proprietary skin care items. Following the Gotta Shop link will get you to a good starting point, from where viewing all of this merchandise will be a quick and simple affair. The bottom line is that this mostly rather silly site bears a few worthwhile items, but mostly only nonessential stuff that only a mother could love.

| ·ACCESSORIES | ·BEAUTY | | |
|---|---|---|---|

**888-831-4474** • **Bella Essentials**                    **BellaMama.com**

If you're in the habit of using all-natural skin care products, you'll be glad to know of this limited line of salves and salts, which stick closely to their all-natural credo, occasionally taking advantage of ingredients common to aromatherapy. Tackling skin problems typically encountered by the expecting or nursing mother, the site offers an extensive ingredients list that explains the advantages of each oil, extract and/or vitamin that will come into contact with your skin. This is only bound to get better.

| ·BEAUTY | ·HEALTH | | |
|---|---|---|---|

**011-44-870-751-8944** • **Blooming Marvellous**            **BloomingMarvellous.co.uk**

Whether true or not, we can at least imagine that checking out this site gives us a glimpse of how expecting mothers dress in the UK. Generally, there doesn't tend to be anything too flashy or daring about this garb; it mostly keeps a balance between quaint and coolly casual, which of course is exactly the qualities that make us curious about the British in the first place. Fortunately, should you find yourself feeling jealous of any of these limey ladies, you can simply click on the $ button to figure out how many good old American dollars it will cost to put these marvelous clothes on your back (they misspelled this one, not us)....

| ·EVENING WEAR ·SWIMWEAR | ·CASUAL WEAR ·FITNESS | ·UNDERWEAR ·NURSING | ·CAREER DRESS |
|---|---|---|---|

**800-590-7802** • **Bravado Designs**                    **BravadoDesigns.com**

Nursing bras in themselves aren't terribly hard to find, but how about one in leopard print? This would seem to be the greatest element of "bravado" encountered on this peculiar site. Its narrow focus on nursing bras and maternity panties makes it fairly simple to shop, a small selection balancing out the oddball navigation so that simply following the Products link will get you where you want to be, or at least show you where you might want to go, whether you're more a traditional underwear or thong type of gal.

| ·UNDERWEAR | ·NURSING | | |
|---|---|---|---|

## BreastFeedingStyles.com

CO Nursingwear • 800-341-2901

Look closely at each of the dresses and shirts in this small catalog and you still may not even notice their common thread: a zipper. Disguised as seams, top-to-bottom opening zippers adorn these clothes for breast-feeding access with easy adjustment while the baby nurses. It's the sort of thing that sounds like it could be a bit dangerous, but the zipper consists of small, plastic threads designed to prevent mishap. Styles range from velvet dresses to cotton T-shirts, but generally stick to the casual end of things.

| | ·CASUAL WEAR | ·NURSING | ·SPECIALTY SIZES | |
|---|---|---|---|---|

## CadeauMaternity.com

Cadeau Maternity • 866-622-3322

Pulling together a bit here and there from well-established fashion traditions, this line of maternity clothing takes its name from the French for "gift," has its designs made in Italy and was founded by a couple of fashion executives with Barney's pedigrees. Bottom line is that these are some quite attractive garments with seasonal flairs added to classic looks, all made of stretch fabrics so as to accommodate a swelling belly.

| | ·CASUAL WEAR | | | |
|---|---|---|---|---|

## ChantelRenee.com

Chantel Renée • 516-695-0788

For the mommy-to-be who lives to coordinate, this unique line of maternity wear features a seasonal series of sets that include matching pieces and accessories. With thematic names like Dangerous Denim, Hawaiian Punch and Upper East Side, these sets intend to promote a feeling of fashionable fun, a sense that is carried through in design of the small but needlessly cumbersome site. Generally, this all stretch-fabric collection is more tasteful than it lets on, occasionally bordering on elegant.

| | ·CASUAL WEAR | ·ACCESSORIES | | |
|---|---|---|---|---|

## ChicAndShowing.com

Chic & Showing • 877-295-6103

By the looks of it, this clothing retailer was created as a place for trend-savvy women to shop for the latest looks during pregnancy. A section referred to as "Cool Pregnant Chick" would reinforce this interpretation. More than just a mall store for mommies, though, this site offers a decent mix of contemporary casual and career designs, wardrobe staples (such as camisoles, yoga pants and slip dresses) and even some athletic apparel tossed in to remind us that cool can include the entire closet.

| | ·CASUAL WEAR | ·CAREER DRESS | ·ACCESSORIES | ·FITNESS |
|---|---|---|---|---|

## 888-891-5933 • Conception Store
### ConceptionStore.com

From conception on through to baby rearing, this store focuses on the tools of the trade, whether they be fertility monitors, pregnancy tests or breast pumps. The goal of these items is to ensure the comfort and health of both mother and child, starting from the moment parenthood is even considered and continuing on into the nursing process. Granted, reproduction has continued unabated for all of human history without the assistance of any of these products, but that doesn't necessarily mean you can't improve the process.

| ·ACCESSORIES | ·HEALTH | ·EQUIPMENT | |
|---|---|---|---|

## 877-372-2848 • Erbaviva
### ErbaViva.com

If you're into naturals, and want your child to be as well, start by checking out this site whose name means "living herbs." Basically, it offers soothing and sweet-smelling salves that are "100% pure, certified organic," so you can indulge yourself with skin and body care products without having to worry about your baby's exposure to any harmful toxins; at least until he or she is born. Even then, some of these bath essences, body rubs and aromatic oils are designated baby friendly, so all you have to do is move out of the city, grow your own uncontaminated food and draw water from a well or mountain spring, and your kid can grow up the way nature, and homeopathy, intended.

| ·BEAUTY | ·HEALTH | | |
|---|---|---|---|

## 877-378-9537 • BabyStyle
### eStyle.com

The eStyle shop covers many different areas for mother and child, but in this case we'd like to direct your attention to the Babystyle section, and particularly the Maternity and Gear subsections. Once inside, shopping proves inconsistent and cluttered, so it'll take a keen eye to accomplish everything you want. However, the products are great, whether you're looking through the sexy, fun clothing or at entirely necessary items like strollers, car seats and home-safety devices. Rounding out the selection is nursing clothes and equipment, because baby's gotta eat.

| ·EVENING WEAR ·FITNESS | ·CASUAL WEAR ·EQUIPMENT | ·CAREER DRESS ·NURSING | ·BEAUTY ·DESIGNER |
|---|---|---|---|

## 888-961-9100 • Fit Maternity & Beyond
### FitMaternity.com

The main concern with clothing, both during pregnancy and after, is achieving the proper fit. The answer, aside from a sizable new clothes budget of course, is fitness. In these pages you will find a complete selection of workout clothes for the new and/or expecting mother, including bike shorts, swimsuits, support socks and even a nursing sports bra. Should you desire a jump-start on regaining your prepregnancy figure, you can also find some support girdles, and if you want to get baby into the act there's always a jogging stroller or two to choose from.

| ·CASUAL WEAR ·EQUIPMENT | ·UNDERWEAR | ·SWIMWEAR | ·FITNESS |
|---|---|---|---|

# Gap.com

**The Gap • 888-906-1104**

If you've gone shopping for clothes in the USA at all in the past 10 years, you know exactly the kind of stuff The Gap has to offer. What you may not have noticed is that they've brought their same clean-cut sensibilities to a line of Maternity apparel. Now, whenever you see a gaggle of fresh-faced kids cavorting across your television screen to celebrate whichever fabric or pattern is popular at the perennial mall store that week, you'll know that, even if yours is a pregnant fresh-faced beauty, you can get it too.

| | ·CASUAL WEAR | ·FITNESS | | |
|---|---|---|---|---|

# GarnetHill.com

**Garnet Hill • 800-870-3513**

If you start looking for the maternity apparel this site doesn't have, you're missing the point. While this selection is small, merely an addendum tacked into a tiny corner of the also limited Women's Clothing section of this catalog, the fact is they carry stuff like Stretch Velour Bootcut Maternity Pants and silk maternity blouses, making this much more than just a worthwhile stop. You'll also find some good sleepwear and underwear, as once you find your way inside the maternity selection, shopping turns out to be blissfully easy.

| | ·CASUAL WEAR | ·UNDERWEAR | | |
|---|---|---|---|---|

# GirlShop.com

**GirlShop.com • 888-450-7467**

Girl Shop brings together a number of chic designer boutiques, but in order to take advantage of the maternity wear available here you'll have to go to the area of the storefront called Power Shop! and search under the Maternity category. Then you'll be treated to an extraordinarily stylish, if small, selection of slick and sexy apparel from the Chiarakruza store (you may also search specifically for this shop). It doesn't get much more sultry than this, pregnant or not!

| | ·EVENING WEAR | ·CASUAL WEAR | | |
|---|---|---|---|---|

# HappyStork.com

**HappyStork.com • No Service Number**

This miserable-looking site represents an entirely happy function: selling Birth Announcements. They feature hundreds of options, ranging from cutesy to your standard, traditional elegance. Should you be so inclined to promote the unutterable adorability of the baby in question, you may opt for an announcement that comes complete with a built-in photo insert slot. Each order may also be personalized to include return addresses and personalized messages, in the typestyle of your own preference.

| ·PERSONALIZATION | | | |
|---|---|---|---|

## 800-466-6223 • iMaternity

# iMaternity.com

A lowercase "i" or "e" at the beginning of a domain name typically connotes a web shop that sprang up as a part of the Great Internet Explosion, never having had any previous footing in the real world. As such, we should maybe hold these sites to a higher technological standard, demanding excellent design and user-friendly navigation. That being said, this site delivers. Follow the link to Maternity Shop and then use the animated menus at the top of the page to fulfill nearly all of your maternity clothing needs. Or, link to Maternity Outlet, where the great thing is that these clothes were all priced affordably to begin with.

| ·EVENING WEAR<br>·SWIMWEAR | ·CASUAL WEAR<br>·NURSING | ·UNDERWEAR | ·CAREER DRESS |
|---|---|---|---|

## 800-808-0555 • Japanese Weekend

# JapaneseWeekend.com

This line of maternity apparel has nothing at all to do with Japan—it was simply named after a dance choreographed by the line's designer. What do the clothes have to do with dance? Nothing, really… well, maybe an element of grace. They are intended to make a woman "feel assured that she looks good while being comfortable from the early months of pregnancy throughout her nursing days." With all kinds of clothes that expand and contract, including a special coat with a built-in sling to carry your baby close, this stuff certainly does so, with grace to spare.

| ·EVENING WEAR<br>·SWIMWEAR | ·CASUAL WEAR<br>·NURSING | ·UNDERWEAR | ·CAREER DRESS |
|---|---|---|---|

## 888-900-2229 • Just Babies

# JustBabies.com

This URL is somewhat of a misnomer, as they don't actually sell babies here. It should say "Just for Babies," but even that would be wrong, as some quite thorough nursing and maternity selections make this place ideal for new and expectant mothers as well as tots. It starts with a great selection of beauty and skin care products, including body oils and lotions for mother and child. More and less practical items include breast pumps, lingerie and books on all kinds of parenting topics, many of which may actually prompt you to come back to peruse the Nursery and Feeding Baby sections.

| ·UNDERWEAR<br>·NURSING | ·ACCESSORIES | ·BEAUTY | ·HEALTH |
|---|---|---|---|

## 800-950-1239 • Little Koala

# LittleKoala.com

The Online Store section of this site offers a decent range of maternity apparel, as well as some nursing accessories, how-to books and skin care items. The best, though, turns up in the Nursing Clothes and Bras & Lingerie sections. From nursing camisoles to support bras and girdles, these sections offer several ways to get your changing body under control, and will make anything you put over them all the better; which is a good thing, as most of the clothes here, despite their fashionable brand-name origins, are typically uninspiring at best.

| ·CASUAL WEAR<br>·FITNESS | ·UNDERWEAR<br>·EQUIPMENT | ·ACCESSORIES<br>·NURSING | ·BEAUTY |
|---|---|---|---|

## LizLange.com

Liz Lange Maternity • 888-616-5777

The former editor of *Vogue* magazine has really kicked up the style of expectant mothers, assembling her own line of maternity wear on this somewhat over-designed but ultimately functional site. Just click on The Collection to view the clothes, both every-day wear and swimsuits, each of which is fantastic. So fantastic, in fact, that some women may be inspired towards pregnancy just to try out some of these fun and sexy garments. Don't worry; sizes are adapted from prepregnancy standards (you may need to check), and some of this stuff is simply made to adapt to a growing body, so it may still fit after the birth of your child, if you're lucky.

| | ·EVENING WEAR ·DESIGNER | ·CASUAL WEAR | ·CAREER DRESS | ·SWIMWEAR |
|---|---|---|---|---|

## LSRMaternity.com

LSR Maternity • 720-876-1815

"LSR" stands for designer and founder Laura S. Rudolph, but it might as well stand for "Light, Stretchy and Racy." This line of "sleepwear with sass" challenges any preconceptions that pregnancy and sex appeal are mutually exclusive with scintillating garments that make heavy use of sheer fabrics. These designs have names like Flirty, Alluring and Shagadellic, just in case the pictures aren't enough to clue you in that this sexy sleepwear isn't necessarily made with sleeping in mind. It's a simple site, with a small selection, which isn't to say there's not a lot to look at....

| | ·UNDERWEAR | | | |
|---|---|---|---|---|

## Maternity-Clothing-Fashions.com

Maternity Clothing Fashions • 866-439-7328

Offering "up to date maternity wear," click on this site's Collection to view a lot of fun and hip clothes that often emphasize your sex appeal while keeping up with current trends. For example, we found some skintight snake print and camouflage pants paired with low-cut tops and textured fabrics. It's not entirely spicy though; just the tops, bottoms, lingerie, swimwear, plus sizes, evening and active wear. The 9 to 5 section features some sedate, office-type attire. To be honest, though, most nonpregnant women don't look this good at work.

| | ·EVENING WEAR ·SWIMWEAR | ·CASUAL WEAR ·DESIGNER | ·UNDERWEAR ·SPECIALTY SIZES | ·CAREER DRESS ·FITNESS |
|---|---|---|---|---|

## MaternityOutfitters.com

Maternity Outfitters • No Service Number

Finding maternity clothes isn't really all that difficult. The hard part is finding clothes that are suitable for work and special nights out (unless you're eager to wear one of those *I Love Lucy*-era poncholike designs that have a giant bow tied across the front). That's why we like this shop. Not only does it offer an elegant selection, but it allows you to lease rather than buy, which means that you'll only own these clothes, which you'll only wear for a few months, for a short while and at a bargain.

| | ·EVENING WEAR | ·CAREER DRESS | | |
|---|---|---|---|---|

## 866-244-2666 • Mommy Chic

### MommyChic.com

As it turns out, for some who visit this site, the question may be whether some of this attire is maybe too chic for a mom-to-be, as this catalog includes short skirts, revealing dresses and at least one instance of a lace tube top. Genuinely, though, there is plenty of tasteful garb running all through this site, including a classic array of knits, elegant evening wear and various snappy professional garments. Let's just say the site is good enough to include items with a touch more daring in the name of selection.

| ·EVENING WEAR | ·CASUAL WEAR | ·CAREER DRESS | ·NURSING |
|---|---|---|---|

## 212-744-6667 • Mom's Night Out

### MomsNightOut.com

Dispelling the notion that pregnancy consists primarily of muumuus and bed rest, this clothing line/boutique lends a touch of glamour to maternity wear with a selection of formal attire capable of dressing any special occasion. Both dresses and gowns, whether or not you perceive a difference, are available in slim selections, and they even offer a selection of bridal apparel. Each frock is well represented with pictures and descriptions, shown complete with accessories (like veils, jackets and wraps), which may be either added to your dress order or purchased separately.

| ·EVENING WEAR | ·ACCESSORIES | | |
|---|---|---|---|

## 800-466-6223 • Motherhood Maternity

### Motherhood.com

This very slick site makes it quite easy to browse and view all manner of maternity apparel, with entire sections devoted to things like pantsuits, leggings and jumpers, in addition to the more standard lingerie, career wear, dresses and jeans. This even holds true for plus sizes. There's nothing spectacularly snappy or up to date here, but you will find a great selection of basics; the kind of stuff equally suitable to wear while running errands or kicking up your feet, all priced to make you a repeat customer.

| ·EVENING WEAR ·SWIMWEAR | ·CASUAL WEAR ·FITNESS | ·UNDERWEAR ·NURSING | ·CAREER DRESS ·SPECIALTY SIZES |
|---|---|---|---|

## 877-512-8800 • Mothers In Motion

### Mothers-In-Motion.com

If you're not a big believer in the notion that the best way to approach pregnancy is with "plenty of bed rest," you'll be happy to discover this site, which trades exclusively in athletic apparel and swimwear for the expecting mother. The gist is that all these items feature their patented "Bioengineered Performance System," which really just means that all garments offer additional sewn-in support to the places a mom-to-be needs it; namely, the abdomen, lower back and inner thighs. Finally, maternity clothes you can sweat in.

| ·CASUAL WEAR | ·SWIMWEAR | ·FITNESS | |
|---|---|---|---|

# MothersBest.com

Mothers' Best • 877-226-2464

Considering how a mother nursing her child is one of the more natural and beautiful interactions available to humankind, it shouldn't be difficult to find comfortable and functional nursing attire, right? Okay, so it's not difficult; at least not with this site around. Offering fitting guides, tips and brand comparisons, this site proves to be one of your better places to locate the right nursing bra, as well as some nursing clothes that provide easy access without disrupting your wardrobe completely. Breast pumps, bottle warmers and other nursing supplies round out a healthy selection.

| ·UNDERWEAR ·SPECIALTY SIZES | ·ACCESSORIES | ·EQUIPMENT | ·NURSING |
|---|---|---|---|

# MotherWear.com

Motherwear • 800-950-2500

One of the great things about breast-feeding is that it requires very little in terms of accoutrements in order to be successful; that is, all the necessary equipment tends to be supplied by mother and child. Of course, this is not to say that nothing else can help the process. At least, therein lies the premise of this site, which offers both apparel and accessories to the nursing mother. Clothes consist generally of tops that provide easy access to the nipple, whether a bra, shirt or swimsuit (and some dresses too), while a supply of pumps and accessories will keep baby happily fed when mom's not around.

| ·CASUAL WEAR ·ACCESSORIES | ·UNDERWEAR ·EQUIPMENT | ·CAREER DRESS ·NURSING | ·SWIMWEAR ·SPECIALTY SIZES |
|---|---|---|---|

# NicoleMaternity.com

Nicole Maternity • 888-424-8228

The home page implies that this maternity clothing line is "Sexy, Stylish, (and) Chic." Well, they aren't kidding. With current looks and sleek designs, nearly every product in this catalog offers proof that this is "not your typical maternity wear." We found snake patterns, scooped necklines and flared pant legs, for starters, and this only out of a dozen or so designs. Even the Clearance section had some great dresses, both formal and casual. It's all easy to see—just follow the link that says Shop and don't look back.

| ·EVENING WEAR | ·CASUAL WEAR | | |
|---|---|---|---|

# OldNavy.com

Old Navy • 800-653-6289

You've probably seen the campy commercials, and so you understand what these guys mean with terms like Performance Fleece or Techno Chino Skirts. Basically, this is trendy, cheap casual wear for anyone from kids to adults. Styles are simple, so any tops mix easily with any bottoms, and a great selection of outerwear will match just about anything you put underneath it. This is a place that makes shopping especially easy, so if you're willing to embrace that Old Navy cookie-cutter charm, then nothing here will disappoint.

| ·CASUAL WEAR | ·SWIMWEAR | ·FITNESS | |
|---|---|---|---|

**877-661-6321** • **One Cool Mama**              **OneCoolMama.com**

Promising to "take you through your pregnancy in style," the "cool mama" part really starts with this site's deference to comfort. By "comfort," of course, they often mean the feeling that you're sexy and chic even as your belly grows (they'll tell you where to stick the word "fat"), but in the midst of various popular designer maternity clothes you can actually find some simply comfortable, relaxing threads. The Basics and Vintage Levi's sections, for example, should keep you cool through several pregnancies with stuff like black turtlenecks and faded jeans. At least, until you want to heat things up….

| ·EVENING WEAR ·FITNESS | ·CASUAL WEAR ·NURSING | ·UNDERWEAR | ·CAREER DRESS |
|---|---|---|---|

**800-217-3750** • **One Hot Mama**              **OneHotMama.com**

This zany site plays host to a maternity and nursing wear shop that started as an online entity and then developed into a brick-and-mortar store in Los Angeles. Literally a mom-and-pop organization, the married couple that owns and operates the shop advocates breast-feeding and involved parenting. And yet they do live in LA, and so have a great appreciation for beauty and fashion. This shows in their product selection, with everything from swimsuits to baby slings proving that good parenting can be synonymous with style.

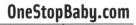

| ·EVENING WEAR ·SWIMWEAR | ·NURSING ·FITNESS | ·UNDERWEAR ·DESIGNER | ·CAREER DRESS ·SPECIALTY SIZES |
|---|---|---|---|

**888-828-2229** • **One-Stop Baby**              **OneStopBaby.com**

A prime example of the sort of small business venture enabled by the internet, this diminutive line of nursing and maternity products gets a strong start with "the best maternity pillow ever," then keeps it up with some skin care and bibs for both baby and mom. The site itself is not very sophisticated, nor are the products within really, but they're useful, available in a wide variety of different fabrics and colors and in most cases well designed. You won't see them elsewhere.

| ·ACCESSORIES ·UNDERWEAR | ·BEAUTY ·EQUIPMENT | ·NURSING | ·CASUAL WEAR |
|---|---|---|---|

**800-460-0337** • **Pumpkin Maternity**              **PumpkinMaternity.com**

Standing proud behind the slogan, "the birth of cool," this store for hip mamas offers seasonal apparel, along with the occasional parental device or skin care item. Pretty much all you need to know in order to imagine the sort of shopping to expect is that the line of clothes was "conceived in the fall of 1996 as designer Pumpkin Wetzel toured Europe with her rock band in a converted fish truck." Shopping isn't ideal, but the clothes just might be, whether you plan to rock or maybe just roll a little bit.

| ·EVENING WEAR ·FITNESS | ·CASUAL WEAR ·DESIGNER | ·CAREER DRESS | ·BEAUTY |
|---|---|---|---|

## PumpStation.com

The Pump Station • 877-842-7867

Known to be the nation's first "lactation center," the Pump Station has been operating successfully in Santa Monica for nearly two decades, steadily growing all the while, so it only makes sense that it would eventually find its way to the web. While you can find quite a bit of quality breast-feeding equipment and a great selection of nursing bras, that's only half of what makes this a great site. Also here is a wealth of information in the form of articles and a selection of helpful books. If you have questions, check here.

| | | •CASUAL WEAR •NURSING | •UNDERWEAR | •ACCESSORIES | •EQUIPMENT |
|---|---|---|---|---|---|

## Puronyx.com

Puronyx • 800-944-4006

Declaring that, "there is no other time in life when comfort counts more," this site offers a proprietary line of Breastfeeding Aids and Maternity Support Products, including maternity compression pantyhose, support belts and the "only comprehensive breast care management system available." Browsing this small selection of products is easy and quick (just follow the link to the Product Catalog), while the rest of the site offers some helpful words and resources on topics such as changing breast shape, nipple irritation, mastitis and other important-to-know information.

| | | •EQUIPMENT | •NURSING | •HEALTH | |
|---|---|---|---|---|---|

## StorkAvenue.com

Stork Avenue • 800-861-5437

A somewhat overly cute and slow-to-use site plays host to this shop that offers some joyous items like birth announcements, baby shower stuff, baby scrapbooks and those hilarious bubblegum cigars that a proud, nonsmoking father might like to hand out upon the birth of his child. After the splash page, you will encounter a small, illustrated village. Each house in the village offers access to a different variety of products; simply roll the cursor over each house and wait for a description of the category to pop up. It's kinda fun, but not so much that you'll want to repeat the experience.

| •PERSONALIZATION | | |
|---|---|---|

## Storkie.com

Storkie Express • 800-771-7867

Birth announcements, baby shower invitations and thank-you cards comprise the bulk of the products available from this creatively constructed catalog. With a special section for twins, and consistently clever designs throughout, the Browse Store link leads to fairly easy shopping, especially if you assume a laid-back approach. Otherwise, you may have to brush up on the semantic distinctions between the words "cute," "precious," "darling" and "adorable," as these black and white, rich color or pastel designs run the gamut.

| •PERSONALIZATION | | |
|---|---|---|

**877-330-5900 • Support Sock Shop**　　　　**SupportSockShop.com**

With a proud declaration, the likes of which you probably never thought you would hear, this site claims to offer "the crème de la crème of compression hosiery." With such a statement, one is forced to expect a lot, and if you're already familiar with the better brand names of support hosiery you might not be disappointed. The rest of us, though, tend to wish the Products page of this site wasn't organized by manufacturer, and may benefit most from the Search option, which at least allows you to narrow things down by key word and price range. If you haven't something specific in mind, this can be a confounding experience.

| ·UNDERWEAR | ·FITNESS | | |
|---|---|---|---|

**410-358-0116 • Tummies Maternity**　　　　**TummiesMaternity.com**

Founded on the earnest desire for maternity apparel that was both fashionable and yet reserved, the Baltimore brick-and-mortar store behind this site had such great word-of-mouth that a web presence was actually requested by potential customers. It's little wonder, as the shop brings together the "modest" designs of some of the better maternity labels out there, including Japanese Weekend, Duet Designs, Noppies and Mommy Chic. Career clothing is the ultimate focus, but some lovely evening wear and lingerie round everything out nicely, so to speak.

| ·EVENING WEAR ·SWIMWEAR | ·CASUAL WEAR ·BEAUTY | ·UNDERWEAR ·SPECIALTY SIZES | ·CAREER DRESS ·DESIGNER |
|---|---|---|---|

**626-308-3626 • Zoee Maternity**　　　　**ZoeeMaternity.com**

The designer of this line for expecting mothers was looking to create clothes that she would wear "even if she wasn't pregnant." The result is a catalog of very stylish maternity apparel in seasonal designs intended to evoke "the essence of modernism and sophistication." Don't think of it as clothing meant to conceal the physics of impending motherhood, though; if anything it's the opposite. The site sums it up best: "Accentuate your belly. Proudly reveal your newfound figure. Celebrate your pregnancy in style."

| ·EVENING WEAR | ·CASUAL WEAR | ·CAREER DRESS | ·DESIGNER |
|---|---|---|---|

NOTES:

# Men's Apparel

Used to be, the most pressing clothing issue for a guy was whether to go with a zipper or button fly. Still an important distinction, men are however starting to get the hang of the whole fashion thing, even if the style in question is tantamount to jeans and a T-shirt. Of course, we're talking about the weekend. Workdays are an altogether different matter, whether you're dressing for business, business casual or coveralls. Then there are nights out, special occasions, clubs and dates. It's at this point that it starts to get complicated, and men tend to want none of it, willing to settle for the sweaters and ties given as gifts by grandmothers and aunts. After all, why bother with crowded shopping malls, the scrambling for open parking spaces and the undefendable smells of the food courts? Who wants to suffer the aggressive attentions of a commissioned sales staff or, conversely, the inattentiveness of a noncommissioned one? Heck, a married man is quite possibly only there to try on clothes his wife picks out, allowing her to make the decisions while he silently navigates the quickest possible route home in his head, hoping to make it back in time for kick-off.

All right, these are stereotypes; some guys truly love to shop, even take pleasure out of crafting a style. They don't mind wading through store after store when they could be on the sofa, watching the game. In fact, they revel in the selection. The web reconciles both perspectives, possessing everything from tuxedoes and blue jeans to polo shirts and boxer shorts. Better yet, with these sites you can quickly assemble a wardrobe befitting any mood or social obligation, with no more effort than a web browsing session. Which leaves the rest of your time open for important things, like sports and electronics.

NOTES:

_____

_____

_____

_____

_____

_____

_____

_____

_____

_____

_____

_____

_____

_____

_____

_____

_____

# TIPS ON BUYING MEN'S APPAREL ONLINE

These suggestions may help prevent frustration and improper fit.

•ORDERING REGULAR SIZES:  Most of us know our sizes for familiar brands, but many clothing lines have differing views on what constitutes a Large, Medium, Small, etc.  When in doubt, look for the manufacturer's site to find a size/measurements chart, or call the customer service number.

•ORDERING SUITS & DRESS SHIRTS:  Purchasing a suit online may oftentimes save you a bit of money, but as standard sizes for such apparel can be unforgiving, most will require additional tailoring, so you'll still have to take them into a local shop for a fitting (some sites offer custom tailoring at the time you order—see the icon legend).

•ORDERING CUSTOM ATTIRE:  Custom tailoring is a great option once you've ascertained your personal measurements (this may most easily be done by a professional tailor, or see the site listed below).  However, once a retailer has put in the time and effort of altering apparel, it's not likely to offer refunds if you're unsatisfied with the items in question.  Before committing to an order, be sure to note the site's return policies with regard to tailored clothing.

# SITES THAT MAY COME IN HANDY

The following URLs may be useful when you shop.

Men's Size Chart: http://www.fibergypsy.com/common/men.shtml
European Clothing Size Chart: http://www.onlineconversion.com/mens_clothing.htm
Taking Measurements for Suits: http://www.bakerprecision.com/measure.htm
How to Tie a Tie:  http://www.tieanecktie.com
Men's Fashion Articles: http://www.askmen.com/fashion/index.html
Formal Attire Glossary of Terms: http://www.sarnotux.com/glossary.asp
A Simple Guide to Buying a Suit: http://www.soyouwanna.com/site/syws/menssuit/menssuit.html#para1.1

>>

## SECTION ICON LEGEND

Use the following guide to understand the rectangular icons that appear throughout this section.

### CUSTOM TAILORING

Any time clothes may be cut to your measurements through an online order, this icon will appear to let you know.

### PROFESSIONAL ATTIRE

Not all as boring as it sounds, this icon highlights a variety of suits and components to a workplace wardrobe, ranging from the fashionable to the functional.

### SPECIALTY SIZES

Bigger, taller and shorter men will be able to find better fits at stores tagged by this icon.

### UNDERWEAR

The perennial question, "Boxers or Briefs?" may be answered with a simple click ... unless you order boxer-briefs.

## >> LIST OF KEY WORDS

The following words represent the types of items typically found on the sites listed in this section.

**ATHLETIC**

A lot of athletic apparel may be found in the Sports & Outdoors section, but this key word can point you to anything from athletic supporters to warm-up suits.

**CASUAL**

In many ways, the word "casual" has become synonymous with "cool." Not always, though. A lot of these clothes are just simple and comfortable.

**DESIGNER**

Whether casual, professional or formal, if the clothes were created with a specific fashionable season in mind, they're pretty much designer.

**FORMAL**

Mostly tuxedoes, this attire will usually sit in your closet, only to resurface on occasion to make you look fine.

**OUTERWEAR**

Trench coats, bomber jackets, windbreakers, rain gear and so on, this stuff protects you from the elements when walls can't.

**SOCKS**

As self-explanatory as a key word can get, yours may have holes in them; have you checked?

**STREETWEAR**

A little tougher to explain than most of these key words, we generally mean Streetwear to be somewhere between designer and casual; stuff that looks a little better than what you watch TV in, but not overpriced.

**SUITS**

The difference between this and Professional Attire is mostly in the attitude. Sure, many suits are fine for work … others are just too cool. Either full suits or specific pieces.

**SWIMSUITS**

Because we try never to jump into water with our pants on, we need a bathing suit.

**VINTAGE**

Not just old threads, these clothes typically consist of classic old threads.

## >> KEY WORD INDEX

Use the following lists to locate online retailers that sell the Men's Apparel you seek.

### ATHLETIC

AbercrombieAndFitch.com
AE.com
APC.fr
Audace.com
BigDog.com
BigTallDirect.com
BowlingShirt.com
CasualMale.com
Daddyos.com
DrJays.com
Everlast.com
InternationalMale.com
Kaufmans.com
KingSizeDirect.com
OneHanesPlace.com
PacSun.com
SauvageWear.com
ShortSizesInc.com
UnderGear.com
UniversalGear.com
Wickers.com

### CASUAL

AbercrombieAndFitch.com
AE.com
AmericanFit.com
APC.fr
ArmaniExchange.com
AWear.com
Bachrach.com
BananaRepublic.com
BenSilver.com
BigDogs.com
BigGuys.com
BigTallDirect.com
BillsKhakis.com
BowlingShirt.com
Buckle.com
CasualMale.com
Daddyos.com
DenimExpress.com

DrJays.com
Fabric8.com
Gap.com
GirbaudOnline.com
Guess.com
GuyShop.com
HotTopic.com
IC3D.com
InternationalMale.com
Izod.com
JCrew.com
JohnSmedley.com
JosBank.com
KarmaLoop.com
Kaufmans.com
KennethCole.com
KingSizeDirect.com
LuckyBrandJeans.com
MarkShale.com
McCulleys.com
NPeal.com
OldNavy.com
PacSun.com
PeruvianConnection.com
Polo.com
ShortSizesInc.com
T-Shirts.com
UnderGear.com
UniversalGear.com
Urbanix.com
URBN.com
XLarge.com

### DESIGNER

APC.fr
ArmaniExchange.com
DiscountDesignerMensWear.com
GirbaudOnline.com
GuyShop.com
MauriceMaloneUSA.com
UniversalGear.com
Urbanix.com

### FORMAL

AscotChang.com
Bachrach.com
BenSilver.com
Bernini.com
BrooksBrothers.com
CTShirts.co.uk
DiscountDesignerMensWear.com
HickeyFreeman.com
JosBank.com
JPressOnline.com
Kaufmans.com
MensWearhouse.com
MyShirtMaker.com
ThomasPink.co.uk

### OUTERWEAR

AbercrombieAndFitch.com
AE.com
AllJacketsAllTheTime.com
ArmaniExchange.com
Bachrach.com
BananaRepublic.com
BigDog.com
BigTallDirect.com
BrooksBrothers.com
CasualMale.com
Danier.com
DiscountDesignerMens
  Wear.com
DrJays.com
Fabric8.com
Gap.com
Guess.com
HickeyFreeman.com
InternationalMale.com
Izod.com
JCrew.com
JosBank.com
Kaufmans.com
KingSizeDirect.com
OldNavy.com

PaulFrederick.com
Polo.com
ShortSizesInc.com
UnderGear.com
Urbanix.com
URBN.com
WilsonLeather.com
XLarge.com

### SOCKS

AE.com
Audace.com
Bachrach.com
BananaRepublic.com
BenSilver.com
BigGuys.com
BigTallDirect.com
BrooksBrothers.com
CasualMale.com
FreshPair.com
Gap.com
GuyShop.com
InternationalMale.com
JCrew.com
JosBank.com
JPressOnline.com
Kaufmans.com
KingSizeDirect.com
MarkShale.com
MensWearhouse.com
OldNavy.com
OneHanesPlace.com
Polo.com
ShortSizesInc.com
ThomasPink.co.uk
UniversalGear.com

### STREETWEAR

ArmaniExchange.com
AWear.com
Daddyos.com
DrJays.com

Fabric8.com
GirbaudOnline.com
GuyShop.com
HotTopic.com
InternationalMale.com
KarmaLoop.com
KennethCole.com
MauriceMaloneUSA.com
PacSun.com
UnderGear.com
UniversalGear.com
Urbanix.com
URBN.com
WilsonLeather.com
XLarge.com
ZootSuitStore.com

## SUITS

AmericanFit.com
AscotChang.com
AWear.com
Bachrach.com
BananaRepublic.com
BenSilver.com
Bernini.com
BigGuys.com
BigTallDirect.com
BrooksBrothers.com
CasualMale.com
DiscountDesignerMensWear.com
HickeyFreeman.com
InternationalMale.com
JosBank.com
JPressOnline.com
Kaufmans.com
KennethCole.com
KingSizeDirect.com
MarkShale.com
MauriceMaloneUSA.com
MensWearhouse.com
MyShirtMaker.com
PaulFrederick.com
ShirtCreations.com
ShortSizesInc.com
ThomasPink.co.uk
Ties.com
ZootSuitStore.com

## SWIMSUITS

Audace.com
BigDogs.com
BigGuys.com
BigTallDirect.com
eBoxersOnline.com
Everlast.com
GuyShop.com
InternationalMale.com
Izod.com
JCrew.com
KingSizeDirect.com
MarkShale.com
OldNavy.com
PacSun.com
Polo.com
SauvageWear.com
UnderGear.com
UniversalGear.com
Vilebrequin.com

## UNDERWEAR

AbercrombieAndFitch.com
AE.com
Audace.com
Bachrach.com
BananaRepublic.com
BenSilver.com
BigDogs.com
BigGuys.com
BigTallDirect.com
BrooksBrothers.com
CityBoxers.com
DrJays.com
eBoxers.com
FreshPair.com
Gap.com
GuyShop.com
InternationalMale.com
JCrew.com
JosBank.com
JPressOnline.com
Kaufmans.com
KingSizeDirect.com
LuckyBrandJeans.com
MauriceMaloneUSA.com
MensWearhouse.com
OldNavy.com
OneHanesPlace.com
Polo.com

SauvageWear.com
ShortSizesInc.com
ThomasPink.co.uk
TopDrawers.com
Uglies.com
Undergear.com
UniversalGear.com
WebUndies.com
Wickers.com

## VINTAGE

BowlingShirt.com
Daddyos.com
FashionDig.com
ZootSuitStore.com

## AbercrombieAndFitch.com

Abercrombie & Fitch • 888-856-4480

Known today primarily for their enormously popular prep-school attire, it's hard to imagine that the Abercrombie & Fitch catalog at one time sold hunting and fishing gear, as well as other such outdoor equipment. In fact, they outfitted Teddy Roosevelt's voyages to Africa and the Amazon, as well as Robert Peary's expedition to the North Pole. To highlight their rugged catalog, their old Fifth Ave. store in NYC featured a log cabin penthouse and a basement shooting range. Of course, that version of the store went bankrupt in the 1970s, leaving rise to their new product line, which can be seen here on the backs of ceaselessly cavorting models. This is a far cry from the masculine glory days of old, to be sure, but girls seem to dig it.

| ·CASUAL | ·OUTERWEAR | ·ATHLETIC | ·UNDERWEAR |
|---|---|---|---|

## AE.com

American Eagle Outfitters • 888-232-4535

As distinctly American as the name would have you believe, this catalog offers a rather down-to-earth collection of clothes for the casual dresser who's got nothing to prove, beginning with sweats and extending to jeans and flannel shirts. Hovering in that suburban gray area between rocker and athlete, none of this stuff is stylish, per se, but neither is it pretentious or overly flashy. Same goes for the prices, which could almost be used as a reference for what simple attire costs these days. Pretty easy to shop from if the pages loaded quicker, a guy's guy will ultimately find this one refreshing.

| ·CASUAL ·UNDERWEAR | ·SOCKS | ·OUTERWEAR | ·ATHLETIC |
|---|---|---|---|

## AllJacketsAllTheTime.com

AllJacketsAllTheTime.com • 800-434-4729

In case the domain name doesn't sink in, a few words on this home page reaffirm that here it's "Jackets. Nothing But Jackets." Yes, that would be leather jackets, bomber jackets, varsity jackets, fleeces and traditional raincoats, for starters. Browsing is quite simple once you decide what you're after and the looks are pretty good, surprisingly, as the site doesn't look all that great. But, hey: what you don't pay for in terms of aesthetic appeal, you don't charge your customers for either. At least, one would hope so.

| ·OUTERWEAR | | | |
|---|---|---|---|

## AmericanFit.com

AmericanFit.com • 201-653-9466

Call us suckers for custom-fit clothing, but we just dig the fact that the internet has brought down the price and availability of tailoring. When we last checked, this site's Men section stuck strictly to pants and shorts—frankly, the custom leather pants would be enough. It's not entirely simple, but the toughest part will probably be taking your own measurements, though you can opt out of that by simply sticking to the perfect waist and inseam, or by measuring a pair of pants you already own and like (their Copy Cat feature). This may even be better than trying stuff on in the store.

| ·SUITS | ·CASUAL | | |
|---|---|---|---|

## 212-966-0069 • A.P.C.

### APC.fr

Only the French could come up with a selection of sleek designer sportswear as desirable as this and make it so difficult to purchase online. You're better off staying away from the Flash version of the site (even our crack consultants couldn't figure it out), and then constantly bear in mind that "Ajouter" means "Add"; in this case you'll be adding to the shopping cart, which isn't specifically called a "shopping cart," but looks like one at least. Your reward will be fine quality clothes as, once again, only the French could muster.

| ·CASUAL | ·DESIGNER | ·ATHLETIC | |
|---|---|---|---|

## 800-717-2929 • Armani Exchange

### ArmaniExchange.com

Let's get something straight right away: this is not a place to shop for finely tailored suits. See, Giorgio Armani isn't so one-sided as his designer suit and couture lines would indicate. Here, he wants you to know that he's down with the young, urban crowd by offering a selection of street-savvy clothes for characters like the Indie Informer, or the Versed Visionare (examples of different schemes available from this A|X brand). To give him credit, these clothes are pretty cool, and nowhere near as expensive as one would expect. Ironically, Armani may have taken fashion up a notch, by taking it down a peg or two.

| ·CASUAL | ·OUTERWEAR | ·DESIGNER | ·STREETWEAR |
|---|---|---|---|

## 310-550-1339 • Ascot Chang

### AscotChang.com

"Some men feel a shirt is just a shirt. This isn't a shirt catalog for them." As if to prove the point, this may be the single most complicated shopping experience on the web, and unless you are absolutely determined to have one of these finest-in-the-world shirts, search elsewhere. If you are intent, here's what you do: first, look in Products, following the right-hand arrows (>) until you see a fabric you like (important: write down the fabric code). Then, study the confusing How To Order diagram, get familiar with your body (tape measure), and tackle the Online Order Form, which will take up the rest of your day.

| ·FORMAL | ·SUITS | | |
|---|---|---|---|

## 888-522-7502 • Audace

### Audace.com

In the world of men's underwear, this online shop serves as an equitable answer to Victoria's Secret—scratch that; it's the men's answer to Frederick's of Hollywood. That's right, in this world it's men who are treated like pieces of meat and, depending on your sensibilities, the detailed images found here may be enough to make you swear off thongs forever. Still, so far as swimsuits and underwear are concerned, you'd be hard-pressed to find a more thorough selection of racy wares. The occasional coding problems may stump you on this site, but once encountered they are easy to avoid.

| ·SOCKS | ·ATHLETIC | ·SWIMSUITS | ·UNDERWEAR |
|---|---|---|---|

## AWear.com
A-Wear • 604-685-9327

To understand A-Wear's concept of "conscious clothing," you need only to consider their term "a-wear-ness." Yes, they seek to enlighten the fashionable with a global understanding of how style fits in with politics, entertainment and commerce ... or something like that. There's an online magazine, and some other stuff that makes the site seem a bit confusing. We'd recommend heading straight for the Catalog, where you can browse some fairly slick shirts, pants, jackets and suits. There's not a lot to sort through, but it's really cool, and it's listed in Canadian dollars. That means this stuff is even cheaper than it looks, making it one of the best deals on the web.

| ·CASUAL | ·STREETWEAR | ·SUITS | |
|---|---|---|---|

## Bachrach.com
Bachrach • 800-222-4722

For casual wear and business attire alike, this clothing line offers mostly standard fare, with the occasional bit of flair thrown in for effect. At least, you can count on it being in there, somewhere. The thing is, each clothing category offers a featured item or two, and then lists the rest of your choices in text form. While these links offer some pretty good looks at this stuff, it's kind of a pain in the ass to filter through them all, so you'd do well to have a particular item of clothing in mind before you try. Better yet, if you like what you see, just Request a Catalog.

| ·FORMAL ·OUTERWEAR | ·SUITS ·UNDERWEAR | ·CASUAL | ·SOCKS |
|---|---|---|---|

## BananaRepublic.com
Banana Republic • 888-277-8953

You might know Banana Republic as that store in the mall that's always teeming with attractive young women. Well, that's because it's pretty damn near impossible to look bad in these clothes, named for the "safari-inspired" collection the store originally sold back in the late 1970s. Lamentably, their safari days have long since been forsaken in favor of the simple, metropolitan styles that have driven their brand to extraordinary franchise success. While this success may result in the crowding of our urban centers by identically clad consumer masses, clamoring for more crew neck sweaters, stretch-wool pants and ribbed tees, the truth is these clothes may be worth it.

| ·SUITS ·UNDERWEAR | ·CASUAL | ·SOCKS | ·OUTERWEAR |
|---|---|---|---|

## BenSilver.com
Ben Silver • 800-221-4671

London, England, and Charleston, South Carolina, have an unlikely association with this tailor/retailer of fine shirts and suits that calls both cities home. Essentially, this stuff has the class to fit both old English and Southern societies, right down to the umbrellas, evening sticks and pocket squares (aka handkerchiefs). Of course, primarily you'll need to shop the selection of shirts, blazers, suits and tuxedoes to make those accessories work. Here you can find all such timeless looks made from modern fabrics.

| ·FORMAL ·UNDERWEAR | ·SUITS | ·CASUAL | ·SOCKS |
|---|---|---|---|

**No Service Number • Bernini**

**Bernini.com**

If you're looking for a known quantity of fashionable Italian menswear, Bernini is virtually guaranteed to hook you up with some elegant threads, in country. Follow the Men's Clothing link to view their selection of tuxedoes, suits, vested suits, blazers and sports coats, each of which is fairly limited in scope, but high in style. It's all pretty simple, none too awe-inspiring on the technical side of things, but this may just be due to the fact that these guys are way more interested in clothes than they are in the internet.

| ·FORMAL | ·SUITS | | |  |

---

**800-642-3647 • Big Dogs**

**BigDogs.com**

Welcome to the official company store of the clothing line that has taken its St. Bernard logo beyond all logical extensions. This one's immediately good for a laugh—we encountered a family of dogs wearing sweatpants and fleeces. But then, once we settled down it turns out that you can find some great deals on simple sportswear, flannel boxers, outerwear and pajamas. This is a far cry from anything you'll see even within miles from designer runways, but this is a family-oriented brand meant for family-oriented individuals. Besides, your kids never care what you're wearing.

| ·CASUAL ·UNDERWEAR | ·SWIMSUITS | ·ATHLETIC | ·OUTERWEAR | |

---

**909-984-8648 • BigGuys.com**

**BigGuys.com**

Behind the proclamation "Size Really Does Matter," this site caters to the heftier among us with a scant but sizable selection of work, dress and casual wear. Keeping jeans from being hard to find, and shirts from being hard to button, affordability is truly the greatest asset here, with prices low enough to warrant just buying everything in sight. There's a little, rather a big, bit of everything to be found here, from suspenders and belts to keep your pants on when you're slimming down and button extenders to keep your shirt from choking you when you slim back up. Here, it's easy either way.

| ·CASUALS ·SUITS | ·SOCKS | ·SWIMSUITS | ·UNDERWEAR | |

---

**800-214-9686 • BigTallDirect.com**

**BigTallDirect.com**

Not just Hawaiian shirts and jumpsuits, though you can find these here, this is a clothing retailer specifically aimed to the man of great girth, height or, as is often the case, both. The only thing below average here is the site's design, though our chief complaint is merely that it lacks imagination and seems hastily assembled. We won't offer too much criticism as quick, easy shopping is possible due to the complete but limited variety of banded bottom shirts, extra-wide socks and a host of wardrobe basics available. This one's all but imperative if you answer to the name "Big Guy."

| ·SUITS ·ATHLETIC | ·CASUAL ·SWIMSUITS | ·SOCKS ·UNDERWEAR | ·OUTERWEAR | |

## BillsKhakis.com

Bills Khakis • 800-435-4254

The of origin of khakis may be traced back a couple hundred years to India, where colonial British soldiers, finding it nearly impossible to keep their white uniforms clean in an unfamiliar environment, took to dyeing them with tea. Who would have thought that this fussiness would breed a whole genre of clothing? Not Bill, founder of this company. His was simply a quest for sturdy, quality khaki trousers, and one that blossomed into this all-tan-all-the-time clothing label. No, you won't find a lot of variety for your wardrobe, but you'll certainly have brown covered once you've shopped here. Oh, and it's all pretty good, too.

| •CASUAL | | | |
|---|---|---|---|

## BowlingShirt.com

BowlingShirt.com • 800-444-1685

Just as you would imagine, this shop has a bowling shirt for you. Its selection runs deep and wide, with some classic looks mixed up with your odd, fun styles. Sections like the Baddabing Mafia Store, Beer Bowl-O-Matic, Vegas Baby Vegas and Nightclub Fashions will turn you on to some of the less predictable fare, while Hawaiian Paradise tends to speak for itself. Hey, you know that bowling shirts can be just as fashionable outside the lanes as in; you just happen to like bowling a lot is all.

| | •CASUAL | •VINTAGE | •ATHLETIC | |
|---|---|---|---|---|

## BrooksBrothers.com

Brooks Brothers • 800-274-1815

Bearing the dubious distinction of having designed the coat Abe Lincoln was wearing when he was assassinated, Brooks Brothers has been around for a long, long time; since 1818 in fact. Their staying power can only be attributed to the exceedingly high quality of their clothes—the term "finely tailored" doesn't seem to do them justice. From sporty shirts to formal suits, and even some socks and underwear, this brand has been a favorite of such far-reaching individuals as studly actor Clark Gable, boxer Jack Dempsey, pilot Charles Lindbergh and beat author Jack Kerouac. Still, it doesn't take a president, or even a cultural icon, to know that you simply cannot go wrong with these clothes.

| | | •FORMAL •UNDERWEAR | •SUITS | •SOCKS | •OUTERWEAR |
|---|---|---|---|---|---|

## Buckle.com

Buckle • 800-522-8090

What you will find here is denim, some T-shirts, shorts, boxers, khakis and cargo pants. Basically, the kind of clothes you can kick around in, the stuff you'd like to be wearing all the time, if anyone cared to ask. Since this site focuses on jeans, they make it really simple for you to find some in your size, or by a particular fit (wide leg, baggy, bootleg, etc.) or brand. This is key, as none of us really want to spend all day shopping for clothes we intend to destroy slowly with a lifestyle of bruising activity and/or couch sitting.

| •CASUAL | | | |
|---|---|---|---|

## 800-767-0319 • Casual Male

**CasualMale.com**

Big and tall shops never look this good, and rarely do they have this much to choose from. Yet, here we are, face to face with a store that allows larger men to savor such things as selection and style. Sure, some of these sections are lacking (most notably sweater vests), but by and large there's variety, and in nearly every case it's easy to browse, good to look at, comes in multiple colors and is fantastically inexpensive. It may be the best extra-large size shop online for the casual, or even dressier, male.

| ·SUITS ·ATHLETIC | ·CASUAL | ·SOCKS | ·OUTERWEAR |
|---|---|---|---|

## No Service Number • City Boxers

**CityBoxers.com**

These guys tell you right away that they're in the business of "Selling the World's Finest Quality Boxer Shorts." With plaids and prints in flannel and chambray, these designs come with underwear-of-the-future sounding model names like the Series 6000, or the presumably more advanced Series 7000. The Swatches page offers a glimpse of everything they have to offer, but begs the question: if these are the finest quality boxer shorts the world has to offer, how come there aren't any available in silk?

| ·UNDERWEAR | | | |
|---|---|---|---|

## 866-797-2701 • Charles Tyrwhitt

**CTShirts.co.uk**

Pronounced "Tirit," this clothier claims to be "England's largest maker of quality shirts through the internet and mail order." It's simple; they sell high-quality button-down collared shirts. You can shop by colors, or by deviations in style (cut-away collars, stripes and special weaves, for example), and one handy feature even allows you to change the sizing and pricing to USA standards. They also offer 3-D views of several shirts, but it's really kind of a laughable feature, as you'll learn next to nothing after wasting time downloading software. See, the great thing about a specialty site like this is that you can get in, get out, and know that in 7-10 days you'll get a dapper shirt in the mail (that's Brit-speak for "stylish").

| ·FORMAL | | | |
|---|---|---|---|

## 888-900-1950 • Daddy-O's

**Daddyos.com**

Where does this store, "where the coolest get their coolness" find inspiration? Well, for the answer we'd have to refer you to the most fashionably dressed of all athletes. That's right: bowlers. No, we haven't gone loco. This site caters to the swingin' hepcats of any community, and it just so happens that the bulk of this coolish catalog is made up of bowling shirts, and pretty cool ones at that. Some feature slogans like "The Lucky Strikes" or "Bowl-A-Rama!" Others have buttons illustrated with pin-up girls. This is timeless hipster attire, and it looks good on everybody.

| ·CASUAL | ·VINTAGE | ·ATHLETIC | ·STREETWEAR |
|---|---|---|---|

## Danier.com

Leather, leather, leather. There's not a whole lot of it here, but it's all you will find, and it's all you will care about once you've perused the selection. Consisting of trench coats, blazers, jackets, bombers and even some pants (for the brave), this selection is not likely to go out of style anytime soon, and if it does you have only to wait a season before it comes back. Sure, some will protest that you're wearing the skin of an animal. Turns out, this is true, and a cow had to die to give you that great jacket. But if you've enjoyed a steak lately, look at it as if you've now made use of more than one part of the animal.

| ·OUTERWEAR | | | |
|---|---|---|---|

## DenimExpress.com

Want jeans, easy and cheap and in your size? This shop is incredible in accomplishing these things with a very simple design and low shipping costs. Represented are Levi's, Lee, Calvin Klein, Polo, Dockers and Carhartt brands (this last one's good for both style and price, if you're willing to try new things). Simply pick a brand, locate a specific style and/or fit (relaxed, straight-leg, etc.), pick your size from a list (apparently a 31" inseam doesn't exist, much to the chagrin of this writer), select a color (or wash) and go.

| ·CASUAL | | | |
|---|---|---|---|

## DiscountDesignerMensWear.com

Whenever you see the words "discount" and "designer" next to each other you may be certain of one thing: somebody, somewhere is cutting costs. Well, the obvious answer with this site is that the retailer skimped on its web design, as it looks just shy of atrocious and operates like a small dog trying to carry a big stick. Still, we're all suckers for a bargain, and in most cases that is exactly what you will find here. More precisely, you will find low-priced Ralph Lauren, Oleg Cassini and Nino Cardi suits and tuxedoes.

| ·FORMAL | ·SUITS | ·OUTERWEAR | ·DESIGNER |
|---|---|---|---|

## DrJays.com

This urban streetwear retailer started in the South Bronx in 1975, which, as they point out, was about the same time that Hip Hop developed in the same part of town. Like many urban streets, traffic is slow on this site, and we encountered several scripting errors that made shopping a hassle from time to time. Generally, though, it all works out, and you'll be able to find some fresh new brands, as well as some metropolitan mainstays. It's a good place to update your gear, and comes complete with a strange combination of slang and corporate-speak: definitely something to behold.

| ·CASUAL ·UNDERWEAR | ·OUTERWEAR | ·STREETWEAR | ·ATHLETIC |
|---|---|---|---|

## 866-326-9377 • eBoxers

### eBoxersOnline.com

Odds are high that this site is not what you'd expect. Yes, there are boxers here, but they will only turn up once you've sorted through some of the silk thongs and erotic underwear. Loungewear and swimsuits round out the selection on this site that is usually more hilarious than it is provocative (whatever your sensibilities, you will no doubt get a laugh in the Ties section). In regard to less-entertaining issues, the site is well-put together and quite simple to use, with product details that go above and beyond the call of duty.

| ·SWIMSUITS | ·UNDERWEAR | | |  |

## 800-777-0313 • Everlast

### Everlast.com

From the guys who make shorts for pro boxers (not to be confused with boxer shorts) comes this site of men and women's athletic apparel. Alternating between offering comfort and support, you can rest assured that these clothes will taking a beating (here's hoping you don't), whether they happen to be spandex shorts, a bathing suit or a ribbed cotton tank. Either way, expect the Everlast logo to be prominently featured somewhere on the clothes, presumably so other people will know just how tough you are.

| ·ATHLETIC | ·SWIMSUITS | | |

## 888-554-4321 • Fabric8

### Fabric8.com

Here's where the freaky turn to find "Crafty Street Couture" and sundry urban attire of "Independent Design." You may end up wondering just what they've been smoking, but if you're planning to go for the type of night out that recommends earplugs and requires booty-shaking, these funky fashions will get you there in style. You'll find several options for browsing, but all lead you to the same silly model photographs and cheeky product descriptions that show consistently how these guys put fun first.

| ·CASUAL | ·OUTERWEAR | ·STREETWEAR | |

## 866-327-4344 • FashionDig

### FashionDig.com

This vintage clothing site devoted to "Exploring 20th Century Style" really doesn't have a lot to offer to a man, as females clearly make up its primary target demographic. However, if you can find the Haberdashery section (try the Shopping Mall link if you don't see it under the Shopping pull-down menu) you will find one of the best selections of men's vintage wear online. Granted, it's tiny, and each item is only available in one size, which means we are more often out of luck than not. However, this site warrants a bookmark as frequent return visits will eventually turn up the perfect fit.

| ·VINTAGE | | | |

# FreshPair.com

With a name meant to remind you that maybe you're running out of days, this site almost makes you want to log on immediately to order some new underwear for overnight delivery. Well, poor planners can do that, as there're plenty of choices here to suit any typical guy's undergarment needs; and get some socks, tees and pajamas while you're at it. Surprisingly well made, with great looks given that almost nobody else will ever see these sub-dud duds, this winning site even has a range of Big & Tall sizes, so as to avoid any constriction in the nether regions. We like to kid, but this one's done right.

# Gap.com

"Welcome to the Gap!" bellows the greeter, like a sentry on duty, the second your foot inches across the threshold that distinguishes you from being just another mall citizen, or a potential Gap shopper. If you've been there, you know the best reason to actually go inside is that you can instantly find the simplest of basic T-shirts, pants, boxers, scarves and whatever, conveniently broken down into the standard sizes, neatly folded and on display so you can pick your preferred color and get the heck out of there before the sales clerk tries to talk you into buying a leather weave belt. Well, all that stuff applies to this site, only you don't even have to get anywhere near the mall to find it.

# GirbaudOnline.com

Just because it's casual doesn't mean it needs to be shoveling-dirt casual. At least, so seems to be the theory behind these designs of Marithé and François Girbaud. The basic attire you'll find here is so elemental, so simple, that the average person will balk at the sticker price and move on. You may want to yourself. But amidst these pants, shirts, sweaters and jackets are items with just enough precision and charm to warrant closer inspection, and this very detail-oriented site accommodates with exquisite looks. You may still leave without buying anything, but your standards may go up in the process.

# Guess.com

You'll probably remember Guess as the brand whose advertisements introduced Claudia Schiffer, Kim Smith and Laetitia Casta to the world. What you may not realize is that Guess makes clothes, and not just for women, either. You can find some pretty cool denim and leather designs here: shirts, pants and jackets mostly. Their catalog is always updated with new, seasonal designs and, as their online selection isn't terribly big, it's no trouble keeping track of it all. If you do find something you like, take heart in the fact that, in your own small way, you've contributed to the rise of the next Guess supermodel.

## 888-450-7467 • Guyshop
**GuyShop.com**

Like its counterpart, GirlShop, this store gathers a collection of hip New York City boutiques, offering a slew of "hard-to-find stuff that you won't see on everyone you know." Basically, this means a lot of hip clothes, made by hip designers you've never heard of, that people outside NYC will typically never see. Which is great, in terms of personal style... except it makes it hard to decide which boutique you'd like to browse through. Never mind, though, because their search function will grab whichever type of clothing (jacket, shirt, shoes, etc.) you want from all the boutiques, and even narrow it down by price range. The result will be a small sampling of cool clothes that are really easy to buy. Just remember: technically, you were never in a boutique.

| ·CASUAL ·SWIMSUITS | ·SOCKS ·UNDERWEAR | ·DESIGNER | ·STREETWEAR |
|---|---|---|---|

## 888-603-8968 • Hickey Freeman
**HickeyFreeman.com**

Founded with the intention of providing men with a clothing range somewhere between custom-tailored and ready-to-wear suits, Hickey Freeman does so by offering a predictably stalwart collection of high-quality clothes in more sizes than—actually, no. Truth is, the sizes aren't that variable, which means for some this will be ready-to-wear stuff, and for others it will require alterations. However, these garments are decently priced for the quality you'll get, so if you know a cheap tailor, or are married to one, it might all make sense in the end.

| ·FORMAL | ·SUITS | ·OUTERWEAR | |
|---|---|---|---|

## 800-892-8674 • Hot Topic
**HotTopic.com**

This one's for all the rockers out there. Actually, this mall shop turned online store should be able to satisfy the needs on any kind of club goer with its edgy apparel and kinky accessories. Punk, gothic, lounge, or dance—even if you're just into looking hip as you loiter in the streets—you can dress yourself here and still have enough cash left over to go to the show (just don't wear a band T-shirt to that band's show). If you missed the show, a big selection of band merchandise serves almost as well as actual memories.

| ·CASUAL | ·STREETWEAR | | |
|---|---|---|---|

## 212-279-8939 • IC3D.com
**IC3D.com**

If you've ever had a problem finding jeans that fit, grab a tape measure and log on to this site immediately. Here you can literally assemble your own pair of custom jeans; and not just blue denim, either. To start with, you have your choice of 13 different fabrics, including leather, camouflage, faux leather, suede, velvet, and two gauges of corduroy. From there, you have a choice of: several colors; different fits for your hips, legs and ankles; copper, brass or nickel rivets/buttons; zipper or button fly; several options for pockets and belt loops; and even the color of thread used to sew it all together. The only hard part is the 11 different measurements you must make of your lower body to order.

| ·CASUAL | | | |
|---|---|---|---|

## InternationalMale.com

International Male • 800-293-9333

For 25 years, now, these guys have "dedicated [their] efforts to creating a distinctive look for fashion-conscious men the world over." The result is a delightful collection of stuff like mesh shirts and thong bathing suits. Seriously, though, this site's prodigious catalog runs the gamut, from tank tops to trench coats, and even some, er, "shape enhancing" underwear. All right, so you may not look like the ripped and bulging models that show off all this gear, but then women have been suffering such body comparisons for years (see VictoriasSecret.com). Just keep reminding yourself: it's about the clothes.

| ·SUITS ·STREETWEAR | ·CASUAL ·ATHLETIC | ·SOCKS ·SWIMSUITS | ·OUTERWEAR ·UNDERWEAR |
|---|---|---|---|

## Izod.com

Izod • 800-365-2678

You've probably heard the urban myth about the baby alligators getting flushed into the sewers, where they eat rats and grow to great sizes, then terrifying the populace. Well, Izod's kind of like that. Rather, this brand, whose name was synonymous a couple of decades back with polo shirts sporting little alligator logos, is back, and bigger than before. By "bigger" we mean they still have polo shirts (though no alligators in sight) but have plenty of other shirts, trousers, sweaters and outerwear to go around. Somewhat perfect for somebody whose last passion for fashion took place in the way back when.

| ·CASUAL | ·SWIMSUITS | ·OUTERWEAR | |
|---|---|---|---|

## JCrew.com

J. Crew • 800-932-0043

Maybe you noticed those exuberant, self-satisfied smiles of J.Crew models while you were tearing apart an old catalog for use as kindling. Then, maybe if you managed to penetrate the upper echelons of the Rugby shirt and chino world, you'd be smiling too. The trick is to select the appropriate seasonal colors to match your hair and skin tones (they've plenty to choose from), while remembering to maintain an—ah, who are we kidding? These classically comfortable styles either suit you, or they don't. If they do, you can find suitable office attire, weekend kick-around clothes and even some decent underwear, all on a well-maintained site that's easy enough to follow. If they don't, then you probably stopped reading at the term, "seasonal colors."

| ·CASUAL ·OUTERWEAR | ·SOCKS | ·SWIMSUITS | ·UNDERWEAR |
|---|---|---|---|

## JohnSmedley.com

John Smedley • 011-44-162-953-4571

Oh, it must have been back in late 18th century Derbyshire when two businessmen, Smedley and Nightingale, inspired by the successes of Sir Richard Arkwright, determined to make sweaters in a garment factory located in the village of Lea. Oh, but isn't this how nearly all success stories begin? Funny as it is (just another reason to be charmed by the British), these are some great sweaters, whether you prefer cotton or wool, with just enough colors and styles to make it interesting, though not too many to cause a headache. Then, if a company's survived centuries on sweaters alone, they have to be good.

| ·CASUAL | | | |
|---|---|---|---|

**800-285-2265** • **Jos A. Bank**                                          **JosBank.com**

For nearly 100 years, Jos A. Bank has offered low prices on quality men's apparel, which they attribute to their practice of purchasing fabrics straight from the factories; but there's no need to concern yourself with all that. All you need to know is what you're looking for, whether it's a sports coat, trousers, business dress (corporate or casual) or a tux. Making it easier is their Suit Builder, which boasts "six simple steps to the perfect suit," and a similarly fashioned Shirt Builder that does it in five. You can also beef up your weekend wardrobe, and even your golf attire, though it will do nothing for your game.

| ·FORMAL ·OUTERWEAR | ·SUITS ·UNDERWEAR | ·CASUAL | ·SOCKS |
|---|---|---|---|

---

**212-687-7642** • **J. Press**                                          **JPressOnline.com**

Just look at the following statement and you'll know precisely whether or not this "premier line of gentlemen's haberdashery, furnishings and accessories" interests you: "Tradition, taste and an eye for the finest fabrics and tweeds available today, has allowed us to cater to a century of the most dignified clients a clothier has known." Essentially, Ivy Leaguers cannot do without such attire; the rest of us may do what we can to avoid it. Either way, the walking shorts, button-downs and ties here are quite easy to sift through, and not terribly difficult to buy.

| ·FORMAL | ·SUITS | ·SOCKS | ·UNDERWEAR |
|---|---|---|---|

---

**866-658-1902** • **Karmaloop**                                          **KarmaLoop.com**

Colorful and eclectic styles are bound to get attention, and when they combine comfort and function, well, that just gives you the best of everything. Most of the gear sold on this stimulating site is made to accommodate dancing into the night, or at least to facilitate movement from sidewalk to sidewalk, and all of it represents a young culture that is entirely wary of the limitless appeal of ever-changing styles. "Fresh" could be the only consistent description of these clothes that originate in the hip scenes of New York, San Francisco, Los Angeles and plenty of other cities.

| ·CASUAL | ·STREETWEAR | | |
|---|---|---|---|

---

**888-761-8255** • **Kaufman's**                                          **Kaufmans.com**

Founded by a sizable former football player, men of great dimensions can find properly sized attire on this store's site, whether they're outfitting for the workplace or the weekend sofa. Some formal attire and workout gear also creep their way in, as the store aims to fit a size of man more than a type. However, while the products are big, the selection is sort of small, so some men still won't enjoy what they see, no matter the size. Hopefully, as time goes by, the selection will expand—in terms of variety we mean.

| ·FORMAL ·OUTERWEAR | ·SUITS ·ATHLETIC | ·CASUAL ·UNDERWEAR | ·SOCKS |
|---|---|---|---|

# KennethCole.com

**Kenneth Cole Productions • 800-536-2653**

Kenneth Cole Productions started off making shoes, but they were so successful that expanding into regular apparel just made sense. Starting with leather, and continuing through some pretty chill casual and business attire (finally some suits with an air of style), this line is well suited to the art of lounging. Then, if you follow the Reaction Online link, you'll find a stash of more casual Kenneth Cole gear (think Miami) that runs off the same commerce engine, so you can shop back and forth without losing your order. Sure, we'd rather see all this stuff together, but both halves of this site make shopping for cool garb quite easy, so we're willing to let it slide.

| | ·CASUAL | ·STREETWEAR | ·SUITS | |
|---|---|---|---|---|

# KingSizeDirect.com

**King Size • 800-677-0249**

For the man who can't find anything in the puny sizes of "regular" stores, this site features your standard, everyday kinds of clothes in bigger, longer sizes. Still, this site is no panacea for the "king size man," as these sizes may still be limited in scope, depending on the selection. However, they do offer some tailoring services on request, so all is not wasted. Take it or leave it, these guys are going for a niche market, and if you happen to fit that market, it may prove worthwhile.

| | ·SUITS ·ATHLETIC | ·CASUAL ·SWIMSUITS | ·SOCKS ·UNDERWEAR | ·OUTERWEAR |
|---|---|---|---|---|

# LuckyBrandJeans.com

**Lucky Brand • 800-964-5777**

If you want jeans that'll stand up to your rugged lifestyle—whether it's the Casual Friday type of rugged or the regular kind—this is a good place to look first. There are a bunch of different blue jean options, including some that aren't blue, and a bunch of other sturdy shirts, jackets, sweats and boxers too. The best part is that the site's set up for the impatient shopper—just click on what you're looking for, find what you want, buy it and get back to the important stuff, like chewing on nails and gambling on sporting events.

| | ·CASUAL | ·UNDERWEAR | | |
|---|---|---|---|---|

# MarkShale.com

**Mark Shale • 888-333-6964**

Clean and simple style is what you can expect from this chic purveyor of mostly casual clothes. Now, if they could only make their website clean and simple. You can narrow down the selection to Men's Apparel, but beyond that the categories are unevenly dispersed, sometimes making their contents explicit, sometimes a little more difficult to fathom. Fortunately, there's not too much to sort through when all is said and done, so it's worth a quick browse to see if these wares are for you.

| | ·SUITS | ·CASUAL | ·SOCKS | ·SWIMSUITS |
|---|---|---|---|---|

## No Service Number • Maurice Malone

### MauriceMaloneUSA.com

Maurice Malone is a Detroit native who began his lately skyrocketing career in design by successfully crafting himself a hat that emulated one he couldn't afford to buy. Perhaps this is why he's been successful both in the high-fashion world and on the street. While his collections offer sometimes experimental, often daring lines of designer suits, the great bulk of his catalog here consists of the MaloneSports and MoJeans lines, both of which offer really cool clothes for any man on the make (especially his line of boxer shorts built with a special condom pocket).

| ·DESIGNER | ·STREETWEAR | ·UNDERWEAR | ·SUITS | |
|---|---|---|---|---|

## 800-527-4407 • McCulley's

### McCulleys.com

When approaching this "largest selection of Scottish Cashmere in the USA," try not to be overly frightened by its tagline: "An Investment in Clothing." After all, you must reserve some shock for when you delve into the site and see some of the sweaters priced up to $600 (and then some) in order to fully make it worth your while. To be fair, some of these are priced in the low hundreds, and the scarves chime in at barely a sawbuck. We would recommend, however, that you try to avoid checking the price of cashmere throws.

| ·CASUAL | | | | |
|---|---|---|---|---|

## 877-986-9669 • Men's Wearhouse

### MensWearhouse.com

Unlike most of the sites featured here, there's a good chance you know what the owner of this men's fashion retailer looks like, as he's regularly seen guaranteeing that "you'll like the way you look" on TV ads. He pops up around the site sometimes, whether you're looking at extremely formal (tuxedoes), casual attire (like sports coats) or the basic elements of professional dress (your daily suit)—but he's easier to ignore. The other best part of this shopping mechanism is that, in addition to simple categories like Dress Shirts and Big & Tall Sizes, you can shop By Occasion, which includes items selected for Job Interviews, Weddings and Semi-Formals.

| ·FORMAL | ·SUITS | ·SOCKS | ·UNDERWEAR | |
|---|---|---|---|---|

## 888-744-7897 • The Custom Shop

### MyShirtMaker.com

At times confusing, the intent here is to offer quality shirts for your business or formal suit, tailored to your own measurements. The truth is, unless you find a branch store near you to get a measurement by their staff, what's really available here is a bevy of dress shirts that size collars to the nearest quarter inch and collars to the nearest half. This actually works fairly well combined with choices in cuff style, fabric, collar style, pocket styles, sleeve placket buttons (or not), front styles, button colors and monogramming. Stopping just shy of personal tailoring, for the price this is about the closest you'll get to the perfect shirt.

| ·FORMAL | ·SUITS | | | |
|---|---|---|---|---|

## NPeal.com

N. Peal • 212-333-3500

What you may not know, but may want to be aware of, is that "N. Peal [is] synonymous with creative design in cashmere knitwear." This is probably due to the fact that their "in house designer works on creating a total image for a discerning fashion-conscious clientele." See, we would have merely stated that these guys offer a fair range of cashmere sweaters that are a bit pricey, but pretty slick, judging by the photos. Then again, we also lack a certain "new body awareness" in our designs.

| ·CASUAL | | | |
|---|---|---|---|

## OldNavy.com

Old Navy • 800-653-6289

If you've seen any of Old Navy's campy commercials, you know that this stuff is basic, colorful and easy to match. Basically, it's great, cheap casual wear for anyone who likes their shopping experience to take less time than an inning of baseball. Because these styles are so simple, any shirts and sweaters will mix easily with their extensive selection of pants (in hundreds of sizes), which should take the guesswork out of matching. This user-friendly site makes every step of your visit easy, so if you're willing to embrace that wacky Old Navy charm, nothing here will disappoint.

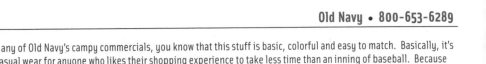

| ·CASUAL ·UNDERWEAR | ·SOCKS | ·OUTERWEAR | ·SWIMSUITS |
|---|---|---|---|

## OneHanesPlace.com

One Hanes Place • 800-671-1674

Once a catalog known as the "Family Showcase of Savings," this simple new visage offers a focus more on what we all (hopefully) wear under our clothes. Mostly popular national brands (Hanes and Champion, for example) dominate the web space here, in sock, brief and boxer form, though you may find some decent workout wear here as well. It's all relatively easy to find, and should prove an inexpensive way to stock up on a lot of basics, so you can focus your precious time buying clothes people will actually see.

| ·SOCKS | ·ATHLETIC | ·UNDERWEAR |
|---|---|---|

## PacSun.com

Pacific Sunwear • 877-372-2786

Making the decision to shop here requires the simplest of thought processes: if you're going to kick back at the beach, you might as well look the part. This shop offers surf- and skate-inspired clothes for doing just that: a bevy of board shorts, swim trunks, tank tops, T-shirts, hoodies and sweaters (for some post-sunset lounging) that trap pockets of sand in just the right way. These looks are more California beach than Mediterranean beach, the biggest distinction being that here you won't have to wade through any bikini briefs or thongs while you shop.

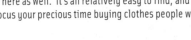

| ·CASUAL | ·STREETWEAR | ·ATHLETIC | ·SWIMSUITS |
|---|---|---|---|

**800-247-8162 • Paul Frederick**  **PaulFrederick.com**

The Paul Frederick line of clothes is known to be a quality set of dress attire, but don't you make the mistake of thinking these are stuffy clothes! Somehow, these guys have managed to blur the boundaries between professional and casual, with breezy designs which will have you looking and feeling more comfortable than anybody else in the office. Of course, the great benefit of this is that you can then easily make the transition into regular life, still looking sharp but with an air of indifference. It's nice to know style can transcend the restrictions imposed by the traditional suit and tie.

·SUITS    ·OUTERWEAR

**800-255-6429 • Peruvian Connection**  **PeruvianConnection.com**

From the mountains of South America comes the inspiration for this seasonal line of clothes that can add a dignified air to any outfit. Mostly cardigans, pullovers and sweater vests, there's not a whole lot here for a man to sort through, but that's part of its charm—in five minutes you'll know if any of these knits, with their sometimes funky patterns and always rich colors, are right for you. If so, break out your pipe and ascot, because you, sir, have achieved cultural refinement.

·CASUAL

**888-475-7674 • Polo**  **Polo.com**

Ralph Lauren's designs may never escape the descriptor, "preppy," but so far as prep attire goes, this may be about as stylish as it gets. Clean lines and simple combinations have become nearly as synonymous with his work as the little pony rider logo that appears throughout his catalog, and sure the ladies seem to like him too. Shopping's about as easy as a day of leisure on Martha's Vineyard, with just enough of a selection to make each category a worthy visit, be it Underwear or Dress Shirts.

·CASUAL        ·SOCKS        ·OUTERWEAR    ·SWIMSUITS
·UNDERWEAR

**858-514-8229 • Sauvage**  **SauvageWear.com**

If you would describe your fashion sense as conservative, you might want to skip this site altogether; these wares are racy as all get out. With plenty of what they describe as "exotic, cutting-edge swimwear," the watchword here is "confidence," as to wear these suits, T-shirts and even underwear is to attract the closest of scrutiny. If you happen to have the chiseled, well-balanced type of body exhibited by these models, you may feel right at home. Otherwise, well, the Women's section of this site is interesting too.

·ATHLETIC      ·SWIMSUITS     ·UNDERWEAR

## ShirtCreations.com

This great site offers a simple and inexpensive means of custom-ordering dress shirts. Begin by selecting a fabric/color (Cotton Striped Voiles or Blue Textured, for example), then move on to collar (including banded or wingtip), pockets (flat round, pleated square), cuffs (square, French) and several tiny details, all quite simple to select and extraordinarily well laid out. For an additional fee you can even enter your own custom measurements, ensuring that the shirt you order here will fit you in every possible way.

·SUITS

## ShortSizesInc.com

Standing in stark contrast to Big & Tall shops (literally and figuratively), here's a fairly mediocre store with a worthy mission: to furnish the man under 5'8" with clothes that fit without need of hem or belt. Except that in many cases the inseam is set, so hemming is required, and the shirts don't vary too much in size either, which may leave many of them looking baggy nonetheless. Bottom line is that while the prices are good and the clothes themselves just fine, this store comes close to servicing the diminutive male, but there's still a short way to go to be perfect.

| ·SUITS ·ATHLETIC | ·CASUAL ·UNDERWEAR | ·SOCKS | ·OUTERWEAR |

## T-Shirts.com

Sure, on this site you can find plenty of popular T-shirts, from popular music shirts to novelty selections (like the classic tuxedo print). But we want to point out the best part about this site: custom tees! Follow the Design Online link to simply Select a Shirt (from ringers and tanks to long sleeves and three-quarter sleeve baseball shirts) and pick a color. But it doesn't end there—you can upload the image of your choice to be printed, front and/or back, positioned by you, sized to your specifications. The whole process takes less than five minutes, and the only even remotely hard part is deciding on an image. Easier than choosing a tattoo though.

·CASUAL

## ThomasPink.co.uk

If you'd like a shirt of poplin or twill, like to know what the differences between the two are (hint: it depends on the warp and weft) or even to know just what the ballyhoo is going on here, anyway, take a look at this UK web site. Chiefly, they offer fine cotton shirts, in classic styles that are "unaffected by the vagaries of fashion." The four principal styles include Casual and Business Casual, with their Black Label collection falling just short of a formal evening line. All you have to do is look over to the right-hand side of the page to the shopping Menswear link, where you'll notice they sell some pretty spiffy ties and boxers as well. Prepare to look sharp.

| ·FORMAL | ·SUITS | ·SOCKS | ·UNDERWEAR |

**888-686-8437 • Ties.com**  **Ties.com**

Surprisingly enough, this site doesn't actually sell ties, but rather those plastic helmets that you can put beer cans into and drink from through straws. Of course, we're joking: these guys have hundreds of ties. With a humorous tone, they let you shop by tie color, designer, pattern, price or category (from Animal to Unusual). They even have directions on how to tie three different knots (including Half-Windsor). True to its name, this place will set you up, whether you want a solid, conservative color, or some kind of freaky cartoon character. Who'd of thought ties could be fun?

·SUITS

---

**No Service Number • TopDrawers.com**  **TopDrawers.com**

We're almost including this one just for its domain name's double meaning. As it turns out, they also offer a decent selection in all varieties of men's undergarment, with good pictures and easy shopping (assuming you have a somewhat decent connection speed). While their primary objective is to sell you quality underwear, whether you're a boxers or brief type of guy, or even of a thong ilk. With plenty of popular name brands and the occasional shape-enhancing pair of briefs (back or front), if nothing else this site will make you ponder the invigorating life of the underwear model.

·UNDERWEAR

---

**No Service Number • Uglies**  **Uglies.com**

If you've ever pondered the abundance of loud, unsightly patterns in the world of boxer short designs, you might just appreciate this brand that easily offers the ugliest of the ugly. These boxers "are so ugly," they tell us, "she'll beg you to take them off." Well, that's one approach, we suppose. The gimmick is that these boxers are made of not one but two or three different horrendous patterns, delivering sort of a Frankenstein's monster effect wherein you might have tie-dye on one side, plaid on the other and paisley in the middle. Use the top bar navigation for the easiest browsing.

·UNDERWEAR

---

**800-853-8555 • Undergear**  **UnderGear.com**

For a site primarily devoted to underwear, this site sure seems to promote the way a man looks in his underwear. To be honest, they have plenty of nonunderwear merchandise: swimsuits, shirts, leather pants, stretch denim jeans and workout gear too. However, ultimately all seems to allude to the same thing: very muscular men vaunting their, uh, bulging mass, all greased up and in the sunlight. Take it or leave it, one thing's for absolute certain: this selection is definitely meant for hotter climates.

·CASUAL
·SWIMSUITS   ·OUTERWEAR   ·STREETWEAR   ·ATHLETIC
·UNDERWEAR

## UniversalGear.com

Universal Gear • 800-204-1844

Looking for some enticing clubwear, or for something to attract notice while you walk down the street? Okay, well, let's just say you can get your tight jeans and short shorts here. The stodgy British tailored suit tradition takes a hit with this decidedly American male outfitter that carries kinky and designer labels that typically call more attention to what's underneath than the clothes themselves. Not for everybody, and not for every body, you're going to have to be extra careful about sizing with this one, or it simply won't fit.

| ·CASUAL ·SWIMSUITS | ·SOCKS ·UNDERWEAR | ·STREETWEAR ·DESIGNER | ·ATHLETIC |
|---|---|---|---|

## Urbanix.com

Urbanix.com • No Service Number

So-called urban style favorites like Sean John, Enyce and FUBU make for a good start to this selection of street-savvy attire described as "Urban Gear in the Digital Millennium." Valuable search filters enable you to search by size, price, brand, clothing type or a combination therein, so you can get a quick glimpse of what they have that will fit you and be gone before you know it. Of course, given the variable bagginess of each particular cut and label, maybe things aren't as cut and dry as it would seem....

| ·CASUAL | ·OUTERWEAR | ·DESIGNER | ·STREETWEAR |
|---|---|---|---|

## URBN.com

Urban Outfitters • 800-959-8794

Urban Outfitters has made a name for itself in the past few years, with franchise stores secured as mainstays in busy shopping districts wherever young people may yearn for cargo pants, hoodies or logo tees. As the name would suggest, all of their products are infused with a metropolitan vibe; this is hard to shake, especially when you're subjected to the pseudo-pop music piped into any one of their international store locations. To simulate this experience, they've thoughtfully opted to broadcast this music online as well. Fortunately, on the web site you can turn it off.

| ·CASUAL | ·OUTERWEAR | ·STREETWEAR | |
|---|---|---|---|

## Vilebrequin.com

Vilebrequin • 212-650-0353

Seeing as these swim trunks come to you straight from St.-Tropez (which is located in France), we can't technically call them Bermuda shorts (Bermuda is located in the southern Atlantic), but that's kind of what they look like, so call them what you will. There's not really a whole lot else to say about this small but winning selection of men's bathing attire, or about this site for that matter. You simply log on, peruse the dozen or so styles/patterns, pick whichever you like, and Add to Shopping Cart. Simple, *voilà*!

| ·SWIMSUITS | | | |
|---|---|---|---|

## No Service Number • WebUndies.com

### WebUndies.com

This site is like a dream come true... that is, if your dream is to be met with laughter every time you take off your pants. Seriously, though, these guys specialize in novelty boxer shorts, some of which bear the familiar likenesses of cartoon characters, others covered in dollar signs, camouflage, smiley faces and the like. You won't find any erotic themes, really (leopard print's about as racy as it gets), but you will find yourself compulsively clicking to check out the options that lie just on the other side of each link.

| ·UNDERWEAR | | | | |
|---|---|---|---|---|

## 800-648-7024 • Wickers.com

### Wickers.com

Of all the specialty retailers listed in this section, this is the one we'd least likely expect—its devotion is to "high performance underwear for active people." Lightweight or heavyweight, this may seem funny at first but it turns out these things are on the level. The secret here is a material called Awatek, which apparently uses the same mystical technology found in thermoses that keeps your juice cold but your soup hot—it keeps you warm in cold weather and cool when it's hot out. This is just what happens when you apply rocket science to your skivvies.

| ·ATHLETIC | ·UNDERWEAR | | | |
|---|---|---|---|---|

## 800-236-9976 • Wilson Leather

### WilsonLeather.com

Opting for this name rather than Wilson Cowhide (a splendid marketing maneuver), it's immediately obvious that this large retailer of leather goods is run by cool heads. Featuring leather jackets worthy of the Fonz, the men's collection here is pretty cool as well. Pants and vests are fairly well represented, and some suede rounds out the selection, which includes a little bit of color other than the traditional black and shades of brown. Including sizes for big and tall men (presumably to meet the demand of Harley-Davidson riders), this simple shopping experience should aptly gear you up for the road.

| ·OUTERWEAR | ·STREETWEAR | | | |
|---|---|---|---|---|

## 818-291-0600 • X-Large

### XLarge.com

Probably best known among youth culture for its affiliation with the Beastie Boys, the truth is that this once frontline urban style shop has been around more than a decade, and most of its early clients have since grown up. Chances are, though, they still check the selection from time to time, as the spirit of the clothes hasn't changed even if the styles have a bit. Seemingly built around the hooded sweatshirt and skate shoe, these pants aren't strictly baggy anymore, but they're still representative of some cool happenings.

| ·CASUAL | ·OUTERWEAR | ·STREETWEAR | |
|---|---|---|---|

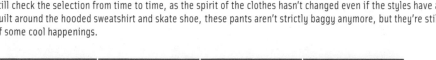

## ZootSuitStore.com

Harkening back to another swingin' hipster era, this store's devotion to zoot suits would be riotously funny were it not so undeniably cool. The boldly colored suits famous for their baggy pants and long jackets were designed for swagger, and all pertinent accoutrements are included, and by this we mean hats with turned-down brims and long watch chains (more commonly used these days with wallets). You needn't go so far as to order a suit, as you'll find some retro-style shirts among the overall selection, but if you do want the full shebang you may as well have it custom-made in your choice of cut (pachuco, double-breasted, etc.) and fabric (satin lapels). Too cool for school.

| | ·SUITS | ·STREETWEAR | ·VINTAGE | |
|---|---|---|---|---|

# Minors (0-18)

Children make up the single most powerful consumer demographic in the nation. Any parent knows how easy it is to succumb to the unabashed desires of a youngster. Advertisers sure know it, and they push hard to make sure kids both desperately want a product and use their influence to convince you to buy it. Why not? Whether we're trying to keep them well-dressed, educated, healthy or just blissfully happy with toys and funny furniture, there's nothing wrong with spoiling them a *little* bit, right? But here's the thing—by shopping for your children's products online you can avoid things like toy stores, candy counters and other impulse stations that become the captivating islands of childish temptation. Stick to the merchants included in this section, and public tantrums may be a thing of the past. Gone. The decision-making process will be placed back in your hands... at least until they're teenagers (and even *they* might find stuff they like here... though you may not always approve).

There is a breadth of quality merchandise out there for children of all ages. You can order the finest products from around the globe, particularly in terms of educational items—some of which are entertaining enough to order for yourself (admit it, you still like to finger paint, don't you?). Of course, before you get that far there're diapers and cribs and breast-feeding and weeks on end without sleep. You can find a lot of good baby resources in here as well, from health-related stuff to cribs and cutesy clothes. Take note, though, that there's a slight overlap with our *Maternity* section. Basically, the distinction is this: if a product or selection is intended to help a mother raise her baby, it will be in *Maternity*. If, however, the focus is on the daily wants and needs of the child, you can absolutely find it here.

NOTES:

## TIPS ON BUYING CHILDREN'S PRODUCTS ONLINE

These suggestions may help prevent whining and disinterest.

•**EUROPEAN SIZES:** Bear in mind that much of the more charming children's clothing comes from Europe and uses a different sizing structure. See the European Clothing Size Chart URL listed below for reference.

•**AGE-APPROPRIATE TOYS:** Take note: toys and games are often constructed for particular age ranges. Some toys are too advanced and even can be dangerous for younger children. Others are meant for younger kids and will deeply embarrass a teenager.

•**TAKE A DEEPER LOOK:** There is truly a bounty of unique products listed in this category. It may be easy to find the typical, cookie-cutter clothes, toys and educational products, but just a little digging on your part may be greatly beneficial to your child's lifestyle and creative development.

## SITES THAT MAY COME IN HANDY

The following URLs may be useful when you shop.

Parenting Tips: http://www.parentingtoolbox.com
Educational Centers: http://www.escore.com
Children's Health Information: http://www.kidshealth.org
Children Shoe Size Measurement: http://www.cadvision.com/shoes4u/HappylandShoeSize.htm
European Clothing Size Chart: http://www.freelollies.co.uk/sizechart.htm
Educational Toy Guide: http://www.toyportfolio.com
Summer Camp Guide: http://kidscamps.com
Public Libraries Directory: http://www.publiclibraries.com
Big Brother & Big Sister Program Directory: http://www.bbbsa.org
Online Encyclopedia: http://www.britannica.com

>> **SECTION ICON LEGEND**

Use the following guide to understand the rectangular icons that appear throughout this section.

### INFANTS & TODDLERS

Easy enough to remember, this icon indicates that a store offers merchandise designed for little ones under the age of 3.

### KIDS

The stores with this icon include toys, furniture, clothes and more for children between the ages of 3 and 12.

### PERSONALIZATION

This icon indicates that a site is prepared to personalize items with names, images, initials or otherwise.

### TEENS

This is a rare enough icon, as most interests of those aged 13-18 are included in other sections throughout the book.

# >> LIST OF KEY WORDS

The following words represent the types of items typically found on the sites listed in this section.

## ACCESSORIES

Even children like to accessorize given the breadth of stuff available on these sites... well, less so the boys. Includes hair accessories, bracelets, watches, belts and backpacks.

## BABY NEEDS

This selection includes strollers, baby carriers, car seats, baby grooming items, high chairs and other common baby equipment.

## BOOKS & MEDIA

These may be educational or simply a diversion for your children in the afternoon. Included is youth fiction, videos and coloring books.

## CLOTHES

Little clothes for small people; bigger and trendier for teens.

## CUSTOM

Some shops offer customization of certain products, whether in the tailoring of clothes or the building of furniture.

## EDUCATIONAL

A key word you can feel good about, stores listed beside it offer products that help a child's development, whether in the guise of games, instructional materials or school supply.

## FURNITURE

Kids' furniture isn't just smaller, it comes in themes and designs that appeal to a younger mindset.

## HEALTH

These shops offer health-related items that are designed specifically for children, ranging from toothbrushes to over-the-counter medication.

## NURSERY

Nursery and layette items include infant clothing and nursery items like changing pads, diaper rash ointment, burping cloths and other stuff you'd find in a diaper bag.

## PARENTS' TOOLS

Products designed to enable a stronger interaction between parent and child, including cultural materials, special needs devices, teaching aids and internet restrictions.

## SAFETY

Protecting your children from themselves and others, these stores offer safety equipment and security devices.

## SHOES

Footwear for little people, from sneakers to tap shoes.

## SPORTS

Sports gear and recreational equipment (tetherball is sort of a toss-up) that'll keeps your kids physically active.

## SUNDAY BEST

The nice clothes that you'll want to get safely back into the closet before the kids find their way into a patch of mud.

## TOYS & GAMES

The stores your kids want you to know about.

## TRAVEL

Stores denoted by this key word offer merchandise that will make it easier to travel with children.

## UNIFORMS

Mostly school uniforms, with a few sports and physical education uniforms thrown in for posterity.

## >> KEY WORD INDEX

Use the following lists to locate online retailers that sell the Children's Products you seek.

### ACCESSORIES

AllAboardToys.com
Alloy.com
AmericanGirlStore.com
BabyCenter.com
BellaKids.com
CartoonNetwork.com
ChildrensPlace.com
Delias.com
FamilyOnBoard.com
FrenchToast.com
GaGaGifts.com
GapKids.com
GirlProps.com
GoJane.com
Gymboree.com
HannaAndersson.com
HearthSong.com
iBabyDoc.com
Journeys.com
LillianVernon.com
LtlThings.com
Oliebollen.com
OshKoshBGosh.com
RainBee.com
RightStart.com
SchoolUnif.com
TotShop.com
TravelingTikes.com
WetSeal.com

### BABY NEEDS

BabyBazaar.com
BabyBox.com
BabyBundle.com
BabyCenter.com
BabyStyle.com
BabyToes.com
BabyUniverse.com

FamilyOnBoard.com
GaGaGifts.com
GapKids.com
GeniusBabies.com
HannaAndersson.com
iBabyDoc.com
InFashionKids.com
Oliebollen.com
OneStepAhead.com
OshKoshBGosh.com
RainBee.com
RedWagons.com
RightStart.com
ShopZoo.com
SoulsShoes.com
TotShop.com
TravelingTikes.com

### BOOKS & MEDIA

AllAboardToys.com
AmericanGirlStore.com
AsiaForKids.com
BabyBox.com
BabyCenter.com
BabyUniverse.com
Campmor.com
CartoonNetwork.com
EnablingDevices.com
ExploratoriumStore.com
FamilyOnBoard.com
GaGaGifts.com
HearthSong.com
ImagineToys.com
LearningCo.com
Oliebollen.com
OneStepAhead.com
RightStart.com
Scholastic.com
SensationalBeginnings.com
SmarterKids.com

### CLOTHES

Alloy.com
AmericanGirlStore.com
Anichini.net
BabyBazaar.com
BabyBox.com
BabyBundle.com
BabyCenter.com
BabyStyle.com
BabyToes.com
BabyUniverse.com
BellaKids.com
BestPromDresses.com
Campmor.com
CartoonNetwork.com
ChildrensPlace.com
CosmicDebris.com
CWDKids.com
Delias.com
FrenchToast.com
GapKids.com
GoJane.com
Golfini.com
GreenBabies.com
Guess.com
Gymboree.com
HannaAndersson.com
HealthTex.com
InFashionKids.com
IsabelGarreton.com
Journeys.com
LtlThings.com
OldNavy.com
Oliebollen.com
OshKoshBGosh.com
PapoDAnjo.com
RainBee.com
SchoolUnif.com
TotShop.com
TractorJeans.com
WetSeal.com

### CUSTOM

BuildABear.com
PoshTots.com
TrendyToosies.com

### EDUCATIONAL

AmazingToyStore.com
AsiaForKids.com
BabyBundle.com
BabyStyle.com
DragonflyToys.com
Edu4Fun.com
EnablingDevices.com
ExploratoriumStore.com
FAO.com
HearthSong.com
iBabyDoc.com
ImagineToys.com
LearningCo.com
LillianVernon.com
MasterMindToys.com
OneStepAhead.com
QuincyShop.com
RainBee.com
RightStart.com
Scholastic.com
SmarterKids.com
ZanyBrainy.com

### FURNITURE

BabyBazaar.com
BabyBundle.com
BabyStyle.com
BabyUniverse.com
BellaKids.com
NotABeanBag.com
PlayFairToys.com
PoshTots.com
QualityTrading.com
RainBee.com
RockingToy.com
SensationalBeginnings.com

## HEALTH

BabyBox.com
BabyBundle.com
BabyCenter.com
BabyUniverse.com
iBabyDoc.com
OneStepAhead.com
RightStart.com
YummiBears.com

## NURSERY

Anichini.net
BabyBazaar.com
BabyBox.com
BabyBundle.com
BabyCenter.com
BabyStyle.com
BabyToes.com
BabyUniverse.com
BellaKids.com
Golfini.com
GreenBabies.com
Guess.com
HannaAndersson.com
HealthTex.com
iBabyDoc.com
InFashionKids.com
Oliebollen.com
OneStepAhead.com
OshKoshBGosh.com
RainBee.com
TotShop.com

## PARENTS' TOOLS

AsiaForKids.com
BabyCenter.com
BabyUniverse.com
DragonflyToys.com
EnablingDevices.com
iBabyDoc.com
LearningCo.com
NetNanny.com
OneStepAhead.com
RightStart.com
RocketCash.com
Scholastic.com

## SAFETY

BabyCenter.com
BabyUniverse.com
CyberPatrol.com
FamilyOnBoard.com
iBabyDoc.com
NetNanny.com
OneStepAhead.com
RedWagons.com
RightStart.com
SchoolUnif.com
SensationalBeginnings.com
TravelingTikes.com

## SHOES

BabyStyle.com
BellaKids.com
Delias.com
GapKids.com
GoJane.com
HannaAndersson.com
InFashionKids.com
Journeys.com
JRayShoes.com
OshKoshBGosh.com
SchoolUnif.com
ShoeBuy.com
SoulsShoes.com
TrendyTootsies.com

## SPORTS

AmazingToyStore.com
Campmor.com
EnablingDevices.com
GopherSport.com
HearthSong.com
IntoTheWind.com
LillianVernon.com
PlayFairToys.com
QualityTrading.com
QuincyShop.com
RedWagons.com
SchoolUnif.com
SensationalBeginnings.com
Sports4Kids.com
TravelingTikes.com

## SUNDAY BEST

Anichini.net
BabyStyle.com
BellaKids.com
BestPromDresses.com
GoJane.com
Golfini.com
InFashionKids.com
IsabelGarreton.com
LtlThings.com
PapaDAnjo.com
SchoolUnif.com

## TOYS & GAMES

ActiveToys.com
AllAboardToys.com
AmazingToyStore.com
AmericanGirlStore.com
BabyBazaar.com
BabyBox.com
BabyBundle.com
BabyStyle.com
BearSt.com
BellaKids.com
BigFunToys.com
BuildABear.com
CartoonNetwork.com
CreativeToymaker.com
DragonflyToys.com
Edu4Fun.com
EnablingDevices.com
ExploratoriumStore.com
FAO.com
Fisher-PriceStore.com
FreeBears.com
GaGaGifts.com
GeniusBabies.com
Gymboree.com
HearthSong.com
iBabyDoc.com
ImagineToys.com
IntoTheWind.com
KBToys.com
Lego.com
LillianVernon.com
MasterMindToys.com
Oliebollen.com
OneStepAhead.com

PlayFairToys.com
QualityTrading.com
QuincyShop.com
RainBee.com
RedWagons.com
RightStart.com
RoboToys.com
RockingToy.com
Scholastic.com
SensationalBeginnings.com
ShopZoo.com
SmallBluePlanet.com
SmarterKids.com
TotShop.com
ToyCollection.com
ZanyBrainy.com

## TRAVEL

AsiaForKids.com
BabyBundle.com
FamilyOnBoard.com
SensationalBeginnings.com
TravelingTikes.com

## UNIFORMS

Frenchloast.com
HannaAndersson.com
SchoolUnif.com

## ActiveToys.com

Active Toys • 877-858-8697

This "largest selection of toy trucks on the internet" makes it simple to find, uh, toy trucks. They basically fall into three categories, with the Roadmax models built to be rounder and thus safer for young children, the Standard Series built with scant detail to keep the costs down and the Pro Series consisting of "small ones just like the big ones." All the trucks here are the products of Bruder, a German toy manufacturer whose scope is not limited to miniature big rigs—that is, it features two or three toy boats as well.

| ·TOYS & GAMES | | | |
|---|---|---|---|

## AllAboardToys.com

AllAboardToys.com • 800-416-7155

Here it is, the "Ultimate Thomas the Tank Engine Store!" "Thomas the what?" you may ask. Well, to those in the know, this popular character comes across in product categories like Audio Cassettes, Videos, Train Sets, Puzzles & Games, Clothes, Furniture and even Luggage. The most promising items, however, will most likely be found in the Books section, as these will best answer any questions as to the origins and purpose of this steam engine with a grin. Can such a character really warrant its own web site? We think it can, we think it can.

| ·TOYS & GAMES | ·BOOKS & MEDIA | ·ACCESSORIES |
|---|---|---|

## Alloy.com

Alloy • 888-502-5569

Sassy attitudes are on display on this all-around lifestyle site. Its shop offers some girlish clothes and accessories shopping by category or brand name, or via a smattering of styles that includes names like Beach Babe, Cool 4 School and Rock Style. Once all outfitting is taken care of, there's a selection of bedding and other bedroom furnishings for the discriminating teenybopper. Of course, anyone who spends more than a couple of minutes at a time on this site will almost immediately outgrow it; at least, we hope so.

| ·CLOTHES | ·ACCESSORIES | | |
|---|---|---|---|

## AmazingToyStore.com

AmazingToyStore.com • 617-924-8500

How did these guys find so many "amazing toys for amazing kids?" By "hand selecting the best toys," of course. Now, they're not all so spectacular, but while none are entirely frivolous, none are entirely unfun either. In fact, to a particularly cerebral child (perhaps one of the "amazing kids" to which they refer), this might just be as great a store as it claims to be. With categories like Puppets, The Mad Scientist, Blooming Artists and Builders & Designers, we certainly won't make any claims otherwise.

| ·TOYS & GAMES | ·EDUCATIONAL | ·SPORTS |
|---|---|---|

## 800-845-0005 • American Girl

### AmericanGirlStore.com

Girls love dolls and, given that they remain unexposed to multimillion-dollar marketing campaigns, they don't tend to care which particular dolls they call their own (so long as ownership is ensured). If you'd like your daughter's dolls to be imbued with a sense of history, you won't do much better than with these plastic pretties. Here you may sort through a selection of girl dolls that each come with a story and dress related to a particular American cultural era. Characters include an early 19th-century New Mexican ranch girl, an escaped slave or the daughter of a revolutionary. Otherwise, you can find books and toys related to a dancing mouse called Angelina Ballerina.

| ·TOYS & GAMES | ·CLOTHES | ·BOOKS & MEDIA | ·ACCESSORIES |
|---|---|---|---|

## No Service Number • Anichini

### Anichini.net

The oldest children's clothing store in Florence, Italy, offers a fine selection of traditional European styles for boys, girls, and babies who prefer the more refined and venerable look of a young monarch on the make. Promising only the highest quality fabrics, Anichini will tailor its orders via an online form where you can enter measurements you take yourself. While it may be wise to take into account the rapid growth of your child against the time it takes to alter an outfit and ship it from Florence, where else can you find custom-fit Italian attire for your kids without making the trip yourself?

| ·CLOTHES | ·NURSERY | ·SUNDAY BEST | |
|---|---|---|---|

## 800-888-9681 • Asia For Kids

### AsiaForKids.com

"Your best resource for language and cultures," this site may be just what you need to help teach your kids that there's more to this planet's history than the eternal struggle between Cowboys and Indians. It proves to be an excellent place to find materials relating to a variety of unique cultures from the planet's largest continent: Asia. Country by country browsing will turn you on to aspects such as food, music, languages and martial arts. Ultimately, the site may prove particularly useful to the adoptive parents of international children as a means for both to keep in touch with a mutually unfamiliar culture, and to ensure none of us lose sight of where we've come from.

| ·BOOKS & MEDIA | ·EDUCATIONAL | ·PARENTS' TOOLS | ·TRAVEL |
|---|---|---|---|

## 877-543-7186 • BabyBazaar

### BabyBazaar.com

Finally, a site pops up wherein you can dress your infant or toddler appropriately for any occasion, whether it be casual, hip or chic. We kid, but this site actually makes such categorical distinctions for your baby's wardrobe (as if babies have wardrobes). It's tough to fault them, though, as this fantastic selection is only exceeded by a bevy of car seats, strollers, carriages and other essential gear. Add to that some assorted baby toys and nursery furniture, and you've got a fairly well-rounded shop, whether you think of it as a bazaar or just plain bizarre.

| ·TOYS & GAMES ·BABY NEEDS | ·CLOTHES | ·FURNITURE | ·NURSERY |
|---|---|---|---|

# BabyBox.com

**BabyBox.com • 800-373-8216**

Selling what they refer to as "unique and high quality baby gifts in elegant gift packaging," this baby gift boutique features interesting if scant selections of stuff like clothes, nursery items, baby blankets, toys and a Bath & Beach section that makes it all worth the visit (think adorable baby swimwear and froggie, doggie and duckie hooded terry wraps). Between the use of microfibers and whimsical designs, these wares more than justify use of the word "unique." We don't know for sure about the packaging.

| | | ·TOYS & GAMES | ·CLOTHES | ·BOOKS & MEDIA | ·HEALTH |
| | | ·PERSONALIZATION | ·NURSERY | ·BABY NEEDS | |

# BabyBundle.com

**BabyBundle.com • 877-620-2229**

Baby Bundle has a riddle for you: in their Everything Baby Needs category (one has to wonder why there even are other sections), would you be more likely to find clothes under the Baby Bedding, Clothes & Blankets or Unique Baby Items subsection? It's a trick question; you'd actually have to look under the Baby Lulu, Pepper Toes, Cotton Caboodle and Wes & Willy category (it's all one category). Slightly less confounding is that carriers and diaper bags are located in the Baby Bjorn Products section. Why bother, you wonder? Simple: there's some neat stuff in this boutiquish baby gift shop.

| | ·TOYS & GAMES | ·CLOTHES | ·FURNITURE | ·EDUCATIONAL |
| | ·HEALTH | ·NURSERY | ·BABY NEEDS | ·TRAVEL |

# BabyCenter.com

**BabyCenter • 866-241-2229**

With a full arsenal of baby-raising equipment to peddle, BabyCenter.com sets out to win your repeat business with technological assistance, community and informative content. To start with, if you enter your baby's due or birth date, the entire site will be customized to feature products and information pertinent to his or her stage of development at any time you log on. If a $5 flat shipping rate doesn't encourage you to stock up on supplies, their extensive list of relevant articles and expert advice might, or the community chats and message boards. They also offer extras like baby-naming software, childcare and doctor finders, a vaccine guide and everything else they can come up with to keep you satisfied and coming back time and again.

| | ·CLOTHES | ·BOOKS & MEDIA | ·HEALTH | ·SAFETY |
| | ·PARENTS' TOOLS | ·ACCESSORIES | ·NURSERY | ·BABY NEEDS |

# BabyStyle.com

**BabyStyle.com • 877-378-9537**

Cool lunchboxes and finger-paint soap are the types of things that might attract you to KidStyle, but when you get there all the colors and clutter might keep you from what you're looking for. The key is to focus on their Toys & Gear and Kids Rooms sections, where you'll find some nifty items that will make your child's lifestyle a little cooler. The bedroom furniture, in particular, includes stuff like the "Sit in a Mitt," a giant, overstuffed baseball mitt that can add flair to any kid's bedroom. There're also things like bedding and rugs that your child might not care about, but you'll like, assuming the rooms aren't too messy to notice such stuff.

| | | ·TOYS & GAMES | ·CLOTHES | ·SUNDAY BEST | ·FURNITURE |
| | | ·EDUCATIONAL | ·SHOES | ·NURSERY | ·BABY NEEDS |

**800-222-9863•  BabyToes.com**  **BabyToes.com**

The proprietors of BabyToes were so successful selling their line of hand-painted baby clothes on the streets of SoHo in New York City that they picked up their operation, moved upstate, and started selling on the internet instead. Made with nontoxic paints, the baby bunting, one pieces and bib overalls created by these artists and their friends are, as they say, "edible." But with cute designs that include frogs, elephants, flowers, friendly insects and big trucks, you might rather use these outfits to clothe your infants than feed them. Virtually any pattern may be painted on every item of clothing, and while there doesn't seem to be a choice in fabric colors, these guys aim to please, so greater choice is just a phone call away.

| ·CLOTHES | ·NURSERY | ·BABY NEEDS | ·PERSONALIZATION |
|---|---|---|---|

---

**877-615-2229 •  Baby Universe**  **BabyUniverse.com**

You may just want to head straight for the Store Directory link on this one, because this selection of baby wares is as large as the name would indicate. To give you an idea, we found five different types of jogging strollers that were made specifically to hold twins. So it goes that we can only imagine how much variety may be found in sections and subsections devoted to clothing, diapering, feeding, health care, bedding, bathing supplies and nursing aids. Fortunately, we only have to imagine; browsing through it all, well, that's up to you.

| ·CLOTHES ·SAFETY | ·FURNITURE ·PARENTS' TOOLS | ·BOOKS & MEDIA ·NURSERY | ·HEALTH ·BABY NEEDS |
|---|---|---|---|

---

**No Service Number •  GUND**  **BearSt.com**

This is the official web seller of GUND, which is probably the best known of the world's plush-toy manufacturers. It turns out to be one site that's even better than it sounds, as teddy bears are just the tip of the iceberg and, truth be told, comprise probably the least-inspired stuffed animals featured here. If category names like Australian Animals, Monkey Business and Jungle Cats don't get you at least a little bit excited, maybe you'll be more impressed with the Harry Potter and Winnie the Pooh selections. Better yet, just follow the Family Album link to view passport-photolike images of all these toys on one undeniably cuddly page.

| ·TOYS & GAMES | | | |
|---|---|---|---|

---

**877-235-5254 •  Bella Kids**  **BellaKids.com**

This Manhattan-based outfitter keeps up with the seasonal styles of Paris, Milan and other European fashion hubs and delivers them to you, fresh from kiddy-sized catwalks. In fact, shipping is free for their entire selection of apparel, shoes, and whatever else you may discover for your infant or toddler on this elegant and easily navigated site. If the age-based sizing doesn't match your child's speedy development, don't fret, online sizing charts will help you ensure the right fit. They also give tips as to the proper attire for different occasions, whether it's school or a formal party, and even have a few suggestions on where else you might like to take your young son or daughter in order to show off their new duds.

| ·TOYS & GAMES ·ACCESSORIES | ·CLOTHES ·SHOES | ·SUNDAY BEST ·NURSERY | ·FURNITURE |
|---|---|---|---|

## BestPromDresses.com

You may miss out on the music-montage worthy afternoon of trying on prom dresses, as popularized by TV and film, but whether you prefer the more elegant or party-girl type of gown, they're all priced to move with this retailer. The "best" implication is surely subjective, but they do offer a bunch of styles to choose from. To achieve the best of both worlds, this site's greatest value may be achieved by trying stuff on in brick-and-mortar stores, then matching your preferred style with a more inexpensive alternative here. Oh, and lest you think it's a once-a-year thing… these dresses work just as well for homecoming.

| ·CLOTHES | ·SUNDAY BEST | | |

## BigFunToys.com

Big Fun  • 877-386-8692

"Shop yourself silly" is the motto of this wild and colorful site that makes online retail more fun than a barrel of sea monkeys. The toys range from the wacky to the sublime, including things like fake mustaches, chemistry sets, stilts, and night-vision goggles. There's also an entire section devoted to practical jokes (in case you need a remote-control fart machine), and an area devoted to kites. Other toys are broken down by age group, then split into categories like Girly Girl, Tom Boy, Brainiac, Goof Ball and Cool Dude, which makes it easy to find items to tickle your child's fancy, whatever it is. A search function might make it easier to find those toys you have in mind coming in, but then you would miss out on all the good stuff you could never imagine.

| ·TOYS & GAMES | | | |

## BuildABear.com

Build-A-Bear Workshop  • 888-560-2327

This site is somewhat of a misnomer. It's not that you can't customize, or "build" a teddy bear, complete with one of several cute outfits (including a football uniform, fishing gear and a bikini)—you can, and easily at that. But, among the many bear options are included pandas and koalas, which are technically not bears. Okay, okay, so we're nitpicking. But what do you say to the fact that among these "teddy bear" options are also included a monkey, bunny, cow, elephant, pony, tiger and turtle? If you're anything like us, you'll say, "Cool!" These dolls are almost as much fun to shop for as they are to own.

| ·TOYS & GAMES | ·CUSTOM | | |

## Campmor.com

Campmor.com  • 800-525-4784

The combined infatuations of television and video games keep a lot of kids voluntarily indoors these days. Campmor.com offers a lot of gear that will inspire them to get out of the house for a change. Parkas, helmets, ski boots and snowsuits are just some of the child-sized active wear available here for your next trip to the slopes. Tents, sleeping bags, and fleeces may be found here as well, great for those backyard camp-outs that help adults reclaim the house for a romantic evening. Or, maybe you just want to get your little angels out of the house for a while so you can practice your own video basketball skills? Whatever your motivation, it's nice to know they'll stay warm this time out.

| ·CLOTHES | ·BOOKS & MEDIA | ·SPORTS | |

## 877-839-1216 • Cartoon Network
### CartoonNetwork.com

Saturday mornings are so over. Thanks to the advent of cable television, we can enjoy animated hilarity morning, noon and night. In particular, the Cartoon Network has salvaged favorites like *Scooby Doo, Looney Tunes* and the *Flintstones*; introduced us to the *Power Puff Girls* and *Dexter's Laboratory*; and given a more sophisticated redux to *Space Ghost*. Sure, we recognize these shows' superiority to the overcommercialized drivel generally served to youngsters nowadays, but sometimes it seems that kids don't want to watch it if they can't wear it. Well, here's the official merchant of the TV channel, complete with toys, clothes and posters that don't necessarily focus on kung-fu robots.

| ·TOYS & GAMES | ·CLOTHES | ·BOOKS & MEDIA | ·ACCESSORIES |
|---|---|---|---|

## 877-752-2387 • The Children's Place
### ChildrensPlace.com

Smart clothes for babies through 12 year olds are the main attraction of this retail-outfit-turned-online-store. All merchandise is designed exclusively for sale through Children's Place, and features the clean, modern styles of a street-smart up-and-comer. While most items seem to go well together, an innovative Mix & Match feature allows you to piece together outfits for view online before you send your kids to school looking like a Crayola™ box gone awry. Still, if mismatching your daughter's patent pleather hair band with her denim pony print dress is the worst these clothes can do, they can't be all that bad.

| ·CLOTHES | ·ACCESSORIES |
|---|---|

## 877-273-1939 • Cosmic Debris Etc., Inc.
### CosmicDebris.com

Do you like Yum Pop, Oopsy Daisy and Emily Strange? If you even know what these are you're probably a girl. These cutesy clothes and accessories usually entail cartoonish character themes, like the morbidly darling Emily Strange, offering different lines of merchandise with different colors and attitudes. All exhibit a certain appeal, especially as these pages tend to involve games that may cause you to forget about shopping altogether. Incidentally, if anybody solves the mystery of Emily's Strange Day, please contact **thepurplebook** to let us in on it. Thanks.

| ·CLOTHES | | | | |
|---|---|---|---|---|

## 877-809-8697 • Toys 2 Wish 4
### CreativeToymaker.com

Anytime a retailer claims to have "selected the world's greatest toys," we turn our skeptical, critical gaze towards its selection and prepare to strike a blow to such braggadocio, in the name of consumer service, you understand. Turns out, these guys have some merit to their claim. Take just one section, for example: Pretend Play. In it you'll find subcategories Spy Tools, Cosmetics and Dress-Up (to keep them out of your closet) and Housekeeping (if for some reason they think pretending to sweep is fun). The subsection Puppets & Marionettes even features its own subcategories, and all in all Pretend Play doesn't even constitute 10% of the site.

| ·TOYS & GAMES | | | |
|---|---|---|---|

# CWDKids.com

While this site may prove terribly slow, and most of the clothes won't be all that appealing to an adult, it might be worth a look if only because sometimes kids like to wear things like dinosaur T-shirts or velveteen dresses. Then, there's the fact that children are likely to destroy whatever clothes they're wearing when they find ways to get into trouble (which is often enough), so it makes sense that you dress them down a bit before sending them out into potentially muddy or grass-staining situations. Some of these clothes are perfect for such times, and the occasional Polo shirt doesn't hurt either.

| ·CLOTHES | | | |
|---|---|---|---|

# CyberPatrol.com

If you cringe the moment your child wanders out onto the information superhighway before you look both ways, the downloadable software application offered here might be for you. Available for Mac or PC, this internet filter keeps the bad guys at bay while your little ones plod happily through a G-Rated web universe. Purchase gets you a 12-month, automated subscription to the service's "Cyber Lists" of trouble spots, which includes daily list updates so new smutty sites won't slip by. You can adjust filter settings to vary between 9 household users, and even set up time restrictions so mischief-making youngsters can't sneak online when they're supposed to be asleep.

| ·SAFETY | | | |
|---|---|---|---|

# Delias.com

This decidedly girly clothes and accessories catalog makes style an everyday occasion, raising the bar on blue jeans and T-shirts with stuff like rhinestones and cutesy logos. They seemed to have mastered the art of demonstrating an innocent appeal, offering a catalog that bridges the gap between parental sensibility and the popularity of role models like Britney Spears. Best of all, the prices are never out of control, especially in the Discount Domain, which is divided into categories all its own, making it, unlike your daughter, both cheap and easy.

| ·CLOTHES | ·ACCESSORIES | ·SHOES |
|---|---|---|

# DragonflyToys.com

Physically challenged and developmentally disabled children tend to have two things in common: they love to expand their horizons and they love to have fun. From sensory exploration games to those espousing hand/eye coordination and just plain education, this site features toys and technology that promotes healthy response and a broader grasp of the physical realm in youngsters with special needs. These games and devices, along with some truly useful daily living aids, may be easily found by creating an individual child profile that will guide you toward only relevant products. The abysmal loading time on this site may try your patience—if so, that's something we can learn from the children.

| ·TOYS & GAMES | ·EDUCATIONAL | ·PARENTS' TOOLS |
|---|---|---|

**888-338-4386 • Edu4Fun**  **Edu4Fun.com**

If you consider yourself or your child a fan of wooden educational puzzles, get ready for a big treat! These guys have full categories available of 3-D Shape Puzzles, Matching Puzzles, Double Sided Puzzles and Language Puzzles (in different languages, featuring alphabets and numbers). You may view them all on the index page, but we wouldn't really recommend it as the page just keeps going on and on and on. And on. Actually, we never imagined there could be so many variations to the simple paint-and-wood-carving-puzzle concept, so kudos to them for that. Frankly, you haven't lived until you've borne witness to the Circular Sorter Educational Toy.

| ·TOYS & GAMES | ·EDUCATIONAL | | |
|---|---|---|---|

**800-832-8697 • Enabling Devices**  **EnablingDevices.com**

This web site represents Toys For Special Children, Inc., which is "dedicated to developing affordable learning and assistive devices to help people with disabling conditions." They proclaim that their products are "not over-designed, nor do they have unnecessary frills," but this might serve to misrepresent the quality of these items. Not merely unimaginative blocks of electronics, these useful, friendly devices simply get the job done in the most intuitive way possible, which in many cases is just what a kid could want, frills or not.

| ·TOYS & GAMES ·PARENTS' TOOLS | ·BOOKS & MEDIA | ·EDUCATIONAL | ·SPORTS |
|---|---|---|---|

**415-397-5673 • Exploratorium Store**  **ExploratoriumStore.com**

Is science cool? Well, based on a thorough analysis of the items contained within this popular San Francisco science museum's web shop, we could only draw one possible conclusion: absolutely yes! It's more than just the incredible ways the physical properties of the universe are illustrated in many of these remarkably fun products (we're talkin' stuff like Lightning Machine, Optical Illusion and Robot kits)—okay, so it's not much more than the educational stuff, but isn't that enough? It's as if all the mad scientists in the world got together and started making toys (which is much better than their usual efforts at world domination).

| ·TOYS & GAMES | ·BOOKS & MEDIA | ·EDUCATIONAL | |
|---|---|---|---|

**800-793-2075 • Family on Board**  **FamilyOnBoard.com**

When traveling with children, you typically deal with three primary concerns: 1) keeping them safe, 2) keeping them comfortable and 3) keeping them quiet. This site addresses all of these needs for both road and air travel, with a brief array of products designed to secure, coddle and/or entertain the kids during the meantime of a vacation. From the simplicity of a harness that stabilizes a baby on your lap during airplane turbulence, to the extravagance of an in-car DVD player, there's not much here, and it's not all easy to shop for, but you'll be glad you did sometime midvoyage.

| ·BOOKS & MEDIA ·ACCESSORIES | ·SAFETY | ·BABY NEEDS | ·TRAVEL |
|---|---|---|---|

## FAO.com
### FAO Schwarz • 800-876-7867

For more than 130 years, FAO Schwarz has been one of the greatest toy stores in the whole wide world. Now, it's one of the best on the world wide web. Its ever-reaching selection is easy to access, either by category, age or brand, and special boutique sections make it easy to browse popular names like Lego, G.I. Joe and Thomas the Tank Engine. You may even sort through FAO exclusive products, like the giant floor piano made famous by the movie *Big*. It might be best if your kids don't find out about this site.

| ·TOYS & GAMES | ·EDUCATIONAL | | |
|---|---|---|---|

## Fisher-PriceStore.com
### Fisher-Price • 608-831-5210

Responsible for the ubiquitous round, bubbly, colorful and oversized toys known to children for generations, the Fisher-Price brand is no stranger to the hands of tots. You pretty much know the kind of stuff you'll find here, from Power Wheels to Sesame Street merchandise. Unfortunately, not every one of their products is available for sale online, so if you're looking for a My First Record Player or something you might be disappointed. Then again, some stuff is only available online. Funny how that is.

| ·TOYS & GAMES | | | |
|---|---|---|---|

## FreeBears.com
### FreeBears.com • 866-340-2327

Alas, unless you win one of their monthly drawings, there are no free teddy bears to be had with this site. Actually, as selling these toys are their *raison d'être* they would be sort of foolish to give them away. Likely, though, the site would survive merely by selling its selection of Disney-related merchandise, bolstered further by its sampling of plush Seaworld, GUND and Winnie the Pooh dolls. Categories like Jungle Animals, Cushy Critters and Bendum Buddies probably don't hurt much either.

| ·TOYS & GAMES | | | |
|---|---|---|---|

## FrenchToast.com
### French Toast School Uniforms • 800-373-6248

We may never know what the term "French Toast" has to do, if anything, with this "School Uniform Superstore," but in time we've learned that it's better simply not to ask. Instead, the focus should be placed on the selection of pleated plaid skirts, cardigans, jumpers, polos and other standard-issue wardrobe items of institutional dress codes. If your child's school does indeed adhere to a uniform policy, chances are good that running a search here will turn up a selection of items especially suited to the school, whether it requires ties, special backpacks or pea coats.

| ·CLOTHES | ·UNIFORMS | ·ACCESSORIES | |
|---|---|---|---|

## 323-653-3388 • GaGa Gifts
## GaGaGifts.com

A relatively small selection of "gifts of whimsy," this site's appeal will largely be to the nostalgic set. Popular items include a cartoonish wind-up alarm clock, blankets with cowboy patterns and a traditional tin jack-in-the-box. Just when you think it's over, you encounter the Click Here to See the Products We Try to keep in Stock link, which of course leads you to the good stuff (in most cases). Not quite what you'd expect from a retailer based out of a hip Los Angeles neighborhood, but it suits us fine, cowpoke.

| ·TOYS & GAMES | ·BOOKS & MEDIA | ·ACCESSORIES | ·BABY NEEDS |
|---|---|---|---|

## 888-906-1104 • Gap Kids
## GapKids.com

Sure, most of this site seems like an excuse to show you yet more pictures from one of The Gap's many ubiquitous (and no doubt expensive) marketing campaigns. Other than making this shopping experience a little slow, there's little trouble caused by these images; you can still easily access the points of interest here: the clothes. Everything that you might expect from this mall store with a shop in nearly every town makes itself readily available online. As their sizes remain fairly simple and consistent, it's a wonder anybody would bother going into one of the stores anymore.

| ·CLOTHES | ·ACCESSORIES | ·SHOES | ·BABY NEEDS |
|---|---|---|---|

## 704-573-4500 • GeniusBabies.com
## GeniusBabies.com

This store would seem to operate under the theory that a stimulating environment will improve a child's creative impulses and brainpower in general. Sounds plausible. And what could it hurt to surround your child with mobiles, colorful playmats, soothing music and thought-provoking toys? Well, this is what you get when a bunch of devoted mommies band together to create a business concerned with the betterment of child rearing—a pretty darn good business. Here's hoping the child-rearing part works as well.

| ·TOYS & GAMES | ·BABY NEEDS | | |
|---|---|---|---|

## 212-505-7615 • GirlProps.com
## GirlProps.com

Cheerfully proclaiming their aversion to the word "cheap," the proprietors of this site would rather view their inexpensive items with a touch of humor. But how else could we look upon the brightly colored wigs and glitzy, glam accessories presumed to go with them? The truth is, some of the fancy bobby pins, poofy hair clips and glitter makeup merely makes us smile a little. Hey, some girls just like to sparkle, just like some girls like to wear a set of feathery wings when they dress up for a night out. Well, this site is for just such a girl.

| ·ACCESSORIES | | | |
|---|---|---|---|

## GoJane.com
GoJane.com • 800-846-5263

Teens and young adults will especially appreciate the low prices and sassy styles represented in this somehow straightforward and funky online shop. The pants for sale are especially fun, but jeans aren't the only things here with flair. Whether it's a homecoming dress, a cool pair of shoes or summery tanks and tube tops, all is represented here with a range of attitude. But it's attitude you don't have to pay extreme prices for, which is great because younger women tend to have less money.

## Golfini.com
i golfini della nonna • 323-782-1410

If you're looking for a place to buy hand-knitted apparel for your infant, you've found it. Here, the i golfini della nonna line of merchandise (translated, "grandmother's little sweaters") is conveniently laid out for your perusal. Though limited in quantity, the selection, which also includes booties, T-shirts, rompers and beanies, offers a variety of colors and sizes for your first-year child. Only one thing may leave you wondering: how do such original clothes, whether you settle upon a lime green cardigan or a pink union suit, still manage to "recapture the feeling of yesteryear?"

## GopherSport.com
Gopher Sport • 800-533-0446

As if the trauma of Phys Ed in school wasn't enough, this site allows you to recreate the experience at home, offering all manner of children's recreational and athletic gear. For starters, you can find many sizes of those ubiquitous red, air-filled balls (known to many as the terror-inflicting "dodge ball"). Then there're big items like climbing-walls, gymnastic stations, bowling carpets, tetherball sets and even those big parachutes that teach youngsters the value of... something or other. Once you've filled your yard with this equipment, you can even get scoreboards and bleachers, invite other parents over and hold a tournament to determine whose kid is best at what.

## GreenBabies.com
Green Babies • 800-603-7508

To avoid any misunderstandings, let it be known that we at **thepurplebook** believe babies to be wonderful and extra-special no matter what color they happen come in. We just happen to be fond of Green Babies because they use 100% organically grown cotton. Yes, newborns up to 24 months of age may be securely nuzzled in these rompers and cushy hats that use toxin-free dyes on top of being ecologically sound. Sure, the kids won't be able to say, "ecological," let alone understand it, but they'll sure understand what cozy means.

## 877-444-8377 • Guess

### Guess.com

Welcome to the site where even the infant models wear too much makeup. They do look pretty good, though that may have something more to do with the clothes they're wearing than anything else. You have to click deep in order to get anywhere, but it's worth it for a great selection of stuff ranging from sweaters and jeans to jackets and girl's swimsuits for starters. In this place, even newborns wear viable styles. As if they already didn't grow up too fast....

| ·CLOTHES | ·NURSERY | | |
|---|---|---|---|

## 877-449-6932 • Gymboree

### Gymboree.com

Gymboree began as an altruistic program aimed to enrich the social development of young children through interactive play and musical exercises. Somewhere along the way they opened retail stores, selling their own brand of bright and colorful clothing through hundreds of franchises in several countries. Now they bring their wares to the web with this artfully designed site. Simply organized by age and gender, these easy-to-view clothes are made to be mixed and matched, though a Gift Center will suggest specific outfits should you have any doubts. If you want to know more about the program, the site points you to local Gymboree Play & Music classes, which only forces you to wonder: what will all the other children be wearing?

| ·TOYS & GAMES | ·CLOTHES | ·ACCESSORIES | |
|---|---|---|---|

## 800-222-0544 • Hanna Andersson

### HannaAndersson.com

If for some reason the apparel on this site looks familiar, that's because these soft fabrics and colorful designs draw inspiration from the clothes worn by Swedish schoolchildren. It's not surprising, then, that this clothing line excels in winter clothes, stuff like long johns, sweaters, mittens and especially a wild selection of knit caps. There's a deep selection, which can make shopping a less than speedy process despite animated menus. It evens out, though, as impulse shopping here could lead you to buy everything you see.

| ·CLOTHES ·NURSERY | ·UNIFORMS ·BABY NEEDS | ·ACCESSORIES | ·SHOES |
|---|---|---|---|

## 800-554-7637 • Healthtex

### HealthTex.com

This is an imaginative and colorfully illustrated site, which unfortunately makes it slow and confusing. As fun as the cartoonish options might seem, we'd recommend steering clear of some of these visual navigation techniques (if you can make sense of Playville Hill, more power to ya). Instead, stick to the right-side menu to track down their selections of affordable, easy to mix-and-match clothes for babies and up. It still may prove a little disorienting as you click deeper, but if you stick to using the pull-down menus that appear you will be able to find the clothes, we promise.

| ·CLOTHES | ·NURSERY | | |
|---|---|---|---|

## HearthSong.com

Stressing the importance of imaginative play among children, this site promises "toys you'll feel good about giving." In a nutshell, you'll find lots of arts and crafts kits, including areas of interest like music, cooking and gardening. Featured are plenty of outdoor activities and, given the appeal much of this will also have to adults, it can prove a great place to seek out family activities. While a kit teaching kids how to make their own soda pop strikes one as a tad less than healthy, in most cases these guys hit the mark.

| ·TOYS & GAMES ·ACCESSORIES | ·BOOKS & MEDIA | ·EDUCATIONAL | ·SPORTS |
|---|---|---|---|

## iBabyDoc.com

Each of the products you will find in this baby-specific store comes recommended by a board-certified pediatrician. Specifically, by the pediatrician who founded the store. His feeling is that, whatever sort of baby product you are looking for there are only really a couple of satisfactory products available, if that. So, if you're going to believe someone just because he's been educated and has experience making sure young children stay healthy and sound, even if he does profit these products might just be what you are looking for.

| ·TOYS & GAMES ·PARENTS' TOOLS | ·EDUCATIONAL ·ACCESSORIES | ·HEALTH ·NURSERY | ·SAFETY ·BABY NEEDS |
|---|---|---|---|

## ImagineToys.com

This site focuses on products for children that "inspire the imagination while building confidence and strong, quick minds." Sounds kinda cool, we guess, if you're into that sort of thing. Shopping by age seems to be the best way to filter out items inappropriate for one child or another, but some helpful categories like Outdoor Toys and Musical Instruments prove invaluable if you want something specific. In particular, they seem to have an overabundance of Ride On toys, so Junior can imagine himself in traffic.

| ·TOYS & GAMES | ·BOOKS & MEDIA | ·EDUCATIONAL |
|---|---|---|

## InFashionKids.com

Promising "great fashion at gentle prices," this New Jersey–based retailer offers a broad range of clothes for babies and older children, featuring what could only be considered dapper dress clothes for boys and darling dresses for girls. Category headings tell the rest of the tale, with fantastic Pajamas, plenty of Shoes, Slippers & Socks, lots of Children's Coats and the ever-popular Swimwear & Water Shoes. The best, though, might be their Halloween Costumes section, which offer some classics, as well as stuff like Superman and Barbie that actually look like the character in question, as opposed to the dreadfully familiar plastic smock with the picture of the character on it. A must see.

| ·CLOTHES ·SUNDAY BEST | ·SHOES | ·NURSERY | ·BABY NEEDS |
|---|---|---|---|

## 800-541-0314 • Into The Wind

**IntoTheWind.com**

This might be the best place online to buy a kite. That is, if you're impressed with such things as a terrific selection of box kites, stunt kites, flying animal shapes and traditional designs (i.e., diamond shapes). Or would it thrill you to notice that there's a healthy sampling of kites that'll fly when there's almost no wind at all? Or maybe you don't like actively battling the wind for position and would rather sit by, sipping a lemonade, watching a windsock or spinner from your porch or patio? From boomerangs to lawn ornaments to the special kite designs that'll soar so high you need binoculars to see them, this site humbly serves your kite-flying needs and then some.

| ·TOYS & GAMES | ·SPORTS | | |
|---|---|---|---|

## 310-833-7768 • Isabel Garreton

**IsabelGarreton.com**

We try to maintain a semblance of objectivity in our site reviews, and we're certainly not trying to sell you any children's clothes (if these entries seem a little lopsided towards the positive, it's because we tossed the bad ones). However, this site is simply great. Great because the girl's and baby girl's dresses are fantastically adorable, especially those meant for special occasions. Simple because... well, it's incredibly easy to pick a winner from these seasonal designs. There is one drawback, though—each dress is part of a limited run, and they all tend to sell out fairly quick. No pressure, but don't hesitate to check this one out.

| ·CLOTHES | ·SUNDAY BEST | | |
|---|---|---|---|

## 888-324-6356 • Journeys

**Journeys.com**

Hip kids need hip shoes or they become just kinda cool kids. That's how it works. Well, from skate shoes to boots and even Heelys (the shoes with wheels embedded in the heels), this shop's got the stylin' footwear youngsters and teens tend to clamor for. Brands like Adidas, Vans, Dr. Martens, Converse, Puma and Timberland in particular stand out, but many more are well represented in this store that's known to reside in a mall or two. Better to shop from them online, though, because food courts just aren't cool.

| ·CLOTHES | ·ACCESSORIES | ·SHOES | |
|---|---|---|---|

## 800-342-6321 • J-Ray Shoes

**JRayShoes.com**

For those of us who think it's never too early to teach our daughters a healthy appreciation for shoes, there's this site, which would seem boring to anybody lacking in such a lust for footwear. Sure, there are plenty of shoes for young boys here too, as well as a hefty selection for babies. But the real meat of the site lies in its sandals, boots and ballerina slippers; really, all kinds of dainty little shoes for the girl with a demanding wardrobe. Simple to use by anyone's standards, your little girl's going to need some more closet space.

| ·SHOES | | | |
|---|---|---|---|

## KBToys.com

KB Toys • 413-496-3000

You've got to hand it to this pillar of the mall toy community—it is thorough. With as large a selection of toys as it has to sell, you would think that particular toys would be tough to find, or that it might take weeks to receive your order. Not so. You can find items based on your child's age, toy name brands, and various toy categories. A Gift Registry lets your child pick out things he or she really wants, so as to avoid the trauma of receiving, say, a Nintendo 64 instead of a Sega Dreamcast. It's maybe not the kind of abject commercial efficiency you always dreamed of, but if convenience, speed, and ease of use count for anything in toy shopping, this successor to the eToys domain might just be your ticket.

·TOYS & GAMES

## LearningCo.com

Broderbund • 319-247-3325

From educational-software specialist Broderbund comes this online store that strives to make all the time your children spend in front of a computer productive for a change (you may continue to waste time online). From fun and games to educational and reference materials, these software packages often feature popular characters like Scooby Doo, Carmen Sandiego and a bunch of kooky Dr. Seuss creations. Other software may not be so kid-specific, but should enable you to make the most out of computer-assisted quality time with the youngsters, especially when bad weather keeps you all from going outside.

·BOOKS & MEDIA    ·EDUCATIONAL    ·PARENTS' TOOLS

## Lego.com

Lego • 800-453-4652

Is it the best toy on the planet? Well, on any given day that would be up to you. Whether you just want a big box full of pieces to assemble into the shapes of your erstwhile imagination, or you're looking for detailed kits to assemble properly into things like remote control cars, dinosaurs or *Star Wars* spaceships, they're all here in the form of Lego's trademark interlocking pieces. Did we say for you? Um, we meant your kids of course. They will love to piece it all together. Then, they might need a little assistance, especially if you get one of the sets that allow them to assemble actual, working, programmable robots. Yeah, robots! Just, at least let the kids help out a little bit.

·TOYS & GAMES

## LillianVernon.com

Lillian Vernon • 800-545-5426

Lillian Vernon created a mail-order empire back in 1951 with a simple ad selling personalized leather belts and handbags. In 50 years, her line of merchandise has made its way to the internet, and expanded to include a vast array of gifts and decorations for the home, and a surprisingly fun selection of products for kids. You may question the catalog's evolution from monogrammed belts to children's water toys, but inflatable waterslides, water balloon machines, and "stay afloat swimsuits" are just some of the things available here that you just simply don't see anywhere else. The site also features educational toys, clothes, and a bunch of other stuff your kids will love, as long as you don't mention where you got it.

·TOYS & GAMES    ·EDUCATIONAL    ·SPORTS    ·ACCESSORIES

## 877-661-2229 • Little Things Mean a Lot

**LtlThings.com**

Not just a jumble of letters, this site representing Little Things Mean a Lot Infant Specialties aims to make special occasions just as formally stuffy for infants as they are for the rest of us. Actually, these satin, cotton and gabardine suits, dresses and bibs are probably as comfortable as they come, particularly those designed for religious ceremonies across multiple religions and denominations. Take, for example, the tiny white satin tuxedo we found. Talk about smooth.

| ·CLOTHES | ·SUNDAY BEST | ·ACCESSORIES | |
|---|---|---|---|

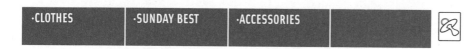

## 888-388-0000 • Mastermind Toys

**MasterMindToys.com**

A confusing jumble of stuff awaits you at MasterMindToys.com, but it's good stuff. They have a great selection of Arts & Crafts materials, from the typical to the sublime (a Make Your Own Lip Balm kit, for example). They also feature a range of other toys that, as they put it, "encourage curiosity and challenge thinking." Sounds pretty cool, huh? They are. With so many smile-inducing toys, from construction kits and puppets to things that fly, if your kid can't find something he likes here, at least you will.

| ·TOYS & GAMES | ·EDUCATIONAL | | |
|---|---|---|---|

## 425-649-1100 • Net Nanny

**NetNanny.com**

Chances are, your child doesn't remember a time before computers crept into our homes, and it's just second nature for them to hop online and have the uncensored world at their fingertips. If this bothers you, this software arms you with technology to shield minors from sites and information that run counter to your childrearing. Like a V-chip for your PC, a personalized filter lets you block out undesirable content, still allowing Junior to make the most of his browsing time. The site also sells family-friendly books, magazines and games, and features content-based reviews of popular movies, TV shows and computer games, so you can prevent your kids from seeing, hearing or egregiously destroying evil in virtually all of its entertaining formats.

| ·SAFETY | ·PARENTS' TOOLS | | |
|---|---|---|---|

## 616-361-1100 • Not-A-Beanbag.com

**NotABeanBag.com**

You see, it may look like a beanbag, and it may act like a beanbag, but no folks, if there's one thing this store wants you to know, it's that its primary product is not a beanbag. Welcome to the "Home of the World-Famous Polymorphic Poof Chair"— not as famous as its bean-filled cousin, it seems. The great and important distinction being made here is that these chairs, pillows and couches aren't filled with polystyrene pellets but with malleable foam that meets the contours of your body and yet manages to retain its original shape. The great benefit to your family's household? When your children inevitably tear one open to see how it works, you won't have to clean up a mess of beans.

| ·FURNITURE | | | |
|---|---|---|---|

## OldNavy.com

Old Navy • 800-653-6289

It's tough to imagine a better match for kids than the clothes offered by Old Navy—their easy-to-mix, colorful styles prove handy in keeping children's wardrobes small but flexible, and with decent prices you get more bang for your buck. Of course, there's a little more to it than that; these goofy styles come and go at about the same clip as your kids' sizes. In other words, these are great clothes for a youngster to grow out of. This is the site to check out if you really want to make it easy on yourself.

| ·CLOTHES | | | |
|---|---|---|---|

## Oliebollen.com

Oliebollen • 877-543-2665

When they were handing out domain names, it seems this seller of "cool things for kids" was last in line. But with excellent design, wacky presentation and amusing illustrations, this site named for a Dutch fried pastry (literally translated, "oil flour balls") won't soon be forgotten. Its proprietor, "a former stay-at-home mom with a stubborn addiction to childish living," is intent on avoiding second-rate mass-market items, offering only handpicked toys, books, clothes and accessories of the highest quality. Classic titles like *Good Night Gorilla* or *The Stinky Cheese Man* are for sale in the Books section, or you can find great furnishings in the cleverly illustrated Olie's Room.

| ·TOYS & GAMES ·NURSERY | ·CLOTHES ·BABY NEEDS | ·BOOKS & MEDIA | ·ACCESSORIES |
|---|---|---|---|

## OneStepAhead.com

One Step Ahead • 800-274-8440

If you're not fond of snooping through great big selections of child and baby items, and would prefer a little selectivity from your retailer, this site might be right for you. Founding mom-and-pop Karen and Ian Scott provide a valuable editorial selection based on their own worldwide research of products. Categories like Child Proofing, Bathtime Fun, On the Go Gear and Diapers & Potty turn up some unique items such as an Auto[mobile] Bottle Warmer, a tot-sized chili pepper costume and the Fun Flushin' Musical potty. Given its relatively small size, this one rules in selection.

| ·TOYS & GAMES ·SAFETY | ·BOOKS & MEDIA ·PARENTS' TOOLS | ·EDUCATIONAL ·NURSERY | ·HEALTH ·BABY NEEDS |
|---|---|---|---|

## OshKoshBGosh.com

Osh Kosh B'Gosh • 800-692-4674

Originally established in 1895 to manufacture hardy clothing for "the working man," by the early 20th century Osh Kosh designs had become just sturdy enough to outfit children as well. Today, guided by the success of their signature product, bib overalls, they feature a variety of clothes and accessories, for infants on through adults. The primary focus, though, is definitely on their kid's line, which has expanded over the century to include swimwear, outdoors wear, and even underwear. With a well-conceived and colorful site, this purveyor of classic Americana will likely meet the rigorous demands of active children for years to come.

| ·CLOTHES ·BABY NEEDS | ·ACCESSORIES | ·SHOES | ·NURSERY |
|---|---|---|---|

## 888-660-6111 • Papo d'Anjo

**PapoDAnjo.com**

We can't figure out exactly what Papo D'Anjo means (something about angels), but we do know that this selection of "classic handmade children's clothing" comes from Portugal. Featuring lots of plaid and floral patterns, stuff like bloomers, short overalls and sundresses with poplin collars will make you wonder about just how strongly these guys place an emphasis on the word "classic," but the styles are updated just enough to prove modern, if in a quaintly European way; just look at the great pictures.

| ·CLOTHES | ·SUNDAY BEST | | |  |
|---|---|---|---|---|

## 303-440-7229 • PlayFair Toys

**PlayFairToys.com**

Once you log on you'll probably doubt it, but we promise that this site plays home to some very cool stuff. We're talking pogo sticks, teepees and fire-engine-shaped beds for starters. Problem is, the site looks like a dud. This lack of visual appeal isn't helped much by the fact that each category link you follow leads to a list of text-based links, which means you have to do a lot of reading and clicking to find what you like (we hate that). But hey—that's the price for leaving the beaten path, and some of this stuff does differ from the norm. It will take some digging, but may be worth it.

| ·TOYS & GAMES | ·FURNITURE | ·SPORTS | |  |
|---|---|---|---|---|

 ★

## 866-767-4868 • Posh Tots

**PoshTots.com**

Boasting, "the most extraordinary children's furnishings in the world," these guys go on to say that they seek "to spark the imagination of children by making their environments engaging and inspiring." Well, we've known sites to pay a lot of lip service to the idea of evoking the imagination; however most don't turn out to be the best children's furniture shop online. Offering decorative themes like Circus, Nursery Rhymes, Castle and Tribeca Loft, the greatest danger of this understandably expensive retailer is that once you've furnished your child's room with this merchandise, the rest of your home will look shabby and dull in comparison.

| ·FURNITURE | ·CUSTOM | | |  |
|---|---|---|---|---|

 ★

## 310-257-9400 • Quality Trading

**QualityTrading.com**

Before the word "quality" leads you to any false conclusions, you should know that these guys specialize in inflatable furniture. Truly. So, maybe this stuff isn't suitable for the living room; there are still plenty of advantages to a sofa that floats. See for yourself, as they also sell a selection of inflatable swimming pools; nothing too big, just some fun in the summertime types of deals. We don't know where this site came from or why it sells the things it does, but if you're a kid, a velour inflatable sofa set just feels right. Truly.

| ·TOYS & GAMES | ·FURNITURE | ·SPORTS | |
|---|---|---|---|

## QuincyShop.com
Quincy • 800-299-4242

Here's a rarity; a retailer that's picky about the makeup of its customer base. As they put it, they "serve customers who love life. Make art, see. Laugh out loud. Write and build." Grammar aside, these guys do really intend to promote intelligence and creativity, as evidenced in their selection of journals, musical instruments, crafts kits, Photographic Tomfoolery, art supplies and games. It's a bunch of great stuff in a pretty darn good shop. Cool kids only need apply.

| ·TOYS & GAMES | ·SPORTS | ·EDUCATIONAL | |
|---|---|---|---|

## RainBee.com
RainBee.com • 877-724-6233

Almost like shopping on another planet, the types of items you find here will be familiar (stuff like young children's toys, furniture and apparel), but none of the names. For starters, the clothing lines featured include ultra-adorable designers like Munki Munki and H. M. Woggle Bug. The Furniture section offers definite high points, in particular with some bunk beds that follow Pirate and Excalibur themes, among others. Best of all, though, might be the toys, which include such nonstandard fare as a puppet theater and animal-shaped playmates. All in all, a toddler's delight, if you're patient enough to navigate into unknown brand territory, as the site offers no other way to browse.

| ·TOYS & GAMES ·ACCESSORIES | ·CLOTHES ·NURSERY | ·FURNITURE ·BABY NEEDS | ·EDUCATIONAL |
|---|---|---|---|

## RedWagons.com
Red Wagons • No Service Number

Could they be any more explicit? Yes, these guys sell little red wagons—specifically, Radio Flyer wagons (the famous kind). But that's not all, as it turns out. The site also features battery-powered ride-ons, tricycles, scooters and bicycles (with or without training wheels), which means they have two-, three- and four-wheeled vehicles for tots covered. Heck, they even have toboggans (should wheels prove too advanced) and, since it all can lead to elements of danger, you can check out the Safety Gear section for some peace of mind.

| ·TOYS & GAMES | ·SAFETY | ·SPORTS | ·BABY NEEDS |
|---|---|---|---|

## RightStart.com
The Right Start • 888-548-8531

The bevy of educational experts RightStart.com has established, from librarians to coaches to pediatricians, can certainly guide you on the development of your child through their regularly featured Q&A columns. But nothing will prepare you for the incredible amount of educational tools, toys, kits, games and gear for sale on this site. Organized by brand, grade, price or age group, every link will lead you to highly entertaining and stimulating products in such fields as science, art, sports and language. Highlights include ant farms, phonics sets and clay for younger kids, with robotics kits, kayaks and steel drums for children with a little more experience in life. Your only complaint may be that there was no RightStart.com when you were younger....

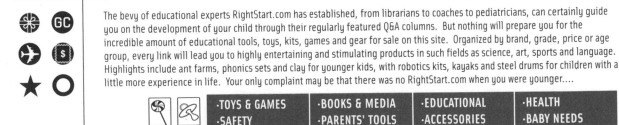

| ·TOYS & GAMES ·SAFETY | ·BOOKS & MEDIA ·PARENTS' TOOLS | ·EDUCATIONAL ·ACCESSORIES | ·HEALTH ·BABY NEEDS |
|---|---|---|---|

## 818-769-5563 • RoboToys

**RoboToys.com**

Boasting "Toys for the Moderne Age," this site might seem out of touch—then, it is Robo Toys. Dedicated to robots across the board, this sci-fi fan's dream store carries everything from Transformers and robot-related videos to robot kits, robot pets, robot models, infrared battle robots and remote control robots. Just when you think you're going to get tired of the word, of the notion, "robot," your eye catches yet something else available from this site that sets your circuits a-whir again, and it's, "robot, robot, robot," all day long.

| ·TOYS & GAMES | | | |
|---|---|---|---|

## No Service Number • RocketCash.com

**RocketCash.com**

Probably one of the most frightening moments for parents is the handing over of a credit card to their child; it is after all easy to imagine a family's entire savings suddenly being invested in forty-pound bags of candy. This company offers a less threatening way to give kids access to internet commerce. Parents can set predetermined amounts for their children to spend with Rocket Cash accounts, which may be used like credit cards at hundreds of online shops. You still may end up with candy, just not a lifetime supply.

| ·PARENTS' TOOLS | | | |
|---|---|---|---|

## 800-638-3330 • The Rocking Toy Co.

**RockingToy.com**

The Rocking Toy Company offers a fantastic selection of rocking horses that are each handcrafted and hand-painted, featuring exquisite detail on such things as saddles, bridles and manes. But it's not all horses here; this selection includes planes and trains for modern rockers, and a ram for... well, if for nothing else variety's sake. For the more casual set you may find rocking chairs here, but no less ornate as they feature character carvings of bears, cats and clowns. A selection rounded out by statuesque, nonrocking carvings ensure you will have no shortage of borderline creepy cartoonish faces with which to scare your young children.

| ·TOYS & GAMES | ·FURNITURE | | |
|---|---|---|---|

## 800-770-4662 • Scholastic

**Scholastic.com**

Chances are, your kids come home from school a couple of times a year all excited about reading and wanting you to buy them books from a little paper Scholastic catalog that was passed out in class. It's a financially motivated service, yes, but if it gets kids excited by reading, maybe it's not entirely bad. Well, if you'd like a go at maintaining that excitement year-round, you can find all the popular favorites here, including the Goosebumps and now legendary Harry Potter series.

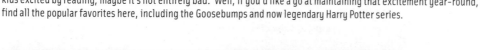

| ·TOYS & GAMES | ·BOOKS & MEDIA | ·EDUCATIONAL | ·PARENTS' TOOLS |
|---|---|---|---|

## SchoolUnif.com

Here's a site brought to you from bizarro-world, courtesy of the Frank Bee Uniform [Company], known to service such clients as the FBI, Secret Service and NASA. Yes, it's all a bit perplexing, especially when you come across items like gas masks and Kevlar body armor. There are actually school uniforms for children in here, we promise, plus Scout uniforms (Boy, Girl, Brownie and Webelo), dance shoes and a selection of ceremonial gowns, in case you need one quick. Does this site get any weirder? The answer to that would be an emphatic "YES—" that is, unless you happen to be in the market for a Mobile Command Center.

| ·CLOTHES ·ACCESSORIES | ·SUNDAY BEST ·SHOES | ·SPORTS ·SAFETY | ·UNIFORMS |
|---|---|---|---|

## SensationalBeginnings.com

Brandishing "toys and tools that celebrate the wonders of childhood," this catalog features "products for infants and toddlers that stimulate their senses while promoting interaction between parent and child." It's really not as dull as it sounds, though it may seem so if you use the navigational tabs at the top of the page (probably the first to catch your eye). Instead, if you stick to Shop by Age or Shop by Category you'll find a vibrant, fun selection of stuff endorsed by a nurse (even if she is the site's founder). Better yet, shop here in the months preceding Halloween and find the best children's costume selection going.

| ·TOYS & GAMES ·SAFETY | ·FURNITURE ·TRAVEL | ·BOOKS & MEDIA | ·SPORTS |
|---|---|---|---|

## ShoeBuy.com

In no other form of apparel is proper sizing so important than shoes. Pants that don't fit may fall down, but if shoes are too tight or loose they can cause blisters or muscular tension—either way, it makes shopping online for shoes a scary proposition. ShoeBuy.com helps you overcome this fear with printable sizing charts and a unique feature that displays the specific fitting characteristics of each model they offer. And, in the Kids section, you'll find a great variety of name-brand shoes. So much, in fact, that you should forego the standard product navigation on the left side and use the Brand, Category, and Department menus located at the top of the page, or your kids might outgrow their shoes before you've bought them.

| ·SHOES | | | |
|---|---|---|---|

## ShopZoo.com

Where would you expect to find "the web's greatest selection of stuffed animals... fuzzy and furry creatures [ranging] from armadillos and bears to giant pandas and tigers to zebras?" Why, the world-famous San Diego Zoo, of course! Well, in their online store, that is. In addition to a varied selection of such cuddly critters as koalas, these guys offer plush versions of slightly more ferocious, creepy and/or prickly animals like a Tasmanian devil, tarantula and porcupine. Whatever the animal, it's nice to know that some of the proceeds go towards the preservation of species and habitats (though one less venomous spider wouldn't really hurt anybody, right?).

| ·TOYS & GAMES | ·BABY NEEDS | |
|---|---|---|

## 800-320-0890 • Small Blue Planet
**SmallBluePlanet.com**

This Small Blue Planet is populated mostly by action figures—literally thousands of them. Now, we're not talking about the G.I. Joe or *Star Wars* figurines to which you're probably accustomed. These figures include ultrarealistic characters like the Israeli Defense Force Weapons Instructor, the British Paratrooper and the SWAT Sharpshooter (even special "hostage" dolls to go with him). But don't start thinking you know what to expect here, or you'll be shocked to discover Yellow Submarine characters (even Ringo), Rockem Sockem Robots, Transformers, DC Comics dolls and a special edition Frank Sinatra Barbie.

·TOYS & GAMES

## 800-293-9314 • Smarter Kids
**SmarterKids.com**

Do your kids want you to shop for toys here? Probably not. But what do kids know anyway? Not much, at least until they start waxing educational with fun but informative toys, the likes of which exist here in abundance. Shopping generally starts by age group, but you can easily bypass that in favor of popular characters, themes and brands, or you can select whichever particular subject (the "Three R's" included) upon which you'd like a child to focus. Add some "Specialty Centers" devoted to Special Needs or Gifted & Talented children, and this site can help your kids get smart, even if you ain't so much.

·TOYS & GAMES ·BOOKS & MEDIA ·EDUCATIONAL

## 323-664-3489 • Souls
**SoulsShoes.com**

Strictly speaking, this one's not a baby-oriented retailer. But if you look past the loafers, slides and other comfort-oriented women's shoes, you'll come across a simple selection of baby booties. This is merely one type of booty, available in three sizes, and offered in barely a dozen colors. Each is constructed with a cushy microfiber and lined with a nusuede trim, and each comes with a matching baby blanket. If you don't like them, you're out of luck. Nevertheless, we think you'll like them, and so do they. In fact, they're so confident, they offer the "Baby Booty Grab Bag," which includes every available color, so your baby's booties can match veritably every outfit. Booty.

·SHOES ·BABY NEEDS

## 800-864-0080 • Sports 4 Kids
**Sports4Kids.com**

Just like it sounds (though not quite like it's spelled), this site caters to the needs of athletically motivated children. With equipment for basketball, baseball, football, soccer and hockey, pretty much all of the Little League team sports are covered, as well as individual games such as tennis, wrestling, snowboarding and golf. From protective gear (including prescription safety goggles) to recreational items (toboggans and skateboards), and uniforms for nearly every appropriate occasion, this site will really help you push that competitive edge (bench warmers sold separately).

·SPORTS

# TotShop.com

From some of our favorite web entrepreneurs comes this site that focuses on designer children's wares, "most of them designed by moms who saw a void in the children's wear marketplace." Basically, the shop consists of "boutiques" featuring designers like Cozy Toes, Koo Koo and Baby A Go Go. Who are these designers? Well, it's not like kids really talk about their clothes on the playground, so in general the labels won't make a difference to anybody. Let's just say that this stuff constitutes just about the most fashion-forward gear you'll find for a toddler. Neat-o.

| | ·TOYS & GAMES ·BABY NEEDS | ·CLOTHES | ·ACCESSORIES | ·NURSERY |

# ToyCollection.com

"Presenting specialty toys from around the world," this online retailer offers us the sort of stuff we don't generally see often enough. The categories alone—like Puzzles & Brainteasers, Construction Toys, Puppets & Soft Toys and Action & Imagination—give us cause to wonder at all the changes technology has brought about. Sure, while robot dogs and video games thrill the tech-enthusiast, small children still appreciate the simpler things life has to offer. This site allows you to indulge such classic sensibilities, at least until they catch a glimpse of Saturday morning commercials.

| | ·TOYS & GAMES | | | |

# TractorJeans.com

To most of us, this is a spacey site with little to offer. However, to a blue jean–minded girl or teen, this could just represent "a galaxy of fashion." As it happens, this galaxy is restricted to young girls, juniors and junior plus sizes, and the selection itself is limited to jeans (and not many, at that). To be fair, the small selection does make an earnest attempt to keep fresh in regard to teen fashions, and so long as the size is right, shopping will be incredibly easy. Just tuck this one in the back of the brain.

| | ·CLOTHES | | | |

# TravelingTikes.com

Here's a fun little site "for kids on the go," whether they get there under their own power or with the help of somebody else. Category names like Car Seats, Strollers, Baby Carriers & Backpacks, Pedal Cars, Trikes and Wagons should pretty much give you the idea, though a few stationary products, like Bassinets/Bouncers and High Chairs may also be found. As if that weren't easy enough, they include shopping by Price and Brand as well, making up for any design deficiency we might otherwise have scored them for.

| | ·SPORTS ·TRAVEL | ·SAFETY | ·ACCESSORIES | ·BABY NEEDS |

## 541-548-6688 • Trendy Tootsies — TrendyTootsies.com

Here you'll find "fun and fashionable shoes for babies and toddlers," which generally means kooky hand-painted designs like cow print (Holstein), leopard print and petroglyphs. The selection is small, so it will only take you a few clicks to view the entire offering, but chances are you'll like at least a couple of pairs, if not in their regular View Line & Order section then on their What's New & Specials page. For a small, independently operated site out of rural Oregon, this one's fantastic.

| ·CUSTOM | ·SHOES | | |
|---|---|---|---|

## 866-746-7938 • Wet Seal — WetSeal.com

What began in the 1960s as a beachside bikini shack has grown immeasurably over the years to the point that it has over 500 stores in 42 states and even in US territories. What could promote such growth, you may ask? Well, for starters, their market is fashionable young women and teens. Add to that their hip, updated selections and slap on a moderate price tag, and you've got a sure-fire success waiting to happen. We can only hope the advent of this online branch will curb their growth somewhat, before the expansion of Starbucks is threatened by this seller of trendy garb.

| ·CLOTHES | ·ACCESSORIES | | |
|---|---|---|---|

## 800-500-4376 • Yummi Bears — YummiBears.com

Here's a product line that aims to please: a spate of nutritional supplements delivered in the form of gummi bears. Sure, kids will probably like eating them (careful, they may want to eat too many of them), but it's parents that would want to refine their kids' nutritional intake (though an easier way would be a reduction of fast food). At any rate, be sure to check the small print, which sets guidelines for dosage (usually "not to exceed...") and take note that the FDA doesn't regulate nutritional supplements.

| ·HEALTH | | | |
|---|---|---|---|

## 888-548-8531 • Zany Brainy — ZanyBrainy.com

It doesn't really take an elite squad of software-reviewing, educational "Kidsultants" to tell you that the toys, books, videos, software, and music available from this exciting children's store will invigorate and entertain your kids. But their stamp of approval for a catalog of stuff that is "hi-quality, non-violent, safe, and incredibly fun" sure doesn't hurt your peace of mind. Ranging from educational to just downright extraordinary, the toys here are perfect if you want your young scientist to grow his own frog, or if your performative tykes need to hone their karaoke skills. These musical instruments, picture books, and learning aids all promise to be "extraordinary," and as easy to find as velociraptor bones in a Mini Excavation Kit.

| ·TOYS & GAMES | ·EDUCATIONAL | | |
|---|---|---|---|

NOTES:

# Pets

Our affinity for animals can be so fickle. Take mice, for example: some of us keep them as pets. Some of us set traps to keep them dead and out of our cereal boxes. Yet others of us use them to feed the giant snakes we keep as pets. Increasingly, the distinction drawn between beastly creatures and pets has more to do with how we feel about them than how they feel about us. Yes, we love to turn animals into our own little unconditional friends—even if they sometimes aren't so little. While cats and dogs remain the most popular pets to keep, birds, reptiles, rodents, fish, horses and even spiders have become veritably commonplace. With the surprising exception of fish, none of these pets can actually at this time be purchased online (try to imagine the havoc a ferret in the postal system might wreak). But you *can* buy the food and hygiene products necessary for keeping these hungry little darlings alive, trained and happy, lest they chew on your nose for sustenance.

Then there're the less essential stuff. We found sites catering to all sorts of fashion tastes, particularly for dogs (who as we all know adore the spring collections). Dressing them up isn't the only way to lavish them with praise and love, of course. Gourmet treats, palatial estates [read: doghouses and furniture] and super fun toys are just some of the material items we can best use to show them a love they most assuredly understand. Mostly, there are the fun items that you can use to form those enduring bonds with the nonverbal members of your family (and parrots, lots of stuff for parrots). Really, if you take a look at everything, you'll eventually come to the same conclusion we have: Noah could have used this section to stock the ark.

NOTES:

## TIPS ON BUYING PET SUPPLIES ONLINE

These suggestions may help prevent frustration and furniture destruction.

•**IS IT EDIBLE?**  Anything you buy for your pets will almost assuredly end up in their mouths at some point, that's why they're called animals.  Be careful, then, about buying something that could be harmful if ingested, whether pointy, indigestible or flat-out poisonous.

•**CONSULT A VET:**  Sure, there's a bunch of health-related merchandise for your pet, and some fun treats, but as you would for yourself, be sure to consult a licensed medical professional before feeding your animals with anything potentially hazardous to their health.

•**ADOPT A PET:**  Now that you've got all this access to great stuff, wouldn't it be nice to add another member to your household?  Check the Pet Adoption link below or contact your local Humane Society or animal rescue to save a lovely creature from a lonely, imprisoned peril.

 ## SITES THAT MAY COME IN HANDY

The following URLs may be useful when you shop.

Pet Info, Resources & Community: http://www.greatpets.com
Pet Health Info & Vet Locator: http://www.petplace.com
Pet Training & Behavior: http://www.greatpets.com
Traveling With Pets: http://www.dogfriendly.com
Pet Adoption: http://www.petfinder.org
Dog Breeder's Index: http://www.animalplaza.com

>> ## SECTION ICON LEGEND

Use the following guide to understand the rectangular icons that appear throughout this section.

### EXOTIC PETS

These sites may or may not include stuff for dogs and cat, but they'll definitely carry supplies for one or more of the following: reptiles, amphibians, insects, critters, fish, birds and then some.

### HEALTH

Highlighting products that promote your animals' continued health, this icon covers everything from pet pharmaceuticals to pet health insurance.

### SUPERSTORE

A lot of pet stores cover all kinds of supplies for all kinds of pets. Defying further distinctions, sites beside this icon are known to cover all their bases, and will often not be associated with any specific animal key words.

## LIST OF KEY WORDS

The following words represent the types of items typically found on the sites listed in this section.

**ACCESSORIES**

Accessories for your pet may include collars, ID tags, aquarium décor, horseshoes and plenty else.

**BIRDS**

You know what birds are, right? They have wings, feathers and beaks... None are sold online, but stuff they like is.

**CATS**

Generally, these sites cover supplies for domesticated housecats, not the much larger, dangerous, predatory types.

**DOGS**

Man's best friend is probably the most commonly featured pet of all, and stuff for your pooch will be found in most of these sites.

**EQUIPMENT**

The types of equipment you'll need for your pet includes but will not be limited to: leashes, feeders, water bowls, scratching posts and habitrail tubes.

**FISH**

You'll want to supply your own water, but everything else you need to raise fish can be located by using this key word.

**FOOD**

This key word indicates that there's food available for one kind of pet or another. Use in conjunction with other key words to locate yours.

**GROOMING**

From brushes and nail clippers to shampoo, this stuff will keep your animal clean and cute (we don't know what it takes to make a lizard clean or cute, but we assume it's in there).

**HABITAT**

Wherever your animal likes to live, whether it's in an aquarium, cage, doghouse or just on a special bed, there's a store here that sells it (no stables).

**HORSES**

Preferably the only pet you try to ride, most of us cannot house a horse, but we can take care of their needs at a stable.

**PET APPAREL**

Most dogs and cats come equipped with a shiny fur coat. Still, some people feel the need to buy them clothes.

**REPTILES**

If there are reptiles that aren't snakes or lizards, we don't want to know. Also included here will be some amphibians.

**SMALL MAMMALS**

Some of these pets are ugly. All are small and furry though, including ferrets, hamsters, gerbils and rabbits.

**TOYS & TREATS**

Sometimes, a toy will be as fun for you as it is for your pet. Mostly, though, it will be something that your pet finds endlessly amusing for reasons we'll never understand. Still, we'll reward them for stellar play with treats.

**TRAINING**

Very important in keeping your relationship with your pet a positive one (not to mention with others), this points you to some essential training supplies for a variety of animals.

**TRAVEL**

Taking your pet on vacation can be tough, but we're apt to do it. These stores offer supplies that will help.

# >> KEY WORD INDEX

Use the following lists to locate online retailers that sell the Pet Supplies you seek.

## ACCESSORIES

13Cats.com
ABirdsWorld.com
AnneWayBernard.com
AudubonWorkshop.com
BestNest.com
CastorPolluxPet.com
CatToys.com
ChiwawaGaGa.com
ClassyPets.com
CleanRun.com
CoolPetStuff.com
CyberCanine.com
DecadentDogs.com
DogDayCafe.com
DogPark.com
DogToys.com
DoverSaddlery.com
FenixResearch.com
FetchPets.com
FoxAndHounds.com
GoTags.com
InTheCompanyOfDogs.com
JakesDogHouse.com
JeffersPet.com
LesPoochs.com
LuxuryDog.com
Morrco.com
PetCareRx.com
PetFoodExpress.com
PetsPreferUs.com
PetTags.com
PetVogue.com
RadioFence.com
SpeedyPetTags.com
TailsByTheBay.com
TheBirdBrain.com
TravelinPets.com
TrixieAndPeanut.com
UpTownPets.com
WagWear.com
YourActivePet.com

## BIRDS

5050PetSupply.com
ABirdsWorld.com
AudubonWorkshop.com
BestNest.com
FenixResearch.com
Lafeber.com
NaturesPet.com
PetClick.com
TheBirdBrain.com
UpTownPets.com

## CATS

13Cats.com
1888PetMeds.com
5050PetSupply.com
All-The-Best.com
CastorPolluxPet.com
CatToys.com
ClassyPets.com
ClickerTraining.com
EarthWiseAnimal.com
FenixResearch.com
FetchPets.com
FoxAndHounds.com
GoodPet.com
GoTags.com
GroomersChoice.com
HealthyPets.com
JakesDogHouse.com
MackiesParlour.com
NaturesPet.com
Pet-Shop.net
PetClick.com
PetRx.com
PetTags.com
PetVogue.com
RadioFence.com
SpeedyPetTags.com
TailsByTheBay.com
TravelinPets.com
TrixieAndPeanut.com
UpTownPets.com

## DOGS

1888PetMeds.com
5050PetSupply.com
All-The-Best.com
CastorPolluxPet.com
ChiwawaGaGa.com
ClassyPets.com
CleanRun.com
ClickerTraining.com
CyberCanine.com
DecadentDogs.com
DogDayCafe.com
DogPark.com
DogSupplies.com
DogToys.com
EarthWiseAnimal.com
FenixResearch.com
FetchPets.com
FoxAndHounds.com
GoodPet.com
GoTags.com
Grobiz.com
GroomersChoice.com
HealthyPets.com
InTheCompanyOfDogs.com
JakesDogHouse.com
LesPoochs.com
LuxuryDog.com
MackiesParlour.com
Morrco.com
NaturesPet.com
Pet-Containment-
  Systems.net
Pet-Shop.net
PetClick.com
PetRx.com
PetTags.com
PetVogue.com
RadioFence.com
SafePets.com
SmallDogMall.com
SpeedyPetTags.com
TailsByTheBay.com
ThreeDog.com
TravelinPets.com
TrixieAndPeanut.com
UpTownPets.com
WagWear.com
YourActivePet.com

## EQUIPMENT

AllPets.com
AudubonWorkshop.com
BestNest.com
CastorPolluxPet.com
ClassyPets.com
CleanRun.com
CoolPetStuff.com
DecadentDogs.com
DogDayCafe.com
DogSupplies.com
DoverSaddlery.com
DrsFosterSmith.com
FerretStore.com
GroomersChoice.com
JakesDogHouse.com
JeffersPet.com
LuxuryDog.com
Pet-Containment-
  Systems.net
Pet-Shop.net
PetCareRx.com
PetFoodDirect.com
PetFoodExpress.com
PetMarket.com
PetSmart.com
PetsPreferUs.com
PetVogue.com
RadioFence.com
SafePets.com
SmallDogMall.com
ThatPetPlace.com
TheBirdBrain.com
ValleyVet.com
WorldPetStore.com
YourActivePet.com

## FISH

PetClick.com
WorldPetStore.com

## FOOD

All-The-Best.com
AllPets.com
DrsFosterSmith.com
FerretStore.com
InTheCompanyOfDogs.com
JeffersPet.com
Lafeber.com
NaturesPet.com
Pet-Shop.net
PetCareRx.com
PetClick.com
PetFoodDirect.com
PetFoodExpress.com
PetMarket.com
PetSmart.com
PetsPreferUs.com
ThatPetPlace.com
TheBirdBrain.com
ThreeDog.com
ValleyVet.com

## GROOMING

All-The-Best.com
AllPets.com
CastorPolluxPet.com
ChiwawaGaGa.com
ClassyPets.com
CleanRun.com
CoolPetStuff.com
CyberCanine.com
DecadentDogs.com
DogDayCafe.com
DoverSaddlery.com
DrsFosterSmith.com
EarthWiseAnimal.com
FerretStore.com
FetchPets.com
GoodPet.com
GroomersChoice.com
HealthyPets.com
JakesDogHouse.com
JeffersPet.com
LesPoochs.com

Pet-Shop.net
PetCareRx.com
PetFoodDirect.com
PetFoodExpress.com
PetMarket.com
PetSmart.com
PetsPreferUs.com
PetVogue.com
SmallDogMall.com
TailsByTheBay.com
ThatPetPlace.com
TheBirdBrain.com
TrixieAndPeanut.com
UpTownPets.com
ValleyVet.com
WorldPetStore.com

## HABITAT

5050PetSupply.com
ABirdsWorld.com
AllPets.com
AudubonWorkshop.com
BestNest.com
ClassyPets.com
CleanRun.com
CoolPetStuff.com
DecadentDogs.com
DogSupplies.com
DrsFosterSmith.com
FerretStore.com
InTheCompanyOfDogs.com
JeffersPet.com
LuxuryDog.com
MackiesParlour.com
Pet-Shop.net
PetCareRx.com
PetFoodDirect.com
PetFoodExpress.com
PetMarket.com
PetSmart.com
PetsPreferUs.com
PetVogue.com
SafePets.com
SmallDogMall.com
SpeedyPetTags.com
TailsByTheBay.com
ThatPetPlace.com
TheBirdBrain.com
TrixieAndPeanut.com
UpTownPets.com
ValleyVet.com
WagWear.com
WorldPetStore.com

## HEALTH

1888PetMeds.com
All-The-Best.com
AllPets.com
CastorPolluxPet.com
CyberCanine.com
DoverSaddlery.com
DrsFosterSmith.com
EarthWiseAnimal.com
FerretStore.com
GoodPet.com
HealthyPets.com
JeffersPet.com
MyPetPrescriptions.com
NaturesPet.com
Pet-Shop.net
PetCareRx.com
PetClick.com
PetFoodDirect.com
PetInsurance.com
PetMarket.com
PetRx.com
PetSmart.com
ThatPetPlace.com
TheBirdBrain.com
ValleyVet.com
WorldPetStore.com

## HORSES

ClickerTraining.com
DoverySaddlery.com
GoTags.com
PetClick.com
UpTownPets.com
ValleyVet.com

## PET APPAREL

ChiwawaGaGa.com
ClassyPets.com
CleanRun.com
CoolPetStuff.com
DecadentDogs.com
DoverSaddlery.com
FerretStore.com
FetchPets.com
Grobiz.com
InTheCompanyOfDogs.com
LuxuryDog.com

MackiesParlour.com
PetFoodExpress.com
PetsPreferUs.com
SmallDogMall.com
TrixieAndPeanut.com
UpTownPets.com
WagWear.com

## REPTILES

FenixResearch.com

## SMALL MAMMALS

5050PetSupply.com
ChiwawaGaGa.com
FenixResearch.com
PetClick.com

## TOYS & TREATS

13Cats.com
5050PetSupply.com
AllPets.com
CastorPolluxPet.com
CatToys.com
ClassyPets.com
CoolPetStuff.com
DecadentDogs.com
DogDayCafe.com
DogPark.com
DogSupplies.com
DogToys.com
DrsFosterSmith.com
FerretStore.com
FetchPets.com
InTheCompanyOfDogs.com
JakesDogHouse.com
JeffersPet.com
Lafeber.com
LesPoochs.com
LuxuryDog.com
MackiesParlour.com
PetFoodDirect.com
PetFoodExpress.com
PetMarket.com
PetSmart.com
PetVogue.com
SmallDogMall.com
SpeedyPetTags.com
TailsByTheBay.com

ThatPetPlace.com
ThreeDog.com
TrixieAndPeanut.com
ValleyVet.com
WorldPetStore.com

## TRAINING

AllPets.com
CleanRun.com
ClickerTraining.com
CoolPetStuff.com
DogDayCafe.com
DogSupplies.com
DrsFosterSmith.com
GroomersChoice.com
Morrco.com
Pet-Shop.net
PetCareRx.com
PetFoodDirect.com
PetMarket.com
PetSmart.com
PetsPreferUs.com
RadioFence.com
SafePets.com
SmallDogMall.com
TailsByTheBay.com
ThatPetPlace.com
ValleyVet.com
WorldPetStore.com
YourActivePet.com

## TRAVEL

5050PetSupply.com
AllPets.com
ChiwawaGaGa.com
CleanRun.com
CoolPetStuff.com
DecadentDogs.com
DogDayCafe.com
DogPark.com
DogSupplies.com
DrsFosterSmith.com
FerretStore.com
FetchPets.com
JeffersPet.com
LuxuryDog.com
PetCareRx.com
PetFoodDirect.com
PetMarket.com
PetSmart.com

PetsPreferUs.com
PetVogue.com
SmallDogMall.com
SpeedyPetTags.com
TailsByTheBay.com
ThatPetPlace.com
TheBirdBrain.com
TravelinPets.com
TrixieAndPeanut.com
WagWear.com
WorldPetStore.com
YourActivePet.com

NOTES:

_____

_____

_____

_____

_____

_____

_____

_____

_____

_____

_____

_____

_____

_____

_____

_____

_____

_____

## 13Cats.com

If keeping cats as pets just isn't enough, and you feel the need to put kitty stuff all over your house and person, this is the site for you. Remarkably, there's less available for your cat here than there is for you, with a few things like the "Cat Dancer" or "Video Catnip" that you can enjoy together. The layout here is fairly easy to understand, but browsing is hindered by having to go back and forth between links, which will leave you playing with a mouse more than your feline. Seriously, it's better you heard that joke from us before entering this site.

| ·CATS | ·ACCESSORIES | ·TOYS & TREATS | |
|---|---|---|---|

## 1888PetMeds.com

"America's Largest Pet Pharmacy" turns out a pretty good web site here. With a bevy of nonprescription medicines and some vaccines that should preclude use of prescription drugs, caring for your hypochondriac pet just got a little easier and a whole lot cheaper. The Online Catalog pull-down menu makes it easy to shop for specific needs like Anxiety Relief, First Aid and Odor Control. But there are a lot of prescription-only products here as well, and you should definitely visit the vet before treating any ailment that's hindering your animal's quality of life.

| | ·DOGS | ·CATS | ·HEALTH | |
|---|---|---|---|---|

## 5050PetSupply.com

Here's a somewhat boutiquish version of your standard pet superstore—not a whole lot of merchandise, but good across the board. Their focus appears to be kennels, crates, cages and other sorts of containment units for dogs, cat, birds and small mammals, but you'll sporadically find stuff that's much more interesting than metal bars meant to restrict your animal's access to the car, room or yard. For example, the Cat Furniture section boasts some scratching posts that include hammocks (to make you jealous), and the Birds section features Playgyms (to make your children jealous). You'll wish there was more.

| ·BIRDS ·HABITAT | ·CATS ·TRAVEL | ·DOGS ·TOYS & TREATS | ·SMALL MAMMALS |
|---|---|---|---|

## ABirdsWorld.com

Well, here's a bit of a different view of pets—the kind you don't keep. The birds referred to in this domain name aren't canaries or macaws, but the wild birds that may peck around your backyard from time to time on the way to their next big flap. The products here allow you to play host to such free-spirited little creatures, with birdhouses, feeders and birdseed to make their visit an enjoyable one (and some binoculars to help you take it all in). When word gets out, your habitat will be the chirp of the bird world.

| ·BIRDS | ·ACCESSORIES | ·HABITAT | |
|---|---|---|---|

## 800-962-8266 • All The Best Pet Care — All-The-Best.com

What does "the best" consist of? The simple answer is all-natural pet care, more specifically "Natural Foods, Supplements and Remedies for Dogs and Cats." Some of the foods boast "human-quality ingredients" (so what are we eating?), and many of them at least claim to be healthier than your typical bag of kibble. Chemicals can sour an otherwise perfectly healthy lifestyle, animal or human so, assuming they work, the arthritic remedies, skin care products and nontoxic flea repellents here are awesome.

| ·DOGS ·GROOMING | ·CATS | ·FOOD | ·HEALTH |
|---|---|---|---|

## 888-738-6388 • AllPets.com — AllPets.com

These guys can sell you just about any necessary item you can think of for your pet, be it a dog, cat, fish, bird, reptile or rodent. But what you may first notice, other than the site's somewhat silly exterior, is a full range of well-written articles that offer fun, informative and/or invaluable advice in pet care, beginning with where you acquire your pet from in the first place. Look deeper, and you'll find a well-constructed online community full of helpful fellow pet owners who are just itching to show you pictures of their precious ones acting "just like people." Pretty good prices too.

| ·EQUIPMENT ·TRAVEL | ·FOOD ·TOYS & TREATS | ·HEALTH ·GROOMING | ·HABITAT ·TRAINING |
|---|---|---|---|

## 540-334-2960 • Anne Way Bernard — AnneWayBernard.com

This one's a bit unusual to be included in this compendium, but as some of us consider our pets as worthy of iconography as anything else, even more so, we just couldn't leave it out. See, Anne Bernard is a painter from Virginia who seems to specialize in pet portraits. If you send her some photos of your pet, she will try to capture its personality for posterity, either as oil on canvas or in a plywood cutout. A sampling of her work appears on the site, along with variable pricing information and tips on best capturing your pet on film. It can be a great way to preserve the memory of a valued family member, or just a fun way to decorate the doghouse.

| ·ACCESSORIES | | | |
|---|---|---|---|

## 812-537-3583 • Audubon Workshop — AudubonWorkshop.com

Turning your yard into a way station for migrating birds (or just hungry ones) can be a great way to enjoy animals without the responsibility entailed in keeping pets. Just sit back with a pair of binoculars, watch them dance and hear them sing. This site makes it easy to attract the attention of our feathered friends with feeders, houses, baths, bird-friendly pesticides and some delicious alternatives to grubs. Better yet, a pull-down menu makes it easy to hone in on your favorite types of birds (bluebirds, doves, hummingbirds, orioles, owls and then some) to find products best suited to selective attraction. You can even attract bats... though we don't know why you'd want to do this.

| ·BIRDS | ·ACCESSORIES | ·EQUIPMENT | ·HABITAT |
|---|---|---|---|

# BestNest.com

BestNest.com • 877-369-5446

Whether you like it or not, critters are going to make use of your backyard. With this site, you can best determine which critters in particular rule, with a general focus on the nice-looking ones, of course. For example, you can attract birds with feeders and baths, which should keep some of the insects away. Or, you can attract the pretty insects, like ladybugs and butterflies. It tends to differ from person to person, as evidenced by the existence here of both squirrel baffles (to keep them varmints from eating your birdseed) and squirrel feeders (to keep those adorable critters coming back).

| ·BIRDS | ·ACCESSORIES | ·EQUIPMENT | ·HABITAT |
|---|---|---|---|

# CastorPolluxPet.com

Castor & Pollux Petworks • 800-875-7518

This site comes complete with a mythology; the story of a dog (Castor) and cat (Pollux) who escape together from the pound only to struggle against a cruel world that lacks foods and treats made from the finest available ingredients. A tragic tale indeed, the shop is of course poised to remedy such a situation, offering an exclusive assortment of everyday pet stuff like collars, chews and cat litter, as well as the foods and treats Castor & Pollux (named for the Gemini twins, of course) longed for. Additionally, you can find some good, naturally made products for your pet's grooming and pest control, as well as a treatment against stains, of which you probably have plenty already.

| ·DOGS ·HEALTH | ·CATS ·TOYS & TREATS | ·ACCESSORIES ·GROOMING | ·EQUIPMENT |
|---|---|---|---|

# CatToys.com

CatToys.com • 877-364-8697

Yes, it's what you think; a store with a strict devotion to keeping kitty entertained. The primary advantage to getting your cat toys here over anywhere else is that these guys have taken the liberty of drawing the products into categories distinguished by your cat's Breed (47 different breeds to be exact) or Personality (from Extremely Active to Couch Potato). As it turns out, most cats pretty much dig the same things, but these distinctions serve to shorten browsing time, one of the best reasons to shop from a niche retailer.

| ·CATS | ·ACCESSORIES | ·TOYS & TREATS |
|---|---|---|

# ChiwawaGaGa.com

Chi-Wa-Wa Ga-Ga • 504-581-4242

Chihuahuas may be the first love of this "dinky store for dinky dogs," but all small pooches, and some slightly larger ones, get attention here (and even ferrets, if yours should be in need of a bomber jacket). What's their angle? "We want you to dress your dear, darling, doggie in a delightful outfit and squeal; jumping up and down, clapping your hands, screaming in an uncontrolled falsetto, 'That is SOOOOOOO CUTE!!!!'" Yup, it's a silly store, but it backs the silliness up with a quite good selection that starts with clothes but includes quality pooch products across the board, from collars and bedding to toys and grooming supplies. Heck, the Costumes and Hats & Ties sections alone are worth the visit.

| ·DOGS ·PET APPAREL | ·SMALL MAMMALS ·GROOMING | ·ACCESSORIES | ·TRAVEL |
|---|---|---|---|

## 866-872-4785 • Classy Pets Boutique

### ClassyPets.com

This bakery/boutique based in Fort Lauderdale, Florida, began with beef-flavored gingerbread men, BBQ sauce–flavored "ribs" and kosher mini-bagels (all for dogs and cats), but have expanded to include equally cutesy pet accessories and apparel. Some of these cat and doggy styles do reach the ranks of elegance, some could only be considered butch. But between kitty tiaras, lavish metal frame beds and crown-shaped feeding dishes, class here is really no less arbitrary than in the human world, just more adorable.

| ·DOGS ·HABITAT | ·CATS ·TOYS & TREATS | ·ACCESSORIES ·GROOMING | ·EQUIPMENT ·PET APPAREL |
|---|---|---|---|

## 800-311-6503 • Clean Run

### CleanRun.com

Want your dog to be the type seen lunging headlong through the air to catch a Frisbee in its mouth, but it's more prone to lie in the grass and chew on flowers? This site's products are aimed specifically at increasing your pooch's agility, with both training programs and equipment designed to push the limits of its speed and flexibility. Most of this stuff is probably the most fun your pet will have all day, and you'll probably end up getting some exercise yourself in the process. What's more, the Store here is a great source of variable length leads, different sizes/types of balls and some Frisbees that'll really get those tired dogs leaping.

| ·DOGS ·TRAVEL | ·ACCESSORIES ·GROOMING | ·EQUIPMENT ·PET APPAREL | ·HABITAT ·TRAINING |
|---|---|---|---|

## 800-472-5425 • Karen Pryor's Clicker Training

### ClickerTraining.com

We don't want to let our pets run wild or out of control, but we don't want to smack them around, either. Clicker training provides a very effective means of noncoercive (all-positive) reinforcement for your dog, cat or horse. It's got something to do with teaching the animal to respond favorably to the sound of a click ... hey, if we could explain it well here you'd have no need for this site. As it stands, here you will find kits devoted to this technique at basic through advanced levels, complete with books, videos and whichever other components are necessary (we're guessing clickers).

| ·DOGS | ·CATS | ·HORSES | ·TRAINING |
|---|---|---|---|

## 800-510-8841 • CoolPetStuff.com

### CoolPetStuff.com

Begging the question, "What constitutes cool pet stuff?" this site responds with a rather lengthy list of items that just might fit the bill for your chill dog or hep cat. Something like an ATV pet seat, or a tennis ball launcher may seem unnecessary for your pooch. On the other hand, automatic feeders and doggy backpacks may prove indispensable (and kinda cool). Sure, not everything you'll encounter here will work in every crowd (a bow tie for cats comes to mind), but it's a fun and varied shopping experience for geeks and the chic alike.

| ·ACCESSORIES ·TOYS & TREATS | ·EQUIPMENT ·GROOMING | ·HABITAT ·PET APPAREL | ·TRAVEL ·TRAINING |
|---|---|---|---|

## CyberCanine.com
CyberCanine.com • 866-686-3626

Just like people, some dogs have allergies and/or a heightened sensitivity to chemical household and cleaning products. This homegrown business was developed to provide organic solutions to this problem in the form of hypoallergenic and nontoxic grooming products, and things like gluten-free dog biscuits. Homegrown or not, though, this site looks about as slick as any other on the web and, having viewed their adorable Customers' Picture section, we're quite glad to know they are around.

| ·DOGS | ·ACCESSORIES | ·HEALTH | ·GROOMING |

## DecadentDogs.com
Decadent Dogs • 866-459-5437

To give you an idea just how decadent a site this is for dogs, treats are located in the section referred to as Fine Dining. Meanwhile, products include the Tick Spritz (listed under Health & Spa), Faux Fur Coats (to cover their real fur) and sunglasses (yes, sunglasses for dogs). Now that we've established the luxurious nature of these items we should probably point out that a lot of these consist of good, healthy, all-natural alternatives to the sorts of things you'll typically find in a pet superstore. That being said, there's probably no health advantage to be gained from owning a dog-sized chaise lounge....

| ·DOGS<br>·TRAVEL | ·ACCESSORIES<br>·TOYS & TREATS | ·EQUIPMENT<br>·GROOMING | ·HABITAT<br>·PET APPAREL |

## DogDayCafe.com
Dog Day Cafe • 866-246-7167

Set up wonderfully for the dog (and occasional cat) on the go, this site offers a good amount of products that take your pet's safety and health into consideration. In particular, you can find some helpful travel items, ranging from a seatbelt/harness for car rides to a variety of travel bowls. There's also plenty of stuff pertaining to all aspects of your pet's home life, including an interesting section regarding Clicker Training, a good, positive reinforcement training technique for dogs. Peculiarly, they don't seem to offer the clickers themselves, which leads us to believe they aren't trying to sell a product, but actually believe the training works.

| ·DOGS<br>·TOYS & TREATS | ·ACCESSORIES<br>·GROOMING | ·EQUIPMENT<br>·TRAINING | ·TRAVEL |

## DogPark.com
DogPark.com • No Service Number

This site wants you to take your dog outside, frequently and for long periods of time. To this end, it sells an interesting variety of outdoor dog accessories, stuff like glow-in-the-dark collars and a tennis ball tosser that keeps your hands from getting all slobbery during a zesty game of fetch. All of their items come with free shipping, and a free treat for your pooch as well. But this site goes beyond just selling you stuff, it will actually tell you good dog-friendly places to go, anywhere from dog parks to canine friendly hotels (for the long-distance traveler). In fact, if it weren't for the lack of food on display, one might almost get the impression that this site was actually operated by dogs....

| ·DOGS | ·ACCESSORIES | ·TRAVEL | ·TOYS & TREATS |

## No Service Number • DogSupplies.com

**DogSupplies.com**

We are going to go ahead and refer to this as a "no frills" site, instead of just saying it looks bad. We say so because we like it so much—for its size and obvious lack of monetary investment, what this shop has to offer dog owners is quality of selection and terrific prices. We don't know if it could even handle the volume of business it probably deserves, but let's see. If you're reading this, log on and buy something, and maybe if enough of us do we can crash their server and slow their delivery time. Okay, okay, go easy on them—but check it out anyway.

| ·DOGS ·TOYS & TREATS | ·EQUIPMENT ·TRAINING | ·HABITAT | ·TRAVEL |

## 877-364-8697 • DogToys.com

**DogToys.com**

Here's a site that doesn't mince words—it sells toys. For dogs. It offers just about anything a dog could hope to get its mouth on: bones, ropes, rubber, rawhide, shags, squeaks, frisbees, fleeces, balls, biscuits, and... biscotti? Yes, well this selection of toys and treats runs the gamut, for sure, but some well-organized navigation won't leave you wondering which way to look. In fact, a special Select by Breed feature recommends toys known to please the instincts and preferences particular to your dog and his whole family. And if you've got a mutt? Don't worry; other browsing features include a search by dog size, and even an option to listen to audio samples of different squeak toys, so you'll still be sure to find the toys you—rather, your dog—will enjoy most.

| ·DOGS | ·ACCESSORIES | ·TOYS & TREATS |

## 800-989-1500 • Dover Saddlery

**DoverSaddlery.com**

You'll have to scroll down the home page of this site to find the Click Here for Menu link (in the left-hand margin). When you do, though, you'll see a fine menu for competitive or show riding, of horses that is. In Tack & Accessories you'll find bridles, reins, bits, breastplates, cavesons and martingales (whatever those are), while in Grooming, Horse Health Care and Stable Equipment you'll find all you need to care for your stallion or nag. Finally, there's apparel to spiff up either the horse or yourself (it's tough to say who'll look better).

| ·EQUIPMENT ·HORSES | ·GROOMING ·PET APPAREL | ·HEALTH | ·ACCESSORIES |

## 800-381-7179 • Doctors Foster & Smith

**DrsFosterSmith.com**

If you find the expert advice of veterinarians reassuring when you're buying stuff for your dog or cat, this site may be where you want to pick up your basic supplies, particularly health supplies. Especially since, it turns out, you can actually vaccinate your pets at home very inexpensively, as well as treat them for mild illnesses and ailments. Basically, the Drs. Foster & Smith have selected products to cover everything from pet furniture to treats & toys, so all items here come with a pro recommendation, valuable enough even if these pros do happen to own the store.

| ·EQUIPMENT ·TRAVEL | ·FOOD ·TOYS & TREATS | ·HEALTH ·GROOMING | ·HABITAT ·TRAINING |

# EarthWiseAnimal.com

Earthwise Animal • 212-579-7170

It's been a long time since dogs and house cats ran loose in the wild (yes, this is obvious). However, long-since domesticated or not, this isn't to say that it's in any way natural for your pet to be fed preservatives, washed with chemicals or taught to fetch plastic. The all-natural, earth-friendly grooming, training and feeding products you'll find here may not be exactly what nature intended for your dog or cat, but they earnestly try to come close, with nutritional supplements and natural remedies that will appeal to your sense of commitment and the animal's sense of smell—after all, their noses know.

| ·DOGS | ·CATS | ·HEALTH | ·GROOMING |
|-------|-------|---------|-----------|

# FenixResearch.com

Fenix Research • 800-993-3649

Well, you do tend to look at them all the time, so they might as well be sort of nice looking.... Oh, we're talking about your pet's food and water dishes. It's easy to opt for the simple, cheap plastic design, and certainly your dog, cat, bird, reptile or critter won't give a lick where it licks, snarfs or pecks. But maybe you do? If so, these are fairly simple and inexpensive, while just a little (a little) nicer-looking than your typical feeder. Shopping is easy and, if such things impress you, you can view the list of celebrity fashions previously produced by this pet bowl designer.

| ·DOGS<br>·SMALL MAMMALS | ·CATS<br>·ACCESSORIES | ·BIRDS | ·REPTILES |
|-------|-------|--------|-----------|

# FerretStore.com

FerretStore.com • 888-833-7738

Just when you think, "Hey, it's about time ferrets got their own store, devoted exclusively to the fuzzy little rodents," the first thing you notice on the home page is, "We're not just for ferrets!" Yes, it's true; while ferrets definitely get the special treatment on this site, all of your typical pets are also represented: dogs, cats, birds, other rodents, reptiles, hermit crabs... you name it. There's generally a little more clicking involved than we like to encounter, and the selection's not as deep as would be nice, but any way you slice it, there's definitely more going on here than you'd expect going in.

| ·EQUIPMENT<br>·TRAVEL | ·FOOD<br>·TOYS & TREATS | ·HEALTH<br>·GROOMING | ·HABITAT<br>·PET APPAREL |
|-----------------------|-------------------------|----------------------|--------------------------|

# FetchPets.com

FetchPets.com • 212-352-8591

Here you can read the "diary entries" of a very large dog from Greenwich Village who is named after Muhammad Ali, or you can shop through a catalog of "[pet] items that combine functionality and great design." Your choice, but you should know that the diary entries tend to be a bit self-involved (aren't they all?), while the items are funky/stylish things like mood collars, rose-petal spritzer and something called "Poochi Sushi." Yes, this isn't your typical doggy shop fare (there is a small cat selection too), but then, would you let it be said that your dog is typical?

| ·DOGS<br>·TOYS & TREATS | ·CATS<br>·GROOMING | ·ACCESSORIES<br>·PET APPAREL | ·TRAVEL |
|-------------------------|---------------------|------------------------------|---------|

**800-735-2299 • Fox & Hounds Ltd.**

**FoxAndHounds.com**

These guys make their own dog (and occasional cat) collars and accessories with the following altruistic appeal: they are "designed with the pet's comfort in mind." That being said, they don't necessarily scrimp on style, what with the suede, studs, glitter, animal prints and rhinestones involved. Actually, they also feature a selection of tiaras, which we must assume have been made decidedly in disregard to the pet's comfort. But, that could just be a touch of pessimism; it's entirely possible that dogs and cats love having twinkling items strapped to their heads for the sole amusement of humans.

| ·DOGS | ·CATS | ·ACCESSORIES | |
|---|---|---|---|

**800-222-9932 • Dr. GoodPet**

**GoodPet.com**

If you don't like chemicals for yourself, odds are good you don't want them for your beloved pet, either. Fortunately, there's this "Natural Pet Pharmacy for Dogs and Cats." As is typical, birds and rodents get the shaft, but for your pussies and pooches you can find a good deal of homeopathics, vitamins and nontoxic flea control. This all should sooth your pet's itching, keep it calm and get it clean. It's a simple site, and never very far-reaching, but it'll generally help put your mind at ease when your pet is not.

| ·DOGS | ·CATS | ·HEALTH | ·GROOMING | ⚕ |
|---|---|---|---|---|

**800-558-1842 • GoTags.com**

**GoTags.com**

If you feel up to taking about two minutes out of your day, you can check this web site and order personalized tags for your dog, cat or even horse. Available in funny shapes, military style or in 22k gold, all you have to do is type in the information (name, address, phone number, etc.) and you'll receive the engraved tags in the mail. Or, you can click on the Fastags link for a set of make-them-yourself IDs that involve cutting out shapes and a little baking (a fun craft you can pawn off on your kids). That's pretty much it, other than collars and leashes, about which we have nothing to say.

| ·DOGS | ·CATS | ·ACCESSORIES | ·HORSES |
|---|---|---|---|

**No Service Number • Grobiz Pet Fashions**

**Grobiz.com**

The proprietors of this site claim to be "experienced in canine couture." As disturbing as this notion is, aside from some bad grammar they seem to know what they're doing. At least, most of these clothes for canines fit into the "disgustingly cute" category, which in pooch apparel is actually a high mark. Hooded sweatshirts, pajamas and sundresses are sure to raise a few chuckles (like them or not, you simply must look at these pictures), but not until you get into the Costuming section will you strike true comedic gold. Here, the proper outfit can convert your dog into a ladybug, dinosaur or bunny rabbit. You know, if you're sick of it just being a dog all the time.

| ·DOGS | ·PET APPAREL | | |
|---|---|---|---|

## GroomersChoice.com

Groomer's Choice Pet Products • 888-364-6242

This site will come in handy, you can be sure. Well designed, and well stocked, it focuses solely on grooming supplies for dogs and cats. Whether you're quite serious about it (wherein you'll find colognes and grooming tables, for example), or you just want to maintain the best health and appearance of your beloved pet (with clippers, shampoos, etc.), you can find expert grooming guides that have plenty of tips to help you along. In fact, you may want to try a few on yourself.

| ·DOGS ·TRAINING | ·CATS | ·EQUIPMENT | ·GROOMING |
|---|---|---|---|

## HealthyPets.com

HealthyPets.com • 800-889-9475

However glossy, popular and effective any product you buy for your pet may be, you will always find pause to wonder: "What would my vet say about this?" Well, if he/she happens to be one of the pet physicians that founded this online venture, they'd probably say, "shop here." Sure, in the human world, a doctor recommending a certain brand name or formula is suspect, very likely receiving some sort of sponsorship or special incentive from a pharmaceutical manufacturer to endorse its product. But, as we like to think this cynical happenstance hasn't infected the world of veterinary medicine... well, check it out regardless.

| ·DOGS | ·CATS | ·HEALTH | ·GROOMING |
|---|---|---|---|

## InTheCompanyOfDogs.com

In The Company Of Dogs • 800-688-8051

The proprietors of this site say they aim to take the "drabness" out of dog accessories, and they ain't kidding. They've plucked from various sources some of the most outlandish and entertaining dog gear available to mankind. Looking for clothes? Avoid the dreaded wet-dog smell by getting your pooch a rain slicker, or just embrace the lavish redundancy of outfitting him with a cashmere sweater. If you're interested in something grander, you can find here miniature (dog-sized) couches, or even a canine cabana (you know, for long weekends). But there's more than just fun stuff here; useful and innovative products, like a self-locking doggy door with an electronic collar key, are featured to remind us that pet ownership is about substance as well as style.

| ·DOGS ·TOYS & TREATS | ·ACCESSORIES ·PET APPAREL | ·FOOD | ·HABITAT |
|---|---|---|---|

## JakesDogHouse.com

Jake's Dog House • 800-734-5253

Jake's got himself a fairly convincing tag line: "Cool Stuff for Cool Dogs." Well, it seems cool dogs may, among other things, be tired of the same old tennis balls; here they come in both mint flavored and giant sized (for larger breeds). This small, simple shop is full of fun toys and treats like Bow Wow Bistro Cigars that'll give your dog some fun and provide you with some macho photo ops. The kicker, though, is that Jake has outfitted this house with a lot of professional Team Logo Gear for your pooch. These collars, leashes and tags won't necessarily make your dog a true fan, but the competition won't have to know that.

| ·DOGS ·TOYS & TREATS | ·CATS ·GROOMING | ·ACCESSORIES | ·EQUIPMENT |
|---|---|---|---|

## 800-533-3377 • JeffersPet.com
**JeffersPet.com**

There is a lot of merchandise available from the Jeffers Pet Catalog; easily enough to overload your senses. It might help to start thinking ahead of time about what you'll choose to buy when you get here, or you'll be bogged down with choices. For instance, if you take a look under Pet Beds, you'll have to choose between round and square beds, collapsible camping beds, burlaps and fleeces, or igloos and hammocks. It sounds great, but sorting through it all can take a while. Even if you're looking for unusual pet items like cat colognes, canine costumes for Halloween, or hoof picks for your horse (should you need one), the same rule applies: the only easy thing to find is selection.

| ·ACCESSORIES ·HABITAT | ·EQUIPMENT ·TRAVEL | ·FOOD ·TOYS & TREATS | ·HEALTH ·GROOMING |
|---|---|---|---|

## 800-842-6445 • Lafeber Company
**Lafeber.com**

Named for the birdbrain—er, veterinary avian specialist that created it, this is a line of nutrient-heavy feeding pellets, cakes, seed and vitamins for tropical birds like parrots and cockatoos. You end up reading more about the Dr. Lafeber than the foodstuffs at first, but you can just skip down the page to the Bird Food & Toys links (either under Lafeber Co. Products or Order Lafeber Products, both work). Chances are, feed your bird this stuff and he'll never shut up; if you want it quiet, by all means, just give Polly a cracker.

| ·BIRDS | ·FOOD | ·TOYS & TREATS | |
|---|---|---|---|

## 800-745-4512 • Les Poochs
**LesPoochs.com**

Right about now, you're wondering just what sort of dog items one might want to purchase from France. Well, the same kinds of thing humans like to buy: fragrances and shampoos. Actually, lots of different grooming supplies are here, with the added feature of a Breed Glossary to let you know which products are appropriate to your dog's skin and hair particularities. Many of the treatments and rinses you'll find here are naturally derived, some hypoallergenic, and you'll even find some organic treats that'll help entice your poochs into their new, sweeter-smelling bath.

| ·DOGS | ·ACCESSORIES | ·TOYS & TREATS | ·GROOMING |
|---|---|---|---|

## 561-691-6930 • LuxuryDog.com
**LuxuryDog.com**

Somewhere along the way we figured out that this site doesn't really cater so much to all dogs; rather, the real focus is on small dogs, specifically those with the type of long, shampooed hair that owners like to tie with ribbons. This is not explicit, and you may see pictures of golden retrievers and other big dogs, and even find some items for such mastiffs. Generally, the feeling that this is for little dogs stems more from the style of this merchandise, stuff like a four-poster iron bed, a pair of angel wings and a tiara. Sure, you could probably manage to make this stuff fit a St. Bernard, but would it look right?

| ·DOGS ·TRAVEL | ·ACCESSORIES ·TOYS & TREATS | ·EQUIPMENT ·PET APPAREL | ·HABITAT |
|---|---|---|---|

## MackiesParlour.com

Mackie's Parlour  •  888-991-7884

This self-proclaimed "truly unique pet boutique" out of Scottsdale, Arizona, delivers with its variety of original, handcrafted products for the dog or cat with more refined tastes. Toys made out of tennis balls and heart-shaped feeding dishes are *de rigueur* here, while more discerning pets might demand a faux mink bed, a doggy tuxedo, or a collar of pearls. Most of the store's merchandise may be personalized, and much of its wares are one of a kind. Even so, the web site offers only an "abbreviated representation" of the brick-and-mortar store's selection. More is available on demand.

| · DOGS · PET APPAREL | ·CATS | ·HABITAT | ·TOYS & TREATS |
|---|---|---|---|

## Morrco.com

Morrco Pet Supply  •  800-575-1451

Is your dog tough? Do you want him to at least look tough? This site lends a little assistance to your watchdog-in-training with spiked collars, leather boots (seriously) and harnesses (as passersby will be grateful you've got the beast contained). If the beast really needs to be contained, there are some muzzles here you might want to look into, and some training tools you should certainly invest in. Usually, though, we've found that a spike collar on any dog (Chihuahuas excepted) will make any trespasser think twice before entering, without the risk of having a trained killer in your front yard.

| ·DOGS | ·TRAINING | ·ACCESSORIES | |
|---|---|---|---|

## MyPetPrescriptions.com

MyPetPrescriptions.com  •  877-666-2501

A simple-to-use drug store for your pets, this online shop doesn't tend to waste anybody's time with flashy advertised specials or featured items. It's simple: look under Prescription Items and you can peruse an alphabetized set of lists of medicines, quickly finding the one you want. Look under Non-Prescription Items and you can similarly peruse a brief list of categories like Anxiety Relief, Flea & Tick and Skin Care to view the selection of available items. The topper is that you can also set up an Auto-Refill program, which means the two minutes it takes to get through this process can keep your pet medicated for months and months to come.

| ·HEALTH | | | |
|---|---|---|---|

## NaturesPet.com

NaturesPet.com  •  201-796-0627

"Modern physics, various Eastern philosophies and ecology all have shown that we live in a unified field." This says it all, does it not? At least, it serves to explain, in part, why this retailer sells "natural and holistic products designed to enhance and extend the lives of your pets." You see, according to the owners of one brand featured here, "animals are herbalist by nature but domestication prohibits them from instinctively seeking the botanical diversity their bodies require." All right, this one does deviate from the beaten path a bit, but you can't shake a stick at natural products and treatments for a variety of animals. Unless, of course, shaking a stick is one of the recommended treatments.

| ·DOGS ·HEALTH | ·CATS | ·BIRDS | ·FOOD |
|---|---|---|---|

## 800-826-5527 • Pet.Innotek

**Pet-Containment-Systems.net**

Are you barbaric enough to still be smacking your dogs to get them to behave? Do you still have a lot of ugly fencing to keep your pooch in the yard? Kind sir or madam, you may be missing the point of technology here! This site offers electric collars that deliver mild shocks to your animals for multiple purposes. You can opt to control excessive barking (not recommended for watchdogs), lay down an invisible fence in your yard (when the dog tries to pass, the collar shocks it) or restrict the pooch's access to certain rooms of the house even when you're not home. The ethical questions will delight your friends, and the collars are only kind of ugly.

| ·DOGS | ·EQUIPMENT | | |
|-------|-----------|---|---|

## 408-541-1300 • Little River Pet Shop

**Pet-Shop.net**

Primarily for dog and cat lovers (and those bearing a special fondness for ferrets), the Little River Pet Shop is all too aware of competitors who possess larger, better-funded online pet stores. Their solution? Offer a wide selection of quality merchandise at lower prices, and provide excellent, personalized customer service. Thus, if their easy site navigation isn't enough to help you find the product you're looking for, simply send out an email and they'll scour their inventories to find it for you on that very same day.

| ·DOGS ·HEALTH | ·CATS ·HABITAT | ·EQUIPMENT ·GROOMING | ·FOOD ·TRAINING |
|---------------|----------------|----------------------|-----------------|

## 800-844-1427 • PetCareRx.com

**PetCareRx.com**

The greatest drawback of using an online pet pharmacy is that you miss out on the kindly old man with the friendly, weathered face that offers reassurance that you're doing what's best for your precious little creature. Well, not this shop, which stands behind the image of just such a man (True veterinarian or an aged model? You be the judge). In terms of friendly reassurance, the site offers a bulletin board where questions may be asked of a team of licensed vets, as well as articles involving common health issues for dogs, cats, birds and fish. Also included are reptiles and small furry animals, though the latter may be recommended to feed to the former.

| ·ACCESSORIES ·HABITAT | ·EQUIPMENT ·TRAVEL | ·FOOD ·GROOMING | ·HEALTH ·TRAINING |
|-----------------------|--------------------|-----------------|-------------------|

## 888-825-9550 • PetClick.com

**PetClick.com**

When you imagine a store proclaiming itself "The All-Natural Pet Source," you pretty much imagine a shoddily put together site that has little to offer. Not so with this food specialist that offers a variety of natural items for all manner of household pets and horses too. Including raw foods, diet foods and nutritional supplements, you get some pretty good descriptions that will make it tough for you to decide. Once you do, however, you can opt for regular delivery, replenishing your pet's natural morsels without a second thought.

| ·DOGS ·FISH | ·CATS ·FOOD | ·BIRDS ·HEALTH | ·SMALL MAMMALS ·HORSES |
|-------------|-------------|----------------|------------------------|

## PetFoodDirect.com

Do not be fooled—behind this web shop's goofy exterior lies the cold, calculating heart of a fully functional product database, and not just for food, as the name would imply. While the layout can leave you scanning endlessly for different menu options, and searches will yield dozens upon dozens of results, those with moderately fast connections should breeze through these pages with just a few well-placed clicks. Basically, if an animal fits in your house you can find products to please it here... and prices to please you.

| ·EQUIPMENT ·TRAVEL | ·FOOD ·TOYS & TREATS | ·HEALTH ·GROOMING | ·HABITAT ·TRAINING |
|---|---|---|---|

## PetFoodExpress.com

This San Francisco Bay–area pet store chain is considerably more "express" when you visit in person, and it turns out they sell a bit more than merely pet food. But we as American shoppers don't care what a store's name is so long as the merchandise is good and the prices are low. Well, folks, we have a winner. Pets of all shapes and sizes get a fair bit of attention, which they like (unless it comes in the form of a Harley-Davidson leather cap for dogs), and the value's tough to beat (which you'll like).

| ·ACCESSORIES ·HABITAT | ·EQUIPMENT ·TOYS & TREATS | ·FOOD ·GROOMING | ·HEALTH ·PET APPAREL |
|---|---|---|---|

## PetInsurance.com

Just like it sounds, this site offers health insurance for your pets, whether they're dogs, cats, birds or exotic (this category ranges from geckos to iguanas, and gerbils to pot-bellied pigs). Working on a reimbursement system, the plans they offer will cover procedures performed by any licensed veterinarian nationwide, to a varying percentage, minus a low deductible of course. Plans are different for different types and size of animals, and it is insurance, so you never really know what you're paying for till disaster strikes. But if you consider that these guys are banking on your pets' long life and good health in order to turn a profit, signing up does at least have a preventative feel about it.

| ·HEALTH | | | |
|---|---|---|---|

## PetMarket.com

The look of this site may be deterrent, but the words are enticing and refreshing: "In this age of the internet where most pet sites are trying to be all things to all four-legged owners, we will remain focused as a pet solution site. As you will soon discover, our site fosters collaboration and discussion about pet remedies and the products that help." Yeah, they're pretty much like the rest in terms of selection and price, etc., but we do get the feeling they have more of an interest in animals and pet ownership than other equitable retailers. Then again, maybe they just have us boggled.

| ·EQUIPMENT ·TRAVEL | ·FOOD ·TOYS & TREATS | ·HEALTH ·GROOMING | ·HABITAT ·TRAINING |
|---|---|---|---|

## 888-889-1814 • Pet Rx                    PetRx.com

This one has loads of useful information and some particularly useful products. If you have a sick animal on your hands, you can find pet medication here. However, this site is not exactly set up for browsing, and you won't know what most of the stuff is anyway. Which is fine, as it turns out, because you can't buy it without a prescription. The good news is that if you enter the contact information of your vet, the PetRx staff will verify the prescription and fill your order. Still, you probably want to restrict use of this one to refilling orders.

| ·DOGS | ·CATS | ·HEALTH | |
|-------|-------|---------|--|

## 888-839-9638 • PetSmart                    PetSmart.com

With enough merchandise and information to raise an animal army, you'd think it would be easy to get lost in this popular online pet store. But excellent organization makes this site easy to use, and a spate of software solutions helps you to weed out the chaff (if you're looking for all-natural pet supplies or travel gear, for example). PetSmart goes even further by offering expert advice, product comparisons and a breed guide that gets specific about your particular dog or cat's behavior and care. And if you're really interested, an interactive food calculator lets you punch in some key information about your pet, then responds with suggestions on how best to regulate his diet—a feature your fat cat might learn to resent.

| ·EQUIPMENT<br>·TRAVEL | ·FOOD<br>·TOYS & TREATS | ·HEALTH<br>·GROOMING | ·HABITAT<br>·TRAINING |
|-----------------------|-------------------------|----------------------|-----------------------|

## 800-497-8933 • PetsPreferUs.com                    PetsPreferUs.com

Many of these pet shop listings toss around the term "unique items" in reference to their catalogs, and most of these are warranted. However, when these guys do it, they mean to say that they have hundreds of unique items. At least, we haven't seen any TV-shaped cat beds, dog breath sprays, ferret knapsacks or hamster potty trainers anywhere else, and we only had time to browse a few of the dozens of categories these guys maintain for each pet they service, which is pretty much every pet you can legally keep in your home (and some that you can't). Don't be put off by the look of this site, it's a good one.

| ·ACCESSORIES<br>·TRAVEL | ·EQUIPMENT<br>·GROOMING | ·FOOD<br>·PET APPAREL | ·HABITAT<br>·TRAINING |
|-------------------------|-------------------------|-----------------------|-----------------------|

## 800-227-4260 • PetTags.com                    PetTags.com

You've got to hand it to specialty sellers; they sure know how to maintain a focus. We won't tell you what it is that these guys sell, specifically, but we will tell you three things about them. First: any of them can be personalized, some on two sides. Second: you can opt for a range of traditional shapes, meaning circles, and a few polygons you've likely grown to expect. Third: if traditional's not your style, tie-dye and cartoon themes (including some Looney Tunes characters) are available. Have we said too much?

| ·DOGS | ·CATS | ·ACCESSORIES | |
|-------|-------|--------------|--|

# PetVogue.com

This one's brought to you by the same people behind CoolPetStuff.com and, as it turns out, much of the stuff considered "cool" on their other site is considered "vogue" here. Go figure. While we'd rather these folks just pick one site and run with it, the non-overlapping selection of one site or the other simply may not be left out if we're to be thorough. These products aim to "spoil" your dog or cat, though in truth they're more geared towards making you say "awww" when you look at them. Still, stuff like cat bow ties and doggie Hawaiian shirts are just too cool—rather, vogue—to pass up.

| ·DOGS ·HABITAT | ·CATS ·TRAVEL | ·ACCESSORIES ·TOYS & TREATS | ·EQUIPMENT ·GROOMING |
| --- | --- | --- | --- |

# RadioFence.com

Electronic devices to help train and control your pet's whereabouts have grown in popularity over the years; so have the moral objections as to the humanity of delivering automated or manual shocks to your animal as a means of negative reinforcement. Whichever side of the electric fence you sit upon, you will surely find something both useful and agreeable on this all-electric site. If you're looking to control barking or curiosity through surges of voltage, fine. Otherwise, there are products like electronic key doggy doors or timed feeders. Hey, it's an electric world, we just live in it.

| ·DOGS ·TRAINING | ·CATS | ·ACCESSORIES | ·EQUIPMENT |
| --- | --- | --- | --- |

# SafePets.com

While this site is called SafePets.com, what most of these products actually do is protect you, your stuff and your patience from the wily nature of your dog, cat or possibly pig. A range of options, for example, is there for you to contain your animal (with both actual or invisible fences). Likewise, you'll find different means of training your pet, including some oh-so-valuable Bark Control systems. They also offer some controlled-entry pet doors, and a few devices designed to keep animals out of certain rooms or away from your valuables. Generally, this is all very useful, and mostly quite humane, but really some of these items may work best as a last resort.

| ·DOGS | ·EQUIPMENT | ·HABITAT | ·TRAINING |
| --- | --- | --- | --- |

# SmallDogMall.com

Like the dogs it caters to, this site is small in scope, with just a few key items that are sized to fit the great big ferocious beast that is trapped in a little, tiny, bouncy body. Thus, the Site Map may be your best bet in navigation, as you can get an idea of the things you'll find all on one page. These things include bags you can carry your pup around in, and party hats to cute them up with (not that they need the help). Then there's several collars and leads, grooming supplies and toys that won't make the little guy fall over when he picks them up.

| ·DOGS ·TOYS & TREATS | ·EQUIPMENT ·GROOMING | ·HABITAT ·PET APPAREL | ·TRAVEL ·TRAINING |
| --- | --- | --- | --- |

**800-955-8247** • Speedy Pet Tags          **SpeedyPetTags.com**

Ironically, this site sells much more than pet tags and, come to think of it, it's not a particularly speedy experience, either. But, it is about as much as you could expect from a discount pet supply store. Items range from some ingenious sanitation products (aren't you dying to know?) to your basic pet necessities. Either way, you can often buy them in bulk, at even greater discounts, or just pick over the items one by one. Now, browsing's not exactly a chore, but neither is it terrific fun, so bring patience or don't come at all.

| ·DOGS | ·CATS | ·ACCESSORIES | ·HABITAT |
|---|---|---|---|
| ·TRAVEL | ·TOYS & TREATS | | |

---

**877-464-3364** • Tails By The Bay          **TailsByTheBay.com**

Specifically, these tails would be by the San Francisco Bay Area, home to the dogs whose owners operate the site. They've thoughtfully included a fairly well-rounded section for cats here, including a nearly unbeatable selection of litter boxes that don't necessarily look like litter boxes. Of course, dog lovers being what they are, pooches will find special attentions, including sections devoted to small dogs and huge dogs, respectively. Whichever animal you shop for, though, you'll find a unique sampling of some fairly classy and useful items, like canopy beds, extravagant cedar doghouses and pet-sized lifejackets.

| ·DOGS | ·CATS | ·ACCESSORIES | ·HABITAT |
|---|---|---|---|
| ·TRAVEL | ·TOYS & TREATS | ·GROOMING | ·TRAINING |

---

**No Service Number** • ThatPetPlace.com          **ThatPetPlace.com**

If you have one pet, you're pretty much going to find very little deviation in price wherever you shop, with a few exceptions where style is a consideration. Here, however, multiple-pet owners can get a bit of a break. In most cases, on this site, if you buy more than two of any item you receive a discount. While this makes little sense in say, dog doors (though you will find a selection here), this can save you loads in the long run on rawhide chews, food and grooming supplies. If you're thinking about adding a new pet or two, you should be aware that they usually offer this discount in a quantity up to 9999.

| ·EQUIPMENT | ·FOOD | ·HEALTH | ·HABITAT |
|---|---|---|---|
| ·TRAVEL | ·TOYS & TREATS | ·GROOMING | ·TRAINING |

---

**888-923-2140** • The Bird Brain          **TheBirdBrain.com**

Here's one for the birds that talk, sing and swing; like parrots, canaries, macaws, lovebirds and cockatoos. Offering toys, perches, cages, food, health supplies, bowls and cleaners, this store is quite comprehensive in its selection. Better still, it proves an invaluable resource, even going so far as to separate items based on the type of bird you own, paying particular attention to its variable needs and interests. Excellent across the board, this is likely going to be the best place to buy bird-care items online for a long time to come.

| ·BIRDS | ·ACCESSORIES | ·EQUIPMENT | ·FOOD |
|---|---|---|---|
| ·HEALTH | ·HABITAT | ·TRAVEL | ·GROOMING |

## ThreeDog.com

**Three Dog Bakery • 800-487-3287**

This site speaks a "pawticular" brand of dog pun–laden English that proves nearly incomprehensible at times, especially when used in conjunction with a very dizzy, albeit colorful, site design. After some digging, we finally realized that this is the retail arm of a dog biscuit bakery, and that the products sold from their "DOGalog" are gourmet treats for your pooch; stuff like canine biscotti, bagels and mini-pizzas. There's no accounting for taste, and animals don't tend to care what their food looks like, but at the very least this stuff promises to be fresh.

| ·DOGS | ·FOOD | ·TOYS & TREATS | |
|---|---|---|---|

## TravelinPets.com

**Travelin' Pets • 866-738-7932**

It only takes a moment to imagine the havoc that might ensue if animals were allowed to roam free on an airplane. As fun and carnival-like an atmosphere as this might be, it's probably for the best that pets are relegated to specialized cages back in cargo. The real question: is it more humane to let them bark and fuss in that cargo space, or to tranquilize them for the voyage…? Here there are no answers, only the carriers that are the specialty of this site, which also features pet car seats and restraints; vest carriers and backpacks (similar to those people use to carry babies); and various pet travel items, like collapsible water dishes.

| ·DOGS | ·CATS | ·ACCESSORIES | ·TRAVEL |
|---|---|---|---|

## TrixieAndPeanut.com

**Trixie & Peanut • 212-979-1603**

Two more dogs immortalized by the internet, Trixie and Peanut's owner put her experience in graphic arts towards this mail-order catalog turned web shop, placing an emphasis on clean design. The results include slick and pretty web pages with more than their share of bugs. However, the products have also been made with keen eyes, and presumably without the potential for technical glitches. Great-looking pet apparel, travel accessories, toys, treats, grooming supplies and beds for dogs and cats include kitty sushi and one of those little wooden kegs that hang from the collar of St. Bernards (really). This is fine fare for the lavish pet owner.

| ·DOGS<br>·TRAVEL | ·CATS<br>·TOYS & TREATS | ·ACCESSORIES<br>·GROOMING | ·HABITAT<br>·PET APPAREL |
|---|---|---|---|

## UpTownPets.com

**UpTownPets.com • 866-775-7387**

Boasting "exclusive items for the discerning pet owner," UpTown Pets essentially offers ways to dress your pets in accordance to particular styles that you may have selected for them. For example, should you be drawn to the Bad Ass section, you will find a bevy of Harley-Davidson–themed merchandise, like bandanas and leads. It's all specific enough that different sections and styles exist for dogs/puppies and cats/kittens, and you may even find stuff for birds and horses (should you need hoof glitter or something similar). Further styles feature colorful names like Nautical, Jet Set and Spoiled, the latter of which certainly suits any pet that would be wearing this stuff.

| ·DOGS<br>·ACCESSORIES | ·CATS<br>·HABITAT | ·BIRDS<br>·GROOMING | ·HORSES<br>·PET APPAREL |
|---|---|---|---|

**800-419-9524 • ValleyVet.com**                               **ValleyVet.com**

Sure, when most of us think of pets we imagine dogs, cats and small animals that won't end up on a grill. But to some, the cows and pigs that nuzzle the ground outside with their snouts are pets of sorts, and for just such folk there is this site. Say you need an electric dehorner, udder treatment or sheep vaccine—it's important to know that the world of internet commerce hasn't forgotten you. There's also a huge section devoted to equine care and riding tack, as well a thorough catalog devoted to "regular" pets. This one is humongous; it will serve you well whether they're meant as pets or livestock.

| ·HORSES ·HABITAT | ·EQUIPMENT ·TOYS & TREATS | ·FOOD ·GROOMING | ·HEALTH ·TRAINING |
|---|---|---|---|

**888-924-9327 • Wagwear**                                      **WagWear.com**

This rather slick dog site could only have come out of New York City. See, their catalog is small, so small in fact that it fits on one page. It's expensive, too, some things costing more than twice that of comparable items. However, if you're in the You-Get-What-You-Pay-For camp, none of this will bother you, as these are some of the sturdiest, most chic items you'll find for your pooch either online or off. From the cut of the clothes to the style of the travel gear, your pet just might end up better dressed than most people you know.

| ·DOGS ·PET APPAREL | ·ACCESSORIES | ·HABITAT | ·TRAVEL |
|---|---|---|---|

**800-569-3397 • WorldPetStore.com**                           **WorldPetStore.com**

A kind of clownish looking, jack-of-all-trades site, what really makes this one stand out isn't that it sells new shells/homes for your pet hermit crab (though, that would certainly do it). What impressed us the most was their selection of fish: live fish. That's right, you can buy pet fish in the mail, from guppies and catfish on through to some small sharks, and a variety of tropicals in between. You may even find a frog or two, if you're lucky (or unlucky, depending on your point of view), and a crayfish (which, of course, looks more like a lobster). We will not, however, recommend their snails to you. You have to draw the line somewhere.

| ·FISH ·TRAVEL | ·EQUIPMENT ·TOYS & TREATS | ·HEALTH ·GROOMING | ·HABITAT ·TRAINING |
|---|---|---|---|

**877-288-2008 • YourActivePet.com**                           **YourActivePet.com**

Does your dog like to run? Probably. Does it like to play in water? Some do. Well, maybe your dog would be into mountain hiking or white-water rafting as much as you are? This site seems to think so, boasting "adventure gear for your pet." Stuff like hands-free leashes, canine boots and doggie life jackets enable you to take your faithful companion with you on your jaunts outdoors (Because, really, where would a dog rather be?). They even offer equipment for something called Skijoring, which gets your pets in on the act of cross-country skiing. Glad you didn't get a housecat?

| ·DOGS ·TRAINING | ·ACCESSORIES | ·EQUIPMENT | ·TRAVEL |
|---|---|---|---|

NOTES:

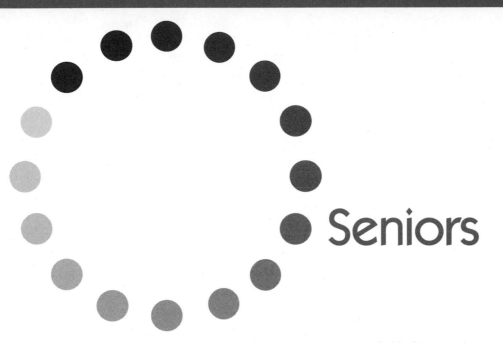

# Seniors

While the media's typical representation of a computer-savvy individual is a geeky teenager, in reality anyone with a few hours to kill can learn to get around a hard drive. While kids have obviously taken to the computerization of the planet faster than most, they absolutely have *not* been the only ones to benefit from this proliferation of technology. The fact is, seniors make for one of the single largest growing groups of computer users, and their presence on the web may be felt more greatly every year—more so, at least, than the slim number of senior-specific sites would indicate.

No, this section serves a different purpose than to segregate the older members of our internet community. These sites are merely devoted to the special needs of seniors, whether it's in deriving a community with shared interests or catering to the physical demands of age. Here may be found health items for the elderly, as well as household items customized to those with ailing health or capabilities. Then there's the occasional grandparenting site, wherein you may find gifts that make more sense than some of the oddball cartoon-character toys that dominate toy store displays.

That being said, one must understand that just about every commerce site by definition caters to seniors. That is, internet shopping is perfect for any person with the decreasing mobility of age, and just because a site isn't listed in this section doesn't mean it's restricted to younger folk. By the same token, these aren't just good places for seniors to shop, but great places to shop *for* seniors.

NOTES:

_____

_____

_____

_____

_____

_____

_____

_____

_____

_____

_____

_____

_____

_____

_____

_____

_____

_____

## TIPS FOR SENIORS BUYING ONLINE

These suggestions may help save time and money.

•**GRANDPARENTING:** This section offers a few sites catering to grandparents, but by and large the best resources for grandparents will turn up in the Minors, Entertainment and Sports & Outdoors sections, many of which boast special children's and/or educational sections.

•**BEWARE OF INTERNET FRAUD:** As with the real world, the internet is littered with unscrupulous individuals who will take advantage of anybody just for a buck. Unfortunately, sometimes an online retailer may be responsible for dubious activities as well. Most of these sites offer secure online credit card transactions, but they may turn around and sell your address, phone number, email address or other personal information to less secure parties. Be wary of unsolicited emails, and keep a watchful eye over your credit card balances after ordering from the web.

•**TAKE A DEEPER LOOK:** Online transactions don't always explicitly mention senior discounts, but especially with regard to travel bookings, they may be available. It may often be worth a phone call to a site's customer service division to find out.

## SITES THAT MAY COME IN HANDY

The following URLs may be useful when you shop.

Caregivers and Resources: http://www.careguide.net
Senior Resources & Community: http://www.seniorsite.com
American Association for Retired People: http://www.aarp.org
Search for Local Senior Discounts: http://www.seniordiscounts.com
Assisted Living & Retirement Community Search: http://www.springstreet.com/seniors/?gate=shousing&popup=on
Health Information: http://www.webmd.com
General Information & Resources: http://www.About.com
Computer Terms Glossary: http://www.WhatIs.com
Internet Terms Glossary: http://www.NetLingo.com

>> SECTION ICON LEGEND

Use the following guide to understand the rectangular icons that appear throughout this section.

### GIFT IDEAS

Our Stationery & Gifts section has much more to offer, but beside this icon you'll find sites offering plenty in the way of gifts designed specifically with the older individual in mind.

### GRANDPARENTING TOOLS

Loving them is easy, relating to them can be a challenge. Here are some sites geared toward finding bonding activities with grandchildren, including some toys that aren't based on cartoon merchandising.

### INDEPENDENT LIVING

Probably representative of the greatest value of this section, sites listed beside this icon offer helpful tools and appliances that make it easier for seniors to live alone while combating common ailments like arthritis, hearing loss and deteriorating vision.

## >> LIST OF KEY WORDS

The following words represent the types of items typically found on the sites listed in this section.

### APPAREL

Clothing will be better found in our Men's and Women's Apparel sections, but some of these sites have decent selections of their own, at times with special considerations.

### HEALTH

Several of these sites offer health-related items, ranging from pill-cutters to orthopedic footwear. More will be found in the Health & Beauty section.

### HOBBIES

Cooking, gardening, puzzles and cards are only some of the hobbies that turn up on these sites. Take a look for yourself.

### HOUSEHOLD

The tools here have usually been designed in order to improve independent living; stuff like easy-grip devices, magnifiers and dressing aids.

### LARGE PRINT

Another alternative for those who love reading but haven't eyes like they used to, this key word will guide you to a selection of books printed with larger lettering.

### MOBILITY

Helping seniors to get around with greater ease, this selection of items includes wheelchairs, canes, walkers and more.

### PERSONAL CARE

These items offer increased personal care and safety for seniors and/or their caregivers, including pill timers, safety rails and monitors.

### SECURITY

Offering psychological security as well as physical, products on these sites offer some element of protection for personal effects, both in and out of the home.

## >> KEY WORD INDEX

Use the following lists to locate online retailers that sell the merchandise you seek.

### APPAREL

CarolWrightGifts.com
Dynamic-Living.com
GoldViolin.com
IndependentLiving.com
LifeHome.com
MaxiAids.com
SeniorCelebration.com
SeniorShops.com
Silverts.com

### GRANDPARENTING

GrandparentsOnline.net

### HEALTH

1800Wheelchair.com
AgeNet.com
CarolWrightGifts.com
DrLeonards.com
Dynamic-Living.com
ElderCorner.com
EnablingDevices.com
GoldViolin.com
IndependentLiving.com
LifeHome.com
MaxiAids.com
SammonsPreston.com
SeniorCelebration.com
SeniorShops.com
SpinLife.com

### HOBBIES

Care4U.com
CarolWrightGifts.com
Dynamic-Living.com
ElderCorner.com
Geezer.com
GiftIdeasForSeniors.com
GoldViolin.com
IndependentLiving.com
LifeSolutionsPlus.com
MaxiAids.com
SammonsPreston.com
SeniorCelebration.com
SeniorShops.com
SeniorStore.com
SpinLife.com

### HOUSEHOLD

AgeNet.com
AidsForArthritis.com
Care4U.com
CarolWrightGifts.com
DrLeonards.com
Dynamic-Living.com
ElderCorner.com
GiftIdeasForSeniors.com
GoldViolin.com
IndependentLiving.com
LifeHome.com
LifeSolutionsPlus.com
MaxiAids.com
SammonsPreston.com
SeniorShops.com
SeniorStore.com

### LARGE PRINT

DoubledayLargePrint.com
GoldViolin.com
SeniorStore.com

### MOBILITY

1800Wheelchair.com
AgeNet.com
Care4U.com
Dynamic-Living.com
ElderCorner.com
EnablingDevices.com
GiftIdeasForSeniors.com
GoldViolin.com
LifeHome.com
LifeSolutionsPlus.com
MaxiAids.com
SammonsPreston.com
SeniorCelebration.com
SeniorShops.com
SeniorStore.com
SpinLife.com

### PERSONAL CARE

AgeNet.com
AidsForArthritis.com
Care4U.com
CarolWrightGifts.com
DrLeonards.com
Dynamic-Living.com
ElderCorner.com
EnablingDevices.com
GiftIdeasForSeniors.com
GoldViolin.com
IndependentLiving.com
LifeHome.com
LifeSolutionsPlus.com
SammonsPreston.com
SeniorShops.com
SeniorStore.com
Silverts.com

### SECURITY

AgeNet.com
Care4U.com
LifeHome.com
SeniorCelebration.com
SOSID.com

NOTES:

# 1800Wheelchair.com

1-800-Wheelchair.com • 800-320-7140

First things first: this site does not strictly sell wheelchairs; they actually offer a pretty thorough selection of senior-specific stuff, including health items and products meant to enhance independent living. That being said, there's not a terrific selection of these things, so the reason you'll want to shop here does turn out to be the wheelchairs (and scooters). Apart from a great selection, both of powered and manually driven chairs, there are some handy accessories (including a fishing rod attachment), and the availability of billing Medicare, because that is what it's there for.

| ·MOBILITY | ·HEALTH | | |
|-----------|---------|---|---|

# AgeNet.com

AgeNet • 888-405-4242

★

Before the web, finding information on the myriad issues relevant to those over fifty was like trying to find an honest politician; not impossible, but in no way easy. Fortunately, sites like AgeNet bring together a wealth of resources to cut through the excess. In addition to financial, health, insurance and legal matters unique to the age group, this site offers a lot of information regarding caregivers and alternative living facilities. More directly, in the Senior Shop you will find a great selection of products to complement the information, from items promoting safety to those lending increased mobility. Just follow the Consumer Information for Seniors and Caregivers link from the home page to get started.

| ·MOBILITY ·SECURITY | ·PERSONAL CARE | ·HEALTH | ·HOUSEHOLD |
|---------------------|----------------|---------|------------|

# AidsForArthritis.com

Aids for Arthritis • 800-654-0707

By focusing entirely on products that "promote joint preservation and energy conservation and reduce pain," this site makes sifting through its vast assortment of arthritic aids quite simple. Sections guide you straight to the products you may seek, whether for Kitchen, Dressing & Grooming, Bathroom, Resting & Relaxation, Comfort & Therapy or more. Given the division of the pages into scrollable frames, we think it would behoove them to include an ergonomic mouse or two, but they still offer one of the better selections online for weary hands.

| ·PERSONAL CARE | ·HOUSEHOLD | | |
|----------------|------------|---|---|

# Care4U.com

Care4U • 877-538-6568

The mission statement from these guys claims, "We will scour the world to find and offer useful, mostly unknown, products that sometimes cost very little but can be of great value to those who use them." Indeed, with a host of assistive functions ranging from playing cards to clipping nails, these products live up to the hype, offering solutions to common problems that may arise from time to time due to arthritis, impaired hearing/vision and decreased mobility.

| ·MOBILITY ·HOUSEHOLD | ·PERSONAL CARE | ·HOBBIES | ·SECURITY |
|----------------------|----------------|----------|-----------|

**732-287-8833 • Carol Wright Gifts**                    **CarolWrightGifts.com**

Can we describe what sort of product range this site offers, exactly? No. Nor can we specifically point out what makes it qualify for the Seniors section. Better just to mention that this catalog offers an erratic smattering of handy products covering nearly all aspects of adult life, with low prices and a remarkable lack of interest in ultracontemporary trends or conventions. If nothing else, it's intriguing to realize that no other site would ever even dream of being like this, let alone try, and we couldn't tell you if this is a good or a bad thing.

| ·PERSONAL CARE ·HOUSEHOLD | ·APPAREL | ·HEALTH | ·HOBBIES |
|---|---|---|---|

**No Service Number • Doubleday Large Print**          **DoubledayLargePrint.com**

Devoted to large-print books, this site offers titles from popular authors such as John Grisham, Louis L'Amour, Mary Higgins Clark and plenty of others, numbering in the hundreds. It's pretty easy to search by title or author (assuming either are to be found), and some subject key words should help narrow your browsing. If you plan to be a repeat customer, membership in the book club requires very little commitment, but returns great benefits, enough that you may be inspired to start a slightly oversized library.

| ·LARGE PRINT | | | |
|---|---|---|---|

**800-455-1918 • Dr. Leonard's**                        **DrLeonards.com**

As seen in our Health & Beauty chapter, this health-related catalog offers an intriguing array of helpful and/or bizarre items for young and old alike. However, probably no single group may take advantage of this site more than the aging, as it devotes a strong focus to a variety of health issues faced by the elderly, including impaired senses and especially arthritis. The proprietors would do well to evaluate the site design, but then excessive clicking may be part of a shrewd scheme to create future customers....

| ·PERSONAL CARE | ·HEALTH | ·HOUSEHOLD | |
|---|---|---|---|

**888-940-0605 • Dynamic Living**                       **Dynamic-Living.com**

The word "dynamic" here can actually take on three different meanings. First, the "dynamic living" characterized by change; in this case the changes that take place in a person's lifestyle as he or she ages, and the adaptation to both internal and outside forces that affect it. Next is "dynamic living" marked by vigor, encouraged here through a variety of products intended to aid those affected by impaired senses, decreased strength, reduced mobility, loss of motor function or any other affliction resulting from surgery, illness or the effects of aging. Finally, there's the interactive "dynamic," represented by the easy navigation, great product descriptions and in-field reports by other seniors who've tested the products and offer honest evaluations of their worth.

| ·MOBILITY ·HOBBIES | ·PERSONAL CARE ·HOUSEHOLD | ·APPAREL | ·HEALTH |
|---|---|---|---|

## ElderCorner.com

Elder Corner • 888-777-1816

Any web store that features a section called "Talking products" is bound to be good, and this one is. It also happens to be one of the rare sites in this section that takes web design into account, offering easy organization and simple browsing techniques that won't necessarily get you in and out in a hurry, but will never likely cause frustration or confusion. Most importantly, though, its wares lengthen the list of independent living aids we've seen, with a particularly good focus on hobbies and recreation, making it also a great site for gifts.

| ·MOBILITY ·HOUSEHOLD | ·PERSONAL CARE | ·HEALTH | ·HOBBIES |
|---|---|---|---|

## EnablingDevices.com

Enabling Devices • 800-832-8697

You'll notice upon entering this site that its specialty is "Toys for Special Children"; in fact, you'll find this one listed in the Minors section. However, we haven't sent you to the wrong place: take a look down to the lower right of the page to find a link inviting you to "Check Out Our Adult/Senior Section." Following this link will lead you to a small but innovative selection of assisted-living products that combine technology with ingenuity to help cope with limited mobility or communications skills in the pursuit of general comfort.

| ·MOBILITY | ·PERSONAL CARE | ·HEALTH | |
|---|---|---|---|

## Geezer.com

Geezer.com • 877-803-1468

A funny name is the least of this site's appeal. The gist is that all of the various items offered for sale here, from clothes to garden decorations, have been made by folks in their golden years. Essentially, the site offers a forum for seniors to hock their wares, even if they don't own a computer. As charming as the product selection (mostly woodcraft, needlepoint and handcrafted jewelry, as well as a few surprises) are the biographies of the venerable artisans, each of who seem to be genuinely enthusiastic about their work. Which is more than can be said about most manufacturers.

| ·HOBBIES | | | |
|---|---|---|---|

## GiftIdeasForSeniors.com

Gift Ideas For Seniors • 303-926-9301

You should know going in that, while there are, as promised, gifts for seniors available from this site, there aren't many, and they don't tend to be all that spectacular. What you can find is a bevy of retirement-, anniversary- and grandparent-themed gifts; some novel, some sentimental (we were disappointed, however, at the lack of "World's Greatest Grandpa" mugs). Perhaps the most endearing item we did find here is a framed newspaper, customized to a person's birth date and featuring the major headlines of the day; here's hoping the world went wild on your giftee's day in question.

| ·MOBILITY | ·PERSONAL CARE | ·HOBBIES | ·HOUSEHOLD |
|---|---|---|---|

## 877-648-8465 • Gold Violin

### GoldViolin.com

This site recognizes the elegance implicit to a long life filled with accomplishment and self-reliance, and thus delivers a product line "designed for heroes." If it sounds sentimental, sure, it is. But the merchandise within tends to be practical and tasteful, with ergonomic household items and streamlined gadgetry intended to help seniors maintain high quality of life without sacrificing independence. Easy-grip pens and large-print items serve to enable those impaired by the wear and tear of age, while things like lightweight luggage and sure-grip kitchen tools make it easier to stay active. Artistically crafted canes and similarly refined items assure us that, when it comes to growing old, "with grace" is more than merely an expression.

| ·MOBILITY ·HEALTH | ·PERSONAL CARE ·HOBBIES | ·APPAREL ·HOUSEHOLD | ·LARGE PRINT |
|---|---|---|---|

## 877-875-5437 • GrandparentsOnline.net

### GrandparentsOnline.net

Here's some toy shopping on the easy for grandparents who would rather avoid both trashy cartoon toy trends and the toy stores that promulgate them. You can shop by age range, strictly for educational toys or for Arts & Crafts sets. The index also features a complete list of toy categories if you're looking for something specific, and to give you an idea, there's an entire Stuffed Toy Index, as well as magic tricks and some "Action/Adventure Dolls (for girls)" that could run circles around Barbie. Good stuff.

| ·GRANDPARENTING | | | |
|---|---|---|---|

## 800-537-2118 • Independent Living Aids, Inc.

### IndependentLiving.com

This site boasts a catalog of "can-do products," and to give you a clear idea of what this means, there is a whole section devoted to talking devices: tape measures, Caller IDs and even pens that scan printed text and read it aloud. There's plenty more, though, from computer accessories to personal care items, with some fun stuff thrown in for, well, fun. The pages are simply laid out, assuming you follow the Products link from the home page, and with a smart selection, browsing this one's easily a worthwhile activity.

| ·PERSONAL CARE ·HOUSEHOLD | ·APPAREL | ·HEALTH | ·HOBBIES |
|---|---|---|---|

## 800-653-1923 • Life@Home, Inc.

### LifeHome.com

This company's full name is Life@Home, Inc., which makes it sound like their purpose is the proliferation of high technology. However, as they put it, their "primary goal is to create a healthier living environment through preventative home modifications." In other words, they kind of work under the assumption that injury or ailment is never far off, and one should prepare to conquer it. Basically, their articles on elderly safety are either backed up by a well-considered selection of products that promote safety and personal care, or overly pessimistic, depending on your point of view.

| ·MOBILITY ·HOUSEHOLD | ·PERSONAL CARE ·SECURITY | ·APPAREL | ·HEALTH |
|---|---|---|---|

## LifeSolutionsPlus.com

LifeSolutionsPlus • 877-785-8326

Words like "ornery" and "stubborn" often get bandied about in reference to senior citizens who work fiercely to maintain their independence, when really a much better word already exists to describe them: "proud." This shop is stocked with useful items that enable seniors with arthritis or other ailments that affect motor skills to perform life's daily rituals like dressing, cooking, cleaning, writing and just plain getting around. Browsing is easy and the prices are low, but satisfaction will be high.

| | ·HOBBIES | ·PERSONAL CARE | ·HOUSEHOLD | ·MOBILITY |
|---|---|---|---|---|

## MaxiAids.com

MaxiAids.com • 800-522-6294

This site features a list of independent living products—nothing too flashy or unfamiliar, just a thorough collection. The best part about it is that, for each type of product, there are generally alternatives, in models if not brand names. Unfortunately, the product descriptions don't do the variety justice, meaning in some cases your choice won't be clear. A link called Product List can make your life hell—avoid it. However, the Product Index, located at the top of the left-hand menu, proves better navigation than the menu itself. Just so you know.

| | ·MOBILITY ·HOUSEHOLD | ·APPAREL | ·HEALTH | ·HOBBIES |
|---|---|---|---|---|

## SammonsPreston.com

Sammons Preston Rolyan • 800-323-5547

This one's unusual in the sense that it offers pictures to help you browse categories, but not to browse products. This would be the biggest flaw of this actually not-so-unusual site for seniors. Offering a similar set of products to many of its competitors, this one at least dresses them well with section names like Getting Around, Resting Comfortably, Pain Relievers, Living Fit and Kitchen & Dining Self Helpers. This well-stocked site offers little but quality merchandise, and should you have the patience you may take advantage of some pretty decent prices.

| | ·MOBILITY ·HOUSEHOLD | ·PERSONAL CARE | ·HEALTH | ·HOBBIES |
|---|---|---|---|---|

## SeniorCelebration.com

Senior Celebration • 800-303-3202

There certainly seems to be a lot of sites that sell ergonomic and/or home safety aids to help counteract the affects of aging, and this site is certainly one of them. But this one's unique in that it really offers the best selection of travel items for active seniors who're taking advantage of retirements by seeing more of the world. Portable door locks and alarms, for example, will increase feelings of security while staying in the hotels or inns of exotic locales. Then there's a light, folding cart that may be used to easily transport any souvenirs picked up along the way, and likewise a folding chair (with footrest!) that provides a place to take a load off wherever one may roam. Who needs an RV?

| | ·MOBILITY ·SECURITY | ·APPAREL | ·HEALTH | ·HOBBIES |
|---|---|---|---|---|

## 800-894-9549 • Senior Shops

Boasting "over 400 gifts and products for seniors," the Senior Shops catalog listings, anything from air purifiers and orthopedic supports to bed rails and heating pads, can get a bit confusing. The home page does loosely categorize them into sections called Feel Better, Hear Better, See Better, Move Better, Handle Better, Work Better and Play Better (obviously the most exciting of the bunch), which help initially. But, once you get deeper, all the products sink into a big mess of letters and words. Still, with patience, there's bound to be something good in such a big selection of stuff, and the descriptions are thorough enough that you won't question what you're getting.

| ·MOBILITY ·HOBBIES | ·PERSONAL CARE ·HOUSEHOLD | ·APPAREL | ·HEALTH |
| --- | --- | --- | --- |

## 303-926-9301 • SeniorStore.com

This is a lot like any of the other sites in this section that sell innovative items and ergonomic designs to help seniors maintain independence and security into longevity—with one exception: this site has a lot more stuff. For example, in addition to large print and mobility aids, this features clothes specially made for those requiring special assistance. But not all of these products pertain to serious health issues—jovial birthday and retirement gifts, for example, proclaim things like "Retired—Under New Management (See Spouse for Details)," and other self-deprecating humor. A Music & Nostalgia section offers items like replica old-fashioned radios and telephones, and vintage toys that tend not to compete in the gaudy displays of today's toy stores.

| ·MOBILITY ·HOUSEHOLD | ·PERSONAL CARE | ·LARGE PRINT | ·HOBBIES |  |
| --- | --- | --- | --- | --- |

## 800-387-7088 • Silvert's

For the majority of us who don't know, Silvert's is the "Easy-Wear Easy-Care Clothing Company." This means their selection of clothes is both easy to take on/off, and easy to wash. While there's certainly nothing complicated or flashy about this catalog of clothes, the stuff's not as tasteless as one might imagine (though, nothing against it, the color blue does seem to be a bit overused). There are quite a lot of clothes here, for men and women, so the right style shouldn't be too tough to find. Ultimately, they offer an easy way to stay independent, or to facilitate assistance for those who require it.

| ·PERSONAL CARE | ·APPAREL | | | |
| --- | --- | --- | --- | --- |

## 800-767-7210 • SOS ID

Medical Emergency Bracelets are nothing new, but for the twenty-four hours a day they are typically going unused, they can surely hamper a person's style. With that in mind, this company has devised a selection of medical emergency jewelry that looks attractive, yet still alerts medical professionals to any pre-existing conditions or needs. Instructional strips fold into bracelets, locket-style pendants, shoe clips and even wristwatches. The only drawback would be the slim chance a corrupt paramedic might pocket the jewelry before reading it.

| ·SECURITY | | | | |
| --- | --- | --- | --- | --- |

# SpinLife.com

If you're getting around on a set of wheels, you may find a lot of stuff here to soup up your ride on this site that puts a nice spin on wheelchair use (sorry—horrible pun unfortunately intended). Whether manual chairs, sport chairs, powered chairs or scooters, all are offered with a variety of options and designs, along with accessories ranging from cushions to "urologicals." Best of all, live customer support is always available, so any questions may be promptly answered, almost before they're asked.

| | | •MOBILITY | •HOBBIES | •HEALTH | |
|---|---|---|---|---|---|

# Shoes & Accessories

Sometimes functional, often frivolous, this section covers a vast spectrum of items, literally enough to adorn your body from head to toe. These minutia accoutrements have the power to transform even a generic wardrobe into an expression of your personality, whether you're punching up a dark suit with a striking tie or cinching a basic summer frock with a unique belt.

Obviously, footwear comprises the most vital and universally sought element found in these listings, so we've highlighted the stores that offer it for the sake of browsing ease. However, we've assembled a very deep selection of headwear, jewelry, bags, belts, gloves and more, so if you've got something more specific in mind it should be easy to find using key word browsing and the indexes at the back of the book.

Whatever your accessorizing needs, with the access granted you by the internet, you really have little excuse not to look fabulous anymore.

NOTES:

## ›› TIPS ON BUYING ACCESSORIES ONLINE

These suggestions may help keep your accessory buying experience from turning sour.

•**SHOES:**  Buying shoes online can be a little scary, given the variety in shapes and sizes demonstrated even by a single manufacturer.  The most important thing to take note of before buying footwear online is the store's return policy.  In most cases, it shouldn't be a problem, but when in doubt don't hesitate to call the customer service number and ask some direct questions.  However, just to be sure, try on your new shoes indoors on clean floors, as ill-fitting soiled shoes will be tough to exchange or return.

•**DESIGNER LABELS:**  Many of our sites offer designer label products, and in most cases the prices will reflect the high stature of such items.   Before purchasing, check to make sure the site is prepared to back up any claims of authenticity, preferably with a guarantee, to make sure you get what you pay for.  If a product proves to be counterfeit or otherwise questionable, contact the seller immediately.

•**WATCHES & FINE JEWELRY:**  Before making a heavy investment, it's a wise idea to educate yourself about the quality and reputation of certain jewelry and watches.  This may require a lot of tedious research, but if you know the market and grading systems it could prove worthwhile to the amount of thousands of dollars in savings.  Additionally, you may wish to inquire into payment options, which often work similarly to car loans.  As always, you'll want to research any store's return policy/guarantees before purchase.

•**EYEWEAR:**  As you obviously can't try them on, get to know the return policies of an eyewear shop before you commit to a set of frames, or you could be stuck with some goofy and expensive glasses.  Also, take note that prescription lenses are in many cases available, but are not necessarily refundable, even if the frames are.

## ›› SITES THAT MAY COME IN HANDY

The following URLs may be useful when you shop for certain accessories.

International/US Adult Shoe Size Conversion: http://onlineconverters.com/shoes.html
International/US Children Shoe Size Conversion: http://littleshoes.com/littleshoes/size-chart.htm
Adult Shoe Size Measurement: http://www.shoestoreusa.com/footfacts/sizechart.asp
Children Shoe Size Measurement: http://www.cadvision.com/shoes4u/HappylandShoeSize.htm
European Shoe Size Chart: http://www.onlineconversion.com/clothing.htm
Universal Currency Converter: http://www.xe.com/ucc
How to Tie a Tie: http://home.earthlink.net/~thetiepages
Current Designs and Trends in Shoes and Handbags: http://www.style.com
Hat Size Measurement and Conversion: http://www.countrycalendar.com/Country_Store/hats/hat_sizes.htm
How to Select a Diamond (Cut, Clarity & Color): http://www.diamondreview.com

>> SECTION ICON LEGEND

Use the following guide to understand the rectangular icons that appear throughout this section.

### FINE JEWELRY

This icon is intended to distinguish between high-end, expensive jewelry and trendier, inexpensive baubles. Distinctions include high karat precious metals and gemstones; rare designer and estate jewelry; and most engagement rings.

### FOOTWEAR

Making it easier to find the most universally worn accessories, this icon represents any or all of the following: athletic shoes, casual shoes, dress shoes, bridal shoes, heels, pumps, slides, sneakers, slippers, sandals and boots, as well as shoe care and accessories.

### MEN'S ACCESSORIES

Used to elucidate which of the entries cater in part or exclusively to male consumers, sites marked with this icon may include dress shoes, ties, cufflinks, hats, pocket squares, wallets, watches, belts, umbrellas, backpacks, travel cases, organizers, briefcases, eyewear, keychains, jewelry and gloves among their wares.

### PERSONALIZATION

Letting us know when the option to mark these wares our own is available, this rare feature usually indicates custom engravings in jewelry, or monogrammed stitching in other accessories.

>> LIST OF KEY WORDS

The following words represent the types of items typically found on the sites listed in this section.

## BAGS & WALLETS

Sites marked by this key word may offer any of the following: backpacks, carry-alls, cosmetics cases, diaper bags, evening bags, handbags, leather bags, totes, travel bags and wallets.

## BELTS

Some are made of leather, others of alligator, cotton, precious metals or string. Most of them will keep your pants up.

## DESIGNER

Representing celebrated designers from places like Italy, France, Japan, Brazil and the streets of New York, this word denotes ultra-fashionable accessories of every description from upscale designer labels (as opposed to nationally recognized brand names).

## EYEWEAR

Sunglasses are the most obvious items covered by this Key Word, but considering that even prescription reading glasses may be worn with a touch of flair; and that contacts may be used to change your eye color; frames, lenses and cases are all represented by this term.

## GLOVES

Keeping your fingers warm or your layered-look cool, this one's pretty self-explanatory.

## HAIR ACCESSORIES

Hair clips, barrettes, jewel encrusted tiaras or just plain rubber bands; when you see this word expect to find something hair-related.

## HATS

Any and all kinds of hats may turn up on sites with this label. Pith helmets and flapper caps are only the beginning....

## JEWELRY

Emerald cufflinks or zircon bindis, if it even appears to be made of metal and stone we've attributed this word to it. Find necklaces, pendants, ring, earrings, cufflinks, body jewelry, chains, bracelets, nose rings, anklets and more.

## KIDS

Most children-oriented sites may be found in the Minors section, but in the cases that these adult accessory sites included a few kids items, we thought we should point it out. Especially with the shoe stores....

## SCARVES & WRAPS

Not tailored enough to be sweaters, not big enough to be blankets, these are the shawls, scarves and pashminas that lend credence to a cool summer breeze.

## TIES

Bowties, ascots, narrow and wide; the everyday noose of the working man is represented in all conceivable colors and patterns.

## WATCHES

Some of the watches overlap into jewelry, as they feature gem stones and precious metals. Some simply don't. Just to be sure, all are identified by this key word, from vintage and pocket watches to the digital and novelty varieties.

# KEY WORD INDEX

Use the following lists to locate online retailers that sell the type of accessories you seek.

## BAGS & WALLETS

AllenEdmonds.com
Annadita.com
AnyKnockoff.com
ArtBag.com
BagEnvy.com
BeniBoutique.com
ChesterHandbags.com
Coach.com
ColeHaan.com
Dooney.com
eBags.com
eLuxury.com
EtienneAigner.com
EuropaCouture.com
FlipFlopTrunkShow.com
Forzieri.com
Fossil.com
Ghurka.com
GinaShoes.com
Holly-Go-Lightly.com
JaneFox.com
JemzNJewels.com
JestJewels.com
JohnstonMurphy.com
Journeys.com
JPGaultier.com
KennethCole.com
LedererDeParis.com
LeSportSac.com
MaxFiorentino.com
MoynaBags.com
NineWest.com
Nordstrom.com
Oakley.com
OsbornAndRobert.com
PacSun.com
Perlina.com
PeterBeaton.com
PilgrimDesigns.com
Portolano.com
RaffaelloTies.com
Rockport.com
SamanthaRoot.com
SearleNYC.com
ShoeBuy.com

SovaLeather.com
SoWear.com
StubbsAndWootton.com
TheSak.com
Timberland.com
ToteLeMonde.com
WilsonLeather.com
YakPak.com
Yoox.com

## BELTS

AlexAndAni.com
AllenEdmonds.com
Annadita.com
AnyKnockoff.com
ArtBag.com
BenSilver.com
Coach.com
ColeHaan.com
Dooney.com
eLuxury.com
EtienneAigner.com
EuropaCouture.com
Forzieri.com
Fossil.com
Ghurka.com
JaneFox.com
JemzNJewels.com
JohnstonMurphy.com
JPGaultier.com
KennethCole.com
LynGaylord.com
MoynaBags.com
Nordstrom.com
OsbornAndRobert.com
PacSun.com
RavinStyle.com
Rockport.com
SearleNYC.com
ShoeBuy.com
SovaLeather.com
SoWear.com
Timberland.com
Vegetarian-Shoes.co.uk
WilsonLeather.com
Yoox.com

## DESIGNER

AllWatchbands.com
Annadita.com
APairOfShades.com
BeniBoutique.com
eLuxury.com
EuropaCouture.com
EyeGlasses.com
Forzieri.com
Giarre.com
JemzNJewels.com
JewelryService.com
JPGaultier.com
Nordstrom.com
PaulFrederick.com
RaffaelloTies.com
RavinStyle.com
SelimaOptique.com
TheWatchMuseum.com
WatchesPlanet.com
Yoox.com

## EYEWEAR

APairOfShades.com
BenSilver.com
Coach.com
eLuxury.com
EyeGlasses.com
Fossil.com
FramesDirect.com
Giarre.com
JPGaultier.com
KennethCole.com
Nordstrom.com
Oakley.com
PacSun.com
PeterBeaton.com
RaffaelloTies.com
SearleNYC.com
SelimaOptique.com
SunglassHut.com
TheSunglassCity.com
Timberland.com

## GLOVES

Annadita.com
Coach.com
Dooney.com
EuropaCouture.com
Forzieri.com
Ghurka.com
JohnstonMurphy.com
Portolano.com
SearleNYC.com
WarmWoman.com
WilsonLeather.com
Yoox.com

## HAIR ACCESSORIES

AlexAndAni.com
eLuxury.com
EuropaCouture.com
GirlProps.com
JaneFox.com
JestJewels.com
MoynaBags.com
Nordstrom.com
RavinStyle.com
SoWear.com
TarinaTarantino.com
WigGirl.com

## HATS

Coach.com
Forzieri.com
HatMonger.com
JaneFox.com
JemzNJewels.com
JestJewels.com
JHHatCo.com
LegendMink.com
MinnetonkaMocc.com
Oakley.com
OFarrellHats.com
PacSun.com
PeterBeaton.com

Portolano.com
RavinStyle.com
ScreamerHats.com
SoWear.com
TheSak.com
Timberland.com
VillageHatShop.com
WarmWoman.com
WigGirl.com
Zappos.com

## JEWELRY

Akteo.com
AlexAndAni.com
AlexWoo.com
AntiqueJewelryExch.com
AnyKnockoff.com
BenSilver.com
BoucherJewelry.com
BruceFrankBeads.com
Cufflinks.com
eLuxury.com
ErwinPearl.com
EuropaCouture.com
Forzieri.com
Fossil.com
GalleryAtTheCreek.com
GirlProps.com
Ice.com
JestJewels.com
JPGaultier.fr
KennethCole.com
Longmire.co.uk
LynGaylord.com
Nordstrom.com
OsbornAndRobert.com
PaulFrederick.com
RavinStyle.com
TarinaTarantino.com
TinaTang.com
WendyBrigode.com
Yoox.com0
Zales.com

## KIDS

APairOfShades.com
BirkenstockCentral.com
eBags.com
EyeGlasses.com
FlipFlopTrunkShow.com
FramesDirect.com

GirlProps.com
HatMonger.com
JestJewels.com
Journeys.com
Keds.com
LacesForLess.com
MinnetonkaMocc.com
Nordstrom.com
PayLess.com
Pell.com
ScreamerHats.com
Skechers.com
TarinaTarantino.com
Teva.com
Timberland.com
YakPak.com
Zappos.com

## SCARVES & WRAPS

AnyKnockoff.com
Baldoria.com
Coach.com
EtienneAigner.com
EuropaCouture.com
Forzieri.com
Ghurka.com
JemzNJewels.com
JestJewels.com
JHHatCo.com
LegendMink.com
MaxFiorentino.com
MoynaBags.com
Nordstrom.com
Portolano.com
RavinStyle.com
SoWear.com
WarmWoman.com
Yoox.com

## SHOES

AldenShop.com
AllenEdmonds.com
Annadita.com
BeniBoutique.com
BenSilver.com
BirkenstockCentral.com
Bootlaces.com
ChurchsShoes.com
Coach.comColeHaan.com
DesignerShoes.com

Dooney.com
eLuxury.com
EtienneAigner.com
EuropaCouture.com
FlipFlopTrunkShow.com
Florsheim.com
Fluevog.com
FryeBoots.com
Ghurka.com
GinaShoes.com
JemzNJewels.com
JohnstonMurphy.com
Journeys.com
Keds.com
KennethCole.com
LacesForLess.com
LargeFeet.com
MinnetonkaMocc.com
NavajoSandals.com
NineWest.com
Nordstrom.com
Oakley.com
OddBallShoe.com
OsbornAndRobert.com
PacSun.com
PayLess.com
Pell.com
RaffaelloTies.com
RavinStyle.com
Rockport.com
SearleNYC.com
ShoeBuy.com
Skechers.com
SohoShoe.com
SoulsShoes.com
StubbsAndWootton.com
Teva.com
TheSak.com
Timberland.com
ToBoot.com
Toffelmakaren.se
Vegetarian-Shoes.co.uk
WarmWoman.com
Yoox.com
Zappos.com

## TIES

Baldoria.com
BeauTiesLtd.com
BenSilver.com
EuropaCouture.com
Forzieri.com
JPGaultier.fr

LedererDeParis.com
LeeAllison.com
NeckTies.com
Nordstrom.com
PaulFrederick.com
RaffaelloTies.com
Ties.com
WildTies.com

## WATCHES

Akteo.com
AllWatchbands.com
AntiqueJewelryExch.com
APairOfShades.com
Coach.com
eLuxury.com
ErwinPearl.com
Forzieri.com
Fossil.com
Ice.com
JestJewels.com
JPGaultier.fr
KennethCole.com
Nordstrom.com
Oakley.com
PacSun.com
SunglassHut.com
Swatch.com
TheWatchMuseum.com
Timberland.com
USAWatchCo.com
WatchesPlanet.com
WorldOfWatches.com
WristWatch.com
Zales.com

## Akteo.com

Akteo Watches • 800-360-2586

If you prefer something a little bit different in a watch, start by looking at this intriguing and unique site. These quirky watches combine slick design with a modest bit of camp, resulting in some very cool but fun faces. If you'd rather do without the camp, don't be discouraged—this site can link you to sister companies Boccia and Teno, which offer incredibly stylish titanium and stainless steel designs, including a compelling and pristine selection of jewelry. This is stuff you won't ever get tired of looking at.

| | ·WATCHES | ·JEWELRY | | |
|---|---|---|---|---|

## AldenShop.com

The Alden Shop • No Service Number

"Since 1884, the Alden Shoe Company has designed and manufactured classic gentlemen's footwear that represents America's tradition of old-school, custom shoemaking at its finest." High quality leather dress and casual shoes abound on this simply assembled site, usually in colors like black, burgundy and walnut brown. As excellent as the shoes are, the sizing makes it all the better, and most are available in the standard range of sizes, but also in widths gauging from A and AAA to E and EEEE. You can't deny the appeal of old school.

| | ·SHOES | | | |
|---|---|---|---|---|

## AlexAndAni.com

Alex and Ani • 800-725-7822

Apparently, Providence, Rhode Island is the "jewelry capital of the world." Hard to say why this would be, and tough to verify, but designer Carolyn Rafaelian Ferlise makes an argument for it here with a collection of crazy, unusual wares. Pattern-printed fashion jewelry and hair accessories are just a start; you can find some interesting "cobra" belts, precious metal coils wound like the underbelly of their venomous namesakes. There's no real clear way to find some of these things, but there's not a huge selection, so it shouldn't take you long to decide whether you can handle this Rhode Island madness.

| ·JEWELRY | ·BELTS | ·HAIR ACCESSORIES | |
|---|---|---|---|

## AlexWoo.com

Alex Woo • 212-226-5533

The difference between this and many comparable jewelry retailers is this: there's no boring jewelry here. Creative designer baubles of semi-precious stones and metals fill these pages with innovation that is sorely lacking from much modern jewelry. As for the site itself, the one major flaw would be a shopping link that is separate from the catalog displays. Fortunately, this consists of a pop-up window that you may easily leave open on your desktop while you browse some intriguing rings, chains, earrings and pendants.

| | ·JEWELRY | | | |
|---|---|---|---|---|

**877-817-7615 • Allen Edmonds**

**AllenEdmonds.com**

This site excels in moderately hi-end leather accessories for men, particularly in the form of some great belts and wallets. Mostly, though, it's all about the shoes. On the Customer Help page, a Glossary of Terms will help you distinguish between Algonquin toes, moc-toes, wing tips, vamps, foxings, bluchers and bals, which will be essential if you're going to browse with any accuracy. Or, you can opt to search by color, which offers unique leather choices like bourbon, chestnut, chili and mushroom in addition to brown and black patent leather. Good stuff.

| ·BAGS & WALLETS | ·BELTS | ·SHOES | |
|---|---|---|---|

**877-768-6400 • JewelryService.com**

**AllWatchbands.com**

The days of strapping designer watches to your wrist with duct tape when the original band breaks are over! Rather, the days of letting watch repairmen overcharge you for the replacements have passed. Here you can find replacement bands for just about every model of just about every known brand, from Timex, Omega, Casio and Swatch to Bulova, Tag Heuer and Gucci. If you didn't like the original band to begin with, you can find easy variations in materials like braided leather, alligator, nylon and rubber. Most you should be able to attach to the watch yourself, without heavy adhesives.

| ·WATCHES | ·DESIGNER | | |
|---|---|---|---|

**No Service Number • Annadita**

**Annadita.com**

Shipped straight out of Italy, this site offers a wealth of designer wallets and handbags sporting lavish labels like Gucci, Prada, Fendi and Armani. Better yet, they're listed at generally affordable prices. How so? Well, aside from the savings incurred by having pieced together an obviously lo-fi web site, the wares assembled here don't exactly consist of the new crop of bags rolled out by these classic brands. However, they're as recent edition as discount designer bags are likely to be, usually not more than a couple of seasons behind. Their value may have depreciated, but they will not go unappreciated.

| ·BAGS & WALLETS ·DESIGNER | ·GLOVES | ·BELTS | ·SHOES |
|---|---|---|---|

**800-809-4190 • Antique Jewelry Exchange**

**AntiqueJewelryExch.com**

Jewelry is a very popular family heirloom, which generally means that the best jewelry time has seen gets handed down through the generations and never again sees the light of a marketplace. Appropriate then, that this is a family owned and operated business, one that seeks out antique and estate jewelry in order to create one of the richer and finer jewelry selections online. Specializing in platinum and watches, they definitely have some lovely items to display in either category, but the rest generally has that character and charm left out of many contemporary catalogs.

| ·JEWELRY | ·WATCHES | | |
|---|---|---|---|

## AnyKnockoff.com

Boasting "trends at affordable prices," this shop specializes in contemporary fashion items that have been made to give the appearance of highly sought after wares. Or, as they say, "Knock offs are affordable products inspired by today's hottest designers and fashion trends. Knock offs, other than similar in look, are in no way affiliated with the designers from which the inspiration occurs." If you're attending the sort of social gathering where someone might point out your possession of a not-so-Gucci handbag, this site will only lead to embarrassment. Otherwise, look Beverly Hills at St. Louis prices and relish the fact.

| | ·JEWELRY | ·BAGS & WALLETS | ·BELTS | ·SCARVES/WRAPS |
|---|---|---|---|---|

## APairOfShades.com

There are three great things about this site. They are, in no particular order: the selection, the product detail and the prices. Heck, even the site design is pretty darn good. Between the long list of designer sunglasses and the big selection of designer frames (you know, for the regular kind of glasses), you might just miss out on their other sundries, like watches and contact lenses. It would be pointless to start naming some of the designer brands you can find here; suffice to say, if you want one in particular you'll probably find it.

| | ·EYEWEAR | ·WATCHES | ·DESIGNER | ·KIDS |
|---|---|---|---|---|

## ArtBag.com

Straight from Madison Avenue comes this father and son team who design and repair fashionable leather handbags for the jet set. Shopping categories like Every Day, Evening, Woven, Quilted, Traupunto and Satchels make it pretty easy to figure out what you like from the site (assuming you know what Traupunto means). Then, there's an Exotic Skins section that features alligator, lizard and such (as opposed to cow skin), and a One of a Kind area that'll have real enthusiasts drooling. The best part, though, is the promised 20% reduction in price for orders placed online.

| | ·BAGS & WALLETS | ·BELTS | | |
|---|---|---|---|---|

## BagEnvy.com

When you're accessorizing, especially when it comes to something like a handbag, the entire joy of parading it before the jealous eyes of your friends will be utterly lost if they can simply find and garner the same design only days later. That's one reason to appreciate this boutique that, in an effort "to avoid the proliferation of [its] bags and to protect their enviable uniqueness," includes in this catalog "only limited quantities of each." They claim to secure their wares from "unusual places" and "obscure designers." Unlikely to pop up around town or not, these are some cool, very funky bags.

| | ·BAGS & WALLETS | | | |
|---|---|---|---|---|

## No Service Number • Baldoria

### Baldoria.com

Offering some of the best in custom-made Italian silk, this site delivers promising statements like, "In Baldoria, the item you choose does not exist until you create it." Of course, the excitement sort of wears off when you realize that this is a tailor of ties, and that there really aren't that many directions you can go with them. Still, these are Italian silk ties, and there are plenty of patterns to sort through before you order. Besides, you can personalize every tie with the embroidered words of your choice.

| ·TIES | ·SCARVES/WRAPS | | | | |
|-------|----------------|--|--|--|--|

## 800-488-8437 • Beau Ties Ltd.

### BeauTiesLtd.com

Granted, bow ties aren't the most popular choice in neckwear, but should you find the occasion to brave or embrace the style, this site will serve you right. Beginning with dozens of color options, you may also find stripes, polka dots and more complex patterns, as well as some really elaborate designs with pictures all over them. Each then lets you choose your neck size; elect freestyle, pre-tied or clip-on; and select assorted widths like slim line and butterfly. To top it off, they automatically select for you coordinated ascots, cravats, cummerbunds and pocket squares, lest you not feel goofy enough already.

| ·TIES | | | | |
|-------|--|--|--|--|

## No Service Number • Beni Boutique

### BeniBoutique.com

Handbags by Louis Vuitton, shoes by Manolo Blahnik; yes, the designer world has a lot more to offer than just dresses and sweaters, but at what cost? Well, thanks to this site, not all that much it turns out. Pioneering the term "Discount Designer Goods," it lets you browse dozens of top name brands, or you can just cruise through the entire selection of handbags. Of course, shoes are always tough to shop for, but search by shoe size and you'll see just those adornments for your feet that will likely fit. Better yet, bearing in mind that different designers use different sizings, they also include the interior length of the shoe as an additional measurement for your consideration. If you think that's good, wait until you see the shoes.

| ·BAGS & WALLETS | ·SHOES | ·DESIGNER | | |
|-----------------|--------|-----------|--|--|

## 800-221-4671 • Ben Silver

### BenSilver.com

London, England and Charleston, South Carolina have an unlikely association with this tailor/retailer of suits and their finest accessories that calls both cities home. Essentially, this stuff has the class to fit both old English and Southern societies, right down to the umbrellas, evening sticks and pocket squares (a.k.a. handkerchiefs). Lest you think the collection stuffy, you should know that belts, cufflinks and shoes make up the bulk of the merchandise you'll come looking for, all predictably classic for those times you just can't get away with anything else.

| ·TIES ·SHOES | ·JEWELRY | ·EYEWEAR | ·BELTS | | |
|--------------|----------|----------|--------|--|--|

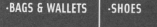

## BirkenstockCentral.com

Birkenstock Central • 800-247-5748

If you're familiar with the brand name there's really little else we need to say here other than to tell you this site's a worthy place to find your next pair of sandals. If you haven't worn Birkenstocks before, we have to tell you: don't be turned off by the sometimes-gaudy looks of this site. The products are top notch, quite possibly the most comfortable footwear you'll find for the price. They offer lines of slip-ons, shoes and clogs as well, along with options including Water Friendly (for the outdoors enthusiast) and Leatherfree (for the true hippie).

| | | ·SHOES | ·KIDS | | |
| --- | --- | --- | --- | --- | --- |

## Bootlaces.com

Bootlaces.com • 011-44-127-930-5623

The good people of Bootlaces "scour the world to find the laces you want." Sound crazy? Well, as long as you don't have to, right? Your task is instead to scour the site, which may take just as long as it's slow and prone to errors. Indeed, the site looks terrible on top of acting that way, but it's got shoe and bootlaces in a wide variety of sizes, length and styles and even some "no-tie laces," which must be seen to be fully understood. Sure, we wish this site was better, but what are you gonna do?

| | | ·SHOES | | | |
| --- | --- | --- | --- | --- | --- |

## BoucherJewelry.com

Laura Mady's Boucher Jewelry • 866-623-9269

Inexpensive, fashionable jewelry can be hard to come by for the cool customer. But discriminating accessorizers on a modest budget should find plenty of good bracelets, earrings and necklaces on this quirky site whose name is apparently French for "butcher" (we don't know why, we're just sayin'). Categories are split into color themes, like Cool Blues, Santa Fe (turquoise and coral), Oceania (deep sea blues and greens) and Royal Blush, which revolves around pinks and reds. You'll probably make return visits.

| ·JEWELRY | | | |
| --- | --- | --- | --- |

## BruceFrankBeads.com

Bruce Frank Beads • 877-232-3775

Who is Bruce Frank? Well, he's an "antique collector by nature" who runs a bead and ethnographic arts gallery in New York as he is "captivated by the intense artistry and skill" these little threaded baubles possess. To be sure, he knows his stuff, so if you scroll to the Online Store link at the bottom of the page, you'll find an exquisite little catalog of beaded jewelry, stuff like necklaces and eyeglass chains, as well as strings of semi-precious stones. The coup de grace, though, is his unparalleled selection of glass beads. Each more beautiful than the last, they're likely to make his obsession your own.

| ·JEWELRY | | | |
| --- | --- | --- | --- |

## 310-446-8084 • Chester Handbags

### ChesterHandbags.com

This line of handbags was created by Tiffany Lerman, daughter of novelist Jackie Collins. While she currently works out of LA, she harkens back to her early days in 1970's London to draw inspiration for these funky bags that have been featured on shows like *Friends* and *Buffy the Vampire Slayer,* and owned by the likes of Cindy Crawford and Annette Bening. As if the allure of '70s London wasn't enough, she attempts to infuse each piece with flashes of color, complimentary textures and clean lines. She succeeds quite nicely, offering great bags to take to the beach or on vacation, or even to stow your baby gear in. Talk about versatile.

| ·BAGS & WALLETS | | | |
|---|---|---|---|

## 888-997-4637 • Church's English Shoes

### ChurchsShoes.com

Some call it stuffy; we call it British elegance. Since 1873, Church's English Shoes has been making footwear for the refined gentleman, and they have kept up with the times enough to offer what are generally referred to as "timeless designs," i.e. those that will suit any occasion in which you are neither wearing blue jean shorts, jogging nor trogging through mud. Here's a tip: go straight to the bottom of the home page to find the Site Map. This way you can view all the shoes at one time, with no trouble, and without having to understand peculiar category names like Blissworth or Bamford.

| ·SHOES | | | |  |
|---|---|---|---|---|

## 888-262-6224 • Coach

### Coach.com

This is a good looking site, but really it's the finishing touches, like the home page's expanding, animated menu, that makes it great. Similarly, the items you'll find here will go a long way in adding those final touches to your wardrobe, whether it's one of Coach's many fine leather items (their specialty), or any of their sunglasses, gloves, scarves, shoes, wallets, belts or hair accessories. Of course, if you're familiar with Coach, you'll know that its first offerings consisted of some finely hewn handbags, a collection they maintain to this day.

| ·EYEWEAR<br>·HATS | ·BAGS & WALLETS<br>·SHOES | ·GLOVES<br>·WATCHES | ·BELTS<br>·SCARVES & WRAPS | |
|---|---|---|---|---|

## 800-695-8945 • Cole Haan

### ColeHaan.com

If you're after some great leather shoes, whether for those high formal occasions, standard dressy affairs, walking in the country or just kicking back at home, this'll be a good place to find them. There's also stuff like briefcases, belts, wallets and handbags, and even some stuff in alligator skin. The wide variety is separated into categories like City, Country, Studio and Resort, and browsing them can take time, though it's usually worth it, given what you'll find. One subcategory you definitely shouldn't miss offers your standard Country and Studio shoes with a twist: these leather shoes actually utilize Nike Air technology. That's right, finally a loafer you can leap in.

| ·BAGS & WALLETS | ·BELTS | ·SHOES | |  |
|---|---|---|---|---|

# Cufflinks.com

Lest you think they merely hold French cuffs together, this site is here to show us all that cufflinks can be. It begins with a bounty of engravable sterling silver and gold designs, some boasting gems, and a bevy of thematic shapes owing to such interests as Sports, Music, Transportation, Local Interests (mostly major US cities), Career Related interests and the Military. Most intriguing, however, are the Functional cufflinks found here, embedded with such useful items as watches, compasses, thermometers, lockets, working levels and abaci. Mix-match two of these, add a pocketknife and you have yourself one handy, well-dressed man.

·JEWELRY

# DesignerShoes.com

Established "for women who leave a larger footprint," this is an excellent source of familiar designer footwear in tough-to-find sizes. En vogue brands like Anne Klein, Steve Madden, Sesto Meucci and Stuart Weitzman are represented here, as are more casual lines like New Balance and Hush Puppies. Sizes vary between a women's size 8 and 14, with widths in AAAAA to WW. A clunky page and menu design offers easy enough shopping by brand or style, but as all sizes aren't represented in all shoes, we highly recommend the Shop by Size option to save both time and disappointment.

·SHOES ·DESIGNER

# Dooney.com

Dooney & Bourke have been at it for a quarter of a century, and in that time they've come to be known for some of the finest handbags on the market. Durable, attractive and just slick, these wares pretty much set a standard for elegance... in the world of handbags that is. They also sell a refined selection of wallets, gloves, shoes, belts and even some very stylish cases for your cell phone, pager, PDA or CDs. The Online Catalog will take you directly to a menu of products for browsing, or you can look to the Site Map for a very detailed catalog of items to head straight for what you want. If only everything that worked so well looked so good.

·BAGS & WALLETS ·GLOVES ·BELTS ·SHOES

# eBags.com

Here's a site that stretches the meaning of the word "bag" to its logical conclusion. Backpacks, handbags and luggage are only the beginning; these guys offer a wide selection of bags and cases for sports, the outdoors, business or travel, and they even build upon their traditional offering of briefcases to include satchels and cases for your laptop, cell phone, pager or PDA, among other things. Simply put, if it can be contained in anything short of a box, these guys will find that container and sell it to you.

·BAGS & WALLETS ·KIDS

## 877-890-7171 • eLuxury

### eLuxury.com

Chances are, you already own several handbags, a couple of belts, a scarf or two and plenty of shoes. To own any more at this point would be simply an indulgence, a luxury if you will. Well, coincidentally, this site has been developed specifically to serve the needs of those of us who want a little extra in our lives. Their products, which also include wallets, hats, gloves and hair accessories, were created by some of the more highly regarded designers of such things in the world (Badgley Mischka handbags, for example). It's easy to shop by product, brand or price range, wherein you will find detailed pictures, thorough item descriptions and great prices. This is a highly functional, utility shopping site… they just happen to sell luxury items.

| ·JEWELRY ·HAIR | ·EYEWEAR ·SHOES | ·BAGS & WALLETS ·WATCHES | ·BELTS ·DESIGNER |
| --- | --- | --- | --- |

## 800-379-4673 • Erwin Pearl

### ErwinPearl.com

Once a designer of fine jewelry, Austrian born Erwin Pearl (not likely his real name) decided after a few very successful years at his trade that the true challenge lay in the pleasing of a broader market with the design of a more fashion-oriented jewelry. Has he succeeded? Well, here you'll find everything from reversible bracelets to gold-tone chains, alongside enamel dog pendants (you read it correctly). It's simply laid out, with not too much to sort through, so let's just say the cream will find its way to the top.

| ·JEWELRY | ·WATCHES | | |
| --- | --- | --- | --- |

## 800-673-3001 • Etienne Aigner

### EtienneAigner.com

If you consider yourself an active woman, Etienne Aigner is aiming its selection of quality accessories directly at you. While they're not from France, as it would seem, but from New Jersey, don't let it throw you; their wares are stylish enough to be imports. Mostly, they deal in leather shoes and handbags, stuff to fit any business attire, and plenty for the casual times as well. You may notice some other intriguing items, as visual menus take advantage of our attraction to shiny objects, but it's when you click on Zoom that you'll suddenly understand some of the more understated items' appeal.

| ·BAGS & WALLETS | ·BELTS | ·SCARVES/WRAPS | ·SHOES |
| --- | --- | --- | --- |

## 412-915-1515 • EuropaCouture.com

### EuropaCouture.com

Claiming to be "the world's largest online boutique featuring exceptional Haute Couture upscale fashions," we can only assume that this site attributes a singular meaning to the word "exceptional." Still, their selection is unique, and it does feature dozens of fabulous designers, so we won't hold them to it. The Premiere Collection is where they house their new items, while items consigned from celebrities, socialites and movie studios populate the Encore Section. If you're not particular, everything can be found in the Entire Collection link, which, given the site's poor design, ultimately makes the most sense.

| ·TIES ·BELTS | ·JEWELRY ·SCARVES/WRAPS | ·BAGS & WALLETS ·SHOES | ·GLOVES ·DESIGNER |
| --- | --- | --- | --- |

# EyeGlasses.com

So, there are obvious benefits to shopping for glasses in a real-world store rather than online; rather, there were. After all, who wants to miss out on the fun of trying on different shades to stylish and often hilarious results? Well, fun with mirrors aside, this site's developed an innovative way to check yourself out. It's simple, really; just email a scanned image of yourself, and then you can "etry" on any pair of glasses they offer (a wide, high quality selection to be sure). Imagine looking at yourself online with any of hundreds of different available styles. And thanks to creative search features, finding variants of any styles, materials, colors, brands and shapes will give you a much better selection than any local store. Always good for a laugh, at least....

# FlipFlopTrunkShow.com

Declaring sandals to be fashionably acceptable year round, this internet boutique puts a bright pink happy face on mules, slides and thongs that, frankly, we just don't see every day. Quality of merchandise ranges from affordable to extravagant (to the extent that sandals may be extravagant), and a few funky accessories are tossed in just to keep a stylistically uniform front. Shopping for footwear's rarely this fun, and hardly this worthwhile.

# Florsheim.com

If you're a guy, and quite picky about what you put on your foot, stylewise, Florsheim offers a huge selection of proprietary designs for your perusal. They've been doing this for over 100 years, so you can generally count on a measure of quality in whichever model suits your fancy. At first glance, it doesn't appear that you can look at a shoe without following one of hundreds of text links. Relax, it's not nearly so time-consuming; just keep an eye on the top left corner of the screen and watch pictures pop up when you roll-over any of the shoe names they offer, whether they're Formal, Dress, Casual or Refined Casual (see if you can spot the difference).

# Fluevog.com

Probably the strangest and coolest thing to come out of Canada since Mounties, this site owes its wares to the creative brain of John Fluevog, formerly of Fox & Fluevog. Seems his former partner, Peter Fox, went on to design Bridal Shoes, while Fluevog... went in a decidedly different direction—actually, we haven't seen such a wide disparity in career course since Sonny & Cher split up. In contrast to the lily-white pumps of Fox, Fluevog displays here some attitude-laden boots and clunky shoes. If you look deep, you may find something lighter, but generally this wickedly stylish footwear better suits a rocker than a bride or a Mountie.

## 800-476-1718 • Forzieri

### Forzieri.com

Italy. The long-standing, global epicenter of fashion is celebrated in this Florence-based store that offers the finest in handcrafted Italian designer accessories. Sure, the site can run kinda slow, but what's the rush if it's Italian? Take your time browsing the ties, ascots and scarves, or cufflinks, tie clips and belts. Or look at handbags and briefcases, what difference does it make? Man or woman, you're sure to find something in your price range or color preference, in your favorite materials, always made by Italy's finest; its designers.

| ·TIES<br>·HATS | ·BAGS & WALLETS<br>·SCARVES/WRAPS | ·GLOVES<br>·WATCHES | ·BELTS<br>·DESIGNER |
|---|---|---|---|

## 800-449-3056 • Fossil

### Fossil.com

Initially a watchmaker, this expansive brand's site still features plenty of cool watches for men and women; in fact a huge selection with product names like Hippie, Titanium and Big Tic. Then there's an interesting assortment of accessories, stuff like bags, belts, wallets and sunglasses, fit for the fashion conscious, yet not at exorbitant prices. Everything here could be easily mixed and matched to accessorize clean-fitting outfits— the kind of stuff people like to wear in order not to feel ostentatious; the kind of stuff that won't require replacement in a few months because it's become horribly passé.

| ·JEWELRY<br>·WATCHES | ·EYEWEAR | ·BAGS & WALLETS | ·BELTS |
|---|---|---|---|

## 800-248-9427 • Frames Direct

### FramesDirect.com

Able to "provide almost any of the 116,000 different frames available in the US," these guys make a pretty good case to support their claim of being the "world's largest online optical store." Having a couple of brands in mind is pretty much the only way you'll find any sunglasses, though, without having to actually browse through those hundred-thousand-plus options. You can also look for frames particular to such activities as golf, skiing and tennis, as well as peruse some contact lens brands and prescription frames for those less than sunny days.

| ·EYEWEAR | ·KIDS | | |
|---|---|---|---|

## 800-826-3793 • Frye

### FryeBoots.com

If you're looking for a pair of boots with a little bit of history, this manufacturer dates back long enough to have stocked both sides of the US Civil War. They've been no less ambivalent in the time since, having supplied boots to servicemen in WWII, and then catering to the counterculture of the 1960s. Perhaps no other contradictory pairing exists though than in their esteemed celebrity clientele, as this footwear has been known to adorn the feet of both Bruce Springsteen and Liza Minelli. Good boots, whichever side you happen to be on.

| ·SHOES | | | |
|---|---|---|---|

## GalleryAtTheCreek.com

Coldwater Creek • 800-510-2808

Small town tastes meet designer flair at this Idaho-based web site that actually features an exceptionally good selection of fine and fashionable jewelry. Each piece here is shown with excellent detail and a great product description, and the site design makes it easy to root around for the best stuff. Still, should you have any problems, instant gratification is on the way with online customer service reps that will respond to your pleas for help while you continue to browse. All this from a place that, according to the About Us section, is overrun with moose (plural). Who knew?

 ·JEWELRY

## Ghurka.com

Ghurka • 800-587-1584

These guys used to just be a "small leather bag workshop;" now they're pretty much huge, with stores all over the US, in Europe and Japan. Some of their bags even get cast in feature films, like *What Lies Beneath* and *Hannibal,* or turn up on the arms of the wealthy and famous. They don't even just make handbags anymore, selling loads of mostly leather accessories like shoes, wallets and stuff as cool as liquor flasks or mundane as business card cases. How, you might ask, does a company grow to such prodigious heights? Got to be the quality, we guess ... and really high prices.

| ·BAGS & WALLETS ·SHOES | ·GLOVES | ·BELTS | ·SCARVES/WRAPS |

## Giarre.com

Giarre • 800-668-5153

Italy and fashion go hand in hand—this we know. But who knew that the best place to buy designer eyewear was this e-store based in Tuscany? All the top designers' wares are featured here: Gucci, Armani, Versace, Prada, Dolce e Gabbana, Bollé, Bvlgari, Chanel, Calvin Klein, DKNY and even Gaultier. Then there are more populist brands like Nike and Ray Ban to give you some perspective. Here's the crazy part, though: this stuff is cheap, way cheaper than all its online competitors. Sure, there's shipping from Italy to consider (though sunglasses are quite light), but as long as a favorable exchange rate holds up, this is the place to buy your chic new shades, no doubt about it.

| ·EYEWEAR | ·DESIGNER | | |

## GinaShoes.com

Gina • 011-44-207-235-2932

There doesn't seem to be an actual Gina involved with this high-end line of shoes and handbags. Rather, this family business currently being run by a second generation of Kurdashes out of London continues an almost half-century of design that was initially inspired by the glamour of 1950's Hollywood actresses. The shoes and bags are phenomenal, and duly expensive, especially when you consider the prices are listed in pounds, not dollars. But with such flair as these shoes display, and the aid of a matching bag feature, you will find yourself hard pressed to leave this site empty-handed.

| ·SHOES | ·BAGS & WALLETS | | |

## 212-505-7615 • GirlProps.com

**GirlProps.com**

Cheerfully proclaiming their aversion to the word "cheap," the proprietors of this site would rather view their inexpensive items with a touch of humor. But how else could we look upon the brightly colored wigs and glitzy, glam accessories presumed to go with them? The truth is, some of the fancy bobby pins, poofy hair clips and glitter makeup merely makes us smile a little. Hey, some girls just like to sparkle, just like some girls like to wear a set of feathery wings when they dress up for a night out. Well, this site is for just such a girl.

| ·JEWELRY | ·HAIR | ·KIDS | |
|---|---|---|---|

## 214-828-0639 • HatMonger.com

**HatMonger.com**

A case could be made that the hats of today lack the character and quality of haberdashery from other eras. If you'd be the person making this case, here's a site that should at long last find you satisfaction. Offering a great wealth of vintage headwear, the selection here spans decades to include: top hats, fedoras, skimmers (a la barber shop quartets), cloches (necessary accoutrements for any flapper) and straw hats in all kinds of shapes and sizes. You just don't see this stuff on peoples' heads anymore, let alone in stores; however, if you're looking to add a feather to your bonnet, this place has got it.

| ·HATS | ·KIDS | | | |
|---|---|---|---|---|

## 704-793-1133 • Holly-Go-Lightly Collection

**Holly-Go-Lightly.com**

From former Gucci designer Cherie Metcalf comes this extremely fun collection of handbags, purses, backpacks and totes. With enticing category names like Romantic, Bohemian, Tropical and Baby-Go-Lightly, you never quite know what you're going to get yourself into, but it can be fun to find out. All of these bags are handmade and, if customer satisfaction is any indication, high quality (one gleeful shopper exclaims, "If only you had shoes!"). Audrey Hepburn fans shouldn't be disappointed with this one.

| ·BAGS & WALLETS | | | |
|---|---|---|---|

## 800-539-3580 • Ice

**Ice.com**

With a name like Ice, you'd expect this site to be very cool, clean and crisp. It's all those things; a very slick site with excellent browsing and search options covering a fine selection, and excellent looks at some equally slickly designed rings, necklaces, bracelets, watches, etc. Despite the good looking wares, though, the prices on this site are far from overblown and, should you find cause to disagree, they're willing to set you up with a monthly payment plan. Think of this as the rare jewelry store that exceeds expectations.

| ·JEWELRY | ·WATCHES | | | |
|---|---|---|---|---|

# JaneFox.com

Buzz by Jane Fox • 516-599-6677

Cute handbags in vibrant colors seem to be quite the valuable commodity, and almost nowhere is that more evident than in this shop. The totes, clutches and other sundry bags here have been far more successfully designed than the pages that proffer them, as the site proves far too clunky and animated for its own good. However, this hasn't seemed to hinder sales, and if you can afford the moderately high prices you should snatch up anything you like without hesitation; others do, and these seasonal items will sell out.

| ·BAGS & WALLETS | ·BELTS | ·HATS | ·HAIR |
|---|---|---|---|

# JemzNJewels.com

Jemznjewels • 800-488-8265

This is a great site for couture accessories of many kinds: bags, shoes, scarves, hats and belts. A bevy of recognizable (and some beyond recognizable) designer brands will immediately command your attention, whether it's Chanel, Prada or Walter Steigner, and most of the items will keep you current and looking good. Better yet is the selection of vintage accessories, mostly handbags, that recall some of the fine designs of the past yet still stand the scrutiny of today's looks; they may even lend you an air of accomplished indifference to passing trends. As quantities are quite slim, you might want to keep this one to yourself.

| ·BAGS & WALLETS ·HATS | ·DESIGNER ·SCARVES & WRAPS | ·SHOES | ·BELTS |
|---|---|---|---|

# JestJewels.com

Jest Jewels • 415-563-8839

Where's a girl to go when she needs a good purse, ankle bracelet, toe ring, hat, animal pin, watch, jewelry box or feather phone? Here, apparently, although where the feather phone idea comes from we may never know. The rest of the stuff, however, is legitimate, and also includes hair accessories, earrings and plenty of other things to keep it interesting. There doesn't seem to be any overriding style; it ranges from girly animal shapes and trendy animal prints to classic (if extraordinarily cheap) pearl strands. Chalk it up to the store's San Francisco and Berkeley, CA locations—they see it all out there.

| ·JEWELRY ·HAIR | ·BAGS & WALLETS ·WATCHES | ·HATS ·KIDS | ·SCARVES/WRAPS |
|---|---|---|---|

# JHHatCo.com

Jackson Hole Hat Co. • 307-733-7687

Getting a cowboy hat from Wyoming is like getting a facelift in Beverly Hills; it just feels authentic. But there's another great reason to buy a hat from this Jackson Hole retailer in particular: customization. You'll find an array of felt cowboy hat designs, ranging in styles from Derby, Fedora and Top Hat to all the various sheriff and outlaw looks you've seen in any movie; and all are available made-to-fit. You may also select from dozens of colors and hatbands, and may adjust the brim size to suit your own bent, pardner.

| ·HATS | ·SCARVES/WRAPS | |
|---|---|---|

## 888-324-6189 • Johnston & Murphy

**JohnstonMurphy.com**

Since 1850, this company founded by an "English immigrant shoemaker... [has coupled] old world shoemaking techniques with new world style and comfort." In other words, they update classic designs to suit the gentleman interested in fine handcrafted leather shoes. Are they good? Well, they'll be the first to clue you in, claiming to have "made shoes for every US President since Millard Fillmore" (President from 1850–1853, if you're curious). You'd think these shoes would be astronomically expensive, as well as their belts, gloves and briefcases, and yet, they're not. Definitely old world.

| ·BAGS & WALLETS | ·BELTS | ·SHOES | ·GLOVES |
|---|---|---|---|

## 888-324-6356 • Journeys

**Journeys.com**

The concept of shoes has certainly evolved over the years, branching out from the strapping of animal skins to the feet, on to various developments that have resulted in contemporary forms like loafers, mules, slides and pumps. This site doesn't sell any of those shoes. Journeys describes its products as "an attitude you can wear," and its selection of boots, sneakers, sandals and platforms doesn't disappoint. This stuff is made for city streets or rowdy nightclubs, whether you go with studs or without, knee-high or steel-toed, you can find some of the top brands in urban footwear from Vans and Durango to Doc Martens. Not for the dainty.

| ·BAGS & WALLETS | ·SHOES | ·KIDS | |
|---|---|---|---|

## 011-33-1-44-68-84-84 • Jean Paul Gaultier

**JPGaultier.com**

Welcome to the fascinating and in some ways flabbergasting universe of French designer Jean Paul Gaultier. Some parts of this website seem designed to bewilder, and while they're certainly fun to explore, to get to the really good stuff you should just follow the Shop Online link from the homepage. There you'll find an easy-to-decipher list of bags, backpacks, belts, ties, sunglasses and umbrellas, each of which bears that coveted Gaultier sensibility that has made him so internationally revered. You'll also discover a lot of things along the way—some very strange—but in the end, who cares as long as he keeps it coming?

| ·TIES ·BELTS | ·JEWELRY ·WATCHES | ·EYEWEAR ·DESIGNER | ·BAGS & WALLETS |
|---|---|---|---|

## 800-428-6575 • Keds

**Keds.com**

Almost synonymous with childish summer romping, these simple sneaker mainstays have kept several generations of girls leaping and dancing almost without an ounce of change, other than to expand around their original design. Stick to the classic white models or branch out into colors and styles, it doesn't matter; simply donning these light, inexpensive shoes and slides will probably put you in that youthful frame of mind. Probably the worst thing you could do is to put these on and then stay inside.

| ·SHOES | ·KIDS | | |
|---|---|---|---|

# KennethCole.com

The full name, Kenneth Cole Productions, is part of a ploy that let Mr. Cole park a big truck on the streets of midtown Manhattan as a movie production crew (the only way to get a permit) so he could display his wares at a shoe show. The maneuver, played at the expense of the Mayor (who even threw in a couple of NYC's finest as security), worked big time, and now the company offers not only highly recognized shoes but also a bevy of belts, handbags, wallets, jewelry, watches, sunglasses and hosiery. But wait, just when you think it's over, follow the Reaction Online link to reveal another stash of even hipper, more vibrant stuff.

| | | ·JEWELRY ·SHOES | ·EYEWEAR ·WATCHES | ·BAGS & WALLETS | ·BELTS |

# LacesForLess.com

Billing itself as "The Shoelace Place," this is a very simply organized site. In fact, everything is simple. You can shop by color, length or style (categories like Athletic, Athletic Neon, Boot, Wide Lace and etc.), and get a good look at the resulting selection. There's the rub, though, as the selection, too, is simple, not very extensive in quality or design. It would be nice if you could find a better choice of, say, materials or widths. Then again, we're talkin' shoelaces here, what do you want?

| | | ·SHOES | ·KIDS | | |

# LargeFeet.com

This is the online version of an Atlanta shoe store that specializes in large, usually hard-to-find shoe sizes. We could tell you about their extensive selection or effective browsing techniques, but instead we'll just mention a sampling of their better known clientele: heavyweight champion Lennox Lewis; football legend Ed "Too Tall" Jones; baseball players Andres Galarraga and Tony Gwynn; and basketball stars David Robinson, Dikembe Mutombo and Shaquille O'Neal. Basically, some of the most prominent big men on the planet find their footwear here.

| | | ·SHOES | | | |

# LedererDeParis.com

Boasting the "finest European hand-crafted goods since 1898," this NYC outfit enters its second century with an incredible and accomplished selection of briefcases, alongside some prim and, for lack of a better word, appropriate handbags. You'll probably find their ties atrocious (no offense if you're a fan), but they also have a few classy pieces of luggage that'll compliment your professional polish. At any rate, do be sure to glance at the ties, at least, especially the one with a frog print. It could make a good gag gift.

| | ·TIES | ·BAGS & WALLETS | | |

## 888-434-8437 • Lee Allison

**LeeAllison.com**

Granted, bow ties aren't the most popular choice in neckwear, but should you find the occasion to brave or embrace the style, this site will serve you right. Beginning with dozens of color options, you may also find stripes, polka dots and more complex patterns, as well as some really elaborate designs with pictures all over them. Each then lets you choose your neck size; elect freestyle, pre-tied or clip-on; and select assorted widths like slim line and butterfly. To top it off, they automatically select for you coordinated ascots, cravats, cummerbunds and pocket squares.

·TIES

## 866-367-6465 • American Legend Mink

**LegendMink.com**

Is there such a thing as too much mink? This is the question you'll be forced to ask yourself after visiting this site. It's not really that there's an overabundance of the stuff—there's no more than a couple dozen items in actuality. No, the reason being is that there's more to this mink than jackets and stoles. There are hats to keep your head warm, a collar to keep your neck warm, a scarf, a shawl, a purse and an ascot. Basically, these guys seem intent on making anything they can think of out of mink, which will certainly win over the hearts and minds of PETA activists.

·HATS    ·SCARVES/WRAPS

## 877-397-6597 • Le Sport Sac

**LeSportSac.com**

Finding the right handbag can be complicated; you may be able to find a great style, but then there's a matter of matching it up with the right color, and vice-versa. The LeSportSac brand feels your pain. They offer several styles for each type of bag in their repertoire, whether it's a tote, backpack, cosmetic case or clutch (for example), and each design turns up in any of a variety of colors and patterns, stopping just short of a create-your-own-bag scenario. In return, all you have to put up with is the repeating LeSportSac logo striping across your new bag. Don't worry, it's not as conspicuous as it sounds... unless you want it to be.

·BAGS & WALLETS

## 011-44-207-930-8720 • Longmire

**Longmire.co.uk**

It stands to reason that the United Kingdom would provide a good source of hi-end cufflinks, and this site does not disappoint. With an array of gems, fine metals (including white gold) and "coloured enamel" designs, some of these are distinctly British, some just plain classy. Of course, clamping your cuffs with such distinguished jewelry doesn't come without a price, and these prices will certainly give one pause. But good looks at some good-looking wares will surely entice the sort of sophisticate who can manage.

·JEWELRY

## LynGaylord.com

**Lyn Gaylord Accessories • 203-853-3264**

The ornate metal work found on this site adds exquisite texture to any outfit, whether in cufflink or belt buckle form. Inspired by 19th century European objets d'art, these pieces come shaped like animals or carved with illustrious scenes and landscapes, in nearly all cases silver. These are the sorts of things you're likely to find in Beverly Hills boutiques, which, as it happens, is where they're typically found.

| ·BELTS | ·JEWELRY | | |
|---|---|---|---|

## MaxFiorentino.com

**Max Fiorentino • 212-327-3553**

Handbags and pashminas go hand in hand. Well, not really, but don't tell that to Max Fiorentino. Here, you'll find all the pashminas you could want, in any of three sizes and a "dazzling array of colors," alongside a large assortment of bags in all kinds of animal styles. The pashminas are easy to shop for, the bags are not. You'll have to browse through several pages of handbags, clutches, cases and backpacks before you've seen them all. And you really should see them all: ostrich, crocodile, deer or otherwise.

| ·BAGS & WALLETS | ·SCARVES/WRAPS | | |
|---|---|---|---|

## MinnetonkaMocc.com

**The Moccasin House • 800-969-6690**

If you've been walking miles in another's moccasins, your sense of perspective may be admirable, but you've been doing a great disservice to your feet. As some of the most comfortable shoes that may ever cover your toes, these may not be this or any season's best look, but when you're talking about walking, sometimes function just has to win out over form. So far as moccasins go, these adhere pretty authentically to Native American traditions, available often in deerskin and mooseride along with the more common leathers. You will even find some fringed suede boots, sheepskin slippers and cool western hats (read: cowboy), all with the greatest of ease. Good site.

| ·HATS | ·SHOES | ·KIDS | |
|---|---|---|---|

## MoynaBags.com

**Moyna • 212-967-0760**

Moyna is Moyna Singh, and she designs not only bags, but also scarves, shawls, hair accessories and obi belts as well. She began her design business after becoming "involved with the design and manufacture of handcrafted home accessories in India," and it shows. Her designs often feature beading or embroidery, usually on vibrantly colored silk, and actually hint at influence from various Asian cultures. A tip to those trolling for handbags: scroll past all the press clippings to find some of the best stuff.

| ·BAGS & WALLETS | ·BELTS | ·SCARVES/WRAPS | ·HAIR |
|---|---|---|---|

## 954-455-5021 • Navajo Sandals

What can we say about Navajo Sandals by Jack Rogers? Not much, actually. He makes Native American inspired sandals in a great variety of colors, yet all with the same design. Of course, it's a great design, and the color combinations all seem to work well; you just have to find one you like and remember to select it in the ordering page. Oh yeah, at the time of this writing there is promised a future of Navajo Handbags as well, you know, if you like to match such things. We suppose they'll be pretty cool too.

·SHOES

## 01 1-44-700-596-8099 • NeckTies.com

**NeckTies.com**

This is not a terrific site, and it doesn't offer any of the best ties on the planet. But for many of us, a tie is just something we wear with our suits to keep us from looking like a con artist or eccentric billionaire. For just such a man this site offer an easily browsed selection of basic ties in all the predictable patterns and colors. What's more is that they also feature a wide selection of specialty and novelty ties, so you may adorn your suit with farm animals or Austin Powers should you so desire. But please don't.

·TIES

## 800-999-1877 • Nine West

**NineWest.com**

These guys have made a pretty good name for themselves by selling a pretty good selection of pretty good shoes at pretty good prices. Actually, most of these shoes are better than that, which brings us to the best part of the site: the Advanced Search feature. Actually, the browsing on this site is above par, especially considering there aren't enough shoes here to make it a miserable chore. However, you can quite easily narrow down the search by shoe size, material, heel height, style and price range, so you may view every shoe suitable to your needs within a matter of moments.

·BAGS & WALLETS    ·SHOES

## 888-282-6060 • Nordstrom

**Nordstrom.com**

It's all about the shoes. Sure, Nordstrom has been selling all manner of men's and women's apparel for nearly a century, but first and foremost its success lies in its huge selection of quality footwear. Here you'll find dozens of your favorite brands in a range of sizes, from sandals to boots, and everything in between. If you don't like shopping by brand, it's easy to browse by function, occasion or even by "trend setting styles." If you want to "try shoes on," go to the store—otherwise, just shop here and save your feet some work.

| ·TIES | ·EYEWEAR | ·BAGS & WALLETS | ·BELTS |
| ·SCARVES/WRAPS | ·HAIR | ·SHOES | ·WATCHES |

## Oakley.com

Oakley • 800-403-7449

It's easy to think of Oakley as a fixture of the past; after all, weren't theirs the shades favored by mulleted sports car enthusiasts and hair band rockers of the mid-eighties? Yes, they were. However, their designs have more than kept up with the times, and their sunglasses are as futuristic as they are popular. The polarized lenses and wrap-around frames that give Oakleys a distinctive and often emulated look remain true to form, but they've managed to keep way ahead of their emulators with some seriously teched out alterations, new looks, footwear and even watches that put their own history to shame.

| ·EYEWEAR ·WATCHES | ·BAGS & WALLETS | ·HATS | ·SHOES |
|---|---|---|---|

## OddBallShoe.com

Oddball Shoe Company • 800-884-4046

Can guys with big feet have any fashion sense? They can if they shop here. Founded by a couple of oversized siblings in the Portland, OR, this exquisitely designed site serves sizes 12–20 with aplomb, featuring popular brands like Converse, Doc Martens, Adidas, New Balance, Vans and plenty more, granting big feet fashionable options where there once were none. They'll even custom order shoes for larger sizes, as this store whose motto is "Where Size Always Matters" boasts once having sold a pair in the size 56.

| ·SHOES | | | |
|---|---|---|---|

## OFarrellHats.com

O'Farrell's Hats • 800-895-7098

Some of us may find it mildly offensive that a site is willing to charge as much as $1500.00 for, of all things, a cowboy hat. You might be more offended to see how awful this site looks and operates. Would it help to mention that these could be the best cowboy hats you'll ever find anywhere? Okay, this is a difficult distinction to swallow, so instead let's just say that these Durango, Colorado-made hats are "works of hat making art to be treasured for a lifetime." In other words, keen status symbols, in certain crowds.

| ·HATS | | | |
|---|---|---|---|

## OsbornAndRobert.com

Osborn & Robert • 800-655-1423

Upon entering this page, you are greeted by the image of a palmy beach, the ocean water sparkling green under a blue sky, an island even appearing on the horizon. Under this image are the words, "Welcome To Style," which pretty much sums up the attitude behind the Florida designed accessories here, which include handbags, jewelry, headbands, belts and, of all things, cummerbunds. It's pricey, but it's got flair, and if you see yourself wiling away the days in a tropical paradise, this selection may just be a suitable match.

| ·JEWELRY | ·BAGS & WALLETS | ·BELTS | ·SHOES |
|---|---|---|---|

## 877-372-2786 • Pacific Sunwear

**PacSun.com**

Making the decision to shop here requires the most basic of thought processes, which seems well suited to their potential clientele. Simply put, if you're going to kick back at the beach, you might as well look the part. This shop offers surf and skate inspired accessories for doing just that: a bevy of beachy shades, hat styles for sun-lovin' folk, sneakers, sandals and watches. These styles consist of the pure California beach look, going well with sun-bleached hair and proving the perfect accents to a wetsuit.

| ·EYEWEAR ·SHOES | ·BAGS & WALLETS ·WATCHES | ·BELTS | ·HATS |
|---|---|---|---|

## 800-247-8162 • Paul Frederick

**PaulFrederick.com**

The Paul Frederick line is known to be a quality set of dress attire, but don't you make the mistake of thinking these accoutrements are strictly old-school! Somehow, these guys have managed to blur the boundaries between professional and casual, with breezy designs that will have you looking at least as cool as anybody else in the office (except maybe those open-collar, blazer and jeans guys). Of course, the great benefit of this is that you can then easily make the transition into regular life; that is, the sort of regular life that warrants cufflinks and a tie.

| ·TIES | ·JEWELRY | ·DESIGNER | |
|---|---|---|---|

## 877-474-6379 • Payless

**PayLess.com**

As it turns out, you only really have to spend a lot of money on shoes that are flashy, daring and/or exceptional. If you want footwear that is simply fashionable and functional, it can be quite inexpensive. At least, that's what you learn when you pay this site a visit. This international shoe source has made finding decent shoes at low prices a no-brainer, with basic categories and subsections clearly delineated. One possible exception might be the Specialty section, in which you'll find slippers, work boots, dance shoes and cleats, but now you know how to deal with that.

| ·SHOES | ·KIDS | | |
|---|---|---|---|

## 800-968-7463 • Pell.com

**Pell.com**

After 50 years as a shoe repair shop, Pell has never really sold its shoe maintenance and repair items except wholesale to retailers and manufacturers. Until now. Here you can find stuff like shoe polish, shoelaces, shoe cleaner and orthopedic insoles. Then there are waterproofing agents, shoetrees and stretchers (which increase the sizes of ill-fitting shoes without having to take them to a shop). For some reason they also sell key rings, and some parts of the site don't work very well. Is there a connection? We don't know.

| ·SHOES | ·KIDS | | |
|---|---|---|---|

## Perlina.com

This sharp looking site may not be interested in the likes of you. They want to sell their wares to "career-oriented men and women with complicated lifestyles and a passion to the finer things in life." What? Oh, we must have mistaken you for someone else. Of course *you* have a passion for fine handbags, backpacks, organizers and wallets, otherwise why would you have read this far into the accessories section? The real question, then, is this: are these products fine enough for your discriminating tastes? That is for you, the discriminating shopper, to decide.

| ·BAGS & WALLETS | | | |
|---|---|---|---|

## PeterBeaton.com

If you're in the market for a lovely straw hat, check out these head toppers designed in Nantucket not by Peter Beaton, but actually by his mother. See, a woman named Darcy Creech started a successful hat design company under her own name, then sold the designs and brand to a larger company. Years later, she decided to return to the hat business and, unable to use her own name, chose to name her new designs after her son, Peter. Straight out of Nantucket, these hats will take you back to the country days of old.

| ·EYEWEAR | ·BAGS & WALLETS | ·HATS | |
|---|---|---|---|

## PilgrimDesigns.com

This small design firm says it "goes beyond the trends to bring you the chicest, most unique handbags." Grammar aside, designer Jill-Anne Partain makes good handbag, using fine fabrics and matching them exquisitely with her inspired designs. The site makes it easy to browse by collection and, each collection being small, you won't waste any time in doing so. Best of all, this site encourages you to do your "shopping at 1:00 am in your pajamas and mud mask," a concept that we whole-heartedly endorse.

| ·BAGS & WALLETS | | | |
|---|---|---|---|

## Portolano.com

Winter's probably the only time of year when accessories aren't merely stylish accentuations of your wardrobe, but imperative objects of attire that you will rue leaving at home. Fortunately, there's a site like this that offers easy access to some wonderful scarves, gloves and knit caps. These are simple, classic designs, but made a sight better than those of generic brands, with materials like leather, suede, cashmere and merino wool. It's not a lot, but it's just about all you need, at least until the rainy season.

| ·BAGS & WALLETS | ·GLOVES | ·HATS | ·SCARVES/WRAPS |
|---|---|---|---|

## 888-286-7071 • Raffaello

**RaffaelloTies.com**

The FAQ page of this site proclaims, "High Quality Designer Ties and Leather Goods are exclusively produced in Italy." While we might take exception to that, the Italian designer ties these guys show us offer a pretty convincing argument. Ermenegildo Zegna, Gucci and Armani are just some of the prestigious names bandied about in their silk tie menus, and that doesn't even include the belts, wallets and briefcases you'll find. There are also some dazzling handbags and scarves for the ladies, and if they don't sell you on the tradition of Italian finery, just wait until you get to the shoes....

| ·TIES ·DESIGNER | ·EYEWEAR | ·BAGS & WALLETS | ·SHOES |
|---|---|---|---|

## 212-965-9626 • Ravin Style

**RavinStyle.com**

If you've always dreamt of having your own personal shopper, and aren't particularly picky about it, check out this cadre of characters. Ravin, Lela and Jackie, you see, are cartoon characters, each representing a certain type of woman. Jackie, for example, goes for the "sleek, city look," while Lela encourages you to "flaunt your feminine side." Website namesake Ravin, meanwhile, simply commands you to "get in touch with your inner wardrobe." Basically, all three entities provide a cutesy means for the real-life proprietors of Ravin Style to display their top picks from current designer collections, which happens to be somewhat worth it, if you don't mind taking advice from a sketch.

| ·JEWELRY ·HAIR | ·BELTS ·SHOES | ·HATS ·DESIGNER | ·SCARVES/WRAPS |
|---|---|---|---|

## 800-762-5767 • Rockport

**Rockport.com**

This brand that is known for successfully combining comfort and style delivers a web site that struggles to bridge the gap between sophisticated design and user friendliness. Nevertheless, there's more of a selection here than one would expect from a single line of footwear, and if you can suffer the pains of flashy animated menus and graphics, you'll find some decent belts and bags on top of it. Atypically, the Men's section has more to offer than the Women's, and it shows—hip women's shoes may never be comfortable.

| ·BAGS & WALLETS | ·BELTS | ·SHOES | |
|---|---|---|---|

## 310-963-8883 • Samantha Root

**SamanthaRoot.com**

In what may be the easiest and fastest way to buy a cute handbag over the internet, Samantha Root brings her simple designs to a simple design (a web page, that is). See, all of her wares fit easily onto one page here, so almost before you get started you've finished looking. Any you like may be selected for better detail and a written description, and purchased in no time at all. If we may risk sounding presumptuous; you are going to wish all internet shopping could be done this way.

| ·BAGS & WALLETS | | | |
|---|---|---|---|

## ScreamerHats.com

The only apt descriptions of this collection must entail copious use of the word "wacky." Comprised almost entirely of wool knits and fleeces, this warm weather headgear comes in wild colors, crazy styles and cutesy conceptual designs. If the Wild & Zany Hats section doesn't particularly thrill you, there's always the Talking Animal Hats category, which, rather than explain, we'll let you explore for yourself. As for the non-wacky items, there's actually a great assortment of hip beanies in normal—rather, usual—colors.

| ·HATS | ·KIDS | | |
|-------|-------|--|--|

## SearleNYC.com

Manhattan arguably has got the highest percentage of fashionably dressed people on the planet. So, in the spirit of New York City style, Searle has brought together a selection of items from local boutiques to add just a little bit of flavor to your wardrobe (unless you're prepared to spend load of money, in which case—anticipate a lot of flavor). There's not much to it—a few sunglasses, some hats, gloves, boots and a variety of scarves—but what you see are some very hip accessories for your wardrobe. After all, your ensemble is only as good as its smallest detail, right?

| ·BAGS & WALLETS ·EYEWEAR | ·GLOVES | ·BELTS | ·SHOES |
|--------------------------|---------|--------|--------|

## SelimaOptique.com

These are the sort of designer sunglasses you might expect to see on a professional athlete, model, actor, pop star or global political activist. In fact, one of the models of specs found here were initially custom-designed for and worn by everybody's favorite rocker/social advocate, Bono of U2. Don't tell him, but this and other of Selima Salaun's engaging optical designs are available at this simple, yet effectively edgy online boutique, and it turns out his shades aren't even the best of the bunch.

| ·EYEWEAR | ·DESIGNER | | |
|----------|-----------|--|--|

## ShoeBuy.com

Offering varieties from "more than 200 brands," this shop has a truly wide and deep selection. This can make browsing a daunting affair, especially if you haven't got anything in particular in mind (in which case you'll want to make heavy use of their Advanced Search feature). What makes the site worthwhile, on the other hand, is that they offer free shipping (at least, as of this writing) and zero tax, so the price you see listed on the pair of shoes you like will be the price that you'll pay, bottom line.

| ·BAGS & WALLETS | ·BELTS | ·SHOES | |
|-----------------|--------|--------|--|

**800-746-3411 • Skechers Footwear**                    **Skechers.com**

Not just for skaters anymore, this Manhattan Beach, CA based shoemaker has gone international, even claiming to be, "the hottest footwear brand in the world." See, what customers in Dusseldorf, Germany are just discovering is that this brand has expanded from its near classic sneaker offering to include boots, sandals and casuals in the lineup. Presumably, you will find them all here, every last design, so you can bypass the somewhat editorial selections of other retailers and just make foreigners envious.

| ·SHOES | ·KIDS | | |  |
|---|---|---|---|---|

**718-464-8603 • Soho Shoe Salon**                    **SohoShoe.com**

This site describes its wares as "fashion forward large size women's shoes." Specifically, they deal in heels, pumps and boots that range in size from 7 to 13, and while they don't have a tremendous size of selection, the quality is comparable to what you'd expect to see in strictly standard sizes. Prices are fair to begin with, but we'd recommend heading straight to the Sale Shoes section, as it seems to be the single largest category on the site, has great looking shoes and prices that are, of course, the as low as you want them to be.

| ·SHOES | | | | |
|---|---|---|---|---|

**323-664-3489 • Souls**                    **SoulsShoes.com**

Stylish loafers? Why that's unheard of, or so we thought before we encountered this little online comfort zone for the foot. We also wouldn't have imagined a need for stylish slippers (other than the fuzzy variety of course), and yet here they are. None of these designs here are really overly hip or anything, they just bear a simple appeal, afforded by an unlikely hint of elegance and the occasional unexpected burst of color. Only one thing could make this soft footwear any more out of the pale; and that's if you elect to have your pair monogrammed.

| ·SHOES | | | | |
|---|---|---|---|---|

**415-626-8899 • Sova Leather**                    **SovaLeather.com**

This is one of those dismal looking sites that offers a great selection and affordable prices, which ultimately is better than a great looking site that overcharges you for the same old stuff (not that we're pointing any fingers). Obviously, what we're talking about here is leather—specifically in the form of bags, belts, luggage, briefcases and wallets. There's also an entire section devoted to Eel Skin and another that bears a unique assortment of hand-painted bags that prove stunning, in the literal sense of the word.

| ·BAGS & WALLETS | ·BELTS | | | |
|---|---|---|---|---|

# SoWear.com

SoWear • 212-677-2257

There are two keen points of interest to this site that claims to be "dedicated to promoting emerging talent in fashion," both owing to the relative obscurity of these young design brands. One is that they offer some very entertaining names: Feeling Pomeranian, Trash-a-Porter and Moi Et Cat, for instance, as well as some others that can't generally be mentioned in polite conversation. The other, more tangible result of this selection is that these designers often try hard to make their mark, so a lot of these items range somewhere between "daring" and "daringly original" on the scale of upbeat couture. In other words, wear these and you will stand out in a crowd.

| ·BAGS & WALLETS ·HAIR | ·BELTS | ·HATS | ·SCARVES/WRAPS |
|---|---|---|---|

# StubbsAndWootton.com

Stubbs & Wootton • 877-478-8227

According to these guys, there may be a lot you don't know about your shoes. For example, do your current shoes "socialize and spectate... enchant and engage?" No? Well, maybe these are qualities only possessed by the slippers, slides and mules presented here. At this writing, they plan to expand to include handbags and (the ever ambiguous term) accessories (how do we get away with it?). One can only speculate as to just how enchanting these items will prove to be, but given the social splendor of these shoes, we'll wait with polite smiles at the ready.

| | ·BAGS & WALLETS | ·SHOES | | |
|---|---|---|---|---|

# SunglassHut.com

Sunglass Hut • 800-786-4527

From the mall to your computer comes this ubiquitous seller of sunglasses, cases and... watches. All the usual suspects are here: Revo, Ray Ban, Maui Jim, Oakley—the list goes on and on. While prices aren't nearly as competitive as the Sunglass Hut would have you believe, the selection is pretty solid, and it's easy to shop by brand (especially the brands everybody wants). Basically, if you know exactly what you want and can't find it somewhere else, come here. Otherwise, even the mall has other options.

| | ·EYEWEAR | ·WATCHES | | |
|---|---|---|---|---|

# Swatch.com

Swatch • 866-379-2824

Back in its heyday, the mid-nineteen-eighties, Swatch became an almost household name, as pretty much every young person just had to have one. Well, not only is Swatch still around, but if anything their designs have gotten even better. Relatively inexpensive, ultra stylish and colorful timepieces are these guys' forte, one from which they never stray, and this site makes it easy to look at them all. Chances are you will look at them all, as they're nothing if not intriguing; nowadays, you're going to want at least a couple.

| | ·WATCHES | | | |
|---|---|---|---|---|

## No Service Number • Tarina Tarantino

**TarinaTarantino.com**

Wanna have some fun? Log on to this site and take a look at the flash version. You'll be treated to a thirty second series of animations designed to delight and amuse with colors and thrills. Well, the fun doesn't stop here. Tarina Tarantino's jewelry is just as delightful, using lots of crystals and eye-catching color. Even the category names are freaky-fun, whether it's Urban Princess, '60s and '70s Wonderland or Glam Rock (you kind of get the idea). It's easy to see why someone like Madonna wears Tarantino designs— and what more testimonial could you want?

## 800-367-8382 • Teva

**Teva.com**

Known primarily as one of the sturdier selections of open-toed footwear, this brand offers plenty of boots, hiking shoes and river shoes to go with their flip-flops and slides. However, sandals are the big order of the day, and rightfully comprise the bulk of the catalog. Their Originals models are bolstered by a selection ranging from Boat Deck Sandals and Hiking Sandals to Running Sandals. The name "Teva" stemming from the Hebrew word for "nature," it's little wonder this footwear is favored by outdoorsy folk; what's the point of wearing a sandal inside?

## 800-843-7251 • Elliott Lucca

**TheSak.com**

The Sak is short for The Sak Elliott Lucca, a line of bags that was started by a couple of guys in the San Francisco Bay Area in the late 1980s (they would be Todd Elliott and Mark Talucci). As the company has expanded with the years, so has its wares, and it now sells a fine assortment of handbags, wallets, cases and purses, each possessing the classic charm that has made the company a success. For a slick and smooth (if occasionally tedious) shopping experience, and a sak to match, don't miss this one.

| ·BAGS & WALLETS | ·HATS | ·SHOES | |
| --- | --- | --- | --- |

## 888-822-7297 • Sunglass City

**TheSunglassCity.com**

If you're the type to demand an element of style at every turn, not just in your eyewear, for example, but in the store from which you buy your eyewear, this one might just live up to your expectations. This slick looking site offers slick looks at some slick specs, with a thorough selection of popular and trendy national brands. Of course, in the battle of surface vs. substance, they've little to offer other than good looks and gear, so if you're looking for a little extra in your browsing experience, look elsewhere.

| ·EYEWEAR | | | |
| --- | --- | --- | --- |

## TheWatchMuseum.com

The Watch Museum • 888-516-2361

Self described as "one of the first world's leading sources of fine horological items," we're going to go ahead and assume what they mean to say is "we have good watches." Actually, they distinguish between Fine Watches and Fashion Watches, with several name brands represented in each, though not so much that browsing becomes tedious, as with some of the other watch sites out there. There's also a Pre-Owned Watches section, but don't mistake it for being the cheap section, as a lot of these merely go for twelve grand rather than twenty thousand. Did we mention this is a high-end retailer?

| | ·WATCHES | ·DESIGNER | | |
|---|---|---|---|---|

## Ties.com

Ties.com • 888-686-8437

Surprisingly enough, this site doesn't actually sell ties, but rather those plastic helmets that you can put beer cans into and drink from through straws. Of course, we're joking: these guys have hundreds of ties. With a humorous tone, they let you shop by tie color, designer, pattern, price or category (from Animal to Unusual). They even have directions on how to tie three different knots (including Half-Windsor). True to its name, this place will set you up, whether you want a solid, conservative color, or some kind of freaky cartoon character. Who'd have thought ties could be fun?

| | ·TIES | | | |
|---|---|---|---|---|

## Timberland.com

Timberland • 888-802-9947

Featuring what is probably a bigger selection than you would expect, this top name in sturdy, comfortable outdoor footwear also offers some durable wallets, belts, backpacks, sunglasses and watches. Also, as it turns out, they make more than just hiking boots, offering sections of Office and Casual shoes, as well as some sporty cross-trainers. Mostly, though, the boots and hiking shoes here should be credited for the brand's enormous success, as they're perfect for the outdoors and more than serviceable in the often more perilous urban wilderness.

| | ·EYEWEAR ·SHOES | ·BAGS & WALLETS ·WATCHES | ·BELTS ·KIDS | ·HATS |
|---|---|---|---|---|

## TinaTang.com

Tina Tang • 212-645-6890

Hollywood couldn't tell a better story. Tina Tang turned her back on a Wall Street career (with Goldman & Sachs no less) to follow her dreams of becoming a designer. Now, this daring spirit has been captured in her collection of chokers, necklaces, bracelets and earrings. She uses handpicked crystal, glass, pearls and semi-precious stones to find a sort of cosmic harmony in her designs, and whether she expresses this with bold colors or elegant silver-work, her "bliss" shines through, for all (including you) to see.

| | ·JEWELRY | | | |
|---|---|---|---|---|

## 877-464-3293 • To Boot

**ToBoot.com**

Actually, this site doesn't offer any boots; rather, no high cut boots may be found here. Instead, there's a selection of well-crafted leather shoes, sandals and slippers. Given that the Weekend Casual section will suit most quasi-formal occasions, you can imagine that the Dress & Black Tie category has some really snazzy pairs, nothing too engrossing or outrageous, just very slick, polished shoes. The Sandals seem somewhat out of place, generally not as comfortable looking as sandals should be, but if you're a master of the universe, sometimes a sandal just has to look imposing.

·SHOES

## 011-46-40-26-94-77 • Toffelmakaren

**Toffelmakaren.se**

If you're in the market for clogs, what better place to get them than from the source? In this case, that means a small family business located in Malmö, Sweden that makes authentic clogs by hand. While we can't figure out in which national currency these shoes are priced exactly (kroners, euros, dollars—our Swedish certainly wasn't good enough to warrant a response), we can say that, should you be inclined to like the real thing, a one-time purchase might be worth the risk of some potentially expensive shoes.

·SHOES

## 212-868-6848 • Tote Le Monde

**ToteLeMonde.com**

Designer Tia Wou sites the "importance of versatility in fashion" as a motivating force behind a lot of her designs. Thus, you will find handbags that turn into backpacks, which can be converted into totes, which may be worn as a shoulder bag, etc. Whether convertible or not, these great designer bags have been favored by high profile women like Cameron Diaz and Ashley Judd, as well as on actresses of several TV shows. If quality breeds success, success should be close behind this selection.

·BAGS & WALLETS

## 800-394-4446 • Prime Time Swiss Watch

**USAWatchCo.com**

Talk about a messy site. First of all, you can't always tell whether some of the dozens of name brands of watches listed on the menu will actually be for sale on this site. Then, if they are, the link sends you to a different site location in a different browser window. However, we wouldn't list it if there wasn't any upside, and here it is: selection, selection, selection. Hundreds of watches with a variety of looks are available, and if you're keen enough you're even likely to score a good deal.

·WATCHES

## Vegetarian-Shoes.co.uk

Vegetarian Shoes • 011-44-127-369-1913

$$$

★ ◎

No cows were killed in the formulation of this website. It sounds silly to say, but when you consider that this footwear retailer offers brands like Doc Marten and Birkenstock, it's actually kind of remarkable. Boots, belts and gloves of fake leather are all over this site from the country where the cows are mad, along with plenty of other types of footwear that appear to be suede, but aren't. It's the perfect answer for those who secretly love the look of animal skin, but have moral qualms about wearing it. Be warned, however, that others may not be able to tell the difference, meaning you may find yourself explaining your accoutrements often.

| | | ·BELTS | ·SHOES | | |
|---|---|---|---|---|---|

## VillageHatShop.com

The Village Hat Shop • 888-847-4287

✈ $

★ ○

Some will protect your head from the cold, some may shade your eyes from the sun; but the foundation of most of the hundreds of hats found here is style, of some sort or another at least. Berets, fedoras and cowboy hats may be found in plentitude, but it's a whimsical selection including things like coonskin caps, leather aviator helmets, propeller-top beanies and wizard caps that makes this site most memorable. Add to that such cultural oddities as Viking helmets and some authentic headwear of the Wan-Nyaka Mossi People of West Africa (Ouagadougou style), and there's practically no hat you won't find here.

| 𝒫 | | ·HATS | | | |
|---|---|---|---|---|---|

## WarmWoman.com

Warm Woman • 800-553-8079

✳ GC

✈ $$

◎

Don't let the name misguide you— this is actually a site to be visited by a cold woman. Essentially, the items listed in this catalog are designed to ward off a chill. Consequently, in the Warm Hands category you'll find gloves and mittens, whereas in Warm Feet there'll be some sheepskin slippers. Then, of course, there's Warm Headwear, consisting of fleece hats, scarves and some scattered earmuffs, each relatively stylish in its own way. While finding a healthy selection of Leg Warmers here was no surprise, we'd never before encountered Wrist Warmers. Talk about thorough.

| | ·GLOVES | ·HATS | ·SCARVES/WRAPS | ·SHOES |
|---|---|---|---|---|

## WatchesPlanet.com

WatchesPlanet.com • 011-6-039-282-3000

We had fun with this site, which is "Devoted to Delivering Your Favourite Time." Their catalog is deep enough, and their pictures detailed enough, that we noticed some pretty striking details; like that each of these dozens of popular brands have their own "favourite times." For example, all the Casio watches are set to 10:58:50, while Fendi seems to prefer approximately 10:08:43. While the ten o'clock hour was the overwhelming winner, some differed, like Omega watches, set to 1:50:38. Maybe we should have noticed other things … like the price.

| | ·WATCHES | ·DESIGNER | |
|---|---|---|---|

## 888-809-3639 • Wendy Brigode

### WendyBrigode.com

This one-time personal stylist for Linda Ronstandt has also worked as a make-up artist and an interior decorator. But it's Wendy Brigode's jewelry designs that will bring you to this very basic site. The earrings, necklaces and bracelets here range in style and quality but, in terms of self-expression, you'll probably be able to find something uniquely your own among these wares, as the differences offered merely serve to enhance their individual qualities. You'd think that a little more money would've gone into the site's design, given the cost of the jewelry; then again, if you're shopping here, you're not interested in superfluous presentation or bargain basement glitter … right?

| ·JEWELRY | | | |
|---|---|---|---|

## No Service Number • wiG

### WigGirl.com

If you groove on the funk, these furryish hats might suit you. Founded "as a reaction to windy San Francisco nights, and the endless need for more party-wear," this one is by and for party folk. The quirky site offers interesting depictions of the headgear, which gets its name from the vaguely hair-like look of the hats (well, they don't look like any hair you'll see on a person at least). Sound weird? It is, a little. The proprietors warn of their wares: "They need to be worn with perseverance and confidence and they need to be accompanied by an honest look in the eyes."

| ·HATS | ·HAIR ACCESSORIES | | |
|---|---|---|---|

## 877-945-3843 • Wild Ties

### WildTies.com

A sure sign that times they are a-changin, this site claims to be "the oldest internet tie store in the world." Most such statements would be used to signify some sort of old-world elegance, or time-tested grandeur but then, this is the internet. The site's product line tends to be "novelty and conversational neckwear." No, you won't find any ascots here, but you may find a Tabasco tie, or one starring the ever-hungry Garfield (the cat, not the president). Easy and funny, this site's tamer selections include solid colors and polka dots; but really, a suit only offers one expressive item of clothing, so sometimes you just gotta go wild.

| ·TIES | | | |  |
|---|---|---|---|---|

## 800-236-9976 • Wilson Leather

### WilsonLeather.com

Opting for this name rather than Wilson Cow Hide (a splendid marketing maneuver), it's immediately obvious that this large retailer of leather goods is run by level heads. Well, their selection of accessories for men and women should also suit some level heads, starting with hats and eking its way down to briefcases, backpacks, handbags, gloves and wallets. Truly, there's plenty to sift through here; they even offer cases for some of your prized electronic gadgets, and even a leather CD case or two (located in the Tech section). Good details and huge pictures top off the shopping experience, which is, without hyperbole, easier than a morning on the farm.

| ·BAGS & WALLETS | ·GLOVES | ·BELTS | |
|---|---|---|---|

# WorldOfWatches.com

These guys promise that you can "Save up to 60% on the world's finest watches." Skeptical? Well, the Advanced Search feature doesn't just include brand names, price ranges and special features, but also a Savings Amount menu, which includes the option "50 Percent OFF or MORE." Sure, sixty percent of their original retail price doesn't mean you'll save that much compared to the competition, but it's a nice gesture and a good start. The prices and selection here make it a good research site, if nothing else.

| ·WATCHES | | | |
|----------|--|--|--|

# WristWatch.com

Not only does this site have one of the huger selections of watch brands online, they have what are arguably the best browsing options as well. While finding a watch suitable to your own personal style will still take a bit of effort, this does offer more categories than merely a brand name hunt. Under Type you can hunt for pocket watches, titanium watches or ones with big numbers, for example. By Activity you may distinguish between such designs as for swimming, photography (which include built-in digital cameras) and survival (which may include internal GPA units). Finally, the Function list includes items like a compass, illuminated face or tide graph, should you need such things in a timepiece.

| ·WATCHES | | | |
|----------|--|--|--|

# YakPak.com

Anyone who regularly has to lug stuff around all day, but is resistant to the idea of owning a briefcase, will delight in YakPak (probably a notion you never considered). Here they feature some pretty solid backpacks, vexed bags (the recently popular kind that have a thick, crossover strap), shoulder bags and, yes, even fannypacks (though we wouldn't recommend wearing these unless you want to risk being labeled "tourist," even in your home town). While selection is somewhat scant, there's really some good stuff here for students, travelers and DJs. Worth checking.

| ·BAGS & WALLETS | ·KIDS | | |
|-----------------|-------|--|--|

# Yoox.com

Here's a site that forces us to focus more than any American likes to. The wide selection of designer and top-brand accessories has obviously been thoroughly organized. Just as obvious, however, is that user-friendliness wasn't a consideration, as the browsing techniques and visual display lack imagination as well as sympathy for the end-user. Patience, though, yields an awesome amount of great looking gear for men and women, up, down and all around.

| ·BAGS & WALLETS ·JEWELRY | ·BELTS ·SCARVES/WRAPS | ·DESIGNER ·SHOES | ·GLOVES |
|--------------------------|----------------------|------------------|---------|

**800-311-5393 • Zales**

You've probably come to us looking for an alternative to this largest of national jewelry chains, which undoubtedly has a brick-and-mortar location somewhere in your vicinity anyway. However, the ubiquity of this retailer could be precisely what makes this site advantageous. Used in conjunction with your local Zales merchant, you can familiarize yourself with prices and selection before you commit to anything, and make pick-ups and fittings an easier affair. Or, you can just compare their prices easily to the competition. Either way, this one's a no brainer.

| ·JEWELRY | ·WATCHES | | |
|---|---|---|---|

**888-492-7767 • Zappos.com**

Self-proclaimed the "Web's Most Popular Shoe Store!" this shop is big enough to be huge, and huge enough that it's tough to make sense of everything. Even complex searches usually result in some excessive browsing, and even zeroing in on one particular pair of shoes results in enough noisy information on the screen to make a person tired. Should you have a focus, though, it can be a very worthwhile site, with good looks at a variety of footwear for men, women and even those who'd rather not classify themselves in such ways.

| ·HATS | ·SHOES | ·KIDS | |
|---|---|---|---|

NOTES:

# Sports & Outdoors

As many of us know, when the Olympics first began in ancient Greece most of the athletes competed completely in the nude. Nowadays, except in the cases of a few naked volleyball encampments, such tanline-free athleticism won't fly. Neither will the adornment of simple sneakers and sweatpants keep you competitive anymore—you need the proper gear; whether protective, supportive, enhancing (like the cleats worn by baseball players) or ritualistic (like those stirrup socks worn by baseball players). Then there are the physical activities that send you into the extreme climactic conditions of high mountains, dense jungles and deep underwater. You'd no less want to go camping without a sleeping bag than scuba diving without an air tank. Of course, technology helps, and often the greatest high-tech gadgets on the planet are meant to aid in modern day action excursions, like Global Positioning Satellite gizmos that can even keep you from getting lost while wandering the Sahara Desert. Not that all physical activities need be so extreme. Last we checked bowling, golfing, fishing and croquet were still considered sports, requiring special equipment and a relaxed attitude. Even yoga can be a strain without a mat.

There's a point here. Unless you intend to run barefoot through dewy fields of grass, your sport and fitness endeavors will require at least a few accoutrements. Whether you're looking into a home gym, a Ping-Pong table, archery sets, hiking boots, bicycles or snowboards, you will find various options within this section devoted to pulling you from the intractable thrall of your television and computer. All of which may be easily ordered … from your computer. Does it sound more active if we call it extreme e-commerce?

NOTES:

# TIPS ON BUYING SPORTS & OUTDOORS EQUIPMENT ONLINE

These suggestions may help prevent frustration and injury.

•**SIZE, WEIGHT & SHIPPING:**  Weights are incredibly heavy by design, and fitness machines can be mighty bulky by necessity.  Either are going to run up shipping costs like you wouldn't believe.  Different retailers have learned to deal with this in different ways.  Whenever possible, opt for a merchant that can get this gear to you cheap, whether they distribute it locally or incorporate shipping costs into their competitive price structure.

•**COLD WEATHER RATINGS:**  Stuff like sleeping bags and snowsuits are designed to keep you warm in cold conditions; however, some for colder weather than others.  Keep an eye on such products' temperature ratings to make sure you don't end up in a 20-degree bag on a minus-20-degree mountain.

•**USE EQUIPMENT WITH CARE:**  We've provided listings in this book for some stores that offer powerful, potentially dangerous equipment.  Whether hunting, climbing, skiing, diving, boxing, hiking, skating or otherwise, please take care not to reap harm upon yourself or others.  In other words: if you don't know or are unsure on how a piece of equipment is properly and safely used, find somebody who does before attempting anything foolish.  Thank you.

•**WARRANTIES & REPAIRS:**  As with all big ticket items, be sure there is a warranty on expensive orders, especially stuff like personal fitness machines that might easily be damaged in some way.  It's not like any of us need another excuse not to exercise....

# SITES THAT MAY COME IN HANDY

The following URLs may be useful when you shop.

Fishing License & Information:  http://www.fishingworks.com
Bike Registration / Theft Prevention: http://www.nationalbikeregistry.com
Personal Fitness & Nutrition Info: http://www.fitnessonline.com
Ski Reports & Gear Reviews: http://www.onthesnow.com
Surf Reports & Real-Time Pictures: http://www.surfline.com
Sports Rules: http://www.rulescentral.com

## >> SECTION ICON LEGEND

Use the following guide to understand the rectangular icons that appear throughout this section.

### ADVENTURE GEAR

Adventures come in many forms. Some will think this icon overused, some will insist we missed a few (we didn't count golf). Basically we defined adventuresome activities as those that pit humans not against each other so much as against nature and the elements. Hence, this icon will lead you to camping equipment, hiking gear and essential tools for climbing, kayaking, diving, skiing, long-distance cycling and plenty of other natural excursions that offer an element of danger.

### APPAREL

Some of the apparel we wear for sports and outdoor activities is skin-tight, some quite bulky and heavy. From waterproof waders and legwarmers to helmets and ski-masks, stores marked by this icon can keep you covered from head to toe.

### PERSONAL FITNESS

Strength, flexibility, cardiovascular health and physical appearance are just some of the reasons we exercise. All kinds of equipment and apparel are available for such activities, and you may find them next to this icon.

### SUPERSTORE

Some stores just have it all, and to try to list everything would just be ridiculous. This is why you won't find some of these stores noted under our index entries; when you see this symbol, just assume it's got whatever sort of sporting equipment or apparel you're looking for and check it out. If in doubt, look at the key words associated with these sites to determine some of the store's strengths.

## >> LIST OF KEY WORDS

The following words represent the types of items typically found on the sites listed in this section.

### CYCLING

Mountain bikes, road racers, cruisers and tandems are only the beginning. All sorts of bikes surface here, along with accessories, parts and safety gear/apparel. Bike enthusiasts can build their own online, or upgrade components, while novices can find good selections of the finished product.

### EQUIPMENT

This quite common key word applies to just about everything that is used for competitive athletics, personal fitness, outdoor recreation, water play, winter sports and anything else that requires more than just your two hands. Use this in conjunction with other key words and/or icons to pinpoint the sort of equipment you seek.

### FAN GEAR

Fans of pro sports can let everybody know about it with jerseys, caps, socks, jackets, pennants, collector's cards, wristwatches and a surprising variety of other items that pay allegiance to your favorite teams and athletes.

### FOOTWEAR

The kind of shoes you wear to work didn't make the cut, but anything you can play in is here: running shoes, cleats, ski boots, sporty sandals, dance shoes and more.

### KIDS

Our Minors section offers a great bunch of child-oriented stores that cover sporting goods, but in this section you'll find a good number of sports-oriented stores that also happen to cater to children.

### OUTDOORS/CAMPING

This is the stuff you take with you off the beaten path. Camping gear includes tents, sleeping bags, backpacks, camp stoves, first aid, trail food, guides and compasses.

### REC ROOMS

Somewhere slightly less rigorous than sports there is recreation, and this key word highlights the sort of recreational items you might keep in your home, stuff like pool tables, Ping Pong tables, dart boards, foosball tables, air hockey tables, poker tables and any number of similar tables and/or boards.

### SOLO SPORTS

Sports you engage in without the assistance of teammates include running, wrestling, golf, racquet sports, archery, fishing and more. These sites cater to the individual athlete.

### TEAM SPORTS

Usually the first activities we think of when we hear the word "sports" are games like basketball, baseball, football, soccer, rugby and hockey. Okay, so rugby's not so common. Neither is lacrosse. Still, if it involves team play, we've listed it here.

### WATER SPORTS

Played in, around, on the surface of or under water, these sports may or may not require you to swim, and quite possibly involve a vehicle of some sort. Included are fishing, boating, water-skiing, wakeboarding, surfing, swimming, body boarding, kayaking, windsurfing and more.

### WINTER SPORTS

Winter sports are typically played on snow or ice, and that's what you'll find here, from skating to skiing and everything related, including plenty of stuff to keep you warm against the elements.

## >> KEY WORD INDEX

Use the following lists to locate online retailers that sell the Sports & Outdoors gear you seek.

### CYCLING

Airborne.net
Altrec.com
BikePartsUSA.com
BikesDirect.com
Campmor.com
DicksSportingGoods.com
EMSOnline.com
FogDog.com
GHSports.com
GIJoes.com
KronanCycle.com
Nashbar.com
Nirve.com
PerformanceBike.com
Plaines.com
SuperGo.com

### EQUIPMENT

ActionVillage.com
ActiveMailOrder.com
Airborne.net
AmericanFly.com
BalazsBoxing.com
BargainSports.net
BassPro-Shops.com
BeAPro.com
BigToeSports.com
BikePartsUSA.com
Blades.com
BowlersParadise.com
Bowling.com
Cabelas.com
Campmor.com
CCS.com
CenturyFitness.com
CheapSkater.com
ChristySports.com
CopelandSports.com
CSSkiEquipment.com
DicksSportingGoods.com
DoverSaddlery.com
eAngler.com

EastBay.com
eBodyBoarding.com
eKickFight.com
EMSOnline.com
FogDog.com
FootLocker.com
GetBoards.com
GIJoes.com
GolfBalls.com
GopherSport.com
JHHE.com
JustBats.com
JWhiteCricket.com
KarateDepot.com
KensingtonTrading.com
Lacrosse.com
LacrosseUnltd.com
Life-Link.com
LiquidGolf.com
MartialArtsSupplies.com
MGear.com
Modells.com
MonsterSkate.com
MooseJaw.com
NordicTrack.com
OceanicWorldwide.com
Overtons.com
PalosSports.com
ParagonSports.com
PerformanceBike.com
PeterGlenn.com
PGATourStop.com
PurePolaris.com
RacquetballCatalog.com
RingSide.com
RugbyImports.com
Ruggers.com
SaddleSource.com
Skateboard.com
SkiBoards.com
Soccer.com
SoccerStore.com
SonomaOutfitters.com
SportEyes.com
SportsFair.com
SportsTeams.com
SportsTutorInc.com

SpringCoAthletics.com
TennisCompany.com
TennisWarehouse.com
TitleBoxing.com
TourLineGolf.com
UncleDansOnline.com
WingSet.com
WorkoutWarehouse.com
WrestlersExpress.com
WWSport.com

### FAN GEAR

BigToeSports.com
CopelandSports.com
CupStuff.com
Distant-Replays.com
EastBay.com
FootballFanatics.com
FootLocker.com
HatWorld.com
Lacrosse.com
LacrosseUnltd.com
MinorLeagues.com
MLB.com
Modells.com
MVP.com
NASCAR.com
NBA.com
NFLShop.com
NikeTown.com
PGATourStop.com
RugbyImports.com
Soccer.com
SoccerStore.com
UpperDeckStore.com

### FITNESS

4Swimwear.com
Adidas.com
Aquajogger.com
Athleta.com

BalazsBoxing.com
BarefootYoga.com
BargainSports.net
BigFitness.com
CapezioRVC.com
CenturyFitness.com
CopelandSports.com
DicksSportingGoods.com
EastBay.com
eKickFight.com
Flying-Carpets.com
FogDog.com
FootLocker.com
GHSports.com
GIJoes.com
Gophersport.com
HuggerMugger.com
KarateDepot.com
MartialArtsSupplies.com
Modells.com
NewYorkYoga.com
NikeTown.com
NordicTrack.com
PalosSports.com
ParagonSports.com
Patagonia.com
RingSide.com
Speedo.com
SportsFair.com
SpringCoAthletics.com
SwimToWin.com
TitleBoxing.com
TitleNineSports.com
WalkingShop.com
Wickers.com
WorkoutWarehouse.com
YogaZone.com

### FOOTWEAR

ActiveMailOrder.com
Adidas.com
Altrec.com
Athleta.com
BackCountryGear.com

BigToeSports.com
Blades.com
BowlersParadise.com
Bowling.com
Cabelas.com
Campmor.com
CapezioRVC.com
CCS.com
CheapSkater.com
ChristySports.com
ClassicSportsShoes.com
CopelandSports.com
Customatix.com
DicksSportingGoods.com
EastBay.com
eKickFight.com
EMSOnline.com
FogDog.com
FootLocker.com
GIJoes.com
LiquidGolf.com
MGear.com
Modells.com
MooseJaw.com
MovementConnection.com
Nashbar.com
NikeTown.com
ParagonSports.com
PeterGlenn.com
PGATourStop.com
Puma.com
RacquetballCatalog.com
REI.com
RingSide.com
RoadRunnerSports.com
RugbyImports.com
Ruggers.com
Skateboard.com
SkiBoards.com
Soccer.com
SoccerStore.com
SonomaOutfitters.com
Speedo.com
SportsTeam.com
SpringCoAthletics.com
TennisWarehouse.com
TitleNineSports.com
Travelcountry.com
UncleDansOnline.com
VenueSports.com
VoiceOfDance.com
WalkingShop.com
WrestlersExpress.com
WWSport.com

## KIDS

ActiveMailOrder.com
Altrec.com
CapezioRVC.com
DiversDirect.com
EMSOnline.com
FootLocker.com
GopherSport.com
JustBats.com
LiquidGolf.com
MLB.com
MooseJaw.com
MovementConnection.com
NikeTown.com
OceanicWorldwide.com
Overtons.com
PalosSports.com
Patagonia.com
PerformanceBike.com
PGATourStop.com
Puma.com
PurePolaris.com
REI.com
SonomaOutfitters.com
Speedo.com
SportsFair.com
SwimToWin.com
TennisWarehouse.com
UncleDansOnline.com
VoiceOfDance.com

## OUTDOORS/CAMPING

Altrec.com
AmericanFly.com
Athleta.com
BackCountryGear.com
BassPro-Shops.com
Cabelas.com
Campmor.com
CoastlineAdventures.com
CopelandSports.com
DicksSportingGoods.com
eAngler.com
EMSOnline.com
FogDog.com
GIJoes.com
MGear.com
MooseJaw.com
OutDrs.com

Patagonia.com
PerformanceBike.com
REI.com
RiverWire.com
SonomaOutfitters.com
TackleDirect.com
TheTentStore.com
TrailFood.com
TrailFoods.com
TravelCountry.com
UncleDansOnline.com
Wickers.com
WingSet.com
WorldWaters.com

## REC ROOMS

CopelandSports.com
DicksSportingGoods.com
GopherSport.com
KensingtonTrading.com
PalosSports.com
ParagonSports.com
SportsFair.com

## SOLO SPORTS

4Swimwear.com
ActionVillage.com
ActiveMailOrder.com
Adidas.com
Altrec.com
AmericanFly.com
BalazsBoxing.com
BargainSports.net
BassPro-Shops.com
BigFitness.com
Blades.com
BowlersParadise.com
Bowling.com
BowlingShirt.com
Campmor.com
CCS.com
CenturyFitness.com
CheapSkater.com
ChristySports.com
CopelandSports.com
CSSkiEquipment.com
Daddyos.com

eAngler.com
EastBay.com
EMSOnline.com
GetBoards.com
GolfBalls.com
GopherSport.com
KarateDepot.com
LiquidGolf.com
MartialArtsSupplies.com
MGear.com
Modells.com
MonsterSkate.com
MooseJaw.com
NikeTown.com
PalosSports.com
ParagonSports.com
Patagonia.com
PerformanceBike.com
PeterGlenn.com
PGATourStop.com
RacquetballCatalog.com
RiverWire.com
SaddleSource.com
Skateboard.com
SkiBoards.com
SonomaOutfitters.com
Speedo.com
SportsFair.com
SpringCoAthletics.com
TackleDirect.com
TennisCompany.com
TennisWarehouse.com
TourLineGolf.com
UncleDansOnline.com
VenueSports.com
WrestlersExpress.com
WWSport.com

## TEAM SPORTS

Adidas.com
BargainSports.net
BeAPro.com
BigToeSports.com
CopelandSports.com
EastBay.com
FootLocker.com
GopherSport.com
JustBats.com
JWhiteCricket.com
Lacrosse.com
LacrosseUnltd.com

Modells.com
NBA.com
NikeTown.com
PalosSports.com
ParagonSports.com
RugbyImports.com
Ruggers.com
Soccer.com
SoccerStore.com
SportsFair.com
SportsTeam.com
SportsTutorInc.com
WWSport.com

## WATER SPORTS

4Swimwear.com
Altrec.com
AmericanFly.com
AquaJogger.com
Athleta.com
BargainSports.net
BassPro-Shops.com
BoatersWorld.com
BoatUS-Store.com
Cabelas.com
Campmor.com
CSSkiEquipment.com
DicksSportingGoods.com
DiversDirect.com
eAngler.com
eBodyBoarding.com
EvolutionSurf.com
FogDog.com
GetBoards.com
GHSports.com
GIJoes.com
MGear.com
Modells.com
MooseJaw.com
OceanicWorldwide.com
OutDrs.com
Overtons.com
ParagonSports.com
Patagonia.com
PeterGlenn.com
PurePolaris.com
RiverWire.com
SailNet.com
SalamanderPaddleGear.com
SonomaOutfitters.com
Speedo.com

SportsFair.com
SwimToWin.com
TackleDirect.com
TeamArena.com
TravelCountry.com
WestMarine.com
WindSurfingSports.com
WorldWaters.com

## WINTER SPORTS

Altrec.com
Athleta.com
BargainSports.net
Blades.com
Campmor.com
CCS.com
CheapSkater.com
ChristySports.com
EMSOnline.com
FogDog.com
GetBoards.com
GHSports.com
GIJoes.com
Life-Link.com
MGear.com
Modells.com
MooseJaw.com
ParagonSports.com
Patagonia.com
PeterGlenn.com
Plaines.com
PurePolaris.com
REI.com
SkiBoards.com

NOTES:

_____

_____

_____

_____

_____

_____

_____

_____

_____

_____

_____

_____

_____

_____

_____

_____

_____

# 4Swimwear.com

4 Seasons Swimwear • 800-352-8868

The swimwear found here isn't exactly the kind of stuff you want to wear to the beach (unless you're a lifeguard, in which case they offer a full section of suits), or to get a tan (except for their small selection of "Tan Thru" suits and the occasional Hunza swimwear). Mostly, though, this is competitive swimwear, including goggles, swim caps and full-body racing suits, bolstered by a selection of kickboards, fins, nose-clips, ear plugs and paddles (all found in Accessories). Best of all, this shop is thong-free.

| | | ·WATER SPORTS | ·FITNESS | ·SOLO SPORTS | |
|---|---|---|---|---|---|

# ActionVillage.com

ActionVillage.com • 847-709-6100

This conglomeration of specialty retail focuses on three activities in particular: skateboarding, paintball and golf. With wide inventories across the board, and the addition of an Auctions section where overstock and customer returns may be found at discount prices, you can find a decent selection of items whether you're looking for a new deck or a paintball gun autococker. All is fairly standard, except that the convergence of these three recreations on one site begs the question: what if they were combined into a single kick-flipping, paint-splattering, long-driving sport?

| | ·EQUIPMENT | ·SOLO SPORTS | | |
|---|---|---|---|---|

# ActiveMailOrder.com

Active Mail Order • 800-588-3911

Here's a skate shop about as well-designed as its wares, which is saying a lot in the context of this extremely style-conscious and self-expressive sport. Whether you buy a board preassembled or by component, you'll find a decently solid selection of brands and designs; plenty at least to rival any local store. The good selection doesn't stop at skating hardware either, but carries over into the Clothes, Accessories and even Shoes sections. A good thing, since stylin' kicks are as important as anything else.

| | ·EQUIPMENT | ·KIDS | ·SOLO SPORTS | ·FOOTWEAR |
|---|---|---|---|---|

# Adidas.com

Adidas • 800-982-9337

You wouldn't think that three parallel slashing stripes would create such a cultural impact as the three raggedy diagonals that comprise the Adidas logo, and yet it's a symbol that proves instantly recognizable the world over. Found on a variety of apparel as well as on shoes designed to outfit such sports as tennis, soccer, running, skating, basketball and that of casually stepping down the street, just about the only way these products can disappoint is to cramp your feet (their shoes are notoriously undersized). One thing's for sure; this well-maintained site and its unmatched selection won't disappoint.

| | | ·FITNESS | ·FOOTWEAR | ·TEAM SPORTS | ·SOLO SPORTS |
|---|---|---|---|---|---|

## 888-652-8624 • Airborne Titanium Bicycles

### Airborne.net

You may be disappointed to find out that this site won't actually get you too far off the ground. Actually, if all goes right, the bicycles sold here should keep you firmly planted on the road. Unless you opt for an off-road bike, which of course will keep you riding in dirt. Jokes aside, a custom-building feature enables you to add to these titanium frames piece by piece, meaning that if you do a little research into the variety of parts located around the site, you'll end up with one heck of a ride. Very worth it.

| ·EQUIPMENT | ·CYCLING | | |  |
|---|---|---|---|---|

## 800-369-3949 • Altrec.com

### Altrec.com

For people who would rather be outside than indoors at any given moment, this store comes fully stocked with the gear to make it tolerable. Whether you want a kayak, skis or some fly tackle, you'll find a decent selection, and if you just want to hike you can outfit yourself pretty well too. Primarily, though, camping gear is the top order of the day, as they have an incredible selection of tents, sleeping bags, backpacks and all the accoutrements. After all, if you are going to be inside, it might as well be inside a tent.

| ·WATER SPORTS ·SOLO SPORTS | ·WINTER SPORTS ·FOOTWEAR | ·OUTDOORS ·CYCLING | ·KIDS | |
|---|---|---|---|---|

## 800-410-1222 • American Fly Fishing Company

### AmericanFly.com

Devotees will tell you that fly-fishing beats all other kinds in terms of skill and enjoyment. This site will tell you the same, with a wide selection of gear and apparel, alongside a great assortment of flies. Of course, hardcore enthusiasts consider the true sport to be in the tying of flies (pitting your cunning and intellect against the most finicky of aquatic creatures). If you like to try your hand at this artistry, you'll find all the tools and materials you need to get started, and even some books on the subject . . . if you need books to outsmart a fish, that is.

| ·OUTDOORS | ·SOLO SPORTS | ·EQUIPMENT | ·WATER SPORTS | |
|---|---|---|---|---|

## 800-922-9544 • Aquajogger

### AquaJogger.com

All right, there's a gist to this very limited but focused site. Everybody knows that low-impact aerobic exercise is the ideal, and can best be achieved by swimming laps over and over. Except that some people are just not very good swimmers. That's where these guys come in, offering buoyancy belts that enable you to float approximately shoulder deep in a swimming pool and engage in any manner of aerobic exercise, whether it be a jogging motion, kicking, flipping, stepping, skiing or whatever. This, they say, "promotes correct posture, supports the lower back, and tones abdominal muscles." Anyway, it sounds good.

| ·FITNESS | ·WATER SPORTS | | |  |
|---|---|---|---|---|

# Athleta.com

Athleta • 888-322-5515

Here's a well-designed site for the activity prone woman, "where shopping is no sweat." With categories like Climbing/ Bouldering, Yoga/Dance, In-Line Skating and Triathlon, you know you can find gear for the type of workout you're about to endure, while other categories like Sports Bras and Maternity remind you that, yes, this store is conscientious of the female body. The great thing, though, is that you don't have to enter each category to access the types of products within. Simply choose Browse Online Store from the home page, and jump straight to your preferred product type. Not bad at all.

| | | ·WATER SPORTS ·FOOTWEAR | ·WINTER SPORTS | ·FITNESS | ·OUTDOORS |
|---|---|---|---|---|---|

# BackCountryGear.com

Backcountrygear.com • 800-953-5499

Promising "equipment for the body, escape for the soul," this retailer specializes in the sort of gear you'd want to have if you were traveling in the wilderness, fifty miles from nowhere. Perhaps it's a sign of the times that this selection includes some packs designed to carry, among other things, a laptop computer (escape for the soul?), but this is only one fringe item that stands aside from the rest, which includes boots, tents, cooking equipment, rugged clothes and lightweight instruments of exploration and survival.

| | ·OUTDOORS | ·FOOTWEAR | | |
|---|---|---|---|---|

# BalazsBoxing.com

Balazs Boxing • 888-466-6765

Behind the amusing tag line "Knock Yourself Out," this site promotes the sport of healthily slapping people around, whether through boxing or the martial arts. This gear ranges from protective equipment and hand-wraps to bags, gloves and even a full-size boxing ring. Package deals make it easy to get started, while a variety of books & videos will keep up your progress until you either no longer possess the mental faculties to read, or you can give it better than you take it, whichever comes first.

| | ·EQUIPMENT | ·FITNESS | ·SOLO SPORTS | |
|---|---|---|---|---|

# BarefootYoga.com

Barefoot Yoga Co. • 877-227-3366

There's no question that yoga is hip, the question here is: are you hip enough for yoga? This is a cool yoga site that'll help you one way or another, with plenty of great rugs and mats, mat bags, lots of clothing (including a line of hemp apparel) and any sundry accessory that might help your stretching exercises. Take it to the beach, or set up in your living room—these guys won't help a beginner in figuring out the tricks of the trade, but they can make anyone look close enough to enlightenment.

| | ·FITNESS | | | |
|---|---|---|---|---|

888-271-7500 • BargainSports.net

**BargainSports.net**

This sporty generalist is not nearly as comprehensive as its competitors, but should you be lucky enough to find your favorite sport in representation, you will most likely find some nice, low prices. Mostly, these would be in baseball, hockey, golf, pogo and snow sports, with some particular values found in their Ice Skating section. You'll probably wish the store was bigger, and maybe one day it will be, but until that time it's at the very least a great place to compare prices against other stores that guarantee low costs.

| ·EQUIPMENT ·TEAM SPORTS | ·WATER SPORTS ·SOLO SPORTS | ·WINTER SPORTS | ·FITNESS |
|---|---|---|---|

800-227-7776 • Outdoors Online

**BassPro-Shops.com**

This, the "World's Leading Supplier of Premium Outdoor Products," acts pretty much as a one-stop shop for that breed of people who take pleasure in tracking down, capturing and/or killing animals for sport (and hopefully for eats as well). Whether you prefer to pit your wits against the likes of fish, waterfowl, deer or wascally wabbits, this shop can hook you up with lures, calls, decoys, camouflage and other sundry sporting equipment. Be careful, though; the great irony here is that the more you buy the less sporting it gets.

| ·WATER SPORTS | ·OUTDOORS | ·SOLO SPORTS | ·EQUIPMENT |
|---|---|---|---|

888-423-2776 • beapro.com

**BeAPro.com**

If you're a baseball player in need of a mitt, this store may or may not be able to help. On the one hand (right or left), they have over 800 different gloves to choose from. On the downside, they have over 800 different mitts to sort through, so choosing can be a rather daunting task. Nevertheless, if you can narrow your focus to glove size and/or position, you'll find a healthy selection for all hands and styles of play. There are also hundreds of bats, dozens of balls, bags, pitching machines and apparel. Essentially, if you dig America's favorite pastime you can get your fix here, statistically speaking.

| ·EQUIPMENT | ·TEAM SPORTS | | |
|---|---|---|---|

888-292-1807 • BigFitness.com

**BigFitness.com**

This site sells pretty much any type of equipment you might expect to find in your local gym, and most of it ships for free. However, those items that don't are what make up the bulk of this gym equipment (begging the question, "who buys weights online?" The answer: "dumbbells," of course). If you don't want to pay exorbitant shipping fees on stuff you're not yet strong enough to lift, there are plenty of more home-oriented fitness products. Like videos, jump ropes or chin-up bars that fit in doorways, tough guy.

| ·FITNESS | ·SOLO SPORTS | | |
|---|---|---|---|

# BigToeSports.com

**Big Toe Sports • 800-244-8637**

Get your kicks at this specialty retailer devoted strictly to soccer (or football, as the rest of the world would have it). Find cleats or indoor boots, a bevy of pads and guards, jerseys, shorts, socks and a whole ranges of goalkeeper gear. This colorful selection extends to balls, goals, practice equipment and replica jerseys from teams most Americans have only barely, if ever, heard of. There's no doubt it's a cool site; well designed and excellently organized. But you really shouldn't kick with your toe.

| | ·EQUIPMENT | ·FOOTWEAR | ·TEAM SPORTS | ·FAN GEAR |
|---|---|---|---|---|

# BikePartsUSA.com

**Bike Parts USA • 877-727-8731**

Billing itself as "your neighborhood bike shop online," one is forced to wonder why someone with a bicycle and a neighborhood bike shop wouldn't rather just ride there in the first place? But, if you're immobilized for some reason, or your neighborhood is lacking, this proves quite handy as a place to pick up various parts, from baskets to chains and everything in between. Pull-down menus make browsing easier than coasting down a 5% grade, though a lack of decent product images may just be the information superhighway equivalent of road burn.

| | ·EQUIPMENT | ·CYCLING | | |
|---|---|---|---|---|

# BikesDirect.com

**BikesDirect.com • No Service Number**

Unlike a lot of the biking sites featured in this collection, these guys don't require you to know all the different specific parts and brands you might want incorporated into your bicycle (what's a derailleur?). Here, you can simply browse between sections for Road Bikes, Mountain Bikes (MTB), Comfort Bikes, Cruisers and Hybrids. These fairly cool bikes won't win any races or break any speed records, but they should be somewhat comfortable, and judging by the pics offered here, look pretty good as well. Easy as can be.

| | ·CYCLING | | | |
|---|---|---|---|---|

# Blades.com

**Blades Board & Skate • 888-552-5233**

This board and skate shop offers a pretty good selection of snowboarding and skateboarding gear, both equipment and apparel. However, we think you'll get more out of the Inline Skating section than anything else. With a really big and well-managed selection of skates, it's easy to browse for some blades that'll get you rolling whatever your speed. They even have a smattering of quads (or, as we old-schoolers call them, roller-skates). And, if wheels ain't your thing, check out the ice skates.

| | ·EQUIPMENT | ·WINTER SPORTS | ·SOLO SPORTS | ·FOOTWEAR |
|---|---|---|---|---|

## 877-690-0004 • BoatersWorld.com — **BoatersWorld.com**

This isn't a shop for most of us, as its entire selection is pretty much geared towards boat owners. But should you be lucky enough to fit this demographic, it should serve you well. Whether you take the boat out for water sports, fishing or just to break out of national waters where you may freely cultivate your interests in nude sun tanning and cockfighting, respectively, this site cannot only provide the necessary equipment to get you out there, but also any necessary for repairs, safety and navigation to ensure you make it back.

| ·WATER SPORTS | | | |
|---|---|---|---|

## 800-937-2628 • Boat U.S. Online Store — **BoatUS-Store.com**

This superstore is a boater's dream, including options for boat insurance and towing service (kind of like AAA for the water) as well as a huge selection of important (and some luxuriously less-important) gear. From Anchoring products to Wood Care and Watersports, the multitudinous categories will get you just about anything you need to set sail or start your engines (sadly, the only boats actually sold here are Dinghies and Inflatables). Perhaps the most fun stuff may be found in the special onboard Electronics sections, which features such scintillating devices as surround sound speaker systems, autopilots and night vision goggles.

| ·WATER SPORTS | | | |
|---|---|---|---|

## 888-969-2695 • A Bowler's Paradise — **BowlersParadise.com**

Do these guys have everything a bowler wants? Well, except for the shirts, yes. At least they seem to. This best bowling site we found is so comprehensive you can probably match one of those nifty bowling gloves to a pair of those nifty bowling shoes, and then find a ball that matches them both. Not that color coordination will help your game, but it's nice to know that it's possible. Another interesting aspect of this site is something we haven't seen elsewhere: if you click on a non-link part of the page you'll find a pop-up, animated menu to the site. Paradise? No, but close to it so far as the web's concerned.

| ·EQUIPMENT | ·FOOTWEAR | ·SOLO SPORTS | |
|---|---|---|---|

## 800-441-2695 • Bowling.com — **Bowling.com**

Yabba Dabba Doo! This may not be the site that all bowlers wish it would be, but that doesn't change the fact that it's loaded with balls, bags and shoes. Pure browsing is impeded by that pesky brand name organization, but within each brand category you will find a healthy list of pictures to skim. This becomes important if you wish to easily locate the clear ball with a skull set in the middle of it (à la the movie *Mystery Men*).

| ·EQUIPMENT | ·SOLO SPORTS | ·FOOTWEAR | |
|---|---|---|---|

# BowlingShirt.com

Just as you might imagine, this shop has a bowling shirt for you. It's selection runs deep and wide, with some classic looks mixed up with your odd, fun styles. Sections like the Baddabing Mafia Store, Beer Bowl-O-Matic, Vegas Baby Vegas and Nightclub Fashions will turn you on to some of the less predictable fare, while Hawaiian Paradise tends to speak for itself. Hey, you know that bowling shirts can be just as fashionable outside the lanes as in, you just happen to like bowling a lot is all.

| ·SOLO SPORTS | | | |
|---|---|---|---|

# Cabelas.com

Stock full of articles and stories about hunters and their predilection for using very large guns with powerful ammo, this site actually seems to be a gamesman's best bet in cruising the web for hunting supplies. Loads of equipment and information is neatly organized— a little better than it should be, actually— so that little patience need be wasted on shopping, and may be better spent out in nature. Big game, small animals, fish or waterfowl, this is one site that'll almost let you forget there's a dirty side to the sport.

| ·WATER SPORTS | ·OUTDOORS | ·FOOTWEAR | ·EQUIPMENT |
|---|---|---|---|

# Campmor.com

Not only is this a good site for campers, but it also offers plenty of fun toys to play with while establishing a temporary residence in the great outdoors; stuff like off-road biking gear, kayaking accessories and climbing essentials. Most of this stuff, however, is good, general use camping equipment: all the basics like tents, sleeping bags and backpacks. Then there are things like insect repellents, durable cold-weather wear, compasses and survival tools, which you can manage to do without, but why would you want to?

| ·EQUIPMENT ·CYCLING | ·WATER SPORTS ·SOLO SPORTS | ·WINTER SPORTS ·FOOTWEAR | ·OUTDOORS |
|---|---|---|---|

# CapezioRVC.com

Encouraging you to "Keep on dancing!" this all-dance, all-the-time site caters to your every step, whether it be ballroom, breakdancing or ballet. Under Footwear you'll find tap shoes, jazz shoes, point shoes and more, while Bodywear includes skirts, leotards, tights, tutus and slinky dresses. Even male dancers can find what they need in terms of dance belts, footed tights and thong leotards (these last will take up to two weeks to make, so be sure to order them ahead of time). Bear in mind you'll be practicing in front of a mirror.

| ·FITNESS | ·FOOTWEAR | ·KIDS | |
|---|---|---|---|

## 800-477-9283 • CCS

**CCS.com**

Shredders delight. Skating (skateboarding, not roller blades) and snowboarding get full attention here, complete with the slightly haughty tone that such endeavors elicit. Only those in the know will have any clue what exactly CCS stands for (we sure don't), but it's little matter when you peruse the boards, tools, accessories and apparel, whether you opt for a custom-built ride or a preassembled one. It's all pretty cool (with the possible exception of the protective gear, though it sure comes in handy when you fall down repeatedly, as everybody does). Either way, it beats scooters.

| ·EQUIPMENT | ·WINTER SPORTS | ·FOOTWEAR | ·SOLO SPORTS |
|---|---|---|---|

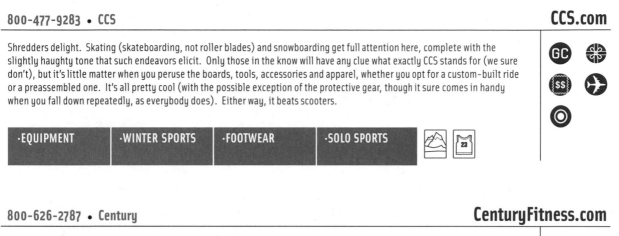

## 800-626-2787 • Century

**CenturyFitness.com**

If you're into any of the following: yoga, boxing, martial arts, strength training or tae-bo, you can fairly easily find the gear you need here. Each department functions as would an individual store, complete with community links and resources. You can easily go back and forth between sections, though, if you want to pile punching bags, medicine balls, weight benches, yoga mats, sparring gear and instructional media all into one order. Of course, some of the bigger, heavier items cost almost as much to ship as to buy, so be sure to check the FAQ section before ordering.

| ·EQUIPMENT | ·FITNESS | ·SOLO SPORTS | |
|---|---|---|---|

## 914-788-1490 • theCheapskater.com

**CheapSkater.com**

As enticing as this name may be, we should clarify that most of the merchandise found on this site is not cheap, bottom-of-the-barrel stuff. Actually, most of these skates— be they for ice-skating, hockey, roller hockey, speed skating (of one sort or another), tricks or just a casual roll (inline or quad)— tend to be pretty high-end. If there's anything cheap, it's that the site doesn't seem to have cost a lot to put together. Still, it gets the job done, which is way better than a site that looks all fancy but delivers squat. This one will do.

| ·EQUIPMENT | ·WINTER SPORTS | ·SOLO SPORTS | ·FOOTWEAR |
|---|---|---|---|

## 888-413-6966 • ChristySports.com

**ChristySports.com**

This chain of Rocky Mountain ski and snowboard shops makes its presence felt online with a store not devoid of charm. Their wares (which include golf clubs for some reason) tend to be split up first by type, then by brand. It's pretty easy to sort through them, with crisp images showing off high marks of quality. The best part really involves travel, though, as you can reserve discount rentals from any of their store locations (Vail, Snowmass and many others), so beginners can get a feel for this stuff before buying.

| ·EQUIPMENT | ·WINTER SPORTS | ·SOLO SPORTS | ·FOOTWEAR |
|---|---|---|---|

## ClassicSportsShoes.com

Classic, retro or old school; whatever you call them, this site specializes in the sale of sneaker designs from the near to distant past. With Adidas, Nike, Puma, Reebok, Converse and Vans, most of the standards are represented. Even Birkenstock sandals pop up for some reason. Unfortunately, variety is limited within each of the brand categories, and surely most of us will go in expecting/hoping to find a particular style that they just don't carry. However, odds are equally good that we'll find one long since forgotten, or never known, that'll satisfactorily take the other's place.

| ·FOOTWEAR | | | |
|---|---|---|---|

## CoastlineAdventures.com

"Equipping you for adventure," these guys don't care if you're hitting the coast, mountains, desert, tundra or deep under the ocean; whatever your course of action they probably have equipment that will keep you from surrendering to the elements. Lots of tough gear, alongside plenty of technologically advanced stuff, fills this store in anticipation of all the environments you as the rugged individual will undoubtedly conquer this year, or maybe next year. Heck, just browsing makes you feel tough.

| ·OUTDOORS | | | |
|---|---|---|---|

## CopelandSports.com

We looked hard to find something funny about this site, for any silly thing we could poke fun at or mock. But, alas there was nothing; it's well designed, its product selection is far ranging and the prices reasonable. It occurred to us that we could tell you then how boring the site is, how uninspiring, how run-of-the-mill. But how can any site be boring if it sells stuff like foozball tables, trampolines and outdoor billiard tables? From standards like baseball and golf, to an excellent Footwear Finder (based on size and activity), these guys have an answer to our every sporting blow, and we almost hate them for it.

| ·EQUIPMENT ·OUTDOORS | ·FAN GEAR ·TEAM SPORTS | ·FITNESS ·SOLO SPORTS | ·REC ROOMS ·FOOTWEAR |
|---|---|---|---|

## CSSkiEquipment.com

The "CS" here stands for "Cool Sports" equipment. Sounds intriguing, right? Well, we tend to be skeptical. However, they did sort of win us over with a bunch of different innertubes that can be towed at high speeds behind a motorboat. And, while they didn't offer any motorboats that we could see, there were some kayaks, canoes and inflatable rafts that looked kinda cool. But, not as cool as the summer sleds, which are like regular sleds except they have wheels so you can ride down hills at breakneck speeds no matter what the season. An odd-looking site, but fun nonetheless.

| ·EQUIPMENT | ·WATER SPORTS | ·SOLO SPORTS | |
|---|---|---|---|

877-287-7883 • CupStuff.com                                    **CupStuff.com**

This is a fan site that focuses partly on the NHL, so you pro hockey fans can avoid any inferiority complex and get your best Colorado Avalanche or Philadelphia Flyers T-shirts. The real story, though, is that the site also caters to CFL fans. That would be the Canadian Football League, home to the Winnipeg Blue Bombers, Edmonton Eskimos and Saskatchewan Roughriders. Talk about underappreciated—most Americans didn't even know they played football in Canada.

| ·FAN GEAR | | | |  |
|---|---|---|---|---|

877-907-4637 • Solemates, Inc.                                 **Customatix.com**

Whether or not you're in the market for new footwear, this one is just incredibly cool; it gives you the chance to design your own shoes. Granted, you have to start with one of their five basic designs—sneakers, slip-ons, runners, skate shoes ("sk8rs" here) and casual/walking boots. But beyond that the choices are almost limitless. Piece by piece, you can choose from dozens of colors for different parts of the shoe, including the laces, soles, tongues and several others. Then you may select from dozens of different logos, in the same dozens of colors, or select the ever important "none." Part color composition, part expression of style, this one warrants hours of your day.

| ·FOOTWEAR | | | | |
|---|---|---|---|---|

888-900-1950 • Daddy-O's                                        **Daddyos.com**

Why would we list this store, "where the coolest get their coolness" in the Sports section? Well, in answer we'd have to refer you to the most fashionably dressed of all athletes. That's right: bowlers. No, we haven't gone loco. This site caters to the swingin' hepcats of any community, and it just so happens that the bulk of this coolish catalog is made up of bowling shirts. Some feature slogans like "The Lucky Strikes" or "Bowl-A-Rama!" Others have buttons illustrated with pin-up girls. Who doesn't want to play a game where looking hip is appreciated?

| ·SOLO SPORTS | | | | |
|---|---|---|---|---|

877-846-9997 • Dick's Sporting Goods                      **DicksSportingGoods.com**

This site is not just huge— it's enormous. It's got pogo sticks, horseshoes and ice-fishing equipment. It has gear for every sport you can think of, and plenty you wouldn't expect: lacrosse, badminton, watertubing and squash, just for starters. If you don't want to shop by sport or game, you can look to their departments to browse categories like Water Sports, Footwear or Hunting Gear. It's actually remarkable how quickly you can track down just what you're looking for in this gigantic selection, and yet you can still browse your way into some entertaining finds. Good Stuff.

| ·EQUIPMENT ·OUTDOORS | ·WATER SPORTS ·CYCLING | ·FITNESS ·FOOTWEAR | ·REC ROOMS | |
|---|---|---|---|---|

## Distant-Replays.com

If you liked sports better the way they were before today's batch of superstars were even born, or if you thought it was a terrible idea for the Houston Astros to give up their colorful home jerseys, this is the fan site for you. Featuring the retro authentic and replica jerseys you just don't see anymore, here you can actually track down jerseys for superstars like Pistol Pete Maravich, Dr. J and Joe Namath. This thrillingly nostalgic selection even includes defunct leagues like basketball's ABA and baseball's Women's and Negro Leagues. The historic selection changes often, so it's worth repeat visits.

## DiversDirect.com

Life below sea level begins with this retailer of scuba gear, snorkels and other underwater equipment. While not terrifically laid out, it's actually pretty easy to browse through the fins, masks and wetsuits presented here. More difficult would be earning your diver's certification, which is required in order to buy some of the more complicated pieces like tanks and regulators. If you know what you're doing, though, you can shop here without so much as getting your feet wet; simply fax your C-Card and ID, and hold your breath while awaiting delivery.

## DoverSaddlery.com

You'll have to scroll down the home page of this site to find the Click Here for Menu link (in the left-hand margin). When you do, though, you'll see a fine menu for competitive or show riding, of horses that is. In Tack & Accessories you'll find bridles, reins, bits, breastplates, cavesons and martingales (whatever those are), while in Grooming, Horse Health Care and Stable Equipment you'll find all you need to care for your stallion or nag. Finally, there's apparel to spiff up either the horse or yourself (it's tough to say who'll look better).

·EQUIPMENT

## eAngler.com

Looking for jigs, flies or waders? Fishing enthusiasts can find rods, reels, lines, lures and pretty much anything you might want to tie in to your tackle, as well as some of the finer river accoutrements like funny hats and vests. They can even set you up online with a fishing license for a few select states, and give you weather and tidal information for regional areas, easily accessed by a clickable map of the US. They also act as a good reference if you're inexperienced, complete with articles, guides and a community of others who're all too willing to share their favorite fish tales.

·EQUIPMENT    ·OUTDOORS    ·SOLO SPORTS    ·WATER SPORTS

## 800-628-6301 • Eastbay Online

**EastBay.com**

Can you make your game better just by shopping from the right place? This shop makes a good case for it. With a fantastic selection that begins with athletic shoes and extends to equipment, apparel and sports fan gear, there may be plenty of things you cannot find here, but you'll probably be satisfied enough with what you can get not to worry about it too much. Navigation isn't immediately obvious, but turns out to be rather easy: within each tabbed section (linked from the top of the page) there are subsections, which may be found through a series of pull-down menus. This here's a good one.

| ·EQUIPMENT ·TEAM SPORTS | ·FAN GEAR ·SOLO SPORTS | ·FITNESS | ·FOOTWEAR |
|---|---|---|---|

## 877-326-2734 • ebodyboarding.com

**eBodyBoarding.com**

For those who like to do it on their stomachs, this bodyboarding specialty shop will prove a great find. Their expected selection of boards, wetsuits, fins and skegs are bolstered by the likes of portable showers, car roof racks and repair kits. They even offer a Buying Guide section that can match your height and weight with different board options, as well as other tips to help novices get on their way (what's a skeg?). Between this, the Webzine and the ultra-helpful Interact section, this should be all a bodyboarder needs.

| ·EQUIPMENT | ·WATER SPORTS | | |
|---|---|---|---|

## No Service Number • eKICKFight

**eKickFight.com**

Here's a site capable of outfitting you to either give or receive a massive beating. Offering headgear, mouthguards and plenty of other protective pads to complement a readily perused assortment of gloves, one would almost get the impression that kickboxing is sort of a pansy sport—almost. If the fine assortment of handwraps doesn't get the tough-guy point across, just remember that when they make a movie about kickboxing, they give it a title like *Bloodsport*. Here's hoping the training materials offered here keep you on the winning side of the tussle.

| ·FITNESS | ·FOOTWEAR | ·EQUIPMENT | |
|---|---|---|---|

## 888-463-6367 • Eastern Mountain Sports

**EMSOnline.com**

The name of these guys is Eastern Mountain Sports, and they pretty much cater to any activity you might pursue on an inclined plane. Whether it's clothing or equipment you need, you can gear up for some generally masochistic mountain biking, thrill-heavy rock climbing and kayaking (which lies somewhere in between). Unfortunately, a boring site makes perusing these products even less fun that hiking around in snowshoes (which you can also pick up here), so save your enthusiasm for higher elevations.

| ·EQUIPMENT ·FOOTWEAR | ·OUTDOORS ·CYCLING | ·KIDS ·WINTER SPORTS | ·SOLO SPORTS |
|---|---|---|---|

## EvolutionSurf.com

Evolution Surf • 888-386-4249

Here is one of the better places (if not the best) to buy a surfboard on the web (many of the surf shops don't even offer boards online). This surf company's batch of high-end boards includes one model crafted of balsa wood, which is perilously expensive but ultra-light and maneuverable. They also feature boards built especially for female surfers, as well as a series of double-enders and high performance models "designed to ride waves from 2 to 20 feet." This is surfing broken down to its barest elements, and quite good.

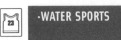

| ·WATER SPORTS | | | | |
|---|---|---|---|---|

## Flying-Carpets.com

flying-carpets • 800-233-1238

With what amounts to a very tiny selection of yoga mats, this site makes a fairly big impression. The premise seems to be that, given the spiritual aspects of yoga, one should sit upon something better than your standard blue vinyl floor mat. Therefore, these unique, hand-made, beautiful alternatives may increase your stretching pleasure. Whatever the case, they look good, and will in most cases out-style your yoga wardrobe, which could distract you from your meditations. Bottom line: upgrade everything if you intend to achieve enlightenment.

| ·FITNESS | | | | |
|---|---|---|---|---|

## FogDog.com

FogDog.com • 800-624-2017

Upon entering this site, the first thing you'll notice is a few select sporting sections like Golf and Wakeboarding. This is all fine and good, except that it distracts you from the wide selection of equipment they offer for nearly every imaginable sport, from racquetball to paintball, and even a few that require no balls at all. They also have an extensive personal fitness section, underlied by some great sports medicine products, which will come in handy when you invariably hurt yourself trying to play all these sports; really, at your age you should know better.

| ·EQUIPMENT ·OUTDOORS | ·WATER SPORTS ·CYCLING | ·WINTER SPORTS ·FOOTWEAR | ·FITNESS |
|---|---|---|---|

## FootballFanatics.com

Football Fanatics • 877-827-8965

Just like it sounds, this is a great site for big football fans that want to advertise their team to all the other loser team's fans. Whether it's an NFL or big college squad, all you need to do is pick your team off of a list and then see what sort of merchandise is available, whether it's a shirt, hat, jacket, coffee mug or commemorative rug (or any number of other common or unusual items). There's even a good amount of autographed merchandise to be seen though, sadly, no body make-up. You'll have to look elsewhere to paint yourself up for the big game.

| ·FAN GEAR | | | | |
|---|---|---|---|---|

## 800-991-6815 • Foot Locker

### FootLocker.com

You almost know exactly what you'll find here before you see it. It's pretty much just like any Foot Locker you'll see in hundreds of malls across the universe, with one big exception: more stuff. Here, they have room for all sizes, all colors and all styles. Especially valuable if you've been to the mall recently but couldn't find precisely what you wanted, you can easily access hundreds of brands, or run searches specifically by size and sport. And this isn't even to mention the fan gear, sporting equipment and apparel. If you ask us, these guys should let their mall leases expire and just run online.

| ·EQUIPMENT ·TEAM SPORTS | ·FAN GEAR ·FOOTWEAR | ·FITNESS | ·KIDS |
|---|---|---|---|

## 800-754-2627 • GetBoards.com

### GetBoards.com

If you're a board sport fan, you will find plenty to sort through on the fairly slick, multi-faceted site. Whether it's on land, water or snow that you prefer to tear it up, this spot very likely caters to your interests (with the marked exceptions of surfing/windsurfing). However, most of us won't even know what all of these sports are; in addition to bodyboarding, snowboarding and skateboarding, represented here is skimboards, wakeboards, mountainboards, skiboards, freeboards and carveboards. If these are unfamiliar, just take a look at the site. They offer excellent looks and full detail on all products—hey, maybe you'll get turned on to something new.

| ·EQUIPMENT | ·WATER SPORTS | ·WINTER SPORTS | ·SOLO SPORTS |
|---|---|---|---|

## 877-428-9447 • GH Sports

### GHSports.com

With a selection made almost entirely of athletic apparel, this site doesn't cater to every conceivable sport, nor does it fully cover all aspects of the activities it does include. However, those in need of some good running, cycling, aerobic, outdoor and equestrian gear should have some luck. Swimmers, however, will find the greatest selection, with plenty of floats, fins, clips, plugs, goggles, prescription goggles, kickboards, caps and suits easily at the ready. No word on what the "GH" stands for.

| ·WATER SPORTS | ·WINTER SPORTS | ·FITNESS | ·CYCLING |
|---|---|---|---|

## 800-578-5637 • G.I. Joe's

### GIJoes.com

Behind the mantra "Go to Joe's, Grab the Gear, Seize the Weekend," this extensive sporting goods store that was founded by a former WWII pilot (hence the name) delivers the goods. All you have to do is follow the View All Sports link to see just how thorough the selection is—they even have a decent selection of skate shoes (a pretty good indicator that all is well). Despite being so enormous, this site is very well put together, with great use of subcategorization and fantastic product detail. No jokes, it's good.

| ·EQUIPMENT ·OUTDOORS | ·WATER SPORTS ·CYCLING | ·WINTER SPORTS ·FOOTWEAR | ·FITNESS |
|---|---|---|---|

## GolfBalls.com

Golfballs.com • 800-372-2557

Here is the site that begs the question: just how many variations of a golf ball can there be? Well, that's tough to say, exactly, but we can tell you that this ultra-niche retailer lists 13 categories comprised of more than 50 brands. Some of the products actually prove intriguing, at least more so than your run-of-the-mill, white, dimpled ball. Take Colored Balls, Illegal Balls, Floaters (to confound water hazards) and Nitelites. Best may be their section of Trick Balls, which promise to either explode or wobble on the green. Add to that the options to Buy in Bulk, a Clearance section and a catalog of used balls, and you have here the absolute best place to buy golfballs online.

| ·EQUIPMENT | ·SOLO SPORTS | | |
|---|---|---|---|

## GopherSport.com

Gopher Sport • 800-533-0446

As if the trauma of Physical Education in the schools wasn't enough, this site allows you to recreate the experience at home, offering all manner of children's recreational and athletic gear. For starters, you can find many sizes of those ubiquitous red, air-filled balls (known to many as the terror-inflicting "dodge ball"). Then there are climbing walls, gymnastic stations, bowling carpets (to simulate indoor lanes), tetherball sets and even those big parachutes that teach youngsters the value of … something or other. Once you've filled your home and yard with this equipment, select from scoreboards and bleachers and invite other parents over to get worked into a frenzy over whose kid is best at what.

| | ·EQUIPMENT ·SOLO SPORTS | ·FITNESS ·KIDS | ·REC ROOMS | ·TEAM SPORTS |
|---|---|---|---|---|

## HatWorld.com

HatWorld.com • 888-564-4287

These guys have your sports-loving head covered. Whether you prefer the NHL, NFL, NBA, Major League Baseball, the NCAA or NASCAR, there's a great chance you'll find a variety of hats here representing your favorite teams and/or stars. Or, you may attempt to combine all your sporting loves into one love with the Create Your Own cap section. While hugely hindered by a poor, complicated design, this does let you choose from a variety of hat styles, generic logos, stitching (colors) and personalized text. Go nuts.

| | ·FAN GEAR | | | |
|---|---|---|---|---|

## HuggerMugger.com

Hugger Mugger Yoga Products • 800-473-4888

Here's a great, slick yoga site with plenty to offer either the yoga enthusiast or neophyte in search of a good start. They have Zabutons and Zafus, for example, though if you know exactly what those are you probably own some already. Categories like Clothing, Lifestyle Products, Multimedia (mostly instructional) and Props & Tools should be pretty easy to fathom, though animated menus that should make navigation easy require a little too much precision to be perfect (only the most advanced yoga fingers might adequately chart them). This may seem a little bland, but every little bit helps.

| | | ·FITNESS | | | |
|---|---|---|---|---|---|

## 888-342-7656 • Jackson Hole Horse Emporium — JHHE.com

If you're going to stop by the Jackson Hole Horse Emporium, surely you won't want to miss The Polo Shop. Where else, after all, are you going to find the high quality saddles, fittings, bits, bridles and halters you need to stay competitive? And that's just for horses. For the rider you can find gloves, braces, boots, spurs, mallets and whips (This is starting to sound like one crazy sport!). Of course, the whole selection is rounded out by the all-time classic Polo Shirt, and a few of those nifty hats like Elizabeth Taylor wore in *National Velvet*.

| ·EQUIPMENT | | | | |
|---|---|---|---|---|

## 866-321-2287 • JustBats.com — JustBats.com

We know, we know. How many variations of bats can there possibly be? Well, not a lot, especially considering we didn't see any cricket bats included to beef up the selection. But there sure are a variety of baseball, softball and tee ball bats to choose from. Then there are a good dozen or so pitching machines and some balls to go with them. Add a couple of fungos and a radar gun, and you've got yourself a whole game of batting practice, all by yourself.

| ·EQUIPMENT | ·TEAM SPORTS | ·KIDS | |
|---|---|---|---|

## 516-867-1608 • JWhiteCricket.com — JWhiteCricket.com

We know what you think about cricket. But truly, this is a sport that's popular in the rest of the world. It's a sport of leisure, a gentlemanly endeavor. Seriously, it doesn't suck. It just happens that this game requires a lot of special, very dapper equipment, all of which may be found on this lovely site. Stuff like bats, gloves, ab guards, elbow guards, leg guards, thigh pads and head gear, all easy to find and purchase. Hey, you don't see baseball players needing all sorts of extra padding, do you? This game can be dangerous ... even if only in a leisurely, genteel, dapper sort of way.

| ·EQUIPMENT | ·TEAM SPORTS | | | |
|---|---|---|---|---|

## 877-216-2669 • KarateDepot.com — KarateDepot.com

The Depot turns out to be a fairly comprehensive martial arts specialty retailer, covering categories like Protective Gear, Training Aids, Weapons and Uniforms with ease. Shopping may be most effectively achieved through use of the Style Specific menu, which includes a lengthy list of techniques like Tai Chi, Muay Thai, Tae Kwon Do, Judo, Kendo, Boxing, Kung Fu and the fan favorite Ninjitsu (complete with one of those nifty black outfits. Books on the fighting arts are also available, even if titles like *Obsessive Mental Attitude*, *The 101 Deadliest Karate Moves* and *How to Develop a Perfect Body* make it somewhat laughable (the book section, not the sport).

| ·EQUIPMENT | ·FITNESS | ·SOLO SPORTS | |
|---|---|---|---|

## KensingtonTrading.com

**Kensington Trading Company • 877-374-8881**

If you're like most people, you commonly lament just how difficult it is to find a decent, regulation croquet set. Well, kind sirs and madams let your grieving stop here. The Kensington Trading Company offers all the finest in the gentle sports: badminton, leisure boule, home skittles and, yes, garden skittles (also commonly referred to as lawn bowling). Yes, you get what you pay for, which turns out to be ludicrous amounts of money. But if the alternative is letting your finely manicured green lawn go to waste, what other choice is there for a gamer of class?

| ·EQUIPMENT | ·REC ROOMS | | |
|---|---|---|---|

## KronanCycle.com

**Kronan Cycle • 866-465-7662**

You've heard of a Swiss Army Knife, but how about a Swedish Army Bike? Well, these bicycles were created from the original designs once used to make bicycles for Sweden's military. To some, the sturdy, simple construction (no fancy gears on these) may only be appealing in that bulky, military-issue sort of way, but something about the clean, classic looks will attract riders who merely wish to cruise at a regular peddling speed.

| ·CYCLING | | | |
|---|---|---|---|

## Lacrosse.com

**Great Atlantic Lacrosse Company • 800-955-3876**

This site, of course, is devoted to lacrosse, the sport that America forgot about. Well, nearly forgot about. Here you can buy a stick complete or assemble one from your favorite shafts, heads and stringing combinations. Then there are the helmets and pads that remind us just how brutally violent this sport can be, alongside other apparel that may be necessary to improve your game. As if that weren't enough to make this probably the best lacrosse site around, these guys even carry fan gear for the NLL. That would be the National Lacrosse League. Yeah, who knew?

| ·EQUIPMENT | ·FAN GEAR | ·TEAM SPORTS | |
|---|---|---|---|

## LacrosseUnltd.com

**Lacrosse Unlimited • 877-932-5229**

Whether what you are looking for is an unstrung head, bodyform turfwear, a titanium shaft or a throat guard, here's a lacrosse niche retailer that can outfit you for a match or just give you the leg up in a rumble. With a better selection than page design, it should nevertheless be easy enough to find what you are looking for, assuming you have a favorite brand. If you're a college player, or just a fan, you may even find select equipment in your team's colors; at the very least you can get the shaft.

| ·EQUIPMENT | ·FAN GEAR | ·TEAM SPORTS | |
|---|---|---|---|

**800-443-8620 • Life-Link Backcountry Essentials**                  **Life-Link.com**

When these guys refer to their wares as "backcountry essentials," they are trying to let you know that this isn't the kind of ski gear you take with you to impress the ladies at your local ski lodge. Here you'll find the stuff of back-country skiing, the type that requires you to trek a ways before finding your run, and to actually climb the slopes while your at it (you'll find no lifts on the other side of the mountain). Gear consists of all-terrain skis, boots and bindings (all tough but light) along with saws, avalanche probes and shovels to let you know that, yes, it can be dangerous out there.

| ·WINTER SPORTS | ·EQUIPMENT | | | |

**800-903-6376 • Liquid Golf**                  **LiquidGolf.com**

Staking its claim as "the first online country club," this pro shop on the web offers some pretty good products and services. Appropriately enough, the more you know about golf, the better the store gets, but if you're still somewhat new to the sport they can still help. With sections for left-handed, ladies and junior gear, it's pretty easy to find all the woods, irons, wedges and putters you'll likely need. If not, a catalog of apparel ensures that if you can't golf like a pro, you can at least dress like one (though in that case you may want to stick to bowling).

| ·EQUIPMENT | ·KIDS | ·SOLO SPORTS | ·FOOTWEAR |

**877-223-4528 • MartialArtsSupplies.com**                  **MartialArtsSupplies.com**

From padded weapons to sparring gear, there's plenty of equipment to be found at this martial arts specialist with which you and your friends may beat on each other and yet be left intact for the next round of practiced violence. They also have a fantastic selection of outfits, from kendo armor to ninja uniforms, which you can order and simply wear to feel cool. Or, if you possess a sense of honor, check out the site's Dojo Directory to find a place where you can learn exactly how the wide selection of other gear here is meant to be used.

| ·EQUIPMENT | ·FITNESS | ·SOLO SPORTS | |

**800-829-2009 • Mountain Gear**                  **MGear.com**

Your journey up from sea level to the sky will probably involve a lot of the equipment sold in this Mountain Gear store. Hiking and climbing tools and apparel can get you up to the top safely and comfortably, while skiing and telemarking (also known as free-heel skiing) gear pretty much serve to get you back to the bottom, fast. Meanwhile, when you are at the top, you may just want to cook, camp, drink water or wear warm clothes; fortunately, this store can outfit you for such extreme activities as well.

| ·EQUIPMENT | ·WATER SPORTS | ·WINTER SPORTS | ·OUTDOORS |
| ·FOOTWEAR | ·SOLO SPORTS | | |

# MinorLeagues.com

Minor Leagues, Major Dreams • 800-345-2421

Despite the name, this retailer actually has mostly Major League Baseball fan gear for sale (plus some NBA, NFL and college branded merchandise). Still, for the fan whose town rallies around a development league, it's one of the few places anywhere (let alone online) to find caps representing teams like the Durham Bulls, Michigan Battle Cats, Toledo Mudhens, Lakewood Blue Claws, Quad City Bandits and others. The site's not perfect, but then, neither are the players. But they're truly in it for love of the game.

| ·FAN GEAR | | | |
|---|---|---|---|

# MLB.com

Major League Baseball • 866-225-6457

This official site of Major League Baseball will give you all the news, stats and scores you desire, but that's only half the story. Look in the Shop and you will find yourself privy to more merchandise than you could ever imagine, from authentic and replica jerseys to branded, Italian leather briefcases. Better yet, you can find all sorts of media related to America's pastime, from books to videos and even streaming audio for a season's worth of games. Hey, we gotta support this thing or they'll shrink the league.

| ·FAN GEAR | ·KIDS | | |
|---|---|---|---|

# Modells.com

Modell's Sporting Goods • 866-835-9129

This store is kind of like about a dozen other sporting goods retailers you might find around the internet; actually, it's exactly like them, right down to the selection and prices. So, if you're fond of The Sport Chalet, Sport Mart, Oshman's, The Sports Authority or Dunham's Sports, this site won't prove any different. That is to say, they offer a little bit of everything, at fair prices, with easy to use organization. So why did we pick this particular site? Because you "Gotta Go to Mo's," of course.

| ·EQUIPMENT ·FITNESS | ·FAN GEAR ·SOLO SPORTS | ·WATER SPORTS ·TEAM SPORTS | ·WINTER SPORTS ·FOOTWEAR |
|---|---|---|---|

# MonsterSkate.com

MonsterSkate.com • 866-287-8337

Behind the motto, "Always Online Never Inline," this snappy retailer makes darn sure that you know not to even ask if they carry rollerblades. This one is all about skateboarding, lest you forget that it's the hippest sport on the planet. They do it pretty well here, too, with a robust selection of the brands that sponsor pros, and some that just offer cool deck designs. If you're unsure as to which best suit your styles and skill level, just spend some time in their online magazine and let the hype choose for ya.

| ·EQUIPMENT | ·SOLO SPORTS | | |
|---|---|---|---|

## 888-208-2258 • Moosejaw

### MooseJaw.com

In addition to its memorable name, this site promises "the best equipment and outerwear in the world, and some nonsense." The latter is not readily apparent, however, as you first notice some great camping, paddling and climbing gear at nice, low prices. They might be referring to the Moose Crap section, which amounts to some tall tales of mountainous mischief, or Mama Toad's Cookin', which features uncomplicated recipes for stuff like watermelon ("Slice it and dice it."); nonsense or otherwise, it's easy to find.

| ·EQUIPMENT ·KIDS | ·WATER SPORTS ·SOLO SPORTS | ·WINTER SPORTS ·FOOTWEAR | ·OUTDOORS |
|---|---|---|---|

## 877-326-2300 • The Movement Connection, Inc.

### MovementConnection.com

If you're going to put some twinkle in your toes, the first thing you'll need is dance lessons. Then, as you tend to the blisters forming on your poor feet, you'll come to realize that you need the proper footwear. Here you'll find it, whether you want ballet slippers, tap, jazz or pointe shoes. The Ballroom Dancesport category even has a nice variety, featuring pumps and sandals in varying colors, for those who might dance competitively. Which brings us to the apparel sections, because some people like to add a little sparkle to go with their twinkle.

| ·KIDS | ·FOOTWEAR | | |
|---|---|---|---|

## 866-690-2381 • MVP.com

### MVP.com

Fan memorabilia is the first thing that will grab your attention upon entering this site. This may be for the best, as their sporting goods catalog is lacking compared to many of the other sites we've seen. Aside from an intriguing As Seen On TV section, little else proves interesting save for some links to sporting news and fantasy sites. These, however, may entice you to return at a later date to grab that special-issue championship jersey or all-star cap, at which point the visibility of all the fan garb will suddenly make sense.

| ·FAN GEAR | | | |
|---|---|---|---|

## No Service Number • NASCAR

### NASCAR.com

This official site of the National Association for Stock Car Auto Racing offers plenty to keep enthusiasts entertained, and a store for those particularly avid fans. Of course, there are no stock cars for sale here, only memorabilia and branded merchandise. Actually, there are some strange items to go along with the regular assortment of caps and T-shirts, like a Jeff Gordon pool cue, Rusty Wallace mouse pad and decks of Dale Earnhardt playing cards. Shop by product or driver to get your NASCAR fix.

| ·FAN GEAR | | | |
|---|---|---|---|

# Nashbar.com

Bike Nashbar • 800-627-4227

This is one of the better bike shops online, except that it doesn't seem to offer the sale of any bikes. Of course, if you really wanted to, you could shop through this selection and assemble your own bike piece by piece, starting with the frame and continuing through to a variety of brakes, chains, derailleurs, fenders, forks, hubs, handlebars, peddles, saddles and wheels. An excellent source of parts and accessories (for safety and/or fun), we'd recommend getting the bike elsewhere and just relying on these guys for upgrades, replacements and repairs.

·CYCLING  ·FOOTWEAR

# NBA.com

National Basketball Association • 800-622-0548

Welcome to pro basketball central. Whether you're a men's hoops fan or like the ladies' game, this site get you what you need to display your allegiance from head to—well, shirt mostly. Of course, there's really much more to the site, including daily scores and player news, with team pages getting you more in-depth. You might not get the straight story on what criticisms Mavericks owner Mark Cuban has to offer about league officiating, but you will be able to vote for all-stars, figure out which games are on TV and buy all the official merchandise you can fit through a basket.

·FAN GEAR  ·TEAM SPORTS

# NewYorkYoga.com

New York Yoga • 212-717-9642

Can inner peace be achieved while looking at a computer screen? This question may be answered with this site, which offers yoga instruction online through streaming video. Classes are available for beginners on through power and advanced users, as well as by particular schools like Anusara, Ashtanga and Hatha on through Pilates and Vinyasa. All you need is a mat (which they conveniently offer for sale), as clothing is optional (assuming you're streaming this into your home). You may need to set your screen saver to activate at wider intervals, or you'll be forced to toggle your mouse in the middle of a stretching exercise; no way to practice a meditation for sure.

·FITNESS

# NFLShop.com

National Football League • 800-635-7467

The best way to navigate this official retailer of National Football League merchandise is to pick your favorite team and then wade through the menu items until you've seen all the clothes, hats, jackets and engraved flasks you can handle. The exception would be in the Books/Videos category, which isn't really all that big and deals with the league in general. Now you may, of course, find replica jerseys featuring the names and numbers of the biggest NFL stars, but what's the fun of that when they offer customized jerseys featuring any custom name and whatever two-digit number you like?

·FAN GEAR

## 800-806-6453 • Nike

### NikeTown.com

If you're one of the few and shrinking number of people on this planet who aren't already well acquainted with the Nike swoosh, well then we're almost sorry to be introducing you to it here. Chances are, though, that you've owned at least one pair of Nike sneakers in your life, or at least coveted the Air Jordans of another. Here you'll find virtually every Nike product available, including the now infamous, personalized Nike iD sneakers. With over 150 pairs of shoes to choose from in the Men's section alone, even those of us who grew up in these shoes have plenty of browsing to do.

| ·FAN GEAR ·TEAM SPORTS | ·FITNESS ·SOLO SPORTS | ·FOOTWEAR | ·KIDS | | |
|---|---|---|---|---|---|

## 888-296-4783 • Nirve

### Nirve.com

This is not a bicycle shop for squares. For starters, here you will find a good proprietary selection of BMX bikes, the best for taking moguls and jumps on dirt tracks. For the extreme rider of smooth surfaces, they offer a series of Freestyle (FS) bikes (all of these bikes bear the Nirve brand name), which can be made to do any number of miraculous, highflying tricks/combinations. Rounding out the selection on a much chiller, primarily stylish tip is their line of Cruisers that, if you think about it, put most cars to shame. This is a fantastically slick, well-executed site for a great line of merchandise.

| ·CYCLING | | | | |
|---|---|---|---|---|

## 800-220-1256 • Nordic Track

### NordicTrack.com

Yes, these are the guys who sold all those cross country ski simulators on television commercials, promising a "total-body workout." Well, what if we told you they sell other machines as well? With strength training units, steppers, bikes and treadmills, among others, it would appear that these machines offer supplemental or alternative workouts to the original skier model. Total, or otherwise, this small selection of machines nevertheless seem like they'll get you into shape in a dozen different ways—assuming they don't just stack up in the garage.

| ·FITNESS | ·EQUIPMENT | | | |
|---|---|---|---|---|

## 510-562-0500 • Oceanic

### OceanicWorldwide.com

With the exception of air, pretty much all the basic elements of scuba diving are covered here: regulators, masks, buoyancy compensators, fins, wetsuits and gauges (of some sort). There are also some less essential items like knives, dive computers and even a Diver Propulsion Vehicle (when swimming slows you down). Meanwhile, you'll notice some snorkel gear, and a mysterious Explorers section. The latter simply offers the same stuff you'll find on the rest of the site, but smaller—you know, for kids.

| ·WATER SPORTS | ·KIDS | ·EQUIPMENT | |
|---|---|---|---|

## OutDrs.com                                                    Eagle Outdoors • 888-782-7542

Welcome to Eagle Outdoors, which is an annoying, hard-to-use, not terribly good looking site that tries but fails to live up to the high standards of the many similar outdoor specialty stores available on the web. However, these guys sell pontoons, and that's pretty cool. Sure, sure, they have a pretty decent selection of other stuff; fishing gear, camping gear, etc. And sure, their prices are pretty good on most items. But, and we can't stress this enough, the Water Craft & Accessories section is where it's at.

| ·WATER SPORTS | ·OUTDOORS | | |
|---|---|---|---|

## Overtons.com                                                  Overtons.com • 800-334-6541

Here's a site that's big, convoluted and great for water freaks. "The World's Largest Water Sports Retailer" offers boatloads of stuff to load into... boats: life vests, diving gear, water-skis, mooring lines, floating trampolines—and that's barely a fraction of the whole. The one thing to watch for is that the site uses a somewhat uncommon navigation technique. A single column menu expands into two, three and four columns to include submenus for each category. Not ideal, but it works.

| ·WATER SPORTS | ·KIDS | ·EQUIPMENT | |
|---|---|---|---|

## PalosSports.com                                               Palos Sports • 800-233-5484

If you're of the mindset that personal fitness is a lot of grueling, hard work, you should definitely pay a visit to this retailer of a veritable bounty of exercise and recreational equipment that proves exercise can be more fun that a big screen TV. Find the Browse the Catalog link to get a look at the long list of standard sporting equipment, and then take notice of decidedly more enticing items like Foam Shapes, Parachutes (not the kind you drop from the sky with) and Wall Mats. This one's for kids and grown up kids alike.

| ·EQUIPMENT<br>·REC ROOM | ·FITNESS<br>·TEAM SPORTS | ·KIDS | ·SOLO SPORTS |
|---|---|---|---|

## ParagonSports.com                                       ParagonSports.com • 800-961-3030

Here's "New York's Finest Sports Specialty Store," which offers a very wide and sometimes deep selection of all the sports items we could come up with off the top of our heads, from Archery to Water Sports with Kayaking somewhere in between. A great organizational effort, easy browsing and some good product looks makes it easy to just cruise around and keep looking, and impressed us in most steps along the way. We'll stop short from calling this a perfect site, but it truly is a good one.

| ·WATER SPORTS<br>·REC ROOMS | ·WINTER SPORTS<br>·SOLO SPORTS | ·FITNESS<br>·FOOTWEAR | ·TEAM SPORTS<br>·EQUIPMENT |
|---|---|---|---|

## 800-638-6464 • Patagonia

### Patagonia.com

Are you ready to get tired of a single word? This outdoor apparel store does everything right— it has great browsing features, great search features, a great selection, great product detail and great looks at each of its items. Yes, it's true, from underwear and hats to wading pants and shoes, this site has virtually no deficiencies whatsoever. This sturdy gear will keep you warm, dry, organized and looking great on top of it all. Yes, as we tried hard to warn you, this one can be summed up in a single word: great.

| ·WATER SPORTS ·KIDS | ·WINTER SPORTS ·SOLO SPORTS | ·FITNESS | ·OUTDOORS |
|---|---|---|---|

---

## 800-727-2433 • Performance Bike

### PerformanceBike.com

A great selection of bikes makes this a good place to get your cycling career started, or at least to help you kick it up a level or two. Otherwise, you can always shop by part, building your dream ride piece by piece, or peruse the Outlet section for good deals. They also feature special store for female riders, and a family store with cool rides for youngsters, including some sturdy strollers and bike-trailers. Finally, repair kits and pumps ensure you won't sweat a flat, or any other bumps in the road.

| ·EQUIPMENT ·KIDS | ·OUTDOORS | ·CYCLING | ·SOLO SPORTS |
|---|---|---|---|

---

## 800-818-0946 • Peter Glenn

### PeterGlenn.com

Snow sport enthusiasts and, in warmer climates, water sport enthusiasts will find plenty to strap on with this Vermont retailer's online shop. The menu devoted to alpine skiing, snowboarding and all the applicable accoutrements for both sports seems to expand with every conceivable click, leading to a startling array of top gear. Meanwhile, wakeboards and water-skis are bolstered by water safety and swimming equipment (all you need is a boat). Or, if you lack $H_2O$ in both liquid and solid form, you can check into their vast selection of in-line skates, though we couldn't imagine why you'd want to.

| ·EQUIPMENT ·SOLO SPORTS | ·WATER SPORTS | ·WINTER SPORTS | ·FOOTWEAR |
|---|---|---|---|

---

## 866-816-0879 • Professional Golf Association

### PGATourStop.com

If you absolutely love professional golf and simply have to let everybody know, there's no better site to find fan gear with which to show off your Tiger Woods devotion than this one. The official store for the Professional Golf Association Tour, this is like the pro pro shop, with everything from shoes and apparel to logoed clubs, bags and barware. You'll even find loads of autographed and unsigned memorabilia, and a slew of videos, books and videogames that pretty much will round out the leftover hours of the day when you actually might not have otherwise thought of golf.

| ·EQUIPMENT ·SOLO SPORTS | ·FAN GEAR | ·KIDS | ·FOOTWEAR |
|---|---|---|---|

# Plaines.com

Plaine's • 888-216-7122

What makes this site great is... well, not much, really. They have a decent selection across the board of bicycle, ski and snowboard products, and depending on the item they have good prices as well. Their navigation is pretty easy to follow, with browsing offering no trouble at all, and there's nothing terribly cool going on here, with the possible exception of Recumbent Bikes (you'll have to see them to understand). So, why are we so down on this site? We're not. It's just not great is all. Just pretty good.

| | | ·WINTER SPORTS | ·CYCLING | | |
|---|---|---|---|---|---|

# Puma.com

Puma • No Service Number

Re-emerging in the popular consciousness, Puma turns in this online outlet for its products, and tries very hard to be quite slick about it. The result: it's a little slow. This is just because they tend to include all of their great looking product presentations for each category on a single page, which can take a [long] while to load. This actually works well, though, for those with a little patience (pick a product type and then go to the bathroom, watch some TV or fix a snack) because once the page is loaded, you can easily scroll through all of your options, assuming they're still in style by then.

| | ·KIDS | ·FOOTWEAR | | |
|---|---|---|---|---|

# PurePolaris.com

Polaris • 800-304-6067

For people who like to tread off the beaten path, but don't like to walk, this retailer devotes its focus to snowmobile, ATV (All Terrain Vehicle) and small watercraft gear. Now, you'll have to track down the actual vehicles elsewhere; here they primarily sell stuff like replacement tires, skis and engine parts. Then there are plenty of decals, chrome and tows to help dress them up. As for dressing yourself up, there's plenty of apparel for flopping about in water, snow and mud, which is what you're ultimately leaving the concrete to do.

| | | ·WATER SPORTS | ·KIDS | ·WINTER SPORTS | ·EQUIPMENT |
|---|---|---|---|---|---|

# RacquetballCatalog.com

RacquetballCatalog.com • 866-443-2777

Topped proudly by the icon of what appears to be a mountain lion playing racquetball, this specialty retailer (which includes sections devoted to squash and handball as well) serves up a pretty thorough selection of indoor court gear. Shoes, racquets and protective eyewear probably make up the bulk of the site but, as is easily ascertained by the lengthy menu, they have plenty more than that to offer. Particularly enticing may be a demo program that lets you try two different racquets for ten days before you decide to buy. If only shoes came with such programs.

| ·EQUIPMENT | ·SOLO SPORTS | ·FOOTWEAR | |
|---|---|---|---|

## 800-426-4840 • REI

**REI.com**

Founded as a consumer cooperative back in 1938, Recreational Equipment, Inc. was primarily created as a means for a group of friends to get quality climbing gear on the cheap. Well, now they can hook you up as well. An extensive store, with loads of great stuff, it's probably best used to find gear for climbing, camping, hiking and snow sports, but they have got way more to offer in all manner of outdoor gear, and great informative articles. If you tend to buy lots of this stuff, you'll want to sign up for membership in the cooperative, whereas everybody stands to benefit from their outlet store.

| ·WINTER SPORTS | ·OUTDOORS | ·KIDS | ·FOOTWEAR |
|---|---|---|---|

## 877-426-9464 • Ringside.com

**RingSide.com**

This site is all about boxing. Whatever your weight class, however unpolished you skills, you can find here plenty of training materials to step up your fight, along with medical gear to repair busted lips, close cuts and reduce swelling. Categories like Gloves, Headgear, Handwraps, Jump Ropes, Mouth Guards, Heavy Bags, Light Bags, Cornermen's Supplies and Boxing Rings should give you plenty enough reason to check this one out, assuming you like to scuffle a bit. Be careful, though, buy a lot and Don King may take an interest.

| ·FITNESS | ·FOOTWEAR | ·EQUIPMENT | |
|---|---|---|---|

## 888-606-5279 • Riverwire.com

**RiverWire.com**

What we've finally stumbled across here is a user-friendly fly-fishing site. You can browse for flies by the type of fish you're after, get some fantastic looks at the lures and then pay great prices for them. The rest of your rig should benefit as well, whether shopping by brand or category for rods, reels and lines; all feature plenty of options and, again, good prices. Add to the mix stuff like waders, small boats and plenty of old and new-fashioned tools, including computer software that prints topographical maps of virtually every fishing spot in the US (contiguous or otherwise). Good site.

| ·WATER SPORTS | ·OUTDOORS | ·SOLO SPORTS | |
|---|---|---|---|

## 800-636-3560 • Road Runner Sports

**RoadRunnerSports.com**

They claim to have well over one million items available to sell, which sounds like a lot, especially given that they specialize almost entirely in running shoes. To be honest, though, we lost count somewhere in the mid-thirties, so we're gonna take their word for it. Surely, they have a whole lot of shoes, in all the major brands, and at great prices too. What's better (or rather, just as good) is that the navigation here is top rate, as is the search functionality. You can also compare shoes side by side, read runner-friendly articles and take a tour through their interesting Endangered Shoes section, which is full of old designs and dwindling supplies. This is a wonderful shop.

| ·FOOTWEAR | | | |
|---|---|---|---|

# RugbyImports.com

Rugby Imports • 800-431-4514

Since we are talking about rugby, the word "imports" here seems redundant. Nevertheless, you should be easily able to track down a selection of balls, training equipment, apparel and some protective gear, which will minimize bruises and breaks even as you reap the scorn of hardcore enthusiasts domestically or abroad. According to the proprietors of the site, "the future of e-commerce and the rugby industry looks promising." Whatever— you must really be an enthusiast to appreciate this one.

| ·EQUIPMENT | ·FAN GEAR | ·FOOTWEAR | ·TEAM SPORTS |
|---|---|---|---|

# Ruggers.com

Ruggers.com • 877-784-4377

"Ruggers" is sort of a cutesy name for the not-so-cutesy sport of Rugby, to which this site owes an unwavering devotion. As such, you'll find plenty of appropriately ugly shirts here, as well as fan gear for teams most of us probably haven't even heard of. Prone to deliver product descriptions like "Hi cuts are worn by players who require maximum ankle support, usually props and hookers" to rate things like boots, tackle bags and scrum machines (whatever those are), it's difficult to say whether this site paints a scarier than necessary picture of this tough-guy sport, or whether it's entirely understated the matter.

| ·EQUIPMENT | ·FOOTWEAR | ·TEAM SPORTS |
|---|---|---|

# SaddleSource.com

Rick's Heritage Saddlery • 800-336-3882

This site has a sometimes maddeningly inconsistent ordering system, at times too difficult even to mess with (especially with regard to their selection of Used Saddles, which would otherwise be the best thing going). However, they also have a great, deep and wide selection of horse riding gear and apparel, from bridles and stirrups to snaffles and other rare things only riders have heard of. You can also get great looks and product descriptions, and the patient rider will tell you it's a wonderful site. We, however, will just tell you that it's there and you can take a look if you like horses.

| ·EQUIPMENT | ·SOLO SPORTS | | |
|---|---|---|---|

# SailNet.com

SailNet • 800-234-3220

This comprehensive boating site goes deep, very deep. Some from its extensive list of categories actually have up to three levels of subcategorization, and there's plenty to choose from all the way. Thus, this selection ranges from Anchors and Sextants to the more obscure Pintles & Gudgeons, Flanged Spade Connectors and Stanchions & Rail Fittings. Fortunately, for those of us who are confused by such language, this site also offers buying guides, articles and resources, so that none are left adrift in a sea of confusion. More like a sea of comfort, actually, as sections like Galley or Cabin & Cockpit play more to a home decorator than a hearty seaman.

| ·WATER SPORTS | | | |
|---|---|---|---|

**800-641-0500 • Salamander**                    **SalamanderPaddleGear.com**

The proprietors of this site are "dedicated to exploring and preserving our natural environment." Preferably via kayak. While they don't actually seem to sell kayaks online, they do have stuff like straps that'll tie one onto your back for hiking purposes. This, combined with an entire section focused on Safety Gear highlights just how rough, tough and simply crazy this outdoors sport can be. But a good look at their list of accessories and apparel makes it sound kind of fun too, and as they donate a portion of all proceeds to preservation groups, we have got to give them props.

| ·WATER SPORTS | | | |
|---|---|---|---|

---

**866-752-3266 • Skateboard.com**                    **Skateboard.com**

Referring to its home page as the Frontside, this site does what it can to live up to its tremendous domain name, mostly by offering a very thorough and detailed selection of decks and hardware from a very wide selection of popular (and even some relatively unknown) brands. Their Shoes and Wearables selections are significantly less complete, though will still prove valuable at least to less discriminating shoppers. Ultimately, this is a pretty cool site, but mainly because skateboarding is pretty cool to begin with.

| ·EQUIPMENT | ·SOLO SPORTS | ·FOOTWEAR | |
|---|---|---|---|

---

**800-784-0540 • Skiboards.com**                    **SkiBoards.com**

If you haven't heard of skiboards, also known as snow skates, it's only because they haven't been around for very long. Essentially, they combine the maneuverability of skiing with the versatility of snowboarding. Shorter than normal skis, and double-tipped (they can go both ways), they're said to be much easier to learn than those other snow sports, enabling even novices to attempt performing tricks with a reduced risk of injury. So if you prefer to hang back in the lodge, nursing a broken leg, drinking hot chocolate and incurring the sympathy of passers-by, you'll be out of luck with this one.

| ·EQUIPMENT | ·WINTER SPORTS | ·FOOTWEAR | ·SOLO SPORTS |
|---|---|---|---|

---

**800-950-1994 • Soccer.com**                    **Soccer.com**

The busy home page of this retailer with an obvious specialty showcases featured products, international news and league headlines; everything but its incredibly large and thorough selection. Behind all the bright colors sit more cleats and indoor boots than we would have thought existed. Then there're pads, guards, balls and socks, plus an entire section devoted to Goalkeeping and a whole inventory of replica jerseys for national, club, women's and major league teams. Just ignore everything, select the Shop link and enjoy the ease offered by the best soccer retailer online.

| ·EQUIPMENT | ·FAN GEAR | ·FOOTWEAR | ·TEAM SPORTS |
|---|---|---|---|

## SoccerStore.com

SoccerStore.com • 800-566-5536

This soccer niche retailer offers plenty in the way of equipment and protective gear... but we've seen it done better. However, when it comes to fan merchandise, these guys are unsurpassed, featuring replica jerseys for international club teams (including various European and Latin American leagues), national teams, local major league teams and special UEFA and World Cup gear. You may not see this stuff as commonly as NFL or MLB merchandise, but you should; simply from an aesthetic viewpoint soccer is better.

| ·EQUIPMENT | ·FAN GEAR | ·FOOTWEAR | ·TEAM SPORTS |
|---|---|---|---|

## SonomaOutfitters.com

Sonoma Outfitters • 800-290-1920

You might not automatically look to California's wine country for sturdy outdoor gear, but, then... here we are. These guys operate a massive brick-and-mortar store, so big it actually takes up two buildings. This means it may actually be easier to shop online, as the pages are simply laid out, and navigation pretty easy to follow. They provide a good range of excellent gear, most of which can't seem to shake a sense of style. It's the perfect place to shop if you are trying to impress a bear or out-dress a park ranger.

| ·EQUIPMENT ·SOLO SPORTS | ·WATER SPORTS ·FOOTWEAR | ·OUTDOORS | ·KIDS |
|---|---|---|---|

## Speedo.com

Speedo • 888-477-3336

Their name is synonymous with those super-tiny, ultra tight men's bathing suits that most men tend to not want to wear. But this site offers a lot more than that; namely, similar suits for women. We kid. While, yes, their selection of suits run from streamlined (for racing) to sturdy (for active swimming), generally you can find plenty of useful gear here for a number of fitness activities, like running or cycling. Last but not least, of course, would be the great selection of goggles, with which you can see just how well those suits fit underwater.

| ·WATER SPORTS ·FOOTWEAR | ·FITNESS | ·KIDS | ·SOLO SPORTS |
|---|---|---|---|

## SportEyes.com

Sport Eyes • 888-223-2669

This retailer of "sports specific eyewear" will appeal to you on many fronts. Primarily, the fact that they offer prescription lenses for the myopic athlete should be enough, but then they'll try to sell you on the notion that you may "look cool while you play." Whether or not this is true, it's hard to complain about a range of products made specifically for ball sports, cycling, fishing, diving, snow sports, swimming and more. Ironically, the layout of their categories makes it hard to see where the actual products come in. Squinting should help.

| ·EQUIPMENT | | | |
|---|---|---|---|

## No Service Number • SportsFair.com

### SportsFair.com

The scope of this sports equipment megamart is said to be "far beyond the familiar sports and activities." While they definitely have the gear for popular games like basketball, baseball and golf, the intriguing selections are in categories like Archery, Badminton, Gymnastics, Inline Hockey, Yolf, Nok Hockey and Walleyball. Yeah, we thought some of these sounded made up too. But that's the point, some of these are unlikely to turn up on any other single merchant's site, reason enough to check these guys out.

| ·EQUIPMENT ·TEAM SPORTS | ·WATER SPORTS ·SOLO SPORTS | ·FITNESS ·KIDS | ·REC ROOM |
|---|---|---|---|

## 800-441-0618 • Complete Sportswear, Inc.

### SportsTeam.com

Any given game, the difference between a team winning and losing can be answered by the question: who wanted it more? Well, traditionally, the art of inspiring motivation has been left up to squads of young ladies with pom-poms and short skirts— that's right, the cheerleaders. These spunky high flyers often don't get enough credit for their acrobatic athleticism, but it never seems to daunt them. Instead, they sometimes seem to view wearing the outfit as a reward in itself. Well, here's where you can get the outfit. Shoes, sweaters and megaphones complete the package, and though this site's ordering page is nearly as bad as it gets, it's tough to find some of this stuff elsewhere.

| ·FOOTWEAR | ·EQUIPMENT | ·TEAM SPORTS | |
|---|---|---|---|

## 800-448-8867 • Sports Tutor

### SportsTutorInc.com

On first glance, this might seem to be a store offering training videos and books on technique. Nothing of the sort. The sort of instruction you can find here is the kind you probably couldn't convince your best friend to give you: endless hours of practice. This site sells machines that'll help you practice sporting techniques over and over until you turn into an athletic machine in your own right. Baseball machines improve hitting or fielding, tennis machines improve backhand or forehand, volleyball machines can set up a spike every time and soccer machines can be made to fling balls at your head. Sadly, they don't seem to offer any machines to retrieve all of these balls when you're through.

| ·EQUIPMENT | ·TEAM SPORTS | | |
|---|---|---|---|

## 800-383-0305 • Springco Athletics

### SpringCoAthletics.com

So, if you've been looking at your backyard and thinking, "Maybe I should set up a pole vault back there…?" now you can. Throwing cages, javelins, hurdles, starter's blocks; this track and field specialist has just about everything short of a track to offer the running, jumping, throwing and leaping fan. That includes shoes and speed suits, as well as training materials and warm-up clothes (you know, for the style-minded). You can even get the necessary equipment to judge a photo finish. That could go in the driveway.

| ·EQUIPMENT | ·FITNESS | ·FOOTWEAR | ·SOLO SPORTS |
|---|---|---|---|

# SuperGo.com

Supergo Bike Shops • 800-326-2453

You can tell this is one of those companies that earnestly put a lot of time, money and planning into the creation of its site, with every intention of making it the best possible bike shop it could be. It's all right, too, with simple browsing and well-presented bikes, components, apparel, accessories and safety gear. Actually, there doesn't seem to be anything wrong here at all, other than the fact that they have a lot of strong competition. Still, a bicycle enthusiast should be able to get out of it exactly what he/she is willing to put in.

| ·CYCLING | | | |
|---|---|---|---|

# SwimToWin.com

SwimToWin.com • 650-328-8561

Competitive swimming finds good representation with this niche retailer. It offers an assortment of goggles, fins, suits, caps, nose clips, earplugs and training materials for those who get their kicks in the water (sorry about that). Browsing is far from ideal, though, as you must wade through a list of text-links within each category, forced to view product images one-by-one (especially frustrating when you don't turn up what you're looking for). Lest you think there is no fun to be had here, though, they do include a Water Toys section.

| ·FITNESS | ·WATER SPORTS | ·KIDS | |
|---|---|---|---|

# TackleDirect.com

Tackle Direct • 888-354-7335

This is a fantastic fishing site. Right away the categories are split between Saltwater, Freshwater and Fly Fishing, which helps more than other online fishing retailers seem to know. The browsing capability lags a bit, as each menu selection offers you merely a text-list of products split by brand, but when you actually get through to the products themselves, the looks and details are exquisite (you'll probably want to open product-links in a new window and keep them open for comparisons). Top it off with flies good looking enough that we almost went for 'em, and it's good enough not to miss.

| ·OUTDOORS | ·WATER SPORTS | ·SOLO SPORTS | |
|---|---|---|---|

# TeamArena.com

Arena • 877-882-7362

Here's a high gloss swimmer site that has a lot of suits for men, women and children, ranging from competitive powerskins to your fitness basics. Then there are plenty of goggles, training equipment, swim caps and even some water polo gear (mostly balls, and suits that can't be ripped off). But this isn't a site we're listing strictly for selection— some very simple navigation and bright design makes this a pleasant, if nearly blinding, online experience capable of making you a stylish swimmer as well as a fast one.

| ·WATER SPORTS | | | |
|---|---|---|---|

**888-276-1727** • the tenniscompany.com

## TennisCompany.com

This is less than ideal in terms of websites, but if you're a tennis freak you certainly won't have any trouble in finding what you need. With even a good selection of tennis socks, the only possible drawback in regard to the gear and apparel sold here is that it's primarily organized by brand, but there's not really enough to make it an issue. The best part is that, despite the fact that there is a good variety of used racquets for sale here, some of the new racquets actually make for the best deals.

·EQUIPMENT   ·SOLO SPORTS

**800-883-6647** • Tennis Warehouse

## TennisWarehouse.com

About as big as you'd expect a store with the word "warehouse" in its name to be, this tennis-specific shop has got a huge and varied selection in anything from balls to shoes to racquets and then some. The navigational menus are actually long enough that you have to scroll down the home page to view them all, which will be preferable to singling out the noisy featured deals that comprise the rest of the page. And, as chances are you will find several racquets you might want, you can opt in for a demo program to try them out a bit before you buy.

·EQUIPMENT   ·KIDS   ·SOLO SPORTS   ·FOOTWEAR

**800-873-6072** • OuTek

## TheTentStore.com

We say it every fifty reviews or so, but there's nothing like a specialty store to set you up right. Finding the right tent for your needs is so incredibly easy here. For starters, categories like Solo, Backpacking, Family, Luxury Family, Screen and Truck Tents (these actually fit in a pickup bed) make it simple to differentiate between different varieties. Then you can further narrow the field by sorting different tent capacities, weight, floor areas and peak heights, so you can skip straight to the right shapes and sizes and be done.

·OUTDOORS

**800-999-1213** • Title Boxing

## TitleBoxing.com

This boxing site brazenly claims, "If we don't have it, you don't need it." They may be right. If not, we won't say anything, because these guys definitely do have a thorough selection of training equipment to help one become quite proficient at beating the snot out of people. While, sure, foremost among this selection is padded gloves and other protective gear, there's also weightlifting equipment, heavy bags and cornermen's supplies (the stuff used to treat contusions and abrasions, presumably caused by someone donning those same padded gloves). A great site for the violent, we'll just go ahead and say, in this context, they're unbeaten.

·EQUIPMENT   ·FITNESS

## Title9Sports.com

Title 9 Sports • 800-342-4448

Frustrated by sports gear that didn't fit right because it had been designed for men, the founder of Title Nine Sports wanted to establish a place where a woman could find athletic apparel that suited the needs of her body's shape and size. The result is a perfect match for active women. A great selection of workout shorts, shoes, tanks and pullovers are easy to find here, all designed for women to suit a variety of sports. This also may be the best place anywhere to buy a sports bra, as they're split based on size and circumstance, with a barbell ratings system to let you know how well other women have enjoyed a particular model.

·FITNESS ·FOOTWEAR

## TourLineGolf.com

Tour Line Golf • 800-530-5767

Before you buy a set of clubs elsewhere, we'd recommend that you check your purchase against this site first. See, among their selections of woods, irons, wedges and putters, which are generally similar to and as complete as those of other online pro shops, these guys offer fantastic deals on used clubs. Having undergone "rigid inspections," these used clubs are guaranteed, so if the brand you seek is of quality, you can expect these to be in good shape. Come to think of it, you can just shop here first.

·EQUIPMENT ·SOLO SPORTS

## TrailFood.com

Trailfood.com • No Service Number

Utilizing some of the freeze-drying techniques enjoyed for decades by astronauts, you just know these light and easy-to-pack meals are going to be the most appetizing thing on the trail. Actually, their liberal use of the word "gourmet" doesn't seem entirely far-fetched when you glimpse a list of their menu items, like Blueberry Cobbler, Honey Mustard Chicken and Chocolate Fudge Mousse. Of course, Breakfast #1 reminds you that this stuff was never prepared in a master chef's kitchen, but it seems ready to serve in a pinch, or at least when you're really hungry and tired from a day of rugged trekking.

·OUTDOORS

## TrailFoods.com

Enertia Trail Foods • 877-363-7842

Specializing in "practical foods for wilderness travel," consisting of "meals with [that] great 'home dried' taste," this site's probably already making your mouth water, huh? To be certain, this trail food isn't just granola. Maybe it'll sound better if we give you samples of this easy-to-pack-and-carry-and-eat-all-without-refrigeration menu: bulgar, chowder, chili, soup, stroganoff, mush. Trust us, when you've been hiking for eight hours and it's a choice between their Sierra Scramble and those infamous red berries, you'll dig into this food like it's sweet ambrosia (do not eat the red berries!).

·OUTDOORS

## 800-643-3629 • Travel Country Outdoors

**TravelCountry.com**

This site has a lot of equipment for outdoors activities like kayaking, climbing, hiki—okay, so far as we're concerned, it's all about the kayaking. Not only do these guys offer a variety of kayaks for different occasions (Did you even know there were different occasions?), but they have plenty of other equipment with which to accessorize the kayak. For the most part, this seems to include gear that'll keep all of your stuff dry in the face of frothing white rapids, but there are some paddles too (to help you get through the sharp rocks sprinkled between the rapids). A good site for tough stuff.

| ·WATER SPORTS | ·OUTDOORS | ·FOOTWEAR | |
|---|---|---|---|

## 888-246-4453 • Uncle Dan's

**UncleDansOnline.com**

Don't make any snap judgments about this site's customer service. When you come across the words, printed in big red letters, "Get out and stay out!" they're simply referring to the great outdoors. See, this Chicagoland retailer "specializes in outdoor equipment and clothing for any adventure." Basically, whatever harsh and/or barren landscape you're heading toward (even if it's just Chicago), this gear can help you weather the worst, with enough camping equipment to get an army across the Alps without the help of elephants.

| ·EQUIPMENT ·FOOTWEAR | ·OUTDOORS | ·KIDS | ·SOLO SPORTS |
|---|---|---|---|

## 800-551-8220 • Upper Deck Store

**UpperDeckStore.com**

The signatures of the greatest athletes on the planet don't come easy or cheap. Actually, wait a second— they come easy, as evidenced by this shop which features autographed photos and souvenirs owing to the likes of Tiger Woods, Randy Johnson, Jerry Rice and Michael Jordan. Expensive is the word, though, especially given the number of legendary figures here (like Larry Bird, Hank Aaron, Jim Brown, Jack Nicklaus and Julius Erving). Hey, if it was this easy to find and cheap as well, what would be the point?

| ·FAN GEAR | | | |
|---|---|---|---|

## 800-676-7463 • eSpikes

**VenueSports.com**

The big question posed by this retailer of cleated shoes (also apparently known as eSpikes.com) seems to be: What do you use your spikes for? These "hard to find shoes and spikes" are primarily for track and field events, including Sprint Spikes, Jump Spikes, Distance Spikes, Multi-Event Spikes and Throw Spikes (you wear them while you throw other things). We couldn't tell you the difference between most of these, which is why we appreciate that these guys make it easy.

| ·SOLO SPORTS | ·FOOTWEAR | | |
|---|---|---|---|

## VoiceOfDance.com

Voice Of Dance • 415-460-5150

If you're wondering where to pick up the uniform of choreographed dance— leg warmers and leotards— look no further than this site, "where dance lives…." Aside from dancer-friendly articles, community boards, a calendar of events and news, the Store section of the site offers plenty in the way of apparel, shoes, music and videos. Men can find dance belts and women may find wispy skirts, and while there's not a lot of any one thing (they may not have the gear you desire for a performance), there's plenty to find here for practice, practice, practice; which, of course, is how you get to Carnegie Hall.

| ·KIDS | ·FOOTWEAR | | |
|---|---|---|---|

## WalkingShop.com

Walking Shop • 800-636-3560

Here is the self-proclaimed "World's Largest Walking Store." Ha ha, no the store itself doesn't walk, rather it sells walking shoes, accessories and apparel (which includes gloves, for some reason). It can be surprising the number of different types of walking shoes that actually exist, but here they are; off road, casual, cross training, street—complete with replacement insoles, reflective clothing and sunglasses. Because despite what anybody might try to tell you, you can't walk without the proper gear.

| ·FITNESS | ·FOOTWEAR | | |
|---|---|---|---|

## WestMarine.com

West Marine • 800-262-8464

If Gilligan had had access to this store, he still probably would've screwed everything up, and not made it off the island. Any moderately proficient boater, on the other hand, should be able to make the most of this "Boating Supply Source." With all kinds of important stuff like rope by the foot, bilge pumps, anchors, engine parts and fasteners, bolstered by all kinds of simply fun stuff, like downriggers (for fishing), water skis and skin-diving gear, it's hard to find complaint here. They even have a good stock of small boats, and can help you secure a loan in order to buy a big one, Skipper.

| ·WATER SPORTS | | | |
|---|---|---|---|

## Wickers.com

Wickers.com • 800-648-7024

Of all the specialty retailers listed in this section, this is the one we'd least likely expect—its devotion is to "high performance underwear for active people." Lightweight or heavyweight, for men and women, this may seem funny at first but if the alternative is wearing Victoria's Secret to climb a mountain, you can sign us up. The secret here is a material called Awatek, which apparently uses the same mystical technology found in a thermos: it keeps you warm in cold weather and cool when it's hot out. This is just what happens when you apply rocket science to your skivvies.

| ·FITNESS | ·OUTDOORS | | |
|---|---|---|---|

## 800-949-7245 • Wind Surf & Paddle Sports

**WindSurfingSports.com**

The first city to pop into mind when thinking about water sports usually isn't Houston, Texas, but that's where this windsurfing, wakeboarding, skimboarding, surf and paddlesports retailer is headquartered. Their selection is wider than it is deep, and browsing is set up by brand name, which for most of these products won't mean much to most of us. However, these guys are unique in that they offer gear for kiteboarding, which is sort of like windsurfing, only with a parachute. Good enough for us.

| ·WATER SPORTS | | | |
|---|---|---|---|

## 800-356-4953 • Wingset

**WingSet.com**

To be sure, whether you're hunting ducks, deer or rabbit, they don't really give a hoot how well you're dressed. On the other hand, if you're the sort to demand classy attire no matter how woodsy the environment, this is the site for you. Offering hunting gear for the high falutin', this site has designer European apparel, hand-crafted duck decoys, stunning boots, splendid fishing tackle and even some special gun cases, among assorted other items. There's no saying the best-outfitted hunter will reap the benefits of fashion, but sometimes it's just better to look good than to shoot well.

| ·OUTDOORS | ·EQUIPMENT | | |  |
|---|---|---|---|---|

## 800-999-3756 • WorkoutWarehouse.com

**WorkoutWarehouse.com**

Here you will find workout machines of various designs, consisting of a variety of popular brands. With treadmills, skiers, climbers, stationary bikes and strength training stations, for starters, it should be a simple matter of determining what physical attributes you'd like to work on (body parts, stamina, weight, etc.) and picking that machine which best suits your needs. Sure, this isn't the way nature intended you to exercise, but those of us who live in cities tend to know very little of what nature wants.

| ·FITNESS | ·EQUIPMENT | | | ⊙ |
|---|---|---|---|---|

## 541-383-0696 • WorldWaters.com

**WorldWaters.com**

It's tough to say which fishing site listed in these pages is best, but this one's at the very least close to it. Its vastly thorough collection falls into the following categories: Bass Fishing, Salt Conventional [fishing], Freshwater Conventional, Fly Fishing, Fly Tying and a Travel section that is amazingly appealing. The one big drawback is that you have to navigate various submenus to get to the products, but this is just testimony to how deep this store's selection can be. Take your time—here it's done right.

| ·WATER SPORTS | ·OUTDOORS | | | |
|---|---|---|---|---|

## WrestlersExpress.com

Wrestlers Express • 800-759-8326

This is not a pretty site, but then, wrestling is not a pretty sport (bear in mind, we're talking about the collegiate, Greco-Roman style, not the fake, jive-talking brand you see on TV, which is actually quite pretty at times).  Mostly, this selection is about singlets, the clingy, efficient uniforms of the sport, which can be found here in Reversible, Custom and Clearance sections.  Then there is some training gear, nutritional/weight loss stuff, protective gear and mats.  It's not great, but like most niche sellers, it gets the job done.

| | ·FOOTWEAR | ·EQUIPMENT | ·SOLO SPORTS | |
|---|---|---|---|---|

## WWSport.com

Worldwide Sport Supply • 800-756-3555

With this site, we come across the unlikely union of wrestling and volleyball, the two and only sports represented by this unusual specialty store.  Each is served moderately well, with the shoes, protective gear and apparel relevant to each sport, as well as balls and nets for volleyball.  The site design is definitely lacking, and it's not a terribly thrilling store to visit, but what the heck: we're going to go ahead and proclaim this to be absolutely the best volleyball and wrestling combined specialty store online or anywhere.

| | ·EQUIPMENT | ·FOOTWEAR | ·TEAM SPORTS | ·SOLO SPORTS |
|---|---|---|---|---|

## YogaZone.com

Yoga Zone • 800-264-9642

From a series of New York City yoga centers comes this dealer of meditative aids.  They offer a great selection of mats (both good looking and comfortable for your rump) and clothing (because it's tough to escape the confines of physical reality if you're not wearing a stylish/sexy top), but even more they offer books, videos, gongs, incense and décor to make your meditative space complete.  Even if you're not seeking the spiritual aspect, you may find plenty of gear here for massage, power yoga and even pilates, which is as hard to explain as it is to pronounce properly.

| | | ·FITNESS | | | |
|---|---|---|---|---|---|

# Stationery & Gifts

Let's get something straight—just about anything can be made into a gift … on the right occasion. Birthdays, anniversaries, retirements and weddings—the list of occasions goes on. More important, there are many different types of recipients. For example, when bestowing a gift upon someone you don't know very well, you may want to buy something simple (like a gift basket) without putting much time into it. Other times, flowers are more appropriate, just to let someone know you're thinking of them. At times you'll want your gift to be extravagant, memorable, personal and truly appreciated.

We've kept all these instances in mind while assembling this section, sure to include everything from the unique/creative gifts to the time-tested, anonymous stand-bys. We've considered the other end of the gift-cycle too—after all, when someone gives a present to you (even if it's one of those obligatory standards) it's only in good grace to reciprocate with a thank-you note or card. That's where the *Stationery* half of this section comes in. From sappy, premanufactured greeting cards to those you design yourself, even personalized multiple mailings may be handled with ease, at a click of the mouse.

This includes invitations or announcements as well. Or, maybe you just want custom letterheads to display your name or monogram on correspondences. What? You don't write letters since you discovered email? Well, maybe if you had personalized stationery and wax seals you'd start again. Actually, you can find pretty much all mail-related items you'd care to, and a pretty decent amount of office supplies too (pens aren't just great gift ideas). Really, there's a lot in here, so much so you may not know where to begin. We'd recommend you start by sending yourself a box of chocolates.

NOTES:

_____

_____

_____

_____

_____

_____

_____

_____

_____

_____

_____

_____

_____

_____

_____

_____

_____

_____

TIPS ON BUYING STATIONERY & GIFTS ONLINE

These suggestions may help prevent frustration and disillusionment.

•**THOUGHTFUL GIFTING:**  There are quite a lot of gifting standards, and this book can help you find a gift quickly and easily. Use key words like Romantic and Creative to find selections of interesting and appropriate alternatives to old stand-bys like flowers and gift baskets.

•**GETTING IT THERE ON TIME:**  Bear in mind that oftentimes even overnight delivery might not get a gift to its recipient on time (due to late day orders and processing delays).  If you want to make sure the gift you send arrives on time, you should probably order it at least a few days in advance (early-birds can probably have a gift sent to arrive on a specific day). Delivery times vary by site, but for true last minute orders, look for the Gift Certificate icon, as most of these sites offer email gift certificates that can be delivered electronically within a matter of minutes.  Sure, the recipient will know that it was a last minute effort, but they won't mind so much if you send them shopping with a great online merchant.

•**GIFT RECEIPTS:**  Obviously, it's a bit gauche to send a gift with the receipt included in the box, but most of these sites offer to include a gift receipt with the item even if they do not offer gift wrapping.  A gift receipt doesn't include the price of an item, but enables the recipient to arrange easy returns and exchanges should there be any problems related to size, color, defective parts or anything otherwise unsatisfactory.

•**STATIONERY PROOFS:**  Personalized stationery is a popular feature offered by several of the sites listed here, and using the web-integrated software solutions of these sites usually works well to get you the look you want on your invitations, announcements or letterheads.  However, there's always a big chance for error when computers are in the mix, so take up these sites on their offers to send you a proof copy of your stationery before they complete the full order.  It will take a bit longer to get everything, but you won't be stuck paying for a stack of misprints.

>> SITES THAT MAY COME IN HANDY

The following URLs may be useful when you shop.

Flower Giving Conventions: http://www.sunmoments.com/toknow-flowers.html
Anniversary Gifting Conventions: http://www.elegantanniversary.com
Giftwrapping Instructions: http://www.craftsnhobbies.com/nmem/categories/birthday-crafts/how-to-giftwrap.html
Keep Track of Special Dates: http://www.lifeminders.com
Locate Addresses: http://www.switchboard.com

>> **SECTION ICON LEGEND**

Use the following guide to understand the rectangular icons that appear throughout this section.

### CONFECTIONS

From boxes of chocolate to tins of hard candy, there is plenty in the way of gift-boxed sweets, including handcrafted pastries and candied fruits and nuts.

### FLOWERS

You already know when it's appropriate to send flowers; with this icon you can find the flowers without hassle.

### GIFT BASKETS

Strictly speaking, the gifts offered by these sites don't always come in baskets. However, the concept remains the same: a bunch of thematically linked gifts bundled together, usually with some kind of bow attached.

### PERSONALIZATION

Want to make sure your gift is not returned? Slap the person's name on it. This icon will point you to plenty of monogramming/engraving options, but in most cases applies to various stationeries.

## >> LIST OF KEY WORDS

The following words represent the types of items typically found on the sites listed in this section.

### CANDLES/SCENTS

The sorts of gifts you can smell through the wrapping paper, it's a little tough to know how good a scent is online, but there's plenty of variety and some delightful sounding names.

### CARDS

Thank you cards, note cards and the ever-popular greeting cards comprise the selections available at sites marked by this key word; some may be personalized.

### CREATIVE GIFTS

These are some gifts that would be appealing to creative people; stuff like kits and instruments requiring a development of skill.

### HOUSEWARMING

These shops offer serviceable to excellent selections of the sorts of gifts you might bring to a housewarming... assuming you've already decided against wine.

### MEMORABILIA

For that special soul who likes to be reminded about those special occasions, items on these sites might recollect some popular cultural events, people and places.

### OFFICE SUPPLIES

From staples to staplers, if it can be squeezed into an office, you'll probably find it in one of these shops, usually manifested as office superstores.

### ROMANTIC

What constitutes Romantic is purely subject to opinion. In our opinions, sites listed under this key word offer gifts that may please your partner.

### STATIONERY

As we see it, stationery includes loose paper, photo albums, journals, cards and anything else that may be written upon with ink.

### TCHOTCHKES

There's no easy way to describe the variety of trinkets represented by this key word, other than to mention that this is what you'll find anytime you enter a store labeled 'Gift Shop.'

### WRAP/MAIL

In some cases these key words will lead you to wrapping paper, sometimes mailing supply, oftentimes both.

## >> KEY WORD INDEX

Use the following lists to locate online retailers that sell the Stationery & Gifts you seek.

### CANDLES/SCENTS

CandleMart.com
CandlesForever.com
CocoonOnline.com
DavenportHouse.com
EssenceDeProvence.com
FireLight.com
GalleryAtTheCreek.com
GoodCatalog.com
Gumps.com
Illuminations.com
JapaneseGifts.com
LadyPrimrose.com
MorningFarm.com
RareCandles.com
Sensia.com
TheBeautifulLife.com
VillageCandle.com

### CARDS

AmericanGreetings.com
AnnouncementsAndMore.com
Bloomin.com
CardStore.com
CardSupply.com
Celebrate-It.com
ChelseaPaper.com
CollageCatalog.com
CurrentCatalog.com
GiftsIn24.com
GreatArrow.com
Gumps.com
Hallmark.com
KatesPaperie.com
MWoodStudio.com
ShagMart.com
Sparks.com
Studio-Z.com
ThePersonalTouch.com

### CONFECTIONS

akaGourmet.com
Bissingers.com
CollinsStreetBakery.com
CookieBouquet.com
CrazyBouquet.com
FortnumAndMason.com
Godiva.com
Kabloom.com
Sees.com
SharisBerries.com
Sparks.com

### CREATIVE GIFTS

Bloomin.com
BotanicalPaperworks.com
BroadwayNewYork.com
CollageCatalog.com
Discovery.com
ExposuresOnline.com
FlaxArt.com
FoundObjects.com
GiftSongs.com
GreatClubs.com
HomeTownFavorites.com
JapaneseGifts.com
Levenger.com
LunarEmbassy.com
LynGaylord.com
MagneticPoetry.com
McPhee.com
ModernArtifacts.com
MousseShop.com
NostalgicImpressions.com
PhotoWow.com
QuincyShop.com
SFMusicBox.com
SharisBerries.com
SofaGarden.com
StarRegistry.com
StickerPlanet.com
UncommonGoods.com
Woodendipity.com
ZipperGifts.com

### FLOWERS

24Roses.com
BBrooks.com
CalyxAndCorolla.com
FlowerOriginals.com
Florist.com
FlowerBud.com
Flowers-International.com
FortnumAndMason.com
FTD.com
GiftTree.com
GoodCatalog.com
Hallmark.com
HarryAnd David.com
HawaiianTropicals.com
Kabloom.com
OrchidSelect.com
ProFlowers.com
SendAnOrchid.com
Sparks.com

### GIFT BASKETS

AAAFruitBaskets.com
AbbottsGiftBaskets.com
akaGourmet.com
BarrelsOfFun.com
CajunTreats.com
CookieBouquet.com
CrazyBouquet.com
DavenportHouse.com
FortnumAndMason.com
FTD.com
GaGaGifts.com
GiftBasketsX.com
GiftTree.com
GoodCatalog.com
HarryAndDavid.com
HillarysGifts.com
MorningFarm.com
ProFlowers.com
RedEnvelope.com
StarTreatment.com
YouGotA.com

### HOUSEWARMING

BarnesAndWagner.com
CocoonOnline.com
CSPost.com
DavenportHouse.com
DecorLine.com
FireLight.com
FoundObjects.com
GalleryAtTheCreek.com
GoodCatalog.com
Gumps.com
HarryAndDavid.com
Illuminations.com
JapaneseGifts.com
LightImpressionsDirect.com
MichaelCFina.com
MorningFarm.com
MousseShop.com
MuseumCompany.com
ObjectsOfEnvy.com
RedEnvelope.com
Ross-Simons.com
SofaGarden.com
Stylocracy.com
SupplyCurve.com
TheBeautifulLife.com
UncommonGoods.com
VintageVending.com
Vivre.com
Wedgwood.com
ZipperGifts.com

### MEMORABILIA

BroadwayNewYork.com
CSPost.com
McPhee.com
VintageVending.com

### OFFICE SUPPLIES

Bittner.com
CollageCatalog.com

ColoradoPen.com
Cross.com
DecorLine.com
DolphinBlue.com
FranklinCovey.com
Levenger.com
Lizell.com
OfficeDepot.com
PenExpress.com
Personalizations.com
Personalize.com
Staples.com
TheRoyalStore.com

## PERSONALIZATION

AbbottsGiftBaskets.com
AmericanGreetings.com
AnnouncementsAndMore.com
ArtfulGiving.com
BarrelsOfFun.com
Bittner.com
BotanicalPaperworks.com
CardStore.com
CardSupply.com
ChelseaPaper.com
CollageCatalog.com
ColoradoPen.com
Cross.com
CurrentCatalog.com
CurrentLabels.com
DreamPapers.com
ExposureOnline.com
FamilyLabels.com
FineStationery.com
FloralOriginals.com
FranklinCovey.com
GaGaGifts.com
GiftsIn24.com
GiftSongs.com
GiftTree.com
Hallmark.com
HarryAndDavid.com
HillarysGifts.com
KatesPaperie.com
MousseShop.com
MWoodStudio.com
MyGatsby.com
ObjectsOfEnvy.com
PaperStyle.com
Personalizations.com
Personalize.com
PhotoWow.com
SFMusicBox.com

StarRegistry.com
StarTreatment.com
ThePapery.com
The PersonalTouch.com
YouGotA.com

## ROMANTIC

24Roses.com
CSPost.com
GiftSongs.com
HawaiianTropicals.com
JapaneseGifts.com
LunarEmbassy.com
MichaelCFina.com
Personalize.com
PhotoWow.com
SFMusicBox.com
StarRegistry.com

## STATIONERY

AnnouncementsAndMore.com
BotanicalPaperworks.com
CardSupply.com
Celebrate-It.com
ChelseaPaper.com
CollageCatalog.com
CSPost.com
CurrentCatalog.com
CurrentLabels.com
DecorLine.com
DolphinBlue.com
DreamPapers.com
FineStationery.com
FlaxArt.com
FranklinCovey.com
FredFlare.com
GiftsIn24.com
GiftsOfGratitude.com
GiftWrap.com
Gumps.com
Hallmark.com
HillarysGifts.com
JapaneseGifts.com
KatesPaperie.com
KozoArts.com
LeDesktop.com
Levenger.com
MuseumCompany.com
MWoodStudio.com
MyGatsby.com
NostalgicImpressions.com

OfficeDepot.com
PaperStyle.com
Papivore.com
QuincyShop.com
ShagMart.com
Smythson.com
Staples.com
Studio-Z.com
SupplyCurve.com
ThePaperCatalog.com
ThePapery.com
ThePersonalTouch.com
TheRoyalStore.com
UncommonGoods.com
Vivre.com
WeArePaper.com

## TCHOTCHKES

BarnesAndWagner.com
CocoonOnline.com
CrystalGiftsAndMore.com
CSPost.com
CurrentCatalog.com
DecorLine.com
FortnumAndMason.com
FoundObjects.com
GoodCatalog.com
Hallmark.com
HillarysGifts.com
JapaneseGifts.com
Lizell.com
LynGaylord.com
McPhee.com
MichaelCFina.com
MousseShop.com
MuseumCompany.com
ObjectsOfEnvy.com
Personalize.com
RedEnvelope.com
Ross-Simons.com
SFMusicBox.com
Stylocracy.com
SupplyCurve.com
TheBeautifulLife.com
UncommonGoods.com
Vivre.com

## WRAP/MAIL

APEC-USA.com
ArtfulGiving.com
BrassPack.com
CollageCatalog.com
CurrentLabels.com
FamilyLabels.com
FredFlare.com
GiftsOfGratitude.com
GiftWrap.com
KatesPaperie.com
OfficeDepot.com
PaperMart.com
R-N-W.com
ShagMart.com
Staples.com
ThePaperCatalog.com
TheRoyalStore.com
USPS.com
WeArePaper.com

## 24Roses.com

24Roses.com • 877-873-6324

A dozen roses is the standard, so why bother, as the name would suggest, doubling it? Well, these guys offer a good incentive; decent prices for twelve, astoundingly better prices for twenty-four. However many you choose to send, you'll get free shipping and a variety of colors to choose from. You can even opt to include some lilies and tulips while you're at it. However, as these guys will remind you, "Roses Whisper What Words Cannot Say." Whatever—you know why you're sending them; this place merely makes it easy.

| ·FLOWERS | ·ROMANTIC | | |
|---|---|---|---|

## AAAFruitBaskets.com

AAA Fruit Baskets • 800-741-8521

These crafty fruit basket specialists know that they'll be among the first you encounter when looking through alphabetic listings to accommodate your gift giving needs... and we've played right into their hands! You may choose between Elegant, Colossal and Grande baskets including bananas, apples, pineapples, grapes and/or whatever else might be fresh. Except for the fact that they don't offer delivery on major holidays or Sundays (the traditional fruit-giving day, is it not?), these guys are a perfect solution to your seed-bearing gift basket needs.

| ·GIFT BASKETS | | | |
|---|---|---|---|

## AbbottsGiftBaskets.com

Abbott's Gift Baskets • 800-741-8521

Okay, it seems like nobody else is going to say it, so we will: there are really very few practical uses left for baskets in modern urban life. However, fill them with candies, fruits, cured meats, cheeses, soaps, wines and other sundry items and you have a lovely gesture all wrapped up and ready to bestow upon strangers, friends or acquaintances alike (however, we'd recommend finding something else to give your romantic interest). This site's got them all, for a plethora of occasions and for a price befitting even enemies.

| ·GIFT BASKETS | ·PERSONALIZATION | | |
|---|---|---|---|

## akaGourmet.com

a.k.a. Gourmet • 800-735-3284

Having trouble finding the right gift? Well, it's a good bet that whomever it is you're trying to find a suitable present for enjoys eating. This site offers a lot of great food—chocolates, cookies, cheesecakes and truffles, for example—in gift form. It's pretty easy to browse by particular item, or by gift-giving occasion (if even the former proves too difficult), and many items are even available as last minute gifts, which may be exactly why you're having a hard time finding something in the first place.

| ·CONFECTIONS | ·GIFT BASKETS | | |
|---|---|---|---|

## No Service Number • AmericanGreetings.com

**AmericanGreetings.com**

You'll have trouble finding what you want on a page, you'll often be unable to use the Back button on your browser and you'll have to sign up for a full year of membership in order to buy anything. Bottom line, though, this site is good for one thing: last minute greeting cards. See, whereas other greeting cards will do you well if you're sending something through the mail, or have thought to order one in advance, with this site you can Create & Print a card right at your computer, meaning in moments you can have a card ready to sign and deliver. This site will undoubtedly frustrate you, but that's what you get for procrastinating.

| ·PERSONALIZATION | ·CARDS | | | |
|---|---|---|---|---|

## 800-753-1434 • Announcements and More

**AnnouncementsAndMore.com**

Half the fun of sending out invitations and announcements is choosing which invitations and announcements to send. As such, it never hurts to have another catalog of choices to browse through, and that's exactly what this site provides. There are also different typesetting styles, return address options and some personalization available. Otherwise, it's not the most efficient means of getting what you want, and some of the add-ons aren't terribly worthwhile, but if you can't find just the right card elsewhere, check it out.

| ·STATIONERY | ·PERSONALIZATION | ·CARDS | | |
|---|---|---|---|---|

## 800-221-9403 • American Printing & Envelope

**APEC-USA.com**

Who knew there was a company out there that specializes entirely in envelopes and similarly constructed mailing products? Well, get ready to meet the American Printing & Envelope Company, "New York's hottest envelope manufacturer." Their selection of mailers, boxes, vellums and glassine envelopes would seem to be enough, and yet they supplement it with mailers specifically suited to compact discs, photos, films and negatives. If only they'd make an envelope suitable to send cookies, we'd be all set.

| ·WRAP/MAIL | | | | |
|---|---|---|---|---|

## 888-274-9225 • ArtfulGiving.com

**ArtfulGiving.com**

Okay, how cool is this? These guys deal strictly in wrapping paper. While this doesn't sound terribly exciting on its own, when you factor in the fact that you can design the paper yourself, it suddenly gets much more interesting. You can add your own text messages to a number of predesigned patterns they offer, but the best bet is a feature that allows you to upload a digital image. Hence, your wrapping can bear a picture of your own face, your entire family, a picture of the gift itself (that'll blow their minds) or any other clever thing you can create, scan or download on your computer.

| ·WRAP/MAIL | ·PERSONALIZATION | | | |
|---|---|---|---|---|

## BarnesAndWagner.com
**Barnes & Wagner Gifts • 866-253-6560**

You've finally found it—"Your Source for Blenko Art Glass." Huh? These are lovely, colorful, hand-blown glass items; everything from vases and decanters to bowls and bubbles. There are also animal and plant shaped glass wares, indescribable aesthetic designs and some peculiar pieces that serve both form and function (like a glass hat that doubles as an ice bucket... actually, it doesn't really make a good hat). The perfect gift for people who like things that can break easily, here's your best glass bet.

| ·TCHOTCHKES | ·HOUSEWARMING | | |
|---|---|---|---|

## BarrelsOfFun.com
**Barrels of Fun • 800-536-7386**

Well, it appears these guys have come up with an innovative response to a burgeoning truth we are all, deep down inside coming to terms with: baskets are fairly useless items. Rather, they propose that you offer gift barrels instead. What? Yeah, barrels, not the wood slatted kind with iron rings that lunatics like to ride over Niagara Falls, but significantly smaller kinds that come with sealing lids and all manner of goodies inside. Find them here for every occasion, and you won't waste one ounce of wicker in the process.

| ·GIFT BASKETS | ·PERSONALIZATION | | |
|---|---|---|---|

## BBrooks.com
**B. Brooks • 888-346-3356**

Flower arrangements are easy. Classy flower arrangements? Not so easy. Unless you get them here: "When you order from these florists you are commissioning an aesthetic—a point of view." Okay, it's a little high-minded for most of us in need of flowers, but then, it keeps us from having to know flowers. See, these guys aim to serve those who "want honesty not contrivance in [their] floral arrangements... [who] understand that arranging with a subtle and graceful hand requires more talent than contrivance." Writing site reviews, of course, involves more contrivance than talent, but we'd rather not get into that.

| ·FLOWERS | | | |
|---|---|---|---|

## Bissingers.com
**Bissinger French Confections • 800-325-8881**

What's more enticing: an offer for a free pound of chocolate with the first purchase, a picture of chocolate dipped strawberries or the term "French Confections?" Well, all three greeted us when we encountered this site, the result being a chocolate feeding frenzy the likes of which should not be seen again. These guys are simply out to make you drool with talk of "luscious chocolate-covered fresh fruits, decadent truffles and hand-crafted chocolate confections." It's best that those with weak wills refrain from viewing the pictures; it's all just too much.

| ·CONFECTIONS | | | |
|---|---|---|---|

## 888-248-8637 • Bittner Fine Pens

**Bittner.com**

If you're tired of scrawling messages on post-its with disposable ballpoint pens, this is the site for you. Fine stationery, elegant journals and fantastic writing utensils capture "the pleasure of writing" on this site that forces us to re-examine the true quality of our laser color printers. Leather bound volumes, fountain pens, textured paper and personalized calligraphy mast-heads are just some of the highlights of the catalog, and just about everything looks worthy of buying in quantities of two....

| ·OFFICE SUPPLIES | ·PERSONALIZATION | | |  |

## 800-894-9185 • Bloomin' Flower Cards

**Bloomin.com**

Perhaps the perfect answer to fruitless greeting cards that will inevitably end up in a trash dump or recycling bin, this site offers a way to maintain the gift card tradition without any of the ecological uncertainty. See, these cards come filled with the seeds of wild flowers and other plants. Simply bury the card once it's served its purpose, and flowers will grow. It's not littering, it's replenishing nature. Especially good for those who're concerned with environmental issues (shouldn't we all be?), the site and the cards may not look great, but you can rest assured they are.

| ·CREATIVE GIFTS | ·CARDS | ·FLOWERS | | |

## 877-956-7393 • Botanical Paperworks

**BotanicalPaperworks.com**

If you're of the do-it-yourself mentality, you'll be thrilled to find some of the out-of-the-ordinary papermaking kits available on this site. Should you have neither the time nor energy required to do this, however, you can find a terrific selection of handmade stationery, envelopes and loose pages as well (made by professionals, not other customers). While their ordering functionality can be a bit frustrating, with so many pretty papers (infused with petals, leaves, grasses and such), there's little else to complain about.

| ·STATIONERY | ·CREATIVE GIFTS | ·PERSONALIZATION | | |

## 888-525-3357 • BrassPack Packing Supply

**BrassPack.com**

Save for a few dot-gov pages, there may not be a less glamorous site online than this seller of packing and shipping supplies. Boxes, tape, labels, envelopes, padding, bubble wrap—you can find a deep and wide selection of just about anything you'll need to send stuff safely through the postal system or into storage. Simply a collection of well-sorted pages with functionally listed pictures, dimensions and quantities, there is no sparkle or glitz, just the occasional incentive. For example, you get a free box shipped with every order!

| ·WRAP/MAIL | | | |

# BroadwayNewYork.com

BroadwayNewYork.com • 800-223-1320

Know a fan of the live theater? Or do they prefer "theatre"? Here either perception of the art form is celebrated, from musicals to comedies, actors or authors. Posters, mugs, shirts and magnets bear logo graphics pertaining to celebrated works, while programs, cast albums and other souvenirs remember particular casts and productions. These gifts will absolutely thrill that friend of yours who's always singing showtunes, reciting lines and referring to obscure performers. Of course, look here and you could always buy them tickets to a show....

| ·MEMORABILIA | ·CREATIVE GIFTS | | |
|---|---|---|---|

# CajunTreats.com

Cajun Treats • 888-772-2586

Every year around Mardi Gras, thousands of people descend upon the Big Easy for wild parties, great jazz and especially tasty food. But why doesn't anyone ever bring the fun to us? Well, gift basket maven Fran Mills aims to do just that, offering gift baskets, New Orleans style, for delivery anywhere. Go to Featured Baskets to see the selection, or customize your own using any of the items found in their Product Catalog. Packed full of Cajun sauces, seasonings, food and drinks, this stuff just barely meets the Post Office's limitations on mailing inflammatory items.

| | ·GIFT BASKETS | | |
|---|---|---|---|

# CalyxAndCorolla.com

Calyx & Corolla • 800-877-0998

First and foremost, when you give the gift of a floral bouquet, it should look impressive. These do, and not in a gaudy way, either. While the florists here match these classy arrangements with what seem to be the perfect pedestals and vases (according to the pictures), you are granted several options with each bunch, including optional vessels or no vessel at all (which will often be dependent on price). The second most important thing to consider when procuring a bouquet is the scent... you'll have to take their word on that one.

| | ·FLOWERS | | |
|---|---|---|---|

# CandleMart.com

Candlemart.com • 877-352-6353

Teaching us all a little bit about the potential of oils and molded wax, this candle-heavy site claims to be the largest online. We won't dispute this, as the lengthy all-text index of their items proved enough to try our patience, but suffice it to say that they have plenty of pillar candles, floating candles, jel candles, ball candles, votives and tealights to go around. While browsing can be a clicking drag, it turns out that each product benefits from enticing details and pictures—if they could download scents they'd be unstoppable.

| ·CANDLES/SCENTS | | | |
|---|---|---|---|

**800-316-4925** • CandlesForever.com

# CandlesForever.com

Aside from the subtle, romantically imbued lighting that just about all of them provide, there are two specific qualities worth looking for in a candle: beauty and aroma. The candles here look better than many, with elegant, understated holders and shapes to compliment a variety of scents. The scents? Well, if names like Baked Apple, Kiwi Pear, Rain Water, Winter Woods and Vanilla Spice don't sound appealing, we don't want to know what does. A lackluster design shouldn't prevent you, or your giftee, from enjoying these products.

| ·CANDLES/SCENTS | | | |
|---|---|---|---|

**510-595-6702** • CardStore.com

# CardStore.com

They've got myriad greeting cards for nearly every occasion, they have invitations and announcements for those times you want to let a bunch of people know about the important events in your life, just about every selection is available folded or as a postcard and they even go so far as to let you arrange a mailing to multiple addresses with personalized greetings (creating an online address book for your future mailings while they're at it), and [gasp] we haven't gotten to the best part yet. That would be the fact that you can upload any image you want for incorporation into any and all of these options. You can spend an entire day here, but you get what you pay for, there is no doubt.

| ·PERSONALIZATION | ·CARDS | | | Ⓟ |
|---|---|---|---|---|

**800-444-2273** • cardSupply

# CardSupply.com

With such event-specific categories as Casino Night; Mystery; Cocktails, Beer & Wine; Formal Fun and Mardi Gras, it's a safe bet your invitation needs can be met with this "Internet's Largest Selection." The same could be said about the announcements, stationery and personalized holiday greeting cards found here. In each section there are several options to choose from, and yet somehow there doesn't seem to be a whole lot of variety. Erring on the side of simplicity, little here makes for a lasting impression and yet it all somehow seems potentially perfect.

| ·STATIONERY | ·PERSONALIZATION | ·CARDS | | Ⓟ |
|---|---|---|---|---|

**877-439-5940** • Celebrate-It!

# Celebrate-It.com

Celebrate what? Whatever. These guys don't care, really; they just want to sell you invitations, announcements, thank you cards and other such stationery. They separate their wares into sections like Baby Showers, Birthday Parties, Graduation Announcements and the ever-mysterious More Stuff, each category offering a scant but appropriate selection. Truly, the spirit and the occasion is up to you; this site is only to be used as a tool, never as a substitute for actual enjoyment.

| ·STATIONERY | ·CARDS | | | |
|---|---|---|---|---|

## ChelseaPaper.com

The Chelsea Paper Company • 888-407-2726

A lot of custom invitation and announcement retailers get the job done, but here's one that does so with aplomb. A great selection of raw materials starts with several dozen occasion-specific categories full of several dozen brand name stationeries, featuring such particular events as adoption anniversaries, bat mitzvahs, wine tastings and commitment ceremonies. The great range of options (tending toward "elegant" far more often than "fun") comes complete with online "proof sheets" that allow you to view how the cards will look once you've contributed your own lines of text.

| ·STATIONERY | ·PERSONALIZATION | ·CARDS | |
|---|---|---|---|

## CocoonOnline.com

Cocoon • 800-842-4352

From a small shop in suburban Chicago comes this web site devoted to small house wares and bric-a-brac that wins one for the little guy. Their charming home décor selection is bolstered by a crazy variety of thematic coasters and an ever-intriguing Baubles section. While the site doesn't cater to your every whim and navigational need, it tries hard to make its tiny selection readily available (keep your eyes open for Next arrows—the catalog's not as tiny as it might seem).

| ·CANDLES/SCENTS | ·HOUSEWARMING | ·TCHOTCHKES | |
|---|---|---|---|

## CollageCatalog.com

Collage • 800-343-3529

Related to The Paper Catalog (listed elsewhere in this section), this store offers a decidedly more stationery-oriented selection of paper, as evidenced by their great selection of writing instruments. Albums, journals and writing sets abound, with a plethora of fine, sometimes handmade, papers to choose from. The bottom line here is that elegant correspondence can be yours, complete with the stuff to make wax letter seals, whether with initials or symbols like angels, clefs, stars and moons.

| ·STATIONERY<br>·CARDS | ·WRAP/MAIL<br>·PERSONALIZATION | ·OFFICE SUPPLIES | ·CREATIVE GIFTS |
|---|---|---|---|

## CollinStreetBakery.com

Collin Street Bakery • 800-292-7400

Even your cartoon-watching kids probably already know that the fruitcake is the perennial joke of all the gift foods, seemingly recycled year after year as nobody admits to eating them and most of us figured they stopped selling them decades ago. Well, if it turns out you actually are looking to buy one, whether for yourself or for another, here's the only place worth looking. With a wider than expected selection that actually promises to taste good, a fruitcake purchased here makes for something more than a gag gift.

| ·CONFECTIONS | | | |
|---|---|---|---|

## 800-766-7367 • Colorado Pen Direct

### ColoradoPen.com

This writing instrument retailer posits the question: "Ironic, isn't it, that we're employing civilization's highest communications technology (the internet) to promote one of the most ancient tools of communication?" To this we say: yes, yes it is. While each of the dozens of brands found here aren't available for online purchase, most are, and the sheer number of pens available is enough to keep you browsing for days. Best bet is to decide early on if you're after a ball-point, roller ball or fountain pen, then choose a price range, as the browsing isn't anything to write home about.

| ·OFFICE SUPPLIES | ·PERSONALIZATION | | | |
|---|---|---|---|---|

## 800-233-2171 • Cookie Bouquets

### CookieBouquets.com

What good are flowers, anyway? They do nothing for nobody. Okay, so maybe this is an utterly over-practical view of these popular gifts. However, be as it may that they please the senses; in time they die, leaving a sort of empty feeling inside. Well, it seems this site has just the thing for that emptiness: cookies. Complimenting the standard floral bouquet, or consisting of a bundle of cookies alone, it's interesting to speculate which item provides the most pleasure—each are known to elicit squeals when given properly.

| ·GIFT BASKETS | ·CONFECTIONS | | | |
|---|---|---|---|---|

## 877-551-1777 • Crazy Bouquet

### CrazyBouquet.com

What could be sweeter or more romantic than a perfectly comprised bouquet, featuring some of the greatest flowers nature has to offer? What could be more brightly colored? Well, how about candy wrappers. Offering a sugary variation on the classic bouquet, this small Oregon retailer assembles tooth-rotting assortments of popular name brand candies into livid expressions of congratulations, gratitude, well wishes and more. Simply click on Bouquets for the short list of options that could but won't last longer than the average lifespan of cut flowers.

| ·GIFT BASKETS | ·CONFECTIONS | | | |
|---|---|---|---|---|

## 800-722-1719 • Cross

### Cross.com

Mightier than the sword, and better than a Bic, Cross pens are the kind you keep around for awhile, the kind that improve your handwriting just by virtue of their quality. Don't get the wrong idea, though. These aren't the ludicrously expensive writing utensils you'd give as a graduation or retirement present. They're actually quite reasonably priced (except when compared to their disposable cousins), and they do the job about as well as any. The Store here offers a variety of different designs, and even offers personalization options, so they make good gifts after all; though you still may want one for yourself.

| ·OFFICE SUPPLIES | ·PERSONALIZATION | | | |
|---|---|---|---|---|

## CrystalGiftsAndMore.com

**Crystal Gifts & More • 866-279-7825**

Know somebody who's enamored of small crystal figurines? At the risk of addicting yourself to these hypnotic trinkets that come in all shapes and sizes, check out this site that offers a well rounded list of options. Between music themes, animal shapes, abstract designs, plants and cultural recreations you may be as surprised as we to see the level of craftsmanship and detail that go into these popular shelf-toppers. (You might equally like this selection if you just happen to enjoy smashing pretty things into prismatic shards).

| ·TCHOTCHKES | | | |
|---|---|---|---|

## CSPost.com

**CS Post & Co. • 888-419-2399**

Reviving the notion of the general store, these guys remember a time when Americans "depended on it for food, supplies and a neighborly news update." Well, this isn't exactly that kind of store, as you'll find none of these things, with the possible exception of the vaguely defined 'supplies,' here. What you will find, however, under Merchandise, is a semblance of style reminiscent of those days of yore. Explicitly found in Antiques, but spanning the entire general catalog you'll find home accessories, body & bath products and miscellaneous items of a certain classy appeal for old-timers and nostalgic folk alike.

| ·STATIONERY ·HOUSEWARMING | ·TCHOTCHKES | ·MEMORABILIA | ·ROMANTIC |
|---|---|---|---|

## CurrentCatalog.com

**Current USA, Inc. • 877-665-4458**

Here's a fine place for the gift giver on a budget. "Where staying in touch is affordable & fun," they offer various kinds of stationary, cards, knick-knacks, photo albums, scrapbooks, journals and then some. It's a bit slow, and it's tough to say that you could look through here and see stuff that you would go out of your way to procure for yourself, which isn't to say this is stuff you would not gladly receive for yourself as a gift. A little patience and an easy-to-please recipient and this one will do it.

| ·STATIONERY | ·PERSONALIZATION | ·CARDS | ·TCHOTCHKES |
|---|---|---|---|

## CurrentLabels.com

**Current Address Labels • 877-755-7940**

If you've actually taken the time to hand-write a letter, the last thing you want to do is further cramp your hand by writing a return address on the envelope. Swooping in to save you from carpal tunnel syndrome is this address stamp and adhesive label specialist that features a full crop of designs that'll add a bit of frivolity and self-expression to the absolute functionality of name, address, city, state and zip code. From pictures of puppies to American flag motifs, and some personalized stationery too, make sure you don't enter any typos when you order from this one.

| ·WRAP/MAIL | ·PERSONALIZATION | ·STATIONERY | |
|---|---|---|---|

**888-470-4950 • Davenport House**

**DavenportHouse.com**

Who knows what the English really give each other as gifts? Maybe American stuff? No matter—if you're going to give a gift to an Anglophile, you want it to at least seem very British. This "English Country Store" has no end of qualifying products, including some very properly English picnic baskets, plenty of serving ware for teatime, gift baskets featuring scones, gift baskets featuring shortbread and a bevy of scented bath & body items native to the United Kingdom. Better yet, you don't have to pay by the pound.

| ·GIFT BASKETS | ·CANDLES/SCENTS | ·HOUSEWARMING | |
|---|---|---|---|

**888-350-2651 • DecorLine**

**DecorLine.com**

Housewarmings, promotions, Mother's Day, Father's Day and weddings just got easier to shop for. An array of gift items can be found in these pastel pages, from decorative boxes and innocuous home accents to cigar accessories and office bric-a-brac. Just about everything here is tasteful, if not compelling. Which is to say that, while any of these items will make for a more than satisfactory gift, little here compliments a personal expression of style. Which makes it a good place to find something 'nice' or 'lovely' for somebody you don't know that well.

| ·STATIONERY | ·TCHOTCHKES | ·OFFICE SUPPLIES | ·HOUSEWARMING |
|---|---|---|---|

**800-889-9950 • Discovery Channel**

**Discovery.com**

You can give somebody something pretty; you can give somebody something sweet. But if that somebody's got a thirsty intellect and a hunger for knowledge, you'd do better to give that somebody something from this science and nature oriented mainstay. Based on the ever-popular Discovery Channel, home of the near-legendary animal documentaries, or "nature shows," you've probably seen Discovery Stores popping up in local malls or promenades. Inside you'll find amazing videos, nifty products and a wealth of fabulous knowledge. Go ahead; pick up something for yourself while you're there.

| ·CREATIVE GIFTS | | | |
|---|---|---|---|

**800-932-7715 • Dolphin Blue**

**DolphinBlue.com**

All these guys really ask is that we "Please be cognizant of the volume of paper being consumed on our globe." If you are ecologically aware, you will definitely appreciate this site, which exclusively sells recycled office supplies. Pretty much comprised of recycled and tree-free bulk printer paper, envelopes, Post-its, organizers, folders and recycled toner cartridges, this stuff all gets the job done, just without additional deforestation or land-fill dumping. Here's hoping they expand the operation.

| ·STATIONERY | ·OFFICE SUPPLIES | | |
|---|---|---|---|

· Stationery & Gifts ·

# DreamPapers.com
Dream Papers • 800-244-5232

Assorted, personalized stationery, invitations, napkins and coasters (yes, you read it correctly) await on this fanciful, simple-to-browse site. Start by clicking on the Dream Gifts link to view all the product headings. A variety of sizes and styles are available in an array of paper goods that include options like monogramming, both embossed and in raised print. Most are elegant, even those they refer to as "playful," so chances are your correspondence will show marked improvement in looks if not in grammar or substance.

| ·STATIONERY | ·PERSONALIZATION | |
|---|---|---|

# EssenceDeProvence.com
Essence de Provence • 402-423-6179

As big fans of the color purple, we could not resist mentioning this site, which has a peculiar devotion to lavender. Of course, their interest is in the flower, and in particular its distinctive scent. Here you may find lavender bath & beauty products (oils and cleansers), decorative items (wreaths) and gourmet foodstuffs, in many cases beautifully packaged and ready to present to a dear one. If it doesn't sound particularly enticing yet, consider this: everything's made of French lavender. Sounds better already, no?

| ·CANDLES/SCENTS | | | |
|---|---|---|---|

# ExposuresOnline.com
Exposures • 800-572-5750

Everybody loves pictures, right? They preserve all those important moments for the ages so we don't have to rely upon our rapidly degenerating, um, you know. Well, this site brings you "products... especially designed to safeguard irreplaceable memories." You'll find frames, albums, picture storage, displays and even mirrors so you can remember what you look like right now. We're not even getting into the "fun" options, like having a picture of your pet's face planted on a painting of a 17th century nobleman. Sound crazy? What if we told you this image could then be printed on a pillow? This one, you'll have to see for yourself.

| ·CREATIVE GIFTS | ·PERSONALIZATION | |
|---|---|---|

# FamilyLabels.com
Family Labels • 954-791-9122

This site simply offers cutesy family address labels that feature illustrated facsimiles of each of your family members. Including pets, and available in black and white or full color, the little cartoon heads will appear under your address on these self-adhesive labels. While it can be difficult to order, requiring you to write down the code numbers of each head as it applies, and then the colors required, should you want them, there's not much to the site, so it won't take you all day. Actually, even if you don't plan to buy anything, it's quite fun just to match the dozens of different heads they feature to friends and family, just for a lark.

| ·WRAP/MAIL | ·PERSONALIZATION | |
|---|---|---|

**888-808-3463 • FineStationery.com**

**FineStationery.com**

This is a great site to find, as they say, fine stationery. Traditional, old guard brands like Crane sit alongside somewhat more adventurous designs from the likes of Stacy Claire Boyd. All the letter sets, invites, announcements and etc. are very well laid out, making it easy to shop by occasion and/or for specific products. The only problem is, it's kind of a slow site, the sort of slow that makes you question the true value of technology. Of course, if the waiting gets to be too much; you can always shop here, then turn off your computer and return to the paper way of life.

| ·STATIONERY | ·PERSONALIZATION | | |  |
|---|---|---|---|---|

**800-821-7112 • Firelight Glass**

**FireLight.com**

These days, candles come in all kinds of wonderful shapes and colors. However, candles are flawed by design: through proper use, they melt away. The glass pieces offered by this site do it a step better—they light a room, but maintain their beauty and shape; these are oil lamps. Beautifully constructed, fill one of these with scented oil and it fills a room not only with shimmering light but also a lovely aroma. Really, it's up to you—give someone a gift that will break as soon as they use it, or give them one of these, which will only break if they drop it.

| ·CANDLES/SCENTS | ·HOUSEWARMING | | |
|---|---|---|---|

**800-343-3529 • FLAX Art & Design**

**FlaxArt.com**

This store, which resides in real life in San Francisco, bills itself as a place "where creative people shop." For our purposes here, though, we think of it as a place to shop for creative people. See, they focus on art and crafts supplies, for people hell-bent and/or serious about creative expression. This translates into some truly inspired gift sets. Take the following, for example: a Balloon Modeling Kit, a Microwave Flower Press, and a Make-Your-Own-Stickers Machine. We're not ashamed to say it: screw other people, we want some of this stuff for ourselves.

| ·STATIONERY | ·CREATIVE GIFTS | | |
|---|---|---|---|

**888-758-4141 • Floral Originals**

**FloralOriginals.com**

So far as pedigreed flower shops go, this one probably wins the prize. Having assembled floral designs for Academy Awards Show ceremonies and Presidential Inaugurations, Gregory Scotte's shop will line you up with some pretty snazzy arrangements. Use the quickshop pull-down menu feature to select the type of bouquet you'd like, or the sort of occasion you're seeking to bedizen, and they'll be delivered, free of any extra charges. Artistically composed, with attention to color and spatial relations, these flowers are meant to impress.

| ·FLOWERS | ·PERSONALIZATION | |  |
|---|---|---|---|

# Florist.com

Florist.com • 800-709-9622

As most online florist shops seem to be the same, we'll tell you that this one is a little bit different. Why is it different? Well, it's a little bit better. Not much, we don't mind mentioning, just a little bit. This has mostly to do with selection, decent pricing and a fairly well designed, browseable store. Of course, if it were perfect we'd tell you so, and there are advantages to shopping at other sites that we won't bother to bring up here. As to why it is that these guys feel the need to slightly surpass the bulk of their competition, we really can't say.

 ·FLOWERS

# FlowerBud.com

Flowerbud.com • 877-524-5400

For fresh-cut, gorgeous bunches of flowers, check out this site that culls buds from farms and nurseries in or around the Portland, Oregon area. A wide variety of flowers are available, each of them brimming with a simple, radiant charm (rather than made ostentatious by ribbons or balloons). Additionally, all bunches are cut to bloom shortly after arrival, so you can look forward to many days of aromatic beauty, especially if you follow the offered Flower Care Tips. Even if you're not terribly selective when it comes to flowers, these guys are, so you can count on high quality every time.

·FLOWERS

# Flowers-International.com

Flowers International • 888-705-9999

When these guys say "International," they mean it. Like, if you need to send flowers to somebody in Senegal, here's where you can do it. In fact, they serve any place where flowers may grow, which turns out to be on 6 continents and their surrounding islands (we'll forgive them for overlooking Antarctica, for obvious reasons). Choosing your flower arrangement is pretty simple: choose a continent, pick a country and select from the variety offered for that region. Just more proof that the internet is somehow making this world a little smaller.

 ·FLOWERS

# FortnumAndMason.com

Fortnum & Mason • 011-44-207-465-8668

From straight out of Piccadilly comes this London mainstay, which began its operation nearly three hundred years ago with the business of selling used candles. That's right, used candles. Well, you have to admire the salesmanship of such a venture, and assume that whatever product they have to offer must at least appear to be of some value. Actually, here you will find a lot of fancy gourmet food items and special teas & infusions, presented in exquisite packaging and as English as the name would allow.

 ·CONFECTIONS ·FLOWERS ·GIFT BASKETS ·TCHOTCHKES

## 888-777-1825 • Found Objects

### FoundObjects.com

Somewhere between funky and cute resides this gift-oriented retailer whose wares are generally too scattered and unconventional to warrant any useful categorization. This makes it a great place to look when you've hit the end of your rope and just don't have a clue what to get for that tough-to-shop-for loved one. Browsing will turn up stuff like Zen stationery, sushi candles, voodoo dolls (plus other helpful items for someone recently made single) and a "Get Lucky" kit (for that same person, once they're ready to mingle again). As it goes, browsing is the only meaningful way of finding anything, so just dive in and see what turns up.

| ·TCHOTCHKES | ·CREATIVE GIFTS | ·HOUSEWARMING | |
|---|---|---|---|

## 800-819-1812 • Franklin Covey

### FranklinCovey.com

If you like to clip, bind, fold, zip or slip things into leather books, bags, briefcases or wallets, this site has a bunch of stuff built to do all these things. A lot of it looks suspiciously alike, but they do offer an interesting feature to prove the differences. Namely, a Design Your Own binder platform gives you choices like the size, style, color, clasp and panel options (as in whether the flaps will contain zippers, folder pockets and/or pen sleeves). Put together your own PDA case, complete with a brass nameplate, or simply opt for an anonymous mustard yellow day planner; whatever keeps you organized.

| ·STATIONERY | ·OFFICE SUPPLIES | ·PERSONALIZATION | |
|---|---|---|---|

## 718-599-9221 • Fred Flare, Inc.

### FredFlare.com

You may need shades to view this bright and colorful site that offers equally bright and colorful paper products for the girl on the go (read: teenagers, and adult women who're funky enough to inspire teenagers). Wild stationary, disposable coasters and outrageous iron-on patches pretty much sum up the thematic concept of this stuff, which originated "off the back of a bike in Soho." You may not find a whole lot of stuff here, but the visit should leave you with a goofy grin, and should maybe not be attempted from the office.

| ·STATIONERY | ·WRAP/MAIL | | |
|---|---|---|---|

## 800-736-3383 • FTD

### FTD.com

Chances are, you remember these guys as the flower company endorsed by football legend Merlin Olsen. Reason enough to shop there, right? Interestingly enough, the "FTD" originally stood for "Florists' Telegraph Delivery" when the company was founded back in 1910 by fifteen florists who agreed to share out-of-town orders for faster and cheaper delivery. The name's since been changed to "Florists Transworld Delivery," to reflect the company's global capabilities, as well at the obsolescence of the telegraph wire. Either way, they sell flowers in bouquet form, "for every occasion."

| ·FLOWERS | ·GIFT BASKETS | | |
|---|---|---|---|

# GaGaGifts.com

GaGa Gifts • 323-653-3388

A relatively small selection of "gifts of whimsy," the "gaga" refers to this store's focus on baby-related gifts. Most products are imbued with a nostalgic air, such as cowboy-patterned blankets and a jack-in-the-box. Your best bet is to customize a gift basket, which makes for an excellent gift for a baby shower or toddler's birthday. Not quite what you'd expect from a retailer that's based out of a hip Los Angeles neighborhood, but it far and away gets the job done.

| | | ·GIFT BASKETS | ·PERSONALIZATION | | |

# GalleryAtTheCreek.com

Coldwater Creek • 800-510-2808

Small town tastes meet designer flair at this Idaho-based web site that actually features an exceptionally good selection of Gifts & Treasures (their description, but we could come up with none better). Each piece here is shown with excellent detail and a great product description, and the site design makes it easy to root around for the best stuff. Still, should you have any problems, instant gratification is on the way with online customer service reps that will respond to your pleas for help while you continue to browse. All this from a place that, according to the About Us section, is overrun with moose (plural). Who knew?

| ·CANDLES/SCENTS | ·HOUSEWARMING | | |

# GiftBasketsX.com

giftbasketsX • 800-443-8724

More like Gift Baskets A-Z, this site covers the gamut of thematically packaged gift items, accommodating different occasions with categories like Sympathy, Sports, Playful, Care Package and Get Well. Various baskets (and sometimes clever basket substitutions) include things like gourmet foods, spa items, coffee, wine and cocktail accessories. Additionally, finding one for a particular person is pretty easy, whether as general as a man or a woman, or as specific as a lover. With names like 'King of the Grill' and "Kama Sutra Lovers," these fulfill all of your gift basket desires.

| | ·GIFT BASKETS | | | |

# GiftsIn24.com

Gifts In 24 • 800-244-5232

The gist of this shop is that you'll receive your order within twenty-four hours, provided it's one of their "selected" items, and you've made your order before a certain hour, between Monday and Thursday. As far as the rest of it goes, they offer plenty of interesting stationery, including cards, invitations and napkins, and seemingly everything is available for personalization. Get it tomorrow, get it next week; that's really not the issue anyway, right? Ultimately, it's selection you really want, and here you'll find it.

| | ·STATIONERY | ·PERSONALIZATION | ·CARDS | |

## 800-914-4342 • Gratitude & Co.

### GiftsOfGratitude.com

These gift boxes aren't designed so much to express any huge gratitude—rather just to say, "Thanks for coming," or something along those lines. They're 3x3 inch boxes, printed or paper-wrapped, that may come with tea inside, or cookies, stationery or potpourri. It's the sort of thing that works perfectly if you're thanking a whole group of people, say for attending your lovely and lavish day party or reception. Scour through dozens of different imprints and designs, and either have them fill it and add an interior note for you, or just order the boxes and do the rest yourself.

| ·STATIONERY | ·WRAP/MAIL | | |
|---|---|---|---|

## 800-725-7664 • P.S. I Love You!

### GiftSongs.com

We think we may have found Air Supply, in case anybody on the planet was looking. This site offers an unusual and not in the slightest bit cheesy service: personalized songs for your loved ones. By personalized, we mean you can type in traits like the recipient's name (phonetically, so there are no snafus) and eye color (Blue, bedroom or shimmering?), and one of the site's dozens of original songs may be altered and recorded to suit a variety of people and occasions. This might work better as a gag gift than one in earnest, but let us tell you, gag gifts do not get any better.

| ·ROMANTIC | ·CREATIVE GIFTS | ·PERSONALIZATION | |
|---|---|---|---|

## 800-931-3620 • giftTree

### GiftTree.com

According to their site, these guys offer "the largest selection of gift baskets in the world." We're pretty thoroughly convinced. Their expansive catalog of items includes flowers, balloons, stuffed animals, wine, golf balls, barbeque tools, bonsai trees, candles, pastries, spa items and plenty of other stuff, all expertly packed together. Any occasion can be met, it would seem, and if you're not quite happy with any of them you can request one to be custom made. In the world of gift basketry, this store's a keeper.

| ·FLOWERS | ·GIFT BASKETS | ·PERSONALIZATION | |
|---|---|---|---|

## 877-625-8421 • Giftwrap.com

### GiftWrap.com

If you've been having trouble finding gift-wrapping supplies and designs by such renowned artists as Anne Geddes or Debbie Mumm, look no further than this specialty shop online. Boasting "one of the largest selections of quality gift wrapping paper, tote bags, ribbons, bows, photo albums, journals, greeting cards and stationery products" anywhere, these products will ensure that, even if the actual gift is of questionable value/taste, it will sure look better than the rest prior to unwrapping. From the goofy to the sublime, this one's legit.

| ·STATIONERY | ·WRAP/MAIL | | |
|---|---|---|---|

# Godiva.com

**Godiva Chocolatier • 800-946-3482**

One has to wonder what exactly these world-renowned chocolates have to do with their legendary nude equestrian namesake. Somehow, we doubt these chocolatiers want you to take the lead of the Lady Godiva's peasantry, who successfully resisted the temptation to witness her bareback ride. Quite the contrary, as these are some sweets worthy of indulgence, and they are in the business luring you to their rich and creamy middles with some smooth, flavorful milk and dark chocolates. At any rate, this site features an online guide to these storied confections... see if you can resist.

| ·CONFECTIONS | | | |
|---|---|---|---|

# GoodCatalog.com

**Good Catalog • 831-649-2489**

They say it's "the thought that counts," but somehow this only seems to hinder rather than help us select the right gift for somebody important. For those times when a simple gift basket or bottle of wine proves too impersonal, this department store styled gift center can help you find, as they say, "unique ideas for you and your home." You can sort categories by price, whether you're looking for lavish or inexpensive, and pretty much anywhere you look you're likely to find something that maybe you wouldn't have thought of yourself. Sure, it begs the question, "does the thought count if you came upon it through well-designed browsing techniques?" Whatever. Ultimately, it's the charge card behind the thought that really counts.

| ·FLOWERS ·HOUSEWARMING | ·GIFT BASKETS | ·TCHOTCHKES | ·CANDLES/SCENTS |
|---|---|---|---|

# GreatArrow.com

**Great Arrow Graphics • 800-835-0490**

Setting up shop in what used to be car factories, including that of the original assembly line product, the Model T, this company puts the spaces to decidedly more creative use. They've developed a slick collection of silkscreen greeting cards, featuring a wide variety for any major holiday or special occasion. But these aren't like your typical greeting cards that feature some silly sort of joke or an even funnier, hackneyed sentiment. Rather, these cards focus on artistically rendered graphic designs, meaning that they may actually be appreciated for more than a momentary viewing instead of barely noticed and cast aside.

| ·CARDS | | | |
|---|---|---|---|

# GreatClubs.com

**Clubs of America • 800-800-9122**

Sure, they love your gift immediately, and are grateful for a good couple of days. But then in almost no time at all they've forgotten how much you care. All right, it's not really like that, but check it out—this site offers you a small selection of monthly gift clubs. Just when they think the gourmet pizzas, microbrews, cigars, flowers or fine wines you've given them have run out, the following month another delightful selection shows up at their door, all year long. The only fear is that they'll get a little too used to it.

| ·CREATIVE GIFTS | | | |
|---|---|---|---|

## 800-436-4311 • Gump's

## Gumps.com

Founded in San Francisco, pretty much on the heels of the Gold Rush, this store could be looked at as a place set up for newly rich individuals to spend their gold. At least, this may explain the high quality of these classy and exotic gifts, which range from decorative items to cards and stationery. Actually, such as the selection is, it could probably suit a number of categories in this compendium, but each seems to look better on other people so we figured right here in the Gifts section it could do no wrong.

| ·STATIONERY | ·CANDLES/SCENTS | ·HOUSEWARMING | ·CARDS |
|---|---|---|---|

GC $$$ ✈ ◉

## 877-490-2355 • Hallmark

## Hallmark.com

More than merely a greeting card company and holiday manufacturer, this site offers all of Hallmark's products for purchase, whether they be flowers, stationery or those little trinkets known only as "gifts." Truly, though, greeting cards are the best reason to shop here, as you can customize fonts and colors, and personalize interior messages. It's especially good if you need to include multiple recipients (such as with thank you cards), since you can simply enter the necessary info and let them do the work for you.

| ·STATIONERY ·PERSONALIZATION | ·FLOWERS | ·TCHOTCHKES | ·CARDS |
|---|---|---|---|

GC $$ ✈ ◉

## 877-456-7700 • Harry and David

## HarryAndDavid.com

Looking for a good gift that a certain somebody isn't likely to receive elsewhere? How about pears? Yep, this tasty fruit may play second fiddle to apples, but that just makes their inclusion in this company's vast array of Gift Baskets, Gift Assortments (boxed items) and Gift Towers (stacks of boxed items) all the more special. There's also plenty more where these came from, with a non-pear variety of fresh fruits, gourmet cheeses and just about any other mouth-watering delicacy you might want to give someone or keep for yourself.

| ·FLOWERS | ·GIFT BASKETS | ·PERSONALIZATION | ·HOUSEWARMING |
|---|---|---|---|

GC ✳ $$ ✈ ◉

## 800-840-3660 • Hawaiian Tropicals Direct

## HawaiianTropicals.com

There are certain types of flowers that people expect to see: roses, tulips, sunflowers, violets and the dreaded carnations. This is a sure fire way to deliver flowers that will surprise and delight whoever is on the receiving end, with arrangements featuring beautiful tropical flowers from the Aloha State. Orchids and birds of paradise make their way into most of these bouquets, and the colors are magnificent. Either a good way to get out of trouble or into good graces; either way, it only gets better with these florals.

| ·FLOWERS | ·ROMANTIC | | |
|---|---|---|---|

$$$ ◉

## HillarysGifts.com
Hillary's • 800-742-6800

Whereas a lot of gift shops will just sort of scatter about products and leave it to you to pick something out, this store recognizes the needs of confounded gift hunters and organizes a host of perfect gifts for any occasion or individual, whether in a brilliantly contrived assortment of gift baskets or some of their more specifically elegant items. As a nice touch, they offer personalization services for many of these home and office trinkets, games, stationery and photo albums, and they won't mention to the recipient just how easy it was for you.

| ·STATIONERY | ·GIFT BASKETS | ·PERSONALIZATION | ·TCHOTCHKES |
|---|---|---|---|

## HomeTownFavorites.com
Hometown Favorites • 888-694-2656

Assembling a catalog of "Old-Time Favorites and Regionally Exclusive Foods," this site has definitely done something right. This is the kind of stuff city folk find "quaint" in rural areas, or that rural folk are surprised not to find in major metropolises. Or, it may just be stuff that has been around seemingly forever, but for some reason or another is tough to track down wherever you live. This proves to be an excellent manifestation of the internet, allowing us to stock up on those foodstuffs we've grown to miss, like Kenyons Clam Cake & Fritters Mix, Moxie soda or Booberry cereal. You're almost guaranteed to find delight in some of this stuff, whatever town you call home.

| ·CREATIVE GIFTS | | | |
|---|---|---|---|

## Illuminations.com
Illuminations • 800-621-2998

Candles come in many forms. On the one hand, there's the molded wax, no frill, straight up and down and tapered if you're lucky. On the other end of the spectrum resides these candles, which are designed to be given as gifts almost more than as a source of light. Lovely wax concoctions and holders populate the site along with the occasional fountain (so you have your choice of fire or water), all capped by some brilliant candle chandeliers. Crisp, clean and easy, this is the bright side of candles.

| ·CANDLES/SCENTS | ·HOUSEWARMING | | |
|---|---|---|---|

## JapaneseGifts.com
JapaneseGifts.com • 817-226-4387

As good as many gift sites are, there's still always going to be a few stinkers dispersed among any store's catalog. This site, on the other hand, is virtually automatic. Maybe it has something to do with the longstanding Japanese design tradition that highly values an elegant, austere beauty, or perhaps the proprietors of this one just have an exquisite eye for great Japanese products (whether kimonos, lanterns, woodblock prints, shoji screens or tatami mats). Either way, it doesn't matter; you could shop here blindfolded and you would still find the perfect gift. Don't miss it.

| ·STATIONERY ·CANDLES/SCENTS | ·TCHOTCHKES ·HOUSEWARMING | ·ROMANTIC | ·CREATIVE GIFTS |
|---|---|---|---|

**800-522-5666** • **KaBloom**　　　　　　　　　　　　　　　**Kabloom.com**

Keeping it simple, keeping it lovely, keeping it pretty darn cheap; this easy to overlook floral delivery site probably deserves more of your attention than you're willing to give. These are flowers, after all, and when flowers are of acceptable quality and maturation they're going to be pretty much the same wherever you get them (in other words, try as you might you'll find no designer flowers). From the standby of roses to a less-typical selection of non-flowering plants, these guys will satisfy without a bang.

| ·FLOWERS | ·CONFECTIONS | | |  |

---

**888-941-9169** • **Kate's Paperie**　　　　　　　　　　　　**KatesPaperie.com**

Putting a little character into personal stationery, invitations and writing journals, this site works simply, if not pristinely, and makes up for any shortcomings with a handy quick-jump menu located at the bottom of most pages (don't miss it). Styles range from elegant to stuff that'll make your kids giggle, and many of the writing sets, invitations and announcements are available for monogramming. The greatest stuff, however, can be found in the Paper section, which offers different colors, sizes, patterns and materials.

| ·STATIONERY | ·WRAP/MAIL | ·CARDS | ·PERSONALIZATION | 𝓟 |

---

**415-351-2114** • **Kozo Arts**　　　　　　　　　　　　　　　**KozoArts.com**

Everybody knows a gift means more if you make it yourself. But the next best thing is if the gift was handmade by somebody else. The photo albums, invitations and journals offered here consist of handmade papers bound with silk to create the most exquisite of stationery gifts. To look at one of these journals, for example, is enough to not want to write in it, for fear that a slip of the pen will ruin something precious. Somebody, at least, put a lot of effort into these creations, and that's a gift that's sure to please.

| ·STATIONERY | | | |

---

**888-382-7673** • **Lady Primrose's**　　　　　　　　　　　　**LadyPrimrose.com**

This site states: "Each of us desires more, but seemingly time does not allow. It is simply a mental adjustment to realize that luxury comes in moments claimed for yourself both within and around you." Of course, then they turn around and offer a whole catalog's worth of luxurious gift items. Mostly spa and bath & body products, along with every other imaginable fragrant product, this stuff looks like it was designed to please the gods on Mt. Olympus, so if your intended recipient has absurdly high standards, these will serve in those luxurious moments.

| ·CANDLES/SCENTS | | | |

# LeDesktop.com

**Le Desktop • No Service Number**

You don't except a web site that sells strictly paper to be cool, or even interesting. And yet, this one definitely is. First of all, the variety of blank pages, note cards and translucents here, while limited, is ultimately quite appealing. Better yet, there are some ecologically sound alternatives to paper culled from fresh tree pulp. Not just standard recycled fare either (though, there are some great, quality recycled papers for sure). In the Tree Alternative section you'll find paper made all or in part from bananas, seaweed and the recycled ingredients of beer.

| ·STATIONERY | | | |
|---|---|---|---|

# Levenger.com

**Levenger • 800-545-0242**

This "Tools for Serious Readers" site actually caters as much to the writers of words as it does those who digest them. Plenty of pens, inks, notebooks and desk accessories go with selections of lighting, desks and chairs to make the writing process comfortable if not fruitful. Errant personal accessories add to the selection, stuff like money clips and watches which have little to actually do with literacy but look good when being revealed by the unfurling of wrapping paper. Either way, good stuff for the word junky in your life.

| ·STATIONERY | ·OFFICE SUPPLIES | ·CREATIVE GIFTS | |
|---|---|---|---|

# LightImpressionsDirect.com

**Light Impressions • 800-828-6216**

If every picture is worth a thousand words, sorting through the accumulated images of a lifetime must be the equivalent of reading the unabridged works of Stephen King: a scary prospect. Thanks to this site's devotion to "archival supplies," things like photo albums, slide storage, scrapbooks and portfolios can make the job of preserving and retrieving your precious photographic memories a lot easier. You can even find some good matting and framing options (for the best shots) and plenty of slide accessories.

| ·HOUSEWARMING | | | |
|---|---|---|---|

# Lizell.com

**Lizell • 800-718-8882**

Need to get something for that special little executive in your life? This site will do the trick. Dozens of quality desktop items—basically the kind of stuff that can distract the office inhabitant from work even if just for a moment—populate this site in various sections, most easily accessed through the handy Gift Ideas link. The best shopping here will be found in the Pen & Ink category, which is replete with great fountain pens, ball-points, rollerballs, mechanical pencils and multifunction pens that consolidate your options. Or, you can just shop by brand name.

| ·TCHOTCHKES | ·OFFICE SUPPLIES | | |
|---|---|---|---|

## 800-586-2729 • Lunar Embassy

**LunarEmbassy.com**

Okay, if somebody tried to sell you an acre of property on the moon, you'd probably call in the straightjackets. On the other hand, call it a gift and it suddenly becomes a romantic gesture, to be cherished for the ages. Well, there's no way to tell how it will all play out when human-kind finally does get around to colonizing outer space, but the proprietors of this site stake a legal claim, by some such authority or another, to the selling of extraterrestrial acres for about $15–20 per. And it's not just the moon, either; you can also buy acreage on Mars, Venus and Io (one of Jupiter's moons). What do you really get? A certificate of ownership and astral coordinates. Truly, this is a gift to behold from afar.

| ·ROMANTIC | ·CREATIVE GIFTS | | |

## 203-853-3264 • Lyn Gaylord Accessories

**LynGaylord.com**

The ornate metal work found on this site works well as a gift, whether in cufflink, belt buckle or vanity mirror (compact) form. Inspired by 19th century European objets d'art, these pieces come shaped like animals or carved with illustrious scenes and landscapes, in nearly all cases silver. These are the sorts of things you're likely to find in Beverly Hills boutiques, which, as it happens, is where they're typically found. To some, this distinction will increase the value of the gift. To these guys, it nearly always does.

| ·TCHOTCHKES | ·CREATIVE GIFTS | | |

## 800-370-7697 • Magnetic Poetry

**MagneticPoetry.com**

Chances are, you've seen magnetic poetry on the refrigerator of a friend and spent a good ten minutes or so scouring the little magnetic tiles for the right words with which to piece together your magnum opus. You then demand that everybody reads your collage of (mostly) adjectives, and insist the owner never alters their order to preserve it for the ages. Of course, it doesn't work that way. Well, here, you can get all the tools to conquer your own refrigerator's blank spaces, or clutter somebody else's, including extra kits featuring words particular to romance or Shakespeare, or other fun magnetic design games (there are a lot).

| ·CREATIVE GIFTS | | | |

## 425-349-3009 • Archie McPhee

**McPhee.com**

Perhaps one of the most hilarious web sites you'll shop from this year, these "Outfitters of Popular Culture" come equipped with some of the most outrageous, kitschy and irreverent novelty items you'll find anywhere. From classics like the Groucho Marx nose-and-glasses disguise to such joyously blasphemous products as the Jesus Christ Action Figure, this site will either anger or entertain you, sometimes both simultaneously. A semblance of style may be uncovered in products like a Leopard Print Flask; on the other hand, none is entirely evident in the full-body Gorilla Suit. Good stuff.

| ·TCHOTCHKES | ·MEMORABILIA | ·CREATIVE GIFTS | |

## MichaelCFina.com

Michael C. Fina • 800-289-3462

There are gifts, and then there are gifts. This site specializes in the latter, with presents you don't just haphazardly dole out to friends, at least, unless your bank balance is written in stanzas. Very high-end merchandise, starting with picture frames and ending somewhere in the stratosphere with items we don't even want to tempt you with, fills these pages with categories like Gifts for Him, Gifts for Her and Entertaining to guide you. This site is a must see for people who're about to attend a cocktail party thrown by, say, the Queen of England. The rest of us may want to skip it.

| ·TCHOTCHKES | ·ROMANTIC | ·HOUSEWARMING | |
|---|---|---|---|

## ModernArtifacts.com

ModernArtifacts.com • No Service Number

Bearing what it describes as "a collection of design-oriented objects for the home, the office and for personal use that have been chosen for the quality and uniqueness of their design," some of the products here are head-scratchers, and some simply make you gasp. All prove to inspire some level of interest, though, and should make great gifts for the stylish individual, the sort of person who might find a calculator dull if it's not constructed of fluorescent, transparent, curved plastic. Sound intriguing? Wait until you see what they do with a simple radio.

| ·CREATIVE GIFTS | | | |
|---|---|---|---|

## MorningFarm.com

Catskill Morning Farm • 845-439-4900

If you're looking to give some rustic, country lovin' folk a nice how-do-you-do, Catskill Morning Farm Online might be up your creek. Sort of the answer to the question, "What if a farm had a gift shop?" these guys promise to bring, "the best of the country to your home." Between the birdfeeders, antique gardening tools and a kazoo for the kids, the quaintness of this catalog is off the charts. Then there are organic foods, all-natural bath products and crooked pottery, all putting a fine polish on the air of clean, fresh, rural living. Well if that don't just beat all....

| ·GIFT BASKETS | ·CANDLES/SCENTS | ·HOUSEWARMING | |
|---|---|---|---|

## MousseShop.com

Mousse • 888-330-5550

What could make better gifts than "unique and/or practical things?" Truly, this stuff is interesting if nothing else, comprised of such a variety of products as to defy categorization. At least, they haven't tried to categorize these inspired designs, which include lighters, personalized jewelry, lunchboxes, bags, stationery, thongs (the kind that go on feet) and towels. Browsing page after page of this scattered merchandise can be a drag, but it's rewarding enough as these items prove that human beings can even make air fresheners look cool.

| ·TCHOTCHKES | ·CREATIVE GIFTS | ·HOUSEWARMING | ·PERSONALIZATION |
|---|---|---|---|

877-305-7201 • **MuseumCompany.com**

**MuseumCompany.com**

You don't typically expect the words "Museum" and "Company" to be seen together. Likewise, you don't typically expect Van Gogh's celebrated painting, Starry Night, to show up on a cutting board. And yet, here we are. See, this site specializes in selling great artwork that has been incorporated into every day items. Hence, Frank Lloyd Wright coasters, Monet-infused umbrellas, and M.C. Escher ties. Not all items feature the work of artists; some simply embrace the style of a past era, like the modern AM/FM Stereo housed in a replica 1930's radio. In any case, lovers of kitsch, or the obsessive devotees of great art, should enjoy surrounding themselves with such unexpected fare.

| ·STATIONERY | ·TCHOTCHKES | ·HOUSEWARMING | |
|---|---|---|---|

800-721-5935 • M. Wood Studio

**MWoodStudio.com**

Graphic designer Melissa Wood won't deny that her work on this catalog of invitations and announcements sort of relies heavily upon the styles of her favorite era, the 1960's; actually she pretty much makes this clear on the opening page. The important thing to understand is that she's referring to the swinging sixties, not the hippie counterculture kind we most prominently remember. Hence, her style has more to do with "the real Vegas" than love beads and suede fringe, which makes for a much more appealing selection, we surmise. There's not much here, but it's a lot of fun.

| ·STATIONERY | ·PERSONALIZATION | ·CARDS | | 🅟 |
|---|---|---|---|---|

888-997-7899 • MyGatsby.com

**MyGatsby.com**

For those of us who never considered that pastels might be blinding, here comes what may very well be, as the ownership claims, "the largest selection [of invitations] online." It's not so much that the gentle looks or genteel stationery on this site in themselves are hard on the eyes. However, with this many choices in what amounts to a single product type, there's really little chance of avoiding a long session of staring at your computer screen as page after page of traditional to contemporary designs float by, especially when you consider personalization options. The easy-to-use Advanced Search filter can help, but like an umbrella in a hurricane, it can only do so much.

| ·STATIONERY | ·PERSONALIZATION | | | 🅟 |
|---|---|---|---|---|

No Service Number • Nostalgic Impressions

**NostalgicImpressions.com**

Are you ready to write letters, old school? Email may have usurped most of the post office's basic business, but one look at these items may inspire you to embrace snail mail once again. For starters, they offer you all the supplies you need to address your letters with a wax seal. You can find initials, as well as symbols like a peace sign, heart, shamrock, yin-yang, lips and many more. Then there are quill pens, as well as other fancy writing tools, and fragranced ink in which to dip them. Even your most dreadful communications will now look incredibly cool.

| ·STATIONERY | ·CREATIVE GIFTS | | |
|---|---|---|---|

## ObjectsOfEnvy.com

Objects of Envy • 866-866-3689

To some, fuel for the argument that our nation owns excessive wealth. To others, a lovely way to drop a dime. We're talking about crystal, glass, porcelain and enamel boxes and figurines, which may be found here in abundance. Shop the categories Murano Glass, Fine Crystal, Extraordinary Glass, Extraordinary Pottery or Limoges ("only porcelain made in the west-central Limoges region of France can be honored with the name Limoges") and find a wealth of trinkets made exclusively for people who like trinkets.

| ·TCHOTCHKES | ·PERSONALIZATION | ·HOUSEWARMING | |
|---|---|---|---|

## OfficeDepot.com

Office Depot • 888-284-3638

For setting up a home office, or just even taking care of stuff like getting envelopes and glue for taking care of day-to-day personal business, these guys promise it all in easy order. In fact, you may even find more than you bargain for, as they offer a whole lot more than merely office supplies, and each category item will lead you to multiple subdirectories, requiring several clicks before you can get a look at most products. They also mandate registering for a password before buying, which we hate, so shop here with an incentive in mind or look elsewhere first.

| ·STATIONERY | ·WRAP/MAIL | ·OFFICE SUPPLIES | |
|---|---|---|---|

## OrchidSelect.com

Orchid Select • 800-430-0133

"For those of elegance… for those of sophistication… for those of passion… for those of style… for those who appreciate the finer things," say the introductory pages. Let's just leave it at this: here's a site for those who bear a little patience. Focusing on what is perhaps the most exotic floral arrangement you'll find, these flowers pretty much live up to the hype. As always they're lovely to look at, and it's tough to go wrong in ordering these as a gift, romantic or otherwise. Really, it's just a matter of choosing from a variety of saturated colors and spidery stems.

| ·FLOWERS | | | |
|---|---|---|---|

## PaperMart.com

Paper Mart Packaging Store • 800-745-8800

Whether or not you want to send something with love is up to you; if you want to send it in a way that it won't break en route, or be subject to the exploratory hands of a corrupt postman, check out this site. Boxes, packaging tape, cushioning (like Styrofoam peanuts) and wrappings are in high supply here, alongside labels, envelopes and gift wrapping that'll enable you to mail stuff with better care than some of the stores featured in this book. Scroll to the bottom of the home page for a more complete menu, or you'll miss out on a lot they have to offer.

| ·WRAP/MAIL | | | |
|---|---|---|---|

## 888-670-5300 • PaperStyle.com

### PaperStyle.com

Whether you're planning a beach party, barbeque, wine tasting, cocktail party or clambake, you'll be able to find the appropriate set of invitations on this slow but well put together site. Even if you're looking for some regular stationery, you will find a great big selection of elegant and/or campy stuff, in most cases easily personalized for no extra cost. But most of these resources are devoted to announcements and invites, and it shows (with options like RSVP envelopes included). In fact, browsing might just inspire you to throw more parties.

·STATIONERY    ·PERSONALIZATION

## 212-334-4330 • Papivore

### Papivore.com

They tell us that a papivore is a "paper lover." Well, creative naming is always a plus, and while it may constitute irony that such a person might look to find paper in an electronic format, these guys do well to satisfy both your parchment lust and your sense of style. While there are no categorical distinctions between stationery, composition books, fancy pens, vellum sheets, gift boxes nor any other specific items, there are only a few pages of products, so browsing all of them is no great undertaking, and worth it for this fully functional and exquisitely neat selection.

·STATIONERY

## 888-598-3278 • PenExpress

### PenExpress.com

Countering the conventional wisdom that you can never find a pen when you need one, this site offers a plethora of fine designs, hundreds of ball-points, rollerballs and fountain pens, accompanied by mechanical pencils and a bevy of ink/refills. Most of these pens may be relied upon for exquisite flow and/or strokes, so when you get down to it, shopping becomes a matter of style. Fortunately, the pictures here are lined up for simple browsing and therefore easy shopping. You may want to write this one down....

·OFFICE SUPPLIES

## 877-547-4438 • Let's Get Personal!

### Personalizations.com

Any gift gets better when it's got the recipient's name engraved, and these guys know it. Offering personalized lettering on such elegant items as pens, mechanical pencils, letter openers and business card holders, these may be in fact more useful for executive types than, say, your grandmother. However, if you do need something good for granny, don't despair. A special message on a picture frame should do the trick, provided you put a picture of yourself in it as well; you know, for that personal touch.

·OFFICE SUPPLIES    ·PERSONALIZATION

# Personalize.com

Personal Creations • 800-326-6626

Taking gift personalization to new and exciting heights, this site seems willing to put a person's name on just about everything. With just a cursory glance we found: a life preserver ring, Afghans, a silver-plated mouse, decorative plates, picture frames, children's furniture, blankets, stuffed animals, music boxes, sweatshirts, more Afghans, jewelry, stepping stones, religious trinkets, mugs, plaques, chocolate body paint, pens, a laundry bag, keepsake boxes, ceramic tiles and memorial stones. And the list goes on.

| | ·TCHOTCHKES | ·OFFICE SUPPLIES | ·ROMANTIC | ·PERSONALIZATION |
|---|---|---|---|---|

# PhotoWow.com

Photowow • 800-453-9333

Some pictures are just too good for a photo album, so we put them in frames. What about the pictures that are too good for frames? Check out this site, and you'll see some very creative responses to this quandary. It's pretty tough to explain some of the things the artists at work here do, but suffice to say that they'll convert a simple image into pop art, a comic book page, a collage and any number of other entertaining, digitally manipulated novelty shots. Then, you can have said image added to a canvas, lamp or other unusual medium. Hey, if it's too good for a frame, maybe it's better suited for a pillowcase?

| | ·ROMANTIC | ·CREATIVE GIFTS | ·PERSONALIZATION | |
|---|---|---|---|---|

# ProFlowers.com

ProFlowers.com • 888-373-7437

Here's another site with a wide selection of floral arrangements to be picked from. What makes this one worthwhile is its many ways to narrow down the field. You can shop by price range, occasion or by whichever sentiment you would like to express (sympathy, congratulations or gratitude, for example). You can also narrow the field based on your estimated price range, and if you follow the More Details link, you can filter by color, style (like elegant or exotic) and, an excellent feature, take into consideration whether the recipient has allergies or perhaps weak olfactory glands. The server sometimes freaks out, but this is generally a good, reliable flower shop.

| | ·FLOWERS | ·GIFT BASKETS | | |
|---|---|---|---|---|

# QuincyShop.com

Quincy • 800-299-4242

Here's a rarity; a retailer that's picky about the makeup of its customer base. As they put it, they "serve customers who love life. Make art, see. Laugh out loud. Write and build." Grammar aside, these guys do really intend to promote intelligence and creativity, as evidenced in their selection of journals, musical instruments, crafts kits, Photographic Tomfoolery, art supplies and games. It's a bunch of great stuff in a pretty darn good shop. If anyone in your life would enjoy these gifts, count yourself lucky.

| | ·STATIONERY | ·CREATIVE GIFTS | | |
|---|---|---|---|---|

## No Service Number • Ribbons & Wraps

### R-N-W.com

If you're as much concerned with the presentation of a gift as the gift itself, you can start your shopping with this gift-wrap specialty store and worry about the rest later. It starts out simply enough, with a very pleasing selection of wrapping paper and ribbons of varying color, width and material— better than your typical selection, but not terribly special. It really gets good when you get to the Bags, Boxes and Tissue section. Here, of course, you can find stuff that will really add an elegant touch to anything you happen to give. Some of these supplies could even make coal seem like a nice gift.

| ·WRAP/MAIL | | | |
|---|---|---|---|

## 888-443-8661 • RareCandles.com

### RareCandles.com

When you start to have trouble telling these various candle sites we've uncovered apart, just remember this as being the one with a hippo-shaped candle. That's not all, this "Manufacturer, Distributor and Wholesaler of Decorative, Novelty and Aromatherapy Candles" also offers werewolf, basketball, potato and snowman-shaped selections. Our favorite, though, may be the Acme Bomb candle, which would surely have exploded on a certain hungry cartoon coyote, but for you it will just melt to reveal a hidden treasure buried inside. These are not your typical candles.

| ·CANDLES/SCENTS | | | |
|---|---|---|---|

## 877-733-3683 • Red Envelope

### RedEnvelope.com

Whether they be celebratory, obligatory, romantic or condolent, Red Envelope lives up to its promise to furnish "gifts for all occasions." Aside from occasions, you can simply browse the different item categories, which encompass all manner of items, from diaper bags to shoeshine kits, without hassle. You may also shop for particular recipients, either by their relation to you, or by their lifestyle. The latter includes types like the Gadget Guru, the Decorator and the Gourmet. This is an excellent shopping site for useful, thoughtful and entertaining gifts.

| ·GIFT BASKETS | ·TCHOTCHKES | ·HOUSEWARMING | |
|---|---|---|---|

## 800-835-0919 • Ross-Simons

### Ross-Simons.com

An almost impossibly large assortment of trinkets and collectible gifts fills the pages of this site, which may be easier to use if you request the company's catalog and strictly order online to expedite the process. Figurines, crystal, ceramics, ornaments and collector's plates; you will find hundreds of these items, and that's just the Gifts section. Table Accessories opens the selection to an even wider variety, though all pretty much of the same taste. Essentially, there's nothing terribly exciting or awe-inducing here, but nothing that bad either.

| ·TCHOTCHKES | ·HOUSEWARMING | | |
|---|---|---|---|

# Sees.com
### See's Candies • 800-347-7337

West Coasters will no doubt immediately recognize the name of this old-time chocolate shop mainstay—now you can let East Coasters in on it with accustom gift box. Featuring all the confections anyone could want, like buttercreams, caramels, nougats, truffles, fruits, nuts and their classic chocolate covered molasses chips, decisions are made excruciating by some mouth-watering imagery (they show you the insides). Don't forget: you're looking for a gift for someone else.

 ·CONFECTIONS

# SendAnOrchid.com
### Send An Orchid • 619-501-9599

What makes orchids so mesmerizing and exotic? Who cares? As a gift, it almost doesn't get better, what with the tall, fragile stalks and delicate pedals sitting languidly atop them. Whether Oncidium, Dendrobim or Moth orchids (bet you don't yet know the difference), you will easily among this selection find the perfect thing to curry favor with, or perhaps apologize to, a woman. The option to upgrade on the default planter or to include an aromatherapeutic candle comes with each flower, and—just like that! —you're done.

·FLOWERS

# Sensia.com
### Sensia • 800-777-8027

For those with a nose to know, here is a site that specializes in aromatherapy-oriented gifts. For starters, they've got many different kinds of incense here, and we're not just talking about the difference between sticks and cones, but aromas ranging from Nag Champa and Sandalwood to a variety of floral and fruity concoctions. You may also find candles, bath oils and massage oils, as well as accessories for all of these scented items. Of course, smelling these items just isn't possible over the wires, so you'll want to have a goal in mind before you start shopping.

·CANDLES/SCENTS

# SFMusicBox.com
### SF Music Box Company • 800-635-9064

Does the San Francisco Music Box Company only sell music boxes? Well, no, actually. Some of these are musical globes, some musical figurines and a few of them musical carousels. Let's face it though, the odds of finding a selection of music-anything this big are staggering enough; the odds that the selection will be this incredible: next to none. Should you doubt the intrinsic beauty and charm of any of these products you have only to click on the Play Me button in the product description to hear the item's typically enchanting, lulling music. Precious.

 ·ROMANTIC | ·CREATIVE GIFTS | ·PERSONALIZATION | ·TCHOTCHKES

## 949-764-0068 • ShagMart

**ShagMart.com**

Here's another site that doesn't offer the huge selection we've come to expect from art shops. Actually, this features just one artist, who goes by the name of Shag, and at any given time most of his scant few selections are sold out. More likely to be found are sets of greeting cards, invitations, stickers, barware and especially wrapping paper bearing his designs, which look like a somewhat demented (it would have to be) blend of cubism and Looney Tunes. Hip kitsch fans will likely appreciate much of this stuff, if they're not, like, over it already.

| ·STATIONERY | ·WRAP/MAIL | ·CARDS | |
|---|---|---|---|

## 888-774-7797 • Shari's Berries

**SharisBerries.com**

Sure, you think, "Chocolate dipped strawberries? Hell, I can do that at home." Well, not these strawberries, buster, these come with a patent. Why? Well, these are the result of proprietor Shari Fitzpatrick's "dream of creating the world's greatest chocolate dipped strawberries." When she bills them as an "edible alternative to flowers," she's not pulling your leg, either, as these berries often come decorated to look like a bouquet of roses. Sound like lunacy? Wait until you see the "Tuxedo Roses." Until you've seen this site, you haven't witnessed what a strawberry can do.

| ·CONFECTIONS | ·CREATIVE GIFTS | | |  |
|---|---|---|---|---|

## 877-769-8476 • Smythson of Bond Street

**Smythson.com**

Originating in London's famous Bond Street, these guys count themselves "the world's foremost stationers, renowned as producers of the highest quality stationery, leather books, accessories and diaries for more than a century." Well, they've left little for us to add. Actually, they haven't really all that much to offer. See, it's the quality of the stuff that's important here, and while in short supply it's as fine as this sort of thing is going to get... though they may take exception to our calling it "stuff" and "things."

| ·STATIONERY | | | |
|---|---|---|---|

## 866-589-1421 • Sofa Garden

**SofaGarden.com**

Just when you thought you knew what comprised a pillow (four corners, rectangular shape, fat in the middle), this site comes along to screw everything up. Specializing in unique and novelty sofa pillows, these guys offer some quite unusual items. Take, for example, pillows shaped like a fried egg or a stack of pancakes. Breakfast not your thing? How about a bundle of asparagus, or a wedge of watermelon? Maybe architecture buffs may prefer a pillow shaped like the head of an Ionic or Corinthian column (sorry, no Doric in sight)? You get the picture, though you could never imagine them all, as these guys are even willing to distinguish between a cabernet and pinot noir wine bottle shape. Weird, but fun.

| ·CREATIVE GIFTS | ·HOUSEWARMING | | |
|---|---|---|---|

## Sparks.com

Sparks.com • 866-232-0960

The greeting card industry has produced a few heavyweights in the vein of lightweight gift gestures. Here's one from off the beaten path. With favorable prices and welcome new varieties, this lighthearted hospitality specialist offers cards, gifts and some flower bouquets that may lack the punch of some of their competitors, but don't lack for any amount of charm. Basically, it's an easy site to add to your bookmarks list, especially if you prefer to offer a greeting that is highly unlikely to be duplicated.

| ·FLOWERS | ·CONFECTIONS | ·CARDS | |
|---|---|---|---|

## Staples.com

Staples • 800-378-2753

Staples brick-and-mortar stores populate the planet with almost as much density as Wal-Mart, often open 24 hours so you can stock up on emergency highlighters, staple removers and rubber bands at 3am (when they're most needed). This site, of course, serves those times when you're not in such a rush, or when you want to avoid the constant crowds and impulse items inside every branch. The site works pretty well, too, with smart categorization and wide variety of run-of-the-mill items. For anything with personality you can do better, but these guys have got the basics down pat.

| ·STATIONERY | ·WRAP/MAIL | ·OFFICE SUPPLIES | |
|---|---|---|---|

## StarRegistry.com

International Star Registry • 800-282-3333

They say there are as many stars in the sky as grains of sand on a beach. Well, naming a grain of sand after yourself or a loved one is utterly absurd. On the other hand, naming a star is something reserved for the likes of epic heroes and demigods... rather it used to be. Here you may name a star and actually have it recorded into the International Registry of Stars, where presumably it will remain for hundreds of years. And assuming your star didn't implode 50 million years ago, it will be easily viewable for ages to come. Upon purchase, you'll receive a detailed map of the sky, pinpointing your star's exact location, complete with telescopic coordinates.

| ·ROMANTIC | ·CREATIVE GIFTS | ·PERSONALIZATION | |
|---|---|---|---|

## StarTreatment.com

Star Treatment Gift Services • 800-444-9059

All right, so you've decided to bestow upon someone the effortless joy of a gift basket. Want to make it the best, most exclusive, highest priced gift basket around? Here you go—this site specializes in the sort of gift baskets that people will actually be astounded and extremely happy to receive. Not to disparage the creative efforts put forth on your average basket, but these really do raise the bar. Take a kid's basket that includes a bowling game, volcano building kit, accordion and candy. Then, there's the tantalizing Secrets of the East basket For Her and a portable putting basket for golf fanatics. Simply put: you cannot do better.

| ·GIFT BASKETS | ·PERSONALIZATION | | |
|---|---|---|---|

## 800-557-8678 • Sticker Planet

**StickerPlanet.com**

This site, it is obvious, offers a world of stickers for your amusement. It's a whimsical site, heavy on the pastels and cutesy through and through. Hardcore sticker enthusiasts will surely be disappointed as the mainstays of the adhesive universe, like bumper stickers and rock music logos, keep a conspicuous absence. Instead, there are a variety of cartoonish stickers (occasionally featuring popular characters), some featuring animals and many devoted to specific holidays or occasions. You have to click on Category to really find anything, but in the end it may serve better to just buy some glue.

| ·CREATIVE GIFTS | | | |
|---|---|---|---|

## 707-964-9448 • Studio Z Mendocino .

**Studio-Z.com**

Featuring very elegant, and yet still unusual designs, this proves to be one of the best places to find unique invitations for tasteful occasions (not so much kid stuff, as the finesse of these cards would probably be wasted on children). Atypical categories like Ladies Who Lunch, It's Not Just the Gym Anymore, The Company of Friends and That Almost Made Me Cry don't necessarily give the whole picture, but manage their own allure nonetheless. The only similar selection that might surpass these invites in quality happens to be found in this site's Stationery collection. It's a masterpiece.

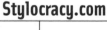
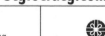

| ·STATIONERY | ·CARDS | | |
|---|---|---|---|

## 888-830-7895 • Stylocracy

**Stylocracy.com**

What makes a stylocracy? Apparently, any place "where style rules." No, it's not Italy, though these designer cocktail and tabletop products might find great acceptance in the famously hip Mediterranean nation. Actually, even if the housewarming you'll be attending is in the relatively square United States, most of these gifts will go over much better than any mediocre bottle of wine. Price ranges vary enough to make this a good site for anybody to check out, and the cool looks of these pages are matched by the unique modern stylings of the wares within.

| ·TCHOTCHKES | ·HOUSEWARMING | | |
|---|---|---|---|

## 888-641-5888 • Supply Curve

**SupplyCurve.com**

This "ahead of the curve online boutique" proves an excellent place to find a variety of gifts that anyone would gladly receive (hint: you might want to pass this one on to a few friends). It starts with an intriguing supply of barware, lighting and beauty/bath products. But the best stuff may be found in the Transglobal section, where you will come across things like Tibetan lanterns, West African masks, Sake sets and Hindu Diety Lunchboxes (for real). Add a few gaudy trinkets and this site's surprisingly comprehensive for its size, proving always that its buyers have great taste.

| ·STATIONERY | ·TCHOTCHKES | ·HOUSEWARMING | |
|---|---|---|---|

# TheBeautifulLife.com

The Beautiful Life • 888-393-1133

A good gift shop is a matter of taste, which is why the sort of gift shop we find here usually fails. Why, then, does this one succeed? Simple: rather than operating under profitable bottom lines of a large company, this shop owes its product selection to the discerning tastes of a single individual, its owner and founder. Consequently, each unique item found in these pages lives up to a set of standards that may change over time, but probably for the better. Best of all, the site feels like that of a larger store, both well-stocked and neatly laid out, thus offering the best of both worlds: selection, and quality selection.

| ·TCHOTCHKES | ·CANDLES/SCENTS | ·HOUSEWARMING | |
|---|---|---|---|

# ThePaperCatalog.com

The Paper Catalog • 800-343-3529

Offering "a variety of handmade, recycled and acid free papers," this San Francisco–based retailer boasts a fantastic selection and breezy shopping. Some papers are textured, some iridescent and many constructed of natural fibers, making them great for wrapping things in particular. There's some fine writing paper as well, and a variety of materials for origami, if you can dig. If you're uncertain about a particular selection, you can simply purchase a small sample or two to help you decide.

| ·STATIONERY | ·WRAP/MAIL | | |
|---|---|---|---|

# ThePapery.com

The Papery • 203-869-1888

According to this site, "if it's quality and it's beautiful, it's bound to be available at The Papery." That being said, it turns out that only products located in the Catalog section are available at The Papery for online ordering, so the selection may not be as great as promised. However, what you can order consists of some fine stationery, often with monograms, or even room for more personalization. The only real problem we found is that once you enter a particular section, it can be difficult to find your way around, so make generous use of the Back button on your browser.

| ·STATIONERY | ·PERSONALIZATION | | |
|---|---|---|---|

# ThePersonalTouch.com

The Personal Touch • 800-733-6313

To varying degrees, everything you can find here may be personalized; hence the name. These products consist of address labels, stationery, cards and ink-stamps. Some may be embossed, some imprinted, several engraved; in most cases it's up to you just how personal you want to get. But literally everything can have your name on it, or at least your initials, so if you like to stake out your property, just to let everybody know whose is what, here you go. Or, if you prefer to bestow stuff upon others... well, you're just something, aren't you?

| ·STATIONERY | ·PERSONALIZATION | ·CARDS | |
|---|---|---|---|

## 800-669-7692 • TheRoyalStore.com

### TheRoyalStore.com

This site makes a pretty staggering claim; that they offer for sale online "any paper product you can think of." Sound like a challenge? Well, before you get too confident in stumping them, beware that they do offer posterboard, vellum, fluorescents, printer/copier paper, placemats and doilies in addition to typical stationery products. They even offer baking cups (the kind often used to make cupcakes and muffins). If you can think of anything that's missing, look for it, it may be there. We, however, concede to their humongous selection.

| ·STATIONERY | ·WRAP/MAIL | ·OFFICE SUPPLIES | |
|---|---|---|---|

## 888-365-0056 • Uncommon Goods

### UncommonGoods.com

Some occasions simply demand giving something memorable, even if only to create a karmic buffer against any more fruitcakes or sweaters coming your way in the near future. This site makes uncommon gifting pretty easy; though don't be misled, here the word "uncommon" isn't just a euphemism for "weird" (you may run across the occasional peculiar item, however). Really, it's just an assortment of coolish, unforeseeable merchandise, ranging from household accents to funky soaps, with some cool lamps and pens to round it out. Oh, and if you have a price range in mind, they'll help you stay within your budget.

| ·STATIONERY | ·TCHOTCHKES | ·CREATIVE GIFTS | ·HOUSEWARMING |
|---|---|---|---|

## 800-275-8777 • United States Postal Service

### USPS.com

First class, postcard, water activated, self-adhesive, rolls, books, flags, liberty and commemorative: it's all about stamps, and this web store hosted by the perennial men in blue may save you a trip to the local post office. Sure, they can get it to you rain, sleet or snow, but a merely a few parking problems and long lines are enough to keep us away. Buy stamps in any denomination, with plenty of available images, from fruits to geese. Of course, the major drawback is now you'll have to pay the ever-rising postage to get your stamps, and a handling fee on top of that. Oh well.

| ·WRAP/MAIL | | | |
|---|---|---|---|

## 800-203-9569 • Village Candle

### VillageCandle.com

This candle shop is all about the scents. Click Buy Online at Our eStore to shop for their variety of sizes and shapes, or for their auto freshening Car Candles. Find votives, squares, tea lights and pillars with ease, starting with the fragrance. It'll be tough enough to choose between Apples'n'Oak, Balsam Fir, Blueberry Cobbler, Cinnamon Bun, Coconut Kiwi, Gingerbread, Honeydew Melon, Juicy Pear, Oranges'n'Cantaloupe, Mulberry Twist, Peony Petals, Spicy Gum Drop, Strawberry Parfait, Tropical Nectar and Wild Huckleberry—and these aren't even half of the options available. Good luck.

| ·CANDLES/SCENTS | | | |
|---|---|---|---|

# VintageVending.com

Vintage Vending • 888-242-6633

Offering "the coolest retro gifts for you and anyone else," most of the stuff for sale on this site would fit in to the general décor of a fifties diner. With classic jukeboxes, tiki bars, neon clocks and old-time candy vending machines, this is as much for preservationists as it is for collectors (if there's a difference). Of course, we advocate visiting any store with a section titled Cool Stuff, and this one's no different. It could be done better, but then if it were too slick it would lose some of its charm. Check this one out even if you're only reading this by accident.

| ·MEMORABILIA | ·HOUSEWARMING | | |
|---|---|---|---|

# Vivre.com

Vivre • 800-411-6515

Vivre is short for *L'Arte de Vivre,* which any Frenchman will tell you (perhaps with a sneer) means, "The Art of Living." Sure, elevating life to the level of art form seems like a lot of pressure, but it makes for good, luxuriant gifting. Note, though, that while these items are, how you say, "Splendid?" they are abysmally laid out on this site. Your best bet is to use the Search feature to narrow down the selection by price range, occasion and product category. Otherwise, you may find yourself suffering from some prolonged and irrational aversion to all things French.

| ·STATIONERY | ·TCHOTCHKES | ·HOUSEWARMING | |
|---|---|---|---|

# WeArePaper.com

We Are Paper • 773-486-9374

This is the paper site for people who love trees—all the pages here have been hand-made using 100% recycled cotton. Well, maybe not 100%, as many of these sheets possess flower, silk, jut and various other inclusions to add texture and style. Pages may be used for "stationery, watercolor, collage, bookbinding, screen printing, invitations, hand lithography, printing, calligraphy, scrapbooking, rubber stamping, packaging, lamp shade material, and more." Possibly your best bet for tree-free paper, you just became earth-friendly.

| ·STATIONERY | ·WRAP/MAIL | | |
|---|---|---|---|

# Wedgwood.com

Wedgwood • 011-44-178-220-4141

Founder Josiah Wedgwood, an 18th-century English potter, friend to both British Royalty and American revolutionaries, aligned himself with some of the renowned progressive, scientific thinkers of his time. Thing is, he managed to combine his variable interests into his creations, which thus sparked a recognition of both beauty and refinement, at the same time striving for that heady realm of technical advancement; a quality still inherent in Wedgwood products, from pottery to trinkets, and all the flatware too. Best of all, this site features an ingenious shopping tool that allows you to find the perfect items for the right people and the right occasion. Classy and easy; that's rare.

| ·HOUSEWARMING | | | |
|---|---|---|---|

## 800-876-1928 • Woodendipity

**Woodendipity.com**

These guys tell us, "For nearly twenty years we have been recognized as the foremost creators of fun-functional folk art in North America...if not the world!" Well, if anybody else in the world made stuff like this, we'd be shocked. Somewhat weird, mostly hilarious, these items are never what you'd expect. Planters come in elephant and basset hound shapes, a birdfeeder is in the form of a monkey and there's just no explaining what you may find in the Surprises category (of course). We will tell you this, though: a little wooden character named Havana Harry holds your humidor and another named Sharkie holds your billiard supplies. Do not miss viewing this one!

| ·CREATIVE GIFTS | | | |
|---|---|---|---|

## 866-227-3722 • You Got a Care Package!

**YouGotA.com**

Somewhere between gift basket and snack pack sits the care package, the perennial parenting tool that says, "As glad as we are to have you out of the house, we feel a bit guilty about it." This site specializes in ready-made care packages for students and campers alike, but also for military personal, corporate travelers, sick friends and anyone else who might like one. Generally full of snacks, occasionally with some appropriate books and toys, some of these items may be customized (choices in magazines, coffee/tea, etc.), but most are simple mouse-click away from being sent, so you can quickly get back to your freshly quiet, empty home.

| ·GIFT BASKETS | ·PERSONALIZATION | | |
|---|---|---|---|

## 323-951-9190 • Zipper Gifts

**ZipperGifts.com**

The credo of this gift shop is this: "Objects are imbued with art and history— make that connection and the objects you choose will enrich your life." While we don't know exactly how such lofty thoughts apply to items like a fish-shaped lighter, we can tell you that anybody who can make paper clips stylish deserves a look. Certainly, these products are eclectic and uncommon, whether it be a feather quill pen or a hand-shaped incense holder. You may shop by categories like Sensuous Home or Personal Accessories, but such names only offer a glimmer as to what you might expect to find inside.

| ·CREATIVE GIFTS | ·HOUSEWARMING | | |
|---|---|---|---|

NOTES:

_____

_____

_____

_____

_____

_____

_____

_____

_____

_____

_____

_____

_____

_____

_____

_____

_____

_____

_____

# Travel

Getting around is *not* like it used to be.  We have increased security, heavier airline restrictions and a heightened sense of awareness when we travel.  All this isn't to say we *shouldn't* get around, it just means we have to plan a little better.  Which is where these sites come in.  Whatever your reasons for traveling, you can reserve a spot well in advance for the best prices (usually) online.  Thus, business trips can be arranged with the greatest expediency, pleasure trips with the greatest possible ease, and those long, red-eye jaunts across time zones … well they can be made as comfortable as possible.  The real payoff is that you can easily and instantly compare prices, thus beating a volatile market at its own game.

Of course, it's not just about getting *to* your destination, but getting around when you get there and having a comfortable, secure place to stay.  Fortunately, most of the major travel sites can accommodate all your needs in one order; reserving rental cars, lodging and sundry travel itineraries for the smoothest of operation—basically, you just show up at the airport with your ID and credit card, and you will be efficiently moved along (unfortunately, long lines will be nearly impossible to avoid these days, so "efficient" may be a subjective term).  Obviously, you'll take more with you than your wallet.  We were just getting to the part about all the great luggage and travel gear available on some of these sites.  There's gear here to outfit the adventure traveler, the spa enthusiast, any backpacking excursion and every cosmopolitan taste.  The more you can fit into the tiniest of spaces the better, and if it happens to be a pretty package, so be it.  So get out there, live it up, love it and send us pictures if you get the chance.

NOTES:

## TIPS ON BOOKING TRAVEL ONLINE

These suggestions may help prevent frustration and vagrancy.

•**BARGAIN FLIGHTS:** If you're browsing for airline tickets and come across a deal that looks too good to be true, don't take too long making a decision. The best online deals go quickly, and in many cases the price you see will be sold out within the hour.

•**ONLINE HOTEL BOOKINGS:** Sometimes, the same hotel will block off a section of rooms specifically for online reservations, while another group will be set aside for phone calls. Occasionally, different prices will be offered as well, so if you're looking for a specific lodging, it might pay to check offline as well as on, especially if there doesn't seem to be a vacancy.

•**BOOK IN ADVANCE:** When all is said and done, travel works the best when you don't save planning for the last minute. However, very occasionally an airline or hotel may run a promotion offering the same ticket class or room size at cheaper rates. If you book early, avoid getting tickets with too many restrictions so you can get the better price if they offer it later; call if you're unsure.

## SITES THAT MAY COME IN HANDY

The following URLs may be useful when you shop.

ATM Locator: http://visaatm.infonow.net/bin/findNow?CLIENT_ID=VISA
Road Trip Planning: http://www.aaa.com
Travel Guide: http://www.fodors.com
Resort Guide: http://www.resortsource.com
Passport Services: http://travel.state.gov/passport_services.html
Currency Converter: http://www.oanda.com/converter/classic?user=pathfinder2
Foreign Entry Requirements: http://travel.state.gov/foreignentryreqs.html
Car Rental Rate Comparisons: http://www.bnm.com
Traveling With Pets: http://www.dogfriendly.com
International Calling Codes: http://www.countrycallingcodes.com

## >> SECTION ICON LEGEND

Use the following guide to understand the rectangular icons that appear throughout this section.

### LODGING

Aside from camping and couch surfing, this icon covers the full range of lodging options, from seedy motels to five star luxury resorts.  Along the way you'll encounter plenty of property rentals and some bed & breakfasts as well.

### TRANSPORTATION

This catch-all icon includes travel by air, land and sea, beginning with flight bookings and continuing on through car rentals, train tickets and cruises.  Check out the associated key words to figure out if a particular site can serve your needs.

### TRAVEL GEAR

Many items can contribute to your travel experience, the most common consisting of luggage, from backpacks to trunks, and some of the most useful being travel-sized appliances and foreign outlet adaptors.  This icon covers anything that you take with you to make the trip run smoother.

## >> LIST OF KEY WORDS

The following words represent the types of items typically found on the sites listed in this section.

### ACCESSORIES

Travel accessories include things like travel-size grooming tools, power adaptors, translation devices, navigation tools and plenty of other devices that may come in handy.

### ADVENTURE

These adventure travel vacations, maps, guides and devices help pit you against nature (with a slight advantage).

### AIR TRAVEL

In rare cases you may find a flight by helicopter, hot air balloon or blimp, but by and large the air travel represented by these sites has to do with airplanes.

### BUS & RAIL

Sure, most modern travel takes place via airplane, but whether due to nostalgia, finances or phobias, many still prefer to stick to bus lines or trains. You may book travel with these sites.

### CAR RENTALS

You may often rent a car directly through the same commerce engine that books your flight and hotel reservations. Otherwise, look at the Sites That May Come in Handy entries in this section to find a site that automatically comparison-shops and links you to the major rental agencies.

### CRUISES

Cruises available for online booking can tour you through the Caribbean or Antarctica, all the way around the globe or just on a short jaunt out to sea and back.

### FOREIGN TRAVEL

Sites marked by this key word specialize in travel to other countries, whether they're country-specific, feature a continent, or just offer heaps of options to get you out of the US.

### HOTELS

From the finest quality to the greatest bargains, just about every hotel on the planet can be booked online from one site or another.

### LUGGAGE

Check it curbside or carry it on, luggage comes in all shapes and sizes, with or without wheels, to be strapped to your back or carried by teams of men. Under this key word you'll find garment bags, toiletry cases, backpacks, trunks and more.

### MAPS & GUIDES

Whether hiking, biking, driving or just sightseeing, you'll need a map to get around, or maybe even a guide to explain where you're going.

### MONEY/SECURITY

As a tourist, you'll be vulnerable to the sketchy thieves and con artists of foreign cultures, even if it's just a different region of the US. These items might help protect your gear.

### PETS

Travel options generally become limited when you wish to bring the animals in your family on vacation. These sites offer a variety of options that should make it easier to take your pets places.

### PROPERTY RENTALS

These listings feature apartments, houses, cabins, villas, cottages, condos, beach-houses and plenty of other desirable properties for short-term rental in locations worldwide.

### RESORTS

A hotel may be seen as a place you stay when you visit a destination; a resort, on the other hand, can qualify as the destination itself. The resorts on these sites let you vegetate, lose weight, party, play, ski, surf and just get pampered.

### TOURS

Touring a destination can be one of the safest, most efficient ways of learning about local history and seeing all the sites.

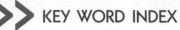

# KEY WORD INDEX

Use the following lists to locate online retailers and booking agencies you seek.

## ACCESSORIES

Amtrak.com
BagKing.com
CampingWorld.com
DeLorme.com
eBags.com
ExOfficio.com
FamilyOnBoard.com
Flight001.com
FreshTracksMaps.com
GoingInStyle.com
InMotionPictures.com
Irvs.com
LaptopTravel.com
LazarsLuggage.com
Luggage.com
Magellans.com
MoriLuggage.com
Pakha.com
RandMcNally.com
REI.com
SamsoniteCompanyStores.com
TeleAdaptUSA.com
Tilley.com
TravelinPets.com
TravelSmith.com
TravelTools.com
TravMed.com
WayPort.net
WorldLanguage.com
WorldTraveler.com

## ADVENTURE

AbercrombieKent.com
AdventurousTraveler.com
BackRoads.com
Butterfield.com
ExOfficio.com
GordonsGuide.com
NatHab.com
REI.com
Tauck.com
Tilley.com

Trails.com
TravelSmith.com
WorldWaters.com

## AIR TRAVEL

11thHourVacations.com
4Airlines.com
AirTreks.com
CheapTickets.com
EconomyTravel.com
Expedia.com
Go-Today.com
HotWire.com
JetBlue.com
OneTravel.com
Orbitz.com
PriceLine.com
Site59.com
TravelNow.com
Travelocity.com
Trip.com
Vegas.com

## BUS & RAIL

Amtrak.com
Greyhound.com
RailEruope.com
Travelocity.com

## CAR RENTALS

4Airlines.com
CheapTickets.com
EconomyTravel.com
Expedia.com
France.com
Go-Today.com
HotWire.com
OneTravel.com
Orbitz.com
PriceLine.com
Site59.com

TravelNow.com
Travelocity.com
Trip.com
Vegas.com

## CRUISES

11thHourVacations.com
AbercrombieKent.com
CheapTickets.com
Disney.com
Expedia.com
i-Cruise.com
OneTravel.com
Orbitz.com
PriceLine.com
Tauck.com
TravelNow.com
Travelocity.com
Trip.com

## FOREIGN TRAVEL

11thHourVactions.com
AbercrombieKent.com
AndrewHarper.com
AsiaHotels.com
BackRoads.com
BarclayWeb.com
Butterfield.com
Concorde-Hotels.com
DriversLicense.net
EconomyTravel.com
EpiCulinary.com
Expedia.com
FiestaAmericana.com
Firmdale.com
France.com
Go-Today.com
HotWire.com
Indo.com
LHW.com
Lodging.com
LondonConnection.com
LondonTown.com

LuxuryLink.com
MandarinOriental.com
MexicoBoutiqueHotels.com
MonasteriesOfItaly.com
NatHab.com
OberoiHotels.com
PassportHelp.com
RailEurope.com
RentVillas.com
Tauck.com
TeleAdaptUSA.com
Travelocity.com
Trip.com
VillasOfTheWorld.com
WorldLanguage.com

## HOTELS

11thHourVacations.com
1800USAHotels.com
4Airlines.com
A1-Discounts-Hotels.com
AccorHotels.com
All-Hotels.com
AsiaHotels.com
BarclayWeb.com
BoutiqueLodging.com
CheapTickets.com
Concorde-Hotels.com
EconomyTravel.com
Expedia.com
ExpressReservations.com
Fairmont.com
FiestaAmericana.com
FindMyRoom.com
Firmdale.com
France.com
Go-Today.com
HotWire.com
ILoveInns.com
Indo.com
LHW.com
Lodging.com
LondonTown.com
LuxuryCollection.com
MandarinOriental.com

MexicoBoutiqueHotels.com
OberoiHotels.com
OneTravel.com
Orbitz.com
Pet-Friendly-Hotels.net
PriceLine.com
QuickBook.com
RelaisChateaux.com
Site59.com
Travelocity.com
Trip.com
Vegas.com
WHotels.com

## LUGGAGE

Amtrak.com
BagKing.com
ClassicLuggage.com
eBags.com
Flight001.com
Ghurka.com
GoingInStyle.com
Irvs.com
LazarsLuggage.com
Luggage.com
Magellans.com
MoriLuggage.com
RandMcNally.com
REI.com
SamsoniteCompanyStores.com
Suitcase.com
TravelinPets.com
TravelSmith.com
TravelTools.com
WorldTraveler.com

## MAPS & GUIDES

AdventurousTraveler.com
AndrewHarper.com
DeLorme.com
FreshTracksMaps.com
ILoveInns.com
Maps.com
MonasteriesOfItaly.com
RandMcNally.com
REI.com
Trails.com
TravelTools.com
Trip.com

## MONEY/SECURITY

FamilyOnBoard.com
Flight001.com
GoingInStyle.com
InsureMyTrip.com
Luggage.com
Magellans.com
RandMcNally.com
REI.com
TravelProtect.com
TravelTools.com
TravMed.com
WorldTravelCenter.com

## PETS

Flight001.com
GoingInStyle.com
Pet-Friendly-Hotels.net
TravelinPets.com

## PROPERTY RENTALS

AsiaHotels.com
BarclayWeb.com
CheapTickets.com
France.com
Indo.com
LondonConnection.com
RentVillas.com
ResortQuest.com
TravelNow.com
Trip.com
VillasOfTheWorld.com

## RESORTS

11thHourVacations.com
AccorHotels.com
AsiaHotels.com
ClubMed.com
Disney.com
Fairmont.com
FiestaAmericana.com
Indo.com
LHW.com
LuxuryCollection.com

OneTravel.com
ResortQuest.com
SpaFinder.com
SuperClubs.com
Travelocity.com
Trip.com
Vegas.com

## TOURS

11thHourVacations.com
AbercrombieKent.com
BackRoads.com
Butterfield.com
EpiCulinary.com
LondonTown.com
LuxuryLink.com
NatHab.com
OneTravel.com
REI.com
RoadTrips.com
Tauck.com
TennisTours.com
Travelocity.com
WorldWaters.com

# 11thHourVacations.com

**11th Hour Vacations • 864-331-1140**

So your practical friends say that to get a good deal you must plan a trip ten years in advance and set your reservations even sooner: there may be some truth to that. But some of us prefer spontaneity, many of us simply too impatient to orchestrate a trip and then wait months and months and months before reaping the benefits. This site serves the 'give it to me now' sensibility, with cruises and packages encompassing a range of global activities. While it won't necessarily barrel you out the door today, it can get you a good deal on a relatively immediate vacation—say, in a couple of weeks. In other words, if you're trying to flee the country ahead of the law, you'll need to look elsewhere.

| ·AIR TRAVEL ·TOURS | ·HOTELS ·FOREIGN TRAVEL | ·CRUISES | ·RESORTS |
|---|---|---|---|

# 1800USAHotels.com

**1800USAHotels.com • 800-872-4683**

If you're looking to quickly ascertain the standard rates of hotels around the world, this site asks little going in and comes back with results, fast. If you're looking for a bargain, it may be possible here; more likely though this will provide an easy means of determining just what constitutes a bargain. However, this site features more than its worth, featuring a menu of links to weather, travel news, travel alerts and currency conversion pages. All together, it's at least worthy of a bookmark.

| ·HOTELS | | | |
|---|---|---|---|

# 4Airlines.com

**4Airlines.com • 800-910-1240**

While their claims of finding the lowest price tickets tend to be thwarted by any amount of comparison-shopping, and their search results appear cluttered and even confusing, there's something about this site that makes it all quite easy. Featuring many more than four airlines (the "4" maybe means "for?"), the site can also hook you up with hotel rooms and car rentals, and at the time of this writing has plans to expand to cruises and vacation deals. Options are nice, even when they come in not-so-pretty packages.

| ·AIR TRAVEL | ·HOTELS | ·CAR RENTALS | |
|---|---|---|---|

# A1-Discount-Hotels.com

**A1 Discount Hotel Reservations • 888-511-5743**

It's remarkable sometimes how a complete and utter lack of frills can make a site all the more valuable. This one's got nearly nothing going for it— straightforward pages, ugly design and text lists abound—virtually no whistles and/or bells whatsoever. However, when you want a cheap hotel room, and want to get through the process quickly, everything here is put into your hands. Its sole bit of helpful coding is a pop-up calendar that enables you to set a date. Otherwise, you must simply enter the site, choose your destination from a long list, select your desired hotel from another list, pick a date and go.

| ·HOTELS | | | |
|---|---|---|---|

## 800-323-7308 • Abercrombie & Kent

### AbercrombieKent.com

Somewhere at the crossroads between adventure travel and luxurious holidays sits this vacation packager with a penchant for tours and cruises. Exotic destinations worldwide provide a backdrop for safaris, river rafting and no shortage of pampering, should you desire it. Essentially, these packages cater to those affluent enough to enjoy the fineries of life, yet still keen enough on the essence of life itself to enjoy mixing it up on a foreign land (or sea). Follow one of their professionally staffed programs, or mix and match their services into a voyage of your own design, and remember to forget about the day-to-day.

·CRUISES    ·ADVENTURE    ·TOURS    ·FOREIGN TRAVEL

## No Service Number • AccorHotels.com

### AccorHotels.com

The Accor group owns more than 3,500 hotels worldwide, known to the public through various brand names like Sofitel, Ibis, Parthenon, Mercure and, uh, Motel 6. Some are resorts, some casinos, right on down to traditional and budget lodgings, but all can be accessed for reservations through this site. Are they worth it? Well, that depends on where you're going, what you want, and obviously how much you're prepared to spend. But with this many hotels in their repertoire, they can certainly put you up in most places you'll go, so it may be worth a look.

·HOTELS    ·RESORTS

## No Service Number • AdventurousTraveler.com

### AdventurousTraveler.com

As the name would indicate, this site offers some essential items for the visitor in search of an adventure; namely, maps and guides to help you find it. Between trail maps, biking maps and glacier guides, these guys cover a wide range of rugged locations that include Death Valley, the Carlsbad Caverns and the Mount Everest Base Camp, along with a few key city guides and foreign language phrases books to aid you along the way. The great irony lies in the fact that while its products make the interesting places of the planet easier to locate, finding these items among these pages can be a lugubrious process to say the least. A cool site, nonetheless.

·ADVENTURE    ·MAPS & GUIDES

## 800-350-0612 • airtreks.com

### AirTreks.com

Round trips are over. Done. At least, they will be once you get a glimpse of this multi-stop travel specialist. Here's how it works: with the help of a virtual map you select a number of cities (at least three, from the entire planet) you would like to fly to, one by one. Then, click on a button marked Get Price, and prepare to push your eyeballs back into their sockets. Not only do they respond with a remarkable Lowest Cost itinerary, but also one with the Fewest Stops and one entitled Most for Your Money, which usually doesn't cost that much more than the cheapest, but throws in a few extra cities along the way. And why not? With this site, flying to just one city and back again simply doesn't make sense anymore.

·AIR TRAVEL

# All-Hotels.com

All-Hotels • 011-44-131-625-1070

Do they really offer rates for all hotels, we wonder? Well, they claim over 60,000, and we got tired of counting at about the 50 mark, so let's just say they have a good head start. They've enough at least to draw distinctions between cheap hotels, discount hotels and discount motels, while offering discount "luxury 5-star accommodations" as well. The site's a no-brainer, both in terms of design and use, with standard search options and a section devoted to Bed & Breakfasts. At any rate, if you can't find your favorite hotel (there is the occasional glaring omission), you'll undoubtedly find ten to take its place.

| ·HOTELS | | | |
|---|---|---|---|

# Amtrak.com

Amtrak • 800-872-7245

A train ride through this nation's amber waves of grain is not as popular as it once was, but the scenic route still bears much of the romance it always has. Even if a plane can get you there (much, much) faster, anyone with time to kill will probably find riding the rails to be a more relaxing and comfortable alternative to long security lines, crowded overhead bins and impatient fellow travelers. Amtrak also offers a small store full of sundry travel items ranging from luggage to games that'll make the dining car a more entertaining and sociable experience. Reservations are the main reason to check this site out, however, and we'd recommend a sleeper car.

| ·ACCESSORIES | ·BUS & RAIL | ·LUGGAGE |
|---|---|---|

# AndrewHarper.com

Andrew Harper Travel • 800-235-9622

Answering the question, "What sort of vacation might James Bond take?" this site operates as a semi-exclusive club aimed towards regular luxury travelers in search of good recommendations and rates. "Sophisticated travelers recognize Andrew Harper as the ultimate authority on luxury travel. Circling the globe incognito for over two decades, he continues to provide his readers valuable inside information on the best luxury hotels and secret hideaways." You can expect nothing villainous, only lavish, ready-made vaunts around the globe, full of only as much intrigue as you bring along yourself.

| ·MAPS & GUIDES | ·FOREIGN TRAVEL | |
|---|---|---|

# AsiaHotels.com

Asia-Hotels.com • No Service Number

With more than 20,000 listings for accommodations in Asia and Australia, this certainly seems to be a good place to book your temporary home on the other side of the world. In particular, if you're planning a beach vacation this site will offer you a variety of spectacular options, ranging from seaside resorts to bungalows that open up into the sand on a private island. Good for finding that gorgeous location, exotic destination and/or your own personal paradise; just pick a country and it's easy browsing from there.

| ·HOTELS | ·RESORTS | ·PROPERTY RENTAL | ·FOREIGN TRAVEL |
|---|---|---|---|

## 800-462-2848 • Backroads

### BackRoads.com

If you're looking for a vacation that makes your heart race and body sweat as you lay your eyes upon the splendor of a foreign land, this site could be for you. An "Active Travel Company," these guys will send you on tours to walk, bicycle, kayak and even ride camels through Africa, Asia, Europe or the Americas, with much of the equipment often included (don't bring your own camel). Mixed in among these activities you may occasionally find golf and cooking classes available (so you may also relax and eat well, respectively), and truly eager travelers may find combinations of activities with which to test their vigor.

| ·ADVENTURE | ·TOURS | ·FOREIGN TRAVEL | |
|---|---|---|---|

## 888-655-2247 • Bag King

### BagKing.com

Starting with an amusingly funky logo and extending to its well-rounded selection, this site makes itself quite useful to the impending traveler. An excellent source of backpacks, garment bags and laptop travel bags in particular, in all of its categories this catalog furnishes a good supply, opting for quality rather than an overwhelming amount of choice. Chances are, you'll find exactly the sort of carry-on or stow away luggage you need within moments, and the price won't make you think twice about leaving home in the first place.

| ·LUGGAGE | ·ACCESSORIES | | | 🧳 |
|---|---|---|---|---|

## 800-845-6636 • Barclay International Group

### BarclayWeb.com

Staking its claim as "one of the world's largest and most reputable collections of hotel alternatives," this site leads you to some fine short-term rentals in popular Western European travel destinations. Renting a villa on Italy's Amalfi Coast, an apartment in Paris's Champs-Elysées or a country cottage in the Isle of Wight (UK), you'll find a variety of prices for as little as one night and as long as each property owner is willing to have you. Note: you must make reservations online a good month or so at least in advance, and pay up front.

| ·HOTELS | ·PROPERTY RENTAL | ·FOREIGN TRAVEL | | |
|---|---|---|---|---|

## No Service Number • Boutique Lodging International

### BoutiqueLodging.com

Hotel chains stretch far and wide; you know what you can expect to find in any particular one, and nearly all of them will book reservations online. But what about the independently owned resorts and hotels that exist in every corner of the planet, the kind that offer knowledgeable, local service, unique style and often better prices than their corporate competitors? Thanks to this site, you can now find a lot of these on the web, complete with pictures, reviews and online bookings. While it does not yet live up to its full potential, its network of individual hotels is growing, and is ready to offer you the greatest of luxuries: options.

| ·HOTELS | | | | |
|---|---|---|---|---|

# Butterfield.com

Butterfield & Robinson • 800-678-1147

If you're not one to travel across the globe just to sit on a bus or take a walking tour of an old museum or cathedral, maybe you'll want to consider one of these Butterfield & Robinson packages. Offering hiking, biking, rafting and kayaking expeditions in exotic locations across the globe, these guys won't let you sit on your haunches, unless perhaps your haunches happen to be on a camel in the Sahara. Or, maybe, snorkeling in Bali is your first choice, or mountaineering in Nepal. Meals and lodging are mostly included in these packages that allow you to scour the world with excursions that may ultimately prove more exhausting than your job.

| ·ADVENTURE | ·TOURS | ·FOREIGN TRAVEL | |
|---|---|---|---|

# CampingWorld.com

Camping World • 866-601-2323

If your idea of camping involves a shower, kitchen, bed, air conditioner, toilet and porch, well you're probably the owner of a Recreational Vehicle. If that's the case, you'll find a whole slew of RV accessories and add-ons here, whether it's equipment to help maintain your vehicle's internal systems (electrical and plumbing, etc.) or just some great lounging gear that'll come in handy whenever and wherever you stop. There are also some games to help pass the time on long rides, and some driving aids (as those games can get distracting). Of course, you'll want to order this stuff before you go.

| ·ACCESSORIES | | | |
|---|---|---|---|

# CheapTickets.com

CheapTickets.com • 888-922-8849

Have these guys got anything more to offer than an alluring name? The best answer we can offer is: maybe? While there's no guarantee that the fares you find here will actually be the best available, you'll at worst pay a typical market price on airline tickets, hotel rooms, car rentals and cruises. As many sites feature both similar promises and prices, this is a good one to use as a comparison, if only to keep everybody honest. Even if it's your final choice, the price you pay is ultimately itemized on your credit card bill next to the words "Cheap Tickets." That should at least be good for your psyche.

| ·AIR TRAVEL ·PROPERTY RENTAL | ·HOTELS | ·CAR RENTALS | ·CRUISES |
|---|---|---|---|

# ClassicLuggage.com

Sterling & Burke LTD • 800-205-7739

What we have here is an atrocious web site that sells some of the best luggage made on this planet. By now, we're used to trading quality of page design for the low prices that usually follow; you won't find that here. These guys feature hi-end British and American luggage from manufacturers like Swaine Adeny Brigg, Papworth, Schlesinger and Sterling & Burke, Ltd., which actually owns and operates the store. If these names don't mean anything to you, you probably don't want to spend this much on travel gear. But, if thought of passing fancy leather luggage, umbrellas and walking sticks to a bellhop warms your sense of decadence, don't let the ugly veneer get in your way.

| ·LUGGAGE | | | |
|---|---|---|---|

## 888-932-2582 • Club Med

**ClubMed.com**

Pampering you for the length of your stay, Club Med resorts have made a name for themselves by offering high levels of hospitality all over the world, from the beach to the ski lodge. Don't be mistaken— these aren't merely places to rest your laurels (unless you choose to). The various resorts offer a bounty of activities for adults and children, ranging from martial arts and scuba diving to climbing and golf. You can browse by location, filter for your notions of fun, or combine the searches and book yourself to the easiest active vacation you're likely to find.

## 800-888-4747 • Concorde Hotels

**Concorde-Hotels.com**

To give you an idea of the worldview possessed by the proprietors of this chain of luxury hotels, the interactive maps that pinpoint their sundry locations are labeled France, Other European Countries and Rest of the World. Indeed, this very continental outlook is consistent in the traditionally lavish accommodations featured within, with hotels boasting gourmet cuisine, spas, golf clubs and casinos. An option deigned Thematic Research makes it easy to find locations bearing such features, or to pick out some intrinsically desirable honeymoon destinations.

·HOTELS  ·FOREIGN TRAVEL

## 800-511-2459 • DeLorme

**DeLorme.com**

Welcome to the world of high-tech travel, where the nuisance of outdated foldaway maps is being made obsolete even faster than your desktop computer. These guys combine the benefits of portable computing and global positioning capability to enable the easy navigation of nearly every locale on the planet, however far you plan to go, however turned around you may feel. Software maps out territory and/or topography on your laptop or handheld device to ensure you have at least a remote idea of where you're heading, whereas GPS receivers will pinpoint your exact location on the map, so you at least know where you're standing when you get lost.

·ACCESSORIES  ·MAPS & GUIDES

## No Service Number • Disney

**Disney.com**

Select the Destinations button on the cartoonish homepage map here to get a decent look at the various resort, theme park and cruise destinations offered by this mainstay in family holidays. One's forced to wonder, while perusing this site, how one of the world's most consistently powerful corporations manages to thrive on what appears to be huge amounts of fluff surrounding miniscule moments of substance. Of course, the wide-eyed grins affixed to the faces of your children will certainly do well to remind you; kids, after all, love fluff.

·CRUISES  ·RESORTS

## DriverLicense.net

International Auto Driver's Club • 718-667-8981

If you're going to drive when you get to your foreign destination, you'd better be certified. Somehow, based on UN conventions, these guys offer a way to get that certification, though seemingly without taking a driving test or proving your abilities. Basically, it only works in conjunction with a driver's license from your own country and, even then, if you drive recklessly or otherwise dangerously, you're going to pay the penalty! It should help clear some of the red tape with its primary purpose "to facilitate the travel of motorists in foreign countries."

·FOREIGN TRAVEL

## eBags.com

ebags.com • 800-820-6126

Here's a site that stretches the meaning of the word "bag" to its logical conclusion. Backpacks, handbags and luggage are only the beginning; these guys offer a wide selection of bags and cases for sports, the outdoors, business or travel, and they even build upon their traditional offering of briefcases to include satchels and cases for your laptop, cell phone, pager or PDA, among other things. Simply put, if it can be contained in anything short of a box, and carted about the planet, these guys will find the right container and try to sell it to you.

·LUGGAGE    ·ACCESSORIES

## EconomyTravel.com

EconomyTravel.com • 888-222-2110

When it comes to this site, cheap is the word. For starters, that would be cheap airfare to destinations in Europe, Africa and the Middle East, along with a few other sundry and exotic locales. Even more impressive, however, may be the car rental rates, which are occasionally low enough to make renting a car domestically seem almost foolish. As with all things, though, discount comes with a price, and here it has to do with a no-frills web design, limited travel opportunities and difficulty in operation. Good deals though.

·AIR TRAVEL    ·HOTELS    ·CAR RENTALS    ·FOREIGN TRAVEL

## EpiCulinary.com

Epiculinary • 888-380-9010

On most travels to a distant land, you may bring back souvenirs and photographs to remind you of your journeys through a foreign culture, but little to help you actually relive the experience. Not so with these tour packages, from which you'll return with the know-how of an authentic regional chef. Whether you're cooking Mediterranean fare on Italy's Amalfi coast or *haute cuisine* in the Provence region of France, you receive cooking instruction wherever you go, along with some fantastic meals, of course. The tours are arranged loosely so you won't wind up spending your entire vacation slaving in a kitchen, but rather working up an appetite traipsing about countryside you'll remember forever through your taste buds.

·TOURS    ·FOREIGN TRAVEL

## 800-644-7303 • Ex Officio

### ExOfficio.com

When this site refers to "travel and adventure clothing," they're not talking about the Hawaiian shirts and Bermuda shorts that comprise the stereotypical uniform of the American tourist. On the contrary, these are simple, durable clothes that prove ideal for active travel because they are "lightweight, quick-dry, anti-microbial, breathable and low maintenance." Even if you're not impressed with the wrinkle resistant styles, sun protective materials and crushable hats, you're certain to appreciate the socks and underwear; maybe not now, but someday, and soon....

| ·ACCESSORIES | ·ADVENTURE | | | |
|---|---|---|---|---|

## 800-397-3342 • Expedia.com

### Expedia.com

Perhaps to guard against being just another web site that wants to book your flights, lodging, car rentals and cruises, Expedia goes a step further by offering different ways of doing so. For example, when it comes to discount air travel, you can either hunt through a list of special (non-refundable, non-upgradeable) prearranged fares, or enter a maximum price you're willing to pay and agree to buy any tickets that fit your specifications. Your lodging, on the other hand, may include hotels, B&B's, condos or even villas. Now, for the spontaneous traveler, you may be able to find real steals on a quick flight out of town, say, tomorrow; just realize that your villa may not yet be ready when you get there.

| ·AIR TRAVEL ·FOREIGN TRAVEL | ·HOTELS | ·CAR RENTALS | ·CRUISES | |
|---|---|---|---|---|

## 800-407-3351 • Express Hotel Reservations

### ExpressReservations.com

Initially established to cut down on lodging costs for travelers in the fashion industry, this site is now open to anyone who likes to stay in quality hotels at discount rates. Unfortunately, it's only available if you're traveling to New York City, Los Angeles or Chicago. Some might argue that these are the only places in the US worth staying, but the value of these discounts certainly warrants expansion. Then, given the typically pricey rates of these three largest American cities, they're easily the right places to start.

| ·HOTELS | | | | |
|---|---|---|---|---|

## 800-257-7544 • Fairmont Hotels & Resorts

### Fairmont.com

"Hotels under the Fairmont banner offer guests an extraordinary place that is created by combining unique architecture and structure, expressive decor and artistry, and magnificent features." These guys get points for consistency, as this site offers most of these things in web form, with excellent pictures of what appear to be outstanding, luxurious hotels and resorts in the Caribbean, Americas and Middle East. Furthermore, descriptions like "nestled in a lush coconut grove oasis" do nothing to alleviate your desire to go there immediately, which is doable thanks to an easy reservation process. Good stuff.

| ·HOTELS | ·RESORTS | | | |
|---|---|---|---|---|

# FamilyOnBoard.com

Family on Board • 800-793-2075

When traveling with children, you typically deal with three primary concerns: 1) keeping them safe, 2) keeping them comfortable and 3) keeping them quiet. This site addresses all of these needs for both road and air travel, with a brief array of products designed to secure, coddle and/or entertain the kids in the meantime of a vacation. From the simplicity of a harness that stabilizes a baby on your lap during airplane turbulence, to the extravagance of an in-car DVD player, there's not much here, and it's not all easy to shop for, but sometime mid-voyage you'll be glad you did.

| | ·ACCESSORIES | ·MONEY/SECURITY | | |
|---|---|---|---|---|

# FiestaAmericana.com

Fiesta Americana • 877-767-2327

This site represents Mexico's largest resort and hotel chain, offering beachside accommodations and lodging close to cultural destinations throughout the expanse of this dynamic North American country as well as in a couple of exciting South American cities. Vacationers in Mexico were among the first to experience swim-up bars, tequila poppers and parasailing, and you'll find such adventurous and raucous activities at many of these resorts. But these hotels aren't strictly about wild times; rather they tend to focus upon comfort and luxury, promising some of the more highly regarded stays in the nation.

| | ·HOTELS | ·RESORTS | ·FOREIGN TRAVEL | |
|---|---|---|---|---|

# FindMyRoom.com

Findmyroom • No Service Number

This one is truly a no-brainer. Essentially, it gives you quick access to over 8,000 hotels, globally, allowing you to check availability in just a few precious moments. You can either browse your way directly to your destination city to view all available options, or you may utilize the Advanced Search feature, setting price and date filters to match your specifications. The listings offer lots of information, but rarely pictures (part of the no-frills, quick-loading aspect of the site). Frankly, we'd rather see a FindMyKeys.com.

| | ·HOTELS | | | |
|---|---|---|---|---|

# Firmdale.com

Firmdale Hotels • No Service Number

This one will only come in handy if you're planning a trip to London. On the other hand, if you are headed to the city on the Thames, here's pretty much the only hotel chain you need to know about. Luxury rooms and below-luxury prices include access to some of the most popular parts of town, including Covent Garden, South Kensington and Soho. Amenities include private dining rooms, gyms and screening rooms, and while the comfort appears to be unbeatable, in the words of the bard, "Let every eye negotiate for itself."

| | ·HOTELS | ·FOREIGN TRAVEL | | |
|---|---|---|---|---|

**877-435-8663 • Flight 001**

# Flight001.com

Billing itself as "A store that recreates the thrill of an international airport with merchandise that addresses every travel need with style and comfort," this travel gear boutique really isn't as complicated as all that. Split into three categories (Pre-Flight, In-Flight and Arrival), it's quite simple to view all of the site's unique, stylish and/or amazing products. Included in their catalog is some light luggage, travel kits, games and accessories, and while we'd love to make fun of it all, even just a little bit, really everything about this store, from concept to products to execution, is too cool. Damn.

| ·LUGGAGE | ·ACCESSORIES | ·MONEY/SECURITY | ·PETS |
| --- | --- | --- | --- |

**800-230-0426 • France.com**

# France.com

Welcome to one of the most popular travel destinations in the world: cultural apex to the literate, romance capital of lovers, origin of the finest wine to heavy drinkers. Access to France in all its glory (and for good measure, Tahiti) is made simple here, with apartment rentals, car rentals and hotel bookings merely a couple of clicks deep. Additionally, you may book day tours to see museums, fashion shows and of course the most popular sites, or opt for night cruises and tours of Paris's famous nightclubs and burlesques; any way you go you'll of course be privy to some of the hautest cuisine on the planet, served by the haughtiest waiters.

| ·HOTELS | ·CAR RENTALS | ·PROPERTY RENTAL | ·FOREIGN TRAVEL |
| --- | --- | --- | --- |

**303-471-5400 • Fresh Tracks Maps Store**

# FreshTracksMaps.com

Wherever the ultimate destination of your next traveling adventure may be is not as important as whether you make it back in one piece. Hence, this site offers old school maps and guide books, along with the more advanced navigational instruments, GPS devices and mapping software that makes it nearly impossible to lose your way even in the few remote landscapes left on the planet. Speaking of which, the proprietors also endorse and contribute to a couple of interesting environmental concerns, so buying from this no-frills site will help satisfy your moral sensibilities as well as your wanderlust.

| ·ACCESSORIES | ·MAPS & GUIDES | | |
| --- | --- | --- | --- |

**800-587-1584 • Ghurka**

# Ghurka.com

These guys used to just be a "small leather bag workshop"; now they're pretty much huge, with stores all over the US, in Europe and Japan. Some of their bags even get cast in feature films, like *What Lies Beneath* and *Hannibal*, or turn up on the arms of the wealthy and famous. You can tell people that as you toss their weather-beaten old carryon items out of the overhead bin to make room for your sleek leather furnishings. After all, something this enviable and valuable you don't want to trust to the burly disregard of the baggage handlers.

| ·LUGGAGE | | | |
| --- | --- | --- | --- |

## Go-Today.com

Go-Today.com • No Service Number

If you've suddenly found yourself facing some free time in the near future, and feel the urge to visit Europe, this site is for you. Whereas spontaneous travel usually entails obscene prices and endless scheduling headaches, here you can find reasonably priced packages to destinations across the continent, airfare inclusive with hotel options at various price ranges. The best way to ensure your vacation's perfection is to plan ahead by as much or more than six months in advance, but in lieu of that this site helps pick up the slack.

| | ·AIR TRAVEL | ·HOTELS | ·CAR RENTALS | ·FOREIGN TRAVEL |
|---|---|---|---|---|

## GoingInStyle.com

GoingInStyle.com • 800-637-8953

With dozens upon dozens of answers to the question, "What might you want to take with you?" this site's useful enough just as inspiration for a travel checklist. Between items of utility and items of luxurious comfort exist a wide range of those that fall in between, stuff like travel air purifiers, exercise equipment, pocket knives and clocks that keep time across multiple time zones. Items are far-reaching enough to be dispersed over ten categories, with Travel Spa and Portable Comforts the most immediately attractive. Adventurer, family vacationer or general roustabout; you're almost guaranteed to find something you'll need, want or just plain like.

| ·LUGGAGE | ·ACCESSORIES | ·MONEY/SECURITY | ·PETS |
|---|---|---|---|

## GordonsGuide.com

GordonsGuide.com • No Service Number

Enticing you with all manner of adventure travels (categories include Cattle Drives, Whitewater Rafting and Houseboat Rentals), all this site is really equipped to do is give you some information on how to arrange for your adventures and set up your bookings at ski lodges, resorts, B&B's and hotels. Listings are detailed and the activities enough to inspire your vacation planning for decades. All in all, this is a good start, guaranteed to get you close to the action. And that is what you want after all, isn't it? The Action?

| ·ADVENTURE | | | |
|---|---|---|---|

## Greyhound.com

Greyhound Lines, Inc. • 800-846-0754

Don't think of it so much as riding along the nation's highways as cheaply as possible while crammed into a metallic barge on wheels; think of it as seeing the homeland rolling by first-hand through the window of a comfortable bus surrounded by a couple dozen fellow Americans. Sure, you don't generally need reservations to ride Greyhound, but securing tickets online may save you a long wait in line, and help you avoid the occasional sell-out (which will save you a long wait in the terminal). It's easy enough to travel the country in such a fashion, if this sort of travel can indeed be called fashionable.

| ·BUS & RAIL | | | |
|---|---|---|---|

**877-468-9473 • Hotwire**                                       **HotWire.com**

If your quest for good bargains includes a disregard for precision planning, this site should be able to find you some fantastic deals on flight, lodging and car rental bookings. Of course, nothing about cheap travel is perfect, and in this case the catch is that, until you make a purchase, you won't know the exact time of travel, the carrier or the name of the hotel you'll be staying in. You can ward against red-eye flights, if that's a concern, but otherwise you may typically expect to end up with times that other travelers have forsaken for one reason or another. Oh, and you'll have an hour to decide if it's worth it. We find it more palatable if you designate such bargain-hunting as "adventurous."

| ·AIR TRAVEL | ·HOTELS | ·CAR RENTALS | ·FOREIGN TRAVEL | |
|---|---|---|---|---|

**No Service Number • iCruise.com**                              **i-Cruise.com**

This claims to be "the internet's leading purveyor of cruise vacation travel, boasting the most complete cruise ship database ever assembled online." Wow, we hope the cruises themselves aren't this dry. Actually, with Adventure Cruises, Luxury Cruises, Discount Cruises and a variety of filters to ensure you find the boat with the best entertainment, spa, food and kids options, they make it easy, which is almost as good as fun. To wit, these cruises go literally all over the world, feeding, pampering and entertaining you all the way, "like summer camp for adults." Okay, we're sold.

| ·CRUISES | | | | |
|---|---|---|---|---|

**800-397-4667 • ILoveInns.com**                                **ILoveInns.com**

This site's not quite like the others. Devoted to Bed and Breakfasts, it's got a very comprehensive listing of information about B'n'B's in US states and territories as well as in Canada. However, here you cannot generally book reservations online (and really, part of the charm of these Inns is an almost anti-technological quaintness). Instead, what you may buy here is membership to the Bed & Breakfast and Country Inn Travel Club. It sounds a bit silly, and it is only worthwhile if you're a constant traveler in need of a homey place to stay, in which case you'll receive discounts and the occasional coupon for a free overnight stay.

| ·MAPS & GUIDES | ·HOTELS | | | |
|---|---|---|---|---|

**No Service Number • Indo.com**                                 **Indo.com**

Few lands are more remote to us, in distance as well as culture, than the thousands of Southeast Asian islands known collectively as Indonesia. Here's your chance to get to know them a little better. This site specializes in hotel and resort bookings all over the archipelago: Java, Jakarta and especially Bali, which is alternately referred to as "Island of the Gods," and "Dawn of the World" (depending on who you want to believe). Beaches, jungles and volcanoes make up most of the geography, but as is the nature of islands, you'll almost always board by the coast, and easily with this excellent resource.

| ·HOTELS | ·RESORTS | ·PROPERTY RENTAL | ·FOREIGN TRAVEL | |
|---|---|---|---|---|

## InMotionPictures.com

In Motion Pictures • 877-383-8646

As if a long flight wasn't uncomfortable enough, airlines have to go and make it worse by showing the most terrible movies ever produced (forcing captive audiences to watch what no one else would). This site wants to free you from this slow form of torture by reserving portable DVD player and DVD rentals for pick-up at the airport. You can rent one-way, dropping them off at your destination, or rent round-trip, taking them back to your hotel room (hotel movie offerings are little better than the airlines'). Or, if you have a long layover, you can simply rent it in the airport and hope not too many people watch over your shoulder. It's a good idea, but participating airports are limited, so unless you're willing to reroute your connections, you may be out of luck.

 | ·ACCESSORIES | | | |

## InsureMyTrip.com

InsureMyTrip.com • 800-487-4722

Yes, it's true, in this world you can insure against almost anything: theft, car accidents, poor health, even death itself. Well you can also insure that vacation you're planning. Why? Because if you're doing it right you're devoting a lot of cash and/or vacation time to a once-in-a-lifetime holiday. Should something come up, say a family emergency or government coup in the country you plan to visit, chances are you may be forced to cancel or postpone your trip. With travel insurance you may recoup your investment, enabling you to travel well another day. This site acts as a broker to many different companies and plans, making it an excellent place to find the right premium for you.

·MONEY/SECURITY | | | |

## Irvs.com

Irv's Luggage Warehouse • 888-300-4787

Recognizing the "lug" in luggage, this "#1 in Chicagoland!" retailer offers a very extensive catalog of suitcases, garment bags, computer cases, tote bags, cosmetic cases, backpacks and even trunks with which to haul your respective load. But this is barely half the story, as pretty much any of these items may be found here with wheels attached as well (which makes the lugging considerably easier). Browsing may be a little cruder than ideal, but a side-by-side Compare Products feature salvages any doubts that good deals are easy to come by with this family-owned operation.

·LUGGAGE | ·ACCESSORIES | | |

## JetBlue.com

Jet Blue • 800-538-2583

Most airlines have plenty to offer: old planes, uncomfortable seats, expensive fares and the back of another passenger's head to stare at for hours on end… oh, and a bag of pretzels. Welcome to Jet Blue, which intends to "to bring humanity back to air travel and to make flying more enjoyable." They do this with a fleet of new planes equipped with leather seats and live satellite television for every passenger. Somehow, prices are still competetive, which probably has to do with a lack of meal service (No airline food? Heaven forefend!) and limited itineraries. Still, if it can get you where you want to go, there may be no better way to travel for the money. Here's hoping their competitors are paying attention.

 ·AIR TRAVEL | | | |

## 888-527-8728 • Laptop Travel

### LaptopTravel.com

If the very thought of wireless communications makes you drool like a hound at a pig roast, this is the site for you, as it is plum full of those little gadgets and cables that make mobility as fun as it is futuristic. From infrared adaptors that can turn your cell phone into a wireless modem to portable computing accessories, this site really offers just about anything you might imagine you need when you're in the middle of nowhere and need to phone, email, fax, scan, print, download or rip whatever it is that's distracting you from nature. Topped off by foreign power adaptors and supplies, should you leave the country, bring a comfortable set of clothes on your trip, because you won't have room for much else.

| ·ACCESSORIES | | | |
|---|---|---|---|

## 877-728-3660 • Lazar's Luggage Superstore

### LazarsLuggage.com

Traveling without the proper luggage can be as difficult as walking up the down side of an escalator, but nowhere near as fun. This sizable travel store specializes in the type of suitcases that have wheels and flip-up handles so they can be effortlessly pulled behind as you stroll the concourse. They also feature a wide range of accessories that add a similar sense of ease to other difficult travel activities like carrying money or maintaining regular hygiene habits. Everything's pretty easy to find, even stuff as specific as Wheeled Garment Bags and Soft Carry-Ons, leading us to believe that, yes, life gets easier upon visiting this store.

| ·LUGGAGE | ·ACCESSORIES | | |
|---|---|---|---|

## 800-223-6800 • Leading Hotels of the World

### LHW.com

When you've got only a few moments to find the best possible hotel located in any particular corner of the world, check this site first. Rather than fill up on all of the possible hotels that can be booked in any old place, this group refuses to include any facility that doesn't meet a very high set of standards. Consequently, if you can find a listing here for the place you would like to visit, you can be fairly certain it's among the best in the entire region, if not the best. From the Caribbean to the Middle East, South American and Africa, there are great hotels to be had all over, right here.

| ·HOTELS | ·RESORTS | ·FOREIGN TRAVEL | |
|---|---|---|---|

## 888-563-4464 • Lodging.com

### Lodging.com

Some people don't like camping out on the sidewalks of a foreign city. Go figure. For such folk, Lodging.com offers an easy means of securing a place to stay before you get there. Start by simply narrowing in on the city in question, starting with the continent, and then by country (any of thousands of cities, even those as rarely visited as Maseru, Lesotho or Koror, Palau). A listing of available hotels will follow, or some bed & breakfasts if you prefer. Book online, and all you'll have left to do is show up.

| ·HOTELS | ·FOREIGN TRAVEL | | |
|---|---|---|---|

## LondonConnection.com
The London Connection • 888-393-9120

"Offering London flats, Paris apartments, and Cotswold Cottages for short-term lets," it's clear there's more to be found on this site than the name lets on.  Established in the UK, and expanding to include France's largest city, essentially this site allows you to live like a local, residing in a short term rental, away from the hotel districts and in the regular mix of the city... even if that mix happens to occur in a great neighborhood.  Search for pads based on criteria like the number of bedrooms and their proximity to tube stops, and you have only to work on that phony accent in order to blend in completely.

| ·PROPERTY RENTAL | ·FOREIGN TRAVEL | | |
|---|---|---|---|

## LondonTown.com
London Town • No Service Number

There are many reasons to be excited about a trip to London, and pretty much all of them are addressed here.  You may learn about different neighborhoods, sights to see, events taking place during your visit, means of getting around, good places to eat (essential), nightclubs, bars, theatre and places to stay.  With these last two in particular the site can be a great help.  Plan your trip far enough in advance and you will find virtually unbeatable rates at some fine area hotels.  Advance booking also helps you get the most coveted tickets to the best shows in town.

| ·HOTELS | ·TOURS | ·FOREIGN TRAVEL |
|---|---|---|

## Luggage.com
LeTravelStore.com • 800-713-4260

Claiming to have been the first all-travel store in the United States, these guys have been at it for more than a quarter century, having over time developed a catalog finely attuned to the needs of modern travelers.  Despite the name, categories like Wheeled Luggage, Backpacks, Shoulder Bags and Packing Organizers offer trim selections at best, however useful.  As it turns out, the real meat of the site is to be found under the Travel Accessories heading, with power converters, money belts, in-flight comfort aids, travel appliances and hostel supplies ultimately making the visit worthwhile.

| ·LUGGAGE | ·ACCESSORIES | ·MONEY/SECURITY |
|---|---|---|

## LuxuryCollection.com
Starwood Hotels & Resorts • 888-625-5144

"Luxury Collection hotels and resorts are distinguished by magnificent décor, spectacular settings, impeccable service and the latest in modern conveniences and amenities. In bustling cities and spectacular resorts around the world, The Luxury Collection provides the definitive hospitality experience for people of superior taste and refinement..." or conversely, "an elite clientele." Is it for you? One gets the feeling that the concierges of these hotels turn their collective noses up at the thought that some of the 'déclassé' among us might just creep through with these online reservations. All the more reason to make them, we figure, and bring a lot of bags along for the ride.

| ·HOTELS | ·RESORTS | | |
|---|---|---|---|

## 888-297-3299 • Luxury Link Traveler

**LuxuryLink.com**

Freely bandying about terms like "the best of the best," this site has been set up to make it easy for you to spend lots of money on decadent and luxurious vacation packages that can put you on a yacht cruising past the French Riviera or in a villa on coastal Italy. If you aren't looking to spend vast amounts of cash but still want to experience such a lavish vacation, they can help with that, too, offering packages for auction and special (often off-season) deals for relatively low prices. Either way, if traveling in style and comfort is your objective, check it out.

| ·TOURS | ·FOREIGN TRAVEL | | |
|---|---|---|---|

## 800-962-4943 • Magellan's

**Magellans.com**

Given the relaxed, not at all pushy look of this site, we were surprised to find just how thorough its selection happens to be. Prepared to equip your travels whether you're going to the outback or to the park, you can find a great supply of travel accessories, appliances, comfort aids and clothing in addition to a fairly standard assortment of luggage. Tops though is the Health & Hygiene section which offers things like dental first aid kits, water purifiers, insect repellent and emergency blankets. Browsing may also be accomplished by Destination (from Afghanistan to Zimbabwe) or Activity (a Cruise to a Peace Corps mission), this is a site not to be missed.

| ·LUGGAGE | ·ACCESSORIES | ·MONEY/SECURITY | |
|---|---|---|---|

## 415-772-8800 • Mandarin Oriental Hotel Group

**MandarinOriental.com**

The Mandarin Oriental Hotel Group started out with a single hotel in Hong Kong. Its success subsequently led them to establish a chain of luxury lodgings in some of the most frequently traveled cities on the globe, as well as a few that are off the beaten path. If you happen to be going to one of these places, particularly some of the great cities of the Far East, you'll do little better in terms of quality than these lodgings, as all strive to fulfill every luxuriant want and need you may have. Anyway, if you can find better digs in the Himalayas, more power to ya.

| ·HOTELS | ·FOREIGN TRAVEL | | |
|---|---|---|---|

## 800-430-7532 • Maps.com

**Maps.com**

How well do you know your way around? Sure, getting lost is one of the most exciting parts of spontaneous travel, but let's face it: however often you hear reference to the world being a "global village," this planet is huge. If you don't have a map, you just might not be making it back anytime soon. Scare tactics aside, these guys can hook you up with maps of cities all over the place, whether for driving, sightseeing or, if you're a purist, you can find a big world map to throw darts at to decide where to get lost next.

| ·MAPS & GUIDES | | | |
|---|---|---|---|

## MexicoBoutiqueHotels.com

Mexico Boutique Hotels • No Service Number

In answer to all the obvious questions that might arise, these guys say of this collection of hotels: "set apart from the rest by their individuality… they are 'boutique' because they are unique… It can be safely assumed that by having been included in this guide they are by definition of an exemplary standard. 'Boutique' presupposes the best in taste, from furnishings to food. It means experiencing something out of the ordinary." Some might argue that Mexico itself is out of the ordinary, but this site does everything to elucidate the beauty that surrounds these fine establishments, which was enough to convince us, even without the excessive language.

| | ·HOTELS | ·FOREIGN TRAVEL | | |
|---|---|---|---|---|

## MonasteriesOfItaly.com

Anacapa Press • 800-528-6398

Imagine staying in some of the most beautiful centuries-old buildings in Italy, rich with history and culture and built in stunning locations.  Now imagine the price for such lodging was well below typical hotel rates.  Sound impossible?  It might be, but this site boasts a book that offers to guide you on how to board in over 400 of the gorgeous monasteries and convents that adorn Italian cities and countryside.  It's a simple purchase, a one-time procurement that could make your stay less expensive and more a vibrant adventure, or you could find yourself sleeping on a wood cot in a drafty room surrounded by silent Italian monks. It's yours to find out.

| ·MAPS & GUIDES | ·FOREIGN TRAVEL | | |
|---|---|---|---|

## MoriLuggage.com

Mori Luggage & Gifts • 800-678-6674

To understand the primary appeal of this site, you have only to scroll through the Shop by Brand pull-down menu located in the top right corner of the screen—there are somewhere around 150 companies here, representing some of the best and the worst in brand name travel (mostly the best).  Unfortunately, not all of these really exist in the inventory.  This is probably irrelevant, though, as most of us are still recovering from the fact that there even are 150 brand names in the travel manufacture racket. Bottom line: this site has a lot to offer, with a fine assortment of quality luggage and accessories.

| | ·LUGGAGE | ·ACCESSORIES | | |
|---|---|---|---|---|

## NatHab.com

Natural Habitat Adventures • 877-745-4648

This site offers vacation packages that take the original concept of an African safari and applies it to all corners of the globe.  You can, for example, find a trip to the Amazon jungle here, a voyage to the Galapagos Islands and journeys to both North and South Poles.  Designed with nature enthusiasts in mind, these packages take you to many of this planet's rich and diverse ecosystems, with a focus on the native animals and vegetation.  Climates may vary, and conditions can be rough at points, but as incongruous as it sounds you can apparently count on one thing: luxurious dining.  Go figure.

| ·ADVENTURE | ·TOURS | ·FOREIGN TRAVEL | |
|---|---|---|---|

## No Service Number • Oberoi Hotels & Resorts

**OberoiHotels.com**

If you're the sort to be cavalier about spending for a single night's board what an average person might spend for a whole month's rent, take a look at these hotels and resorts that "are synonymous the world over for providing the right blend of service, luxury and quiet efficiency." What are you paying for? A host of traditional and high-tech amenities (some suites include butler service as well as broadband connections), opulent settings and stellar accommodation in places such as the Middle East, Sri Lanka, Indonesia, India and Australia.

| ·HOTELS | ·FOREIGN TRAVEL | | |
|---|---|---|---|

## 800-929-2523 • OneTravel.com

**OneTravel.com**

All this technology is supposed to save us time, right? Well, this site does its best, offering quick and easy bookings of rooms, car rentals, flights and vacation packages. In fact, you can set everything you need for a standard trip up in less than ten minutes, and this includes time you may waste looking around for a mid-booking snack. You may find better prices elsewhere, but the big secret of online travel booking is that most of them access the same databases to find the same rates and fares. What these guys do offer is the "Farebeater Ultra" search, which scours any additional deals or restrictions that might knock the price down (usually not by much though). If you want to get it done already, this is your next and only stop.

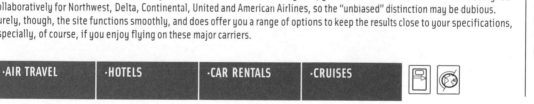

| ·AIR TRAVEL ·RESORTS | ·HOTELS ·TOURS | ·CAR RENTALS | ·CRUISES |
|---|---|---|---|

## 888-656-4546 • Orbitz

**Orbitz.com**

Featuring "the Orbot," an "unbiased flight search engine," this site searches through the fares of over 450 airlines to find you the best, most convenient itineraries in a very short amount of time. That being said, you should be aware that this site was designed collaboratively for Northwest, Delta, Continental, United and American Airlines, so the "unbiased" distinction may be dubious. Surely, though, the site functions smoothly, and does offer you a range of options to keep the results close to your specifications, especially, of course, if you enjoy flying on these major carriers.

| ·AIR TRAVEL | ·HOTELS | ·CAR RENTALS | ·CRUISES |
|---|---|---|---|

## No Service Number • Pakha

**Pakha.com**

If you've tried to nap on an airplane recently, you probably ended up looking to booze for comfort, as you certainly couldn't find any in the linens provided by the airline. If such things are important to you, Pakha specializes in, "The simple joy and decadence of your own pillowcase, napkins, tray covers, blanket and shoe bag while in flight." Yes, you can carry-on a set of items that exceed the quality of first class, never again having to weigh sanitation issues against exhaustion when settling in for a fair night's sleep on a long flight. Unfortunately, airlines do not yet let you bring your own chair.

| ·ACCESSORIES | | | |
|---|---|---|---|

## PassportHelp.com                    American Passport Express • 800-841-6778

Here's the scenario: you've got tickets to leave the country in two days and you've just realized that you have no passport. What do you do? Glad you asked. Thanks to this wonderful technology we call the internet, sites like this one can expedite what is usually a long, bureaucratic process requiring long lines and hours' worth of paperwork to get you a new passport in as little as one day. Of course, they're not doing it for free, and in most cases their fees severely magnify the cost of getting it done through straightforward government interaction (to varying degrees based on how quickly you need it), but in the end, you may just decide that speed and convenience are worth it to escape these shores.

| | •FOREIGN TRAVEL | | | |
|---|---|---|---|---|

## Pet-Friendly-Hotels.net                    Pet Friendly Hotels • 866-568-7027

While many of the lodging reservations sites listed in this book will incidentally book you with pet-friendly hotels, this is the only one that specifically weeds out all the animal prohibitive establishments, making it much easier for pet owners to locate suitable accommodations for that vacation with your favorite animals. It simply operates like any other site, requesting your destination date and the length of your stay, and then responding with available pet-friendly lodging in the specified location. From your pet's point of view, at least, it beats a kennel.

| | •HOTELS | •PETS | | |
|---|---|---|---|---|

## PriceLine.com                    Priceline.com • 800-774-2354

These pioneers of the "name your own price" phenomenon are perhaps best known for reviving the career of William Shatner. At least, that's how they're known to people who've never used this service. Once you've tried them out you'll remember either incredible savings or inconveniently arranged flight, hotel or car rental bookings. That's because, while you may name the maximum budget for each element of your travels, you cannot name much else, and yet you must pay in advance. In fact, your only leeway turns out to be the actual dates of travel, and even these the site may try to convince you to change (for a better chance at cheap prices). All we can say is that, when naming your price, make it low enough to make it worthwhile.

| | | •AIR TRAVEL | •HOTELS | •CAR RENTALS | •CRUISES |
|---|---|---|---|---|---|

## QuickBook.com                    Quickbook • 800-789-9887

Some hotel sites have it all, some boast only the best. These guys focus on making it simple for you to find something you want, a novel idea if not the right one. Like most similar sites, you are asked to enter a destination, date and length of stay, as well as a less common price range filter. However, understanding that this isn't always the way you want to shop, they offer hotel types like Hip Hotels, Family Fun, Seaside Favorites and the Premier Collection, allowing you then to break it down by US city. They won't furnish you with pages upon pages of options, but they might just satisfy, in short order.

| | •HOTELS | | | |
|---|---|---|---|---|

## 800-462-2577 • Rail Europe

**RailEurope.com**

One of the more popular ways of getting about Europe is the Eurorail system. As much as merely getting you around, the romance of riding a train across the changing countrysides is enough a part of a European jaunt to be considered tradition. This site offers regular and student rates on passes that vary regionally and by duration, and additionally a pass for British Rail (as the UK's not covered by the general pass). Covering seventeen countries and most of the western continent, it can be pricey, but when properly executed well worth it.

| ·FOREIGN TRAVEL | ·BUS & RAIL | | | |
|---|---|---|---|---|

## 800-275-7263 • Rand McNally

**RandMcNally.com**

As you might expect from one of the better-recognized names in road maps, this site offers a bevy of fantastic resources for road trippers (and not just maps). The Travel Store doesn't offer a lot in terms of name brand variety, but between the guidebooks, GPS devices, map software, travel games and luggage featured here, all angles are covered; if anything does seem to be missing, it will almost undoubtedly turn up in the Travel Necessities category, which is big enough to be a whole other site unto itself.

| ·LUGGAGE | ·ACCESSORIES | ·MONEY/SECURITY | ·MAPS & GUIDES | |
|---|---|---|---|---|

## 800-426-4840 • REI

**REI.com**

Select the link marked REI Adventures on this popular outdoor activity retailer's web page, and you'll find plenty of uses for any gear you might have accrued elsewhere on the site. Small group activity travel packages range from cycling, hiking, paddling and climbing to combinations therein, taking place in locations all over the world, including Africa, the Pacific Islands and even Antarctica. Additionally, the tours are well staffed, as exemplified by a Galapagos Island cruise that puts you in touch with the native animals per the instructions of a naturalist equipped to educate as well as guide. These are vacations worth remembering.

| ·LUGGAGE ·MONEY/SECURITY | ·ACCESSORIES ·MAPS & GUIDES | ·ADVENTURE | ·TOURS | |
|---|---|---|---|---|

## 800-735-2478 • Relais & Chateaux

**RelaisChateaux.com**

Having achieved the near impossible task of making a web site seem classy, this turns out to be one of the better ways to book luxurious lodgings around the world. A hotel chain based in Europe, the Relais chain owns over 450 beautiful properties globally, many of them featuring gloriously indulgent amenities (some even have golf courses). Browsing by country is easy, but the best way to search is via their Reserve By Criteria feature, which allows you to pinpoint those services and activities important to you to narrow it down. We'd recommend selecting those most important to you first (location is a good start) and utilizing the Number of Results button; as good as these hotels are, none of them offer everything ... yet.

| ·HOTELS | | | |  |
|---|---|---|---|---|

# RentVillas.com

Rentvillas.com • 800-726-6702

On certain European vacations, you opt to make the most of your time and money by hustling about from city to city, country to country, taking in the important popular sites at light speed, leaving out the ones that merely stand to get in the way. Other European vacations are a bit more elegant. All arguments of quality versus quantity aside, this site makes it simple to find a grand short-term property rental by region in Greece, Italy, France, Spain, Portugal and Great Britain, where you may relax and take in the atmosphere, culture and/or climate that makes the area worth visiting to begin with.

| | ·PROPERTY RENTAL | ·FOREIGN TRAVEL | | |
|---|---|---|---|---|

# ResortQuest.com

Resort Quest • 877-588-5800

The very notion of North American travel may pale in comparison to that of a voyage to Europe, Africa or Asia, but the truth is that proximity to home doesn't make a resort vacation any less enjoyable. On the contrary, given the benefits of price and language, spending a little time in a home not so far away from home may be just the ticket, or so says this proprietor of, it just so happens, North American vacation rentals. Made especially worthwhile to beach, skiing, golf and tennis enthusiasts, this site has a way of making domestic travel an enviable proposition.

| | ·RESORTS | ·PROPERTY RENTAL | | |
|---|---|---|---|---|

# RoadTrips.com

Roadtrips • 800-465-1765

Sports fans who want to get a feel for life on the road may do just that with this site that offers prepackaged tours of events and venues in the realms of professional Baseball, Football, Basketball, Hockey, Racing and Golf. Traveling city to city in style, you're promised good seats and first class accommodations, whether taking an extended road trip or simply catching an all-star game. If you want to root root root for your home team on the go, they'll also allow you to set up a custom itinerary, even if you intend to follow the US National Soccer team to points abroad.

| | ·TOURS | | | |
|---|---|---|---|---|

# SamsoniteCompanyStores.com

Samsonite • 800-262-8282

Samsonite was originally founded (under a different name) back in the 19th century to manufacture trunks that would be sturdy enough to withstand the rigorous travel of the Gold Rush. Presuming your own travels will be slightly less physically demanding, one can only surmise that this stuff will last you a long time over great distances. Their selection includes Jantzen backpacks, travel accessories, briefcases and adaptors for the bizarre power outlets and modem lines of different countries. Not least, of course, is the luggage, which by now sets industry standards for durability, though you'll want to carry-on any gold you may find.

| | ·LUGGAGE | ·ACCESSORIES | | |
|---|---|---|---|---|

## No Service Number • Site 59

### Site59.com

If you're ready to go pretty much now, and you haven't any interest in waiting on stand-by, check out this site that specializes in last minute deals. Simply enter your starting point and destination, and the site promptly returns you several days' worth of reasonable options that may include airfare, hotel and/or rental car. Or, if you're not picky, you may browse by date and/or activity to find good deals to just anyplace that isn't home. Set up to work most efficiently with two traveling adults makes this the perfect site to book that spontaneous romantic weekend. Good stuff.

| ·AIR TRAVEL | ·HOTELS | ·CAR RENTAL | |
|---|---|---|---|

## 800-255-7727 • Spa Finder

### SpaFinder.com

On the far end of the spectrum from adventure vacations is a week at a spa, where relaxation is a disciplined art form, and you are guided from massage to recreation to treatment to dinner, usually in a bathrobe. Spas, of course, range in purpose and location, but this site can guide you to them all, whether you're looking for a golf retreat on the beach or a weight loss clinic in wine country. Some will pamper you, some accost you with healthy activities and some will just let you cruise. We recommend the pampering kind; you can always work yourself sweaty at home.

| ·RESORTS | | | | |
|---|---|---|---|---|

## 888-627-3887 • Suitcase.com

### Suitcase.com

Easy to remember and easy to use, this site offers a vast selection of reasonably priced name brand luggage, including Tumi, Samsonite, Hartmann and many others. Customers are probably best served by the Search By Model link, which let's you know the entire array of options available, from Wheeled Carry-ons that range in size incrementally from eighteen to thirty inches, to garment bags, totes, duffels and backpacks. You'll also find smaller items like toiletry kits, organizers and briefcases (for laptops or otherwise) in good supply, and an erratic set of travel items that round out the catalog.

| ·LUGGAGE | | | | |
|---|---|---|---|---|

## 877-467-8737 • Super Clubs

### SuperClubs.com

These guys introduce a new term to your beach resort holiday: Super Inclusive. What this means is that you pay one up-front fee to cover food, lodging, activities, amenities (which includes alcohol) and even airfare if you desire. In return they cover literally everything, transporting you, feeding you, coddling you and entertaining you for the entire length of your stay, with nearly no restrictions (meaning midnight, 2 AM and 4 AM snacks to your stomach's content). Better yet, tipping is off limits, meaning you'll know the exact cost of your vacation going in, and can forget about money entirely for the duration, a vacation unto itself.

| ·RESORTS | | | | |
|---|---|---|---|---|

## Tauck.com

Tauck World Discovery • 800-788-7885

Boasting "enriching adventures," what these guys are really selling is a spate of lavish vacation packages that involve cruises, sightseeing, safaris and cultural experiences in favored destinations around the world. What do we mean by favored? Well, there's Paris, of course, a Mediterranean voyage on Aristotle Onassis's old yacht and a cruise down to Antarctica. Okay, so the South Pole maybe isn't "favored" per se, but how else can you take a leisurely exploration of the seventh continent?

| ·CRUISES | ·ADVENTURE | ·TOURS | ·FOREIGN TRAVEL |
|---|---|---|---|

## TeleAdaptUSA.com

Teleadapt • 877-835-3232

If you travel abroad, you are quite likely to find that wherever you go there's a bunch of funny holes in the walls. That's because our standard two and three prong plugs do not match the differently-volted power outlets other countries have adopted. Some of the phone lines are even more confounding. Nevertheless, converters exist for almost anything, and whether it's the product you need to power your laptop battery, mobile phone or hair dryer, chances are the right adaptor and/or transformer may be procured here, wherever you may roam.

| ·ACCESSORIES | ·FOREIGN TRAVEL | | |
|---|---|---|---|

## TennisTours.com

Championship Tennis Tours • 800-468-3664

Aficionados of the sport that always begins with "Love All," have good reason to visit Melbourne, Paris, London and New York each year—but only if you can secure tickets. This site sets it all up for you, from airfare and hotel bookings to seats on Wimbledon's Center Court. Tour all the grand Slam tourneys or just your favorites, and opt for additional cruises and tours between matches. Bearing in mind that these are some of the most expensive spectator seats in professional sports, the site also offers access to some of the less prestigious tours, where you may watch the elite tennis player in the world go head to head for less.

| ·TOURS | | | |
|---|---|---|---|

## Tilley.com

Tilley Endurables • 800-363-8737

If your exploits are truly to be memorable, you're likely to find yourself in some rugged situations. While you yourself may be tougher than leather, how're your clothes going to hold up? This site specializes in sturdy apparel made not only to survive in rough conditions, but to keep you relatively comfortable in the process. Their rain repellant hats come equipped with secret pockets; wrinkle resistant clothes promise to "keep out creepy crawlies"; socks prevent blisters and are guaranteed to last three years without a hole; and their bacteria, odor and stain resistant underwear "will nether chafe nor bind." Quick drying, lightweight and durable, these are clothes worthy of adventure.

| ·ACCESSORIES | ·ADVENTURE | | |
|---|---|---|---|

## 206-286-0888 • Trails.com                    Trails.com

If your hunger for new hiking, paddling skiing and biking trails exceeds your local grasp, a subscription to this site will grant you access to more than 30,000 electronic trail descriptions in locations spanning the United States and Canada. Should you forego a subscription, you may still browse by region or by activities as explicit as sea kayaking, back country skiing, snowshoeing and relaxing in hot springs (which tends to require a bit of hiking first), then peruse a selection of guides which include topographic maps and trail reviews, available to you to purchase in print or via download.

| ·ADVENTURE | ·MAPS & GUIDES | | |
|---|---|---|---|

## 866-738-7932 • Travelin' Pets                    TravelinPets.com

It only takes a moment to imagine the havoc that might ensue if animals were allowed to roam free on an airplane. As fun and carnival-like an atmosphere this might be, it's probably for the best that pets are relegated to specialized cages back in cargo. The real question: is it more humane to let them bark and fuss in that cargo space, or to tranquilize them for the voyage…? Here there are no answers, only the carriers that are the specialty of this site, which also features pet car seats & restraints; vest carriers & backpacks (similar to those people use to carry babies); and various pet travel items, like collapsible water dishes.

| ·LUGGAGE | ·ACCESSORIES | ·PETS | |  |
|---|---|---|---|---|

## 866-476-8771 • TravelNow.com                    TravelNow.com

Like many of the travel sites (and there are a lot) that populate the web, this one offers air travel, car rentals and hotel bookings. There's nothing standout about these services, though you may strike a good deal or two. What you'll really want to keep an eye on though is their listing of vacation properties. See, it turns out, sometimes it may be cheaper to rent a villa, condo or apartment for a week than to stay at a hotel—really! Especially if you're visiting a city with notoriously bad cuisine, having your own kitchen and dining space can make a huge difference in your holiday experience. Of course, you can forget about room service.

| ·AIR TRAVEL | ·CAR RENTALS | ·CRUISES | ·PROPERTY RENTAL |  |
|---|---|---|---|---|

## 888-709-5983 • Travelocity.com                    Travelocity.com

If you can see through the clutter on the home page, you will ultimately realize that this convoluted site earnestly intends to give you all the options you may be looking for in terms of straightforward travel. Really, there's only a problem if you get easily frustrated answering lots of questions or doing any amount of actual thinking. Otherwise, for the patient folk among us, we can eventually book flights, hotel rooms, car rentals, rail travel, vacation packages and cruises with satisfactory results. And, while the great offers that distract us from the opening page don't usually apply to real life, if a good one does happen to catch your eye … well maybe clutter ain't always bad.

| ·AIR TRAVEL ·RESORTS | ·HOTELS ·BUS & RAIL | ·CAR RENTALS ·TOURS | ·CRUISES ·FOREIGN TRAVEL |  |
|---|---|---|---|---|

# TravelProtect.com

CSA Travel Protection • 800-873-9855

What, insure the best time of your life? Sounds crazy, right? Not as these guys would have it. They offer policies that will help you recoup the expenses of your trip should something happen. Specifically, things like trip cancellation, trip interruption, baggage loss, emergency medicine and rental car damage are covered to varying degrees, as well as a few other unlikely but potentially disastrous occurrences. Premiums are based on the ages of travelers, and plans cover groups of up to 6 people (though, for more than six, something can be worked out). Costlier vacations lead to higher premiums, but if you've saved up for years for the perfect island vacation, you don't want to blow it if, say, the island sinks or something.

| ·MONEY/SECURITY | | | |
|---|---|---|---|

# TravelSmith.com

Travel Smith • 800-995-7010

If Indiana Jones were to shop online, this might be the spot. A travel gear shop that has it all, from clothes to luggage and any accessories in between, it offers a Shop-By-Destination feature that makes it simple to find stuff you might need for a hiking trip, to relax on the Mediterranean or to go on safari. Aside from items like amphibious sneakers, you can also find a wealth of products for the business traveler or standard vacationer. Either way, you'll find sturdy hats and tough jackets that'll make you at least look like an adventurer, alongside some nifty gadgets that'll make you feel like one.

| ·LUGGAGE | ·ACCESSORIES | ·ADVENTURE | |
|---|---|---|---|

# TravelTools.com

Travel Tools • 317-876-5594

While this site is designed with the business traveler in mind, there are plenty of car-related travel items that the rest of us can appreciate. Humanity will thank you to skip the contraption that fastens a laptop to your steering wheel, but a portable car battery charger wins points in an emergency, heated massage cushions will keep your back from cramping up on a long drive and noise-canceling headphones will help drown out the teeth-grating din of children at play in the confined space of an airplane. Sure, the electric tongue cleaner seems frivolous, but it's just one of many unique products to be found on this elementary site.

| ·LUGGAGE | ·ACCESSORIES | ·MONEY/SECURITY | ·MAPS & GUIDES |
|---|---|---|---|

# TravMed.com

Travel Medicine • 800-872-8633

We tend not to dwell upon what could go wrong on our vacations, and if we do we usually wind up overpacking. Well, here you'll find "Information & Products for Safe Travel" that offer suitcase-friendly solutions to problems you may encounter. Water filters, first aid kits and insect repellents will probably address most of your concerns, but should anxiety have established a firm grasp you can find more specific items like a smoke hood designed to give you some breathing room in case of fire, or a skin stapler, should there not be enough time to apply your suture kit.

| ·ACCESSORIES | ·MONEY/SECURITY | | |
|---|---|---|---|

## 800-874-7266 • Trip.com

### Trip.com

This site is so slick as to be almost overwhelming; that is, how comfortable can you be that you're getting a good deal from something so pristinely designed? Well, it's easy to get comfortable pretty quick, as these guys offer easy solutions to flight, car rental and hotel booking, and pretty much all the resources you'll likely need to prepare for your trip. We're talking international street maps, airport maps, currency converters and even a list of holidays set up for each country. Only when you're logging off will you truly realize how much information these guys have made available in such a tidy package.

| ·AIR TRAVEL ·RESORTS | ·HOTELS ·PROPERTY RENTAL | ·CAR RENTALS ·FOREIGN TRAVEL | ·CRUISES ·MAPS & GUIDES |
|---|---|---|---|

## No Service Number • Vegas.com

### Vegas.com

Generally speaking, we don't give specific cities preferential treatment. However, generally speaking, Las Vegas is not a normal city. An unlikely mélange of dry heat, gambling, spectacle and lavish water usage, in Vegas you'll find people of all ages, from all walks of life, achieving new highs and lows and swept up in the sensory overload. This site attempts to make some sense of it all, from a safe distance, providing all manner of resources from bar & club guides to events calendars, and of course discount advance bookings in all the major and minor casinos, often packaged with airfare. You want to go and they want you to come. Sounds like we have a winner!

| ·AIR TRAVEL | ·HOTELS | ·CAR RENTALS | ·RESORTS |
|---|---|---|---|

## 888-728-4552 • Overseas Connections, Inc.

### VillasOfTheWorld.com

This site can connect you with a selection of more than 2000 villas located on coastlines and in countrysides the world over. And when we say "villa," we don't mean glorified shacks either; these short-term rentals have been rated either First Class, Deluxe or Luxurious, though we could scarcely hazard a guess as to what marks such distinctions. Actually, we did find a villa or two that possessed thatched roofs, but as they were located on a private island in the Pacific, we're assuming them to be high-end regardless.

| ·PROPERTY RENTAL | ·FOREIGN TRAVEL | | |
|---|---|---|---|

## 877-929-7678 • Wayport

### Wayport.net

Many travel sites will be of most use to you when you're away from home, when you're least likely to have access to the web. This site takes care of all that, offering (limited for the moment) high speed internet access from airports, hotels and eventually through wireless applications to be taken with you just about anywhere. Frequent travelers can opt for a monthly membership, wherein every time you travel you can keep things like currency converters and translating dictionaries at your fingertips. For the occasional voyager, prepaid uses make the experience relatively hassle free. Get it while it lasts.

| ·ACCESSORIES | | | |
|---|---|---|---|

## WHotels.com

W Hotels • 888-625-5144

This growing line of luxury, "concept" hotels populates many of the major cities in the world, and offers just about anything a modern traveler could want. What does the modern traveler want? Well, as these guys have it, great restaurants, hip lounges, cafés, fitness centers and internet connections in all the rooms. These rooms, by the way, offer the plushest of amenities, backed by a staff dedicated to fulfilling your individual needs. Basically, this is several steps above a Best Western and, for contemporary-minded folk, about as good as it gets.

| ·HOTELS | | | |
|---|---|---|---|

## WorldLanguage.com

WorldLanguage.com • 800-900-8803

If someone were to approach you outside the airport of a foreign land and loudly utter the words "Oensk velkommen til mitt land!" you might have reason to worry. However, with a few key purchases from this site, you'd recognize them as Norwegian greetings, and be able to respond, "Takk You. Hvor er det nærmeste stedet å å kjøpe en hamburger?" See, these guys focus on learning and translating foreign languages, whether with dictionaries, instructional materials or electronic devices (very cool). With a little help from such tools, you can seek out a hamburger in any of hundreds of languages (even Estonian, Farsi and Papiamento) spoken around the world. No guarantee you'll find one though.

| ·ACCESSORIES | ·FOREIGN TRAVEL | | |
|---|---|---|---|

## WorldTravelCenter.com

WorldTravelCenter.com • 800-786-5566

When all is said and done, most likely you won't have needed insurance for the big vacation. But where some might see a waste of funds, others will discover peace of mind. Offered by this site are quotes for a variety of vacation insurance policies, foreign and domestic, that cover such things as lost baggage, canceled flights, unused hotel deposits, rental car damage and emergency medical expenses. You can rate policies against each other from a variety of brokers featured on the site (with a bit of creative web viewing) to find the one that best suits your vision of a dream voyage.

| ·MONEY/SECURITY | | | |
|---|---|---|---|

## WorldTraveler.com

World Traveler • 800-314-2247

Nothing in particular stands out about this site, and indeed it's not very memorable. In most cases, if you need a specific type of luggage, you may find a wide selection here, both in terms of quality and price. If you're less certain than that, you can simply Shop by Activity, whether it is on a business trip, camping trip, leisurely visitation or full-blown vacation that you intend to embark. The products, while fully functional, are about as thrilling as the site itself, which means employing the price range filter will keep you from spending money on what amount to minor frills. All in all it's good, just not that good.

| ·LUGGAGE | ·ACCESSORIES | | |
|---|---|---|---|

541-383-0696 • WorldWaters.com

**WorldWaters.com**

If you're an avid fisherman (or woman), chances are you've got your best local fishing hole down cold— you know the fish, you caught their parents, and the bait you have is what's for dinner. Maybe you've hit all the good spots for as far as your car can drive, and there's just very little sport left to be had. Maybe you need a new spot, someplace far away, where the fish are mean, wily and show great disdain for tourists. This fishing site offers fishing travel deals for deep sea fans, river anglers and anybody in between— whether guided trips, on a boat or just some place scribbled on a map. Bring your tackle or rent it when you get there, this is a fantastic way to plan a vacation and to make fishing a challenge again.

| ·ADVENTURE | ·TOURS | | | |
|---|---|---|---|---|

NOTES:

# Weddings

It's getting much easier to arrange for the best party of your life (and the ceremony that precedes it) by using some of the capabilities offered by web merchants. In this section, we've compiled those online stores in particular that cater to the traditional (and some not so traditional) standards maintained by proponents of wedded bliss. We're talking stuff like engraved invitations, place settings, flower girl dresses and the little bride and groom figurines that stand atop wedding cakes. It's not all *easy* to find, but it's out there, within reach of your computers, including plenty of options you might not yet have considered.

As an added feature we've included a list of **thepurplebook** sites that offer fine bridal registries, just so you know about them. Online bridal registries have become one of the most convenient ways for your guests to procure gifts, and offer the added benefit of mailing gifts straight to your home so you can avoid the hassle of carting away stacks of prettily wrapped boxes from your reception (rather, from forcing friends and family to do so). Besides, in the days leading up to the event you can go online and see what has and has not been purchased yet . . . sort of like peeking at gifts in your parents' closet before your birthday.

Truthfully, no one site will probably satisfy you in this section, and even if you take a bit from each of them you might find it lacking (we know how demanding you can be). But we believe at the very least these selections should make for a good first step in getting the rest of your life underway. If not real life, then for the gaudy, spectacular ritual that precedes it; your wedding.

NOTES:

_____

_____

_____

_____

_____

_____

_____

_____

_____

_____

_____

_____

_____

_____

_____

_____

_____

TIPS ON PLANNING WEDDINGS ONLINE

These suggestions may help prevent stress and disappointment.

•**ORDER EVERYTHING WAY AHEAD OF TIME:** Whether it's personalized invitations or the perfect gown, for whatever reasons many items in this section take a long time to deliver. Since pretty much everything is going to require extra time and work to make it perfect, order well in advance to avoid needless additional stress.

•**REQUEST SAMPLES:** Oftentimes, you can get sample proofs of personalized invitations, swaths of fabric and examples of confections and other small favors. Take advantage of this, or request it if you're uncertain, to avoid wasting time and expense.

 SITES THAT MAY COME IN HANDY

The following sites offer Bridal Registries.

Amazon.com
Chiasso.com
CrateBarrel.com
Gaiam.com
KitchenEtc.com
MaxwellSilverNY.com
NeimanMarcus.com
Pier1.com
RestorationHardware.com
Ross-Simons.com
Sears.com
StacksAndStacks.com
TableTools.com
UnicaHome.com
Williams-Sonoma.com

BedBathAndBeyond.com
Cooking.com
Fortunoff.com
Gumps.com
MarthaByMail.com
MichaelCFina.com
Pfaltzgraff.com
PotteryBarn.com
RetroModern.com
SaksFifthAvenue.com
Spiegels.com
SurLaTable.com
Target.com
Wal-Mart.com

>>

## SECTION ICON LEGEND

Use the following guide to understand the rectangular icons that appear throughout this section.

### GOWNS

There may not be a more important dress in a woman's life, so we designed this icon to make retailers of bridal gowns easy to spot.

### INVITATIONS

Whether somebody attends your wedding surely has more to do with their availability than the look of your invitations.  But this icon points you to a variety of invitation designs, just in case....

### NONTRADITIONAL & UNIQUE ITEMS

Most of us think of weddings as involving a white gown, a black tuxedo, heavenly music and a garter to toss.  If you're thinking of going with something a little different, you might want to follow this icon.

## LIST OF KEY WORDS

The following words represent the types of items typically found on the sites listed in this section.

### ACCESSORIES

Including jewelry, handbags and hair accessories, there are dozens of items here scattered throughout dozens of sites to accessorize both bride and groom.

### BRIDAL ATTIRE

Aside from the gown, the bride is likely to be wearing special lingerie, veils and headpieces; even some fancy gloves to complete her outfit. Find them here.

### CEREMONY

Ceremonies are typically marked by flower baskets, ring pillows, guest books and sundry other items that add to the romantic atmosphere. This key word points you to solutions to your ceremony needs.

### DECORATIONS

This one tends to speak for itself. Use it in conjunction with key words like Ceremony and Reception to figure out just what you may be decorating.

### FAVORS

Thanks to years of hallowed tradition, wedding guests have come to expect wedding favors when they dine. There's a great variety of stuff like bubble bottles, cake boxes, disposable cameras, picture frames, candles and other trinkets for your guests to play with and/or take home.

### KEEPSAKES

Making the occasion tangibly memorable, keepsakes include cake toppers, garter belts, champagne glasses, ring pillows and tussy mussies.

### PARTY ATTIRE

This refers to the clothes your wedding party will be wearing, in most cases dresses for bridesmaids and flower girls.

### PARTY GIFTS

This refers to the gifts typically given in appreciation to your wedding party, including stuff like flasks, jewelry, humidors and jewelry boxes.

### RECEPTION

A lot goes into the post-nuptial party, and most of it may be found next to this key word, from place settings to centerpieces, and plenty else.

### SHOES

Bridal shoes, from heels to sneakers, exist in charming supply in this section, though if you can't find the perfect pair here, look to the Shoes & Accessories section.

### THE GROOM

Typically, this key word refers to tuxedoes, with some different interpretations of formal wear thrown in for the stylish or unfashionable, depending on how you look at it.

## >> KEY WORD INDEX

Use the following lists to locate online retailers that sell the Wedding Merchandise you seek.

### ACCESSORIES

AmericanBridal.com
BachelorettePartyShop.com
BlissWeddingsMarket.com
Bridalink.com
BridalPeople.com
BridalPortfolio.com
BrideSave.com
BridesOnTheGo.com
Cufflinks.com
DavenportHouse.com
eWeddingShoes.com
ExclusivelyWeddings.com
FavorsByLisa.com
ForeverMoments.com
MarilynsKeepsakes.com
MomsNightOut.com
MyGlassSlipper.com
PerfectDetails.com
ReceptionStuff.com
RomanticHeadlines.com
TammyDarling.com
TheKnot.com
VintageWedding.com
WeddingExpressions.com
WeddingHelpers.com
WedThings.com

### BRIDAL ATTIRE

BridalPeople.com
BrideSave.com
eWeddingShoes.com
ExclusivelyWeddings.com
ForeverMoments.com
MyGlassSlipper.com
PerfectDetails.com
RomanticHeadlines.com
TammyDarling.com
TheWeddingShopper.com
VintageWedding.com
WeddingExpressions.com
WesternWeddings.com

### BRIDAL GOWNS

BrideSave.com
ChinaBridal.com
ForeverMoments.com
MomsNightOut.com
VintageWedding.com
WeddingExpressions.com

### CEREMONY

AmericanBridal.com
Bridalink.com
BridalPeople.com
BridalPortfolio.com
BridesOnTheGo.com
DavenportHouse.com
eWeddingShoes.com
ExclusivelyWeddings.com
FavorsEtc.com
MarilynsKeepsakes.com
PerfectDetails.com
ReceptionStuff.com
RomanticHeadlines.com
TheKnot.com
ThePartyBlock.com
TheWeddingShopper.com
WeddingExpressions.com
WeddingPetals.com
WedThings.com
WesternWeddings.com
WrapWithUs.com

### DECORATIONS

AmericanBridal.com
BlissWeddingsMarket.com
ChinaBridal.com
IslandWeddingShop.com
MarilynsKeepsakes.com
ReceptionStuff.com
RomanticHeadlines.com
TheKnot.com

ThePartyBlock.com
WeddingExpressions.com
WeddingFavorites.com
WeddingLinens.com
WeddingPetals.com
WedThings.com
WrapWithUs.com

### FAVORS

AmericanBridal.com
BellaRegalo.com
BlissWeddingsMarket.com
Bridalink.com
BridalPeople.com
BridesOnTheGo.com
DavenportHouse.com
ExclusivelyWeddings.com
FavorsByLisa.com
FavorsEtc.com
FByS.com
GroomStop.com
IslandWeddingShop.com
MarilynsKeepsakes.com
PeachTreeCircle.com
ReceptionStuff.com
RomanticHeadlines.com
TheKnot.com
TheWeddingShopper.com
UniqueFavors.com
WeddingExpressions.com
WeddingFavorites.com
WeddingFavors.com
WeddingPetals.com
WeddingTulle.com
WedThings.com
WesternWeddings.com
WrapWithUs.com

### INVITATIONS

1stExpressions.com
AmericanBridal.com
BotanicalPaperworks.com
BrideSave.com
ChinaBridal.com
DempseyAndCarroll.com
FavorsEtc.com
MyGatsby.com
PaperStyle.com
RomanticHeadlines.com
ThePartyBlock.com
WeddingHelpers.com
WeddingOrders.com
WeddingTulle.com

### KEEPSAKES

AmericanBridal.com
BridalPeople.com
BridesOnTheGo.com
DavenportHouse.com
FavorsByLisa.com
MarilynsKeepsakes.com
PeachTreeCircle.com
ReceptionStuff.com
TheKnot.com
TheWeddingShopper.com
WeddingFavors.com
WedThings.com
WrapWithUs.com

## PARTY ATTIRE

Anakha.com
BestBridesmaid.com
BridalPortfolio.com
BrideSave.com
Bridesmaids.com
ChinaBridal.com
ForeverMoments.com
MensWearhouse.com
MomsNightOut.com
VintageWedding.com
WesternWeddings.com

## PARTY GIFTS

AmericanBridal.com
Bridalink.com
BridalPeople.com
BridesOnTheGo.com
Cufflinks.com
DavenportHouse.com
ExclusivelyWeddings.com
FavorsByLisa.com
GroomStop.com
MarilynsKeepsakes.com
PeachTreeCircle.com
RomanticHeadlines.com
TheKnot.com
TheWeddingShopper.com
WeddingExpressions.com
WedThings.com
WesternWeddings.com

## RECEPTION

AmericanBridal.com
Bridalink.com
BridalPeople.com
BridesOnTheGo.com
Confoti.com
DavenportHouse.com
ExclusivelyWeddings.com
FavorsByLisa.com
FavorsEtc.com
IslandWeddingShop.com
MarilynsKeepsakes.com
PerfectDetails.com
ReceptionStuff.com
RomanticHeadlines.com
TheKnot.com

ThePartyBlock.com
TheWeddingShopper.com
UniqueFavors.com
WeddingExpressions.com
WeddingFavors.com
WeddingLinens.com
WedThings.com
WesternWeddings.com
WrapWithUs.com

## SHOES

BridalPeople.com
BrideSave.com
eWeddingShoes.com
ExclusivelyWeddings.com
MyGlassSlipper.com
PerfectDetails.com
TheWeddingShopper.com
WesternWeddings.com

## THE GROOM

Cufflinks.com
ExclusivelyWeddings.com
GroomStop.com
MensWearhouse.com
TheWeddingShopper.com
VintageWedding.com
WesternWeddings.com

# 1stExpressions.com

1stExpressions.com • 888-732-3560

This, "Your Complete Source for Fine Printing" really does have a lot of wedding invitations and related stationery to offer, which means there are a great deal of outlandish and unbearably cheesy designs here. Conversely, some of them are fantastic, and thanks to a fairly detailed Refine Search filter, you can separate out only the relevant themes, styles, colors, papers and price ranges. Of course, there's no option to distinguish the hip from the hopeless, so be sure to warm up your wincing muscles.

| ·INVITATIONS | | | |
|---|---|---|---|

# AmericanBridal.com

American Bridal • 800-568-3398

This is a very well organized site, featuring cool stuff for wedding ceremonies, receptions and bridal party gifts. At times, however, it may be a little too regimented, requiring repeated clicking to finally view the details of a product. All is forgiven, though, at least in our eyes, as the variety and quality of products surpass such petty wants as quick navigation. Add to it the list of wedding resources and a Shop by Price feature, and we're suddenly grateful for the efforts and details the proprietors of this site have provided.

| ·DECORATIONS<br>·PARTY GIFTS | ·CEREMONY<br>·INVITATIONS | ·RECEPTION<br>·ACCESSORIES | ·FAVORS<br>·KEEPSAKES |
|---|---|---|---|

# Anakha.com

Anakha • 212-367-8051

One of the many great things about this site devoted to bridesmaid dresses is its variety of browsing options. Start by clicking the first menu option, Dress Search. This will take you to a flower shaped menu directing you to shop by Type of Wedding, Style or Silhouette, Fabrics and more. Our favorite is the Bridesmaids Personality feature, the personalities including Groovy & Sexy, Artistic & Cutting Edge, and Undoubtedly Chic. The product descriptions match the attitude; with sentences like, "we should not have to tell you if you can wear this dress," meant as cheeky encouragement. The dresses usually appear in multiple views, and when you see them, the term "never a bride" will have decidedly less sting. Great site.

| ·PARTY ATTIRE | | | |
|---|---|---|---|

# BachelorettePartyShop.com

BachelorettePartyShop.com • 847-622-4317

Just when we thought there was no altruism left in online retail, we come to this site, which was "founded back in 1998 when the owners decided that the women of this world needed a place to purchase hilarious bachelorette party items." Featuring a variety of party games, gag gifts, favors and decorations, this stuff ranges from the risqué to the ridiculous, and we will tastefully neglect to mention anything in particular here. Actually, truth be known, there's not even anything tasteful in the Food & Drink section.

| ·ACCESSORIES | | | |
|---|---|---|---|

**No Service Number • Bella Regalo**  **BellaRegalo.com**

In planning a wedding, some opt for an air of pronounced elegance, while others choose to stay close to tradition. But how many among us just want to make it interesting? Despite the name of this site, the items featured here tend to be unique more than elegant, which makes them stand out. For example, here, if you look for place settings, favors and confections, you might turn up some plantable place cards, miniature topiaries and decorated sugar cubes. A bit deviant from the norm, but that's exactly what we like about it.

·FAVORS

**888-217-5655 • BestBridesmaid.com**  **BestBridesmaid.com**

Let's face it: the perfect wedding gown is probably the single most important part of any wedding, so you don't really want to waste your precious time trying to find the proper dresses for your bridesmaids. This site offers a couple dozen simple, elegant, classic designs, each viewable on one page for the some of the quickest, easiest shopping selections you'll find anywhere. Ironically, while the ordering process may take no more than a few minutes, delivery can take more than two months, so you'll want to order well ahead of time in consideration of alterations. Also, while the color options are as varied as that of a jelly bean jar, you don't get to see most of the colors, a big drawback.

·PARTY ATTIRE

**516-364-4086 • Bliss!**  **BlissWeddingsMarket.com**

The retail arm of online wedding magazine *Bliss!* the proprietors of this site vaunt a creative approach to nuptial events, stating, "more engaged couples than ever realize that their wedding day is not only a rite of passage but also a public expression of their personality as a couple." Hence, they advocate a selective reinterpretation of customary ceremonies, picking out the best parts and discarding the rest. To this end, the magazine portion of the site offers plenty of intriguing ideas and guidelines, whereas a thoroughly stocked catalog includes unique and stylish favors, stationery (including personalized labels) and bridal accessories, without veering too far from the classy course of tradition.

·DECORATIONS ·FAVORS ·ACCESSORIES

**877-956-7393 • Botanical Paperworks**  **BotanicalPaperworks.com**

If you're of the do-it-yourself mentality, you'll be thrilled to find some of the out-of-the-ordinary papermaking kits available on this site. Should you have neither the time nor energy required to do this (who does, with a wedding to plan?), you can find a terrific selection of handmade invitations, guest books and even plantable favors (made by professionals, not other customers). While their ordering functionality can be a bit frustrating, with so much pretty paper (infused with petals, leaves, grasses and such), there's little else to complain about.

·INVITATIONS

# Bridalink.com

Bridalink Store • 800-725-6763

The name makes little real-world sense, but this is a "Wedding Superstore," with the "guaranteed lowest prices," so we'll give them a little credit. Actually, all manner of trousseaux and wedding gifts fill these assorted pages. From centerpieces to favors and even those little wedding-themed disposable cameras that inspire certain guests towards bursts of newfound creativity (move aside, Annie Leibovitz!), this site has just about every little thing you need to throw a wedding in the right direction.

| ·CEREMONY ·ACCESSORIES | ·RECEPTION | ·FAVORS | ·PARTY GIFTS |
|---|---|---|---|

# BridalPeople.com

BridalPeople.com • 877-520-0259

Boasting "1000's of Bridal Necessities," this shop indeed offers a range of ceremony, reception and bridal shower accessories that includes but is not limited to: headpieces, flower girl baskets, ring-bearer pillows, bridal shoes, wedding gloves, guest books, garters, money bags, cake toppers and potpourri-filled bras—you know, all of the customary favorites. Favoring elegance over attitude, this may not be the best place to shop for quirky bridal accents, but for white weddings it will more than suffice.

| ·CEREMONY ·BRIDAL ATTIRE | ·RECEPTION ·SHOES | ·FAVORS ·ACCESSORIES | ·PARTY GIFTS ·KEEPSAKES |
|---|---|---|---|

# BridalPortfolio.com

Bridal Portfolio • 972-562-9779

This online cohort of a Dallas bridal boutique will show you a lot of gorgeous gowns and accessories. Unfortunately, none of this is really available online, so unless you live in proximity of Texas, to search through them would just be to set yourself up for a fall. However, if you ignore everything else and just shoot straight to the Gallery section you'll find an assortment of wedding albums, but more importantly you will see some darling flower girl dresses. Now, it doesn't do to have the flower girl's duds show up the beauty of the bride, so only shop here if you've already got a killer gown for yourself.

| ·PARTY ATTIRE | ·CEREMONY | ·ACCESSORIES |
|---|---|---|

# BrideSave.com

BrideSave.com • 888-321-4696

In the hunt for that all too precious wedding gown, a woman is likely to scour every magazine, catalog and wedding album she can get her hands on, in her head a firm notion of perfection, in the end spending countless hours and viewing hundreds of dresses. This site, on the other hand, offers a paltry 2,600 or so to choose from. Filter by such variations as color, fabric, type of neckline, sleeve style, bodice décor, train length and/or specific designer and you can within moments get a look at several ideas, if not perfect fits to your unerring vision. With the time you save you may choose to sort through the hundreds each selections of shoes, headpieces, bridesmaid dresses and invitations.

| ·PARTY ATTIRE ·ACCESSORIES | ·INVITATIONS ·BRIDAL GOWNS | ·BRIDAL ATTIRE | ·SHOES |
|---|---|---|---|

**212-647-9686 • Bridesmaids.com**                    **Bridesmaids.com**

Even though it may go against timeless tradition to do so, you might consider selecting dresses for your bridesmaids that they may actually want to wear again someday. For such dresses, this can be a great site to visit. While there isn't an overwhelming amount to sort through, the dresses are fantastic, featuring designs by Nicole Miller, Bari Jay and Wtoo, among others. A wide (viewable) color selection and decent prices make it easy to find something your entourage, and more importantly you, will appreciate.

| ·PARTY ATTIRE | | | |
|---|---|---|---|

**800-637-7785 • Brides On The Go**                   **BridesOnTheGo.com**

The splash page of this site makes it look like you need to select a menu link to move on; the truth is, wherever on the page you click, you will simply move on to a second page, and a different menu. This befuddling inconsistency stays with you for most of the site, with slow loading pages and a selection that doesn't quite live up to the promise of that first page's menu. Actually, we probably wouldn't bother to even tell you about this one, except for the spectacularly ornate selection of Garters & Hankies they possess. Oh yes, those, and the honeymoon-essential musical g-string, which plays (what else?) "Here Comes the Bride." Both terrible and hilarious.

| ·CEREMONY ·ACCESSORIES | ·RECEPTION ·KEEPSAKES | ·FAVORS | ·PARTY GIFTS |
|---|---|---|---|

**800-436-8091 • China Bridal**                       **ChinaBridal.com**

From the traditional to the not-so-traditional (check the section called Las Vegas Wedding), this site offers a lovely assortment of Chinese wedding accoutrements. Okay, so the Vegas option essentially has nothing to do with China, but most of this stuff does. Foremost are the fantastic bridal gowns, which include rich embroidery and gorgeous tailoring. Invitations and paper decorations featuring customary and/or lucky characters and symbols fill out the selection, whether you're embracing or deviating from your own family's traditions.

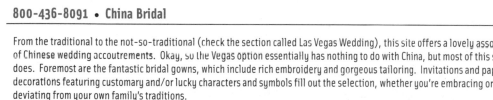

| ·PARTY ATTIRE | ·INVITATIONS | ·DECORATIONS | ·BRIDAL GOWNS |
|---|---|---|---|

**650-569-3220 • confoti**                            **Confoti.com**

If you think the name of this one is strange or inventive... you have no idea. Derived, of course, from the word confetti, less obvious is the influence of the word 'photo' on this easily available domain name. Simply put, these guys make confetti out of your favorite photographs. One might question the wisdom of tossing a shower of tiny images that will ultimately be swept up by a broom and tossed in the trash, but you cannot question the ingenuity that led to this freakish niche. If you opt not to upload your images for reproduction, you may still find some beautifully rendered wedding confetti that easily looks better than the primary and pastel colors typically found.

| ·RECEPTION | | | |
|---|---|---|---|

## Cufflinks.com

**Cufflinks.com • 877-283-3565**

Lest you think they merely hold French cuffs together, this site is here to show us all that cufflinks can be. This begins with a bounty of engravable sterling silver and gold designs, some boasting gems and a bevy of thematic shapes owing to such interests as Sports, Music, Transportation, Local Interests (mostly major US cities), Career Related interests and the Military. Most intriguing, however, are the Functional cufflinks found here, which embed such useful items as watches, compasses and thermometers. We suggest consulting with the bride before getting anything too interesting, though.

| ·PARTY GIFTS | ·THE GROOM | ·ACCESSORIES | |
|---|---|---|---|

## DavenportHouse.com

**Davenport House • 888-470-4950**

Select the Weddings section of this "English Country Store" (if that's not too obvious) and you'll be greeted with the option of browsing through categories like Elegant Receptions, Guest Favors, Ceremony and Gifts for various members of the wedding party. Inside, the items prove to be, well, English and elegant, which is to say pleasing to genteel folk. From Stunning Centerpieces to Lasting Memories, these items won't make for a party that rocks, but it'll sure make the photos come out looking real nice.

| ·CEREMONY ·ACCESSORIES | ·RECEPTION ·KEEPSAKES | ·FAVORS | ·PARTY GIFTS |
|---|---|---|---|

## DempseyAndCarroll.com

**Dempsey and Carroll • 800-444-4019**

This stationery company offers some fine products, but above all else its wedding invitations and announcements stand out. Actually, they feature appropriate styles and materials for a wide range of pre- and post-nuptial activities, from bridal shower invitations to reception place cards and on to a gorgeous wedding album. Though selection is limited, everything here is worthwhile, presuming high elegance and timeless traditional style impresses you. What makes it so classic? Engraved paper. Yes, that's right; even the paper is impressed.

| ·INVITATIONS | | | |
|---|---|---|---|

## eWeddingShoes.com

**eWeddingShoes.com • 877-823-1500**

Not surprisingly, this somewhat girly-looking site is set up to serve the interests of, well, girls. Rather, it's meant to accommodate the dreams of any girl who's grown up into a ravishing bride-to-be, a woman of some taste who demands that her wedding should be exactly as she has always envisioned: with she at the sparkling center. To this end, it's not just categories like Sandals & Slides, Pumps & Mary Janes, Flats and Slingbacks that prove alluring, but a selection of gloves, garters and tiaras as well, with some Flower Girl dresses for cuteness's sake. Basically, this is all stuff men do not want any part of.

| ·CEREMONY | ·BRIDAL ATTIRE | ·SHOES | ·ACCESSORIES |
|---|---|---|---|

## 800-759-7666 • Exclusively Weddings

**ExclusivelyWeddings.com**

Who will prefer to shop for wedding favors and accessories here rather than elsewhere? Well, if the site is to be believed, only "discriminating brides." The rest of you can stick to hand-whittled cake tops and crayon-drawn invitations, apparently. This place offers an elegant, if inexpensive, assortment of things like garters, wedding party gifts and invitations. Pretty much it encompasses all of the little material details that need to be procured between the proposal and the "I Do," and even some "reception sneakers," for discriminating post-nuptial joggers. Talk about thorough.

| ·CEREMONY ·BRIDAL ATTIRE | ·RECEPTION ·THE GROOM | ·FAVORS ·SHOES | ·PARTY GIFTS ·ACCESSORIES |
|---|---|---|---|

## 866-567-5472 • Favors By Lisa

**FavorsByLisa.com**

This looks like a great site: clean design, beautiful images of great products. So, it has the sort of ordering page where you have to remember the item number and name of the item and manually type it in to the Order Info page along with your credit card number— it's kind of a pain, but it ultimately works. Well, the real infuriating thing is that some of these wedding gifts and accoutrements don't offer a title or item number, so like it as much as you want, trying to order it can be a very confusing process. Direct all complaints to Lisa, and maybe it will get better.

| ·RECEPTION ·KEEPSAKES | ·FAVORS | ·PARTY GIFTS | ·ACCESSORIES |
|---|---|---|---|

## 877-597-0234 • Favors Etc.

**FavorsEtc.com**

Part of the fun of weddings is that everybody gets to throw stuff at each other; the bride throws a bouquet at the ladies, the groom throws a garter at the guys, and the entire cadre of guests gets to throw stuff at the newly married couple as they run off to their honeymoon. This last bit is where this site comes in. The traditional rice, of course, has been known to kill birds (mostly pigeons, but it can get messy, nonetheless), so this site offers great alternatives like birdseed, almonds and flower petals. A fourth option is bubbles, which look the coolest but do take away the fun of throwing things.

| ·CEREMONY | ·RECEPTION | ·FAVORS | ·INVITATIONS |
|---|---|---|---|

## 800-320-2664 • Favors by Serendipity

**FByS.com**

Between pear-shaped candles, daisy-shaped seedpods and tuxedoed strawberries, this site offers wedding favors above and beyond the creative call of duty (the latter may attribute their formal attire to white and dark chocolates). Many of these innovative pieces have been made to slip right into any central design scheme, while others fit in to particular ideas offered by the site, including Medieval, Ocean, Butterfly and Cinderella themes, which contribute dolphin cake toppers and Victorian goblets. This one stands out.

| ·FAVORS | | | |
|---|---|---|---|

## ForeverMoments.com

On first impression, this site seems like a throwaway. But if you delve into their catalog of dresses for brides, bridesmaids and flower girls, you'll notice (after a potentially slow download), that this may just be the best place to find beautiful bridal attire on the web. The site's design and navigation is simple at best, but for such important occasions it offers that which is most important to your selection: great pictures. Scan through an index of lovely images and when you see one with potential, click on it to see a nearly full-page photo that well-illustrates the dress's shape and scope. With nearly every size available, the days of searching through endless magazines may be over.

| | ·PARTY ATTIRE | ·BRIDAL ATTIRE | ·ACCESSORIES | ·BRIDAL GOWNS |
|---|---|---|---|---|

## GroomStop.com

They're renting tuxes, seating your guests and standing by you in your most nerve-wrecked hour, and all your groomsmen and ushers expect in return is a token gift, and maybe a wild bachelor party. The party part is up to them, but the gifts fall into your hands— don't worry; they just happen to be this site's specialty. Its charm doesn't lie in originality; this catalog includes all the same things found elsewhere: flasks, pocketknives, cigar accessories, golf toys and barware. The difference is that here you'll find a much bigger selection of each of these items than anywhere else, and that's enough to make even the stripper happy.

| | ·THE GROOM | ·FAVORS | ·PARTY GIFTS | |
|---|---|---|---|---|

## IslandWeddingShop.com

Everybody's got a different idea of what constitutes paradise. To some, it's marriage, for others it involves an island. Here's a site that caters to the cross-section of these folk, offering a bevy of beachy favors and accessories. Sand dollars, cockleshells, starfish and sea glass comprise several sections of reception accents to match such things as sand castle centerpieces and lighthouse place settings. You'll find all the stuff here that you would at any analogous site; only this stuff is perfect for the sun-drenched among us.

| | ·DECORATIONS | ·RECEPTION | ·FAVORS | |
|---|---|---|---|---|

## KitBiz.com

If you think all the stuff leading up to the planning of the wedding is complicated, wait until you try to legally change your name! Between your driver's license, social security card, insurance papers, credit cards, bank account, voter registration and passport, the bureaucracy alone can be enough to make you embrace the notion of a common law marriage. This site has assembled kits complete with all the paperwork you'll need to expedite the process. Aside from a bride name change kit, they offer one for both bride and groom, divorce name changes if things turn sour and prenuptial kits if you think things might go sour. It's all about easy.

| | | | |
|---|---|---|---|

**800-263-5808 • Marilyn's Wedding Keepsakes**  **MarilynsKeepsakes.com**

Given the size of the operation, combined with the overwhelming enthusiasm and desire for perfection of all parties concerned, those customers who're planning a wedding are very special, needy customers indeed. In response, wedding salesmanship has evolved into a unique art form, pitching merchandise with its own very specific, sacrosanct yet jubilant tone. This site has that tone down to a science. Tasteful, gentle, genteel— frankly, the site is a little boring. But it's very efficient, and some within this very solid selection of ceremony and reception-oriented products even actually come close to running the risk of being too interesting to be fit for a wedding.

| ·DECORATIONS ·PARTY GIFTS | ·CEREMONY ·ACCESSORIES | ·RECEPTION ·KEEPSAKES | ·FAVORS |
|---|---|---|---|

**877-986-9669 • Men's Wearhouse**  **MensWearhouse.com**

Unlike most of the sites featured here, there's a good chance you know what the owner of this men's fashion retailer looks like, as he's regularly seen guaranteeing that "you'll like the way you look" on TV ads. He pops up around the site sometimes, whether you're looking at extremely formal tuxedoes or some of the less stuffy alternatives, but he's easier to ignore online than on the tube. The best thing about this site in regards to a wedding is that you can easily outfit groomsmen in different corners of the country in matching attire, and odds are they'll be able to visit a local store for alterations.

| ·PARTY ATTIRE | ·THE GROOM | | |
|---|---|---|---|

**212-744-6667 • Moms Night Out**  **MomsNightOut.com**

Dispelling the notion that pregnancy consists primarily of muumuus and bed rest, this clothing line/boutique lends a touch of glamour to maternity wear with a selection of formal attire capable of dressing any special occasion. Both dresses and gowns, whether or not you perceive a difference, are available in slim selections, and they even offer a selection of bridal apparel. Each frock is well represented with pictures and descriptions, shown complete with accessories (like veils, jackets and wraps), which may be either added to your dress order or purchased separately.

| ·PARTY ATTIRE | ·ACCESSORIES | ·BRIDAL GOWNS | |
|---|---|---|---|

**888-997-7899 • MyGatsby.com**  **MyGatsby.com**

For those of us who never considered that pastels might be blinding, here comes what may very well be, as the ownership claims, "the largest selection [of invitations] online." It's not so much that the gentle looks or genteel stationery on this site in themselves are hard on the eyes. However, with this many choices in what amounts to a single product type, there's really little chance of avoiding a long session of staring at your computer screen as page after page of traditional through contemporary designs float by, especially when you consider personalization options. The easy to use Advanced Search filter can help, but like an umbrella in a hurricane, it can only do so much.

| ·INVITATIONS | | | |
|---|---|---|---|

# MyGlassSlipper.com

My Glass Slipper • 866-933-7463

This Cinderella reference applies to the "Shoe and Accessory" salon of Hannelore's Bridal Boutique, "one of the nation's largest bridal salons," meaning simply that they offer couture bridal footwear, and some inexpensive options as well. In fact, you can shop by either of these distinctions, further filtering your options by heel height for easy retrieval of just the sort of shoes you're looking for, which, given the depth of their selection, you may presume they have. Additional items like purses, garters and cake tops exist in smaller supply, as do an assortment of pre-dyed shoes for bridesmaids—but then, they'll wear what you want them to wear.

| | ·BRIDAL ATTIRE | ·SHOES | ·ACCESSORIES | |
|---|---|---|---|---|

# PaperStyle.com

PaperStyle.com • 888-670-5300

Whether you're planning a formal wedding, or a casual one, you'll be able to find the appropriate set of invitations on this slow but well put together site. Even if you're looking for some regular stationery, you will find a great big selection of elegant and/or campy stuff, in most cases easily personalized for no extra cost. But most of these resources are devoted to announcements and invites, and it shows (usually with RSVP envelopes included). In fact, browsing might just inspire you to invite more people.

| | ·INVITATIONS | | | |
|---|---|---|---|---|

# PeachTreeCircle.com

Peachtree Circle • 770-455-1800

If you're looking for wedding charms, this is a great place to start. If you haven't until now thought to look for them, here's what they are: small metal charms in symbolic shapes like that of an engagement ring, baby carriage or shamrock. As per Victorian tradition, these charms are baked into the wedding cake attached to ribbon, which are then tugged by members of the bridal party, pulling out charms that portend their futures (in the case of the charms above; impending engagement, pregnancy or good luck, respectively). This site has them all, plus plenty of alternate shapes like a frog, binoculars and a slice of cheese, which ought to throw anybody for a loop.

| | ·FAVORS | ·PARTY GIFTS | ·KEEPSAKES | |
|---|---|---|---|---|

# PerfectDetails.com

Perfect Details • 650-576-4927

Seeking to play a role in "defining your style," this simple, visually oriented site serves a simple purpose: accessorizing the bride. Different parts of the body are highlighted, with sections devoted to gloves, shoes, wraps, garters, tiaras and other headwear. Each item is terrifically luxurious, and appropriately expensive, and all sections feature bizarre little quotes like, "Tiaras flirt with the eye." Peculiarly aggressive, it may be just what you need to get things done; or it could be your worst nightmare.

| | ·CEREMONY ·ACCESSORIES | ·RECEPTION | ·BRIDAL ATTIRE | ·SHOES |
|---|---|---|---|---|

## 800-404-4025 • Forever & Always Company

### ReceptionStuff.com

Internet home to the Forever & Always Company, this site has its ups and downs, but generally offers an interesting array of products, particularly under Bridal Accessories. You never know quite what to expect in any particular section or subsection, nor how much of it, which either makes for surprising shopping or sets you up for disappointment. We found some truly distinctive cake toppers and a lavish, frilly wedding certificate (as alternative to the stuffy, official-looking kind). What can you find?

| ·DECORATIONS ·ACCESSORIES | ·CEREMONY ·KEEPSAKES | ·RECEPTION | ·FAVORS |
|---|---|---|---|

## 972-769-8432 • Romantic Headlines

### RomanticHeadlines.com

In terms of bridal apparel, this homegrown site offers everything but the dress, the fact of which may not be lost on the groom. Established by the Jenkinses, a Dallas couple intent on showing off both his web design prowess and her homemade headpieces, this simple shop has expanded to include everything from jewelry on down to lingerie, hosiery and shoes, as well as some accessories for both ceremony and reception. Whether or not each product is an original Jenkins design or pieced together from other collections becomes unimportant, as it's all pretty nice, and hardly ever boring.

| ·DECORATIONS ·PARTY GIFTS | ·CEREMONY ·INVITATIONS | ·RECEPTION ·BRIDAL ATIRE | ·FAVORS ·ACCESSORIES |
|---|---|---|---|

## 908-696-8484 • Tammy Darling

### TammyDarling.com

Not nearly as cutesy as it sounds, this site specializes in two things: handbags and headpieces, and most of it is quite distinctive. The notable exceptions are to be found in Veils, which are your standard white tulle, variety only existing in lengths. On the flipside, most of the handbags may prove a little too much to go with most gowns, heavy with funky textures and dangling with crystals. Ultimately, it's the tiaras, combs and hairpins that are just right, differing from the norm but maintaining a sense of classic elegance.

| ·BRIDAL ATTIRE | ·ACCESSORIES | | |
|---|---|---|---|

## 877-843-5668 • The Knot

### TheKnot.com

This is a store that began with a business plan, some venture capital and ties to AOL, and if they get their way they will dominate the online wedding retail market. Why haven't they collapsed like so many other similarly conceived dot-coms? Credit the fine selection that sits behind a very slick veneer, which has been strategically assembled to cover your every wedding need, or whether the impersonal feel just doesn't capture that wedding spirit you so ardently desire. It's quite easy to tell; buy something or leave forever, either way it should take under five minutes.

| ·DECORATIONS ·PARTY GIFTS | ·CEREMONY ·ACCESSORIES | ·RECEPTION ·KEEPSAKES | ·FAVORS |
|---|---|---|---|

# ThePartyBlock.com

ThePartyBlock.com • 800-205-6400

Personalized napkins and coasters seem to be the most popular items available from this smallish but erstwhile retailer. Actually, this is just the sort of shop we love to tell you about, as its small business credibility shines through with endearing customer service and an uncomplicated selection of quaint to tasteful place settings, decorations and wedding cake accessories (like cake toppers, boxes and serving utensils). Sites like this make it easy to avoid corporations.

| | ·DECORATIONS | ·CEREMONY | ·RECEPTION | ·INVITATIONS |
|---|---|---|---|---|

# TheWeddingShopper.com

The Wedding Shopper • No Service Number

Laying out the fine distinctions between Bridal Lingerie and Honeymoon Lingerie, this site proves to be much better than it first looks, its smallish selection managing to offer some tasteful choices and its prices well under control. Aside from pre- and post-nuptial unmentionables, there are dedicated sections to wedding favors, essential (if mundane) reception items, stationery, bridal party gifts and plenty other of the fine details and keepsakes that make and maintain memories (yes, cameras too).

| | ·CEREMONY<br>·BRIDAL ATTIRE | ·RECEPTION<br>·THE GROOM | ·FAVORS<br>·SHOES | ·PARTY GIFTS<br>·KEEPSAKES |
|---|---|---|---|---|

# UniqueFavors.com

UniqueFavors.com • 800-756-6184

"The elegant touch, the perfect memento." This site breaks a lot. That being said, if you can handle the occasional page error, you should be able to find some pretty darn lavish place card holders and picture frames here. Surprisingly, this ornate metalwork happens to maintain a modicum of elegance with somewhat comical designs, as cardholders shaped like chairs and shoes stand beside picture frames shaped like wacky cars without flinching. Unlike the site, this somehow works, providing memorable wedding favors, if not interesting conversation pieces.

| | ·RECEPTION | ·FAVORS | | |
|---|---|---|---|---|

# VintageWedding.com

A Vintage Wedding • 800-660-3640

Some people like to don multicolored spandex and recite their vows while leaping out of a plane; some like to eek out a slightly more traditional wedding ceremony. This site is for the latter. Featuring some gorgeous gowns, tuxedos and accessories, these items were designed in an era long since gone and are rich in romantic appeal. In a way, the site itself is vintage. For one thing, you have to scroll way, way down the home page before you can find the navigation menu. Secondly, the archaic ordering page is even tougher to find, and a pain to fill out. This site would be dusty, were it possible, but is still valuable.

| | ·PARTY ATTIRE<br>·BRIDAL GOWNS | ·BRIDAL ATTIRE | ·THE GROOM | ·ACCESSORIES |
|---|---|---|---|---|

## 888-659-5085 • Wedding Expressions
### WeddingExpressions.com

Feeling a little uptight about the planning of your wedding? Shop with these guys and "You can relax knowing you are dealing with one of the largest wedding retailers in the Midwest." Now that our east and west coast readers have moved along, we may speak in earnest: this site spans a pretty wide matrimonial cross section, including favors, gifts, gowns and decorative items for both ceremonies and receptions. The catch? It's tough to find anything that really stands out. Let's just say that this otherwise excellent retailer caters to uncomplicated tastes.

| | | | | |
|---|---|---|---|---|
| ·DECORATIONS ·PARTY GIFTS | ·CEREMONY ·BRIDAL ATTIRE | ·RECEPTION ·ACCESSORIES | ·FAVORS ·BRIDAL GOWNS | |

## 714-505-5799 • WeddingFavorites.com
### WeddingFavorites.com

If one goal of your reception is to impart upon your guests just how fashionable you truly are, you'll appreciate the trinkets, stationery and accents offered by this retailer of "stylish favors for weddings and bridal showers." Some pretty original stuff, like silver-plated fortune cookie boxes, sandalwood fans and seashell napkin rings indicate the type of creative merchandise you might find here but in no way represents the tone of the entire catalog. Anything you'll find here is merely a matter of taste, except for the bride and groom teddy bears; they're just for cuteness' sake.

| | | | | |
|---|---|---|---|---|
| ·DECORATIONS | ·FAVORS | | | |

## 651-493-0884 • Keepsake Favors
### WeddingFavors.com

Strictly speaking, these guys offer more than just wedding favors; they have sections for pretty much any kind of party you can think of, from Baby Showers to Quinceañeras. But who cares? We're talkin' about weddings, and that means cakeboxes and candies, and placecards for the reception. Okay, so there's not a whole lot going on in the Wedding Favors section. But remember those other sections we were talking about? Many of them offer things that are non-specific enough to work at a wedding. A little creativity goes a long way here, and that may be what your guests appreciate most.

| | | | | |
|---|---|---|---|---|
| ·FAVORS | ·RECEPTION | ·KEEPSAKES | | |

## 800-274-0675 • The Wedding Helpers
### WeddingHelpers.com

A dreadful looking site, and none too fun to navigate either, there are certainly better places to find cake toppers, wedding-themed disposable cameras and other reception décor; probably on sites that aren't likely to give you a headache. We're listing this one, however, for one very interesting and helpful service that's relatively easy to find: a state-by-state offering of name-change kits. Whichever state you claim residency (or Washington, DC), you may be shocked when you see just how many name change forms are contained within these kits—we're talking dozens here. It won't be fun filling all of them out, but if the alternative is finding all the forms on your own, it's worth the hassle.

| | | | | |
|---|---|---|---|---|
| ·ACCESSORIES | ·INVITATIONS | | | |

# WeddingLinens.com

Weddinglinens.com • 845-426-3300

**\$\$\$**

The odds that you're going to buy wedding linens—stuff like tablecloths, chair covers, tiebacks and chair tassels—are slim. After all, what are you going to do with such stuff once the ceremony has ended (and what's the point of a chair tassel anyway?). With these questions in mind, this site has been set up to rent you these items, long distance if need be. Thus you may dress your reception in satins, silks, velvets, damasks, laces, brocades, lamours, taffetas and other fabrics available in dozens of colors and/or patterns, without having to worry about the logistics of storage afterwards. The cost may not be all that different, however.

| ·DECORATIONS | ·RECEPTION | | | |
|---|---|---|---|---|

# WeddingOrders.com

WeddingOrders.com • No Service Number

**\$**

The unusual thing about this site is that it's really an umbrella for about a dozen different websites, so each category under the Shop Online link leads to a different place. As if this weren't confusing enough, each of these different sites offer the same overlapping array of products, yet have the audacity to send you to a third, secure ordering location, without letting you order from all sites at once. Here's hoping they do it better in the future. In the meantime, we'll have to find satisfaction in some interesting items and a none-too-difficult navigational design.

| ·INVITATIONS | | | | |
|---|---|---|---|---|

# WeddingPetals.com

Petalfetti • 706-332-4888

**\$\$**

There's nothing quite like the hurling of confetti through the air to lend a festive atmosphere to any moment. Of course, one must eventually wonder: who's going to clean all this up? This site proposes a more ecologically sensitive alternative in the form of flower petals and herbs. They call it Petalfetti, "For Fairy Tale Endings," and it may sound silly to say, but it's sure aromatic. Stowed in paper cones or glassine envelopes, the rose petals, rosemary and lavender make for elegant missiles as bride and groom embark upon their new married life.

| ·DECORATIONS | ·CEREMONY | ·FAVORS | | |
|---|---|---|---|---|

# WeddingTulle.com

Wedding Tulle • 408-396-1365

**\$\$**

★

Because having too many options is never a problem for the picky bride, we refer you to this small but worthwhile seller of invitations, place cards and favor packaging. There's not a lot of merchandise here, in fact there's very little, and yet somehow it seems capable of satisfying a wide range of customers. If every online retailer were this efficient, in terms of style, this book would be a lot shorter. A beacon of hope for the exasperated wedding planner, don't visit this one first, or its charm will be lost on you.

| ·INVITATIONS | ·FAVORS | | | |
|---|---|---|---|---|

**888-338-8818 • WedThings.com**

## WedThings.com

This site says, "our team of buyers shop the world to bring you the newest and most elegant essentials for your big day." Well, say what they will, at the center of it all is simply a woman whose life obsession is weddings, and not just her own. It seems she has devoted her life to the study of ceremonies, receptions and wedding magazines, attending any nuptials she can and clipping newspaper announcements of the ones she can't. It's borderline creepy, but here is why it's a good thing: she genuinely wants to make your wedding perfect. All of these items— trousseaux and gifts— have basically passed through her judgmental eye, so you know going in it's going to be all right.

| ·DECORATIONS ·PARTY GIFTS | ·CEREMONY ·ACCESSORIES | ·RECEPTION ·KEEPSAKES | ·FAVORS | |
|---|---|---|---|---|

**888-273-7039 • Renton Western Wear**

## WesternWeddings.com

Perhaps the only bridal-related site to feature a section called Wedding Hats, it's pretty obvious what clientele this shop is here to serve. Men by far take the least amount of risk by shopping here, as the cowboy influenced formal gear surpasses nearly every other tux you could find in terms of style, and that's not even including the boots. Women's gowns and accessories seem dazzlingly beautiful for the hard-working frontier woman, but given that this is internet shopping, most tastes can be better suited elsewhere, and should be. Good shopping for the slim few and rugged among us.

| ·THE GROOM ·PARTY ATTIRE | ·CEREMONY ·SHOES | ·RECEPTION ·BRIDAL ATTIRE | ·FAVORS ·PARTY GIFTS | |
|---|---|---|---|---|

**800-962-0891 • Wrap With Us**

## WrapWithUs.com

Scattered, but something different, this selection features a lot of items that will make you wonder just what some people are thinking! But along with the bad comes the good, and plenty of original products in between. Bear in mind that there's a second menu of favors, decorations, place settings and reception accessories far down the homepage (below the FAQ link, long after the first menu ends). This isn't the easiest of places to shop, but if you know that looking hard enough will bear fruit, test your patience with this erratic but promising catalog.

| ·DECORATIONS ·KEEPSAKES | ·CEREMONY | ·RECEPTION | ·FAVORS | |
|---|---|---|---|---|

NOTES:

_____

_____

_____

_____

_____

_____

_____

_____

_____

_____

_____

_____

_____

_____

_____

_____

_____

_____

# Women's Apparel

Yes, it's entirely stereotypical to say that women love shopping for clothes. On the other hand, we're talking about a stereotype that fuels a multibillion-dollar industry. Women's apparel simply exists in greater number and richer variety than that of men or children, includes more separate pieces and garners much more attention. So let's just say that, despite what a woman may or may not like to do, when it comes to buying clothes she has got nothing but options available.

Besides, unless you're a nun you probably like to wear clothes that make you feel comfortable, keep up-to-date and, well, make you look good. Here we've assembled a terrific selection of clothing retailers for women. Inside, you'll find designer threads, professional attire, luxurious gowns, slinky skirts, and the imperative blue jeans. This, plus you'll find the clothes that go under the clothes, the appropriately named intimate attire.

Whatever your style, whatever your size, if you work in an office or in a piano bar this section can help you to find apparel appropriate to morning, noon and night. You'll even find some clothes that are inappropriate no matter the time of day. Hey, we're just telling you where to look; personal style is up to you....

NOTES:

_____

_____

_____

_____

_____

_____

_____

_____

_____

_____

_____

_____

_____

_____

_____

_____

_____

_____

## TIPS ON BUYING WOMEN'S APPAREL ONLINE

These suggestions may help prevent frustration and buyer's remorse.

• **RETURN POLICIES:** Of course, the biggest concern about buying apparel online is whether it will actually fit you well. Before purchase, take note of the site's return policy. When you receive the goods, leave the tags on and don't throw away the packaging until you are sure you want to keep the garment. (Note: most lingerie and swimsuits are nonreturnable, for reasons that are obvious. Take special care with the purchase of these items).

• **SIZING ISSUES:** Trying to determine the proper fit of any given garment can be tricky, especially for those of us who typically fall between sizes. Each clothing line has a different idea of just what constitutes a standard size. Whenever you are uncertain about a fit, take a look as the site or line itself may offer some hints as to achieving perfect fit. Take note, for example, that European sizes tend to run smaller, whereas "generous" sizes run larger than standard.

## SITES THAT MAY COME IN HANDY

The following URLs may be useful when you shop.

Fashion Show Video & Pictures: http://www.virtualrunway.com
Style News & Trends: http://www.style.com
Misses Size Chart: http://www.clearwaterknits.com/info/misses.html
Women's Size Chart: http://www.fibergypsy.com/common/women.shtml
European Clothing Size Chart: http://online conversion.com/womens_clothing.htm
Bra Fitting Guide: http://www.fittingtips.com/classes/Class-BraSize.htm
Glossary of Lingerie Terms: http://www.lingerie-glossary.com

>> **SECTION ICON LEGEND**

Use the following guide to understand the rectangular icons that appear throughout this section.

### CUSTOM TAILORING

Look for this icon when you want to make sure the clothes fit you better than they do a mannequin. Custom Tailoring is available from several sites, but you'll need to take accurate measurements first.

### INTIMATE APPAREL

There's a heavy overlap between this icon and the key word Lingerie, for obvious reasons. The big difference? This icon highlights shops that offer the sort of lingerie a man may wish to buy for his wife or girlfriend. Enough said.

### PROFESSIONAL ATTIRE

Not all as boring as it sounds, this icon highlights a variety of suits and components to a workplace wardrobe, ranging from the fashionable to the functional.

### SPECIALTY SIZES

Virtually any shop you visit, no selection will include clothes for all sizes. Consequently, this icon is here to point out stores that include but are not necessarily limited to a wider range of sizes, including Plus Size, Petite, Tall and more.

>> LIST OF KEY WORDS

The following words represent the types of items typically found on the sites listed in this section.

## ATHLETIC

This indicates a selection of clothes wherein the primary function isn't to make you look pretty. Some sturdy, lightweight attire from sports bras to bicycle pants is available here as well as in the Sports & Outdoors section.

## CAREER

Women don't typically face dress codes as stringent as those directed at men, but this can lead to uncertainty as to what may be best to wear in the workplace. We think these sites offer some good options.

## CASUAL

Casual clothing covers a wide range of moods. At one end of the spectrum is the ultra-comfy sweat suit, on the other is khaki pants and a polo shirt. You'll find your definition of casual in here somewhere.

## DESIGNER

Sometimes clothes have a stronger identity than those of us who wear them. However, if you've got the means and the taste to wear these designer duds, you can probably get by without personality.

## FORMAL

Some clothes make you look so good they warrant a special occasion. For those events where even glamorous may not be elegant enough, check out these stores that offer selections of formal dress.

## HOSIERY

From socks to pantyhose, these sites can keep your feet and legs warm, comfortable, smooth and/or toned.

## LINGERIE

Some of this involves intimate apparel (stuff like corsets, teddies, garters, bustiers, etc.), but in all cases you should be able to find bras and panties, even the kind that are designed to be comfortable and supportive more so than tantalizing.

## OUTERWEAR

This key word is here to remind us that the primary purpose for clothing is to keep us warm and protect us from the elements. Rain coats, overcoats and even light jackets should be easy to find here.

## SLEEPWEAR

What you choose to sleep in (or without) is your own business, but we offer this key word to point out stores that sell pajamas, nightgowns and some robes for convenience's sake.

## SPORTSWEAR

Somewhere in between casual and dressy exists this key word, highlighting somewhat upscale everyday attire.

## SWIMWEAR

Some is designed for swimming, some for tanning and some just for showing off your physique. From bikinis to one-pieces, it's all here, in a variety of styles and intentions.

## >> KEY WORD INDEX

Use the following lists to locate online retailers that sell the Women's Apparel you seek.

### ATHLETIC

AbercrombieAndFitch.com
Alight.com
Athleta.com
Becoming.com
BostonProper.com
Fitigues.com
Gap.com
JustMySize.com
LandsEnd.com
Newport-News.com
OldNavy.com
OneHanesPlace.com
PlusSize.com
Title9Sports.com

### CAREER

Alight.com
AnnTaylor.com
APC.fr
Avenue.com
BananaRepublic.com
BostonProper.com
BrooksBrothers.com
CasualCornerGroup.com
CTShirts.co.uk
DesignerOutlet.com
Elisabeth.com
FashionDig.com
JCrew.com
JustMySize.com
LandsEnd.com
LongTallSally.com
MarkShale.com
MyCashmere.com
Net-A-Porter.com
Newport-News.com
PeruvianConnection.com
PlusSize.com
Silhouettes.com
SizeAppeal.com
StyleShopDirect.com
ThomasPink.co.uk

### CASUAL

AbercrombieAndFitch.com
ABLambdin.com
Alight.com
AmericanApparel.net
AnnTaylor.com
Anthropologie.com
APC.fr
ArmaniExchange.com
Avenue.com
AWear.com
BananaRepublic.com
Bebe.com
Becoming.com
BeniBoutique.com
BetseyJohnson.com
BostonProper.com
BrooksBrothers.com
Buckle.com
BuiltByWendy.com
Cache.com
CaraBella.com
CasualCornerGroup.com
CTShirts.co.uk
Danier.com
DesignerOutlet.com
Elisabeth.com
FashionDig.com
Fitigues.com
Gap.com
GirlShop.com
GoJane.com
Guess.com
HotTopic.com
IC3D.com
JCrew.com
JustMySize.com
KarmaLoop.com
KennethCole.com
LandsEnd.com
LongTallSally.com
LoveYourPeaches.com
LuckyBrandJeans.com
MarkShale.com
MauriceMaloneUSA.com

MaxStudio.com
MyCashmere.com
Net-A-Porter.com
Newport-News.com
OldNavy.com
PeruvianConnection.com
PlusSize.com
PurpleSkirt.com
RavinStyle.com
SearleNYC.com
ShopBop.com
Silhouettes.com
SizeAppeal.com
SoWear.com
StyleShopDirect.com
ThomasPink.co.uk
Title9Sports.com
TopTops.com
Ujena.com
WetSeal.com
WhiteAndWarren.com

### DESIGNER

APC.fr
ArmaniExchange.com
BeniBoutique.com
BetseyJohnson.com
BuiltByWendy.com
DesignerOutlet.com
Elisabeth.com
FashionDig.com
GirlShop.com
GloriaDelRio.com
KennethCole.com
LuxuryOutwear.com
MauriceMaloneUSA.com
Net-A-Porter.com
PieceUnique.com
PurpleSkirt.com
ShopBop.com
StyleShopDirect.com
TopTops.com

### FORMAL

BetseyJohnson.com
Cache.com
Elisabeth.com
FashionDig.com
GirlShop.com
GoJane.com
Kiyonna.com
PieceUnique.com
StyleShopDirect.com

### HOSIERY

AlexBlake.com
Azzuma.com
BareNecessities.com
BellaLingerie.com
FigLeaves.com
Fredericks.com
FreshPair.com
Kiyonna.com
LegWearDirect.com
LingerieAtLarge.com
MaryGreen.com
OneHanesPlace.com
Splendour.com
StockingShopping.com
ThePinkSlip.com
Trashy.com
VictoriasSecret.com

### LINGERIE

3WishesLingerie.com
AgentProvocateur.com
Alectra.com
AlexBlake.com
Alight.com
AmericanApparel.net
Azzuma.com
BareNecessities.com
BeautifulTonight.com

Becoming.com
BellaLingerie.com
BraSmyth.com
Bravissimo.com
CelebrityOnAir.com
DesignerOutlet.com
Eberjey.com
FigLeaves.com
Flexees.com
Fredericks.com
FreshPair.com
Frisk-Me.com
Gap.com
GirlShop.com
HeatherBloom.com
HerRoom.com
HippieSkivvies.com
HotTopic.com
Inchant.com
JCrew.com
JustMySize.com
LingerieAtLarge.com
MaryGreen.com
Net-A-Porter.com
Newport-News.com
OldNavy.com
OneHanesPlace.com
PlusSize.com
PurpleSkirt.com
RavinStyle.com
SeamlessBody.com
SearleNYC.com
Silhouettes.com
SizeAppeal.com
Splendour.com
StockingShopping.com
ThePinkSlip.com
Trashy.com
VictoriasSecret.com

## OUTERWEAR

AbercrombieAndFitch.com
Alight.com
AnnTaylor.com
Anthropologie.com
APC.fr
Athleta.com
Avenue.com
AWear.com
BananaRepublic.com
Bebe.com
BostonProper.com

BrooksBrothers.com
Buckle.com
BuiltByWendy.com
Danier.com
DesignerOutlet.com
Elisabeth.com
FashionDig.com
Gap.com
GirlShop.com
GoJane.com
Guess.com
JCrew.com
KennethCole.com
LandsEnd.com
LoveYourPeaches.com
LuckyBrandJeans.com
LuxuryOuterwear.com
MaxStudio.com
Net-A-Porter.com
Newport-News.com
OldNavy.com
PeruvianConnection.com
PlusSize.com
PurpleSkirt.com
RavinStyle.com
SearleNYC.com
Silhouettes.com
SizeAppeal.com
SoWear.com
StyleShopDirect.com
Title9Sports.com
WetSeal.com

## SLEEPWEAR

AbercrombieAndFitch.com
Anthropologie.com
Azzuma.com
BananaRepublic.com
BareNecessities.com
BeautifulTonight.com
BellaLingerie.com
BraSmyth.com
DesignerOutlet.com
Eberjey.com
FigLeaves.com
Fredericks.com
FreshPair.com
Gap.com
GirlShop.com
HeatherBloom.com
HippieSkivvies.com
HotTopic.com

Inchant.com
JCrew.com
JustMySize.com
LandsEnd.com
LingerieAtLarge.com
LongTallSally.com
MaryGreen.com
Net-A-Porter.com
Newport-News.com
OldNavy.com
PlusSize.com
RavinStyle.com
Silhouettes.com
SizeAppeal.com
Splendour.com
TheCatsPJs.com
ThePinkSlip.com
Trashy.com
VictoriasSecret.com

## SPORTSWEAR

Alight.com
AnnTaylor.com
Anthropologie.com
APC.fr
ArmaniExchange.com
Avenue.com
AWear.com
BananaRepublic.com
Bebe.com
Becoming.com
BeniBoutique.com
BetseyJohnson.com
BostonProper.com
BrooksBrothers.com
Buckle.com
BuiltByWendy.com
Cache.com
CaraBella.com
CasualCornerGroup.com
CTShirts.co.uk
Danier.com
DesignerOutlet.com
Elisabeth.com
FashionDig.com
Fitigues.com
Gap.com
GirlShop.com
GoJane.com
Guess.com
HotTopic.com
JCrew.com

JustMySize.com
KennethCole.com
Kiyonna.com
LandsEnd.com
LoveYourPeaches.com
LuckyBrandJeans.com
MarkShale.com
MauriceMaloneUSA.com
MaxStudio.com
MyCashmere.com
Net-A-Porter.com
Newport-News.com
OldNavy.com
PeruvianConnection.com
PieceUnique.com
PlusSize.com
PurpleSkirt.com
RavinStyle.com
Silhouettes.com
SizeAppeal.com
SoWear.com
StyleShopDirect.com
ThomasPink.co.uk
WetSeal.com
WhiteAndWarren.com

## SWIMWEAR

AbercrombieAndFitch.com
ABLambdin.com
Alight.com
Athlcta.com
BananaRepublic.com
Becoming.com
BramaSole.com
Bravissimo.com
CaraBella.com
CelebrityOnAir.com
CyberSwim.com
EverythingButWater.com
ExquisiteSwimwear.com
FigLeaves.com
Fredericks.com
Gap.com
GirlShop.com
GloriaDelRio.com
GoJane.com
Guess.com
JCrew.com
LandsEnd.com
LongTallSally.com
LoveYourPeaches.com
MaliaMills.com

Net-A-Porter.com
Newport-News.com
OldNavy.com
OndadeMar.com
PlusSize.com
RavinStyle.com
SauvageWear.com
SizeAppeal.com
ThePinkSlip.com
Title9Sports.com
Trashy.com
Ujena.com
VenusSwimwear.com
VictoriaSecret.com
VixSwimwear.com

NOTES:

# 3WishesLingerie.com

Your imagination may not be able to keep up with this lingerie retailer that has perhaps the most enticing specialty selection of all: costumes. Sexy renditions of cheerleaders, construction workers and Little Red Riding Hood are only the beginning. They have entire sections full of different Mermaids, Genies, Pirates and French Maids, along with any other character fetish you might possess (browsing here, you'll probably pick up a couple of new ones along the way). An outrageous selection of wigs can only add to the fantasy, and a complete array of sizes ensures anyone can play. Truly, this is dangerous.

| ·LINGERIE | | | |
|---|---|---|---|

# AbercrombieAndFitch.com

Known today primarily for their enormously popular prep-school attire, it's funny to think that the Abercrombie & Fitch catalog at one time sold hunting supplies, fishing gear and other such outdoor equipment. They even had a happy client in Amelia Earhart, who most likely never looked to them for camisoles or bikinis. Of course, that version of the store went bankrupt in the 1970's, leaving rise to their new product line, which does in fact offer camisoles and bikinis, as well as plenty of other durable but cute apparel. This site makes it easy, offering great looks and easy navigation; a far cry from their Fifth Ave. location that once boasted a shooting range, but a fine way to shop, nonetheless.

| ·SLEEPWEAR ·SWIMWEAR | ·ATHLETIC | ·OUTERWEAR | ·CASUAL |
|---|---|---|---|

# ABLambdin.com

Probably one of the better places to find jumpsuits, this catalog of "Swim & Resortwear" is "delighted to offer all you'll need for the sun season, along with plenty of items that just indulge your fancy for whimsy and fun!" Of course, plenty of this revolves around swimsuits, including petite and "extended" sizes, though cover-ups and some stylishly relaxed sportswear probably make up the bulk of the catalog (especially, as we said, the jumpsuits). If the word "leisure" is in your summer vocabulary, don't miss this one.

| ·SWIMWEAR | ·CASUAL | | |
|---|---|---|---|

# AgentProvocateur.com

Describing its wares as, "a combination of serious eroticism and naughty exhibitionism" to promote "a sexy superhero feeling," Agent Provocateur delivers on all counts. The London boutique, made famous for controversial window dressings that have prompted complaints to the local constabulary, has turned its line of screamingly sexy lingerie—it walks the fine line between sleaze and mystique—into a highly sought brand by embracing the power of public spectacle. Each range of intimates they feature corresponds to a sordid and kinky scenario which ultimately attracts your attention to the gorgeous and tantalizing corsets, bustiers, et al. that ornament the players. Browsing may take you a while, but you won't be bored. We promise.

| ·LINGERIE | | | |
|---|---|---|---|

## 888-755-9449 • Alectra

### Alectra.com

"Thongs" and "Plus-sized" aren't two terms that typically go together, but this shop changes that, offering a wide range of elegant intimate apparel for full-figures. Camisoles and chemises, along with teddies, boy-cut panties and garter belts round out the selection, well enough discouraging an over-tendency towards modesty. Shopping is quite simple, and the images appealing, making this a site not to miss if the excessively brief straps and cover-nothings prove too restrictive, especially if you are having trouble tracking down a good transparent nightgown.

| ·LINGERIE | | | |
|---|---|---|---|

## 818-501-4771 • AlexBlake.com

### AlexBlake.com

For those of you who know that legs are for more than just walking, here's a store that specializes in fine hosiery, whether sheers, tights or socks, be they knee high, thigh high or go, as they say, all the way up. You can shop through a dozen or so brands or browse by style; either way it's set up conveniently for quick shopping. They also offer reviews for each item (though good luck finding a single critical remark) and a glossary of terms so you can better get to know terms like control top, run guard and gusset: quite useful.

| ·LINGERIE | ·HOSIERY | | |
|---|---|---|---|

## 516-367-1095 • Alight.com

### Alight.com

Sizes 14 to 28w will probably not do better than to check out the selection of this all-encompassing women's apparel site. There's loads of great, stylish stuff here—we mean stylish; well made and good looking. It doesn't matter if you favor a modest approach to dressing, or if you embrace a tight sensuality; these clothes manage to be complimentary without being patronizing. While every item isn't always available in every combination of size and color, the site's entries make it quite clear, so on top of everything else the site is easy to use.

| ·CAREER ·ATHLETIC | ·SWIMWEAR ·OUTERWEAR | ·LINGERIE ·CASUAL | ·SPORTSWEAR |
|---|---|---|---|

## 213-488-0226 • American Apparel

### AmericanApparel.net

Getting back to basics is this "most passionate and innovative wholesale blank T-shirt manufacture and distributor in the world." A thorough selection of classic designs begins with the short sleeved tee and includes different varieties of tanks, cap sleeves, tube tops, long sleeves, crop tops, halters, raglans and more. Color schemes vary between earth tones and pastels on top of the fairly universal blacks and whites, and expanding ranges have come to include simply sexy shorts, bras and panties. Best of all, a strongly adhered to anti-sweatshop policy ensures your everyday wear will suit your ideals.

| ·CASUAL | ·LINGERIE | | |
|---|---|---|---|

## AnnTaylor.com

Ann Taylor • 800-342-5266

Fans of Ann Taylor will definitely appreciate this site, which brings all the grace of her clothing online. If you're not familiar, now's your chance to catch on to this elegant brand that's maintained a satisfied customer base for over 50 years now. The Shop by Occasion categories tell you all you need to know about the clothes: Suits That Work, Work Casual, Weekend Casual and Special Occasion. The Color Glossary will give you a quick look at the available shades from season to season, and the Fabric Glossary will give you tips on cleaning and care. All that's left is that inimitable Ann Taylor style.

| | ·CAREER | ·SPORTSWEAR | ·OUTERWEAR | ·CASUAL |

## Anthropologie.com

Anthropologie • 800-309-2500

Drawing influence from different cultures around the globe, the designers of the exclusive line of clothes for Anthropologie are always careful to accommodate the changing fashions of contemporary urban America. The result is a youthful and stylish selection of sweaters, skirts, tops, pants, dresses and jackets, each with bright colors and a subtle hint of flair, if that's possible. Think of it as a funky Banana Republic, except, as each design is in limited supply, everyone won't be wearing it. This is a good thing.

| ·SLEEPWEAR | ·SPORTSWEAR | ·OUTERWEAR | ·CASUAL |

## APC.fr

A.P.C. • 212-966-0069

Only the French could come up with a selection of sleek designer sportswear as desirable as this and make it so difficult to purchase online. You're better off staying away from the Flash version of the site (even our crack consultants couldn't figure it out), and then constantly bear in mind that "Ajouter" means "Add"; in this case you'll be adding to the shopping cart, which isn't specifically called a "shopping cart," but looks like one at least. Your reward will be fine quality clothes as, once again, only the French could muster.

| | ·CAREER ·CASUAL | ·DESIGNER | ·SPORTSWEAR | ·OUTERWEAR |

## ArmaniExchange.com

Armani Exchange • 800-717-2929

Let's get something straight right away: this is not a place to shop for finely tailored suits. See, Giorgio Armani isn't so one-sided as his designer suit and couture lines would indicate. Here, he wants you to know that he's down with the young, urban crowd by offering a selection of street-savvy clothes for characters like the Style Slayer, or the Party Princess (examples of different schemes available from this A|X brand). To give him credit, these clothes are pretty cool, and not as expensive as one would expect. Ironically, Armani may have taken fashion up a notch, by taking it down a peg or two.

| ·DESIGNER | ·SPORTSWEAR | ·CASUAL | |

## 888-322-5515 • Athleta

**Athleta.com**

Here's a well-designed site for the activity prone woman, "where shopping is no sweat." With categories like Climbing/Bouldering, Yoga/Dance, In-Line Skating and Triathlon, you know you can find gear for the type of workout you're about to endure, while other categories like Sports Bras and Maternity remind you that, yes, this store is conscientious of the female body. The great thing, though, is that you don't have to enter each category to access the types of products within. Simply choose Browse Online Store from the home page, and each category has a series of sub-headings that allow you to jump straight to that category's selection of Hats, Sports Tops and Swimwear. Not bad at all.

| ·SWIMWEAR | ·ATHLETIC | ·OUTERWEAR | |
|---|---|---|---|

## 800-441-1362 • Avenue

**Avenue.com**

Do not be confused by the cadre of waifs pictured on this site; the clothes shown here are sized 14 and above, making for a somewhat misleading, but generally high quality plus-size shop. From swimwear to outerwear, their motto is "nothing should stop you," probably intended to erase any discrepancies between the images and actual sizes. Most of the clothes, to be fair, are shown without a model, and most are actually pretty fine. If you ask us, the Clearance section is your best bet, as great clothes go for great prices.

| ·CAREER | ·SPORTSWEAR | ·OUTERWEAR | ·CASUAL |
|---|---|---|---|

## 604-685-9327 • A-Wear

**AWear.com**

To understand A-Wear's concept of "conscious clothing," you need only to consider their term "a-wear-ness." Yes, they seek to enlighten the fashionable with a global understanding of how style fits in with politics, entertainment and commerce... or something like that. There's an online magazine, and some other stuff that makes the site seem a bit confusing. We'd recommend heading straight for the Catalog, where you can browse through some cosmopolitan tops, bottoms, jackets and dresses. There's not a lot, but it's really cool, and it's listed in Canadian dollars. That means this stuff is even cheaper than the prices show, making it one of the best deals on the web.

| ·SPORTSWEAR | ·OUTERWEAR | ·CASUAL | |
|---|---|---|---|

## No Service Number • Azzuma

**Azzuma.com**

This retailer of "fine imported lingerie" focuses almost exclusively on some scintillating designs form France, begging the question: how do the French ever get anything accomplished? Shopping by brand name opens up to pages full of almost impossibly sexy imagery, which certainly shows the lingerie to fine effect but the problem is; while artistry is implicit in these photos, functionality is not. As a result, not every available item is pictured, merely samples from any particular selection. In most cases this will not matter, as this is fine apparel and will suit the discriminating shopper, but if you must absolutely see what it is you're going to get, you might do better elsewhere.

| ·SLEEPWEAR | ·LINGERIE | ·HOSIERY | |
|---|---|---|---|

# BananaRepublic.com

Banana Republic • 888-277-8953

Even if you're a fan of Banana Republic, and own lots of apparel from the catalog or one of its many stores, you probably never knew that it got its name from the "safari-inspired" clothes it originally sold back in the late nineteen-seventies. That's because they've long since expanded to become the purveyor of a simple metropolitan style, selling clothes today all over the US. While the safari styles are for the most part gone, the quality of the clothes remains intact, with a line as flexible as it is strong. Wear it out for coffee, or relax on the sofa, it doesn't matter what you do if you look jaunty doing it.

| ·CAREER ·OUTERWEAR | ·SWIMWEAR ·CASUAL | ·SLEEPWEAR | ·SPORTSWEAR |
|---|---|---|---|

# BareNecessities.com

BareNecessities.com • 877-728-9272

As the name would indicate, this site focuses on the basics of lingerie: bras, panties and hosiery. Shopping is easy, with a search function that allows you to specify style, size and/or any of a couple dozen highly recognizable brands. While the occasional camisole may pop up, don't count on it; the three-item focus here makes it easier to shop, and that's the point. Despite some advice they may offer on finding the perfect bra, there's no question as to where you should begin your visit here: the Clearance section.

| ·SLEEPWEAR | ·LINGERIE | ·HOSIERY | |
|---|---|---|---|

# BeautifulTonight.com

Beautiful Tonight • No Service Number

Here's one that gets to the point. While the selection of lingerie on display here is slight, it's all high-end, recognizable brands and therefore (presumably) top-quality. Without a doubt these items are very, very sexy. A pull-down menu makes it simple to browse the products quickly (though, in truth, most eyes will linger a bit), so if you don't find anything you're wild about at first glance, it's probably worth another look. We figure stuff this expensive can't help but to deliver, both literally and figuratively.

| ·SLEEPWEAR | ·LINGERIE | | |
|---|---|---|---|

# Bebe.com

Bebe • 877-232-3777

Bebe clothes have been seen on the likes of Madonna, Julia Roberts, Britney Spears, Anna Kournikova and pretty much every single other actress, singer or model who's been photographed in the last five years (see for yourself in The Scene section). But don't take this to mean these clothes are strictly for the woman with a $1500 a day clothes habit. Bebe designers simply take "the look" of the moment and translate it into their own hip brand of stylish, sexy and, more importantly, affordable apparel and accessories.

| ·SPORTSWEAR | ·OUTERWEAR | ·CASUAL | |
|---|---|---|---|

## 800-980-9085 • Becoming
### Becoming.com

A delicate matter leads to a genuinely appreciated shop with Becoming.com, a store dedicated to breast cancer survivors. Outfitting women who have undergone mastectomies and/or chemotherapy, the selection here features lingerie, swimwear and athletic gear designed to accommodate prosthetics, without sacrificing a truly feminine grace and style. The prosthetics may be found here as well, along with some wigs/headwear and of course a general selection of dresses and other apparel that promote comfort to the body, both inside and out.

| ·SWIMWEAR ·CASUAL | ·LINGERIE | ·SPORTSWEAR | ·ATHLETIC |
|---|---|---|---|

## 877-808-3322 • BellaLingerie.com
### BellaLingerie.com

This site takes a rather democratic approach to the development of its catalog, offering only the best-selling lingerie items of some of the world's top brands. Consequently, its limited and ever-changing selection is white-hot, featuring stuff that will tantalize men and make women feel sexy. Shopping can be done in almost no time at all, despite a somewhat slow loading time, though guys shopping for their significant others may want to take their time about it... you know, to make sure they get it right.

| ·SLEEPWEAR | ·LINGERIE | ·HOSIERY | |
|---|---|---|---|

## 650-592-5787 • Beni Boutique
### BeniBoutique.com

There's not a whole lot to this site: limited selections, low prices, dozens of the most prestigious designers in the world and— did we mention the low prices? That's right, this is your source for "discount designer goods," which of course includes dresses, skirts, blouses and pretty much whatever else they can get a hold of. If you don't like the stuff from Helmut Lang, Christian Dior or Vivienne Tam, perhaps you will like the clearance items by such luminaries as Michael Kors, Chanel or Anna Sui. See, this is just the tip of the iceberg.

| ·DESIGNER | ·SPORTSWEAR | ·CASUAL | |
|---|---|---|---|

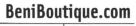

## 877-464-3293 • Betsey Johnson
### BetseyJohnson.com

If you're in the market for clothes worthy of rock stars, Betsey Johnson's got credentials. A veteran of the Andy Warhol set, she's been designing under "her own set of rules" for decades now, dressing members of The Velvet Underground and, more recently, The Dixie Chicks. Funky, crazy, bright and flashy merely describe the web site; these clothes defy description. Suffice to say she has managed to stay fresh with the times, but don't take our word for it. Some of her biggest fans include clients like Salma Hayek, Susan Sarandon, Madonna and, well, Prince. Warning: this one's not for the understated.

| ·FORMAL | ·SPORTSWEAR | ·CASUAL | ·DESIGNER |
|---|---|---|---|

## BostonProper.com

Boston Proper • 800-411-4080

Boasting designer clothes for the "active, affluent woman," what the purveyors of this catalog/web store are neglecting to say is that these clothes are sexy beyond compare; seriously sexy. Not to be confused with trashy, these clothes are a classy, tasteful kind of sexy, based on trim lines and elegant designs rather than overexposed flesh. This is stuff you can wear out to tennis, to lunch or out on the town—it just happens to be very appealing. There's even evening-appropriate attire, as well as intimates for post-evening moments. The site is slow to load, but the great views and details (you may view multiple colors and angles of each item) make it well worth the wait.

| | ·CAREER ·CASUAL | ·SPORTSWEAR | ·ATHLETIC | ·OUTERWEAR |
|---|---|---|---|---|

## BramaSole.com

Bramasole • No Service Number

Where can you find the type of swimsuit worn by the capricious women who frolic upon the beaches of the French Riviera? Well, here, for one. You might also see this high-end line, mostly bikinis, in your favorite fashion magazines, not surprising given the sexy cuts possessed by even their Classics selection (their one-piece string ensemble, for example). Still, none of this stuff is entirely too skimpy, at least given to reason, even though—like most such designer bathing apparel—it is generally intended for athletic figures.

| ·SWIMWEAR | | | |
|---|---|---|---|

## BraSmyth.com

Bra Smyth • 800-272-9466

The name of this site conjures images of a burly, sweaty man with a hammer and an anvil pounding away at iron breastplates, presumably to be worn by Valkyrie or Amazon women warriors. Of course, the intimate apparel featured here is much more delicate than all that; a slight but seemly selection of lingerie and sleepwear that combines high quality and comfort. Beautiful mid-to-high-end designer bras in particular should strike your fancy, ranging from soft cup to those that offer fuller support, with or without an underwire. Sleepwear abounds, ranging from nightshirts and nightgowns to robes, pajamas and chemises, all either sexy or soft or both. Finally, a discount site features great prices on older styles that still hold up over time, so to speak.

| | | ·SLEEPWEAR | ·LINGERIE | | |
|---|---|---|---|---|---|

## Bravissimo.com

Bravissimo • 011-44-192-645-9859

Welcome to "the company that is committed to celebrating your curves!" Namely, in terms of "a wide range of pretty lingerie in D-JJ cup." Not every item is represented in this full range of sizes, and you unfortunately won't be able to tell which is until you've already selected it, chosen a color and sized it out. Actually, in a lot of ways the shopping here can get complicated and cumbersome, but as this may be the only online retailer to outfit this upper range of sizes with quality undergarments, we'll give them the benefit of the doubt.

| | | ·SWIMWEAR | ·LINGERIE | | |
|---|---|---|---|---|---|

## 800-274-1815 • Brooks Brothers

**BrooksBrothers.com**

Bearing the dubious distinction of having designed the coat Abe Lincoln was wearing when he was assassinated, Brooks Brothers has been around for a long, long time, since 1818 in fact. Their staying power can only be attributed to the exceedingly high quality of their clothes—the term "finely tailored" doesn't seem to do them justice. Best suited for professional types, you'll be pleased to know that femininity doesn't receive a blind eye from this fashion fundamental. Aside from Presidents, Brooks Brothers has been seen on women ranging from Katherine Hepburn to Queen Latifah. You simply cannot go wrong here.

| ·CAREER | ·SPORTSWEAR | ·OUTERWEAR | ·CASUAL |
|---|---|---|---|

## 800-522-8090 • Buckle

**Buckle.com**

What you will find here is denim, and those clothes that go with denim (which, it may surprise you to learn, includes bikinis). It being so difficult to find good jeans, it's nice when a store takes the time to give these staples of the American wardrobe the special treatment. And these guys are eager to help you buy jeans from them, offering tips on matching different jean types to your body type, as well as guides to finding the perfect pair based on style and fit. This site makes it easy, which is all we ask.

| ·SPORTSWEAR | ·OUTERWEAR | ·CASUAL | |
|---|---|---|---|

## No Service Number • Built By Wendy

**BuiltByWendy.com**

The fashion press seems to adore the designs of Wendy Mullin, with pretty much unanimous praise for her edgy (or, as some would have it, "cute") designer streetwear. Known to use amateur models (friends and such) for her runway shows, Wendy seems to pass the savings along to the customer, as the prices for these girl-friendly clothes are pretty decent indeed. Whatever your take on her more eclectic items (T-shirts with an embroidered deer design come to mind), you will certainly find the majority of her exclusive tops, pants, skirts and dresses original, if not outstanding.

| ·DESIGNER | ·SPORTSWEAR | ·OUTERWEAR | ·CASUAL |
|---|---|---|---|

## 800-788-2224 • Caché

**Cache.com**

If you're the sort of person who loves both a sale and a great party, this noisy but user-friendly site has a cocktail dress for you. In fact, there's a whole stretch of evening wear options, as well as some less glamorous clothes in which to hit the town, from tops to bottoms and jackets and sweaters. Thanks to some crafty web design, it's all fairly easy to find, especially if you stick to the Shop Caché pull-down menu. You should be sure to scour The Sale Room, as it sometimes has an even bigger selection than the regular sections of the store (and cheaper of course).

| ·FORMAL | ·SPORTSWEAR | ·CASUAL | |
|---|---|---|---|

## CaraBella.com
**Carabella Collection • 800-227-2235**

Offering one of the largest selections of bathing attire we've seen online (particularly in bikinis), this site is large, cumbersome, occasionally confusing and yet somehow manages to get the job done. Aside from swimwear and a huge catalog of sarongs, there are a lot of sexy dresses, from evening gowns and cocktail dresses to beach-friendly wraps and skirts. Ironically, while the name translates from the Italian words for "expensive" and "beautiful," these clothes almost couldn't cost less. Finally, a shop that misleads you in a beneficial way.

| | ·SWIMWEAR | ·SPORTSWEAR | ·CASUAL | |
|---|---|---|---|---|

## CasualCornerGroup.com
**Casual Corner Group • 800-662-8042**

Appealing to a customer base that is "multidimensional, feminine and self-confident," the Casual Corner catalog is "all about style." Basically, what you'll find here is a sharp selection of casual and career-oriented clothing that alternates between demure and alluring, without resorting to the old "less is more" pretense. Different sections of the store cater to petite and plus sizes, though most sizes are included in the central catalog. Particularly enticing are the sale items, which are every bit as appealing as the merchandise in the Must Haves section, but at a fraction (usually less than half) of the already low original price.

| | ·CAREER | ·SPORTSWEAR | ·CASUAL | |
|---|---|---|---|---|

## CelebrityOnAir.com
**CelebrityOnAir.com • No Service Number**

Here's where you'll find the swimsuits of Carol Wior, aka "Slimsuits." These are slimming and supporting suits that help promote hourglass shapes with compression and underwires. As one of their mottoes says, "Shape & Slim, Forget the Gym!" as these suits promise to reduce waistlines by at least an inch and "lift the buttocks at least 1/2 inch," which is probably more gratifying than comfortable. You'll also find the official swimsuit of the Mrs. America Pageant, along with some pareos and other cover-ups for beach visits, and some undergarments that utilize the same "control" designs.

| | ·SWIMWEAR | ·LINGERIE | | |
|---|---|---|---|---|

## CTShirts.co.uk
**Charles Tyrwhitt • 866-797-2701**

By CT Shirts, they mean, Charles Tyrwhitt (pronounced "Tirit") shirts. And by that, they mean, "England's largest maker of quality shirts through the internet and mail order." It's simple; they sell high quality button-down collared shirts. You can shop by color, or by the few slight deviations in style, and one handy feature even allows you to change the sizing and pricing to USA standards. Thus is it easy to get in, get out, and know that in 7–10 days you'll get a dapper shirt in the mail (that's Brit-speak for "stylish").

| | ·CAREER | ·SPORTSWEAR | ·CASUAL | |
|---|---|---|---|---|

## 800-291-2943 • CyberSwim.com

# CyberSwim.com

Looking for an alternative to bathing suits that are "designed to look good on a seventeen year old runway model?" Well, this site is looking for you. Featuring a line of swimwear called Miraclesuits, it touts mostly one-piece suits that are made to contour and support your body. Turns out, these suits are available in dozens of styles, either in Misses, Women's or Plus sizes. Browsing options include Custom Fit to suit your body and/or lifestyle, and Suit Styles for options like tankinis, bandeaus, or maillots. Talk about your Miraclesuit variety.

| ·SWIMWEAR | | | |  |

## 877-932-6437 • Danier Leather

# Danier.com

This is where you look if you're in the market for some sexy leather and suede. The quality of designs here are hard to match, with coats and jackets obviously standing out, although there are some pretty slick skirts and scintillating tops here as well. Of course, no self-respecting, stylish leather shop would be lacking in tight leather, and these guys have plenty to offer in that department, with a variety of colors and styles and even some short shorts. Great pictures, decent prices and a respectable Plus Size selection make this one a winner.

| ·SPORTSWEAR | ·OUTERWEAR | ·CASUAL | |  |

## 800-923-9915 • DesignerOutlet.com

# DesignerOutlet.com

Here is a word you will learn to love: overstock. This place offers you great selections of designer brand apparel at huge discounts, more than half off in some cases. You can shop by designer, by specific clothing item (very specific) or price range, or choose to narrow down your browsing between eveningwear, corporate attire, weekend clothes, workout gear and lingerie. All of this merchandise is overstock, but don't let that make you think it's all stuff nobody else wanted to buy—that's what the Basement Area is for.

| ·CAREER ·OUTERWEAR | ·SLEEPWEAR ·CASUAL | ·DESIGNER ·LINGERIE | ·SPORTSWEAR |  |

## 800-691-9101 • Eberjey Intimates

# Eberjey.com

This site, whose name means "joy" in an obscure Nigerian dialect, offers "a lot of lingerie and sleepwear that encompasses every aspect of femininity and fun without compromising fit." In other words, its very limited selection of sexy intimate attire aims to complement even "small, flat-bottomed girls" without any problem. Ironically, their clientele includes Pamela Anderson, Liv Tyler and none other than Jennifer Lopez. Just evidence of their claim that these designs are adaptable to "any kind of booty."

| ·LINGERIE | ·SLEEPWEAR | | |  |

# Elisabeth.com

Elisabeth • 800-683-7330

From fashion mainstay Liz Claiborne comes the Elisabeth line of elegant plus-size office attire and active wear ... and it's about time. The loading time on this site is abysmal, so if you've got a slow connection you may just want to skip it altogether. But if you have either a fast connection or a superior devotion to style, the quality of clothing here will be worth a wait. Whether you're shopping for dresses, skirts, jackets or full outfits—all are made from beautiful fabrics and decidedly add splendor to any wardrobe—the sex appeal registers off the chart. It's just hard to go wrong with Liz Claiborne.

| | | ·CAREER ·CASUAL | ·FORMAL ·DESIGNER | ·SPORTSWEAR | ·OUTERWEAR |
|---|---|---|---|---|---|

# EverythingButWater.com

Everything But Water • 888-796-6661

If you're a fan of the *Sports Illustrated* swimsuit issue (a fan of the suits, we mean), you may enjoy a feature on this site that shows select pictures from the magazine and lets you click on them to purchase the suit in question (look in Editorial). On the flipside, a feature called Fit Solutions will key you in on choosing a suit best suited to your own body style. Generally, though, most of your shopping will take place in the Specialty and sultry Collections sections, each of which employs different browsing techniques (by brand and page-by-page, respectively), or in Essentials, where you'll find the simple, solid color one-pieces and sarongs that flatter anybody on any beach in any season.

| ·SWIMWEAR | | | |
|---|---|---|---|

# ExquisiteSwimwear.com

Exquisite Swimwear.com • No Service Number

In this case, the exquisite swimwear consists of Israel-based design firms, notably Seaspray, Gideon Oberson and Pilpel. What can you expect? Well, they proudly proclaim, "no g-strings here, just captivating swimwear." In other words: simple and fashionable. Make no mistake; though, you can find some revealing bikinis here, if that's your thing, and some pretty sexy one-pieces as well. Only thing is, either may take a while, as the navigation forces you to browse first by brand, then by specific brand line. If you've got the time, this one should eventually be worth it.

| | ·SWIMWEAR | | | |
|---|---|---|---|---|

# FashionDig.com

FashionDig • 866-327-4344

This clothing site devoted to "Exploring 20th Century Style" aims to satisfy those with vintage cravings. You can browse through the Mod Shop, the Fabulous Fifties or the always intriguing Couture, and you'll easily be met with some truly fashionable attire that is just outdated enough to appear fresh and new. The one big problem: most of the stuff, cool as it is, exists here in a quantity of one and probably won't fit you. However, the site at least warrants a bookmark, as frequent return visits will potentially turn up a perfect fit.

| | ·CAREER ·OUTERWEAR | ·FORMAL ·CASUAL | ·DESIGNER | ·SPORTSWEAR |
|---|---|---|---|---|

## 866-751-2589 • FigLeaves.com

# FigLeaves.com

No doubt you spotted the reference and have figured out that this British online retailer specializes in those garments we use to hide our personal parts, particularly in the form of bras, briefs and hosiery. Of course, there're some other accoutrements here, as any decent lingerie store would provide, but this stock tends to focus on comfort and function, rather than specifically sexy, stand-alone undergarments. The site's layout can be drag to browse, with 70-plus brands to sort through. Fortunately, the Bra, Brief and Legs Finders lets you quickly narrow things down by size, material, style and occasion (if "plunge" can be considered an occasion). That reminds us; keep an eye out for half-off items.

| ·SWIMWEAR | ·SLEEPWEAR | ·LINGERIE | ·HOSIERY |
| --- | --- | --- | --- |

## 800-235-9005 • Fitigues

# Fitigues.com

This line of "comfort driven clothing," developed by a husband and wife team in Chicago has, in their words, "become more of a lifestyle than a brand." The concept? That "The best parts of the day are spent in comfortable clothes baking cookies and reading the Sunday paper." So, keep your clubs and your high society shindigs; these cute clothes are meant for the living room or possibly the deck, playing with the dogs and the kids, and—dare we say—shopping online over a lazy weekend?

| ·SPORTSWEAR | ·ATHLETIC | ·CASUAL | |
| --- | --- | --- | --- |

## 888-888-9328 • Flexees

# Flexees.com

The online retail arm of the Maidenform brand of women's underthings, this site's a great place to find bras without any hassle or waste of time. Aside from an array of categories like Crop Tops, Demi Bras, Strapless Bras and Push-Up Bras, there are sections devoted to Panties and Shapewear. Browsing is simple, the pictures clear and ordering easy. Even better, if there's any question on which sort undergarment suits a particular item of clothing, follow the What to Wear Under What You're Wearing link, which can point you to bras appropriate for clothes like tight sweaters, sheer blouses and halter tops.

| ·LINGERIE | | | |
| --- | --- | --- | --- |

## 602-760-2111 • Frederick's of Hollywood

# Fredericks.com

Just to avoid any confusion, this is Frederick Mellinger we're talking about here, the silky smooth proprietor of Frederick's of Hollywood. Maybe you're familiar with the slightly less than chaste line of intimate apparel that goes by this brand? Things like peignoirs, chemises, teddies, corsets, bustiers, garters, boots, stiletto heels, stick-on bras, crotchless panties and, ahem, wigs. Sure, there's some more standard fare, including somewhat more regular lingerie (if sexy can be considered regular), and some daring dresses as well. Most items here come in all sizes, standard and plus, and with drop-down menus in the Shop section, it's all incredibly easy to find those, um, items you've been looking for.

| ·SWIMWEAR | ·SLEEPWEAR | ·LINGERIE | ·HOSIERY |
| --- | --- | --- | --- |

# FreshPair.com

With a name meant to remind you of the pleasure inherent to putting on clean, new undergarments, this site almost makes you want to log on immediately to order some for overnight delivery, which of course is possible here. Surprisingly well made, with great looks given that almost nobody else will ever see these sub-dud duds, this winning site offers Bras, Hosiery, Socks and Sleepwear, the latter of which inexplicably includes pictures of models watering a lawn in nighties. We like to kid, but this one's done right.

| ·SLEEPWEAR | ·LINGERIE | ·HOSIERY | |
|---|---|---|---|

# Frisk-Me.com

Were you to ask, this punk-influenced collection isn't underwear, it's "innerwear," though the distinction seems to be more in the attitude than anything else. (Ain't it always?) There's certainly a rocker element here, made all the more apparent by the abundance of tattooed models displayed on the Shop page. Some of the this stuff you could probably get away with wearing as risqué tops in certain clubs, some would probably cause problems in most cities. But, ultimately, all of it is unique, and this is the best place to find it.

| ·LINGERIE | | | |
|---|---|---|---|

# Gap.com

If you've gone shopping for clothes in the USA at all in the past 10 years, you know exactly the kind of stuff The Gap has to offer. This makes it a perfect choice for online shopping. As their sizes adhere to a pretty fixed standard, it's simply a matter of picking your favorite cut and colors from the set of styles that follow close on the heels of current trends (or so they'd have you believe, at least). Jeans, skirts, pants, shirts, sweaters and everything else they have to offer, it's all easy, and best of all it's cheap.

| ·SWIMWEAR ·ATHLETIC | ·SLEEPWEAR ·OUTERWEAR | ·LINGERIE ·CASUAL | ·SPORTSWEAR |
|---|---|---|---|

# GirlShop.com

Girl Shop brings together a number of chic designer boutiques and makes their exclusive offerings available online. Consequently, you can find just about anything under the sun here (ever hear of thong clips?), and thanks to the About the Designer sections, you can learn a little about what you're getting yourself into. You may want to go straight to the search function, where you can sort things out by price, category and brand name. They've even solved two of the bigger problems of selling items from multiple stores by including different sizing charts for each designer, and by gathering your order from all the boutiques into one place for a single shipping cost. This is the next best thing to a day of shopping in a hip neighborhood.

| ·FORMAL ·LINGERIE | ·SWIMWEAR ·SPORTSWEAR | ·SLEEPWEAR ·OUTERWEAR | ·DESIGNER ·CASUAL |
|---|---|---|---|

## No Service Number • Gloria DelRio

## GloriaDelRio.com

What should you expect from a model-turned swimsuit designer who hails from Rio de Janeiro? Not much. We mean, of course, that if you're to log on to this site devoted to designs "inspired by the hot white sands of Copacabana and Ipanema," you will find some minimalist fare to say the least. But this site's got more than you'd expect, as the Brazilian designer manages to squeeze some slightly more reserved pieces between the thongs and string bikinis that command your immediate attention. It turns out, less isn't the only thing that can mean more.

| ·SWIMWEAR | ·DESIGNER | | |
|-----------|-----------|---|---|

## 800-846-5263 • GoJane.com

## GoJane.com

Teens and young adults will especially appreciate the low prices and sassy styles represented in this somehow straightforward and funky online shop. The pants for sale are especially fun, but jeans aren't the only things here with flair. Whether it's a homecoming dress, a cool pair of shoes or summery tanks and tube tops, all is represented here with a range of attitude. But it's attitude you don't have to pay extreme prices for, which is great because younger women tend to have less money.

| ·FORMAL ·OUTERWEAR | ·CASUAL | ·SWIMWEAR | ·SPORTSWEAR | ⇅ |
|--------------------|---------|-----------|-------------|---|

## 877-444-8377 • Guess

## Guess.com

You know this one. Here's the online store to help you satiate your lust for the brand that made household names of Claudia Schiffer, Laetitia Casta and, well, Anna Nicole Smith. Okay, so nobody's perfect, but this is a pretty damn good site, easy to figure out, and a pleasure to shop from. You won't necessarily find everything you could in one of their stores, but there's a decent range of mid-to-high-end apparel here, and some pretty cool accessories as well. But you want to know about the jeans, right? Well, they have plenty of them, and even a Jean Guide, to help take all the guesswork out of shopping.

| ·SWIMWEAR | ·SPORTSWEAR | ·OUTERWEAR | ·CASUAL |
|-----------|-------------|------------|---------|

## 626-577-7140 • HeatherBloom.com

## HeatherBloom.com

The online representation of an intimates store located in Old Town Pasadena, California, the products here aren't as seamy or sultry as some of the lingerie we've seen on other sites. This selection tends to promote the comfort of the woman wearing it, both physically and in terms of exhibition. Don't think this stuff isn't sexy, though—it's simply intended to compliment the natural state of a woman's body rather than snap or truss it into shape. Though the visually based navigation can be mildly confusing, if you start in Daywear and just keep clicking on pictures you like, you'll get the hang of it.

| ·SLEEPWEAR | ·LINGERIE | | |
|------------|-----------|---|---|

# HerRoom.com

Her Room • 800-558-6779

This site promises the sort of day-to-day underwear a woman will likely buy for herself (as opposed to the ultra-sheer, nonsupportive and/or excessively strappy lingerie a husband or boyfriend likes to procure). An incredible amount of detailed information accompanies each listed item, and they've organized it in such a way that it actually enhances browsing, rather than hinders it. Hence, their selection enables you to see how bra or panties might fit (or not fit) with various different necklines or hems with multiple views and thorough descriptions.

 ·LINGERIE

# HippieSkivvies.com

Hippie Skivvies • 877-544-5566

"...When ya gotta hide the hippie inside." Yep, tie-dye is back, only now you can put it in a place where few have to see it. Panties come French-cut, boy-cut and in thong form, while camisoles come in full coverage or cropped (to bare the midriff). This all turns out to be quite sexy, perhaps more than it should be. There're also some boxer shorts and a robe, and if any of these don't thrill your need for rainbow colors, you can find a tie-dye kit, enabling you to have at all those dreary clothes you used to like. Cool, man.

·SLEEPWEAR | ·LINGERIE

# HotTopic.com

Hot Topic • 800-892-8674

This one's for all the rockers out there. Actually, this mall shop turned online store should be able to satisfy the needs on any kind of club-goer with its edgy apparel and kinky accessories. Punk, gothic, lounge, or dance—even if you're just into looking hip as you loiter in the streets you can dress yourself here while still have enough cash left over to go to a show (just don't wear a band T-shirt to that band's show). If you missed the show, a big selection of band T-shirts serve almost as well as actual memories.

·SLEEPWEAR | ·LINGERIE | ·SPORTSWEAR | ·CASUAL

# IC3D.com

IC3D.com • 212-279-8939

If you've ever had a problem finding jeans that fit, grab a tape measure and log on to this site immediately. Here you can literally assemble your own pair of custom jeans; and not just blue denim, either. To start with, you have a choice of thirteen fabrics, including leather, camouflage, faux leather, suede, velvet, and two gauges of corduroy. From there you have a choice of: several colors for each fabric; different fits for your hips, legs and ankles; copper, brass or nickel for rivets and buttons; zipper or button fly; several options for pockets and belt loops; and even the color of thread used to sew it all together (label-free if you so desire). The only hard part is the 11 different measurements you must make of your lower body to order....

 ·CASUAL

## No Service Number • Inchant.com

### Inchant.com

Possessing lingerie "for all your romantic moods, from every day to risqué," as we saw it, the bulk of this catalog seems to primarily cater to the risqué more often than not. The big exception to this (no pun intended) is the selection of bra sizes, which start at the minimum and extend into a range most people probably don't even know exist (we're talking about the letter G). There is also a wide selection of plus-size lingerie here, both in underwear and intimate apparel, ranging from modest to the delightfully obscene.

| ·SLEEPWEAR | ·LINGERIE | | |
|---|---|---|---|

## 800-932-0043 • J. Crew

### JCrew.com

Articles have been written upon how to look like a J. Crew model. The simple enough answer is to fit yourself into some of these classically comfortable clothes, and wait for that exuberant, satisfied smile to spread across your face. There's nothing here you'd really want to wear into the finer establishments on the planet, but for those days when you're not scheduled to dine at the ambassador's house, this stuff is great for playing, exploring and just kicking around, letting your taste speak for itself. The items here are well organized and frequently updated, so it'll be easy to come back often to check out their new coats, sweaters and tops. If you don't, your friends will first.

| ·CAREER ·SPORTSWEAR | ·SWIMWEAR ·OUTERWEAR | ·SLEEPWEAR ·CASUAL | ·LINGERIE |
|---|---|---|---|

## 800-261-5902 • Just My Size

### JustMySize.com

For women who have trouble finding comfortable or complimentary sizes without sacrificing elegance or price, this shop for tall, petite and full-figured women will provide a welcome presence on the e-commerce horizon. A balanced mix of tasteful apparel and popular brands, anything from intimates and hosiery to casual clothing, may be easily found using the Product Index pull-down menu featured universally throughout the site. Workout gear and classic styles for dressier occasions are also easy to sort through and, while the selection is limited, thorough product descriptions and good prices make it a palatable experience for any dedicated shopper.

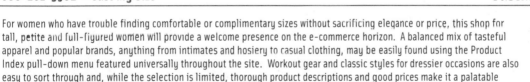

| ·CAREER ·ATHLETIC | ·SLEEPWEAR ·CASUAL | ·LINGERIE | ·SPORTSWEAR |
|---|---|---|---|

## 866-658-1902 • Karmaloop

### KarmaLoop.com

Before you see it on the high runways of Paris or Venice, or it shows up in The Gap's new season of clothes, you oftentimes see it wandering the streets of the city, worn by the young people who're daring enough to explore the edges of fresh fashion. That's the appeal of this site, which brings together budding and established designer labels from an urban dance culture that extends to all corners of the earth. Most of this gear is made to accommodate dancing into the night, or at least to facilitate movement from sidewalk to sidewalk, and all of it represents a young culture that is entirely wary of the limitless appeal of ever-changing styles.

| ·CASUAL | | | |
|---|---|---|---|

## KennethCole.com

**Kenneth Cole Productions • 800-536-2653**

Kenneth Cole Productions began its run as a tasteful shoe brand, instilling enough enthusiasm in their customers that the transition into quality apparel seems to have taken place without a hitch. Starting with leather, and continuing through their entire line of apparel, you can expect to find stuff that is sexy without being inelegant, and some of it is even kinda fun, especially if you follow the link to Reaction Online. This is a stash of more relaxed Kenneth Cole gear (think Miami) that runs off the same commerce engine, so you can shop back and forth without losing your order.

| ·SPORTSWEAR | ·OUTERWEAR | ·CASUAL | ·DESIGNER |
| --- | --- | --- | --- |

## Kiyonna.com

**Kiyonna • 888-549-6662**

Boasting "Sophisticated Style, Sizes 14+," this maker of "stylish and contemporary clothing" avows a need for the fashion industry to recognize and serve a plus-sized niche. Certainly, even just since they began operations in 1996, the industry has taken notice, no doubt in part due to the efforts of Kiyonna's founding partners. So, we're forced to ask the question: why isn't there more here? Browsing is easy, but only by virtue of the fact that you may view the entire catalog within five minutes of logging on to the site, with slim selections of blouses, skirts, dresses and hosiery available. Good stuff, but maybe it's now turn for this brand to pay more attention to the industry.

| ·FORMAL | ·HOSIERY | ·SPORTSWEAR |
| --- | --- | --- |

## LandsEnd.com

**Lands' End • 800-963-4816**

Lands' End actually started out as a mail order yacht supply company (it turns out the misplaced apostrophe was initially a typo). Somehow, they ended up selling clothes, luggage and home furnishings, though how this happened is poorly documented. Nevertheless, their range of clothes covers just about every size known to woman, and thorough searches will find some pretty stylish wares. The site's layout may not be ideal, but if you keep your eye out for a View All link in the bottom right corner of product pages, you'll suddenly notice the selection is much bigger than a first glance indicates. Look elsewhere for sailboat fittings.

| ·CAREER<br>·ATHLETIC | ·SWIMWEAR<br>·OUTERWEAR | ·SLEEPWEAR<br>·CASUAL | ·SPORTSWEAR |
| --- | --- | --- | --- |

## LegWearDirect.com

**LegWearDirect.com • 877-534-3472**

Promising "designer legwear at half the price," these guys actually deliver. How? Well, it turns out that this company manufactures tights and various socks for fashionable labels available internationally. Here, you can buy the same items; just without the labels (who knew a little stitched piece of cloth cost so much?). If you want to show off your exquisite tastes by brandishing such labels, move right along, a boutique surely awaits. If, however, you just want the quality, this is about as inexpensive as quality gets.

| ·HOSIERY | | | |
| --- | --- | --- | --- |

## 866-285-2743 • LingerieAtLarge

## LingerieAtLarge.com

So far as plus-sized lingerie stores go, this one doesn't offer the greatest variety, nor the sexiest, or even the most elegant, though in each of these three aspects this selection is near the top. What it does offer that stands out more than anything is a section replete with kinky costumes for the full-figured fetishist, whether you prefer a vinyl-clad nun, bar maid or police officer. No less playful but decidedly more dangerous is the enigmatic Wild Side category, which at this time is better left unexplained, in deference to minors.

| ·SLEEPWEAR | ·LINGERIE | ·HOSIERY | |
|---|---|---|---|

## 011-44-208-649-9009 • Long Tall Sally

## LongTallSally.com

Seeing as most supermodels are almost by definition tall, we tend not to think of clothes for tall women as difficult to locate. However, understanding that pant legs are usually measured to standard sizes, this site's inclusion here owes to the fact that the strong selection of fashionable trousers here might be by some quite appreciated. As it happens, the entire catalog fits the style-minded sizes 8–20, lending a potential boost to any tall woman's wardrobe, in particular the long and lean.

| ·CASUAL | ·SPORTSWEAR | ·CAREER | ·SWIMWEAR |
|---|---|---|---|

## 888-274-7499 • Love Your Peaches

## LoveYourPeaches.com

Implying the desire to "shake your tree," this line of apparel named for a Steve Miller song follows to a T its motto, "no boundaries." As the founder/designer puts it, she started this oftentimes quite revealing plus-sized catalog, "because it's a wonderful thing to be free." This heartfelt sentiment is carried out to great aplomb with a well-ordered selection of clothes, from cotton sweaters to stretch denim. Best may be the swimwear section, though, which offers several different fabrics and styles, each cut to order, whether one-piece, skirted bikini or thong.

| ·SWIMWEAR | ·SPORTSWEAR | ·OUTERWEAR | ·CASUAL |
|---|---|---|---|

## 800-964-5777 • Lucky Brand

## LuckyBrandJeans.com

"Sturdy" is the word best and most often applied to this brand that seems to rise in popularity every year. Other words come to mind: comfortable, classic, easy—between the excellent customer service and durable designs, there's not a whole lot more you could ask for from a jean manufacturer, except maybe something to wear with the jeans. Thus, Lucky offers a line of similarly hardy attire, the sort of clothes you would like to be wearing if you ever get stranded in the wilderness, on the side of the road or in a bar. The site's simple to navigate, and it gives you a great look at the abundance of cotton, wool and other relaxing fabrics that you can wear through even the least relaxing of situations.

| ·SPORTSWEAR | ·OUTERWEAR | ·CASUAL | |
|---|---|---|---|

## LuxuryOuterwear.com

Alexandros • 877-300-8784

PETA enthusiasts will want to skip this one, seeing as furs are the main—actually, the only—attraction here. Specifically, Alexandros Furs, featuring collections by Halston, Ekso and Mark Montano, if these names ring a bell. You can shop for jackets, stoles, capes or coats by clicking on the Fur Basics button, but the site's clumsy design might be enough to discourage you from continuing. Still, it's a good place to find those enviable furs that should at least stave off that pesky vegetarian crowd for another season.

| ·OUTERWEAR | ·DESIGNER | | |
|---|---|---|---|

## MaliaMills.com

Malia Mills • 800-685-3479

Malia Mills was still a waitress the first time one of her bikinis made an appearance in the *Sports Illustrated* swimsuit issue; she was pretty well through with that gig when, just a few years later, Valeria Mazza and Tyra Banks wore her cheetah prints on the cover. Now, of course, she devotes all of her time to the bikinis you will find on this completely unpretentious site. The cool thing about her designs is that they're sold as separates, so you never get stuck with one piece you like and one you'd just like to throw back. The Style Dictionary turns out, then, to be the best way to shop, as it lists a picture of each type of top and bottom, letting you click through to choose from different fabrics before buying. Skip the one-pieces this year.

| | ·SWIMWEAR | | | |
|---|---|---|---|---|

## MarkShale.com

Mark Shale • 888-333-6964

Keeping it clean and simple, this chic line of apparel ranges from quiet to colorful, all of it finely cut from quality fabrics. Now, if they could only make their website clean and simple. You can narrow down the selection to Women's clothing, but beyond that, the categories are unevenly dispersed, sometimes making their contents explicit, sometimes a little more difficult to fathom. Fortunately, there's not too much to sort through, so you can get through most of the catalog without too many frustrating side effects.

| | ·CAREER | ·SPORTSWEAR | ·CASUAL | |
|---|---|---|---|---|

## MaryGreen.com

Mary Green • 800-359-7455

When it comes to lingerie, men and women often find themselves in disagreement. Walking the line of compromise is this proprietary line of bedroom attire. She will like most of this stuff because it is "cute." He will dig it because it's "sexy." Both will like it because it's generally quite affordable. Many combinations of silk, satin, lace and ribbon conspire for a plethora of playful dressing options in several colors and cuts. A pair of silk panties packaged to look like a rose at the end of a long stem caps the selection as a romantic gesture with a bit of bite. Fun stuff.

| | | ·SLEEPWEAR | ·LINGERIE | ·HOSIERY | |
|---|---|---|---|---|---|

**No Service Number • Maurice Malone**

## MauriceMaloneUSA.com

Maurice Malone is a Detroit-native who began his lately skyrocketing career in design by successfully crafting himself a hat he couldn't afford to buy. Perhaps this lends to the ability of his work to simultaneously capture the favor of both the urban street-set and the high couture crowd. While his collections offer sometimes experimental, often daring lines of designer suits, the great bulk of his catalog here consists of the MaloneSports and MoJeans lines, both of which aptly display the colorful, funky flair for design that has garnered Malone international attention. This stuff is cool, letting you maintain your street-cred while still managing to look sexy and expressive.

| ·SPORTSWEAR | ·CASUAL | ·DESIGNER | |
|---|---|---|---|

**888-334-4629 • MaxStudio**

## MaxStudio.com

For up-to-date fashions, this slick site offers hip casual, professional and evening wear for competitive prices. Simply roll-over the By Category or By Outfit graphics for menus to guide your browsing (click on The Latest for new, seasonal items). Of course, the omni-present Sale category will immediately catch your attention, as well it should since the proprietors of this site seem to have short attention spans; the clothes don't spend a long time in The Latest section before being greatly reduced in price. Actually, the Sale items far outnumber current styles, and as nothing here is terribly outmoded, you can find some excellent deals on some great designer garb. Check back often, this site's a winner.

| ·SPORTSWEAR | ·OUTERWEAR | ·CASUAL | |
|---|---|---|---|

**866-378-1239 • MyCashmere.com**

## MyCashmere.com

When you've got to go with what you feel, let's face it, very few things in the universe feel as good as cashmere. Here you'll find cashmere to suit nearly every occasion simply select Play Days (casual), Business Chic (professional) or Special Occasions (activewear) to browse through a small but charming collection of modern cashmere designs. Or, you can stick to classic form by choosing from an array of brightly colored pashminas, perfect for those long, romantic strolls on a brisk autumn night. Because, though your escort may not know just what the word 'pashmina' means, sometimes a guy's just got to go with what he feels as well.

| ·SPORTSWEAR | ·CASUAL | ·CAREER | |
|---|---|---|---|

**011-44-147-332-3032 • Net-A-Porter.com**

## Net-A-Porter.com

There are always those designers who are just on the fringe; hard to find and only known in tight circles, but who are making incredible clothes. That's what makes this site so great. Here, you are given access to the catalogs of dozens of hip, young designers—people whose work you just won't see anywhere else... along with a few you already adore. What's more is that you can read about all of them to get an idea of who they are and what they're all about. Then follow the seasonal or sale item links to get shopping.

| ·CAREER ·LINGERIE | ·SWIMWEAR ·SPORTSWEAR | ·SLEEPWEAR ·OUTERWEAR | ·DESIGNER ·CASUAL | |
|---|---|---|---|---|

## Newport-News.com
**Newport News • 800-759-3950**

For great prices on fashion and footwear, the diligent shopper will probably find some gems here, although a lukewarm selection might leave you cold. Still, leather rarely comes this cheap, and between clothes, shoes and accessories, there's bound to be something you like here (especially the intimates and swimwear), or at least something comfortable to wear to a ball game or a barbecue. Browsing is simple, and though the category names may keep you guessing, the detailed pictures really do say it all.

| ·CAREER ·SPORTSWEAR | ·SWIMWEAR ·ATHLETIC | ·SLEEPWEAR ·OUTERWEAR | ·LINGERIE ·CASUAL |
|---|---|---|---|

## OldNavy.com
**Old Navy • 800-653-6289**

You've probably seen the campy commercials, and so you understand what these guys mean with terms like Performance Fleece or Techno Chino Skirts. Basically, this is trendy, cheap casual wear for anyone from kids to adults. Styles are simple, so any tops mix easily with any bottoms, and a great selection of outerwear will match just about anything you put underneath it. This is a place that makes shopping especially easy, so if you're willing to embrace that Old Navy charm, then nothing here will disappoint.

| ·SWIMWEAR ·ATHLETIC | ·SLEEPWEAR ·OUTERWEAR | ·LINGERIE ·CASUAL | ·SPORTSWEAR |
|---|---|---|---|

## OndadeMar.com
**Ondade Mar • 866-663-2627**

Daring and colorful bikinis stock this site to the point that you simply don't expect there to be anything else. Multiple views of each suit tantalize on many levels, but primarily with eye-catching patterns and designs ranging from delightfully cute to devastatingly sexy. You may view all of the suits with a rollover flash feature from the home page, but as it turns out, if you follow the Shopping link, all appear in better detail on a single page without requiring you to move your mouse. Either way, this is the easiest way to suit up for a summer full of tanning.

| ·SWIMWEAR | | | |
|---|---|---|---|

## OneHanesPlace.com
**One Hanes Place • 800-671-1674**

Once a catalog known as the "Family Showcase of Savings," this simple new visage offers a focus more on what we all (hopefully) wear under our clothes. Mostly popular national brands (Hanes, Playtex, L'eggs and Wonderbra, for example) dominate the web space here, in sock, bra and panty form, though you may find some decent workout wear as well. It's all relatively easy to find, and should prove an inexpensive way to stock up on a lot of basics, leaving more time open to focus on the clothes people will actually see.

| ·LINGERIE | ·HOSIERY | ·ATHLETIC | |
|---|---|---|---|

## 800-255-6429 • Peruvian Connection
### PeruvianConnection.com

Taking inspiration from an "ancient Andean textile tradition," this company's designers deliver the mountains of South America in the form of a fine selection of sweaters, coats, dresses and wraps. Beautiful patterns provide the foundation for most of these clothes, though knitted fabrics and simple forms play important roles as well, lending to fashionable attire fit for any style-minded, active woman. Simply select the current season, your preferred language and country to get started, and follow the simple browsing categories through this small but enchanting catalog.

| ·CAREER | ·SPORTSWEAR | ·OUTERWEAR | ·CASUAL |
|---|---|---|---|

## 310-444-0452 • Piece Unique
### PieceUnique.com

If you're a collector, or a fashion eclectic, you'll probably get pretty excited about some of the vintage haute couture styles to be found on this difficult but functional site. Reading like a Who's Who of fashion, high-end designers like Chanel, Gucci and Versace dominate the list of consignments here. Clothes are split between Recent Garments and Vintage (usually from the 1960-80's), but the useful categorization ends there. You'll have to scour through a list of named items, rooting yet deeper to see images. Who can complain, though, for prices this low on some of the finest clothes ever made?

| ·DESIGNER | ·SPORTSWEAR | ·FORMAL | |
|---|---|---|---|

## No Service Number • PlusSize.com
### PlusSize.com

As part of an overwhelmingly larger web site, this one lists among its categories Outdoor Living, Office & Business and Auto. Don't be distracted, though, the obvious true focus of this site is plus-sized apparel. Literally hundreds and hundreds of products, from swimwear and lingerie to hosiery and active wear provide more options than most stores of any kind, ranging from stylish to ultra-functional. Of course, the drawback of this is endless clicking to view all these choices, and search functions unfortunately aren't strong enough to make it easy. Then, between easy and well-stocked, we will take well-stocked.

| ·CAREER ·SPORTSWEAR | ·SWIMWEAR ·OUTERWEAR | ·SLEEPWEAR ·CASUAL | ·LINGERIE ·ATHLETIC |
|---|---|---|---|

## 888-404-9643 • PurpleSkirt.com
### PurpleSkirt.com

Brought to you by the obviously overactive imagination of all-around entertainer Tracey Ullman (and friends), this could be looked at as nothing more than a ploy to get other people to dress like her. However, it is not. Actually, it's a seriously good selection of tops, bottoms and dresses from some of the more popular new and established designers, and then a bunch of stuff that the founders of the site just happen to like. It's all pretty fresh fashion too, thanks to a constantly updated catalog, or as Ullman puts it, "We'll have new stuff every few weeks, because we're all so fickle."

| ·DESIGNER ·CASUAL | ·LINGERIE | ·SPORTSWEAR | ·OUTERWEAR |
|---|---|---|---|

## RavinStyle.com

Ravin Style • 212-965-9626

If you've always dreamt of having your own personal shopper, and aren't particularly picky about it, check out this cadre of characters. Ravin, Lela and Jackie, you see, are cartoon characters, each representing a certain type of woman. Jackie, for example, goes for the "sleek, city look," while Lela encourages you to "flaunt your feminine side." Website namesake Ravin, meanwhile, simply commands you to "get in touch with your inner wardrobe." Basically, all three entities provide a cutesy means for the real-life proprietors of Ravin Style to display their top picks from current designer collections, which happens to be somewhat worth it, if you don't mind taking advice from a sketch.

| ·SWIMWEAR ·OUTERWEAR | ·SLEEPWEAR ·CASUAL | ·LINGERIE | ·SPORTSWEAR |
| --- | --- | --- | --- |

## SauvageWear.com

Sauvage • 858-514-8229

If you would describe your fashion sense as conservative, you might want to skip this site altogether; these wares are racy as all get out. With plenty of what they describe as "exotic, cutting edge swimwear," the watchword here is "confidence," as to wear these suits, T-shirts and even underwear is to attract the closest of scrutiny. If you happen to have the tanned, toned and lithe type of body exhibited by these models, you may feel right at home cruising the beach in these skimpy suits. Otherwise... the locations of these photo shoots look pretty fun.

| ·SWIMWEAR | | | |
| --- | --- | --- | --- |

## SeamlessBody.com

SeamlessBody.com • No Service Number

Banking on the theory that what a woman wears under her clothes shouldn't be visible to the general public, Seamless Body features a very specific online catalog of, you guessed it, seamless undergarments. These intimates, or Body Wraps as they call them, go a bit further than your average bra and panties, though, offering shape and support for women of all sizes, in various colors so as to be virtually undetectable. Buying them from the site can prove tricky, so just click on the BuyIt! link immediately from the home page to avoid any annoyance or confusion. Next stop, tight clothes.

| ·LINGERIE | | | |
| --- | --- | --- | --- |

## SearleNYC.com

Searle • 212-730-7717

NYC, of course, stands for New York City, the irrefutable style center of the United States and, thanks to this site, its vantage point for fashion can now be shared with places like Dubuque, Portland and Pittsburgh. Coats will especially grab your attention, with a wide enough selection that you may want 2 or 3 (if you can afford them). In the Ready to Wear section you'll find plenty of chic activewear, including sweaters, jackets, jeans, skirts and tops, all in updated styles, colors and fabrics. A woman wearing these clothes will feel confident and sexy wherever she lives, just like New York intended.

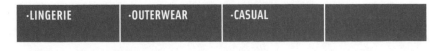

| ·LINGERIE | ·OUTERWEAR | ·CASUAL | |
| --- | --- | --- | --- |

## 877-746-7267 • ShopBop.com

### ShopBop.com

This site's got more character in its name than in its design, but given its propensity for delivering very now designer fashions, you won't give this a second thought. Diane von Furstenberg, Betsey Johnson, Marc Jacobs and Cynthia Rowley are only a smattering of the designers whose wares are sampled here. While no single label's selection is large enough to cause browsing issues, a bright and clean presentation gives the impression at least that this is the best stuff available. Some of it's bound to be just that, whether it's well-cut jeans, cute tops or something for your dog....

| ·DESIGNER | ·CASUAL | | |
|---|---|---|---|

## 888-651-8337 • Silhouettes

### Silhouettes.com

For the full-figured lady of slightly conservative tastes, this thorough and well-designed site offers easy browsing through a selection of clothes ranging from underwear to outerwear. Don't get the wrong idea—it's not that this stuff isn't sexy. In most cases it's quite so. This catalog simply tends to opt for elegant over funky, making it a valuable source for professional attire, as well as stuff like simple sundresses. The biggest drawback would have to be a sometimes excruciatingly slow loading time, most likely due to poor data management of their gorgeous and detailed photos which, some might say, are worth their wait in gold.

| ·CAREER<br>·OUTERWEAR | ·SLEEPWEAR<br>·CASUAL | ·LINGERIE | ·SPORTSWEAR |
|---|---|---|---|

## 866-627-7325 • SizeAppeal.com

### SizeAppeal.com

The term "Size Appeal" here is complimented by sections named coolappeal, sexappeal, chicappeal and workappeal, which should start to give you an idea of this apparel catalog's range. Seeming to understand better than anyone that confidence is the most alluring aspect of style, the founder of this site offers esteem in the form of fashionably cut fabrics, with often titillating results. Railing against the overzealous modesty of other plus-sized lines of clothing, funky and sexy attitudes combine here for one hell of a sassy selection.

| ·CAREER<br>·SPORTSWEAR | ·SWIMWEAR<br>·OUTERWEAR | ·SLEEPWEAR<br>·CASUAL | ·LINGERIE |
|---|---|---|---|

## 212-677-7604 • SoWear

### SoWear.com

There are two keen points of interest to this site, which claims to be "dedicated to promoting emerging talent in fashion." Both facets owe to the relative obscurity of these young design brands. One is that it offers some very entertaining names: Feeling Pomeranian, Trash-a-Porter, Moi Et Cat and some others that can't generally be mentioned in polite conversation, for instance. The other, more tangible result of this selection is that these designers often try hard to make their mark, so a lot of these clothes range somewhere between "daring" and "daringly original" on the scale of upbeat couture. In other words, wear these and you will stand out in a crowd.

| ·SPORTSWEAR | ·OUTERWEAR | ·CASUAL | |
|---|---|---|---|

# Splendour.com

The founders of this site took all the excitement buzzing around online retail to the next level; rather than just start a web merchant devoted to selling women's lingerie, they set out to develop a whole new line of lingerie, specifically to sell online. The results, with such titillating names as the Frontless Bra and the Hands-Free Bra, aren't as overtly prurient as they sound. They merely exhibit a comfortable sensuality, leaving it to the wearer to determine when or where the attire might be appropriate.

| | | ·SLEEPWEAR | ·LINGERIE | ·HOSIERY | |
|---|---|---|---|---|---|

# StockingShopping.com

Hosiery shopping rarely gets easier than with this leg-centric specialty store. Categories initially split between Misses Sizes and Full Figure Sizes, but beyond that you can simply browse specific sections for Knee Highs, Thigh Highs, Tights, Anklets, Pantyhose and Garter Belts. In each you'll find a fairly thorough array of options, from fishnets to black seams, though in truth the low prices are a bigger reason to shop here than variety. And lest you think the rest of your body ignored, Bodystockings are also available, and just as sheer.

| | | ·LINGERIE | ·HOSIERY | | |
|---|---|---|---|---|---|

# StyleShopDirect.com

All kinds of designer and brand name clothes can be found here, so many in fact that you'll probably find yourself a little disoriented upon entering the site. However, the selection of contemporary casual attire and sportswear they offer makes it worth the effort it takes to browse it all, especially if you're looking for a bargain. With this in mind, you can shop by price range, though you never know what items will show up. You can also shop by Designer & Brand, if you see ones you like (Todd Oldham jeans for example), or by Color & Pattern if you're trying to put together an ensemble. Probably the best ways to browse, however, are by Trends & Looks or by Category, either of which will give you a good idea of what this store has to offer.

| | ·CAREER | ·FORMAL | ·DESIGNER | ·SPORTSWEAR |
|---|---|---|---|---|
| | ·OUTERWEAR | ·CASUAL | | |

# TheCatsPJs.com

Are you looking for some "unique pajamas and lounge wear?" Look no further. This San Francisco-based outfit makes PJ's with crazy patterns, like one featuring different cuts of sushi, another with pictures of pinup girls, and the somewhat self-explanatory Pajama-a-Go-Go. The attention-getting sleepers have shown up on TV shows like *Buffy the Vampire Slayer* and *Will & Grace*, and will likely pop up wherever camp is adored. It's a fine example of small business owners finding a niche market, and turning it completely inside out.

| ·SLEEPWEAR | | | |
|---|---|---|---|

## 866-816-7465 • Pink Slip

**ThePinkSlip.com**

From the same intimates store that frequently distracts the denizens of Grand Central Station in New York City comes this equally engrossing web site. Like its brick-and-mortar counterpart, many of the top lingerie brands are available here, the purpose of each to make women look and feel sexy. Well, they've succeeded so far, as is evidenced by the too-steamy-for-words, ahem, product images. As they offer a quick, regular rotation of products, chances are they'll continue to do so well into the future.

| ·SWIMWEAR | ·SLEEPWEAR | ·LINGERIE | ·HOSIERY |
|---|---|---|---|

## 888-336-1192 • Pink

**ThomasPink.co.uk**

This one is all about fine, classic shirts, "unaffected by the vagaries of fashion." In other words, buy it now, wear it until the seams come apart, which is likely to take some time, given the quality of these garments. Shirts come in a variety of colors and three styles: fitted, tailored and Black Label (their top end product). If shirts aren't enough for you, check out their shirt-dresses, essentially following the same style, just not stopping at your waist, of course. With limited options, shopping is easy, provided you find the shopping menu on the right hand side of the page.

| ·CAREER | ·SPORTSWEAR | ·CASUAL | |
|---|---|---|---|

## 800-342-4448 • Title 9 Sports

**Title9Sports.com**

Frustrated by sports gear that didn't fit right because it had been designed for men, the founder of Title Nine Sports wanted to establish a place where a woman could find athletic apparel that suited the needs of her body's shape and size. The result is a perfect match for active women. A great selection of workout shorts, shoes, tanks and pullovers are easy to find here, all designed for women to suit a variety of sports. This also may be the best place anywhere to buy a sports bra, as they're split based on size and circumstance, with a barbell ratings system to let you know how well other women have enjoyed a particular model.

| ·SWIMWEAR | ·ATHLETIC | ·OUTERWEAR | ·CASUAL |
|---|---|---|---|

## 847-673-9116 • TopTops

**TopTops.com**

All you'll find here is tops; strictly speaking, Custo-Barcelona brand T-shirts. You may have seen some of these on TV, in movies or on certain rock stars, or you may just appreciate them here for their obvious hip and sexy appeal. Either way, there aren't a lot of them to choose from, even as they change by season. Actually, there's not a lot of them, period, and they're quite likely to sell out in most sizes. Obviously, the really good ones will go first, so if you see something you like, and it fits you, don't hesitate.

| ·DESIGNER | ·CASUAL | | |
|---|---|---|---|

## Trashy.com

Trashy Lingerie • 310-659-4550

With a name like Trashy Lingerie, there's not a whole lot we can really say that you haven't already figured out for yourself; rather, there are certainly no surprises here. With whole sections devoted to Leather, Lace and Vinyl, it's quite easy to pick your poison, though you may be surprised to learn that there's a pretty lavish selection of robes and pajamas here as well, featuring plenty of silk, satin and the like. In many cases, the word "sultry" falls considerably short of adequately describing these designs, and the pictures are something else altogether. Should prove a lot of fun.

| ·SWIMWEAR | ·SLEEPWEAR | ·LINGERIE · | ·HOSIERY |
|---|---|---|---|

## Ujena.com

Ujena • 800-448-5362

Sexy beachwear. That's all you really need to know about this site. Bikinis, one-pieces and cover-ups reign here, and while you'll find some dresses, tops, intimates and active wear as well, it never really strays far from that sexy, South Beach Miami type of style. In other words, it's a great place to outfit yourself if you never plan to be more than half a mile from the coast. Be warned, though, most of this stuff doesn't leave a lot to the imagination; if, however, you like to "flaunt it," this stuff will absolutely do the trick.

| ·SWIMWEAR | ·CASUAL | | |
|---|---|---|---|

## VenusSwimwear.com

Venus Swimwear • 888-782-2224

This is a swimwear label that grew out of a line of bodybuilding leotards... and yet, for some reason it's only the bikini collection that has expanded and thrived. A good combination of styles and fabrics, you can either focus on one from dozens of particular patterns you like, or select between such distinctions as Brazilian, Camkini, Halter, Tonga, and Triangle tops or bottoms. Or, you can cut to the chase and simply select to browse anything available in your size. Great looks, easy shopping and low prices make this one a perennial spring shopping location.

| ·SWIMWEAR | | | |
|---|---|---|---|

## VictoriasSecret.com

Victoria's Secret • 800-970-1109

What can be said about Victoria's Secret that hasn't been said a million times before? Their ubiquitous presence has literally set a standard for modern lingerie, and their seasonal catalogues have become a cultural staple pleasing to both men and women. Featuring some of the most beautiful women in the world, and some of the finest intimate fashions, as well as some swimwear and evening attire (lest we forget), the site does well to complement the famous catalog, and even allows you to quickly browse through its pages, new and old. You know, in case your postman made off with your copy.

| ·SLEEPWEAR | ·LINGERIE | ·HOSIERY | ·SWIMWEAR |
|---|---|---|---|

## No Service Number • Vix Swimwear

### VixSwimwear.com

This brand makes no pretense—its swimwear line comprised almost strictly of bikinis is intended for "athletic women and teenagers." While both populations tend to consist almost entirely of the swimsuit models seen wearing these designs in myriad magazines, we presume there must be a market somewhere. If you should happen to fall into it, you'll be favored with some terrific solids and prints, at pretty decent prices. However, take note; if you sift through the Press link, you may find access to some different options, even the occasional one-piece.

| ·SWIMWEAR | | | |
|---|---|---|---|

## 866-746-7938 • Wet Seal

### WetSeal.com

What began in the 1960s as a beachside bikini shack has grown immeasurably over the years to the point that it has over 500 stores in 42 states and even in US territories. What could promote such growth, you may ask? Well, for starters, their market is fashionable young women and teens. Add to that their hip, updated selections and slap on a moderate price tag, and you've got a sure-fire success waiting to happen. We can only hope the advent of this online branch will curb their growth somewhat, before the expansion of Starbucks is threatened by this seller of trendy garb.

| ·SPORTSWEAR | ·OUTERWEAR | ·CASUAL | |
|---|---|---|---|

## 877-887-7707 • White And Warren

### WhiteAndWarren.com

These makers of "luxurious, fine quality knitwear" have a scant, but seemly collection of colorful sweaters and tees, and a slick website that shows them to great effect. Actually, the site just may be a little too slick for the small selection displayed, providing a bevy of features that might be of value to a large catalog, but merely prove distracting here. Still, it's nice to take advantage of the excellent looks these guys give of their clothes, especially the Zoom and Examine features, and of all the colors, which will show up bright no matter what your browser settings.

| ·SPORTSWEAR | ·CASUAL | | |
|---|---|---|---|

NOTES:

_____

_____

_____

_____

_____

_____

_____

_____

_____

_____

_____

_____

_____

_____

_____

_____

_____

_____

# Charity

This book has been built on the premise that the internet can make shopping both easier and more fulfilling, with greater access to more things.  However, we recognize that fulfillment is less a function of objects acquired than it is about making a positive impact upon the world around us.  To this end we've included this section, which doesn't offer any great deals or valuable merchandise.  Instead, the ease and access offered here pertains to charitable opportunities: specifically, those donations that can be made online.

It should be noted that this section does not represent every charity available on the web.  There are probably many we didn't get to, and many we should have.  However, these sites are representative of a wide range of popular causes, including but not limited to the following: homelessness, disaster relief, environmental preservation, animal assistance, disease cure & prevention, children's needs and human rights.

Everybody has different concerns and priorities with regard to charitable contributions, and hopefully each may be met through this listing of sites.  Truly, the feeling that you've in some small way helped to make the world better is an indescribable feeling, one that makes donation entirely worth it.  But should you require some more pragmatic justification, consider this: most contributions come with a receipt and tax voucher that you may use as an itemized deduction.  Better yet, a contribution in somebody else's name makes a great gift.  We hope you find this section valuable.

NOTES:

_____

_____

_____

_____

_____

_____

_____

_____

_____

_____

_____

_____

_____

_____

_____

_____

_____

_____

# SECTION ICON LEGEND

Use the following guide to understand the rectangular icons that appear throughout this section.

### CHILDREN'S CHARITIES

This icon indicates that a charity focuses on the needs of children in particular, whether it relates to health, poverty, domestic abuse or educational concerns.

### ANIMAL CHARITIES

One focus of animal-related charities aims to protect an endangered species from extinction; another tries to protect a populous species from abuse. There are plenty of organizations focusing on different animal issues found here.

### ENVIRONMENTAL CHARITIES

The bulk of these charities attempt to preserve the natural resources of the planet from pollution, industrialization and other ecological threats through public policy influence and/or grass roots mobilization.

### HEALTH CHARITIES

Despite the advancements of modern medicine, countless health issues remain a great cause for concern. Activities of these organizations raise funds for research into cures, focus on public policy/awareness and/or attempts to increase the quality of life of those afflicted.

### PEOPLE IN NEED

If we're shopping online we pretty much by definition have it good. Knowing that others in the world, even in our own communities, sometimes need a little assistance, this bunch of charities work to combat poverty, end famine, provide disaster relief and much more.

### CHARITY NETWORKS

These sites offer donation collection services for hundreds, sometimes thousands of different charitable organizations spanning dozens of general and specific causes. Granting a place for those organizations that might not otherwise afford an online presence, these sites can guide you quickly to the charity that matters most to you.

### DOMESTIC ISSUES

The US Constitution provides for a system of checks and balances with our federal governments, but as the price of influence has gone up over the past 200 years, charitable organizations have sprung up to provide a voice strong enough for government officials to hear, tackling a range of domestic civil and legal issues.

# AAH-USA.org

Action Against Hunger is an organization that works to combat famine and prevent disease in areas around the globe that are undergoing natural or manmade crises.

# ACLU.org

This site allows you to contribute to and join the American Civil Liberties Union, and keeps you abreast of contemporary issues and organized activism relating to civil rights.

# ALZ.org

This Alzheimer's Association site collects donations to support continued research into a cure for the disease, and to offer support to those afflicted and their families.

# AmericanHeart.org

The American Heart Association accepts donations on this site to aid in their mission to "reduce disability and death from cardiovascular diseases and stroke."

# AMFAR.org

This American Foundation for AIDS Research site offers information and accepts donations to support AIDS research, prevention, education and public policy awareness.

# Amnesty.org

Amnesty International uses this site to gather support for its international efforts to uncover and prevent human rights abuses, offering information and collecting donations.

## ASPCA.com

The American Society for the Prevention of Cruelty to Animals is one of the nation's foremost organization in promoting and protecting the needs of animals big and small.

## Audubon.org

The National Audubon Society supports conservation and restoration of nature, particularly in relation to wildlife, through gifts, membership and merchandise sales.

## AvonCrusade.com

This charitable branch of the cosmetics company focuses on raising money for breast cancer research, as well as care and support for its victims, taking online donations.

## BreastCancerInfo.com

This Susan G. Komen Breast Cancer Foundation web site helps to gather donations to research a cure, and provides plenty of information and resources as well

## Cancer.org

The American Cancer Society operates this site, accepting donations to help further its cause of providing research into the prevention and treatment of cancer.

## CharityWave.com

This site assures that 100% of your online donation will go to one of hundreds of charities "evaluated for public accountability" across all categories.

# CityOfHope.org

City of Hope operates a medical research center dedicated to discovering cures to cancer, AIDS, diabetes and other dire illnesses; donations gladly accepted.

# ConservationFund.org

This is a large and efficient organization that has had success in converting financial contributions into protection for wildlife habitat and watersheds.

# CovenantHouse.com

The Covenant House provides shelter and services to homeless and runaway youths in cities domestically and internationally, in part with the help of donations to this site.

# Diabetes.org

This American Diabetes Association web site collects contributions and sells merchandise to support research into diabetes and support for its sufferers.

# DogsForTheDeaf.org

Under the About Us menu, this site accepts donations to support its mission to rescue dogs and train them to assist the deaf and hearing impaired.

# DWB.org

Doctors Without Borders sends doctors worldwide to provide urgent medical relief to victims of natural or manmade catastrophe; donations fund supplies and transportation.

## EarthShare.com

Make a donation or purchase logoed merchandise to help support a variety of local environmental nonprofits that subsist under this fundraising organization.

## EGPAF.org

The Elizabeth Glaser Pediatric AIDS Foundation takes donations to support research into child-related prevention and treatment of HIV, AIDS and other pediatric diseases.

## FreshAir.org

Your donations to the Fresh Air Fund sponsors nature excursions for inner-city children who otherwise have limited access to the beauty of the outdoors.

## GildasClub.com

Inspired by and named for comedienne Gilda Radner, this organization takes donations to help provide places for cancer sufferers and their families to find emotional support

## GlobalChild.org

Established to help children survive the traumas of war, the Global Children's Organization offers programs intent on ending the cycles of violence.

## GreaterGood.com

This site links you to many online retailers, wherein a commission on your purchases will go to your choice of charities, including the Humane Society and March of Dimes.

# GreenPeace.org

Working the world over to promote healthy environmental policies and to protect natural ecosystems, Greenpeace accepts help in the form of donations or monthly membership.

# GuideDogs.com

Guide Dogs for the Blind accepts donations to support programs to train seeing guide dogs and provide them to visually impaired people in need.

# H4HA.org

The Hugs for Homeless Animals organization takes donations to assist their work to find homes for unplaced pets, including support of shelters and humane societies.

# Habitat.org

Building homes for the impoverished worldwide, Habitat for Humanity collects gifts and sells merchandise here, and takes applications for volunteer vacations.

# Heifer.org

Contributions to this organization allow the procurement of farm animals and assistance to impoverished families worldwide to help promote self-sufficiency.

# IndependentCharities.org

This site has researched hundreds of charity web sites and selected those national and international groups deemed "high quality" across all categories, listing and rating them.

## JustGive.org

Making it easy to discover a cause you favor, this online network of over 800,000 charities aims to make the donation process efficient and satisfying.

## MichaelJFox.org

This foundation, started by the television star, funds aggressive research into Parkinson's Disease, with the objective of finding a cure within the next ten years.

## MillionMomMarch.org

With product purchase or donation you may support this grassroots movement to prevent gun violence through advocacy of gun control laws and large public demonstrations.

## MODimes.org

Founded by FDR to combat Polio during the great depression, the March of Dimes works today to prevent birth defects, accepting donations in all denominations.

## Mouse.org

Contributions to this organization go towards helping the New York City Public School System keep abreast of technological advancements in the classroom.

## MusicAid.org

Link to a music retailer through this site and proceeds from your purchases are donated to organizations that fund educational programs for kids in less-developed nations.

# NAACP.org

Aside from organizational news and information, this National Association for the Advancement of Colored People site takes member dues to support civil rights efforts.

# Nature.org

The Nature Conservancy is an ambitious project aimed at protecting millions of acres of natural lands around the planet; you may donate once or join as a member

# NCCF.org

This National Childhood Cancer Foundation web site collects donations and sells merchandise to raise money for research and to support care for sick children.

# NetworkForGood.org

This site was established to increase the awareness and funds for hundreds of thousands of charities that might not otherwise have a web presence, including local organizations.

# Oceana.org

Oceana is an organization created "with the sole purpose of protecting the world's oceans," both from pollution and environmentally destructive fishing practices.

# PloughShares.org

The Ploughshares Fund administers grants with the objective to support "initiatives for stopping the spread of weapons of war, from nuclear arms to landmines."

## RedCross.org

The site for this trusted international charity accepts donations to support its constant human and natural disaster relief efforts and offers information on giving blood.

## SaveTheChildren.org

Working to help impoverished, neglected and undereducated children in 45 countries, including our own, this site seeks help in the form of donation and child sponsorship.

## UNICEFUSA.org

This US arm of the United Nations Children's Fund helps support the global organization's efforts to save children's lives through donations and gift card sales.

## VH1SaveTheMusic.com

This entertainment channel's Save the Music campaign uses donations to purchase instruments to protect nationwide public school music programs from elimination.

## VolunteerMatch.org

Linked to more than 20,000 non-profit organizations nationwide, this site offers searches for local volunteer opportunities in fields from public broadcasting to homeless aid.

## WCS.org

The Wildlife Conservation Society accepts donations and membership pledges to support its efforts to save wildlife and the natural lands it inhabits

# WildlifeWayStation.org

This Wildlife Waystation site offers several opportunities to support the preservation of at-risk and endangered species through sponsorship and purchasing merchandise.

# Wish.org

With a donation to the Make a Wish Foundation you can help grant the wishes of terminally ill children "to enrich the human experience with hope, strength, and joy."

# WMF.org

The World Monument Fund works on a member donation basis to protect global art and architecture from the wear of time and the environment.

# WorldWildlife.org

The World Wildlife Fund offers the sale of gifts, membership pledges and one-time donations to help support its efforts to protect endangered spaces and species.

# thepurplebook product index

## a

### accents (for the home)
AngelaAdams.com, 190
AnnieGlass.com, 191
Anthropologie.com, 191
Ashford.com, 230
AvalonGarden.com, 192
BallardDesigns.com, 192
BedBathAndBeyond.com, 193
Bellacor.com, 193
BlindsGalore.com, 194
BombayCo.com, 194
BraidedRugs.com, 194
Chiasso.com, 196
ColonialBrass.com, 197
Comina.com, 197
Costco.com, 232
CrateBarrel.com, 198
DeadlyNightShades.com, 199
DecorateToday.com, 199
DecorLine.com, 469
DelawareRiverTrading.com, 199
DesignerStencils.com, 200
DesignStand.com, 200
DomenicaRosa.com, 201
DresslerStencils.com, 201
DWR.com, 201
eBay.com, 233
ExposuresOnline.com, 202
Exterior-Accents.com, 202
Eziba.com, 202
FrontGate.com, 203
GivingTreeOnline.com, 205
GraciousStyle.com, 205
GreatWindows.com, 205
Guild.com, 205
Gumps.com, 477
HomeDecorators.com, 206
HomeFiresUSA.com, 206
ICanDigIt.net, 206
IndoorWaterFountains.com, 207
Laura-Ashley.com, 208
MarimekkoFabric.com, 209
MarthaByMail.com, 210
MaxwellSilverNY.com, 210
MelinaMade.com, 210
MossOnLine.com, 211
Organize-Everything.com, 211
Palazzetti.com, 212
Pier1.com, 212
PierreDeux.com, 213

PlowHearth.com, 213
PotteryBarn.com, 214
RestorationHardware.com, 215
RetroModern.com, 215
Ross-Simons.com, 487
RueDeFrance.com, 216
SmithAndHawken.com, 217
SmithAndNoble.com, 218
SofaGarden.com, 489
SouthwestCountry.com, 218
Spiegel.com, 218
SurLaTable.com, 219
TotemDesign.com, 220
Umbra.com, 221
UncommonGoods.com, 221
UnicaHome.com, 221
UproarHome.com, 221
URBN.com, 222
VintageWoodWorks.com, 222
Wedgwood.com, 494
YowlerSheppsStencils.com, 223
zGlow.com, 224

### accessories, 367-405
*See also* belts; children's accessories;
eyewear and sunglasses; gloves;
hair accessories; handbags and
wallets; hats; infants' and toddlers'
accessories; jewelry; men's
accessories; scarves and wraps;
shoes; teens; ties; watches;
women's accessories

### action figures
McPhee.com, 481
SmallBluePlanet.com, 321
*See also* toys

### acupuncture
AWorldOfGoodHealth.com,
161

### Africa
*art and collectibles*
Efendos.com, 234
TheAfricaStore.com, 46
*food*
AfricanHut.com, 88
AsiaMex.com, 90

### airline tickets. *See* travel

### alcohol. *See* spirits

### allergy or asthma relief
NationalAllergySupply.com, 175
Sneeze.com, 178

### alternative health
AWorldOfGoodHealth.com, 161
DrugStore.com, 168
Gaiam.com, 235
healing.about.com, 155
Health4Her.com, 171
holisticenetwork.org, 155
KokoGM.com, 237
NaturoPathica.com, 175
OnlineMagnets.com, 176
Origins.com, 176
StressLess.com, 179
TonyTina.com, 180
VitaCost.com, 180
*maternity*
Erbaviva.com, 255

### alternative lifestyle
Gaiam.com, 235
HuggerMugger.com, 430
KokoGM.com, 237
Vegetarian-Shoes.co.uk, 402

### animation cells
Art4Sale.com, 30
Cartoon-Factory.com, 33

### antiques
AntiqNet.com, 29
Antiques.co.uk, 29
CollectorOnline.com, 34
CSPost.com, 468
iCollector.com, 38
RubyLane.com, 44
TIAS.com, 46

### apparel. *See* children's apparel;
maternity, apparel; men's
apparel; teens, apparel;
women's apparel

### appetizers
AllenBrothers.com, 89
ComtesseDuBarry.com, 97
HolidayFoods.com, 104

Kosher.com, 107
OmahaSteaks.com, 112
StonewallKitchen.com, 118
The-Golden-Egg.com, 119

### appliances
AltEnergy.com, 190
ApplianceAccessories.com, 191
Appliances.com, 191
BathClick.com, 192
BBQGalore-Online.com, 193
BedBathandBeyond.com, 193
Bodum.com, 194
ChefStore.com, 196
CompactAppliance.com, 197
Costco.com, 232
Damianco.com, 232
DreamRetail.com, 233
Efendos.com, 234
FrontGate.com, 203
IdeaWorksOnline.com, 207
KitchenEtc.com, 207
RepairClinic.com, 215
Russell-Hobbs.com, 216
SafeHomeProducts.com, 216
Sears.com, 241
Spiegel.com, 218
StacksAndStacks.com, 218
SurLaTable.com, 219
TableTools.com, 219
Williams-Sonoma.com, 223

### archery
GopherSport.com, 310, 430
ParagonSports.com, 438
*See also* sports, solo sports

### aromatherapy
AromaLeigh.com, 161
AWorldOfGoodHealth.com, 161
BeautyHabit.com, 162
BlissWorld.com, 163
BlueMercury.com, 163
CarolsDaughter.com, 164
Caswell-Massey.com, 165
CosmeticsMall.com, 166
eBubbles.com, 168
Elemis.com, 169
Fresh.com, 170
FrontierCoOp.com, 170
Jurlique.com, 172

# • Product Index •

# • Product Index •

# • Product Index •

# • Product Index •

# • Product Index •

# • Product Index •

# • Product Index •

# • Product Index •

# • Product Index •

# thepurplebook company index

## #

| | |
|---|---|
| 11th Hour Vacations | 11thHourVacations.com 504 |
| 13Cats.com | 13Cats.com 334 |
| 1800USAHotels.com | 1800USAHotels.com 504 |
| 1-800-Wheelchair.com | 1800Wheelchair.com 160, 360 |
| 1-888-PetMeds | 1888PetMeds.com 334 |
| 1BookStreet.com | 1BookStreet.com 56 |
| 1stExpressions.com | 1stExpressions.com 540 |
| 24Roses.com | 24Roses.com 460 |
| 3 Wishes Lingerie | 3WishesLingerie.com 564 |
| 301 Wine Shop & Club | 301Wines.com 88 |
| 4 Seasons Swimwear | 4Swimwear.com 416 |
| 4Airlines.com | 4Airlines.com 504 |
| 50/50PetSupply.com | 5050PetSupply.com 334 |
| 877Spirits | 877Spirits.com 88 |

## a

| | |
|---|---|
| A Birds World | ABirdsWorld.com 334 |
| A Bowlers Paradise | BowlersParadise.com 421 |
| A Common Reader | CommonReader.com 64 |
| A La Zing | ALaZing.com 89 |
| A Pair of Shades | APairOfShades.com 376 |
| A Pea In The Pod | APeaInThePod.com 252 |
| A Vintage Wedding | VintageWedding.com 550 |
| A World of Good Health | AWorldofGoodHealth.com 161 |
| A.G. Ferrari Foods | AGFerrari.com 88 |
| a.k.a. Gourmet | akaGourmet.com 460 |
| A.P.C. | APC.fr 273, 566 |
| A1 Books | A1Books.com 56 |
| A1 Discount Hotel Reservations | A1-Discount-Hotels.com 504 |
| AAA Fruit Baskets | AAAFruitBaskets.com 460 |
| AB Lambdin | ABLambdin.com 564 |
| Abbott's Gift Baskets | AbbottsGiftBaskets.com 460 |
| AbeBooks.com | AbeBooks.com 56 |
| ABed.com | ABed.com 190 |
| Abercrombie & Fitch | AbercrombieAndFitch.com 272, 564 |
| Abercrombie & Kent | AbercrombieKent.com 505 |
| Acca Kappa | ShopAccaKappa.com 178 |
| AccorHotels.com | AccorHotels.com 505 |
| Action Against Hunger | AAH-USA.org 596 |
| ActionSportsVideos.com | ActionSportsVideos.com 57 |
| ActionVillage.com | ActionVillage.com 416 |
| Active Mail Order | ActiveMailOrder.com 416 |
| Active Toys | ActiveToys.com 300 |
| Adidas | Adidas.com 416 |
| Adobe | Adobe.com 130 |
| ADS Technologies | ADSTech.com 130 |
| AdventurousTraveler.com | AdventurousTraveler.com 505 |
| Afro World | AfroWorld.com 160 |
| AgeNet | AgeNet.com 360 |
| Agent Provocateur | AgentProvocateur.com 564 |
| Aids for Arthritis | AidsForArthritis.com 360 |
| Airborne Titanium Bicycles | Airborne.net 417 |

| | |
|---|---|
| AirTreks.com | AirTreks.com 505 |
| Akteo Watches | Akteo.com 374 |
| Alex and Ani | AlexAndAni.com 374 |
| Alectra | Alectra.com 565 |
| Alex Woo | AlexWoo.com 374 |
| Alexandros | LuxuryOuterwear.com 582 |
| AlexBlake.com | AlexBlake.com 565 |
| Alibris | Alibris.com 28, 57 |
| Alight.com | Alight.com 565 |
| All The Best Pet Care | All-The-Best.com 335 |
| AllAboardToys.com | AllAboardToys.com 300 |
| Allen Brothers | AllenBrothers.com 89 |
| Allen Edmonds | AllenEdmonds.com 375 |
| All-Hotels | All-Hotels.com 506 |
| AllJacketsAllTheTime.com | AllJacketsAllTheTime.com 272 |
| Alloy | Alloy.com 300 |
| AllPets.com | AllPets.com 335 |
| AllPosters.com | AllPosters.com 28 |
| AllTea.com | AllTea.com 89 |
| Altrec.com | Altrec.com 417 |
| Alzheimer's Association | ALZ.org 596 |
| Am I Pregnant? | Am-I-Pregnant.com 252 |
| AmazingToyStore.com | AmazingToyStore.com 300 |
| Amazon.com | Amazon.com 57, 230 |
| Ambrosia | AmbrosiaWine.com 89 |
| American Apparel | AmericanApparel.net 565 |
| American Blind & Wallpaper | DecorateToday.com 199 |
| American Bridal | AmericanBridal.com 540 |
| American Civil Liberties Union | ACLU.org 596 |
| American Diabetes Association | Diabetes.org 598 |
| American Eagle Outfitters | AE.com 272 |
| American Fly Fishing Company | AmericanFly.com 417 |
| American Foundation for Aids Research | AMFAR.org 596 |
| American Girl | AmericanGirlStore.com 301 |
| American Heart Association | AmericanHeart.org 596 |
| American Legend Mink | LegendMink.com 389 |
| American Light Source | AmericanLightSource.com 190 |
| American Passport Express | PassportHelp.com 522 |
| American Printing & Envelope | APEC-USA.com 461 |
| American Red Cross | RedCross.org 603 |
| AmericanFit.com | AmericanFit.com 272 |
| AmericanGreetings.com | AmericanGreetings.com 461 |
| Amnesty International | Amnesty.org 596 |
| Amtrak | Amtrak.com 506 |
| Anacapa Press | MonasteriesOfItaly.com 520 |
| Anakha | Anakha.com 540 |
| Anastasia Beverly Hills | Anastasia.net 160 |
| Ancient Art Online | AncientArt.co.uk 28 |
| Anderson Butik Swedish Imports | AndersonButik.com 90 |
| Andrew Harper Travel | AndrewHarper.com 506 |
| Angela Adams | AngelaAdams.com 190 |
| Anichini | Anichini.net 301 |
| AnimeDVDStore.com | AnimeDVDStore.com 57 |
| Ann Taylor | AnnTaylor.com 566 |

# • Company Name Index •

## b

# • Company Name Index •

# • Company Name Index •

# xyz

# thepurplebook url index

# • URL Index •

# • URL Index •

# • URL Index •

NOTES:

NOTES:

_____

_____

_____

_____

_____

_____

_____

_____

_____

_____

_____

_____

_____

_____

_____

_____

_____

_____

NOTES:

NOTES:

_____

_____

_____

_____

_____

_____

_____

_____

_____

_____

_____

_____

_____

_____

_____

_____

_____

NOTES:

# thepurplebook™

## submissions & feedback

### Submission Guidelines

Here at **thepurplebook** we've viewed over 10,000 online retailers, and we're just getting warmed up. If you know of a site you think we haven't seen, or may have undergone improvements since our last visit, please include the following information in an email addressed to *submissions@thepurplebook.com,* or fax this page to (310) 385-8022. Please be sure to include the site URL in the email's subject line. [Note: We will only consider sites operating with secure, functional online ordering capabilities. If a site has been recently updated or redesigned, please indicate the launch date of its current incarnation, so that we may be sure to re-evaluate it].

**Company Name:** _____

**Site URL:** _____

**Categories:**

- ___ Art & Collectibles
- ___ Entertainment
- ___ Epicurean
- ___ Gadgets & Electronics
- ___ Health & Beauty
- ___ Home & Garden
- ___ Lifestyles & Megastores
- ___ Maternity
- ___ Men's Apparel
- ___ Minors
- ___ Pets

- ___ Seniors
- ___ Shoes & Accessories
- ___ Sports & Outdoors
- ___ Stationery & Gifts
- ___ Travel
- ___ Weddings
- ___ Women's Apparel
- ___ Charity
- ___ Other/Misc: _____
- _____
- _____

**Comments:**
_____
_____
_____

**Feedback:**

If you have additional comments, questions, corrections or suggestions, please send an email to: *feedback@thepurplebook.com.*
Thank you in advance for your input!

**www.thepurplebook.com**